OCEJWCD Study Companion

Oracle Certified Expert Java EE Web Component Developer

Exam 1Z0-899

Third Edition

Charles Lyons

Published by:
Garner Press, PO Box 382, Beckenham, BR3 3UU, United Kingdom.
http://www.garnerpress.com

OCEJWCD Study Companion
(Oracle Certified Expert Java EE 6 Web Component Developer Exam 1Z0-899)

Third Edition

ISBN: 978-09551603-4-9

The publisher would be grateful if any apparent errors are submitted as errata via our website: http://www.garnerpress.com/errata.

Table of Contents

Chapter 17: Tag Libraries and the JSTL 445

Chapter 18: Custom Tags 479

Chapter 19: Tag Files 525

Introduction

This book is written as a study guide. It isn't meant to be an exhaustive reference to the entire Java EE platform, since that could fill volumes. It also wasn't written with the complete beginner in mind, although many of the topics give a sufficient grounding in the basic theory in order to affirm why things work as they do. There are few code examples, and most of the 'snippets' of code provided require supplementary code to work correctly. Instead, examples are supplied only to emphasise the key ideas being discussed. The reader is encouraged to adapt these examples for themselves, as the best way to 'get good' for any exam is to be practical, build tests and see what happens.

The J2EE 1.4 edition of the exam brought many new features, and added more topics than were removed from the exam objectives compared to its predecessor. In particular, there was a strong emphasis on tag libraries and the Expression Language. As a result, these chapters are longer than others and contain more in-depth discussions. Even if you've never used the Expression Language or created your own tag libraries, these chapters provide a comprehensive guide with a learning curve which isn't too steep. The next evolution was Java EE 6; these exam versions have added major topics including annotations and modular deployment, and asynchronous requests to support AJAX.

To pass the Oracle Certified Expert means you really need to understand every topic in detail, and practical experience is exceedingly helpful. All the content you need is in this book, along with each chapter ending with questions designed to test what you can recall, or indeed what you may have learnt for new, from the chapter. To begin with, it doesn't matter if you get some answers wrong (although if you're getting them right, that's great!). Use the questions at the end of the chapters to find gaps in your knowledge – then go back over the chapter and fill in the gaps, then try the questions again. Repeat this process until you get them all right. Many of the end of chapter questions are similar in style to the performance-based exam questions, though the questions in this book are deliberately slightly harder to ensure knowledge really has sunk in. Once it has, it's a good idea to put it to use: build and deploy example code!

General advice is to pick out the important points in each chapter and note them down separately – just the process of writing notes down or typing them into a word processor may help you remember them. Also, as you read on you'll find many similarities between topics in different chapters; these are worth noting down, as a set of consolidated rules will help you make sensible guesses if you find yourself stuck in the exam. For example, one note you might make is:

> Accessing variables from each of the four scopes always uses the <ins>same</ins> method signatures but on <ins>different</ins> classes:

```
Object getAttribute(String name)
Enumeration getAttributeNames()          (not in JspContext)
void removeAttribute(String name)
void setAttribute(String name, Object value)
```

The four classes are: JspContext (page scope - JSPs only), ServletRequest (request scope), HttpSession (session scope - HTTP only) and ServletContext (application scope).

There are two basic requirements you need to fulfill to pass the exam: you need to have a *good understanding* of the way the container works and how all the Web components work in collaboration; secondly, you also have to *rote learn* syntax, API details and deployment descriptor elements. The latter might seem pointless: developers 'on the job' have access to tools and documentation to ensure they are kept well-informed, so why bother learning all this stuff? However, you might be pleasantly surprised to find that the increased speed at which you can write Web applications after learning the important API is worth the effort put in here!

Free Mock Exam

Included with this book is a subscription to one free online mock exam. This reflects the style and presentation of questions in the real exam, though are deliberately more challenging so you have to think carefully about all the exam material. You can access the mock exam by following the instructions found here:

`http://exams.garnerpress.com/scwcd`

Your author recommends that you leave mock exams until you've finished all the chapters in this book and completed all the questions correctly. Doing mock exams too early won't help you assess your performance, since you'll already be clued-up on the questions when you come to cover the material in the chapters. Instead, use the questions in the chapters to affirm your knowledge, and only when you've finished the entire book, try mock exams. Then recap the topics for which your answers were incorrect. By this stage, you should be almost at, or even over, the pass mark. Most importantly, you should feel comfortable that you can build and deploy a Web application and recall the important API details. Then you're ready to take the exam for real!

Other Resources

In addition to this book, having the following resources at hand is recommended:

- **The offical exam objectives**
  These are given in Appendix A of this book, along with references to the chapters which best cover each objective.
- **Your own notes**
  Nothing beats making your own structured notes, closely following the exam objectives.
- **The Java EE 6 API documentation**
  This is available for viewing and download at `http://docs.oracle.com/javaee/6/api/`. The API documentation contains all the interfaces, classes and methods that you could *possibly ever* need to know. This book provides a condensed summary of those API details you need to know specifically for the exam.

In addition, you may want to refer to these official documents:

- **The Servlet 3.0 specification (under JSR 315)**
  This is available at `http://jcp.org/en/jsr/detail?id=315`
- **The JSP 2.0 specification (JSR 152)**
  This is available at `http://jcp.org/en/jsr/detail?id=152`
- **The JSTL 1.2 specification (JSR 52)**
  This is available at `http://jcp.org/en/jsr/detail?id=52`

These can be useful for checking facts, but even these specifications themselves can omit details which sometimes only practical experimentation reveals the answers to—so if in doubt, whip out your Web server and deploy some test code! Be aware however that every container has its own proprietary extensions and 'features' (AKA bugs); something working in one container may not in another! Your author has been frustrated many times by such 'incompatibilities' in otherwise portable code.

If you haven't already got a Java Web server which you can run examples on, there are two popular options: the latest Java EE 6 version of Sun's Glassfish (at the time of printing, v3.1) which is a fully-fledged open-source Java EE 5 server, or Tomcat 7.0 which is just a Web container. You can download these, respectively, from:

`http://glassfish.java.net/public/downloadsindex.html`

`http://tomcat.apache.org/download-70.cgi`

Download Bundle

All of the code examples found in this book are available for download from:

`http://www.garnerpress.com`

The bundle is located under the Downloads section for this book in the catalogue. The bundle takes the form of a deployable WAR; full instructions and WAR listing can be found in the `readme` file inside the WAR. Please note that, to keep the book condensed, the code examples referred to in Chapter 18 are *only* contained in the download bundle–there is no printed copy.

Exam Format

The OCE Java EE Web Component Developer exam (1Z0-899) is comprised of 57 questions, of which you must answer 35 correctly (61%) to gain a pass, in a time limit of 2 hours. You should *aim to spend no more than 2 minutes per question on average*. Like the Programmer exams, there are no grades assigned–you simply pass or fail. The exam uses two question types:

- Multiple choice (answer one or many; number of correct answers is supplied)
- Drag and drop

This book includes nearly 350 end-of-chapter test questions, in both the multiple choice and drag-and-drop formats.

NOTE: There have been reports of typographical errors in real exam questions, including extraneous backslashes and quotations in code exhibits. Unfortunately the only advice possible is to use common sense and not immediately assume that "compilation error" is the correct answer in such cases (generally these options are only tested on Programmer exams, as this exam is designed to test Java EE undestanding, not code quality).

Feedback and Corrections

Errata for this title is online at: `http://www.garnerpress.com/errata`.

You can pose any questions you have about the content of the book, or send constructive criticism, to `errata@garnerpress.com`.

About the Author

Charles Lyons is an independent software, design and computer administration consultant based near London, UK, with over a decade of programming experience in a wide variety of fields and applications ranging from microprocessors and machine code to the Web, three-dimensional graphics and modelling, and client- and server-side programming using PHP, C/C++ and of course Java.

He is completely self-taught, and after a brief period as a Web designer his interest quickly spread to server-side programming in PHP, before eventually discovering Java. Combining Java Enterprise technology with the Web was a natural progression, finally culminating in this book, which is derived from his own experiences, and mostly from learning by his mistakes and misconceptions!

He holds an MA in Mathematics from the University of Cambridge; after graduating he consulted on a number of programming and design problems with a variety of clients and mainstream programming languages. He presently dedicates his working week (which we hear extends across all 7 days!) as Operations Director at ConnetU, a London-based Internet hosting provider specialising in mission-critical server, cloud and network infrastructures for individuals, SMEs and larger corporations.

Through this work, in addition to being a programmer, he has built a considerable skillset in server management and carrier-grade network design and operation.

His relationship with the exam extends back to February 2004, when he sat the SCWCD 1.4 beta exam, using this 5-hour opportunity to scrutinise real exam questions; this is conveyed through the style of questions presented in this book. Since the First Edition of this book in 2006, with the Second Edition in 2009, he has helped many thousands of readers worldwide to pass the Java EE Web exams!

Java has given me a lot of power over the years; it's the ideal middle ground between inextensible prototyping languages and frameworks, and lower level C/C++/Assembly. There's so much to learn, and the most exciting and rewarding part of it all is the feeling of accomplishment from tackling something new... and succeeding! I hope that you find the skills and knowledge you obtain in this book useful in your career.

I would like to thank everyone who has helped with the production of this book – the patience of everyone involved has been much appreciated. This includes my thanks to the many readers who have taken the time to send me feedback and errata. I would also like to thank the reader for choosing this book over others – I hope that you won't be disappointed. Good luck for all that follows!

P.S. You can join my LinkedIn network (recommendations and success stories always welcome!) at `http://www.linkedin.com/in/charleslyons`.

Are you ready for the OCEJWCD journey?

Turn the page to begin...

I PART 1

The Java EE Environment

Chapter Overview

1. **Networks and HTTP**

   Discusses the basics of networks and the Internet.

2. **The Java EE Platform**

   Briefly examines how Java EE interacts with networks and the Internet before examining the purpose of Web applications and WAR files.

In this chapter you'll:

- ▶ Review the fundamentals of networks.
- ▶ Acknowledge the use of IP addresses and resolving DNS.
- ▶ Learn the difference between URIs, URNs and URLs.
- ▶ Understand HTTP basics.

1 Networks and HTTP

Networks aren't a focus of the Sun Certified Programmer for Java qualification, so passing that exam doesn't guarantee that you know anything about networks. If you do, that's great (and you can probably skip over the elementary overview given in this chapter); if you're not familiar with networks, don't worry – this chapter should explain practically everything you need to know. The most important concepts to understand are the protocols which connect client machines with servers. This chapter, although deviating from the structure and objectives of the exam slightly, will give you an important grounding for the rest of the book, as well as for the rest of your Java EE career.

The Internet

The Internet represents the ultimate of networks: it connects a selection of top-level DNS servers, a whole array of Web hosting servers (as well as those offering services such as financial transaction processing) and millions, even potentially billions, of home and business users. We won't concern ourselves with most network issues, such as IP address resolution and DNS lookup, but instead more with the methods with which data is communicated between machines – the connecting roadway without the start and end destinations as it were.

The majority of the work which we'll do with Java EE will be designed for use on the Web, which might just explain the title of the exam you're sitting: Web Component Developer. However, this doesn't have to be the case – the Java EE platform (in its business component capacity, using technology such as Enterprise JavaBeans) is flexible enough to manage internal and private network communications and data storage as well.

1 IP Addresses

The Internet is irrefutably a large place. As time has moved on, the Internet has reached some of the farthest and most obscure places on the planet, so much so that I don't think I'm stretching my neck out when I say that it has encompassed the world. Everyone from large corporations to the individual home user makes use of the Internet everyday for research, electronic monetary transfers, purchasing items from eBay, or just to find the cheapest local supplier of DIY consumables like nails and screws!

So, I want to find 1.5 inch self-tapping screws in my local supplier's catalogue–but I've got a problem, how do I know where to go? I really want to contact the supplier's computer to check their stock count, but there are *so many* computers on the Internet, just how do I find the right one? The answer comes in the **Internet Protocol** (**IP**). IP is a specification which defines addresses for each individual computer attached to the Internet–the version of IP currently in widespread use is IPv4 (version 4), which limits the number of machines concurrently attached to the Internet to just over 4.2 billion machines.

NOTE: You might think that 4.2 billion machines is enough at any one time–however, with the increased number of business and so-called 'always on' Internet connections, available IPv4 addresses are becoming scarce. As a result, a new specification, **IPv6**, provides support for 3.4 x 10^{38} machines which, unless the population really rockets or everyone gets several palm tops, laptops, desktops and servers, and connects simultaneously, should be ample.

IP addresses are just numbers; each computer in the world is assigned its own unique number which never changes (unless you're a home user whose ISP farms out IP addresses on demand, as with dial-up). An IPv4 address is comprised of four parts, with each part being a number between 0 and 255. Each part is separated by a '.' character. For example: `123.123.123.123` is a valid address, as is `0.132.78.12`. However, `152.354.882.21` is *not* valid since 354 and 882 are both greater than 255. IPv4 addresses consume 32 bits (not that you needed to know that!).

IPv6 addresses are distinguished in that they have eight parts, and each part must be a *hexa*decimal number between 0 and FFFF (decimal 0 and 65,535). Therefore IPv6 addresses consume 128 bits. The second distinguishing factor is that IPv6 uses the ':' character between parts. For example: `3F4:8A4D:992:0:FE12:419:19:417A` is a valid IPv6 address.

NOTE: IPv6 is a relatively new version of the protocol. As a result, it is only just starting to see major adoption.

Domain Name System (DNS)

Right, so I know that my local supplier has the IP address `102.17.206.192` for instance. Now, what do I do with that? I could just type it in my browser right now, and (fingers-crossed), I'll be connected to the right machine. Excellent!

But what happens next week, when I need to look up my supplier's catalogue again. Unfortunately, my memory's not that good – I'm just not able to remember the number `102.17.206.192` for very long (made worse by the fact that everyday I visit over a *dozen* different sites commonly, each with its own very distinct IP address).

Instead, I'd find it much easier to remember a sensible *name*, like `nailsandfixings.com`. Thankfully, someone thought of this idea already, and the **Domain Name System (DNS)** was born. DNS provides a mapping between domain names like `nailsandfixings.com` and IP addresses like `102.17.206.192`. So now, when I type `nailandfixings.com` into my browser, it uses the DNS to **resolve** (or **look up**) this human-readable name into the numeric IP address. The browser then uses the IP address to connect to the correct machine.

URIs, URLs and URNs

Domain names and IP addresses are all very well, but what if my supplier's server is managed by a hosting company, and there are lots of websites on it? In order to contact that machine, I must have used a single IP address – and that address is probably going to (but doesn't have to) be the same for every website on that machine. But I'm not interested in the other websites, just the one with the 1.5 inch self-tapping screws on it! Also, I might want to request *different resources* on my supplier's website – a catalogue index, a product page, a purchasing page, a picture of the screws I'm about to buy, etc. Still, with only one single IP address, how can I get hold of these different resources?

What to do? The answer comes in **Uniform Resource Identifier**s (**URI**s). URIs provide a mechanism to distinguish things belonging to one entity from those belonging to another. For example, my supplier's catalogue belongs to a different company or person than the eBay homepage does.

URIs themselves are abstract quantities – you can't create a URI directly. However,

URIs do have two common concrete forms: **Uniform Resource Locator**s (**URL**s) and **Uniform Resource Name**s (**URN**s).

The general format for a URI (as defined in RFC 3986, January 2005) is:

```
scheme:hierarchy[?query][#fragmentid]
```

where the bracketed sections are optional. For a URL, the hierarchy is composed of two further parts:

```
//authority/path
```

where `authority` represents, according the RFC specification, 'a naming authority so that governance of the name space defined by the remainder of the URI is delegated to that authority'. In practise, the authority is a server name or address, optionally containing user and port information. `authority` therefore takes the general form:

```
[user@]host[:port]
```

The `path` previously referred to is the location of the resource within the authority, which for all practical purposes, is the server. The user information may include usernames and passwords (this is deprecated due to security concerns sending passwords in plain text), but a detailed discussion is deferred to the RFC 3986 specification.

Now, we're all familiar with the construction of a typical URL:

```
http://www.nailsandfixings.com:8080/catalogue?part=4563
```

Here, `http` is the scheme, `www.nailsandfixings.com` is the authority (with port `8080` specified) and `/catalogue` is the path, `part=4563` is the query string, and there is no other optional data. Other valid schemes include `ftp`, `news` and `gopher` to name but a few.

The structure of a URN may be unfamiliar to you—but it is really simpler than a URL:

```
urn:namespace:otherdata
```

The scheme for a URN is always `urn`. The `namespace` is specific to a single entity or organisation, and the `otherdata` is chosen by that organisation. As an example, RFC 3121 defines a set of URNs for use within the Organization for the Advancement of Structured Information Standards (OASIS). The namespace assigned to that organisation is `oasis`. An example of one such possible URN is quoted in RFC 3121:

```
urn:oasis:names:tc:docbook:dtd:xml:docbook:5.0b1
```

The reason why URLs are chosen as the preferred URI is really a matter of popularity.

The necessity to put content on the Web began the domain name registration process. Every domain name can be registered to only one entity, and that makes the domain name the perfect identifier for each person or organisational body on the planet. But, URNs don't include domain names as part of their syntax, and there is no other unique registration process for a URN namespace. So, in order to make use of the uniqueness of domain ownership, URLs are the preferred medium for identifying a resource.

Finally, to return to resource identification, the URL to my supplier's catalogue might be `http://www.nailsandfixings.com/catalogue/` while eBay's homepage is `http://www.ebay.com`. Clearly, these names are quite different; if both resources were to reside on the same server, with the same IP address, it would still be obvious from the URL which resource I was intending to access.

NOTE: For the exam, and life in general, you need to be familiar with URLs and understand that they are a subset of the wider URI category (although in practise no other URI subset is frequently used). Chapter 20 briefly uses the less-common URN.

The Client-Server Model

The two most important parties in the transfer of networked information are the computer requesting information (the **client**), and the machine assigned with the duty of providing that information (the **server**). I say the most important parties since if we consider the average internal network, there would also be hardware like switches, routers and firewalls (located somewhere in the middle of the transfer) present. Across the Internet, data might pass through a multitude of different Internet Service Provider's (ISP) routers and relay servers (often called **nodes** on the connection path), making the whole situation rather clouded if we don't simplify the model by looking only at the two endpoints which we care about: in other words, the client at one end, and the server at the other. You should be pretty familiar with these two terms; they are used frequently and consistently throughout this book as well as in all other technical literature. See Figure 1.1.

1

Figure 1.1

Client-Server Model

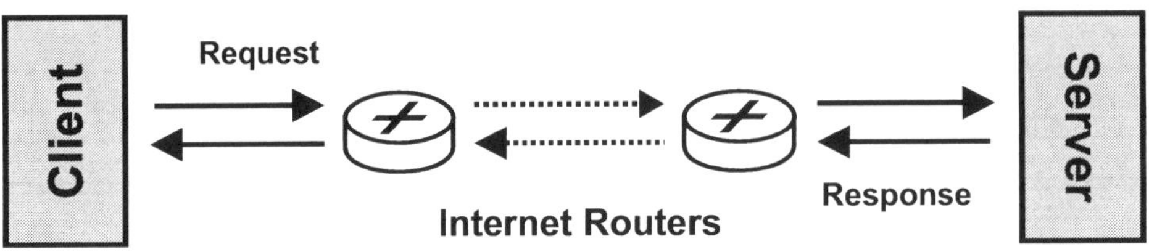

The Transfer of Data and Network Protocols

In order to get digital data from one endpoint to another, we pass streams of binary data (typically electrical pulses) through some sort of connection. The connection could use a solid copper wire, fibre optics, radio waves on a wireless network, or even waves in the microwave spectrum sending communications to orbiting satellites. Whatever hardware transmission mechanism is chosen doesn't concern us: for our purposes the end neglects the means. What is important, however, is the software aspect of the system; while we are generally free to choose any compatible hardware for transmission, the arrangement and ordering of bits and bytes in the transmitted message is crucial. The rules by which data is ordered and packaged for transmission, and how it is unravelled and read at the other end, is a called a **protocol**.

Protocols in General

If you like visual images of things at work, you can think of an automatic cardboard-boxing machine in a factory as a form of protocol. Consider a machine from the 'Neat & Tidy Box Company'. If we put our Neat & Tidy machine into 'box' mode, and switch it on, it will package a line of products up in its own certain way. If we now put our Neat & Tidy boxer into 'unbox' mode and request it retrieve the products from the boxes again, it will do so successfully. However, suppose now that one of the machines breaks, and the company chooses to replace it with a cheaper model from another company, the 'Bodge It & Box It Company'. This machine will probably operate in its own way, independent of that of the other brand (especially since it is a bargain at half the price). Now we attempt to 'unbox' the products previously packaged with the Neat & Tidy machine with our new auto-boxer. Instead of cutting the tape and unfolding the cardboard, the machine cuts down too far, and crushes the box as it tries to remove the product. In this model, the two machines each represent different protocols: they have different operational mechanisms and are completely incompatible.

This illustrates the point well. If we didn't care about protocols at all, then data would be packaged up in one way at one end, and unpackaged differently at the other – leading to a mess of bits and bytes which the receiver can't understand. So, unless we are operating between two self-contained machines (on a private network for instance), we can't just invent a method of data transmission and hope it will work. On the contrary, we need to use standard, well-accepted, protocols to achieve what we want. This couldn't be more true than in cyberspace due to the sheer volume of network traffic.

Standard Protocols

There are lots of well-established protocols around. The most common in networking is **TCP/IP**, an amalgamation of the **Transmission Control Protocol** (**TCP**), which is responsible for the packaging and unpackaging of data between the client and server, and the **Internet Protocol** (**IP**) which is a method of describing the location of the end points (destination of the message) along the connection pathway. We discussed the IP addressing system earlier.

TCP is a low-level protocol; it is used essentially just to connect two machines together and provide a way of data exchange – it is far from the best way for most applications though. In order to maximise the ease and accuracy with which data can be moved from one machine to another, it is necessary to build on top of the low-level protocols, and one of the best advances in technology which achieves this is HTTP, or the **Hypertext Transfer Protocol**.

The Hypertext Transfer Protocol (HTTP)

Even if you have no technological background in HTTP, you will have met it. Nearly every connection to a website made over the Internet uses it, or at least a derivative of it. The reason for HTTP's success as a Web protocol is that it was designed exactly for this purpose: it allows clients and servers not only to pass resources backwards and forwards, but to query each other, append supplementary data and information, and get feedback information with regards to whether a transfer will succeed or not.

For the exam, we will need to know several aspects of HTTP, including:

- Requests and responses
- HTTP Methods
- HTTP Status Codes
- Cookies

Requests and Responses

When a client needs to get a resource on a server, it must first makes a **request** for it. It does this by sending a packet of HTTP data, part of which contains the identification (typically the URL) of the resource being requested. Once the server receives the request, it will attempt to send the requested data back to the client in the form of a **response**. The response will most likely contain more data than the request did by nature: at its most basic, the request only consists of location data (such as a URL), whereas the response contains all the bytes from the requested resource. In the case of an executable or music file, there may be millions of bytes, inevitably making that response a whopping 10,000 times larger than the request might be! Of course the difference in magnitude between the request and response suggests that it is much more likely that errors and corruptions (such as bits being lost over the connection) will occur in the response generated from the server to client, and this is why some larger files don't work after a long download–as annoying as it is. The reverse is true when we consider file uploads: the request will be larger than the response, so inevitably, more errors will occur between the transfer from client to server. The occurrence of this situation is rarer.

Headers and Bodies

Figure 1.2

HTTP Request/ Response Composition

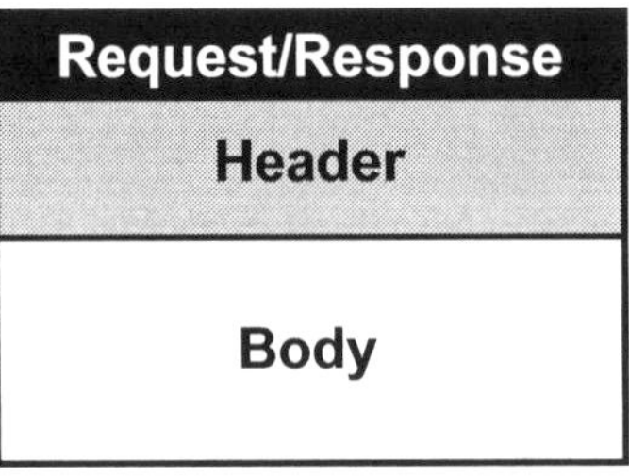

Both requests and responses have two sections to them: the first section is the **header**, and the second is the **body**. This is shown in Figure 1.2.

The header contains metadata about the resource being requested. Metadata is data which describes the resource itself, without resorting to supplying any part of the resource. Information contained in the header includes, among other things, the version of the HTTP standard being used, the language the user communicates in, and in a response, the size of the resource being returned (this is how download programs determine the percentage already transferred and the amount still left).

The body of a request is typically empty, although there are some types of requests which have a body which is not empty (e.g. POST). We will consider each of these next, as having a knowledge of each is an exam objective.

HTTP Versions

Before we continue, we must consider that there are several versions of the HTTP standard, much like Java has gone through various stages of development in its life. The HTTP versions which we should be mostly concerned with are 1.0 and 1.1. These are conventionally written (as well as coded for) as HTTP/1.0 and HTTP/1.1, and this is how I will refer to them when necessary.

In essence, HTTP/1.0 defines the basic HTTP transfer protocol needed for communication, and we can be pretty sure that all machines on the Internet support it (for the purposes of building services for the average home and business user, we can guarantee it). The only HTTP methods available in HTTP/1.0 were `GET`, `POST` and `HEAD` (see below for the full HTTP/1.1 set), and HTTP/1.0 doesn't support the Informational status codes. The majority of browsers and modern services will also support HTTP/1.1, which provides an expanded set of header fields and facilities. For the exam, we can be safe in the assumption that the Java EE platform will transparently negotiate HTTP versions for us.

HTTP Methods

When a request is dispatched to a server, it could be for any number of reasons. For example, the client might just want to get hold of the resource (such as a web page, text file or image) and display it to the user of the machine, or alternatively the user might want to update some information on the server, such as subscription options for a mailing list. At the extremes, the user may have privileges to upload to and delete whole files from the server. Each of these represents a distinct action, and is called a **method** of data transfer. All of the HTTP methods are typically stated in block-capitals, a convention adopted from the original HTTP technical documents. For the new edition of the exam, we are required to know all seven of the HTTP methods that Java provides support for.

NOTE: **Terminology alert!** HTTP methods are not to be confused with Java's methods despite sharing the name 'method'. Unfortunately, servlets provide ample room for this type of confusion since they map Java methods directly to HTTP methods. Where necessary, I will try to make the distinction clear.

The GET Method

The GET method is used to request the retrieval of a resource from a server. This is the most commonly used method of all, and hence we have covered it first. A GET request is typically initiated when the user types a resource URI into the browser window, or when they click a link in a web page. Owing to the nature of how most users go about visiting Web resources, this is the most common example of an HTTP method, and for this reason it comprises over 95% of the total HTTP Web requests.

GET requests are typically used when (a) the client is requesting a resource be returned from a certain location on the server and (b) the client does not wish to provide any additional parameters or information to upload.

A GET request does not contain any HTTP body data since the only data that is required by the server, to return the requested data, is the URI to the resource. It may however supply some supplementary data using attributes encoded in the URI, in the form of a query string, using a question mark to begin the sequence, and ampersands to separate the parameters. A typical example of an encoded URL with a query string is:

```
...form?email=jsmith@domain.ext&comments=Excellent%20site
```

This assumes a resource called `form` exists on the server, and also assumes that the user is sending attributes with the names `email` and `comments`, and that the values assigned to these attributes are `jsmith@domain.ext` and `Excellent site` respectively. The equals sign is used to assign the value to the attribute name, and the ampersand is used as the separator between attributes. Note that the space in the URL has been replaced with the character encoding `%20`. This is because a space is a URL syntax character, and therefore cannot be used in arbitrary places such as resource names or query strings. However, we don't need to know anything about intermediary URL character encodings, as both the client's browser and the Java EE Web container handle the conversions for us.

The POST Method

Sometimes the client will need to pass information to the server for processing. This might be a lot of data, or just a few fragments, and the information might include login information, session data or the user's input from a feedback form. In fact, by using HTML forms (or the newer XForms), a web page author has the flexibility to create any form he wishes–allowing the user to supply as much data as required, and only data of the required type (e.g. an option from a list or a text input).

The POST method is used primarily when there is lots of data to be transferred, in situations where we could use a GET request with an appropriate query string, but it would turn out to be so long that the URI would then become unwieldy! We can also use the POST method when uploading files; after all, you wouldn't want megabytes of data in a query string, would you? Instead of including data in the visible URL, as a GET request does, the POST method makes use of the body of the request (recall that for the GET method the body is empty). It places all the data to the sent, including the name/value **parameter** pairs which might otherwise appear in the query string, in the request body. We won't worry about the precise structure of a POST request, but the exam mandates that we concentrate on how to retrieve request parameters, so we will discuss this at the appropriate juncture.

We can supply extra parameters with a GET request, but instead of including them in the body of the request (which, recall, must always be empty for GET), they are encoded into the URL being requested – in the query string (see left) using a question mark to begin the sequence, and ampersands to separate the parameters

Essentially, we use POST over GET in two situations:

- **Large amounts of data to transmit**
  It is unsightly to include lots of long data encoded in the URL. Instead of the user seeing the URL to the page, they would see lots of attributes with long values if GET were used. In the situation where you have a large count of attributes, or values which extend way off the visible range of the user's navigation bar, consider the use of POST.
- **'Hiding' data**
  Sometimes it is useful to hide data from the user. By not exposing the information in the visible URL, the average user won't even know it's there. This is advantageous since it prevents the user visiting the page again in the future – they can only bookmark the visible URL, so any data included in the body of the request when the POST method is used is effectively hidden. This means they couldn't submit the same details repeatedly, for instance, if they used a feedback form (although refreshing the page just after submitting a form would resend the data).

There are, however, situations where we are transmitting supplementary parameters, and yet a GET request is preferable. These are few and far between, but the most common example is a page containing search engine results. Once the user has performed a search, they might want to come back to the results later (by bookmarking the page or including it as a hyperlink from another site), so it is sensible to include their search criteria *in the bookmarked URL*. For example:

```
...searchResults?s=Java%20Enterprise%20Edition%20Web%20hints
```

We've used the `s` parameter to specify the search criteria, in this case `Java Enterprise Edition Web hints` (after the container has replaced the `%20` encodings for us). Returning to this URL would presumably return the same set of results as the first time it was visited (although due to reindexing of the search engine's database, this isn't guaranteed to be true).

Contrary to some unfounded beliefs, despite the information being concealed in the body of the request and not exposed, the data is not secure. It is no harder to extract `POST` data from the request than it is to read a text file from your computer. If security is your concern, use `POST` in conjunction with the **Secure Sockets Layer** (**SSL**) encryption suite, an integral part of Secure HTTP (HTTPS).

The HEAD Method

Occasionally it might be useful for the client to obtain all of the headers for a resource, before getting hold of it. Recall that the header contains metadata about the actual resource. The browser might, therefore, want to find out the length of a file that a user has requested to be downloaded (from the HTTP `Content-Length` header) and therefore calculate, and present to the user, how long it would take to transfer. If we used a `GET` request, the file would start being transferred before we got any of the headers, and that would be a waste of bandwidth if the user decides it will take too long and terminates the connection.

Similarly, the client might look at the language of the page using the HTTP `Content-Language` header, and if the page is not in the user's chosen language, notify them and present them with the possibility of skipping it. After all, there's no point in trying to read a page in a language you have no hope of comprehending.

The OPTIONS Method

As we said earlier, not all servers will support all the HTTP methods. The `OPTIONS` method will return a response which contains a list of all the methods supported by a server and the resource being requested.

Of course, since we are mainly asking for a response containing the required data, we don't really need a body in the request. However, the HTTP specification does not mandate whether a body should be used or not; instead it leaves it open for future modification. This is to allow extra query data to be sent to the server in the future if necessary.

The PUT Method

The PUT method is, as its name implies, used to place resources onto the server—effectively constituting an upload process. Essentially, the body of a PUT request would contain the data of the resource being uploaded, and an extra header, the Request-URI header field, is used to identify the location on the server to which the resource is to be uploaded to.

Although we don't need to know or use the following status codes in the exam, they are useful to know for future reference. A typical response would reply with a 200 ('OK') status code if the resource is successfully stored (typically overwriting a previous file), a 204 ('No Content') code if the resource was not placed on the server, and a 201 ('Created') response if the resource is new to the server (i.e. a new file had to be created for the resource to be stored in).

A PUT request differs from a POST request in that it contains the Request-URI header field. While POST can contain supplementary data in its body, it doesn't give the server any direct knowledge about where to store that information. Instead, a PUT request delivers the storage location in the Request-URI header, so the server knows exactly where to save the data to. A PUT request is not recommended for simple data (i.e. attribute) transfer, however, since its body contains only a continuous stream of binary data.

NOTE: There are issues of security with POST, but in particular PUT and DELETE. They are considered to be dangerous since in theory they enable the user to interact directly with the server, adding, modifying or even removing data from it. Hence, if you do decide to use PUT or DELETE, you should always configure an appropriate level of security before allowing clients to use these HTTP methods (see Chapter 21). Thankfully, if you don't actually want to use these methods, the default implementation of a servlet doesn't process them anyway, so you don't need to do anything or consider the security implications.

PUT can also be thought of as another form of FTP, since it enables the transfer of a file from a client machine to a server, but this can be misleading since FTP is a *stateful* protocol designed exclusively for file transfer (we contrast stateful with stateless protocols in Chapter 9).

The DELETE Method

Just as we can save resources to the server (using PUT), we can remove resources from the server using the DELETE method. Once again, there are serious security considerations surrounding the use of this method, so it should be used sparingly.

The `Request-URI` header field is used to contain the URI path to the resource that is to be deleted from the server. This is a 'mirror image' operation to that of the `PUT` method. Since it is not sending data to the server, the body of a `DELETE` request is typically empty.

The TRACE Method

Sometimes it is useful to make sure that the server is functioning correctly, or that a Java component such as a servlet has been installed and is operating under normal conditions. If a client needs to verify this, it can use the `TRACE` method.

Using `TRACE` is like looking in a mirror: what the request sends to the server, it gets reflected back exactly in the response. This enables the client to send a set of known request headers and attributes, and ensure that what it gets back matches what it sent. This method is typically used for debugging purposes, to ensure that the server is receiving the full request, and responding appropriately.

Although the new exam asks us to know all the HTTP methods, this is probably the least commonly used, since it is only of interest to system engineers, and not generally to programmers or the client.

The CONNECT Method

This is currently reserved for future use in the RFC 2616 (HTTP/1.1) specification.

HTTP Status Codes

HTTP is particularly powerful because it not only gives a simple way to transfer information across a network, but it gives some feedback as to how the request has been processed as well. This feedback comes in the form of HTTP status codes, some of which we've already seen when we discussed the HTTP methods, and others which you'll have come across when 'surfing the Net'.

Each status code is sent in an HTTP response, and is used by the client to determine what to do next. For example, a status code indicating a successful return of data will cause the response to be displayed, but one indicating a resource not found will be reported as an error to the user.

Each status code is a number which is three digits long. The first indicates the status code class, and the last two are used to identify the exact status type within the general category. There are five classes of status code:

- **Informational (1xx)**
  These are reported during a connection with the client, but do not signify the termination of the request. E.g. 100 indicates that the server is continuing to process the request–hence its name: 100 ('Continue').
- **Successful (2xx)**
  These indicate that the request has been successfully completed. There are several of them, the most common being 200 ('OK'), indicating a complete response has been correctly assembled.
- **Redirection (3xx)**
  A redirection status code indicates that the requested resource has been moved somewhere else, and no longer resides at the requested location. The Java EE Web container provides some convenience mechanisms to perform redirection without having to set status codes directly.
- **Client Error (4xx)**
  These are generated and returned when an error has occurred on the part of the client making the request. For example, the resource can't be found because the user has incorrectly specified its URL. Another common reason for a 4xx being returned is that the user is not authorised to access a resource, or the user agent is not using a correct protocol definition.
- **Server Error (5xx)**
  Just as a client can cause an error in a request, the server can fail to respond correctly–either because of a malfunction, or a temporary lack of resources required to complete the required transaction. They might also indicate a permanent 'Service Unavailable' problem.

Cookies

Cookies are very widely used on the Internet to maintain persistence of a user's settings between visits to a website. We cover them here because they are a basic concept, but we will only put them to practical use later when we discuss sessions in Chapter 9.

Fundamentally, cookies are small text files stored on the client machine. They contain information sent from the server, and they are therefore a form of temporary persistent storage on the client side. They are classified as 'temporary' since their integrity cannot be guaranteed. The user is free to modify them or delete them as they wish, and quite often a flush of the browser's cache will consist of removing the hundreds of cookies which have accumulated over time. The user agent may also not support cookies, or the user may have disabled them.

NOTE: The availability and integrity of cookies can *never* be guaranteed. They are a convenience to enable websites to maintain relatively unimportant information for short periods of time. Good developers should always ensure that cookies are not fundamentally required for use of a website and that an alternative is provided in case the cookie mechanism fails.

A website would typically use cookies to store preference information, or insensitive user information (such as a username to be used for maintaining insignificant login state). When the user first interacted with the site, the preferences would be stored in the cookie; in subsequent interactions, the information could be recalled from the cookie and used again.

Security

Originally, users and developers alike were concerned that cookies would provide a way to take advantage of a user's machine and breach its integrity. However, the security model applied to cookies is in fact very strict.

Cookies are stored based upon the domain, sub-domain and (optionally) path to the resource which saved data into them. A browser normally saves each website's cookies in a new file. This results in information from one website being stored completely separately from the information saved from another. You can even prevent pages from one path from accessing pages from another path within the same website, if you really want or need to be that restrictive.

Common Uses

There are several situations in which cookies are commonly used. These are mostly in terms of presentation: a site might save the user's colour preferences from their first visit so that these can be used again later. Even though the data integrity of a cookie cannot be guaranteed, it doesn't matter in this context, since the user can simply select their presentation again.

Another use is for maintaining a persistent login: sites often offer a 'remember me' option so that users don't have to log back in every time they visit. This can only be used for fairly insignificant purposes since the user might delete the cookie or change its contents. Some form of extra security would have to be imposed to prevent the modification of the login details.

Arguably the most important use for cookies is to maintain data about a session. We will discuss this use in more detail when we cover sessions later in Chapter 9.

Revision Questions

1 **Which of the following statements best describes the HTTP POST method?** **(choose two)**

- A It is the most commonly used document retrieval method.
- B It is usually reserved for sending large amounts of data.
- C No response is returned when this method is used: only a request is submitted.
- D HTML forms most often make use of this mechanism.
- E The body of the request is always empty.

2 **Match the following HTTP methods with their correct descriptions:**

Method	Description
GET	Returns the response headers for the POST method.
POST	Retrieves a resource; supplementary data must be provided within the URL
HEAD	Requests that a resource be removed from the server.
DELETE	Designed for transmitting potentially large amounts of data to the server; requests made using this method cannot be fully bookmarked by the client's browser.
PUT	Places a resource on the server
	Returns the response headers for the GET method.

3 **The HTTP HEAD method is defined to use the headers of which other method?** **(choose one)**

- A GET
- B POST
- C PUT
- D DELETE
- E OPTIONS

4 **Which of the following are HTTP/1.0 methods?** **(choose two)**

- A GET
- B POST
- C PUT
- D DELETE
- E TRACE

5 **A status code lying in the 4xx block represents what category of response?** **(choose one)**

- A Successful
- B Server error
- C Client error
- D Informational
- E Redirection

6 **The status code to describe a resource as being temporarily unavailable is most likely to be:** **(choose one)**

- A 404
- B 200
- C 102
- D 503
- E 403

7 **The best method to use for debugging purposes would be?** **(choose one)**

- A GET
- B PUT
- C HEAD
- D OPTIONS
- E TRACE

8 **Which of the following present considerable security risks?** **(choose two)**

- A GET
- B POST
- C PUT
- D TRACE
- E DELETE

9 **The primary use of a cookie is to:** **(choose one)**

- A Provide a database for the storage of business transactions
- B Enable the developer of a website to maintain long-term persistent storage with the client
- C Provide a temporary data store with the client for use across multiple requests
- D Allow data to be shared between multiple servers and hosts
- E Gain extra information about the client

10 **For a Web developer, the best uses of a cookie are?** **(choose two)**

- A To provide secure storage of usernames and passwords
- B To provide for serialisation of shopping baskets in an online store
- C To store session identification data
- D To save and retrieve user preferences such as language settings and colour schemes
- E To authenticate the client machine between sessions

1 Answers to Revision Questions

1 **Correct answers: B, D**

A is incorrect since this describes the GET method. C is incorrect: all HTTP methods return a response. E is incorrect; in order to send extra data, the body of the request must contain content. While the body *may* be empty, this is usually not the case (unlike GET which is always empty).

2 **Correct answer:**

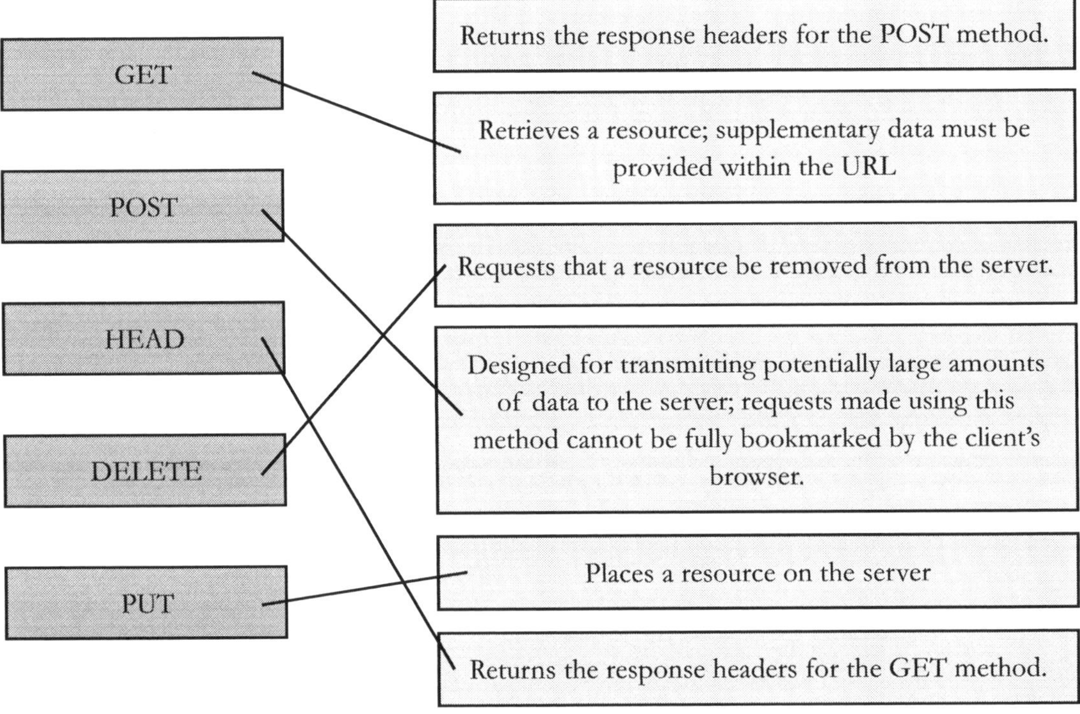

3 **Correct answer: A**

4 **Correct answers: A, B**

5 **Correct answer: C**

6 **Correct answer: D**

A is incorrect since a 404 represents a permanent 'Not Found', implying that the resource doesn't exist. B is incorrect – this represents 200 'OK'. C is incorrect since all 1xx are informational only (and not instructive). E is incorrect, since 403 represents 'Forbidden' meaning that the current client is not permitted to access that resource (but it does exist!)

The error code 503 actually stands for 'Service Unavailable'. In general, all 5xx codes represent internal server errors such as overloading or maintenance downtimes, and all 5xx codes should be accompanied by a notification of whether the problem is temporary or permanent.

7 **Correct answer: E**

TRACE is designed specifically for debugging because it reflects the original request back as a response to the client. Inconsistent data would indicate a problem.

8 **Correct answers: C, E**

A is incorrect since GET can provide only simple textual data as part of the URL. The requested resource will ignore this data if does not expect it. B is incorrect, since although POST can be used to upload files, its primary use is not to modify files on the server, but instead to provide the server with information data. D is incorrect because, if the server is operating correctly, TRACE only reflects the original request; this action does not normally constitute a security threat.

Both PUT and DELETE provide a way to change the file configuration on the server; unauthorised use may lead to the uploading of malicious code or viruses.

9 **Correct answer: C**

A is incorrect: a cookie is only a temporary storage device for *simple textual* (not binary) data. B is wrong because the cookie is not designed for long-term storage. D is incorrect – a cookie can be used only on one specific website for security reasons. E is wrong because a cookie is inherently not permitted to access any part of the client's machine – this prevents cookies being used for malicious data gathering.

10 **Correct answers: C, D**

A and E are both wrong since the integrity of cookies cannot be guaranteed; cookies are not secure – anyone with access to the client machine might be able to steal them and use them to illegitimately authenticate themselves. B is incorrect – cookies can contain only simple textual data, not large amounts of binary data.

In this chapter you'll:

- Review basic Java EE terminology.
- Learn about the purpose of the Web container.
- Use application contexts.
- Understand the basics of WAR file packaging.
- Be introducd to the components we'll be discussing in the rest of the book.

2 Java EE Architecture

In many ways the **Java Enterprise Edition (Java EE)** platform is a natural extension from the standard Java platform into the network environment. Enterprise Java is specially designed for servers, providing many advantages, including the ability to run distributed applications across different JVMs (and hence different physical servers). To accomplish this mammoth task, it requires a whole new programming architecture which alleviates some of the less interesting (putting it mildly) tasks from the server programmer. This allows application developers to run applications on one server, or across an entire cluster of load-balanced servers. Additionally, the Java EE platform provides 'out of the box' support for all standard network protocols, including HTTP discussed in the last chapter. You couldn't get all that with a Java SE download could you?

There are two main uses of the Java EE platform in industry:

- To provide business services such as database storage and transaction processing for clients operating on a network;
- To provide Web front-ends and business services to clients using the biggest network of all: the Internet.

Most of the former is about programming EJB technology to interface with client machines on a network using standard protocols such as Java's Remote Method Invocation (RMI). The latter involves not only EJB technology to build solid business logic, but Java's Web component technology to build practical front-ends for users surfing the Web.

It is this Web component technology which the SCWCD exam concentrates on; if you want to get certified with EJB technology, consider the Sun Certified Business Component Developer exam.

Terminology

Before we can start using Java EE concepts, there are certain key terms to define.

Web Components

2

A **Web component** is defined in the Java EE specification to be either a servlet or a JSP (presumably also the newer filters). Static resources such as HTML documents, images and other files available to the client such as PDFs and executables are not considered Web components, although they may be deployed alongside components. Additionally, metadata about the application itself, as well as all supporting classes, JAR libraries and private configuration files are not considered Web components.

Web components fall under the general category of Java EE components, as do EJB components and application client components, neither of which we will discuss further.

Web Applications

A **Web application** is a collection of Web components, chosen or designed to fulfill the requirements of a particular website or online service, along with other deployment and configuration data. For example, a catalogue application would combine the power of many different Web components: servlets might be used to process complex requests and JSPs for providing HTML or XML responses. It might also contain static resources such as images to be downloaded by the client, and private configuration data such as passwords for database access.

A Web application is known also as a Web (application) module; 'module' here refers to Java EE modules which collectively form a Java EE application. In this book we will only look at stand-alone Web applications, but in reality we can combine Web application modules, EJB modules and application client modules, as required, to form complete Java EE applications.

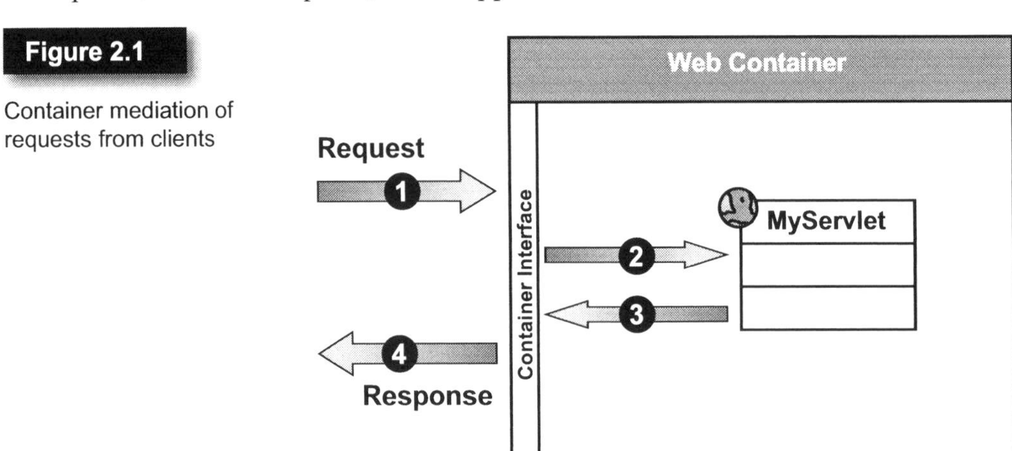

Figure 2.1

Container mediation of requests from clients

Web Containers

We've already said that the server handles many of the menial tasks of a developer for us. In order to provide these extra services, and to implement additional features such as security (the subject of Chapter 21) and filtering (Chapter 7), the container has to manage applications in a 'sandbox'. On the server, these sandboxes are called **containers**. Each Java EE module type has its own container, so there are separate ones for EJBs, applets, application clients, and the particular focus of our studies, the **Web container**. The Web container is where all Web applications (and hence components contained in the applications) are managed and executed.

Normally there will be only one Web container per Java EE server, and this container will enclose every application installed.

No two components in a container can communicate directly with one another. Instead, all communications must pass through the container interface. This enables the container to make decisions about the request being made; for example, 'is the current client permitted to access the resource being called, given the current security constraints?' Similarly, all external requests (for example, from a Web client) are also directed to the container, which then makes decisions about processing. The container even stands between clients and static resources such as HTML documents and images deployed in the container. This container mediation process is shown in Figures 2.1 and 2.2.

NOTE: *All* communications within or into a Web application are *always* moderated by the Web container. This allows the container to transpose its own services (such as protocol management and security) on top of those created by the application developer.

Figure 2.2

Container mediation of requests between components in the same application

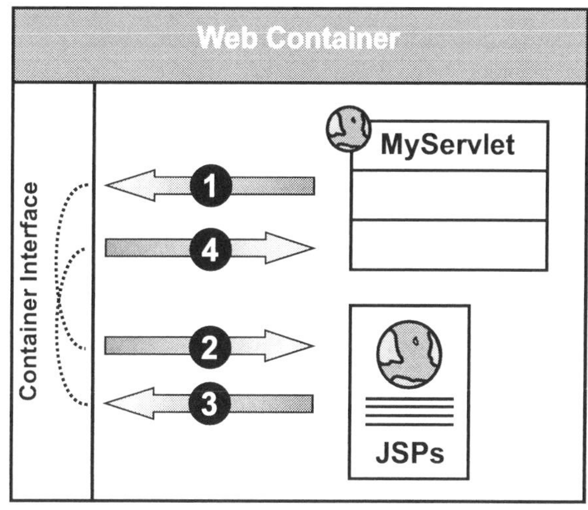

Web Application Contexts

2

All applications are run in the same container, since to start a new container for every application would eat up so much server memory and processor resources that the server might crash. But, you're saying, what about components in one application having the same name as those in another? For example, consider a compiled servlet class called `Router` executing in both of two applications. The container would load the `Router` servlet in one application and then go to load it in the other. If the two were the same, there would be no problem, but one might be a newer edition than the other, or even more probably, completely different. Which one does the container use as the `Router` class?

To prevent this problem from occurring, there is a virtual 'divide' between one application and another. This is achieved by assigning each application its own unique **context root**, often abbreviated to simply its **context**, which is a path name relative to the Java EE server's root. The context is assigned to the application the first time it is deployed. When a request is made from a client to a resource falling under this exact path, the container processes the request and knows which application to look in for the required resources.

Now that we have *logically* (not physically) isolated components in one application from those in another, the container can run a new `ClassLoader` for each application. Hence, classes loaded by the container for one application are completely insulated from those in any other application. The class responsible for class loading is `java.lang.ClassLoader`, found in the core Java API.

Communication between Applications

This solution may seem to present another problem however: since the classes in one application are loaded using a different `ClassLoader` (in a different 'context' as it were) then how can classes (including complied servlets and JSPs) in one application 'talk' to those in another–how can one resource call another in a different application to request its help? Surely classes loaded with one `ClassLoader` cannot 'see' classes loaded by another?

Bring on the solution–the good old container. Since the container intervenes in *every* call between components (as well as from external clients), the container knows when a component from one application is calling another from a different application. It can then act to execute the resource being called separately, process the data returned from it, and send this data back to the calling component. This is a slightly more cumbersome process for the developer than calling an object instance directly (as in a stand-alone client application), but the benefits for a server far outweigh this minor inconvenience (don't get frustrated with the extra typing; tell yourself that it's for your own good, and if that fails, for the good of your application). We will see how to communicate between applications in Chapters 4 and 6.

NOTE: The servlet specification recommends that classes be loaded from the application before looking in the container's shared stores; Tomcat uses the order `/WEB-INF/classes`, `/WEB-INF/lib`, then shared container classes. However, this behaviour is not guaranteed; classes at the container-level may be loaded in preference to those at the application-level. This will always be the case for core Java classes (e.g. those in `java.*` and `javax.*`) and container implementation classes. Be aware that naming conflicts between classes at the container- and application-levels can cause problems.

Figure 2.3

The virtual divide created by the unique context roots of each application

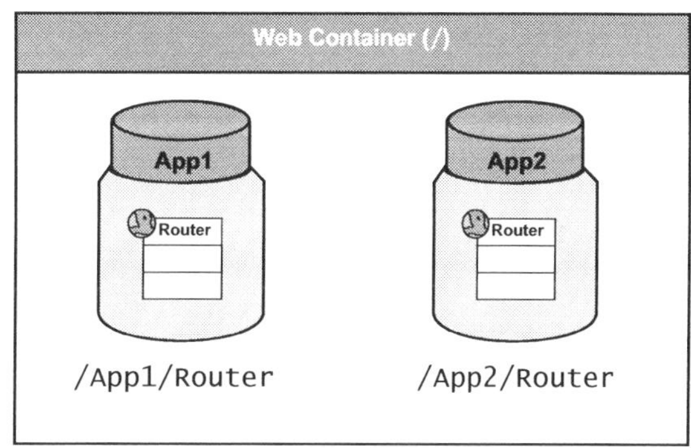

Figure 2.4

Communications between applications pass through the container interface

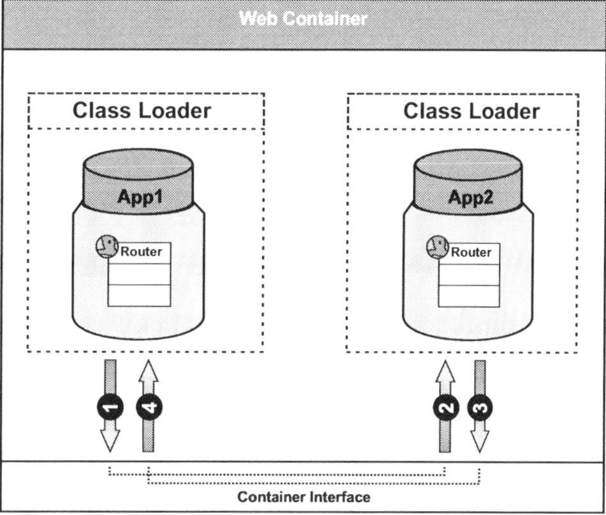

Packaging Applications

There are two possible methods to use when deploying an application to the server:

- Upload all files unpackaged to the server, creating directories where necessary and arranging files separately.
- Package all related application files together into a single **Web application archive (WAR)** file and upload this single file.

The first approach promotes the development and testing phases of an application's life cycle, since it is easy to make modifications to single files and upload these separately. The latter combines all files for a single application together–and as such is much easier to manage if multiple uploads need to be made, or if the bundle is being distributed as a complete application. The second approach should always be followed when the application has been tested and no further changes need to be made.

The exam objectives require that we have a solid understanding of the WAR file structure–and it's easy marks. Expect 2-3 questions (or more if you're lucky) on the exam to be on the structure and deployment of an application. Out of the total of 69, that's a good 3-4% on average, so don't throw these easy marks away by not learning the material. Not much thinking involved–honest!

WAR Files

A Web application archive (WAR) is similar to a JAR file in composition, but it has a well-defined content structure as we shall see shortly. A WAR is used to contain all the files for a single application, as well as the metadata which describes the application to the container. When deployed, a WAR file is given a context root, and at this point, we can consider the WAR file to *be* the Web application, as there is a one-to-one mapping between applications and WAR files: each WAR file represents one application, and one application is represented by only one WAR file.

WAR files can be built using a standard JAR tool (they have the same file format), but should be named with a `.war` extension and not the normal `.jar` extension.

In a complete Java EE application, many WAR files, with other supporting JARs, may be combined into a single **enterprise application archive (EAR)** file which becomes the entire Java EE application to be deployed. If only one WAR file makes up the complete Java EE application, then an EAR is not required.

Context Paths

The context root is unique for each application. It also acts as a URL path from the root of the Java EE Web server to the application running inside the container. Files deployed which are not contained in a WAR are added to the 'default' context, which is at the root of the Web server. This is another reason why WARs are advantageous – all related files are contained under the same context.

For example, if the Java EE Web server's default path was set to `http://domain.ext/` and the context for an application is `/shop/catalogue`, then the full URL to the application's root would be: `http://domain.ext/shop/catalogue`.

For clarity, a certain set of notations have been devised for context-based URLs. For example, one servlet can call another using one of two URL formats:

- **Relative URLs**
  Paths of this nature have no opening forward slash, and are interpreted relative to the path of the calling servlet. For example, `config/data.xml` called from a servlet at the location `/shop/catalogue/` would result in the following file being accessed by the servlet: `/shop/catalogue/config/data.xml`.

- **Context-relative URLs**
  These paths are based upon the context of the application, not the location of the servlet. Context-relative paths always begin with a forward-slash. For example, if `/config/data.xml` was referenced from a servlet at location `/shop/catalogue/` (or in fact *any* servlet at *any* location), the file accessed is `/config/data.xml` from the application's root.

When an application is deployed, the context root is also given with a forward-slash. This time the path is relative to the 'default' context, which is simply the Java EE Web server's pre-configured root. Thus, a context root of `/products` on a server with Java EE root `http://www.wholesaler.com/` results in the newly deployed application being located (and hence accessed) at `http://www.wholesaler.com/products/`.

NOTE: Any path which is relative to the context of the application, in the case of a component, or relative to the root of the Web server, in the case of a deployed application, *begins with a mandatory forward-slash.*

WAR Structure

A WAR file is deployed to a context relative to the Web server. Inside the WAR, static and JSP files can either be stored in the WAR root, or in other subdirectories inside the WAR. When appended to the context root for the application, the path of a resource inside the WAR becomes the URL of that resource.

For example, consider Figure 2.5. For a client to access the `photo.gif` file contained in the `/pages/images` directory inside the WAR of an application installed to the `/pr-app` context, the following URL would be used: `/pr-app/pages/images/photo.gif` (relative to the Web server's root). Other public paths (relative to the Web server's root) are shown alongside.

Note that Figure 2.5 depicts only the paths to static resources like images and HTML files which do not leverage the power of dynamic processing. As we shall see in subsequent chapters, dynamic resources are mapped to public URLs rather differently from static resources, whose public URL is determined simply by their location (path) in the WAR.

Figure 2.6 shows also a special directory with the name `WEB-INF`. This is required for a WAR to be valid, which is just as well since the container makes heavy use of it. Essentially, it is the presence of this directory and its required contents which differentiates a WAR file from a standard JAR file. Since it is a special case, it deserves a section to itself.

The WEB-INF Directory

All public directories in a WAR map to a URL path accessible to clients. However, the `/WEB-INF` directory is private in nature, accessible only to the Web container in which the application is deployed; although the container is able to access it in its

Public content of a WAR archive

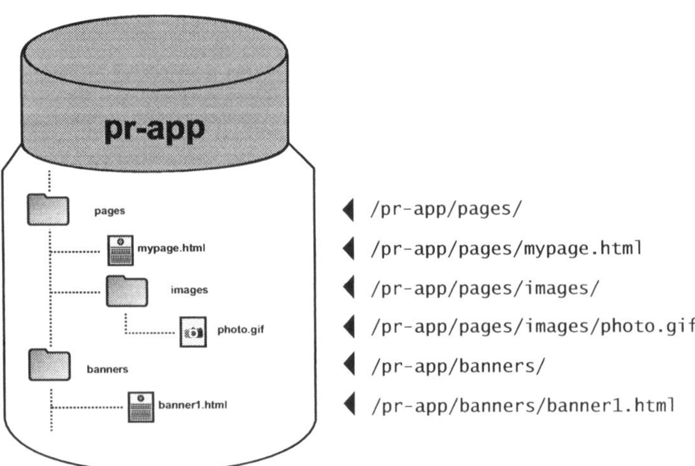

entirety, other applications cannot. Outside the application archive, this directory simply appears not to exist.

This makes it useful for a number of things. Top of the list comes configuration data storage, for example, password files for databases and configuration information about the deployed application can be stored here. We certainly don't want the former to be accessible by the client as this would constitute a breach of security of our server. The latter *could* be displayed to the client, but it isn't very useful – the Internet's a large and confusing enough place as it is, let's not add to it any further! Additionally, your next-door neighbour closet hacker might just use it to gain information about the site which may allow him to find a loop-hole in an apparently otherwise robust design.

The second most popular suggestion for its use is for fragment files. I have to watch what I say here since a new JSP feature is officially known as JSP Fragments, but in this case I'm talking about fragments of, for instance, an HTML page. For example, suppose all pages in the site have a common banner design. Each page could import this banner to save having to code for it explicitly everytime it's used, but in order to do so the banner can only be a code snippet, and not a complete page. We assume that the importing servlet/JSP will fill in the other details on the page for us. If a client could get hold of the banner it wouldn't be much use to them: the HTML code would be incomplete and pretty useless on its own. To conceal the banner's existence from the outside world, it is placed in the `/WEB-INF` directory.

NOTE: In general terms, if a resource is to be used internally within the application only, and at no time needs to be directly accessible to other applications or the client, put it in the `/WEB-INF` directory inside the archive.

Figure 2.6

Private content of a WAR in /WEB-INF/

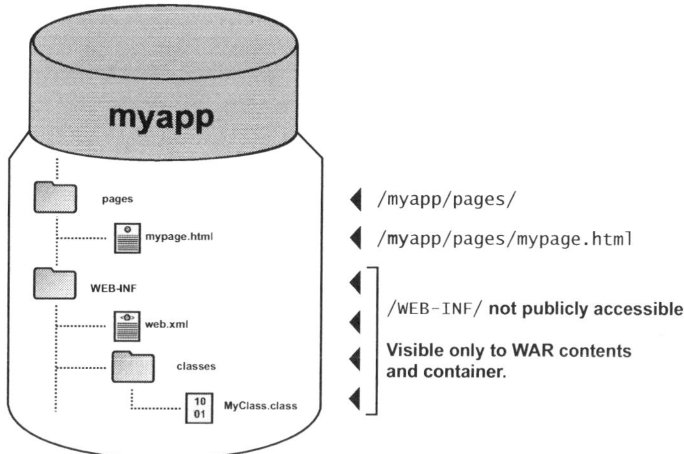

2

We are generally free to put private content directly in, or in any subdirectory of, the `/WEB-INF` directory and name the files whatever we please. These files are then accessed from components in the same application, using request dispatching mechanisms and static inclusion techniques which we discuss at several points later, by specifying the context-relative path `/WEB-INF/` followed by the path inside the `/WEB-INF` directory to the required resource. Figure 2.6 includes a visual reminder that this directory is application-private.

However, as with anything in computing there are exceptions (nothing to do with `java.lang.Exception` though!). There are a few reserved directories inside the `/WEB-INF/` private path which are used for special functions. These are:

- **/WEB-INF/classes/**
  Used for the storage of all compiled Java classes required by the application. This directory is automatically included in the `ClassLoader`'s `classpath` when the application is deployed, so no further work is required by the developer to use classes contained herein.
- **/WEB-INF/lib/**
  Place JAR libraries of classes in this subdirectory. As with the `classes` subdirectory, the `ClassLoader` will automatically look for classes in the JAR files here without further intervention from the developer.
- **/WEB-INF/tags/**
  Used for the storage of JSP tag files; Chapter 19 is dedicated to the subject of tag files, while Chapter 20 looks at their deployment into the WAR.

NOTE: The first two directories given previously are for *all* forms of classes. This includes compiled servlets, JavaBeans and any other useful utility classes required by the application. Servlets must be compiled into `.class` files and placed into these directories to work. URL-to-servlet mappings are made in the deployment descriptor. Additionally, classes located in `/WEB-INF/classes/` must be in subdirectories such that the path of each class matches its package declaration.

Figure 2.7 shows a summary of the standard `/WEB-INF` directory structure.

The Deployment Descriptor

As well as the previous `/WEB-INF` subdirectories, the `/WEB-INF/web.xml` file is required to be present in every application archive. This is the XML-formatted deployment descriptor (sometimes informally referred to as the 'DD') for the

Figure 2.7

Summary of /WEB-INF/ directory structure

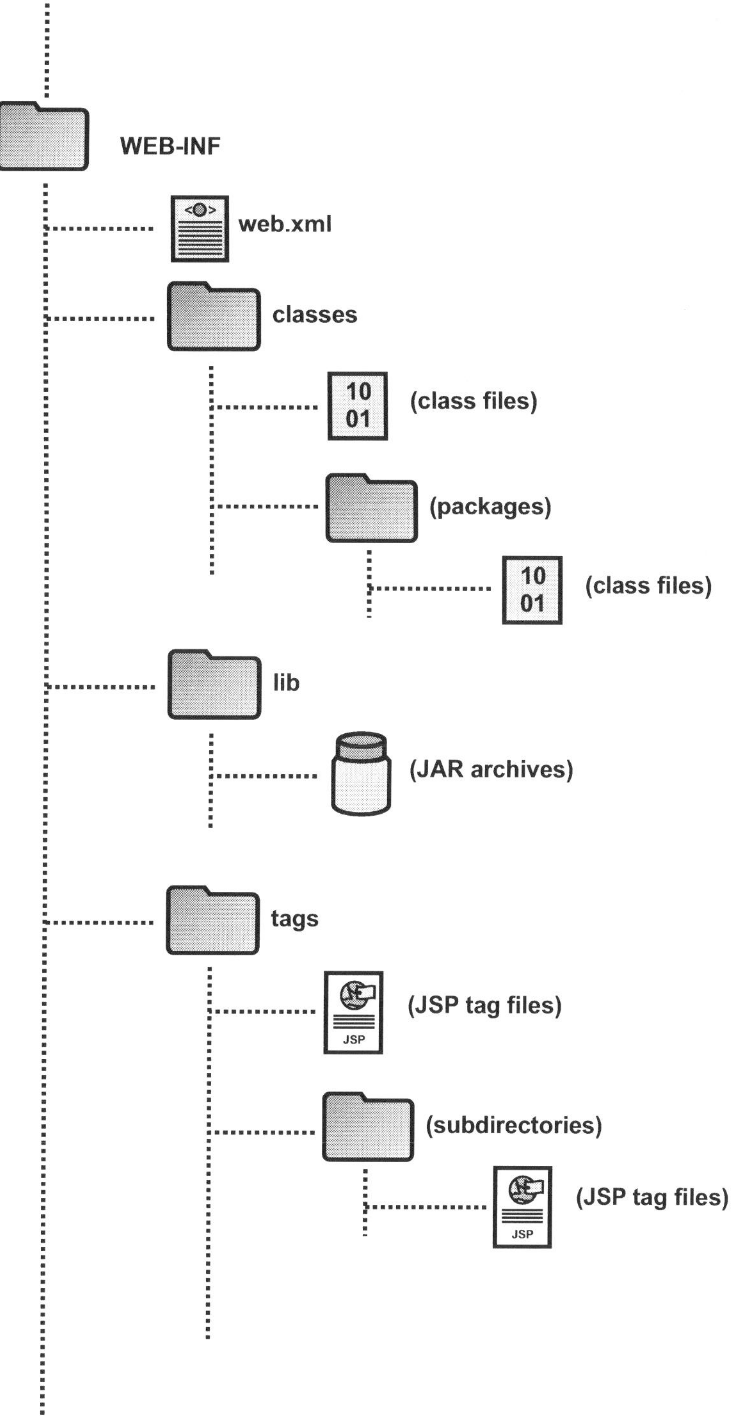

application, and provides metadata information about the application and WAR to the container.

We discuss the deployment descriptor syntax required for the exam in Chapter 10. A beginner's book would likely choose to introduce some deployment descriptor syntax as servlet and JSP concepts are introduced. However, since I assume that you already have some Java EE knowledge, I have not favoured this method here. Instead a whole chapter is devoted to the topic of descriptor syntax, which should help you to revise it thoroughly and consolidate any loose ends you may have in this area. I would hope also that the chapter acts as good reference material as well, so that when you've finished the exam and come out with the mark that reflects what a shining programmer you are (I don't give money-back guarantees by the way), you won't simply toss the book aside and let it gather dust.

Key Java EE Web Components

Before we round off this chapter, let's look briefly at the key types of component which we'll be packaging inside WAR files to build a Web application. Practically the entire rest of this book concentrates on these technologies in this order:

- **Servlets**
  The key building block for any Web application. Servlets are effectively Java classes on the Web server. Combined with the power of the container, they take care of protocol-dependent issues, leaving the developer to concentrate on the application and the component-specific code that makes the servlet do its job. Servlet technology is the subject of Part II.
- **JavaServer Pages**
  JSPs are essentially dynamic documents. A JSP is written like a standard HTML or XML document, but with embedded Java syntax allowing dynamic content to be inserted with ease. JSP components are typically used to create front-end templates for returned data. JSPs are the subject of Part III.
- **Tag Libraries**
  Tag libraries are essentially Java classes which encapsulate standard functionality required by multiple JSP components. If a set of JSPs must each perform a similar task as part of their document processing, then tag libraries are usually a convenient solution. They promote reuse of standard code. Standard and custom tag libraries are also the subject of Part III.

Finally we end the book by taking a look at some extension material such as the Web application security model and some standard Java EE design patterns.

Revision Questions

1 **A Web container...** **(choose three)**

- A is a unit used to execute a single Web application;
- B is a unit which contains all Web applications deployed on the server;
- C provides the interface between components in one application and components in another;
- D provides the interface between components in the same application;
- E is an archive file used to contain all the components in an application.

2 **The role of a Web application's context root is?** **(choose one)**

- A To distinguish components in one application from one another
- B To distinguish components in one application from those in another
- C To allow different applications to be deployed to the same location on the server
- D To secure private directories from unauthorised access
- E To specify the location of the deployment descriptor

3 **The common mechanism for packaging a Web application is?** **(choose one)**

- A The Enterprise archive (EAR)
- B The Web application archive (WAR)
- C The Web module file
- D A Resource Adaptor archive (RAR)
- E The deployment descriptor

4 **An example of a context-relative URL is:** **(choose one)**

- A index.jsp
- B ../documents/mydoc.pdf
- C context/images/logo.gif
- D /catalogue/prices.xml
- E ./downloads/update.exe

5 **The private directory (accessible only by the container and to components in the application) in a WAR is:** **(choose one)**

- A /WAR-INF/
- B /META-INF/

2

- C /private/
- D /WEB-INF/
- E Any directory being marked as private in the deployment descriptor

6 The location of the deployment descriptor is? **(choose one)**

- A /META-INF/web.xml
- B /WEB-INF/deploy.xml
- C /WEB-INF/web.xml
- D /web.xml
- E /deploy.xml

7 The location in a WAR for storing individual Java class files is? **(choose one)**

- A /classes/
- B /library/
- C /WEB-INF/classes/
- D /WEB-INF/lib/
- E /WEB-INF/library/
- F /WEB-INF/components/

8 The location in a WAR for storing JARs of packaged classes is? **(choose one)**

- A /WAR-INF/jars/
- B /META-INF/
- C /private/
- D /WEB-INF/lib/
- E Any directory being marked as private in the deployment descriptor

9 What is special to the container about the following path in a WAR: /secure/catalogue.jsp? **(choose one)**

- A catalogue.jsp can only be accessed by components in the same application
- B catalogue.jsp can only be accessed by components in the same Web application container on the same server
- C HTTPS (secure HTTP) communications must be established with the client in order to access the resource catalogue.jsp
- D Authentication is required before catalogue.jsp can be accessed
- E Nothing is special, it's just another public resource

Answers to Revision Questions

1 **Correct answers: B, C, D**

A is incorrect because the container manages all Web applications within a server instance; each application does not normally have its own container. E is incorrect since the container is a large software architecture running on the J2EE server, not just a single archive.

2 **Correct answer: B**

A is incorrect since the context root applies to the *entire* application and not to individual components within an application. C is incorrect because the context root also becomes the basis of the URL at which the application resides – each application must have its own unique context root and hence URL location. D is too specific: private directories must be configured as part of the application's configuration – they are not dependent on the application's context root. E is wrong since the context root points to the WAR as a whole, not the deployment descriptor – the container first locates the WAR for a given context root, and *then* must search within the WAR for the deployment descriptor.

3 **Correct answer: B**

An EAR is a collection of various types of J2EE modules, so A is incorrect. C is wrong, since a 'Web module file' per se does not exist. The deployment descriptor lies within the application; it does not contain it, so E is incorrect. D is incorrect as RARs contain data support classes (like JDBC database drivers) as part of the J2EE Connector API.

4 **Correct answer: D**

A is a URL relative to the current directory so is incorrect. B is a relative URL which points to mydoc.pdf in the documents directory (a sibling of the current directory). C is a relative URL which points to a sub-directory inside the current directory. E is also a path relative to the current directory.

5 **Correct answer: D**

A, B and C are not treated as special directories by the container – instead they have public visibility. E is incorrect; the deployment descriptor does not provide any such functionality for paths in an application

6 **Correct answer: C**

A, D and E do not point to the WAR's /WEB-INF directory. B points to a resource in the private /WEB-INF directory, but not the deployment descriptor.

7 **Correct answer: C**

8 **Correct answer: D**

9 **Correct answer: E**

A and B are wrong – only the /WEB-INF directory is private. C is incorrect – there is no evidence that an HTTPS connection is mandated (a path alone cannot indicate this). D is also incorrect – while declarative security can be enforced for the /secure (or any other) directory in the WAR, this is not enabled by default.

I suppose this was a bit of a trick question, but you never know if the exam itself may contain a trick or two, so watch out!

PART 2

Servlets

Chapter Overview

3. **Servlet Basics**

   Introduces the essential interfaces and classes in the Servlet API.

4. **Servlet Contexts**

   Examines how servlets can communicate with the container to obtain information about the Web application they are executing in.

5. **Requests and Responses**

   Detailed coverage of how (especially HTTP) requests are handled and how responses can be generated; includes HTTP headers and cookies.

6. **Request Dispatching and Wrappers**

   Building cooperating components is very useful, often necessary. This chapter reveals how to convey requests between different components.

7. **Filters**

   Use filters to implement 'pluggable' behaviour for handling requests.

8. **Asynchronous Requests**

   Learn the techniques to successfully build rich client-side applications.

9. **Sessions**

   Use these to persist user state across multiple HTTP requests.

10. **Application Deployment**

    Deploy Web applications using the Deployment Descriptor.

11. **Modular Deployment**

    Introduces annotations and Web Fragments as powerful tools.

12. **Resource Injection**

    Lets the container take the strain of managing external resources.

In this chapter you'll:

- Learn what servlets are.
- Be introduced to the Servlet interface and the two main abstract classes.
- Discover the servlet lifecycle.
- Understand how requests are processed and responses generated.
- Clarify how delegation occurs for HTTP requests.

3 Servlet Basics

Servlets lie at the heart of every Java Web application. They are normally responsible for most of the processing required by the application – for example, updating a database with information received from a client, displaying the current date and time amongst page content, or mediating a complete request and servicing an appropriate response.

Some beginners may be misled into believing that programming servlets is a radical change from programming objects in Java – that servlets are something mystical and wonderful. The truth is that a servlet is quite simply a special type of class, one that implements the `javax.servlet.Servlet` interface (its still wonderful in its own way though). A servlet is constructed in *just the same way* as a conventional Java class implementing an interface. Before the servlet is deployed, you must convert it to Java bytecode using the standard Java compilation tools, and it is this bytecode class which is then distributed with the application, normally into `/WEB-INF/classes/`, or when packaged into a JAR with other servlets/classes, into the `/WEB-INF/lib` directory of a WAR. So you see, a *servlet is a Java class* and a *servlet instance is a Java object* – if you're happy with Java objects, and I hope you are, then there's nothing surprising there!

A small application may rely on one single servlet to do all the dynamic processing for the entire Web tier – in this sense, a servlet can be considered to represent the entire Web application as the processing part of the application. However, more generally, a servlet is just one small (but still highly important) part of a much larger architecture. The ideal servlet is a component which is designed to handle only one particular type of task, and to do that job as well as possible; this servlet should interact with other servlets (each with their own purpose) to accomplish more complicated processing.

Generic Servlets

A servlet at its most basic must implement the `javax.servlet.Servlet` interface, and don't you forget it. However, most servlets provide similar basic coarse-grained functionality, so to save us having to write the same maintenance code for every servlet, there is one abstract class of particular interest: `javax.servlet.GenericServlet`.

The `GenericServlet` class implementation is protocol-independent, so it doesn't matter if it has to respond to HTTP or FTP requests, raw TCP/IP requests, or a protocol which we made up last week. This gives the entire servlet model an enormous

Figure 3.1

Servlet class hierarchy

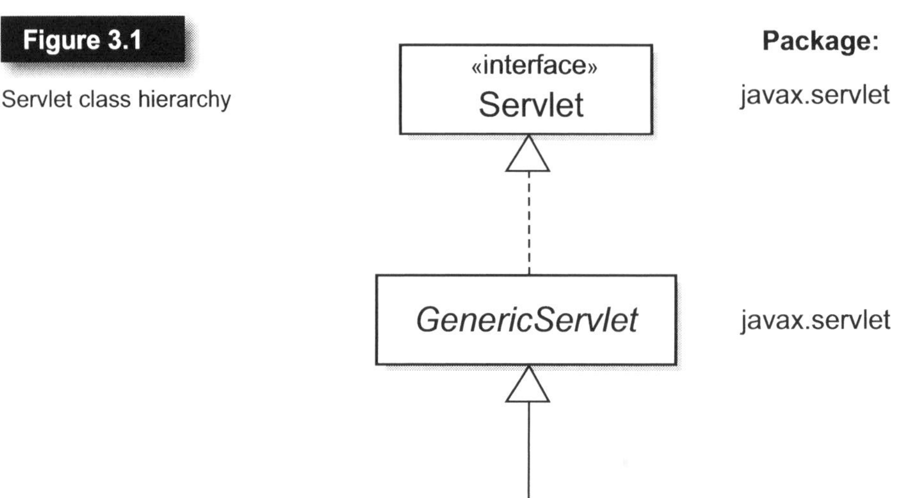

3

amount of flexibility, as it isn't tied to a single protocol or implementation like other languages usually are.

In a Web application however, the lack of any protocol-dependent processing in a class means we have to do more typing and add even more maintenance code to any subclass we create. Since HTTP is the most well known and widely used protocol on the Web, the API also includes one more abstract subclass of `GenericServlet`: `javax.servlet.http.HttpServlet`. Note that this class resides in the `javax.servlet.`**`http`** package. This is because all HTTP-based servlets are types of servlet fit for a specific task only (i.e. involvement in *HTTP* transmissions) and do not fit the protocol-independent nature of the core servlet specification.

This hierarchy of interfaces and classes is shown in Figure 3.1. Generally developers find themselves subclassing `HttpServlet`. For this reason, the exam concentrates more on the methods in this class than either of its parent classes and we cover it exclusively in the next section.

Servlet Life Cycles

The life cycle of an object describes the sequence of steps that the object goes through during its existence. A simple example would be a helper object in a client application: it is created (instantiated) to do a task, performs that task (through method calls and attribute updates), and is then discarded and ultimately destroyed by Java's garbage collector.

However, there are more stages to the life of a servlet because it has to execute inside the Web container, which in turn imposes additional requirements on the life cycle. Since the exam is pretty hot on candidates knowing what life cycles are and how to deal with them, it's something we really ought to concentrate on now. There are also important life cycles for other objects; we'll discuss those elsewhere when appropriate.

At run time, a servlet goes through the following five stages (just learn them):

1. Before the servlet class can be used, it must be **loaded** by the application's class loader. This is normally performed the first time the servlet class is required.
2. If the container is to be able to call the servlet, it must be **instantiated** like any other Java object. The container does this by calling the default (no-argument) constructor, which typically has an empty implementation (often the compiler-generated default constructor will suffice).
3. Next the container updates the servlet with information; this is called **initialisation** of the servlet, and is performed through the `init` method.
4. Now the servlet is 'alive and kicking' on the server, it can actually do some processing. This stage of its life is referred to as its **service** period, since it is now able to *service requests* by delivering appropriate responses.
5. Finally the servlet can be **destroyed**.

This is summarised graphically in Figure 3.2.

The last stage is only normally performed when the server is shut-down, the application is undeployed, or there are no requests to a servlet for a long period of time (although destruction of the servlet is extreme even for this case). Normally a single servlet instance runs without respite from the moment the application is started to the moment it is undeployed. This helps to conserve resources since if the servlet had to be instantiated and initialised for every request, we would soon run out of memory on a busy server, and the application would grind to a halt. Sometimes a small pool of servlet instances are maintained by the container, each request then being serviced by one of the available instances which isn't already servicing a different request. The use of a pool is not recommended (and in fact should be avoided) since it requires more memory; instead, a single instance is normally used. If a container receives multiple requests simultaneously, it will use the *same* service implementation of the *same* servlet concurrently to service the request. Inevitably there are a number of concurrency and threading issues here, but it is not appropriate to discuss these yet. However, a brief word of caution is appropriate: always ensure that service method implementations are safe from concurrent thread access; most problems can often be avoided by always using

3

Figure 3.2

Servlet life cycle

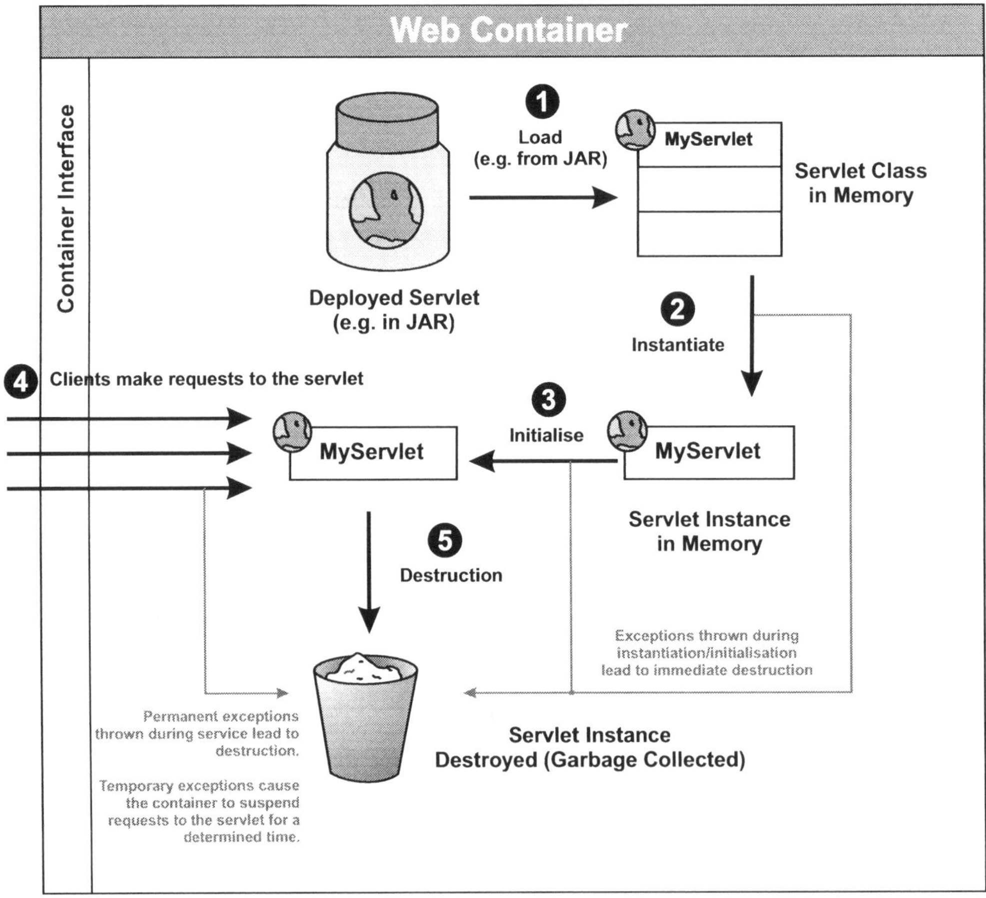

variables which are *local to the service method* and *never* using instance variables which may change over time.

Now we'll look at the above five stages in more detail.

Servlet Class Loading

Each application has its own class loader; it uses this to search for and load classes from the Web application archive's `/WEB-INF/classes` directory, and from JAR files within `/WEB-INF/lib/`. Since servlets are just ordinary Java classes, they are loaded in just the same way as regular classes by the container before being instantiated for the first time. Recall that due to different applications having different class loaders, a servlet in one application cannot communicate with a servlet in another directly–calls must pass through the container interface. Also recall that servlets stored in the application *should* (but do not have to) take priority over servlets at the container level (i.e. those installed directly in the container and not in a specific application) due to the order in which the class loaders are invoked.

Servlet Instantiation

Each servlet must be instantiated by the container in a generic way, since the container does not know what protocol(s) the servlet actually supports. In a client application, the constructors of each class normally contain different sets of arguments which help to instantiate the object with some default values for that instance. However, since the container does not know what the servlet it is instantiating does, it uses the *default* (no-argument) constructor to create a servlet instance. The setting of parameters is not performed here. You should either provide an explicit no-argument constructor, or omit any/all constructors from the servlet class.

The container will use a mechanism similar to the `newInstance()` method of the servlet's `Class` object to get a new instance; this is the reason why a servlet must always have a no-argument constructor and why initialisation is performed after (and not at the same time as) instantiation.

Initialisation

There must be some way for the container to communicate configuration information to the servlet, and as we know, this isn't through the constructor. Instead, each servlet must provide an implementation of the following method defined in the `Servlet` interface:

- **`void init(ServletConfig)`**
  This method should be implemented by a concrete `Servlet` class to initialise that servlet to its default state. Initialisation (configuration) information for the servlet can be found in the `ServletConfig` class, a discussion of which can be found in Chapter 4.

The `GenericServlet` class implements this method and saves the `ServletConfig` parameter as a private attribute inside the servlet. It also defines one more initialisation method:

- **`void init()`**
  A no-argument initialisation method. Subclasses should override this method in preference to `init(ServletConfig)` for convenience. This method is called after the `GenericServlet`'s implementation of `init(ServletConfig)` completes. This enables us to concern ourselves with our own configuration, without worrying about the storage of the `ServletConfig` object.

3

The saved `ServletConfig` object can later be retrieved (either in the no-argument `init` method, or later in the servlet's life) using this `GenericServlet` method:

- **`ServletConfig getServletConfig()`**
  Returns the `ServletConfig` object stored during the call to the `GenericServlet`'s implementation of `init(ServletConfig)`.

These initialisation processes are summarised in Figure 3.3.

Initialisation Exceptions

During the configuration stage of a servlet's life, i.e. when the `init(ServletConfig)` method is called by the container, the servlet can throw exceptions. This might be for a number of reasons, the most common being because a required persistent storage mechanism is offline and configuration information cannot be retrieved, or required initialisation parameters cannot be found, or are not valid.

Whatever the reason, all of the `init` methods can throw a `ServletException` to signal that some error occurred during configuration. If this is the case, the container will not continue to initialise and run this instance of the servlet. Instead, the instance will move directly to the last stage of its life and the garbage collector (without passing 'go'!). The `destroy` method which we examine shortly, will not be called if an exception was thrown.

Figure 3.3

Initialisation of a GenericServlet

`GenericServlet` implements `init(ServletConfig)` which it inherits from `Servlet`.

This implementation first **stores a local copy** of the `ServletConfig` used for initialisation. This instance can later be retrieved via `getServletConfig()`.

It then **delegates** all processing to the no-argument `init` method, which has an empty implementation in `GenericServlet`.

Subclasses **should override** `init()` to provide initialisation processing, but not `init(ServletConfig)`.

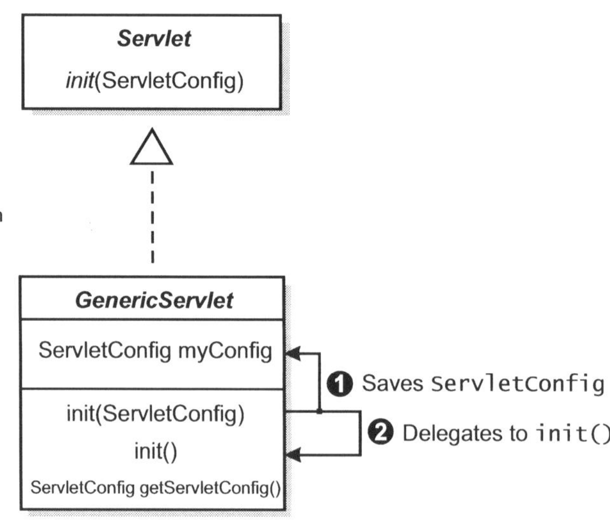

The container will then have to reinstantiate a different instance and try again. If it is expected that the service which wasn't available will not be available for some further time, then the `init` methods can throw an `UnavailableException`, a subclass of `ServletException` which marks a component as being 'offline' for a given period. An `UnavailableException` contains details of how long a temporary problem is likely to persist, or whether the problem is permanent, in which case the container will not try to reinstate a servlet and the component will be removed permanently from service until the application is redeployed. Some containers may try to reinstantiate a servlet if a `ServletException` is thrown; others instead mark the component as permanently unavailable.

The destroy Method

We defined the last step of the servlet's life as destruction; however, just as occurs with the standard J2SE garbage collector, we can never really be sure when a servlet instance has been destroyed and its memory allocation released. Instead, all we can be sure of is when the container *requests* that the servlet be destroyed. At this point in the servlet's long life, the container calls the following method on the `Servlet` object:

- **`void destroy()`**
  Called after the container has removed a servlet from service. This method is invoked to give the servlet a chance to release some extra resources, such as connections to persistent storage mechanisms (databases) and any references to costly JavaBean helpers it may have used.

The `destroy` method takes no arguments and throws no exceptions – it doesn't have to, given that sometime after the method completes the servlet will no longer exist anyway (at the garbage collector's convenience of course!).

As we said earlier, this method will not be called when an exception is thrown during initialisation, since it is assumed that the source of the exception was that all of the required resources were not configured – in which case they will not be available to be released anyway.

NOTE: An invocation of `destroy()` *indicates* that a servlet is being removed from service. It does not actually mean that the instance will be garbage collected immediately, and in the case of an exception being thrown at initialisation, it will not be invoked.

Request Servicing

For a stand-alone object in a client application, the service process would normally involve using a variety of methods, each of which accomplishes a different task. However, since the container must know the signature of the method across *all* servlet instances providing any protocol support, the `Servlet` interface defines one single method used for servicing requests:

- **`void service(ServletRequest, ServletResponse)`**
  This method is called when a request (of any type and of any protocol) is made to the servlet. This is the only service-oriented method which the container is aware exists for any servlet.

Service Exceptions

A `ServletException` (or `UnavailableException` subclass) may be thrown from any service methods, in the case that the servlet in unable to service a given request temporarily or permanently.

If the failure is permanent, an appropriate `UnavailableException` will be thrown. The container will remove the servlet from service, calling the `destroy` method, and not create any more instances. Instead, any further requests for that servlet will return a 404 ('Not Found') HTTP status code, giving the client the impression that the servlet simply does not exist!

If the failure is temporary, the exception thrown will be `ServletException` or an appropriately formatted `UnavailableException`. In which case, the container may ask the client to try again later, and report a 503 ('Service Unavailable') HTTP status code. For a temporary situation, the component is not removed from service, but instead the container does not allow it to receive requests for the specified unavailable time. After this time, the container allows the servlet to continue servicing requests where it left off. If a pool of servlets exists, request servicing might be delegated to another servlet in the pool.

Some containers will automatically treat any service-related exceptions, of whatever type or duration, as permanent errors. This doesn't seem wise, but if that's the way things are, we'll just have to live with them.

As well as the standard `ServletExceptions`, the service method may throw an `IOException` because a resource (such as a database) could not be accessed or a stream threw an uncaught exception. `IOExceptions` are treated as temporary exceptions. An appropriate status code will be returned as the response. Figure 3.4 summarises the exceptions in the Servlet API.

Figure 3.4

Servlet exceptions class hierarchy

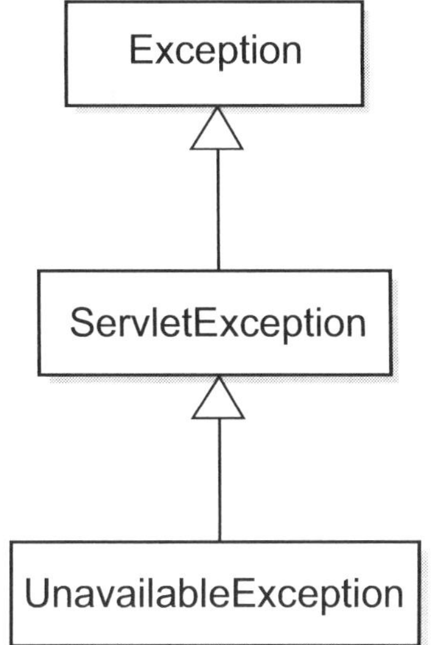

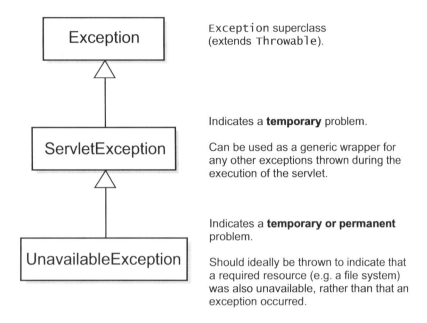

`Exception` superclass (extends `Throwable`).

Indicates a **temporary** problem.

Can be used as a generic wrapper for any other exceptions thrown during the execution of the servlet.

Indicates a **temporary or permanent** problem.

Should ideally be thrown to indicate that a required resource (e.g. a file system) was also unavailable, rather than that an exception occurred.

HTTP Servlets

Although the generic servlet API described in the previous section is designed to handle data conveyed over any protocol, practically very few Web containers support anything other than HTTP(S), the most well known and widely used protocol on the Web. For this reason, the API includes the abstract class `javax.servlet.http.HttpServlet`. along with an number of other helpful classes in the `javax.servlet.http` package. We will discover many of these throughout the book.

HTTP Request Servicing

An HTTP request has data associated with it which is uncommon to a variety of other formats. For example, HTTP can use cookies to store temporary data on the client, and use this mechanism to establish sessions (the subject of Chapter 9). For this reason, the following two interfaces exist in `javax.servlet.http`:

- `HttpServletRequest extends javax.servlet.ServletRequest`
- `HttpServletResponse extends javax.servlet.ServletResponse`

Both of these interfaces encapsulate useful information exclusively for HTTP.

3

As discussed previously, the container will always call the `Servlet`'s `service` method, as listed in the previous section. However, for an HTTP-based servlet, this isn't really sufficient, since a request can be in any one of the seven HTTP methods (e.g. GET, POST, PUT) and to make matters worse, the request and response objects used are not of types `javax.servlet.ServletRequest` and `javax.servlet.ServletResponse`, but of the protocol-dependent `javax.servlet.http.HttpServletRequest` and `javax.servlet.http.HttpServletReponse`, respectively.

Thankfully, `javax.servlet.http.HttpServlet` implements many of the `GenericServlet`'s methods concretely, an example of one being the standard `Servlet`'s `service` method. It also adds the following protected access method:

- **`protected void service(HttpServletRequest,HttpServletResponse)`**
  Delegation of processing responsibility is passed from the standard `service(ServletRequest,ServletResponse)` method to this one, explicitly casting the parameters to the HTTP variants in the course.

Now we *could* override this method in a subclass, with the knowledge that the request and response objects we are getting have already been cast to their HTTP variants. However, the `HttpServlet` class goes further to define concrete protected methods for each of the HTTP method types; for example, there's the `doGet` method for processing a GET request and the `doHead` method for HEAD requests. The protected `service` method scans the headers in the incoming HTTP request for the HTTP method type being used, and delegates processing further to the appropriate one of these methods.

This results in us being able to use a servlet method which is dependent upon both the *protocol* being used for communication with the client and the HTTP *method* used in the request. This makes our task very much shorter indeed.

Figure 3.5 shows a summary of the delegation procedure through which an HTTP and a non-HTTP request pass.

HttpServlet doXxx Methods

We saw the HTTP methods in Chapter 1. As a quick test, you should be able to recall all seven of them now. Turn the book over and have a go; the answers are given in Table 3.1.

Figure 3.5

HTTP Request Servicing Delegation Procedure

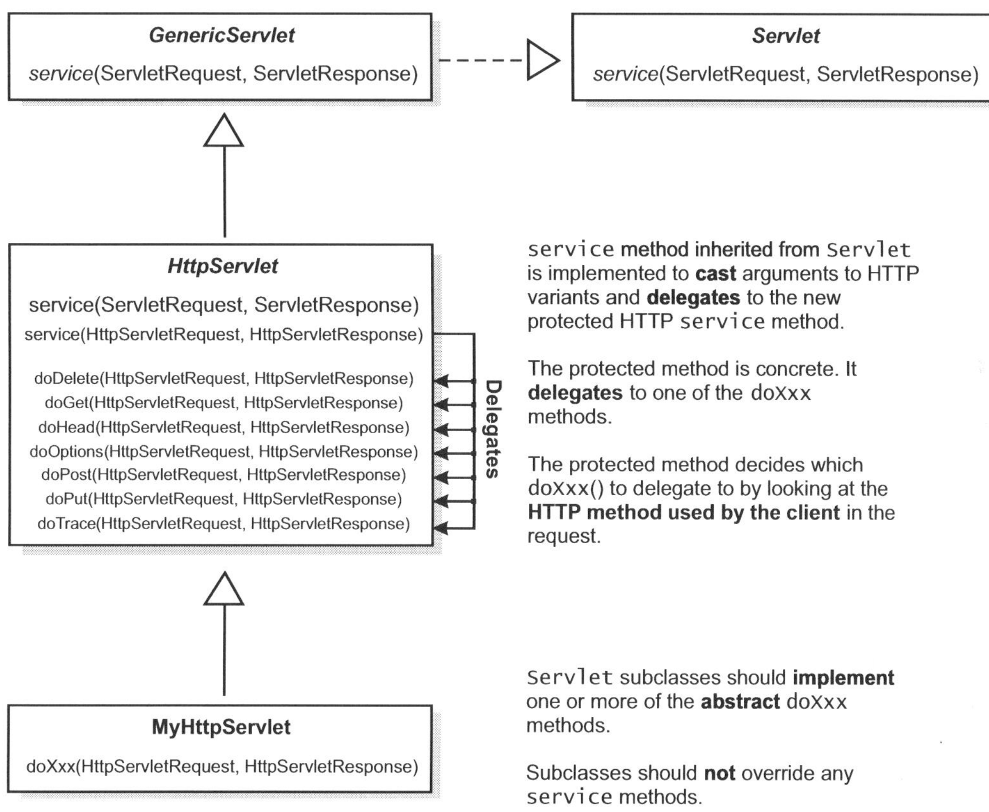

To summarise the discussion so far, an HTTP request to an `HttpServlet` subclass goes through a number of different steps:

1. A call to the public `service(ServletRequest, ServletResponse)` method by the container;
2. Delegation of this call to `HttpServlet`'s protected `service(HttpServletRequest, HttpServletResponse)` method;
3. The protected `service(HttpServletRequest, HttpServletResponse)` method then delegates to the appropriate `doXxx` method, depending on the HTTP method used for the request.

We will be concentrating on step 3 in this section.

3

Table 3.1 HTTP Method to HttpServlet Method Mappings

HTTP Method	Invoked HttpServlet Method Signature
GET	`doGet(HttpServletRequest, HttpServletResponse)`
POST	`doPost(HttpServletRequest, HttpServletResponse)`
HEAD	`doHead(HttpServletRequest, HttpServletResponse)`
PUT	`doPut(HttpServletRequest, HttpServletResponse)`
DELETE	`doDelete(HttpServletRequest, HttpServletResponse)`
OPTIONS	`doOptions(HttpServletRequest, HttpServletResponse)`
TRACE	`doTrace(HttpServletRequest, HttpServletResponse)`

There is a one-to-one mapping between an incoming HTTP method request type and the method in the `HttpServlet` class to which that request will be forwarded. This mapping is shown in Table 3.1.

If we let `Xxx` replace any particular HTTP method name in Table 3.1, then we can derive a general header of each method – needless to say, this and all the method names need to be learnt:

```
protected void doXxx(HttpServletRequest, HttpServletResponse)
throws ServletException, IOException
```

Apart from the method name, this header is the same as the protected `service` method found in the `HttpServlet` class. Note that all these methods are *concrete* with default implementations, although there is a prescribed subclassing routine.

Subclassing the doXxx() Methods

When you construct your own HTTP-based servlets, and extend `HttpServlet`, you are advised to implement one or more of the `doXxx` methods instead of overriding any of the `service` implementations. These are the exact guidelines laid down in the specification and the API documentation:

- Always override one of the methods for GET, POST, PUT or DELETE operations, most normally GET and/or POST.
- Any of these methods not overridden will cause an HTTP error to be returned as the response. In the case of HTTP/1.0, this will be the 400 'Bad Request' status code, and in the case of HTTP/1.1, this is the 405 'Method not Allowed' status code.

- The `doHead` method default implementation returns a header by delegating processing to the `doGet` method and then ignoring the body. This is a resource-intensive process; if you suspect that your clients are likely to make frequent use of HEAD requests, it is far better to provide your own implementation which returns the headers only, and does not process the body. Bear in mind however, that the HEAD method is defined to return the headers for the *GET* method, and no others. If the `doGet` method is not overridden, the `doHead` method should return the appropriate status code: either 400 for HTTP/1.0 or 405 for HTTP/1.1.
- The default `doOptions` and `doTrace` methods do not need to be overridden, unless for the latter you have specific requirements for a trace procedure.

Why use protected methods? To put it simply, the container always communicates with the servlet's public `service` method (the one with non-HTTP parameters). All the delegation of responsibility takes place within the implementations of methods *inside* the `HttpServlet` class. To reflect this encapsulation, all methods which are not exposed to the container and other external influences are given protected accessibility. When you subclass the `HttpServlet` class, you can either give the methods public accessibility (a *less* restrictive access modifier is always permitted on overrides) or protected accessibility, which is preferred.

Revision Questions

1 **All servlets implement which interface?** **(choose one)**

- A java.servlet.Servlet
- B javax.enterprise.Servlet
- C javax.servlet.Servlet
- D java.servlet.HttpServlet
- E javax.servlet.http.HttpServlet

2 **Which of the following are methods of the Servlet interface?** **(choose two)**

- A public void init()
- B public void init(ServletConfig)
- C public void service(HttpServletRequest, HttpServletResponse)
- D public void service(ServletRequest, ServletResponse)
- E public int service()

3 **Which abstract class can be extended to create a protocol-independent servlet?** **(choose one)**

- A javax.servlet.http.HttpServlet
- B javax.enterprise.ServletWrapper
- C javax.servlet.ServletAdapter
- D javax.servlet.GenericServlet
- E javax.servlet.ServletContext

4 **What methods does the abstract class in Question 3 declare, which are not found in any superclasses or implemented interfaces?** **(choose one)**

- A public ServletConfig getConfig()
- B public ServletContext getServletContext()
- C public void init()
- D public void init(ServletConfig)
- E public String getInitParameter(String)

5 **When extending GenericServlet, which of the following methods must be overridden?** **(choose one)**

- A public void destroy()

B public void service(ServletRequest, ServletResponse)

C public void init()

D public void init(ServletConfig)

E public ServletContext getServletContext()

6 **Place the five stages of the servlet life cycle in the correct order:**

Destruction

Instantiatation

Service

Class loading

Initialisation

7 **If a ServletException, and not a subclass, is thrown during execution of a Servlet's init method, what will happen?** **(choose two)**

A The container will immediately invoke destroy() and release the Servlet instance for garbage collection.

B The container suppresses the exception and invokes the service method as normal.

C The container attempts to invoke the init method again.

D The container immediately releases the Servlet instance for garbage collection, without invoking any other methods.

E The container attempts to instantiate and initialise another Servlet instance.

8 **Which checked exceptions are thrown by the service method?** **(choose three)**

A ServletException

B UnavailableException

C UnavailableServletException

D IOException

E Exception

3

9 **Which checked exceptions are thrown by destroy()?** **(choose one)**

- A DestructionException
- B ServletException
- C IOException
- D JspException
- E None

10 **Which abstract class or interface must be extended or implemented to provide an HTTP servlet?** **(choose one)**

- A javax.servlet.Servlet (interface)
- B javax.servlet.GenericServlet (interface)
- C javax.servlet.GenericServlet (abstract class)
- D javax.servlet.http.HttpServlet (abstract class)
- E javax.servlet.http.GenericHttpServlet (abstract class)

11 **Which of the following methods of the javax.servlet.http. HttpServlet class should be overridden by the servlet developer?** **(choose two)**

- A public void service(ServletRequest, ServletResponse)
- B protected void service(HttpServletRequest, HttpServletResponse)
- C protected void doGet(HttpServletRequest, HttpServletResponse)
- D protected void doOptions(HttpServletRequest, HttpServletResponse)
- E protected void doTrace(HttpServletRequest, HttpServletResponse)
- F protected void doPut(HttpServletRequest, HttpServletResponse)

12 **For a GET request, and assuming no exceptions are thrown, place the following HttpServlet methods in the order they are invoked, directly or indirectly, by the container:**

protected void service(HttpServletRequest, HttpServletResponse)
public void service(ServletRequest, ServletResponse)
public void init()
public void init(ServletConfig)
protected void doGet(HttpServletRequest, HttpServletResponse)

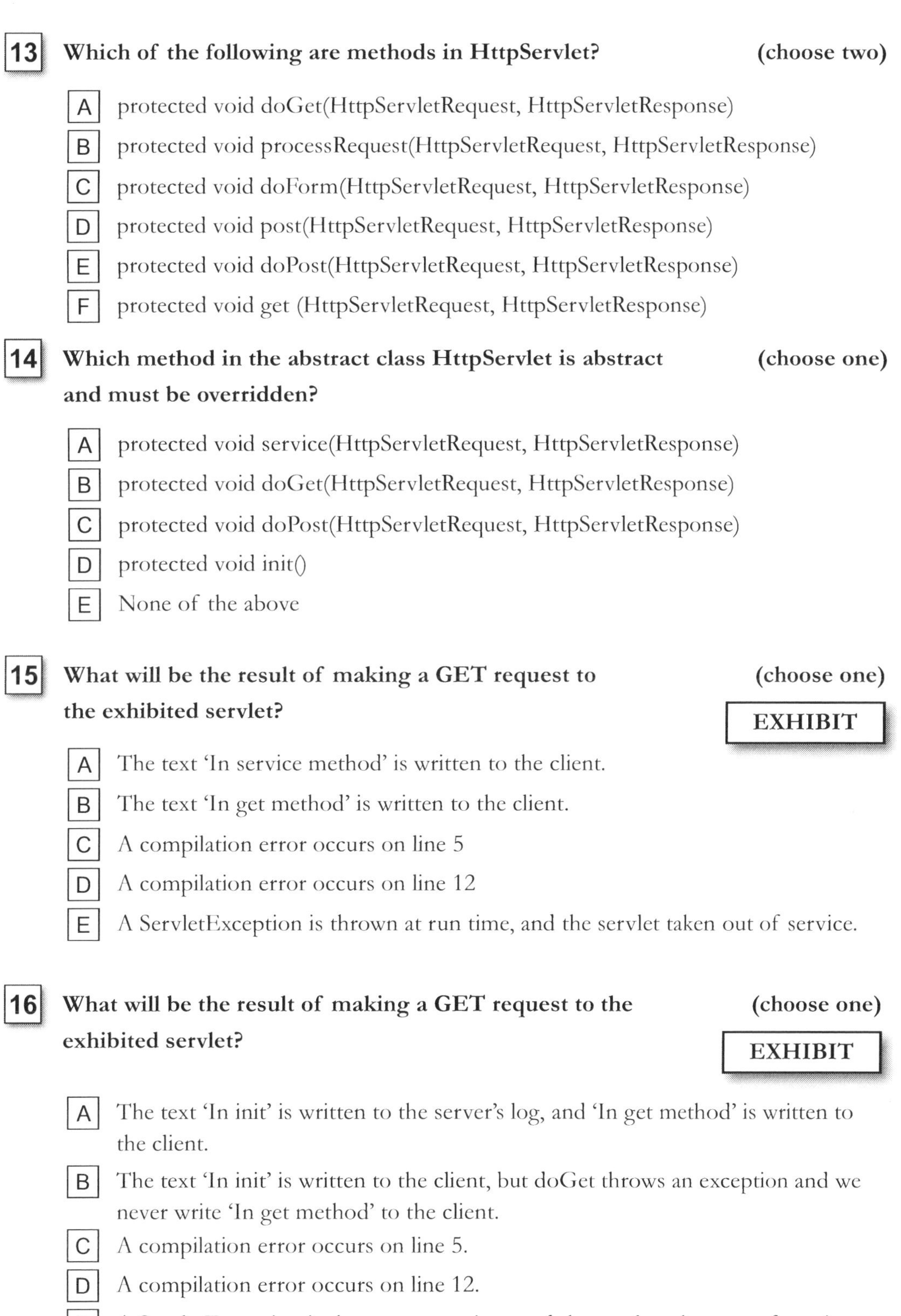

13 **Which of the following are methods in HttpServlet?** **(choose two)**

- A protected void doGet(HttpServletRequest, HttpServletResponse)
- B protected void processRequest(HttpServletRequest, HttpServletResponse)
- C protected void doForm(HttpServletRequest, HttpServletResponse)
- D protected void post(HttpServletRequest, HttpServletResponse)
- E protected void doPost(HttpServletRequest, HttpServletResponse)
- F protected void get (HttpServletRequest, HttpServletResponse)

14 **Which method in the abstract class HttpServlet is abstract and must be overridden?** **(choose one)**

- A protected void service(HttpServletRequest, HttpServletResponse)
- B protected void doGet(HttpServletRequest, HttpServletResponse)
- C protected void doPost(HttpServletRequest, HttpServletResponse)
- D protected void init()
- E None of the above

15 **What will be the result of making a GET request to the exhibited servlet?** **(choose one)**

EXHIBIT

- A The text 'In service method' is written to the client.
- B The text 'In get method' is written to the client.
- C A compilation error occurs on line 5
- D A compilation error occurs on line 12
- E A ServletException is thrown at run time, and the servlet taken out of service.

16 **What will be the result of making a GET request to the exhibited servlet?** **(choose one)**

EXHIBIT

- A The text 'In init' is written to the server's log, and 'In get method' is written to the client.
- B The text 'In init' is written to the client, but doGet throws an exception and we never write 'In get method' to the client.
- C A compilation error occurs on line 5.
- D A compilation error occurs on line 12.
- E A ServletException is thrown at run time, and the servlet taken out of service.

Exhibits

NOTE: Throughout all chapters and in the exam, exhibits which do not start at line 1 deliberately have some code (e.g. imports) omitted. You can assume the omitted code will not be the cause of any compilation error. Due to space considerations, some lines are wrapped; in this case, the second line is a continuation of the first and therefore has the same line number.

Q.15

```
1. import javax.servlet.*;
2. import javax.servlet.http.*;
3. import java.io.*;
4.
5. public class MyServlet extends HttpServlet {
6.   public void service(HttpServletRequest req,
                         HttpServletResponse resp) throws IOException {
7.     Writer out = resp.getWriter();
8.     out.write("In service method");
9.   }
10.
11.  public void doGet(HttpServletRequest req, HttpServletResponse resp)
                                                   throws IOException {
12.    Writer out = resp.getWriter();
13.    out.write("In get method");
14.  }
15.}
```

Q.16

```
1. import javax.servlet.*;
2. import javax.servlet.http.*;
3. import java.io.*;
4.
5. public class MyServlet extends HttpServlet {
6.   public void init() {
7.     /* Invoke GenericServlet's log method */
8.     log("In init");
9.   }
10.
11.  public void doGet(HttpServletRequest req, HttpServletResponse resp)
                                               throws ServletException {
12.    Writer out = resp.getWriter();
13.    out.write("In get method");
14.  }
15.}
```

Answers to Revision Questions

1 **Correct answers: C**

2 **Correct answers: B, D**

3 **Correct answers: D**

4 **Correct answer: C**

5 **Correct answers: B**

B is the only abstract method.

6 **Correct answer:** Class loading, Instantiation, Initialisation, Service, Destruction.

7 **Correct answers: D, E**

8 **Correct answers: A, B, D**

Note that UnavailableException is a subclass of ServletException

9 **Correct answers: E**

No need for any exceptions – we are removing the instance anyway!

10 **Correct answers: A**

Only Servlet **must** ever be implemented – the others are just convenience classes. The *appropriate* (but optional) classes to use are C if you want a protocol-independent servlet, or D for an HTTP-specific servlet.

11 **Correct answers: C, F**

It is not recommended that doOptions() or doTrace() be overridden as they already have suitable default implementations; the API states 'there's no need to override this method'. doGet() and doPut() may, but do not have to, be overridden – at the developer's discretion.

12 **Correct answer:** public void init(ServletConfig), public void init(), public void service(ServletRequest, ServletResponse), protected void service(HttpServletRequest, HttpServletResponse), protected void doGet(HttpServletRequest, HttpServletResponse)

13 **Correct answers: A, E**

14 **Correct answers: E**

No methods in HttpServlet are abstract, even though the class is! However, good practise dictates that one of the doXxx() methods be overridden, even though they have default implementations.

15 **Correct answers: A**

Because we have overridden service(), so delegation never gets to doGet(). Never override service() in HttpServlet!

16 **Correct answers: D**

We haven't declared/caught the checked IOException thrown by getWriter() and write().

In this chapter you'll:

- Discover what an application context is.
- Use the ServletContext API.
- Store and retrieve application-scoped (context) attributes.
- Obtain streams to static resources and RequestDispatchers.
- Learn how to use servlet initialisation parameters for configuration.
- Utilise listeners to be notified of application-wide events.

4 Servlet Contexts

We established early on that all applications have their own context root, unique from any other application's, and that servlets wishing to communicate with other components (inside or outside of their own application) need to make use of the container's interface.

In order to access container-level services, the servlet must first own a copy of the application's `ServletContext`, which is a type of object used to provide the servlet with a view to its Web application.

Each Web application has only one `ServletContext`, and one `ServletContext` belongs to only one application. In essence, a `ServletContext` object represents the application as a whole, at its given context root. In fact, many of the methods that the `ServletContext` provides are designed for retrieving and manipulating (but never modifying) the context root of the application.

We use an application's `ServletContext` to communicate between components in the same application. From one application's `ServletContext` we can also obtain references to other `ServletContexts`, and hence other applications, running on the same server, allowing communication to take place between components in different applications. All in all, `ServletContext` is a pretty important object to have around!

A servlet can use the context for a number of purposes:

- Retrieve information about the location of the application in which it is being executed;
- Dynamically query the Java EE server to find another application currently running on the server, and acquire its associated `ServletContext` object;
- Retrieve and modify application-scoped attributes and initialisation parameters;
- Obtain handles on `InputStreams` for the importation of static resources contained in the application;
- Create a `RequestDispatcher` object which can then be used to forward/include other dynamic resources into the current output stream.

Note that everything in this list is about (a) interfacing with the container, (b) accessing resources. By the end of this chapter you should feel comfortable with each of these topics, and be able to give answers to related questions in the exam with no hesitation.

We will also discuss the `ServletConfig` object, the parameter required for the initialisation of servlets, at the end of the chapter.

The Interfaces

4

ServletContext

Note that this is an *interface*, as with so many Java EE API components. When we obtain a `ServletContext` object, we are actually acquiring an object of a subclass which *implements* this interface, and not a *direct* instance of `ServletContext`. This is true in much of the server architecture because it promotes a separation of data from data type. The implementation class will be specific to the vendor and its container; the good news is that we don't ever have to worry about the concrete implementation as long as we know the contract which that class must fulfil. A contract is an agreement, in this case between the container API and the developer that states that any `ServletContext` objects will do exactly what they 'say on the tin'. The objects can't be instances of the interface (since only concrete classes can be instantiated), but they must at a minimum perform the functions declared in the interface. While the theory behind this is too much for the exam, it is worthwhile to have an appreciation of some of the Java EE lingo – especially if you wondered how 'instances' of an interface can be passed to methods as arguments. The `ServletContext` instance for the application is created by the container when the application is first started; the container automatically configures the context using data contained in the deployment descriptor.

Context (Application-Scoped) Attributes

During the course of developing an application, there may arise situations where it is appropriate to publish a set of variables within the application itself – so that they are accessible to all components in the application. An example of such a use might be in a hit counter. When the client visits the first page on the website, that page updates the relevant variable in the application. All other resources can then read this variable and use it in their pages to relay to the user how many other visitors there have been in total. Notice that in this example, the counter is only incremented on the opening page of the site, while every other Web component just reads its value. It is equally likely in some applications that other components would want to modify that variable, or even remove it from the application entirely.

Variables at this level are called **context attributes**, since they are stored in the application's context. Recall that there is only one `ServletContext` instance per application, and every servlet component has access to it, so the context is a very convenient place to store variables accessible to *every* component in a single application.

There are many other attribute types available in Java EE as well, each at a different scope. When we talk about **scope**, we are concerning ourselves with how available an attribute is to other components: in the above case, the counter attribute had **application scope** since any component in the application could access it. The application level is the least restrictive scope, in terms of the number of components which can access it simultaneously.

Other scopes include the **request** scope, the **session** scope and the **page** scope; these are the subject of other chapters.

NOTE: There are no container-scoped variables. If data needs to be accessible *between applications*, consider a persistent storage mechanism such as a file store or a database.

Attributes have a single `String` as an identifier, and take any `Object` as a value. They are accessed via the following methods in the `javax.servlet.ServletContext` interface:

- **`Object getAttribute(String name)`**
  Returns the `Object` value associated with the attribute identified by `name`. `null` is returned if no attribute of the given name exists.
- **`Enumeration getAttributeNames()`**
  Returns a `java.util.Enumeration` of all the names of attributes currently bound into the context.
- **`void removeAttribute(String name)`**
  Removes the attribute specified by `name` from the context.
- **`void setAttribute(String name, Object value)`**
  Binds the given `Object` value to the attribute identified by `name`. If this attribute already exists, the value of the attribute will be overridden with the new `Object` parameter. Passing `null` as the value is equivalent to calling the `removeAttribute` method.

When an object is added to an attribute (of any scope), the process is referred to technically as **binding**; i.e. an object is bound into a scoped attribute with a given name.

NOTE: A Java EE server will only guarantee to keep context attributes available when the container is 'alive'. Context attributes, because of their scope, are not to be considered an alternative to persistent storage mechanisms such as databases. The developer should only store information in a context attribute when it is temporary (i.e. it might as well be modified or removed by another resource later during the application's life).

The specification recommends that developers use the same naming system for attributes (of any scope) as for packages – i.e. the 'reverse domain name' rule. This avoids conflicts with other developer's components which you may use in your application. For example, if your domain name was `myself.co.uk`, then your attribute name would begin with `uk.co.myself`, with a suffix of your choice – for example `uk.co.myself.info.telephonenum`. Because a domain name can be registered to only one entity at one time, this ensures that no two developers' work can occupy the same name. Knowledge of this naming scheme is not required for the exam, but an awareness of it is worthwhile.

Obtaining Context Information

There are three methods used to access information about the current application context in which the components are running:

- **`String getServletContextName()`**
  Returns the name of this Web application, as declared in the application deployment descriptor's `<display-name>` element, or `null` if this element is not declared.

- **`String getRealPath(String path)`**
  The `String` parameter represents the context-relative path of a resource in the current application. This method returns a `String` which is the actual directory path to the file on the server. The actual value returned will be dependent upon the server's configuration and file system, but for resources contained in a WAR, this method returns `null`.

- **`Set getResourcePaths(String path)`**
  The `String` parameter is a context-relative partial path inside the application. This method searches the supplied path and returns a `java.util.Set` containing `String`s listing all resources and *immediate* subdirectories. Note that this is only a shallow directory enumeration, so only one level of files is returned.

Additionally, there is one important method which allows access to **foreign contexts** – i.e. the contexts of *other applications*:

- **ServletContext getContext(String appURL)**
  Returns the ServletContext object for the Web application identified by the supplied URL, which is relative to the root of the Java EE server, and must begin with a forward slash (/). In effect it is the context path of the other application; for example, an application deployed with the /shop/catalogue context would have a URL relative to the Java EE server root of the same: /shop/catalogue.

Note that this last method may return null if the container blocks communications between applications for security reasons; for example, if multiple applications from different vendors or clients were installed on a single server, one application should not be allowed to access another client's resources. This is a typical configuration for Java Web containers hosted on shared servers.

Gaining the context to another application allows us to forward requests to components in other applications. We will look more closely at this in Chapter 6.

Accessing Static Resources

The ServletContext provides an overview of the application and its contents. Some of the resources in the application are likely to be static, that is, the response they return never changes between requests.

A servlet may wish to access a static resource for a number of reasons. One possible situation is when the servlet needs to read a configuration text file within the application (or within a different application if a foreign context is obtained). Another is when a static file, such as an HTML document or an image, needs to be included in the response. Either of these can be achieved using the following two methods:

- **java.net.URL getResource(String path)**
  The String parameter must begin with a forward slash (/), and is relative to the current application's context root. The returned URL object can be used to examine the resource and its path, or to obtain an InputStream, although this is more quickly and efficiently accomplished via the next method.

- **java.io.InputStream getResourceAsStream(String path)**
  Acquires an InputStream through which the resource, identified by the context-relative path, can be read.

The InputStream can either be used by a servlet to simply read the content from the file and make decisions based upon that data, or the servlet can write the data straight out to the response. We will see a better way of achieving the writing of static resources to the response output in Chapter 6 when we look at RequestDispatchers.

NOTE: These methods for accessing static content output the content found in the file *directly*. This means that if these methods are used to read a JSP or similar dynamic document, the actual *source code* as it appears in the document will be output, and not the dynamic rendition of that source code. This is a type of 'trick' question that those thoughtful examiners might like to throw in for good measure. `RequestDispatchers` provide the solution to this problem.

The following method is used to obtain the **Multipurpose Internet Mail Extensions** (**MIME**) type for the resource:

- **`String getMimeType(String path)`**
  Returns the MIME type of the resource identified by the context-relative `path`. Examples of the returned `String` would be `text/plain` for a plain text file, `text/html` for an HTML document, and `image/jpeg` for a JPEG image.

The MIME type of a resource is usually determined automatically by the container, as one of its many helpful services. The default assignments of the container can be overridden using the deployment descriptor for the application, as discussed in Chapter 10.

Obtaining RequestDispatchers

`RequestDispatcher` objects are used to communicate between components in the same Web container. A `RequestDispatcher` instance is obtained from the `ServletContext` for the application containing the component receiving the request; as a result, the `ServletContext` interface contains the following two methods:

- **`RequestDispatcher getRequestDispatcher(String path)`**
  Returns a `RequestDispatcher` for the resource located at `path`, or `null` if this isn't possible.

- **`RequestDispatcher getNamedDispatcher(String name)`**
  Returns a `RequestDispatcher` for the resource identified in the deployment descriptor with the logical `name`.

See Chapter 6 for a discussion of how `RequestDispatchers` are put to use.

Context Initialisation Parameters

At deployment time, the server Administrator or application Deployer can configure name/value pairs of parameters which provide the components within the application with installation-specific information. Each of these pairs is called a **context initialisation parameter**, because they can be used to provide servlets and other components with additional configuration information when they are in the initialisation stage of their life. Note that *context* (as opposed to servlet) initialisation parameters are available to *every* component within the application, without restriction.

Initialisation parameters by nature cannot be modified by components within the application. They are configured when the application is deployed, but are read-only thereafter. A typical use of a context initialisation parameter is to configure a specific application's title: in the instance that the same basic application (such as an online shopping basket) were sold to multiple clients, then each could name the application after their own site and not a generic name that the application ships with. Another typical example is when an administrator or webmaster makes their name and e-mail address available in case of technical support enquiries. An initialisation parameter can be used to store the name and address so that all components in the application know where to find them.

All context initialisation parameters are configured in the deployment descriptor, which we discuss further in Chapter 10. The following two methods of the `ServletContext` interface are used by components to access the value of these parameters:

- **`String getInitParameter(String name)`**
  Retrieves the value of the context initialisation parameter identified by `name`, or `null` if that parameter does not exist in the deployment descriptor.

- **`Enumeration getInitParameterNames()`**
  Returns a `java.util.Enumeration`, containing `String`s which represent the names of all context initialisation parameters in the application's deployment descriptor.

ServletConfig

The `ServletContext` object is used to provide all servlets in an application with a view to that application. Each servlet 'sees' the same `ServletContext`, which would make configuring each servlet separately by this method very clumsy.

Instead, a means by which the container can initialise *individual* servlets is required, and this is provided by the `ServletConfig` interface, each instance of which provides a specific servlet with its own servlet-dependent initialisation details. This occurs using the `init` method of a `Servlet` subclass which is invoked directly after the servlet is instantiated (see the *Servlet Life Cycles* section in the previous chapter).

Servlet Names and Contexts

The `ServletConfig` interface defines a method that can be used by a servlet to acquire its logical name, as found in the deployment descriptor:

- **`String getServletName()`**
  Returns the logical name of the servlet instance, or if one is not assigned, its class name.

You may also have been wondering, through the beginning of this chapter, how a servlet can obtain a reference to the application's `ServletContext`. The answer is, that the container provides a one-off opportunity for the servlet to grab a handle on this instance during the initialisation stage. In fact, the application's `ServletContext` is encapsulated in the servlet's `ServletConfig` object:

- **`ServletContext getServletContext()`**
  Returns the `ServletContext` object, providing the servlet being initialised with its view to its application.

Because the `ServletContext` object is often needed during the service stage of a servlet's life, but is only provided by the container during initialisation, it is normal for a servlet to store its own internal reference to the context as a private instance variable. We will see exactly how the `GenericServlet` class deals with this issue later in this section.

Servlet Initialisation Parameters

Recall from the previous section that an application can have *context* initialisation parameters which provide static information for every component in the application; for example, a custom name for the Web application. Often enough, a servlet requires its *own* initialisation parameters, which are private to it alone – for example, the location of a configuration XML document in the WAR or the path/address and name of a database table specific to that servlet.

These servlet initialisation parameters are accessed using the following two methods of the `ServletConfig` interface:

- **`String getInitParameter(String name)`**
  Gets the servlet initialisation parameter value with the given parameter name, as specified in the deployment descriptor.

- **`java.util.Enumeration getInitParameterNames()`**
  Returns a `java.util.Enumeration` of the names of all available servlet initialisation parameters.

NOTE: One area which the exam preys on is the potential confusion between *context* and *servlet* initialisation parameters. To make matters more confusing, the names of the *methods* for each type of parameter are the same, but they are located in *different classes*. Make sure you know that they are different, and what the difference is, as well as where and how each might be used.

All servlet initialisation parameters are contained in the Web application's deployment descriptor, inside a `<init-param>` element under the `<servlet>` element. Just to be confusing, context initialisation parameters are also declared in the Web application's deployment descriptor, but inside a `<context-param>` element under the root element `<web-app>`. Deployment descriptor syntax is the subject of Chapter 10. Servlet initialisation parameters can also be configured using annotations, detailed in Chapter 11.

GenericServlet Support for Contexts

Initialisation

The `GenericServlet` class handles the storage of the `ServletContext` object for us, by overriding the `init(ServletConfig)` method, storing the *`ServletConfig`* object locally, and then providing convenience methods for accessing all of the configuration properties, including the `ServletContext`, the servlet's name and the initialisation parameters. This allows us to access all of the servlet's configuration details, including its initialisation parameters, in the service stage of its life as well as during initialisation. The `GenericServlet` class provides the no-argument `init()` method, to be overridden by subclasses, which is invoked after the `init(ServletConfig)` method. We looked at this initialisation procedure in the last chapter; Figure 3.3 summarised it.

Convenience Methods

The `GenericServlet` class provides the following convenience methods for accessing the `ServletContext`:

- **`ServletConfig getServletConfig()`**
  Returns the `ServletConfig` that the `GenericServlet` stored when it was initialised.

4

- **`ServletContext getServletContext()`**
  Returns the `ServletContext` for this servlet's application; equivalent to `getServletConfig().getServletContext()`.
- **`String getInitParameter(String name)`**
  Returns the value of the initialisation parameter called `name`; equivalent to `getServletConfig().getInitParameter(name)`.
- **`Enumeration getInitParameterNames()`**
  Returns the `java.util.Enumeration` of all initialisation parameter names for this servlet; equivalent to `getServletConfig().getInitParameterNames()`.
- **`String getServletName()`**
  Returns the logical name of this servlet, as configured in the deployment descriptor; equivalent to `getServletConfig().getServletName()`.

Context Listeners

Each `ServletContext` goes through a three-stage life cycle:

- **Initialisation**
  This is performed when the application is deployed, and before any servlets, filters or JSPs are initialised (all of these components may need to access the context).
- **Lifetime**
  This is the period during which the context provides the interface between the application and its components – the stage where the object actually does something useful.
- **Destruction**
  The context is only destroyed when either the server is shut down or the application is undeployed. Otherwise, a single instance of the context exists throughout the entire lifetime of the deployed application.

You can implement certain listener interfaces (then declare the implementation classes in the deployment descriptor for the Web application) in order to receive notification when different stages of this lifecycle are reached. We discuss them now.

ServletContextListener

For one reason or another, it may be necessary to receive event notification when a `ServletContext` is changing from one state to another in its life cycle. If so, creating a class which implements `ServletContextListener` could just be the answer.

The `javax.servlet.ServletContextListener` interface declares two methods:

- **`void contextInitialized(ServletContextEvent event)`**
  This method is called after the `ServletContext` has been instantiated for the application, but before any components (e.g. servlets and filters) are initialised.

- **`void contextDestroyed(ServletContextEvent event)`**
  This method is notified before the `ServletContext` has been sent for garbage collection, but after all components (e.g. servlets and filters) have been destroyed.

You may be wondering how exactly we can command an application to use a listener class since there are no programmatic methods for adding listeners to classes as there are in, say, the AWT and Swing GUI classes on the Standard Edition platform. The answer lies in the configuration of the deployment descriptor at deployment time. Listener classes are declared using the `<listener>` element in the deployment descriptor, which we discuss in Chapter 10, or by using the `@WebListener` annotation detailed in Chapter 11. For now, just *learn* the above method headers and purposes, no matter how gruelling that may seem.

The ServletContextEvent Class

Each of the listener methods receives an event object which it can use to determine various properties about the event which occurred – the reason for the method being called. An instance of the `ServletContextEvent` class will be passed to the listener methods, as can be seen from the method signatures above.

Seeing as all context listener methods are only interested in one thing, the `ServletContext` of the application, this is all the `ServletContextEvent` class needs to provide access to:

- **`ServletContext getServletContext()`**
  Returns the `ServletContext` which changed state when the listener method was called.

Additionally, this class has one constructor, but because we will not be creating instances of the class, just receiving them, we don't need to worry about it.

4

ServletContextAttributeListener

The exam also requires that we know how to monitor the state of context attributes, which as you'll recall are scoped at the application level. The listener classes for other scoped attributes are discussed in other chapters as appropriate. It may help during the revision process to see all the listener classes (from all the scopes) together since they are all very similar.

In order to receive notification that a context attribute has in some way changed, we need to create a class implementing the `javax.servlet.ServletContextAttributeListener` interface, which defines three methods:

- **`void attributeAdded(ServletContextAttributeEvent event)`**
  This method is called when a new name/value attribute pair is added to the set of context attributes already in the system. The parameter can be interrogated to find the name of the new attribute, and what its value is.
- **`void attributeRemoved(ServletContextAttributeEvent event)`**
  When an attribute is removed from the set of context attributes, this method is called. The parameter can be interrogated to find the name and *old* value of the parameter being removed.
- **`void attributeReplaced(ServletContextAttributeEvent event)`**
  The value of an attribute can be overwritten as well as removed entirely from the context. When overwriting occurs, this method is called with a parameter which reflects the name and *old* value of the attribute being changed. The new value can be found, if required, by looking up the attribute in the `ServletContext` object using the supplied event argument.

The exam may throw in a question or two asking what the parameters represent in the above methods: for example, in the case of an attribute replacement, the parameter encapsulates the name of the attribute being changed, and its *old* value (not the new one it has now). Thinking through this logically, it makes sense: if the old value were not available to be retrieved here, then it would be lost forever because the new value would have overwritten it already. However, the new value is now contained in the attribute set, so by the time this listener method is called, it has access to everything about the attribute: its name, old value and new value. Don't get caught out by easy questions on the exam asking you to identify what values will be retrieved from the event object during an attribute modification (they're most likely to use a code snippet or two to test this).

The ServletContextAttributeEvent Class

This class extends the basic `ServletContextEvent` class discussed previously. It therefore inherits the following method from its parent:

- **`ServletContext getServletContext()`**
  Returns the context object which the attribute being modified belongs to. This context can be used to find the new value for an attribute where appropriate.

It defines two new methods:

- **`String getName()`**
  Returns the name of the attribute being added, removed or replaced.

- **`Object getValue()`**
  Returns the appropriate value of the attribute being modified: in the case of addition, this is the new value; for removal, this is the old value before the attribute was deleted; for replacement, this is the old value before overwriting occurred.

Revision Questions

1 **A servlet context is a container-managed object that implements which interface?** **(choose one)**

- A javax.servlet.Context
- B javax.servlet.ServletContext
- C javax.servlet.http.ServletContext
- D java.enterprise.WebContext
- E None of the above

2 **Context attributes provide which scope of attribute storage?** **(choose one)**

- A Application
- B Client
- C Session
- D Request
- E Page
- F Local

3 **Context attributes for the application myApp can be accessed by what components in the Web container?** **(choose one)**

- A All components in all applications.
- B All components in the myApp application only.
- C Only those components participating in a single request within the myApp application only.
- D Only the servlet that added the context attribute can access, modify or remove it.
- E Only components configured to be in the same security group in the deployment descriptor.

4 **Which methods does ServletContext provide relating to context initialisation parameters?** **(choose two)**

- A public String getInitialisationParam(String)
- B public Enumeration getInitParamNames()
- C public String getInitParameter(String)
- D public Enumeration getInitParameters()
- E public void setInitialisationParameters(Map)
- F public Enumeration getInitParameterNames()

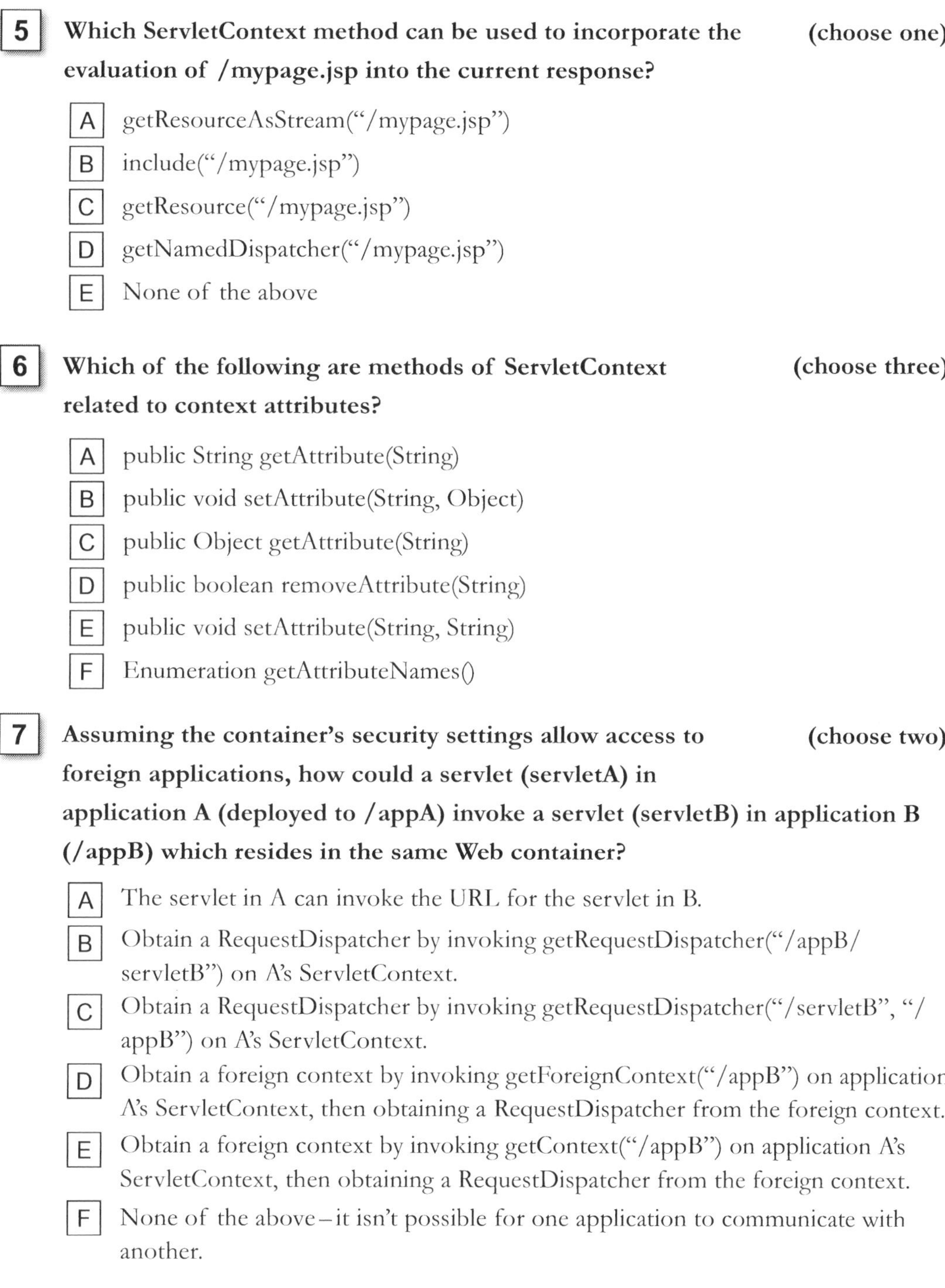

5 **Which ServletContext method can be used to incorporate the evaluation of /mypage.jsp into the current response?** **(choose one)**

- A getResourceAsStream("/mypage.jsp")
- B include("/mypage.jsp")
- C getResource("/mypage.jsp")
- D getNamedDispatcher("/mypage.jsp")
- E None of the above

6 **Which of the following are methods of ServletContext related to context attributes?** **(choose three)**

- A public String getAttribute(String)
- B public void setAttribute(String, Object)
- C public Object getAttribute(String)
- D public boolean removeAttribute(String)
- E public void setAttribute(String, String)
- F Enumeration getAttributeNames()

7 **Assuming the container's security settings allow access to foreign applications, how could a servlet (servletA) in application A (deployed to /appA) invoke a servlet (servletB) in application B (/appB) which resides in the same Web container?** **(choose two)**

- A The servlet in A can invoke the URL for the servlet in B.
- B Obtain a RequestDispatcher by invoking getRequestDispatcher("/appB/servletB") on A's ServletContext.
- C Obtain a RequestDispatcher by invoking getRequestDispatcher("/servletB", "/appB") on A's ServletContext.
- D Obtain a foreign context by invoking getForeignContext("/appB") on application A's ServletContext, then obtaining a RequestDispatcher from the foreign context.
- E Obtain a foreign context by invoking getContext("/appB") on application A's ServletContext, then obtaining a RequestDispatcher from the foreign context.
- F None of the above – it isn't possible for one application to communicate with another.

8 **During initialisation of a servlet, the container creates an instance of which interface?** (choose one)

- A javax.servlet.Config
- B javax.servlet.Configuration
- C javax.servlet.ServletConfig
- D javax.servlet.http.HttpServletConfig
- E javax.servlet.GenericConfig

9 **Assuming a context parameter has been configured in the deployment descriptor, with name apptitle and value 'My Ecommerce Website', what will the servlet code shown in the exhibit output?** (choose one)

EXHIBIT

- A The text 'My Ecommerce Website'.
- B The text 'null'.
- C Nothing is written to the client.
- D A compilation error occurs on line 7.
- E An exception is thrown at run time.

10 **A servlet is required that can iterate through each of the initialisation parameters configured for it. What lines would be inserted instead of lines 9 and 13 in the exhibit?** (choose two)

EXHIBIT

- A line A: enum = getServletConfig().getInitParameterNames();
  line B: value = getInitParam(name);
- B line A: enum = getInitParamNames();
  line B: value = getServletConfig().getInitParameter(name);
- C line A: enum = getServletConfig().getInitParameterNames();
  line B: value = getInitParameter(name);
- D line A: enum = getInitParameterNames();
  line B: value = getServletConfig().getInitParameter(name);
- E line A: enum = getServletConfig().getInitParameterNames();
  line B: value = getServletContext().getInitParameter(name);

11 **Assuming the MyContextListener (implementing ServletContextListener) is configured correctly in the deployment descriptor, what method, if any, will be invoked on this listener when the application is first deployed?** **(choose one)**

- A public void applicationReady(ServletContextEvent)
- B public void init(ServletContextEvent)
- C public void servletContextInitialized(ServletContextEvent)
- D public void contextInitialized(ServletContextEvent)
- E No methods are invoked.

12 **If an application contains a class which needs to receive event notification that context attributes have been modified, what listener interface should that class implement?** **(choose one)**

- A javax.servlet.ContextListener
- B javax.servlet.ServletContextListener
- C javax.servlet.AttributeListener
- D javax.servlet.ServletAttributeListener
- E javax.servlet.ServletContextAttributeListener

13 **An application needs to ensure that a certain context attribute (named important) is never removed from scope. A crude solution uses a listener which adds the attribute back into the scope if it is removed; the implementation which achieves this is in the exhibit. Assuming this listener is correctly configured in the deployment descriptor, what will be the result of using this class as specified?** **(choose one)**

EXHIBIT

- A It works acceptably, adding the attribute back into the context as required.
- B Compilation error on line 8
- C Compilation error on line 9
- D Compilation error on line 12
- E A runtime exception is thrown.

4

14 **When the attributeReplaced method is invoked on a ServletContextAttributeListener, what does the getValue() method of ServletContextAttributeEvent return?** **(choose one)**

- A null.
- B The new String value for the attribute.
- C The old String value for the attribute
- D The new Object value for the attribute.
- E The old Object value for the attribute.

15 **What are the possible results of making a request to the exhibited servlet?** **(choose two)**

EXHIBIT

- A The text 'Visitor number 1' is always written to the client.
- B The text 'Visitor number x' is written to the client, where x is the number of invocations of the servlet performed since the application was deployed.
- C A compilation error occurs on line 6
- D A runtime error occurs on line 8
- E A compilation error occurs on line 15.

16 **Suppose the deployment descriptor contains the declaration in the exhibit. What code inserted in the exhibited servlet on line 7 will retrieve this data and insert it into the lang variable, without throwing an exception?** **(choose one)**

EXHIBIT

- A lang = getServletConfig().getInitParameter("language");
- B lang = getInitParameter("language");
- C lang = getServletContext().getAttribute("language");
- D lang = (String) getServletContext().getAttribute("language");
- E lang = getServletContext().getInitParameter("language");

17 **During initialisation of an HttpServlet, the container creates an instance of which interface?** **(choose one)**

- A javax.servlet.Config
- B javax.servlet.Configuration
- C javax.servlet.ServletConfig
- D javax.servlet.http.HttpServletConfig
- E javax.servlet.GenericConfig

Exhibits

Q.9

```
import javax.servlet.*;
import javax.servlet.http.*;
import java.io.IOException;

public class MyServlet extends HttpServlet {
    public void doGet(HttpServletRequest req,
                      HttpServletResponse resp)
                      throws ServletException, IOException {
        String title =
            getServletConfig().getInitParameter("apptitle");
        resp.getWriter().write(title);
} }
```

Q.10

```
public class MyServlet extends GenericServlet {
    public void service(ServletRequest req, ServletResponse resp)
                        throws IOException, ServletException {
        Writer out = resp.getWriter();
        Enumeration enum = null;
        // line A
        while(enum.hasMoreElements()) {
            String name = (String) enum.nextElement();
            String value = null;
            // line B
            out.write(value + "\n");
        }
} }
```

Q.13

```
public class MyAttributeListener implements
                        ServletContextAttributeListener {

    public void attributeAdded(ServletContextAttributeEvent scae) {}
    public void attributeReplaced(ServletContextAttributeEvent scae) {}

    public void attributeRemoved(ServletContextAttributeEvent scae)
                throws ServletException {
        ServletContext context = scae.getServletContext();
        /* Restore the attribute */
        if(scae.getName().equals("important")) {
            context.setAttribute(scae.getName(), scae.getValue());
        }
    }
}
```

Q.15

```
import javax.servlet.*;
import java.io.IOException;

public class MyServlet extends GenericServlet {

  public void service(ServletRequest req, ServletResponse resp)
                throws ServletException, IOException {
      ServletContext context = getServletContext();
      Integer counter = (Integer) context.getAttribute("hitcounter");
      if(counter == null) {
          counter = new Integer(1);
      } else {
          counter = new Integer(counter.intValue() + 1);
      }

      context.setAttribute("hitcounter", counter);

      Writer out = resp.getWriter();
      out.write("Visitor number: " + counter);
  }
}
```

Q.16

In the deployment descriptor:

```
<context-param>
  <param-name>language</param-name>
  <param-value>en</param-value>
</context-param>
```

Servlet code:

```
protected void doGet(HttpServletRequest rq, HttpServletResponse rs) {
  String lang = null;
  // insert statement
}
```

Answers to Revision Questions

1 **Correct answer: B**

2 **Correct answer: A**

Client and Local storage doesn't even exist!

3 **Correct answer: B**

For A, we commented in the chapter that there are no container-scoped attributes, which is what this would imply. C is incorrect as this is the job of request-scoped attributes. D and E are utter rubbish!

4 **Correct answers: C, F**

All others don't exist!

5 **Correct answer: E**

A would cause the contents to be inserted literally/unevaluated, B does not exist, C returns a URL which at best gets an InputStream, D is Wrong because the argument is not a logical name. Should instead consider getRequestDispatcher("/mypage.jsp"), then invoke include() on that.

6 **Correct answers: B, C, F**

D is wrong – the return type should be void. A is incorrect as the return type should be Object, not String; E is incorrect as the second (value) parameter should be of type Object and not String.

7 **Correct answers: A, E**

Note that A is feasible, but won't communicate directly with the servlet – indeed, communication would leave and then re-enter the container to gain access to the resource this way. This method could be used to include the results of a foreign URL target, including resources residing outside the container.

8 **Correct answer: C**

9 **Correct answer: B**

We are accessing a **context** parameter with **initialisation parameter** methods! Null is returned by the getInitParameter method, which is in turn written as 'null' to the Writer.

10 **Correct answers: C, D**

A is wrong: no getInitParam method, B is wrong: no getInitParamNames method; E is wrong: we obtain the context init. param value and not the servlet value – probably won't exist.

11 **Correct answer: D**

12 **Correct answer: E**

13 **Correct answer: B**

None of the listener methods are permitted to throw any checked exceptions! Other than that, this listener would work as required. However, due to multithreading issues, and the lack of guarantees as to when exactly this listener is invoked, this is a bad design solution. This listener might be invoked at any time in the future after the attribute's removal, even after several other components in the container have been invoked, making this a pretty useless 'solution'!

14 **Correct answer: E**

All *attributes*, in any scope, store Java Object values. Remember that attributes are local to the server, so are most useful if they have the most abstract Java type (an Object). They would be much less useful if they could contain only Strings – as request parameters from the client can. We get the *old* value here, because the new value can be obtained from the existing ServletContext, as attributeReplace() is invoked after the change in attribute value has occurred.

15 **Correct answers: B, D**

This acts as a hit counter, with the counter value stored in the hitcounter context (application-scoped) attribute. Line 8 might cause a ClassCastException to be thrown if the hitcounter attribute is not an Integer at run time – this question didn't put any constraints on the type of the hitcount variable (although we would *expect* it to be an Integer). A is wrong, since it will only display 1 on the first invocation, when hitcounter is null. Lines 6 and 15 are fine, so C and E are wrong.

16 **Correct answer: E**

A and B are incorrect as they obtain a servlet, and not context, initialisation parameter. C and D access scoped attributes, not an initialisation parameters (although D would be valid because getAttribute() returns an Object, so the cast is required, but would of course fail, raising a ClassCastException, if in fact the attribute was not of type String at run time).

17 **Correct answer: C**

Note that this is the same for *all* servlets, regardless of which subclass they implement or what protocol(s) they support.

In this chapter you'll:

- Recap how (specifically HTTP) requests and responses are encapsulated.
- Examine the key interfaces implemented by the container for this encapsulation.
- Be introduced to the important methods on these interfaces.
- Read HTTP request headers and set response headers.
- Examine HTTP request query parameters and body data.
- Obtain an OutputStream or PrintWriter to send data to the client.
- Implement listener interfaces used to receive notifications when requests and request-scoped attributes change.

5 Requests and Responses

The purpose of any OO software program is to abstract details of the real world into a computer-friendly application, composed of objects, defined by classes and interfaces (which are just special types of class), and primitive data types. In the case of the HTTP request-response model, there are four entities involved: the client and the Web container are clearly two of them, with the encapsulation of large amounts of data as part of the request and response being the others. Requests can get pretty large: the number of headers permitted is unbounded, and if using POST methods or the like, the size of the request body is also unbounded. Reasonably, the total length of all headers and requests should be kept as small as possible or the request might never get to the destination intact, but if you want to see a network meltdown caused by large volumes of traffic, you could always try to overload your office network if you're bored one afternoon (just don't tell the boss I said that – I'll deny it!).

Objects, by definition, encapsulate data about an entity. What better way to model a request than as an object with a class; similarly, why not also model a response as an object as well? Now, for every request we've got these two objects which encapsulate all the details of the request, and all the information we send in the response, but how are these created? The answer lies in the container once again. When a request is received by the container, it wraps all the data found in that request into an object, and provides an empty response object which we can fill as we please. It then forwards the request and response objects to the appropriate resources, like filters, servlets and JSPs. By the time the component code we've written gets to see the request and response objects, they already contain all the data we could possibly ever need to access: headers in the request, the request body and its content type (if any), the client's original URL, the IP address of the client and more. Similarly, after we've modified the response object and passed it back to the container, the container unwraps the encapsulated response data, converts it back into a stream of HTTP data and sends it off down the network. You can see why a container-managed object is needed to encapsulate the request: if the container supplied an `InputStream` for the HTTP request, or an `OutputStream` for the response, we'd end up spending more time writing code to manage the HTTP streams than actually providing the services we want to!

Figure 5.1 shows the extensibility provided by the encapsulation; an application doesn't need to know anything about the protocol being used by the time it receives an appropriate request/response object, since the object could be created from a request of

Figure 5.1

Encapsulation of Protocol Requests/Responses into Objects

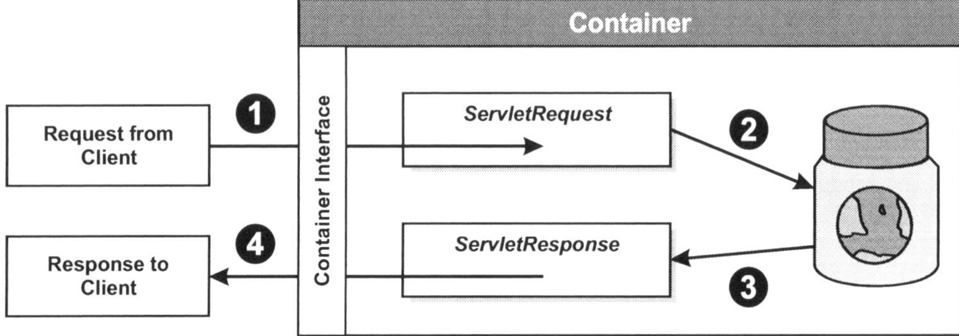

1. The client passes the (typically HTTP) request to the Web server. The request is delegated by the J2EE server to the Web container. As the request passes through the container's interface, all the details it contains are encapsulated into a ServletRequest object. Hence, a generic request is converted into a Java object.

2. The new ServletRequest object is passed to the Web application which services the request. The application can access all the useful data contained in the original request from the client using this object.

3. The application uses an instance of the ServletResponse interface to construct a valid response. A valid ServletResponse instance is made available to the Web application ***by the container*** as part of step 2 (applications do not create their own instances).

4. As the response travels back out of the container to the client, the container's interface converts the ServletResponse object back into a response suitable for the protocol (typically HTTP) used by the client.

any protocol recognised by the Java EE server. Hence, we've added a major level of abstraction which makes application code highly portable (always a good thing!).

It's time to put a face (or a class!) to the objects we've mentioned so far. In fact, since we don't care about what the class is but just the contract it defines, the exposed API contains only interfaces. It is up to the Java EE implementation to supply the classes which implement these interfaces, and to the container to instantiate these classes. All we care about is the behaviour guaranteed by the interfaces, which for request objects are:

- **`javax.servlet.ServletRequest`**
  Encapsulates all client data found in the request to a resource in the Web container. Note that, as with `Servlet` and `GenericServlet`, this does not imply any particular protocol, but instead represents a generic request. Interfaces or classes defining specific protocols should extend this interface.

- **`javax.servlet.http.HttpServletRequest`**
  Encapsulates all the data found in an HTTP request to the container. This interface extends the more generic `ServletRequest`. Since most requests will be of this type, this interface provides a number of additional and useful methods for interrogation of HTTP requests.

Similarly, the interfaces defined for responses are:

- **`javax.servlet.ServletResponse`**
  Encapsulates all data being sent from the server. In particular, an object of this type is used by Web components to establish the properties of a response without defining the details or protocol used to transmit that response–these details are taken care of by the container. Responses which are protocol-specific can use subinterfaces or subclasses to provide specific behaviour.
- **`javax.servlet.http.HttpServletResponse`**
  Provides Web components with useful HTTP-specific response capabilities, principally the addition of convenience methods for altering common response headers and for manipulating cookies. This interface extends `ServletResponse`.

The exam requires us to know at least some of the methods which these interfaces define, so we'll look at each in turn (in the order they appear above) before looking at how to transfer processing of the request between different resources in the next chapter. Those methods which the exam isn't likely to ask about, and aren't stated in the objectives, are headed as 'Not an Exam Objective' and as such you can ignore those sections. Unfortunately, this isn't relatively many of the sections, so you'll still need to do some gruelling learning! These sections were included primarily for completeness, but also to allow you to recap the services offered by the container and its request objects–you never know, you might just see a method that'll be of great use in your next project!

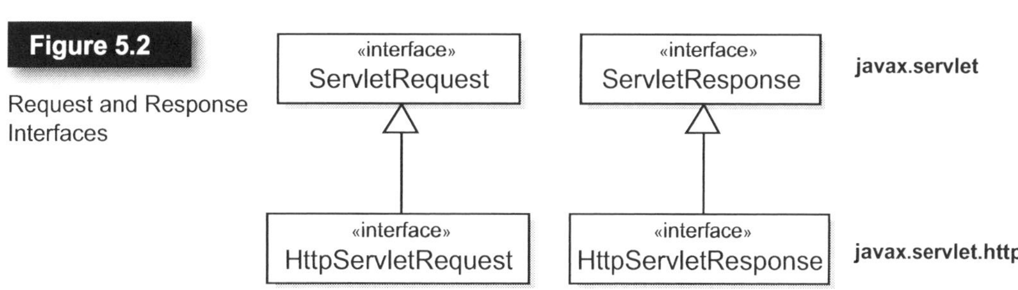

Figure 5.2

Request and Response Interfaces

The Interfaces

For clarity and quick reference, I've grouped the methods exposed by all the interfaces by purpose. The exam concentrates on a few use cases for these methods, so if you know the categories of methods defined in the generic request interfaces, and those in the HTTP-specific interfaces, you'll be halfway there already.

5 ServletRequest

This is the basic interface which must be implemented by the container for all objects encapsulating request data.

Request-Scoped Attributes

In the last chapter we looked at context attributes, scoped at the application level. These are accessible by every component in the deployed application. Often this is too extreme; instead of providing application-wide data we only want to send data to components servicing a particular request. The appropriate scope is called the **request scope**, and the attributes themselves are the **request attributes**. A request attribute is only visible between components involved in the current request; this works by storing the attributes in the `ServletRequest` object for the current request. Every component that processes the request is passed the request object as an argument to its service method, and after the request is fulfilled and the response object returned to the container and ultimately to the client, the request object's contents are destroyed. Thus, every request attribute is also eradicated, meaning that the next request made from a client will not contain those attributes–components in other requests do not 'see' the request attributes.

Since attributes only exist inside the Web container, and hence are protocol independent, the requisite methods are in the generic `ServletRequest` interface:

- **`Object getAttribute(String name)`**
  Returns the value of the attribute identified by the `name` parameter.

- **`Enumeration getAttributeNames()`**
  Returns an `Enumeration` of all request-scoped attributes existing in this request.

- **`void removeAttribute(String name)`**
  Removes the request-scoped attribute identified by the `name` parameter from this request. Once called, the attribute will no longer be available to subsequent components involved in servicing this request.

- **`void setAttribute(String name, Object value)`**
  Sets the attribute identified by the `name` parameter to the `Object` passed in the `value` parameter. After calling this method, the attribute will be available to all other components involved in servicing this request (unless later removed).

Note that these method headers match up exactly with the context attribute methods found in the `ServletContext` interface. Notice also how attribute values are all `Object`s. Since attributes exist only in the Web container (and are not transmitted to the client), the most useful form of storage possible is an `Object`, which in turn could be anything from a primitive wrapper like an `Integer`, to a `Collection`, custom class or JavaBean. On the contrary, *parameters* received from the client (see the *Request Parameters* section below) can only have `String` values, as this is the only suitably flexible mechanism for communication *outside the container* to clients which may not be Java-compatible.

Request Protocol and Transmission Data (Not an Exam Objective)

Although 'request headers' per se belong to the realms of specific protocols, namely HTTP, all requests carry certain metadata properties – information which describes the data in the request or the data required from the response. Components can access this data using the following methods:

- **`String getCharacterEncoding()`**
  Returns the character encoding used in the body of this request, or `null` if not specified or there is no body.

- **`int getContentLength()`**
  Returns the size, in bytes, of the request body, or `-1` if not specified.

- **`String getContentType()`**
  Returns the MIME type of the request body, or `null` if not known.

- **`Enumeration getLocales()`**
  The client may specify a list of locales, principally a set of languages, that they prefer to obtain content in (in HTTP, this uses the `Accept-Language` header). If this data is contained in the request, this method returns an `Enumeration` of `java.util.Locale`s representing those requirements, otherwise this method returns an `Enumeration` containing only the server's default `Locale`.

- **`Locale getLocale()`**
  Returns the client's preferred (primary) `Locale`, from the complete `Enumeration` of all `Locale`s, or the server's default `Locale` should the client not specify one.

5

- **`String getProtocol()`**
  Returns a `String` containing the name and version of the protocol being used for the request–for HTTP 1.1 this is `HTTP/1.1`.

- **`String getScheme()`**
  Returns the scheme used for this request. This is the string before the `://` in a complete URL. For example, `http`, `https`, `ftp`, `news` etc.

- **`boolean isSecure()`**
  Returns `true` only if the channel used for communication with the client employs some form of encryption, such as SSL and Secure HTTP (HTTPS).

- **`void setCharacterEncoding(String enc)`**
  Allows your code to override the character encoding specified by the user. This overrides the character encoding used in the instantiation of a `Reader` obtained from a call to `getReader()`, and the encoding used for request parameters.

The exam is unlikely to ask you about any of these methods, they are given here for completeness. The exam concentrates more on making use of attributes, parameters and input streams for request bodies than anything else.

Request Parameters

When a client needs to convey information to the server, other than in the standard protocol headers, it can use a set of name/value parameters. In HTTP requests, these can take two possible forms: either they are included in the body of, for instance, a POST request, or are included in the URL as extra string data:

```
http://domain.ext/resource?param1=val1&param2=val2...
```

The question mark (`?`) delimits the scheme and path to the resource from the **query string**, which is the ampersand-separated (`&`) list of parameters. In this example, the parameter with the name `param1` has the value `val1`, while `param2` has value `val2`. Note that parameters may only be string-based values: you can't (easily) send an object as a parameter. The reason for this: a good network protocol should be transparent to the types of client and server being used. It would be no good having an Internet protocol (such as HTTP) which required the client to be a Java application, and the server to use Java EE software–all those .NET, CGI, Perl and PHP applications out there would be totally useless as they wouldn't understand Java's serialised objects. Aside from the numerical primitives (and even those can differ between languages and platforms), the only data type common across all languages is the textual string, so there you have it–complete platform-independence.

Protocols other than HTTP may use alternative techniques for declaring parameters, but the concept of a parameter is assumed to be generic enough to warrant being part of this interface. The methods are:

- **`String[] getParameterValues(String name)`**
  Returns an array of all values possessed by the request parameter `name`. This is particularly applicable to HTTP, where parameters may have multiple values (for example, a list of all the options selected on a form). If the parameter specified does not exist, `null` is returned. If the parameter has only one value, an array (of length 1) containing only that value is returned.

- **`String getParameter(String name)`**
  Returns the value of the request parameter `name`, or `null` if that parameter does not exist in the request. If the parameter has multiple values, only the first value is returned. In general, use of the `getParameterValues` method is preferred since it returns all assigned values and not just the first.

- **`Enumeration getParameterNames()`**
  Returns an `Enumeration` of all parameter names which exist in this request, or an empty `Enumeration` if no parameters exist.

- **`Map getParameterMap()`**
  Returns a `java.util.Map` implementation containing parameter names as keys against their values. This is useful when you don't know the names of parameters, but want to iterate through both the names and their values as `Map.Entry` objects.

Note that parameters, once sent in the request from the client, cannot be modified by the application unlike request-scoped attributes: *parameters are read-only*. Don't ever confuse attributes with parameters!

Requested Resource Information (Not an Exam Objective)

Since these aren't as important as the others, and are highly unlikely to be featured on the exam, only headers and brief descriptions (mostly copied from the API documentation) are supplied:

- **`String getLocalAddr()`**
  Returns the IP address of the interface on which the request was received.

- **`String getLocalName()`**
  Returns the name of the IP interface on which this request was received.

- **`int getLocalPort()`**
  Returns the port of the IP interface on which this request was received.

- **`String getServerName()`**
  Returns the host name of the server to which this resource was sent. For example, in
  `http://www.domain.ext:8080/resource`, the returned value would be `www.domain.ext`. It may also return the resolved IP address of the server.

- **`int getServerPort()`**
  Returns the server port number to which the request was sent; for example a request to `http://www.domain.ext:8080/resource` would cause `8080` to be returned. The default HTTP port is `80`.

Client Information (Not an Exam Objective)

Again, only signatures and brief descriptions (from the API) are given:

- **`String getRemoteAddr()`**
  Returns the IP address of the client or last proxy that sent the request.

- **`String getRemoteHost()`**
  Returns the fully-qualified name of the client or last proxy that sent the request. If the server chooses not to resolve the hostname from the IP address, for example, to improve performance, this method returns the dotted-string form of the IP address—e.g. `127.0.0.1`.

- **`int getRemotePort()`**
  Returns the IP port number of the client or last proxy that sent the request.

Reading Request Bodies

If the request has a body, it would be pretty useful for the application to read its contents—and more precisely, pretty useless if it couldn't! This is especially the case in `POST` and `PUT` operations using HTTP, where the body may contain byte streams representing entire files which are being uploaded. Applications using other protocols, such as FTP, will also depend on these methods.

- **`ServletInputStream getInputStream()`**
  Returns a `java.io.InputStream` subclass (which adds a `readLine()` method) suitable for reading data in binary form from the request body.

- **`Reader getReader()`**
  Returns a `java.io.Reader` suitable for reading textual data from the request body. The `Reader` is preconfigured with the character encoding established by calling `getCharacterEncoding()`, which will either be the encoding specified by the client, the server's default, or an encoding set explicitly by your application's code using `setCharacterEncoding()`.

NOTE: Both of these methods may throw a `java.io.IOException` if an error occurs constructing the stream. More importantly, it is only possible to obtain one of these objects – it is generally assumed that the application will be interested either in binary or text data and not both. Invoking both methods on the same `ServletRequest` object will cause an `IllegalStateException` to be thrown.

Request Dispatching

We will look at the `RequestDispatcher` interface and its uses in the next chapter. An appropriate `RequestDispatcher` object is obtained by a call on the request to this method:

- **`RequestDispatcher getRequestDispatcher(String path)`**
  Returns a `RequestDispatcher` appropriate for including or forwarding to the resource at the specified `path`. This path may either be relative to the current servlet or relative to the application context by including a starting forward slash (`/`).

You will recall that `ServletContext` has a similar method for obtaining a `RequestDispatcher`. However, the `ServletRequest` version allows paths *relative to the current servlet* to be specified in addition to those relative to the context root. The `ServletContext` version only allows paths relative to the context root (and starting with the `/`).

HttpServletRequest

This interface extends `ServletRequest` to provide methods applicable specifically to the HTTP protocol. Most applications will choose to use `HttpServlets` along with `HttpServletRequests` as most clients will use HTTP and these classes combined provide the best level of support for HTTP-based applications, generally requiring less application code to achieve the design goals.

Request Headers

The idea of a request header, although it might seem a pretty generic way to specify request information, is in fact specific to the HTTP protocol. For this reason, the `ServletRequest` interface makes no mention of 'headers' per se. Instead, methods relating to headers are found in this interface, and are:

- **`Enumeration getHeaders(String name)`**
  Returns an `Enumeration` of all the values given to the header with the specified name. This is particularly applicable to HTTP, where headers may have multiple values in a comma-separated list – for example, a list of different languages for which the client will accept responses. As an alternative to a comma-separated list, multiple instances of the same header may be declared, each with a different value. If the header specified does not exist, an empty `Enumeration` is returned.
- **`String getHeader(String name)`**
  Returns the first value (should there be multiple) of the header called `name`, or `null` if this header does not exist in the request.
- **`Enumeration getHeaderNames()`**
  Returns an `Enumeration` of `String` objects, each of which is the name of a header existing in the request.
- **`int getIntHeader(String name)`**
  Convenience method which converts the value of the header called `name` into an integer value before returning. If no header called `name` exists, `-1` is returned. If the header cannot be converted to a number, because it contains non-numerical characters, a `NumberFormatException` is thrown.
- **`long getDateHeader(String name)`**
  Convenience method which converts the value of the specified header into a `long` integer representing the number of milliseconds in UTC ('Coordinated Universal Time'), which starts from 1st January 1970 GMT. This is compatible with the standard `java.util.Date` and `java.util.Calendar` classes. If the header with the specified name does not exist in the request, this method returns `-1`.

Oh, and by the way, all header names are case-*in*sensitive.

Request Protocol Data and Resource Path (Not an Exam Objective)

Since these methods do not constitute an exam objective, only signatures and brief descriptions are supplied:

- **`String getContextPath()`**
  Returns the context part (see below) of the request URI.
- **`String getMethod()`**
  Returns the name of the HTTP method which was used to make this request.

- **`String getPathInfo()`**
  Returns the extra path information associated with the request URI. This is the URI which follows the servlet path but precedes the query string. Returns `null` if the request URI does not have any extra information.

- **`String getPathTranslated()`**
  Returns extra path information after the servlet name but before the query string, and translates it into a real path.

- **`String getQueryString()`**
  Returns the query string appended to the URL of the resource in the request URI, or `null` if there is no query string.

- **`String getRequestURI()`**
  Returns the complete request URL, which goes from the end of the host name to the end of the resource name, excluding the query string. This will always begin with a `/` indicating the root of the host server (and not the context of this application).

- **`StringBuffer getRequestURL()`**
  Reconstructs the URL used by the client to make the request, using all the other methods exposed by the `ServletRequest` and `HttpServletRequest` interfaces. The returned URL will contain a scheme, host server name, port number and path to the resource on the server, but does not contain the query string.

- **`String getServletPath()`**
  Returns the section of the request URI from the context of the application to the mapped path to the servlet. The returned value will be the part of the URI which caused the servlet to be invoked as a result of the URL mappings in the deployment descriptor, and not the actual path to the component in the application. For example, if the request URI was `/catalogue/view?p=12` and the invoked servlet was mapped to `/catalogue/*` in the application, the value returned from this method would be `/catalogue/`.

Each of these methods returns a specific part of a request URL. Each of these parts is shown in Figure 5.3 for a servlet mapped to the `/path` in the application with context root `/myapp`. Hence, `getContextPath()` would return `/myapp`, `getServletPath()` returns `/path`, `getPathInfo()` returns `/resource` and `getQueryString()` returns `name=value`. The `getRequestURL()` method returns a `StringBuffer` containing the complete URL as shown.

5

Figure 5.3

The Parts of an HTTP Request URL

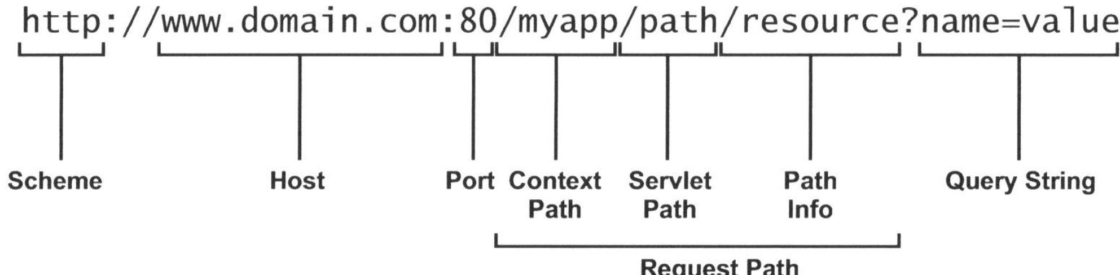

Security-Related Methods

For an explanation of each of these methods, and how to use them, see the *Programmatic Authorisation with Servlets* section in Chapter 21:

- **`String getAuthType()`**
  Returns the name of the mechanism used to authenticate the current client, or `null` if the client is not authenticated.

- **`String getRemoteUser()`**
  Returns the username of the client, or `null` if the client is not authenticated.

- **`Principal getUserPrincipal()`**
  Returns the `java.security.Principal` which represents the current client, or `null` if the client is not authenticated.

- **`boolean isUserInRole(String role)`**
  Returns `true` if, and only if, the current client is both authenticated and is in the role called `role`.

Cookies

When an HTTP request is made, the container helpfully retrieves all cookie data stored on the client, instantiating a new instance of the `javax.servlet.http.Cookie` class for each cookie encountered. Note that the container automatically takes care of any cookies containing session management information such as the `jsessionid` (see Chapter 9), so you don't need to examine these yourself as you might in other lower-level languages. However, if you need to use other custom cookies look no further than this method:

- **`Cookie[] getCookies()`**
  Returns an array of all `javax.servlet.http.Cookie` instances created by the container for all cookies sent by the client with this request. If there were no cookies in the request, `null` is returned.

Session Management

We will look at what sessions are, and how to use `HttpSession` objects in Chapter 9. There are several methods declared by the `HttpServletRequest` interface that allow servlet code to access the current session. Note that session objects are always retrieved from the request object, the reason being that the `HttpSession` object is dependent on the client's session identifier (called `jsessionid` in Java EE) which is either stored in cookies or in the request URI – and both of these data are available only from the `HttpServletRequest`.

- **`String getRequestedSessionId()`**
  Returns the session ID (`jsessionid`) as specified by the client. This may not be same as the session ID used by the valid session in the application, if the application invalidated the session or replaced it with a new one. Returns `null` if no session ID was supplied.

- **`HttpSession getSession()`**
  Returns the current valid session object, or if one does not exist, creates a new one. Equivalent to calling `getSession(true)`. This method never returns `null`.

- **`HttpSession getSession(boolean create)`**
  Returns the current valid session object. If one does not already exist, and the `boolean` argument is `true`, a new one is created; otherwise, if `false`, `null` is returned.

- **`boolean isRequestedSessionIdFromCookie()`**
  Returns `true` if the session ID (`jsessionid`) was located in a cookie on the client machine.

- **`boolean isRequestedSessionIdFromURL()`**
  Returns `true` if the session ID (`jsessionid`) was found as part of the request URI.

- **`boolean isRequestedSessionIdValid()`**
  Returns `true` if the session ID found in the request is still valid for the session object found in the container. If, since the request was made, the session has been invalidated or replaced, this will return `false`.

The most significant of these methods are the `getSession()` and getSession(boolean) variants; these allow servlet code to get a handle on the HttpSession object which represents the client's current session. As we will see in Chapter 9, this object can be used to store session-scoped attributes, which is a pretty common requirement of most applications.

ServletResponse

5

An implementation of this interface constitutes an encapsulation of the most basic properties of a response over any protocol. Most appreciably, it provides output streams for application components such as servlets to write content to the client.

Response Streams

The output streams provide a way to send data to the client transparently of the protocol being used. While the transmission 'over the wire' from the server to the client might use any number of valid protocols (such as sending data bytes as TCP 'packets'), it is the container which takes care of these details. All we need to do is get an output stream to write data to the container's interface and trust that everything will be taken care of! This interface provides two types of output streams: the good old java.io.OutputStream which is used for the transmission of binary data, and a java.io.Writer which is used for character (textual) data. Only one of these may be used; attempting to obtain both raises an IllegalStateException.

- **ServletOutputStream getOutputStream()**
  Returns an OutputStream used to return binary data to the client. Throws IllegalStateException if a Writer has already been obtained via a call to getWriter().

- **PrintWriter getWriter()**
  Returns a Writer suitable for sending character data to the client. Throws IllegalStateException if a binary OutputStream has already been obtained via a call to getOutputStream().

- **void flushBuffer()**
  Flushes the buffer being used (either an OutputStream or Writer), sending all the current contents to the client and committing the response.

- **int getBufferSize()**
  Returns the buffer size used for the response, or 0 if no buffering is used.

- **boolean isCommitted()**
  Returns true if the response is committed. See below for the definition of commitment.

- **`void reset()`**
  Clears any data in the buffered output and any headers or status codes (in the case of HTTP). In effect, this method reverts the `ServletResponse` back to the state which it was in when the first component in the container received it. Throws `IllegalStateException` if the response is already committed, and you're just too late to reset!

- **`void resetBuffer()`**
  Clears any data on the buffer. If the response has been committed, or buffering isn't being used, this method throws `IllegalStateException`.

- **`void setBufferSize(int size)`**
  Sets the size of the buffer: this is the number of bytes which are to be written before the buffer is flushed and the response committed. The buffer will be at least as big as the `int` argument, but may be larger (due to buffer pooling optimisations in the container).

A response is said to be committed when there's no turning back. In other words, once the container has actually started sending data back to the client, it's too late to abort the response – unless you can physically cut the transmission cable in the seconds before the data reaches the client's terminal! I'm guessing you can't run or cut cables that fast, so that isn't a terribly viable option.

Once a response is committed, the data already sent cannot be retrieved or removed from the buffer (hence all the reset methods throw an exception), but in addition any headers or HTTP status codes set cannot be changed. Once the container commits a response, it writes all headers to the client as well – it doesn't have much of a choice since headers always occur before the data in the body. This can present a problem: if a component being processed late in the request cycle discovers that it needs to send an error status code, but the response has already been committed because previous components wrote data to the stream, it can't! What should have been an error is received by the client as only half of a correct response, as the execution was halted wherever the error occurred.

There are two solutions to tackle this seemingly annoying problem: the first is by adjusting the buffer size. Making the buffer size larger means the data won't be sent to the client until more data has been received, thus prolonging the time which the components have to fill out a complete response (or raise an error). However, be advised: making the buffer large increases the amount of memory used on the server, which can degrade performance. The second solution is to use a response wrapper, which acts as a 'middle-man', like an extra buffer between the component and the container. This is essentially the same as using the container's response object directly, but it adds an extra layer of control. We will look at this in more detail in the next chapter.

Response Protocol and Transmission Data

Some data is protocol-independent. For example, the character encoding used for textual response streams, the MIME classifier given to the content type, and the size of the returned data. These can all be modified using the following methods:

- **`void setCharacterEncoding(String enc)`**
  Sets the character encoding of the response stream; examples are `UTF-8`, `UTF-16` and the default `ISO-8859-1`.

- **`String getCharacterEncoding()`**
  Returns the character encoding established explicitly by the `setCharacterEncoding` method, or the default `ISO-8858-1` if no explicit call has been made.

- **`void setContentType(String type)`**
  Sets the MIME content type of the response and, optionally, the character encoding used for the data. Typical values are `text/html` for HTML, `application/xml` for XML and `text/plain` for plain (unformatted) text. Character encoding is appended as follows: `text/html;`**`charset=UTF-8`**. The semicolon is used to delimit the MIME type from the `charset` definition. See also the comment on setting the encoding and calling `getWriter()` below.

- **`String getContentType()`**
  Returns the content type currently established using `setContentType()`, or `null` if it has not been specified.

- **`void setLocale(Locale locale)`**
  Provides a hint to the client as to the locale of the response–principally, the language and encoding being used. The language of the resource is passed to the client as a header if the protocol supports it, while the encoding is used for the response `Writer` (but not for `OutputStream` since this is binary and doesn't have an 'encoding' as such). Locales are often mapped to encodings: for example, the Chinese language requires a more sophisticated character set than French, which in turn is more complex than English. However, if the character encoding has been set explicitly already or subsequently, the encoding implied by the locale is ignored. See also the comment on setting encoding and calling `getWriter()` below.

- **`Locale getLocale()`**
  Returns the `java.util.Locale` preconfigured for this response, or the Web container's default.

- **`void setContentLength(int size)`**
  Sets the number of bytes in the response. This is an optional, but advised,

operation. Some (Java as well as non-Java) HTTP servers, especially those involved with dynamic responses, do not set the content length because they don't know the length of the total response at the time it is committed – components are still executing code which might add more data. If possible, provide support to set the correct content length; this can be achieved using filters and wrappers, which we look at later on.

Note that `setContentLength()` has no accessor ('getter') counterpart unlike all other methods, so don't get caught out!

Also, note that setting the encoding (either via the `setCharacterEncoding` method or indirectly as part of the `setContentType` or `setLocale` methods) only has an effect before the `getWriter()` method is *first called*. This is because the `Writer` is established using the encoding supplied by these methods; changing the character encoding wouldn't be much use after the `Writer` was already streaming data in that format! If using an `OutputStream` obtained by a call to `getOutputStream()`, the encoding is returned to the client in the headers but does not affect the data passed to the binary stream. Since it is independent of the binary `OutputStream`, the character encoding may be changed after a call to `getOutputStream()`, but before the response is committed – remember, commitment is final for all headers!

The HttpServletResponse Interface

This interface adds support for HTTP headers and status codes, URL rewriting used for session management, and the ability to supply cookies to the client.

Response Headers

The following methods provide support for adding HTTP response headers:

- **`void addHeader(String name, String value)`**
  Adds the header with the supplied `name` and sets it to the supplied `value`. If this header already exists, the value is appended to the set of values for this header. Otherwise the header is newly created.

- **`void setHeader(String name, String value)`**
  Sets the header with the supplied `name` to the supplied `value`. The distinction between `addHeader()` and this method is that this method overwrites any existing value(s) for the header rather than appending to existing ones.

- **`boolean containsHeader(String name)`**
  Returns `true` if the response currently contains a header called `name`, otherwise returns `false`.

- **`void addIntHeader(String name, int value)`**
  Convenience method: adds a header with an integer value to the response. Equivalent to the call: `addHeader(name, Integer.toString(value))`.
- **`void setIntHeader(String name, int value)`**
  Convenience method: sets the header with an integer value in the response. Equivalent to the call: `setHeader(name, Integer.toString(value))`.

- **`void addDateHeader(String name, long value)`**
  Convenience method: adds the header with a value formatted as a date. The `value` should be the number of milliseconds in UTC–since 1st January 1970 GMT. This is not a straight-forward mapping, since the date format will depend on the protocol and version of protocol being used. In addition, HTTP allows three formats of date and time (see below).
- **`void setDateHeader(String name, long value)`**
  Convenience method: sets the header with a value formatted as a date. The value should be the number of milliseconds since 1st January 1970 GMT.

Any of these methods invoked after the response has been committed are ignored (they do *not* throw `IllegalStateException`).

The date-related convenience methods are particularly useful, taking the number of milliseconds since 'the epoch' and converting them to valid HTTP dates, which have three possible formats (not that you need to know these for the exam):

- `Sun, 06 Nov 1994 08:49:37 GMT`
- `Sunday, 06-Nov-94 08:49:37 GMT`
- `Sun Nov 6 08:49:37 1994`

The preferred format is the first; the second is obsolete, while the third is discouraged. All times are in GMT, which is considered to be equal to Coordinated Universal Time (UTC) used commonly by computer-time formats.

HTTP Status Codes and Redirection

The status code of the response can be set using the following method:

- **`void setStatus(int code)`**
  Sets the HTTP status code (often abbreviated to 'SC') to the integer value. This value should be one of the constants declared in the `HttpServletResponse` interface, for example `SC_ACCEPTED` (200), `SC_NOT_FOUND` (404) or `SC_FORBIDDEN` (403), amongst many others.

In addition, the interface defines several other convenience methods which set the appropriate response header and do other actions:

- **`void sendError(int code)`**
  Used by component code to signal that an error has occurred and that an appropriate error page in the application should be displayed. The status code used is technically unrestricted, but to be meaningful should be one of the 400 or 500 ranges of codes which indicate client and server errors respectively. Certainly sending an error with status code 200 ('OK') wouldn't be advisable! When this method is called, the container sets the status code, clears the buffer so none of your response is committed and presents the client with the appropriate error page in the application, should one exist (otherwise the container uses the Java EE server's default for that status code).

- **`void sendError(int code, String message)`**
  Signals an error, as with `sendError(int)`, but provides an additional error message as the `String` parameter. This can optionally be displayed in error pages to provide information about a specific problem.

- **`void sendRedirect(String path)`**
  Sets the status code to 302 ('Found') or 307 ('Temporary Redirect'), clears the buffer and signals to the client to redirect their response somewhere else. The `String` parameter should be a URL which points the client to the new location. If the URL parameter begins with a `/`, it is interpreted as being relative to the current application context. Otherwise, it is interpreted as relative to the current request URI (not necessarily the URI of the component which raised the error, a common programming blunder).

Invoking any of these methods after the response has been committed results in an `IllegalStateException` being raised.

URL Rewriting

How and when to use rewriting is discussed in more detail in Chapter 9, but we introduce the methods used to achieve it here as they are part of `HttpServletResponse`:

- **`String encodeURL(String url)`**
  Encodes the URL supplied by the `String` parameter, adding the session ID (`jsessionid`) if applicable and appropriate. The value returned is suitable for all purposes except for URLs required for a redirect.

- **`String encodeRedirectURL(String url)`**
  Encodes the URL supplied by the `String` parameter, adding the session ID (`jsessionid`) if applicable and appropriate. The value returned from this method is suitable for use in the `sendRedirect(String)` method, and may be different from that returned from `encodeURL(String)`.

By 'applicable and appropriate' in the above method declarations, I mean that the URL will only be encoded if:

- The client currently has a valid session in this application and session tracking is turned on ('applicable'),
- The method for transferring the session ID is in the URL, and not via cookies or secure certificates ('appropriate').

Cookies

Use the following method to add a cookie to the response. This cookie will be available on the client's machine, assuming that it supports cookies, until the expiry date you set.

- **`void addCookie(Cookie cookie)`**
  Adds an instance of `javax.servlet.http.Cookie` to the response, indicating to the container to include HTTP code for the client to create a new cookie with the supplied settings.

Request Listeners

In the last chapter we look at using listeners which were called during the life cycle of the `ServletContext`, and as a result of context (application-scoped) attributes changing. Responses don't have, or need, any listeners–let's get that clear now. Response objects are completely under your control while they're executing in your application. Additionally, a request/response pair of objects can travel only down one execution path at once, and cannot be concurrently accessed by different threads like a `ServletContext` can. Each section of application code will be totally responsible for the request and response objects passing through it, so a set of global listeners aren't really necessary.

All this leaves us with is two types of listener for the request object: a life cycle listener, and a request-scoped attribute listener.

ServletRequestListener

This is the life cycle listener. What strikes me is that requests are so short-lived that a life cycle listener really seems unnecessary; on a machine with a fast processor, or if you're lucky enough many fast processors, the `ServletRequest` will be both started and finished with the blink of an eye.

Figure 5.4

Request Event Classes

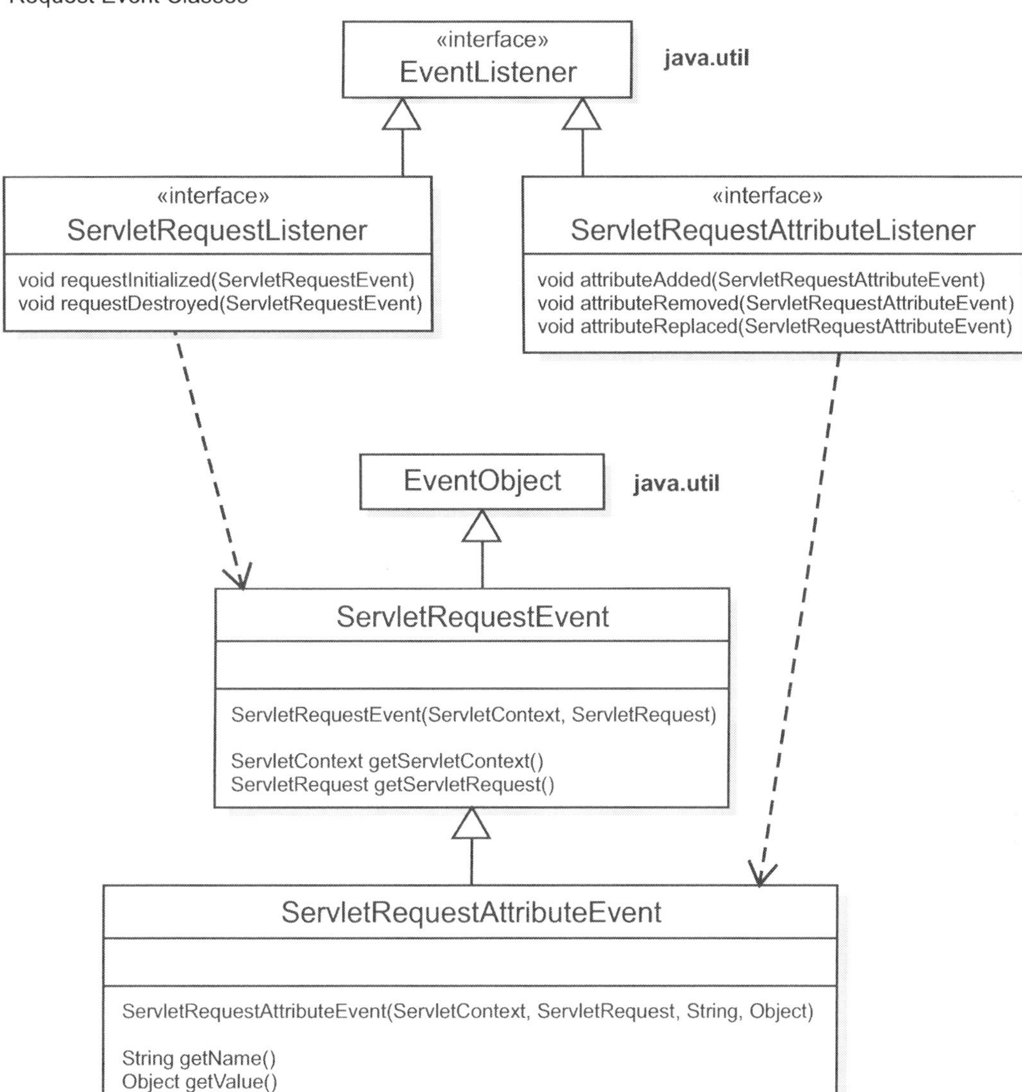

There is no listener for `ServletResponse` objects, but then because requests and responses go hand-in-hand, you can assume that if a request is coming into scope in the application that a response also is, and similarly when a request leaves the application towards the container, the response is leaving as well—so all is not lost if you want to keep track of a response object.

As with all listeners, a concrete class which implements this interface must be declared in the deployment descriptor if it is to be instantiated and registered by the container. This interface defines two methods:

- **`void requestInitialized(ServletRequestEvent event)`**
  Invoked by the container when the request is coming into the scope of the application for which this listener is configured. Again, this doesn't imply that the request object has been newly instantiated, but the container guarantees that all previous state will have been cleared.

- **`void requestDestroyed(ServletRequestEvent event)`**
  Invoked by the container when the request is leaving the application. This method doesn't actually imply that the request object is going to be garbage collected, but instead that its contents will be cleared. The container may choose to recycle request objects, and to keep a small pool for incoming requests, to improve performance. You could use this method to clear out object references stored in request-scoped attributes, but a good container will do that anyway!

The ServletRequestEvent Class

The methods above both take a container-generated instance of this event class. This class defines two methods which are of particular interest:

- **`ServletContext getServletContext()`**
  Returns the application context for the application into which the listener is installed, and in which the request object has changed.

- **`ServletRequest getServletRequest()`**
  Returns the request object which changed, causing this event to be fired. The returned value could equally be an instance of `HttpServletRequest`; if this is critical to what you are trying to achieve, you should cast the result. If you're not sure what class of request is being returned, use the `instanceof` operator:

```
ServletRequest req = event.getServletRequest();
if(req instanceof HttpServletRequest) {
    HttpServletRequest httpReq = (HttpServletRequest) req;
    // Process 'httpReq' as an HttpServletRequest
} else {
    // Process 'req' as a generic ServletRequest
}
```

ServletRequestAttributeListener

If you're concerned with knowing when request-scoped attributes change, implement this interface and declare the implementation class in the deployment descriptor. The container invokes the following methods as attributes change value in any request inside this application:

- **`void attributeAdded(ServletRequestAttributeEvent event)`**
  Invoked by the container when a new attribute has been added to a request in the application. The request object, and the name and value of the new attribute can be retrieved using the `event` parameter.
- **`void attributeRemoved(ServletRequestAttributeEvent event)`**
  Invoked by the container when an attribute is being removed from the request. The `event` argument can be queried for the old name and value of the attribute, before it was removed.
- **`void attributeReplaced(ServletRequestAttributeEvent event)`**
  Called when an attribute's value has been overwritten with a new one. The `event` object returns the name of the affected attribute, and its old value. If you need to know the new value as well, query the attributes of the request object obtained from `event.getServletRequest()`.

The ServletRequestAttributeEvent Class

This class extends `ServletRequestEvent`, and provides two extra methods alongside those used for retrieving the affected `ServletContext` and `ServletRequest`:

- **`String getName()`**
  Returns the name of the attribute which changed, causing this event to be fired.
- **`Object getValue()`**
  Returns the value of the attribute which changed: if the attribute was newly added, this will be the new value; if it was removed or replaced, this will be the old value before the attribute was altered.

5

Revision Questions

1 **Which of the following pairs of interfaces define the container's contract for requests and responses?** **(choose two)**

- A javax.servlet.Request and javax.servlet.Response
- B javax.servlet.ServletRequest and javax.servlet.ServletResponse
- C javax.enterprise.HttpRequest and javax.enterprise.HttpResponse
- D javax.servlet.http.HttpRequest and javax.servlet.http.HttpResponse
- E javax.servlet.http.HttpServletRequest and javax.servlet.http.HttpServletResponse

2 **What is the simplest line of code which must be inserted on line 9 of the exhibit to initialise the lang variable with the value of the language request-scoped attribute?** **(choose one)**

EXHIBIT

- A lang = req.getAttribute("language");
- B lang = (String) req.getAttribute("language");
- C lang = (String) getAttribute("language");
- D lang = req.getParameter("language");
- E lang = (String) req.getParameter("language");

3 **Assuming the servlet in the exhibit is the only component to modify the hitcounter request-scoped attribute, and that it is invoked only once per request, what are the possible results of making a request to this servlet?** **(choose one)**

EXHIBIT

- A The text 'Visitor number 1' is always written to the client.
- B The text 'Visitor number x' is written to the client, where x is the number of invocations of the servlet performed since the application was deployed.
- C A compilation error occurs on line 6.
- D A runtime error occurs on line 7.
- E A compilation error occurs on line 14.

4 **A servlet needs to store data in the request scope. Which ServletRequest method is the correct one to invoke?** **(choose one)**

- A setAttribute(String, String)
- B setAttr(String, Object)
- C setAttribute(String, Object)
- D setParameter(String, Object)
- E setParam(String, String)

5 **During debugging an application, a developer needs to write out all request attributes to the client, formatted as the MIME type 'text/plain'. What lines inserted in the exhibited servlet will achieve this?**

EXHIBIT

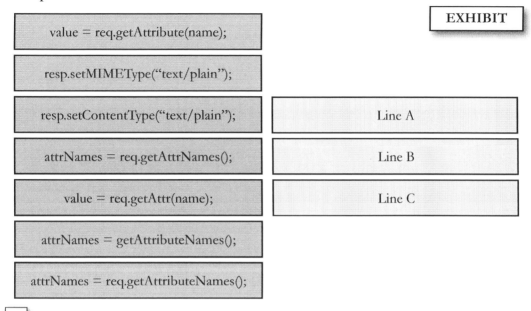

- value = req.getAttribute(name);
- resp.setMIMEType("text/plain");
- resp.setContentType("text/plain");
- attrNames = req.getAttrNames();
- value = req.getAttr(name);
- attrNames = getAttributeNames();
- attrNames = req.getAttributeNames();

Line A

Line B

Line C

6 **Assuming the request contains a parameter name with value 'John' and auto-flushing of reponse is 512 bytes, what is the effect of making a GET request to the servlet in the exhibit?** (choose one)

EXHIBIT

- A The text '<p>Welcome John</p>' is written to the client with text/plain MIME type.
- B The text '<p>Welcome John</p>' is written to the client with text/html MIME type.
- C The client is redirected to the resource at the context-relative path /servlet2.
- D A compilation error occurs on line 8.
- E A runtime error occurs on line 12.
- F A runtime error occurs on line 14.

7 **A servlet is sent XML data as the body of an HTTP POST request. What method on ServletRequest would be the best one to invoke to obtain the data?** (choose one)

- A getBody()
- B getReader()
- C getContentStream()
- D getContentBody()
- E getBodyStream()

5

8 **Which of the following fragments, assuming no errors occur as a result of the omitted servlet code, obtain the value of the request parameter called selected and writes all its values to the response stream?** **(choose two)**

A
```
out.write(req.getParameter("selected"));
```

B
```
String[] s = req.getAllParameters("selected");
for(int i=0; i < s.length; i++) {
   out.write(s[i] + ",");
}
```

C
```
Map m = req.getParameterMap();
out.write(m.get("selected"));
```

D
```
Map m = req.getParameterMap();
String[] s = (String[]) m.get("selected");
for(int i=0; i < s.length; i++) {
   out.write(s[i] + ",");
}
```

E
```
String[] s = req.getParameterValues("selected");
for(int i=0; i < s.length; i++) {
   out.write(s[i] + ",");
}
```

9 **What method is used to obtain the set of Cookies provided by the client?** **(choose one)**

- A String[] getCookies() on ServletRequest
- B Cookie[] getCookies() on ServletRequest
- C Cookie[] getCookies() on HttpServletRequest
- D String[] getCookies() on HttpSession
- E Cookie[] getCookies() on ServletContext

10 **Which class encapsulates cookie data?** **(choose one)**

- A java.lang.String
- B javax.servlet.Cookie
- C javax.enterprise.Cookie
- D javax.servlet.http.Cookie

11 **A servlet is required to output different content depending on the user's preferred language – this is the first value extracted from the HTTP Accept-Language header. If this header has the value 'fr', what is the result of issuing a GET request to the exhibited servlet?** **(choose one)**

EXHIBIT

- A The Content-Language response header is set to 'fr' and the text 'Bonjour' is returned to the client.
- B The text 'Bonjour' is returned to the client, but the Content-Language response header is not set.
- C The text 'Welcome' is returned, and the 'Content-Language' response header is set to 'en'.
- D A runtime error occurs on line 24.
- E A compilation error occurs on line 25.

12 **Which of the following methods should be used to obtain all the values for a particular request header?** **(choose one)**

- A String getHeader(String) on ServletRequest
- B String getHeader(String) on HttpServletRequest
- C Enumeration getHeaderNames(String) on HttpServletRequest
- D String[] getHeaders(String) on HttpServletRequest
- E Enumeration getHeaders(String) on HttpServletRequest

13 **Which of the following methods on HttpServletRequest can be used to convert a request header into a fully-formatted java.util. Date object?** **(choose one)**

- A getHeader(String)
- B getIntHeader(String)
- C getDateHeader(String)
- D formatHeader(String, Class) where Class is 'Date.class'
- E None of the above

5

14 **The exhibited servlet incorporates the contents of a text file /myfile.txt into the response stream, amongst other text. The file contains the text 'quotation'. What happens when this servlet receives a request?** **(choose one)**

EXHIBIT

- A '<h3>Excerpt from file</h3><div>quotation</div>' is written to the client.
- B A compilation error occurs on line 7.
- C A compilation error occurs on line 13.
- D A runtime error occurs on line 11.
- E A runtime error occurs on line 13.

15 **Which of the following code fragments causes the client to be redirected to the context-relative /servlet2 resource? You may assume request and response contain the HttpServletRequest and HttpServletResponse objects respectively, and that 'return' causes the servlet's service method to exit.** **(choose two)**

- A response.sendError(HttpServletResponse.SC_TEMPORARY_REDIRECT);
  response.setHeader("Location", response.encodeRedirectURL("/servlet2"));
  return;
- B response.redirect("/servlet2");
  return;
- C response.setHeader("Location", response.encodeRedirectURL("/servlet2"));
  response.setStatus (HttpServletResponse.SC_TEMPORARY_REDIRECT);
  return;
- D response.sendRedirect("/servlet2");
  return;
- E response.setHeader("Location", request.encodeRedirectURL("/servlet2"));
  response.setStatus (HttpServletResponse.SC_TEMPORARY_REDIRECT);
  return;

16 **Which method can be used to perform URL rewriting?** **(choose one)**

- A rewriteURL(String) on HttpServletRequest
- B encodeURL(String) on HttpServletRequest
- C prepareURL(String) on HttpServletResponse
- D encodeURL(String) on HttpServletResponse
- E rewriteURL(String) on HttpServletResponse

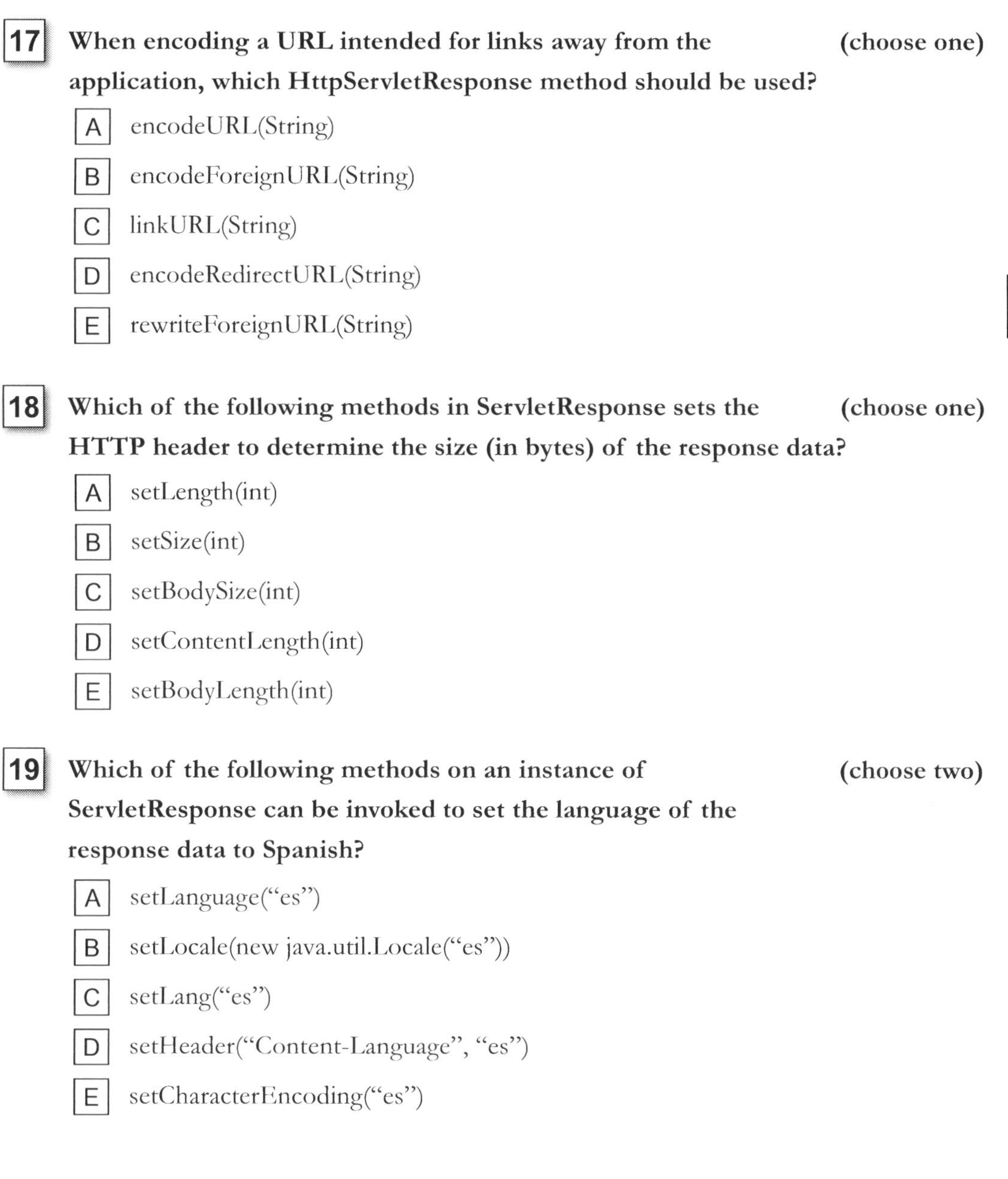

17 **When encoding a URL intended for links away from the application, which HttpServletResponse method should be used?** (choose one)

- A encodeURL(String)
- B encodeForeignURL(String)
- C linkURL(String)
- D encodeRedirectURL(String)
- E rewriteForeignURL(String)

18 **Which of the following methods in ServletResponse sets the HTTP header to determine the size (in bytes) of the response data?** (choose one)

- A setLength(int)
- B setSize(int)
- C setBodySize(int)
- D setContentLength(int)
- E setBodyLength(int)

19 **Which of the following methods on an instance of ServletResponse can be invoked to set the language of the response data to Spanish?** (choose two)

- A setLanguage(“es”)
- B setLocale(new java.util.Locale(“es”))
- C setLang(“es”)
- D setHeader(“Content-Language”, “es”)
- E setCharacterEncoding(“es”)

5

20 **A redirection servlet needs to redirect the client to another resource, but also needs to indicate the minimum time the client should wait before issuing the redirect request. It can do this using the Retry-After HTTP header, which takes either the number of seconds to wait or an HTTP date as its value. The servlet needs to make the client wait 20 seconds. Which method invocations on HttpServletResponse would cause an existing value of this header to be overwritten with the new one?** **(choose three)**

- A response.setHeader("Retry-After", 20)
- B response.setHeader("Retry-After", "" + 20)
- C response.setHeader("Retry-After", Integer.toString(20))
- D response.setIntHeader("Retry-After", 20)
- E response.addHeader("Retry-After", 20)

21 **Which of the following status code methods exist in the HttpServletResponse interface?** **(choose three)**

- A setStatusCode(int)
- B setStatus(int)
- C sendError(int)
- D sendErrorCode(int)
- E sendError(int,String)

22 **An application developer needs to listen for request life cycle events in the Web container. What listener interface should be implemented?** **(choose one)**

- A javax.servlet.RequestListener
- B javax.enterprise.RequestListener
- C javax.servlet.ServerRequestListener
- D javax.servlet.ServletRequestListener
- E javax.servlet.http.HttpServletRequestListener

23 **What method on the request listener interface is invoked when a new request is created?** **(choose one)**

- A void requestCreated(ServletRequestEvent)
- B void requestInit(ServletRequestEvent)
- C void requestInitialized(ServletRequestEvent)
- D void requestReady(ServletRequestEvent)

24 **An application developer needs to listen for attributes being modified on an HttpServletRequest object. What listener interface should be implemented?** **(choose one)**

- A javax.servlet.RequestAttributeListener
- B javax.enterprise.AttributeListener
- C javax.servlet.ServletRequestAttributeListener
- D javax.servlet.http.HttpServletRequestAttributeListener
- E javax.servlet.AttributeListener

25 **Which of the following are not methods in the ServletRequestAttributeEvent class?** **(choose two)**

- A ServletContext getServletContext()
- B ServletRequest getServletRequest()
- C String getName()
- D ServletRequest getRequest()
- E Object getValue()
- F String getValue()

Exhibits

Q.2

```
import javax.servlet.*;
import javax.servlet.http.*;
import java.io.*;

public class MyServlet extends GenericServlet {

    public void service(ServletRequest req, ServletResponse resp)
                throws ServletException, IOException {
        String lang = null;
        // insert line
        if(lang != null && !lang.equals("en")) {
            throw new ServletException("Unsupported language");
        }
    }

}
```

Q.3

```
import javax.servlet.*;
import java.io.*;

public class MyServlet extends GenericServlet {

    public void service(ServletRequest req, ServletResponse resp)
                throws ServletException, IOException {
        Integer counter = (Integer) req.getAttribute("hitcounter");
        if(counter == null) {
            counter = new Integer(1);
        } else {
            counter = new Integer(counter.intValue() + 1);
        }

        req.setAttribute("hitcounter", counter);

        Writer out = resp.getWriter();
        out.write("Visitor number: " + counter);
    }
}
```

Q.5

```
import javax.servlet.*;
import java.io.*;
import java.util.Enumeration;


public class MyServlet extends GenericServlet {

    public void service(ServletRequest req, ServletResponse resp) {
        Enumeration attrNames = null;
        // Line A
        Writer out = resp.getWriter();
        // Line B
        while(attrNames.hasMoreElements()) {
            String name = (String) attrNames.nextElement();
            Object value = null;
            // Line C
            out.write(name + " : " + value + "\n");
        }
    }

}
```

Q.6

```
import javax.servlet.*;
import javax.servlet.http.*;
import java.io.*;

public class MyServlet extends HttpServlet {

  protected void doGet(HttpServletRequest rq, HttpServletResponse rp)
                 throws IOException, ServletException {
      String name = rq.getParameter("username");
      rp.setContentType("text/plain");
      PrintWriter out = rp.getWriter();
      out.println("<p>Welcome " + name + "</p>");
      rp.setContentType("text/html");
      out.flush();
      rp.sendRedirect("/servlet2");
  }

}
```

Q.11

```
public class MyServlet extends HttpServlet {

    public void doGet(HttpServletRequest req, HttpServletResponse)
                throws ServletException, IOException {
        String lang = req.getHeader("accept-language");
        if(lang == null) {
            lang = "en";
        }
        StringBuffer output = new StringBuffer();
        if(lang.startsWith("fr")) {
            output.append("Bonjour");
        } else if(lang.startsWith("de")) {
            output.append("Gut morgan");
        } else if(lang.equals("en-au")) {
            output.append("G'day mate");
        } else {
            output.append("Welcome");
        }
        resp.getWriter().write(output.toString());
        resp.flushBuffer();
        resp.setHeader("Content-Language", lang);
        return;
    }
}
```


Q.14

```
public class MyServlet extends GenericServlet {

    public void service(ServletRequest req, ServletResponse resp)
                throws ServletException, IOException {
        InputStream srm =
             getServletContext().getResourceAsStream("/myfile.txt");
        PrintWriter out = resp.getWriter();
        out.println("<h3>Excerpt from file</h3><div>");
        if(srm != null) {
           ServletOutputStream outBin = resp.getOutputStream();
            for(int i=srm.read(); i >= 0; i = srm.read()) {
                outBin.write(i);
            }
        } else {
            out.println("No file available");
        }
        out.println("</div>");
    }
}
```

Answers to Revision Questions

1 **Correct answers: B, E**

2 **Correct answer: B**

A is incorrect – it doesn't cast from Object type to String. C is incorrect – it retrieves a context attribute. D is incorrect – it retrieves a parameter and not an attribute (although this line is legal, since getParameter() returns a String). E is the same as D, but includes an explicit, and unnecessary, cast (getParameter() already returns a String).

5

3 **Correct answer: A**

This is an incorrectly implemented hit-counter. Since the request attributes are cleared for each new request, and we are told this servlet is invoked only once per request, hitcounter will always be null when we get to line 7. Hence, we always set it to 1. Line 7 cannot cause a ClassCastException to be thrown because we are told in the question that no other components modify the hitcounter attribute – so it must be either an Integer as modified by this servlet, or null. B is wrong, since it will always display 1 on every invocation, as hitcounter is null for each new request. Lines 6 and 14 are fine, so C and E are wrong. As we said, we guarantee that hitcounter is either an Integer or null, so D can never happen.

4 **Correct answer: C**

5 **Correct answer:**

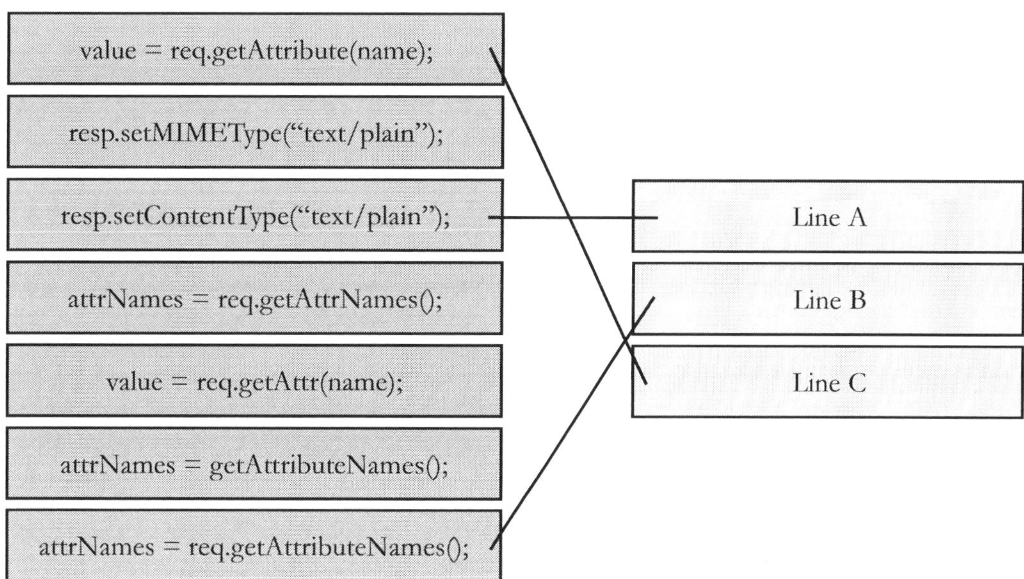

Note if A had contained an encoding as well as the MIME type, it would *have* to occur before B, otherwise setContentType() could not set the encoding since it is invoked after getWriter()!

5

6 **Correct answer: F**

It is illegal to invoke sendRedirect() or any header methods after the response is committed; out.flush() causes commitment. D is wrong–remember that all request *parameters* have String values, so no casting is needed here (unlike with attributes, which would have to be cast from Object to String). A and B are both wrong because the error is handled by the container and takes priority over the content written to the response buffer (but note that if the error didn't occur, A would be the correct answer, because after getWriter() is invoked, setContentType() has no effect). E is wrong–although setContentType() has no effect after getWriter() is invoked, it doesn't throw exceptions.

7 **Correct answer: B**

This returns a Reader, ideal for handling text data, such as XML. Note that the only other valid method is getInputStream(), but this isn't the best choice as it's used to read binary data.

8 **Correct answers: D, E**

The question asks for *all* values for the selected parameter, and A only gets the first, so that's wrong.B uses the nonexistent getAllParameters() method, C writes out the String[] string representation (usually a hash code or memory address) stored as a value in the Map; it doesn't write out each entry.

9 **Correct answer: C**

A and D are wrong–returning String[]. B is wrong–correct return type, but the generic ServletRequest interface doesn't host this method–cookies are specific to the HTTP protocol (and hence specific to HttpServletRequest). D is wrong–getCookies() isn't found on HttpSession because cookies are sent by the client on each request, and not stored in the session. E is clearly incorrect because cookies exist on an individual user basis, so it would be highly inappropriate to use the shared ServletContext for storage.

10 **Correct answer: D**

11 **Correct answer: B**

The response is committed by flushing the buffer on line 23, so line 24 has no effect. Hence the response header isn't set, making A incorrect, and D is wrong because these methods don't throw an IllegalStateException if the response has already been committed. The request header has the value 'fr' given in the question, so line 14 is executed, and the text 'Bonjour' is output to the response. C is wrong–getHeader() would return null here, if the attribute test was case-sensitive. But, all headers are case-insensitive, so 'Accept-Language' is the same as 'accept-language'. E is wrong–it is perfectly valid, although here unnecessary, to use the return keyword in void method.

12 **Correct answer: E**

Note that getHeaders() returns an Enumeration, unlike getParameterValues() which returns a String[]. It is easy to be caught by this discrepancy in the API. A is wrong as headers are specific to the HTTP protocol, and therefore reside in HttpServletRequest.

13 **Correct answer: E**

A returns the String for the value of the header, while B attempts to cast it to a primitive int, so both are incorrect. D doesn't exist, and C might look promising, but does in fact only return a long (this can be used to initialise a Date object, passing the long value to Date's constructor).

14 **Correct answer: D**

You cannot invoke getWriter() and then invoke getOutputStream(). This throws IllegalStateException, as only one type of output stream can be obtained per request..

15 **Correct answers: C, D**

A is wrong – sendError() commits the response and doesn't allow the header to be set. B is incorrect – there is no redirect() method. E is wrong – encodeRedirectURL() is on the Response object, not the Request object.

16 **Correct answer: D**

17 **Correct answer: D**

This method is different from encodeURL() in that it includes logic to determine whether the session ID needs to be included in the URL. We don't want to expose the ID to applications other than our own, so where this occurs, the ID is omitted.

18 **Correct answer: D**

19 **Correct answers: B, D**

Although HTTP headers are not an exam objective, we can eliminate A and C since they are invalid methods, and E because 'es' isn't a valid MIME type. We know that B is correctly formatted, and so is D, and therefore we choose those options as they are the only ones which remain. This is useful exam technique if surprised by a seemingly unobvious question.

20 **Correct answers: B, C, D**

A is wrong – the argument for setHeader() is a String, not an integer primitive. addHeader() is wrong as we want to *overwrite* an existing value (if there is one). "" + 20 is the same as the String "20", and therefore B is valid; C is also valid, and does the casting performed by setIntHeader() explicitly. D does the casting implicitly as part of the setIntHeader() implementation.

21 **Correct answers: B, C, E**

22 **Correct answer: D**

Note that none of the others exist.

23 **Correct answer: C**

24 **Correct answer: C**

Note that none of the others exist.

25 **Correct answers: D, F**

D has the wrong method name, F has the wrong return type – recall that all scoped-attributes have Object (not just String) values.

In this chapter you'll:

- ▶ Use objects of the RequestDispatcher interface to pass processing between various components of a Web application.
- ▶ Learn the difference between forwarding to and including other components.
- ▶ Obtain a foreign RequestDispatcher to communicate with other Web applications in the same server.
- ▶ Use wrappers to modify methods of request and response objects, and then pass wrapper instances through a RequestDispatcher.

6 RequestDispatcher & Wrappers

A critical requirement of any dynamic Web application is to be able to include the output generated by one resource into the output stream of another. For example, a template page provides the layout for the site, but the content which fills that layout is usually derived from the runtime results of other servlet or JSP resources. Similarly, it is common for one central servlet to require the services or the output of other servlets in the application. It is therefore essential that we establish a mechanism for forwarding control between resources. In addition, it is sometimes necessary to override the behaviour of the container's standard request and response services. We can do this by using wrappers in conjuction with `RequestDispatcher`s.

The RequestDispatcher Mechanism

The focus of this section is the `javax.servlet.RequestDispatcher` interface.

In Chapter 4, we looked at the `getResourceAsStream` method of the application's `ServletContext` instance. We said that it was useful for reading static content and, optionally, writing it to the response stream. The emphasis here is on *static* content. If you use this method to invoke a *dynamic* resource such as a JSP, you'll end up with the source code forming the output to the response. Not only is this highly undesirable and very confusing for the end user, but it could at worst constitute a security issue as well–especially if you're in the bad habit of hard-coding passwords as literals in your pages!

On the contrary, the `RequestDispatcher` is an object obtained from the container at run time. All calls to other resources in the application are mediated by the container; it therefore follows that we must have some channel for delegating control to other resources, and inevitably this will involve communicating with the container. The channel is provided by the `RequestDispatcher`, which is obtained using the following methods of `ServletContext`:

- **`RequestDispatcher getRequestDispatcher(String path)`**
  Obtains a `RequestDispatcher` object suitable for passing control to a resource at the given path within the current application. This path must be context-relative, and hence begin with a forward-slash (/). A single `RequestDispatcher` can be used to delegate control only to resources in the current application.

- **`RequestDispatcher getNamedDispatcher(String name)`**
  Obtains a `RequestDispatcher` suitable for passing control to the resource with the supplied logical `name`. A **logical name** is one configured in the deployment descriptor. All servlets must have logical names; configuration of names for JSPs is optional. The parameter is just a string *name* as described by a `<servlet-name>` in the deployment descriptor, and not a path.

As we saw earlier, the `ServletRequest` interface also provides a relevant method:

- **`RequestDispatcher getRequestDispatcher(String path)`**
  Returns a `RequestDispatcher` appropriate for including or forwarding to the resource at the specified `path`. The key difference between this method and the `ServletContext` method with the same signature is that this `path` may be relative to the current servlet (omitting the starting forward-slash) as well as relative to the application context (including the starting forward-slash, `/`).

6

The **`RequestDispatcher` mechanism** (often referred to as simply the RD mechanism) can be used to delegate execution to both dynamic and static resources. Clearly its true power lies with the former, but if used with static resources, the container simply reads the content and buffers it to the output. This is effectively the same behaviour as exhibited using the `getResourceAsStream` method of the `ServletContext` interface. It is therefore advantageous to use the RD mechanism wherever possible since it reduces the likelihood of errors and confusion arising from the classification of resources as either dynamic or static.

At this point I feel I must also mention the JSP `include` directive, which in JSP pages looks a little like this (see Chapter 13 for the full explanation):

```
<%@ include file="..." %>
```

This is a type of inclusion specific to JSPs, and is performed at *translation time* and not at run time unlike both the static stream and RD mechanisms mentioned above. For the exam you should be aware of these three types of inclusion and the differences between them. In general, `RequestDispatcher`s present the most versatile option–if you've got a choice on the exam between different inclusion mechanisms, it's a pretty safe bet that the RD mechanism will be at least one correct answer.

Figure 6.1 shows a summary of the classes, methods and the invocation procedures involved in using `RequestDispatcher`s.

The RequestDispatcher Interface

The container provides a concrete implementation instance of this interface

Figure 6.1

RequestDispatcher Mechanism

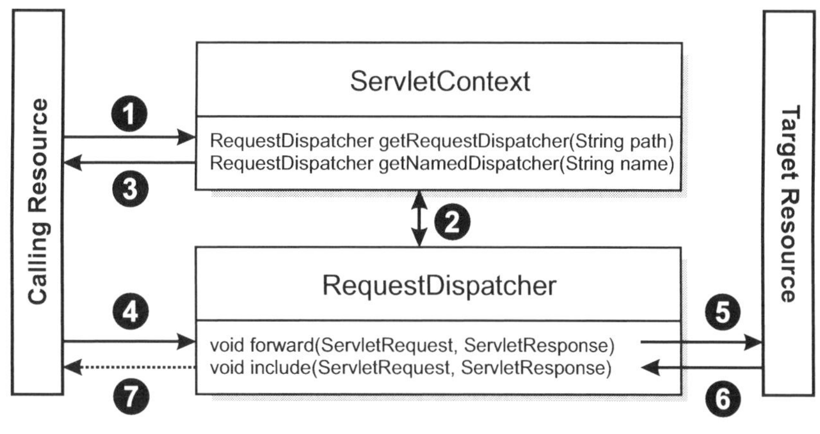

`forward` **operations cause the response to be committed and the stream closed during this step.**

1. The calling resource invokes the application's ServletContext instance to obtain a suitable RequestDispatcher.
2. The ServletContext uses the container's interface to create a new appropriate RequestDispatcher.
3. The ServletContext returns the newly created RequestDispatcher.
4. The calling resource calls the required method on the RequestDispatcher returned from step 3.
5. The RequestDispatcher uses the container's interface to invoke the target resource.
6. The target resource returns control to the RequestDispatcher
7. In the case of an include, control returns to the calling resource. For forwarding operations, the method returns, but the calling resource is not permitted to make any further changes to the response

when the `getRequestDispatcher` or `getNamedDispatcher` methods are invoked. As with most other container-derived services, we aren't interested in the implementation, but just in the contract specified by this interface:

- **`void forward(ServletRequest req, ServletResponse resp)`**
  Causes the `ServletRequest` to be forwarded to the other resource. Uncommitted output in the response buffer is automatically cleared. This allows one servlet to do some processing before another generates the response. Once this method is called, control is completely delegated to the second resource; the first gives up its right to change any data returned in the response to the client. This method must be invoked before the response has been committed or an `IllegalStateException` is thrown. Recommended practise is to invoke this method before any calls to `getOutputStream()` or `getWriter()` as only one of these may ever be invoked during a single

request, or an `IllegalStateException` is thrown (see page 101). The resource being forwarded to may in general call one or other of these methods, but which one is unknown to the caller, so to use either in arbitrary calling code would be unwise.

- **`void include(ServletRequest req, ServletResponse resp)`**
  Causes the runtime evaluation of the second resource to be included in the response. This method may be invoked unconditionally (for example, the response may already have been committed). However, the included servlet may not make any changes to the response status code or headers (attempted changes are simply ignored). Once the second resource returns from its evaluation, control returns to the same position in the first resource and execution of the first continues.

6

A source of confusion for many beginners is that they expect the `RequestDispatcher` methods to contain a third parameter, specifying the name or path of the resource being forwarded to. However, recall that the `RequestDispatcher` instance is created *based on* the second resource's location. You can't use the same RD instance to forward to a different resource; instead, each RD can be used to pass control to one single endpoint only, and this endpoint is inherent in that instance. The container creates instances of its `RequestDispatcher` implementation based on the values passed to the `getRequestDispatcher` and `getNamedDispatcher` methods – if you want to target a different resource, you must obtain a separate dispatcher instance using these methods.

Using RequestDispatchers

We've briefly mentioned what `RequestDispatcher`s are and what they do, and looked at their API definition. Here we give the details of the process which must be followed to obtain and use an actual RD instance.

First, decide which method you want to use to get a handle on the target resource: either specify a path within the application, or give the logical name of the resource. For the former, you would use the following code in a `GenericServlet` implementation:

```
ServletContext context = getServletContext();
String path = "/myresource";
RequestDispatcher dispatch = context.getRequestDispatcher(path);
```

Alternatively, using the logical name:

```
ServletContext context = getServletContext();
String name = "myservlet1";
RequestDispatcher dispatch = context.getNamedDispatcher(name);
```

As you can see, both methods rely on first obtaining the `ServletContext` for the application. The first line of the snippets above both assume that you're using a `GenericServlet` implementation (such as `HttpServlet`); if not, then replace that line by the correct code to obtain the instance. Similarly, the second line literal declaration can be replaced by a runtime value, obtained from a scoped attribute for example.

Once you've got the instance in the `dispatch` variable (or whatever you decide to call it), you can forward to the second resource as follows:

```
dispatch.forward(request, response)
```


Including the second resource is just as easy:

```
dispatch.include(request, response)
```

The difference between forwarding and including is a simple one: when a request is forwarded to a second resource, the response must be sent, committed and the *stream closed* before the `forward` method returns (the helpful container will take care of all this for us). Additionally, the response should not already have been committed before `forward()` is called. For this reason, a call to the `forward` method is usually the last in a servlet's service method, and the servlet does not write much (if any) content to the response (to prevent it from committing) prior to invoking `forward()`.

Although a `forward()` requires that the first resource refrain from making any subsequent changes to the committed response stream, it does not cause servlet methods to return. If you require processing of the servlet to terminate after the forward, you will need to provide an explicit return in your servlet code:

```
public void service(HttpServletRequest req,
                    HttpServletResponse resp) {
    ...
    if(condition) {
        /* Plan: forward and then exit this method */
        // Assume RequestDispatcher called 'rd' already obtained
        rd.forward(req, resp);
        return;
    }
    ...
    // Assume we create a RequestDispatcher called 'rd' here
    rd.forward(req,resp);
    ...
}
```

In this example, if `condition` is `true`, the first `forward()` is invoked. After the second resource has done its processing and written to the response, the `forward` method will return. At this point, the response has most likely been committed by the forwarded resource writing data to the response. If we'd omitted the explicit `return` statement from above, the subsequent `rd.forward()` would be executed and an `IllegalStateException` would be thrown since the response is committed.

NOTE: We could also have got round this problem by using an `else` block to enclose the second `rd.forward()`. Whatever method you use, be careful about commitment after calling `forward()`, and never call more than one `forward()` in a request processing chain!

6

On the contrary, *including* a resource requires that the stream remains open when the method returns, such that further content can be written to the client. An included resource is not permitted to modify any response headers (any attempted modification is ignored). As a result of this behaviour, multiple `include` methods can appear anywhere within the request processing chain of servlets and JSPs, wherever you need some external content to be written into the response's output buffer.

Foreign Context RequestDispatchers

Okay, so the RD mechanism is really useful, but as it stands it doesn't allow resources in other applications to be utilised. However, since all applications are run in the same container and the RD mechanism always uses the container as a mediator, it is just as easy to utilise resources external to the calling application.

The difference in procedure is in the acquiring of the `ServletContext`. Rather than obtaining a `ServletContext` for the current application, we get a foreign context, as shown in Chapter 4:

```
ServletContext thisContext = getServletContext();
ServletContext foreignCtxt = thisContext.getContext("/myapp");
```

We make use of the `ServletContext` interface's `getContext` method, to which we pass the context-root path of the foreign application running in the current container. This path is relative to the Java EE server root, so in the above example, the foreign application is deployed under the `myapp` directory in the Java EE root and with the context name `/myapp`. See the Chapter 4 for more details of the `getContext` method.

We can now use this new context to obtain a `RequestDispatcher` for a resource in the foreign application; for example:

```
RequestDispatcher fd = foreignCtxt.getRequestDispatcher("/cat");
```

This would return a dispatcher for the resource located at `/cat` under the `myapp` application. The full path of that resource from the Java EE root would be: `/myapp/cat`.

NOTE: Although it is possible to utilise other applications in the same container, it is *never* possible to forward or include resources in a *different* container (e.g. running on a separate server or in a separate container instance). Additionally, security restrictions in the container may prevent foreign contexts from being obtained, in which case it will not be possible to utilise applications even if they reside in the same container.

Additional Request Attributes

When a request is forwarded or included using the `RequestDispatcher` mechanism, the container may change the URI paths in the request object to reflect the new path. This section briefly outlines those changes – and unfortunately these are an exam objective, so learn the gritty details!

When a request is forwarded to a second resource, the paths in the request object reflect the path used to obtain the `RequestDispatcher` – i.e. the path of the resource being forwarded to. However, since a call to `getNamedDispatcher(String)` does not take a URI parameter (but instead a logical name), the paths in the request object for a `RequestDispatcher` obtained in this way must be the same as those in the original request.

Similarly, when a resource is included, the paths in the request object passed to that resource reflect the path to the second resource – i.e. the URI passed to the `getRequestDispatcher(String)` method. The exception is once again when `getNamedDispatcher(String)` is used to obtain a RD, in which case the paths in the request object remain unaffected from the original request object.

Of course, we might need the second resource to find out about the original path URIs that were used to make this request. When the container changes the paths in the request object, it keeps a copy of the old values of the paths in request attributes so, if required, they are available to the second resource.

During an include, the container sets the following request attributes (their values reflect the methods of a similar name in the `HttpServletRequest` object):

- **`javax.servlet.include.request_uri`**
- **`javax.servlet.include.context_path`**
- **`javax.servlet.include.servlet_path`**
- **`javax.servlet.include.path_info`**
- **`javax.servlet.include.query_string`**

If the request is subsequently included again, the container will overwrite the values of these attributes for that include. If the `getNamedDispatcher(String)` method is used to obtain the `RequestDispatcher`, these attributes must not be set.

During a forward, the container will set the following request attributes:

- **`javax.servlet.forward.request_uri`**
- **`javax.servlet.forward.context_path`**
- **`javax.servlet.forward.servlet_path`**
- **`javax.servlet.forward.path_info`**
- **`javax.servlet.forward.query_string`**

These attributes always reflect the original request information, regardless of whether the container forwards or includes the request any further. If the `getNamedDispatcher` method was used to obtain the `RequestDispatcher`, these attributes must not be set.

Wrapping Requests and Responses

Sometimes it will be appropriate to modify the services offered by the request and response objects yourself, for example to control the buffering of data with more sophistication than is possible already. Since you can't subclass the request and response objects directly (the implementation classes are container-dependent anyway), you must use a wrapper instead.

The wrapper classes both implement the appropriate interface, allowing them to be used directly as a request/response object. All method calls on the wrapper are, by default, delegated to the encapsulated request/response (which may be the container's object or another wrapper). This is depicted in Figure 6.2.

Clearly this isn't much use as it stands: a wrapper which just delegates all the time isn't any more use than the encapsulated object is on its own, and it just uses more memory, so what's the point? Notice that all the wrappers are already concrete classes, so extending them and overriding some of the methods wouldn't be too hard–certainly easier than implementing a new class from the interfaces! Plus, since all the methods are defined just to delegate, we don't actually *have* to do anything to get a fully working request/response class. The beauty of the wrapper is that you can extend it, override only the methods you're interested in providing custom behaviour for, and still use it just like the original request/response object (since it implements the requisite interface). Wonderful–now all that's left to do is use them!

That's all there is to it:

1. Extend the wrapper and provide an appropriate constructor which calls the `super` constructor;
2. Override the methods you want to provide custom implementations for;
3. Set the `ServletRequest` to the container's object in your application's code;
4. Pass this new wrapper to all method calls you make, in place of the container's version.

This is the same for all wrappers, regardless of whether they're requests, responses, HTTP or not. The API definitions for each wrapper class are given next, but they're pretty similar and all self-explanatory.

Figure 6.2

Wrapper Pattern Delegation

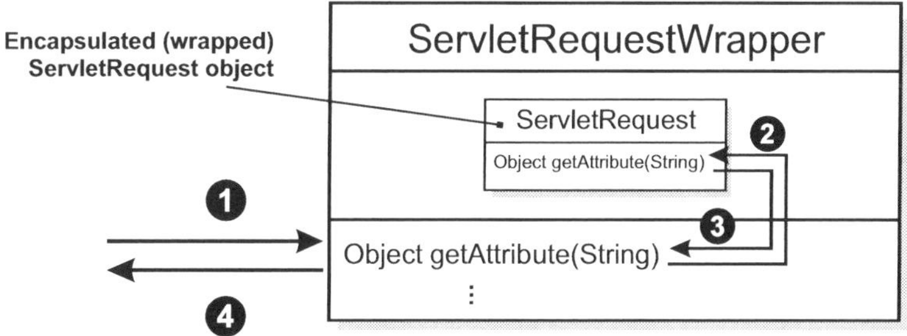

1. The wrapper object's getAttribute(...) method is called.
2. The wrapper's getAttribute(...) method is implemented to delegate to the same method - i.e. getAttribute(String) - in the wrapped ServletRequest object.
3. The wrapped object method returns.
4. The wrapper method returns the value directly returned by the wrapped object's method.

getAttribute(String) wrapper method implementation:

```
Object getAttribute(String name) {
    return wrappedRequest.getAttribute(name);
}
```

6

Figure 6.3

Request Wrappers

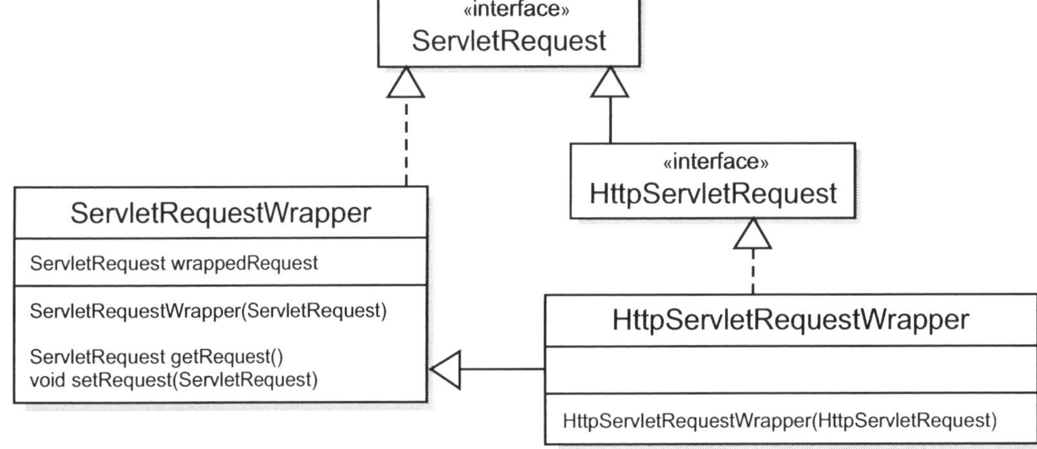

Figure 6.4

Response Wrappers

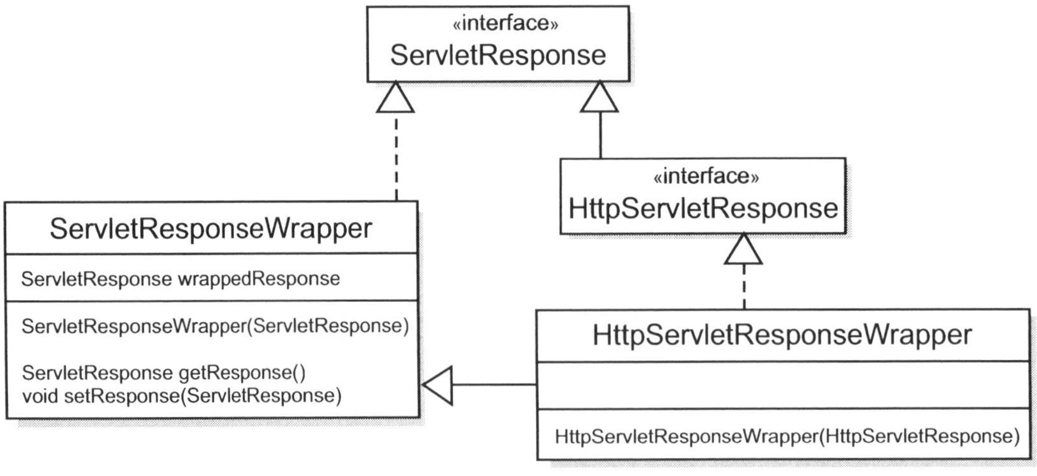

Request Wrappers

There are two classes: the generic `javax.servlet.ServletRequestWrapper` and the HTTP-specific `javax.servlet.http.HttpServletRequestWrapper`.

The ServletRequestWrapper Class

This class has the following header:

```
public class ServletRequestWrapper implements ServletRequest
```


Since it's concrete, it implements all the methods in `ServletRequest` that we've already seen, and their default behaviour of course is to delegate to the encapsulated `ServletRequest`. The constructor sets the encapsulation:

```
public ServletRequestWrapper(ServletRequest encapsulatedReq)
```

This constructor will throw an `IllegalArgumentException` if the argument is `null`, but that's only logical since the wrapper isn't much of a wrapper if it contains nothing to wrap!

This class defines two extra methods used to modify the encapsulated request:

- **`ServletRequest getRequest()`**
  Returns the request object encapsulated in this wrapper.
- **`void setRequest(ServletRequest encapsultedReq)`**
  Sets the encapsulated request object to the one provided in the argument.

The HttpServletRequestWrapper Class

This class has the following header:

```
public class HttpServletRequestWrapper
       extends ServletRequestWrapper
       implements HttpServletRequest
```

This wrapper extends `ServletRequestWrapper`, so brings much of the functionality with it – including methods for storing the encapsulated request object. As a result, all methods newly implemented in this class are from `HttpServletRequest` interface, so no further discussion is warranted. This is the constructor:

```
public HttpServletRequestWrapper(HttpServletRequest wrappedReq)
```

Despite taking the `HttpServletRequest` class as its parameter, the object is actually stored internally in the `ServletRequestWrapper` class as a `ServletRequest`. As a result, it must be cast to `HttpServletRequest` if it's to be used as such. You therefore have to use an explicit cast in servlet code:

```
HttpServletRequest orig=(HttpServletRequest)wrapper.getRequest();
```

Response Wrappers

There are two classes: the generic `javax.servlet.ServletResponseWrapper` and the HTTP-specific `javax.servlet.http.HttpServletResponseWrapper`.

The ServletResponseWrapper Class

This class has the header:

```
public class ServletResponseWrapper implements ServletResponse
```


Since it's concrete, it implements all the methods in the `ServletResponse`, and provides a constructor:

```
public ServletResponseWrapper(ServletResponse encapsulatedResp)
```

This constructor throws an `IllegalArgumentException` if the argument is `null`. It also defines two new methods:

- **`ServletResponse getResponse()`**
  Returns the encapsulated `ServletResponse` object.

- **`void setResponse(ServletResponse encapsulatedResp)`**
  Sets the encapsulated response object to the argument. This may, of course, be an implementation of any subinterface of `ServletResponse` as well (including `HttpServletResponse`).

The HttpServletResponseWrapper Class

The header is:

```
public class HttpServletResponseWrapper
       extends ServletResponseWrapper
       implements HttpServletResponse
```

Since this class extends `ServletResponseWrapper`, it only needs to define the methods added newly in `HttpServletResponse`, which are those we've already discussed. This wrapper encapsulates, you've guessed it, an object of type `HttpServletResponse`:

```
public HttpServletResponseWrapper(HttpServletResponse wrapped)
```

This constructor, just as with the other wrappers, will throw an `IllegalArgumentException` if the argument is `null`.

Despite encapsulating an `HttpServletResponse`, this class uses it parent's storage mechanism which is of type `ServletResponse`. It is therefore necessary to explicitly cast the object retrieved from the `getResponse` method as follows:

```
HttpServletResponse r=(HttpServletResponse)wrapper.getResponse();
```

Wrappers and the Exam

What do you actually need to know for the exam? You need to have an awareness of what the wrappers are, including an understanding of the wrapper pattern, and what they're for. You also need to be able to apply that knowledge to a theoretical situation: for example, what are some practical uses of wrappers in filters? You should also learn the headers of the classes and constructors. Apart from forgetting the casting for the HTTP variants, all the method headers are pretty predictable, so you might as well get a feel for them while you're here.

Since the exam is particularly hot at ensuring you know how to use wrappers, we will dedicate some of the next chapter to looking at how to use them alongside filters to control buffering and commitment of the response.

Wrappers and RequestDispatchers

Much of the discussion which follows can be applied equally well to filters, a servlet technology which we will look at in the next chapter. Our goal here is to get a feel for the way that the request and response wrapper classes can be used in conjunction with the `RequestDispatcher` mechanism.

Usually, a wrapper is used to provide an extra layer of buffering between the client (through the container's interface) and a Web component. By creating a wrapper which contains its own internal buffer independent from the output stream supplied by the container, we can cause a Web component to unknowingly write data to our wrapper's stream. Other components can then examine this data as they find appropriate, and even modify response headers since the response hasn't been committed (remember, we're not writing to the container's output stream, so we haven't actually sent data to the client). Once we're totally satisfied with the contents of the stream in the wrapper, we can write the entire lot to the container's response stream, finally committing the response. The advantages of such a system are obvious if considerable mediating of data (for example, moderation of the posts in chat rooms) is to be performed by some Web components or filters.

By far the most common use of a wrapper is to override the stream behaviour of a request/response object as we just looked at. However, they can also be used to override other request/response methods as well. For example, suppose we wanted to provide a certain Web component with the same constant value for a request header (and guarantee that the header is always present). We can easily override the `getHeader` method in a request wrapper, delegating to the wrapped object unless our special header is being requested, in which case our wrapper can return the constant value. For example:

```
public class MyWrapper extends HttpServletRequestWrapper {
  // constructor taking HttpServletRequest argument omitted

  public String getHeader(String header) {
    if("myheader".equals(header)) {
      return "something";
    }
    return ((HttpServletRequest)getRequest()).getHeader(header);
  }
}
```


In this example, we first check to see if the header being requested is called `myheader`; if so, we always return the string `something`, regardless of whether the client has sent this header or not. Otherwise, we delegate to the wrapped request's `getHeader` method, casting the object returned from `getRequest()` to `HttpServletRequest` in the process. An alternative implementation might return a standard (default) value only if the client's original request does not already declare a value for that header:

```
public String getHeader(String header) {
    /* Get the wrapped request's header value */
    HttpServletRequest req = ((HttpServletRequest)getRequest());
    String reqVal = req.getHeader(header);

    /* Only return the default value "something" for
       the header "myheader" if the wrapped request does
       not contain it (returns null to getHeader(...) method) */
    if("myheader".equals(header) && (reqVal == null)) {
        return "something";
    }

    /* Otherwise return value obtained from wrapped request */
    return reqVal;
}
```

An even more exciting use of wrappers is to provide a new API to Web components. For example, suppose we want to return an XML document to the client. We might create a response wrapper which adds relevant DOM (Document Object Model) methods; for example, at its most basic the wrapper might return an instance of the `org.w3c.dom.Document` interface used to construct XML documents:

```
public class XMLWrapper extends ServletResponseWrapper {
    private org.w3c.dom.Document xmlDoc;

    public XMLWrapper(ServletResponse response) {
        super(response);
        // Instantiate the xmlDoc variable to
        // construct a new XML document
    }

    public org.w3c.dom.Document getDocument() {
```

```
        return xmlDoc;
    }
}
```

I don't intend to go into the details of creating XML documents here (it isn't relevant, and it certainly isn't on the exam), but looking at the pseudocode comments, we can see that this wrapper creates a new XML document and provides the `getDocument()` method for other components to obtain that document (to edit or add to its contents). Web components receiving the response object can use this wrapper by casting it to the `XMLWrapper` data type; as an example, let's look at a servlet which makes use of this wrapper:

```
public class MyServlet extends GenericServlet {
  public void service(ServletRequest req, ServletResponse res) {
    /* We assume that resp is in fact our wrapper */
    XMLWrapper xmlResp = (XMLWrapper)res;

    /* We can now obtain the response document */
    org.w3c.dom.Document doc = xmlResp.getDocument();

    // now we can do things with the document;
    // for example, add some elements/attributes
    // or edit the DOM already there.
  }
}
```

Unfortunately, this design is a mixed blessing: on the one hand it provides a neat way to add extra methods to the request/response objects, but for it to be successful, you've got to be *absolutely sure* that the servlet is definitely receiving an instance of the `XMLWrapper` class and not any other `ServletResponse` object, or the cast will fail at run time (and you'll be left with a nasty exception to handle). You could use an `instanceof` test to pre-empt the cast failure, but that means extra code!

Once we've created a wrapper for whatever task, the next question is what to do with it (this is where filters do things slightly differently from `RequestDispatcher`s). If we're including another resource or forwarding the request from one component to another using the RD mechanism, we must pass the wrapper into the `RequestDispatcher`'s method and not the original request object. Thus:

```
public void service(ServletRequest req, ServletResponse resp) {
  ServletRequestWrapper myWrapper;
  // Assume the wrapper gets instantiated

  /* Get the RequestDispatcher from the context */
  ServletContext con = getServletContext();
  RequestDispatcher rd = con.getNamedDispatcher("component2");

  /* Include the other resource using the wrapper */
  rd.include(myWrapper, resp);
}
```

6

We make use of the wrapper in just the same way as we would a normal request/response object, because the wrapper itself implements the appropriate interface (a wrapper is a `ServletRequest` or `ServletResponse`).

Now let's consider our `XMLWrapper` response object. The wrapper establishes its own `Document` instance which it stores, but we haven't provided anyway so far for the document's contents to be written to the container's response stream. We could do this by using a Front Controller servlet, which is the first component 'seen' by any request from the client (see Chapter 22 for details of this pattern). Since all requests will go through this `ControllerServlet`, this is the perfect place to create our new wrapper and to pass it to all subsequent calls to other components so that we guarantee that they receive our `XMLWrapper` instance and not some other `ServletResponse` instance. Typical servlet code would be:


```
public class ControllerServlet extends GenericServlet {
  public void service(ServletRequest req, ServletResponse res) {
    /* The URL of the resource to be forwarded to - this could
       be the result of a conditional decision */
    String url;
    // initialisation of 'url' omitted

    /* Get a RequestDispatcher for this URL... */
    ServletContext con = getServletContext();
    RequestDispatcher rd = con.getRequestDispatcher(url);

    /* Create the XMLWrapper */
    XMLWrapper xmlResp = new XMLWrapper(resp);

    /* ...and forward to the resource */
    rd.forward(req, xmlResp);

    // here we should copy the contents of the Document
    // in the wrapper into the output stream of the
    // original response object.
  }
}
```

To find out what's going on, just follow the comments. We assume that the local `url` variable contains the context-relative URI of the resource to forward control to. Usually, a Front Controller will find this URI by some conditional set of rules (for example, the type of HTTP method being used for the request, or the presence of a header), or a parameter supplied by the client which specifies the resource being requested. We then obtain the appropriate `RequestDispatcher`, create a new `XMLWrapper` instance wrapping the response passed to the `service` method. We then forward on to the second resource, which will see the `XMLWrapper` in place of the original `ServletResponse` object.

When the `forward` method returns, we take the `Document` contained in the wrapper, and write the XML tree to the output stream of the original response.

Normally of course, forwarding to a second resource prevents the calling servlet from modifying the output stream or its headers (after the method returns the response should have been committed and the stream closed). However, since we are using a wrapper, the container's response object won't have been committed and the response stream to the client will still be open. By giving the wrapper its own internal stream distinct from the container's, commitment is no longer an issue, and our `ControllerServlet` can easily write the data from the `XMLWrapper`'s `Document` into the original `ServletResponse`'s output stream (finally committing the response at this stage). We look at an example of using a custom response wrapper to 'dodge' commitment by using its own internal stream in the next chapter.

NOTE: Although a Front Controller servlet can be used to perform wrapper control, this task is best left to filters (the subject of the next chapter). Using a filter, we can decide whether we want to use the `XMLWrapper` wrapper or not just by adding/removing a declaration from the deployment descriptor, which makes them more portable components.

Revision Questions

1 **A servlet with logical name compA in the deployment descriptor, needs to pass processing of the current request to another servlet with logical name compB. Which of these method and parameter sets would be the best to invoke on the application's ServletContext instance to achieve this?** **(choose one)**

- A void forward("compB", "compA")
- B void invoke("compB")
- C RequestDispatcher forward("compB", "compA")
- D RequestDispatcher getNamedDispatcher("compB")
- E RequestDispatcher getRequestDispatcher("compB")

6

2 **Which methods on which interface(s) can be used to obtain a RequestDispatcher for the resource at path /accounts/preferences.jsp?** **(choose three)**

- A getNamedDispatcher(String) on ServletContext
- B getRequestDispatcher(String) on ServletContext
- C getNamedDispatcher(String) on ServletRequest
- D getRequestDispatcher(String) on ServletRequest
- E getRequestDispatcher(String) on HttpServletRequest

3 **Which methods on which interface(s) can be used to obtain a RequestDispatcher for a relative URL?** **(choose two)**

- A getNamedDispatcher(String) on ServletContext
- B getRequestDispatcher(String) on ServletContext
- C getNamedDispatcher(String) on ServletRequest
- D getRequestDispatcher(String) on ServletRequest
- E getRequestDispatcher(String) on HttpServletRequest

4 **Study the exhibit. What are the possible outcomes when this servlet is compiled and executed?** **(choose two)**

EXHIBIT

- A The text '<p>Included file:</p><div>' is written to the client.
- B The text '<p>Included file:</p><div>FILE</div>' (where FILE is the contents of /include.txt) is written to the client.
- C A runtime error occurs on line 7.
- D A runtime error occurs on line 8.
- E A compilation error occurs on line 7.

5 **Having already obtained a RequestDispatcher, which method should be invoked to pass processing of the request to a second resource, such that the calling component relinquishes control over the response?** **(choose one)**

- A void invoke(ServletRequest, ServletResponse)
- B boolean invoke(ServletRequest, ServletResponse)
- C void forward(ServletRequest, ServletResponse)
- D boolean forward(ServletRequest, ServletResponse)
- E void include(ServletRequest, ServletResponse)
- F boolean include(ServletRequest, ServletResponse)

6

6 **Study the exhibit. This is the first servlet called during the request. What are the possible outcomes when this servlet is compiled and executed?** **(choose two)**

EXHIBIT

- A The text contents of the /include.txt file is written to the client
- B The text '<p>Included file:</p><div>FILE</div>' (where FILE is the contents of /include.txt) is written to the client.
- C A runtime error occurs on line 9.
- D A runtime error occurs on line 10.
- E A compilation error occurs on 7.

7 **Study the exhibit. This is the first servlet called during the request. Assuming the /WEB-INF/banner.jsp resource exists, what is the result of compiling and executing this servlet?** **(choose one)**

EXHIBIT

- A The file /WEB-INF/banner.jsp is evaluated and written to the response.
- B The file /WEB-INF/banner.jsp is written literally (unevaluated) to the response.
- C A runtime error occurs on line 9.
- D A runtime error occurs on line 11.
- E A compilation error occurs on 7.

8 **Study the exhibit. This is the first servlet called during the request. Assuming the /WEB-INF/banner.jsp resource exists, what is the result of compiling and executing this servlet?** (choose one)

EXHIBIT

- A The text '<p>Included resource:</p>' is written to the response, followed by the container's evaluation of the /WEB-INF/banner.jsp file.
- B A runtime error occurs on line 8.
- C A runtime error occurs on line 11.
- D A runtime error occurs on line 13.
- E A compilation error occurs on line 8.

9 **A servlet requires a RequestDispatcher for a resource deployed to /catalogue in another application with context root /public. What invocation chain should be invoked on a ServletContext instance to obtain the appropriate RequestDispatcher?** (choose one)

- A getRequestDispatcher("/public/catalogue")
- B getNamedDispatcher("/catalogue", "public")
- C getRequestDispatcher("/catalogue", "public")
- D getContext("public").getRequestDispatcher("/catalogue")
- E getContext("/public").getRequestDispatcher("/catalogue")

10 **Study the exhibit. This is the first servlet called during the request. What are the possible outcomes when this servlet is compiled and executed?** (choose two)

EXHIBIT

- A The resource /catalogue/display.jsp in the application with context root /admin is included in the current response.
- B A runtime error occurs on line 7.
- C A runtime error occurs on line 8.
- D A runtime error occurs on line 10.
- E A compilation error occurs on line 7.

11 **Study the exhibit. What possible output will be written to System.out during the course of execution of this servlet?** **(choose three)**

EXHIBIT

- A Start Before forward
- B Start Before forward After forward
- C Start Before forward After forward End
- D Start End
- E A runtime exception occurs on line 7

12 **Forwarding a request to a second resource using a RequestDispatcher causes which of the following scoped attributes to be set?** **(choose one)**

- A request_uri
- B javax.servlet.include.path_info
- C javax.servlet.forward.request_url
- D javax.servlet.forward.servlet_path
- E forward_path

13 **Study the exhibit. Given that the MyController servlet is bound to the Controller logical name in the deployment descriptor, and the application is deployed to the / context, what will be the value of the servletPath variable in MyController after an invocation of MyServlet?** **(choose one)**

EXHIBIT

- A " (empty string)
- B '/'
- C 'Controller'
- D '/Controller'
- E null

14 **Which standard classes can be extended to act as wrappers for an HTTP request object?** **(choose two)**

- A javax.servlet.RequestWrapper
- B javax.servlet.ServletRequestWrapper
- C javax.servlet.ServletResponseWrapper
- D javax.servlet.http.RequestWrapper
- E javax.servlet.http.HttpServletRequestWrapper

15 **Which method on HttpServletResponseWrapper should be invoked to obtain the wrapped response object?** **(choose one)**

- A HttpServletResponse getWrapped()
- B HttpServletResponse getEnclosed()
- C HttpServletResponse getResponse()
- D ServletResponse getWrapped()
- E ServletResponse getResponse()

16 **Study the exhibit. This class is compiled and used in a RequestDispatcher forward. The page forwarded to invokes setStatus(404) on this wrapper. What is the result?** **(choose one)**

EXHIBIT

- A The status code of the response is set to 404.
- B Nothing happens.
- C A runtime exception occurs
- D A compilation error occurs.

17 **Study the exhibit. This wrapper is used in a RequestDispatcher include invocation. The included resource tries to obtain the itemcode request-scoped attribute; what is the result?** **(choose one)**

EXHIBIT

- A An unspecified object representing the item's code.
- B The String 'myvalue'.
- C null.
- D A ServletException is raised on line 8.
- E A compilation error occurs.

18 **Study the exhibit. This class is compiled and used in a RequestDispatcher include. The included page obtains the order request-scoped attribute; what is the result?** **(choose one)**

EXHIBIT

- A An unspecified object representing the current order.
- B The string 'myattr'.
- C null.
- D A ServletException is raised on line 8.
- E A compilation error occurs.

Exhibits

Q.4

```
import javax.servlet.*;
import java.io.*;

public class MyServlet extends GenericServlet {
  public void service(ServletRequest req, ServletResponse resp)
              throws ServletException, IOException {
    resp.getWriter().write("<p>Included file:</p><div>");
    RequestDispatcher rd = req.getRequestDispatcher("/include.txt");
    rd.include(req,resp);
    resp.getWriter().write("</div>");
  }
}
```

Q.6

```
import javax.servlet.*;
import java.io.*;

public class MyServlet extends GenericServlet {

  public void service(ServletRequest req, ServletResponse resp)
              throws ServletException, IOException {
    resp.setBufferSize(1024);
    resp.getWriter().write("<p>Included file:</p><div>");
    RequestDispatcher rd = req.getRequestDispatcher("/include.txt");
    rd.forward(req,resp);
    resp.getWriter().write("</div>");
  }
}
```

Q.7

```
public class MyServlet extends GenericServlet {

  public void service(ServletRequest req, ServletResponse resp)
              throws ServletException, IOException {
    RequestDispatcher rd =
                 req.getRequestDispatcher("/WEB-INF/banner.jsp");
    if(rd != null) {
      rd.forward(req,resp);
    }
    resp.sendRedirect("/success.jsp");
  }
}
```

Q.8

```
public class MyServlet extends GenericServlet {

  public void service(ServletRequest req, ServletResponse resp)
                throws ServletException, IOException {
    resp.getWriter().write("<p>Included resource:</p>");
    resp.flushBuffer();
    RequestDispatcher rd =
                    req.getRequestDispatcher("/WEB-INF/banner.jsp");
    if(rd != null) {
      rd.forward(req,resp);
    }
    resp.setContentType(“text/html”);
  }
}
```

Q.10

```
public class MyServlet extends GenericServlet {

  public void service(ServletRequest req, ServletResponse resp)
                throws ServletException, IOException {
    ServletContext foreignContext =
                    getServletContext().getContext("/admin");
    RequestDispatcher rd =
       foreignContext.getRequestDispatcher("/catalogue/display.jsp");
    if(rd != null) {
      rd.include(req,resp);
    }
  }
}
```

Q.11

```
public class MyServlet extends GenericServlet {

  public void service(ServletRequest req, ServletResponse resp)
                throws ServletException, IOException {
    RequestDispatcher rd =
        getServletContext().getRequestDispatcher("/other.jsp");
    System.out.print("Start ");
    if(rd != null) {
      System.out.print("Before forward ");
      rd.forward(req,resp);
      System.out.print("After forward ");
    }
    System.out.print("End ");
  }
}
```

Q.13

MyServlet:

```
public class MyServlet extends GenericServlet {
    public void service(ServletRequest req, ServletResponse resp)
                        throws IOException, ServletException {
        RequestDispatcher rd =
            getServletContext().getNamedDispatcher("Controller");
        if(rd != null) {
            rd.include(req,resp);
        }
    }
}
```


MyController:

```
public class MyController extends GenericServlet {
    public void service(ServletRequest req, ServletResponse resp) {
        String servletPath =
           req.getAttribute("javax.servlet.include.context_path");
    }
}
```

Q.16

```
public class MyResponseWrapper extends HttpServletResponseWrapper {
    public void setStatus(int sc) { }
}
```

Q.17

```
public class MyRequestWrapper extends HttpServletRequestWrapper {
    public MyRequestWrapper(HttpServletRequestWrapper wrap) {
        super(wrap);
    }
    public Object getAttribute(String name) {
        return "myvalue";
    }
}
```

Q.18

```
public class MyRequestWrapper extends HttpServletRequestWrapper {
     public MyRequestWrapper(HttpServletRequestWrapper wrap) {
         super(wrap);
     }
     public void getAttribute(String name) {
         return "myattr";
     }
}
```

Answers to Revision Questions

1 **Correct answer: D**

Although none of these can be used to invoke the servlet directly, A, B and C are invalid methods, while E has a path and not logical name parameter. The only possibility left is D which obtains a RequestDispatcher for a named component.

2 **Correct answers: B,D,E**

A and C are for logical names (not paths).

3 **Correct answers: D,E**

D is the correct answer – this method provides relative URL mapping against the current servlet. E is also correct, since this method is inherited from ServletRequest by HttpServletRequest.

4 **Correct answers: B,D**

If the file /include.txt exists, B will happen. Otherwise, rd will be null, and a NullPointerException is raised on line 8, so D will happen. Execution cannot terminate midway through a method, so A is wrong; req is non-null, and getRequestDispatcher() doesn't throw any exceptions, so C is wrong. Similarly, line 7 is correct, so E is wrong.

5 **Correct answer: C**

6 **Correct answers: A,D**

D will happen if /include.txt doesn't exist, and therefore rd is null. When forward() is invoked, it clears the current buffer, so the '<p>Included file:</p><div>' text is lost forever. As a result, B is wrong, and only the text in A will be written. When this method returns, the response should be considered committed and closed, so the response is already sent and any further content written won't be sent to the client. There is no error on line 7, making E incorrect. Also, getRequestDispatcher() never throws any exceptions, instead choosing to return null, and the container guarantees req is never null, so together these make C incorrect.

7 **Correct answer: D**

D is correct because forward() causes the response to be committed, and trying to send an error or redirection after commitment causes an IllegalStateException to be thrown (note however that HTTP headers set after commitment are ignored, but do not raise an exception).

8 **Correct answer: C**

C is correct because forward() throws IllegalStateException if the response has already been committed, which is exactly what flushBuffer() does.

9 **Correct answer: E**

E is correct. A is wrong – this retrieves the resource at /public/catalogue in the current application. B and C have an incorrect number of parameters. D does not include the mandatory / in the getContext() argument.

10 **Correct answers A,C**

A is what happens if the application /admin exists and security settings are appropriate. If not, foreignContext will be null, and line 8 throws a NullPointerException.

11 **Correct answers: A,C,D**

This question was written to test your understanding of include() and forward(), namely that they never cause the service() method to return automatically. It is tempting to think that once forward() ends, the service() method will also end automatically. However, you must always include an explicit return if you want to abort processing of the current service(). Hence only C and D are possible if no exceptions occur; the only line which can cause an exception is the forward() in line 11, so A is also a possibility in this case. Nothing in line 7 will ordinarily throw an exception.

12 **Correct answer: D**

A and E are wrong. B is valid, but is used for includes, not forwards. C is incorrect; the correct version ends in request_uri not request_url. D is correct, though not often used.

13 **Correct answer: E**

E is correct since a getNamedDispatcher() invocation doesn't set the additional request parameters. If the getRequestDispatcher() method had been used, the answer would have been A, since the context_path never ends with a /, and therefore '/' maps to ''. B, C and D are all incorrect as this attribute is never set and is therefore null.

14 **Correct answers: B,E**

A and D don't exist, and C is used to wrap responses, not requests. Note that B is correct since an HttpServletRequest is also a ServletRequest, so B can be used as a wrapper (although this is inappropriate).

15 **Correct answers: E**

A, B and D don't exist. C is wrong, as the method is inherited from ServletResponseWrapper and therefore has a return type of ServletResponse, not HttpServletResponse.

16 **Correct answer: D**

The (Http)ServletResponseWrapper class(es) don't have a no-argument constructor; the only constructor they have takes a single (Http)ServletResponseWrapper object. Since we haven't declared an explicit constructor, the container creates the default no-argument one which tries to invoke the no-argument super() constructor, which doesn't exist. Hence a compilation error occurs; we should have declared a constructor like:

```
public MyResponseWrapper(HttpServletResponseWrapper wrap) {
   super(wrap);
}
```

If this error hadn't occurred, the answer would have been B; nothing can happen, since our overridden method has an empty implementation.

17 **Correct answer: B**

B is correct, since we overrode getAttribute() to always return the string 'myvalue'—all request attributes (even ones which don't exist in the original wrapped request object) will now appear to have this value. If we hadn't overridden this method, the answer would be A or C depending on whether the attribute actually existed. D is incorrect—this method isn't even declared to throw the checked ServletException. There are no errors in the code, so E is incorrect.

18 **Correct answer: E**

E is correct because we've attempted to override the getAttribute method with a return type of void, when it should have been Object.

In this chapter you'll:

- Learn what a Java EE filter is.
- Understand how filters can be chained together, and how to choose a suitable order for filters in a chain.
- Be introduced to the lifecycle of a filter.
- Create new filters with the Filter API.
- Use wrappers as part of the processing of a filter.

7 Filters

The Filter API was added late in the lifetime of Java EE. Near the end of the chapter we look briefly at 'life before filters', discussing how the job of filters used to be achieved using `RequestDispatcher`s, but why this old technique is no longer appropriate. For the rest of this chapter we look at what filters are and how to use them.

The Filter Mechanism

A diagram can be used to describe the filter mechanism much more easily than words can; consult Figure 7.1.

Essentially, a filter stands between a client and a component within the container. A filter is a 'pluggable', reusable class which intercepts and mediates all relevant requests and responses. More commonly, a filter examines only the headers.

A filter, like a servlet, is just a special type of Java class, implementing the `javax.servlet.Filter` interface. However, the method by which filters are made 'pluggable' leads to a slightly different life cycle and deployment procedure.

Figure 7.1

Filter Invocation

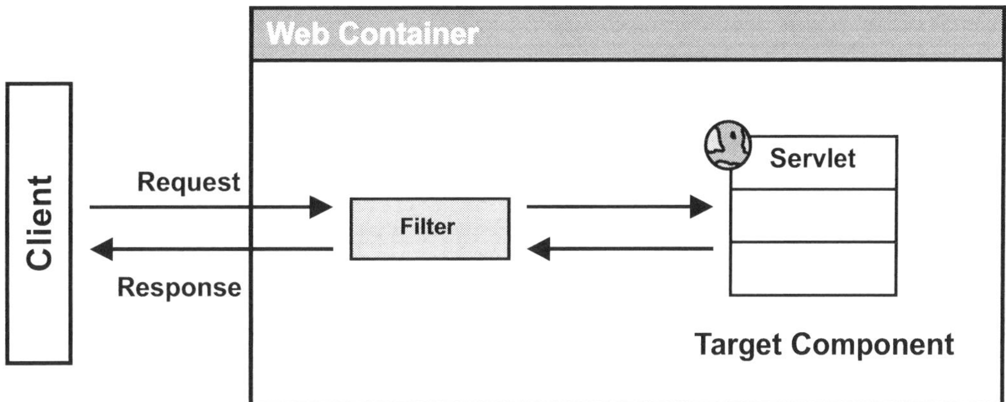

Why use Filters?

Filters stand between the client's request and the target component, as well as the responses sent back from components to the client. They may also, as of the Servlet 2.4 specification, be invoked by `RequestDispatcher forward()` and `include()` calls.

Filters are distinct from servlets: filters take part in the *process* of making a request to a target resource; they are not resources which can be *served* to the client (such as the response from a servlet or from a static HTML page). For example, a typical filter might be used for one or many things: image compression to reduce the amount of bandwidth required for transmission to the client, encryption or caching. Each of these applications manipulates a stream of data 'on the fly'. The data is being *modified* by the filter as part of the response process; the filter does not *create* that data.

Filters intercept requests and responses made between the client and target resource. They are therefore useful for security – to ensure that the client is authorised to access the requested resource. If so, the request can be allowed to pass; if not, the filter can block the request and respond to the client with an error code. Similarly, filters can be used to log requests/responses and any errors returned to the user.

A filter is a lightweight component, making as few changes as necessary to the request/response data to achieve its goal. Since a filter is 'pluggable' by design, removal of it should not cause the application to come crashing down. For example, removal of a logging filter is a transparent action to the client: from an administrative point of view, it is useful to have, but it doesn't actually affect the application by its removal. Similarly, if a compression or encryption filter is removed, the data are still transmitted, but in their plain uncompressed form; the data, however, are still valid. You may think that authentication is a bad use of filters. However, if the filter is removed, the application still functions correctly, the only difference being that anyone can now access the resources since requests can no longer be blocked.

NOTE: The key idea with filters is that they should never act as a target *resource*. Rather, they are always transparent components which sit *between* resources. For example, a filter should not actually construct an HTML page and return this to the user; if the filter were 'unplugged', that resource would no longer be available and the application would have lost its integrity.

Filter Chains

Being able to place a single filter in the request/response process is useful: we could use that filter to do everything we could possibly require. But, that design solution is far from elegant–if we ever wanted to remove a particular function (like authentication or logging) from the application, we'd have to alter the filter's code.

What if, instead, we could 'gang' several filter classes together, so they're executed one after the other? That would allow us to use different filters, each with its own atomic task, and to 'unplug' those filters at will without affecting the rest of the application. This is exactly what the Web container provides: a **filter chain**. Filter chains are declared in the deployment descriptor along with the URL of the target resource to which that chain applies. Each filter can be considered as a single link in the chain–when the container first receives the request, it passes control to the first filter in the chain. Once that filter has finished executing, it passes control to the second filter etc., until the last filter passes control to the target resource. See Figure 7.2.

Any filter may choose not to execute the next filter in the chain, but instead to serve the response directly. This could be useful in, for example, an authentication filter which denies the client access–the filter can block the request from reaching the target resource simply by returning a 403 ('Forbidden') status code straight away. See Figure 7.3.

Since filters can be chained together, it is inappropriate to have a single filter which compresses, encrypts and logs responses, while also authenticating and logging requests. It is much better to have three, or even four, separate filters: one for

Figure 7.2

Filter Chains

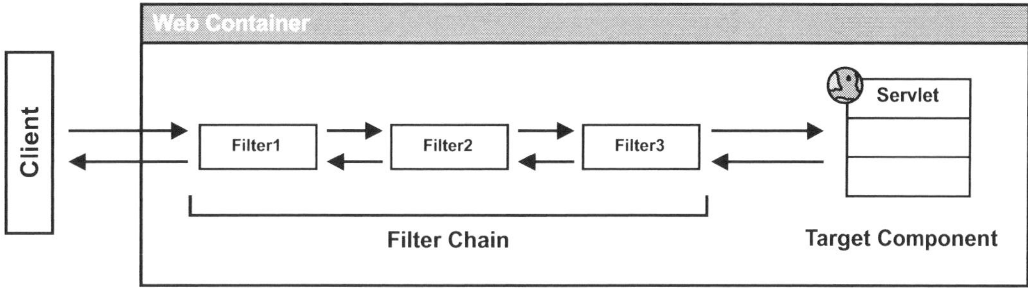

Figure 7.3

Filters Rejecting Requests

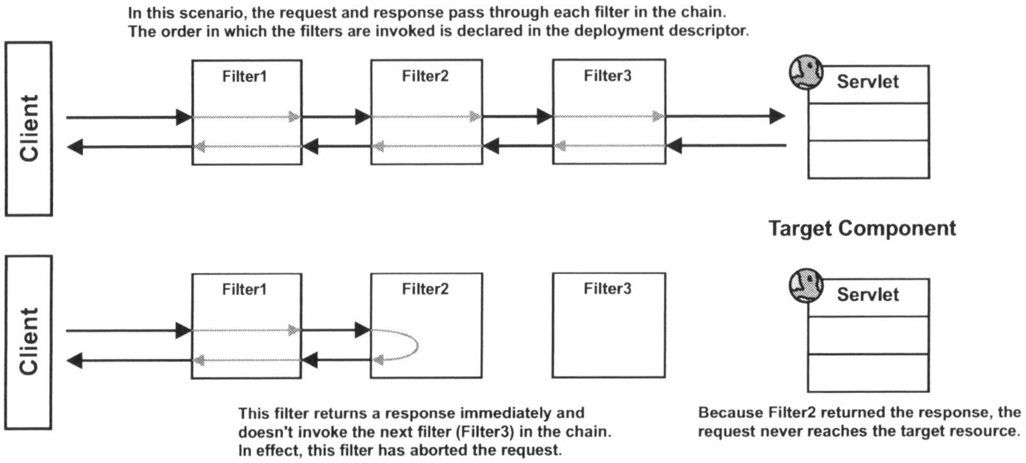

In this scenario, the request and response pass through each filter in the chain.
The order in which the filters are invoked is declared in the deployment descriptor.

Client
Filter1
Filter2
Filter3
Servlet

Target Component

Client
Filter1
Filter2
Filter3
Servlet

This filter returns a response immediately and doesn't invoke the next filter (Filter3) in the chain. In effect, this filter has aborted the request.

Because Filter2 returned the response, the request never reaches the target resource.

logging activity, one for authenticating requests, and another for compressing and encrypting response data.

This modularisation of filters leads to a more robust application. Each filter is responsible for its own function, so for any problems occurring with compression, for instance, we know which exact filter is to blame. Similarly, if one filter is 'unplugged' from the chain (e.g. because it malfunctions or is no longer required), all others still maintain their function without any rewriting of code. This helps to reduce maintenance costs, and exemplifies Java's code reuse policy.

Suitable Filter Ordering

This topic is not on the exam, but for interest I've included something on what I consider to be appropriate ordering here. By ordering, I mean the order in which filters are executed in the chain. This is declared in the deployment descriptor. Consider Figure 7.4 which shows a chain of four numbered filters.

For this example, we will assume that each of these four filters has one of the following functions:

- Security (authentication and authorisation);
- Logging;
- Compression;
- Encryption.

Now let's try to order them to fit the pattern in Figure 7.4. Quite clearly, if a client does not pass the authentication stage, then it cannot be allowed to pass to the next stages, so the authentication filter must appear somewhere near the client end of the chain. However, we may want the responses returned by unauthorised requests to be logged as well as those for authorised requests. Thus, since everything is to be logged, the logging filter should go in position 1. Therefore the authentication filter goes in position 2.

Now consider the compression and encryption. Depending upon your requirements, these filters could be interchanged between positions 3 and 4 (another example of why the modular design of filters is beneficial). For our purposes we shall assume that the entire response (after compression) is to be encrypted, and since it is the response which is being altered, the compression must occur first on the response's trip back to the client. Hence, the encryption filter must go in position 3 and the compression in position 4.

The completed layout is shown in Figure 7.5. Notice how the security filter is placed very near to the client: if the client is not authenticated or authorised, there is no need to continue with any further processing down the chain and to the final resource. In Chapter 21 we will look at even better ways to declaratively specify security constraints such as this but which are managed by the container.

Figure 7.4

Example Filter Chain

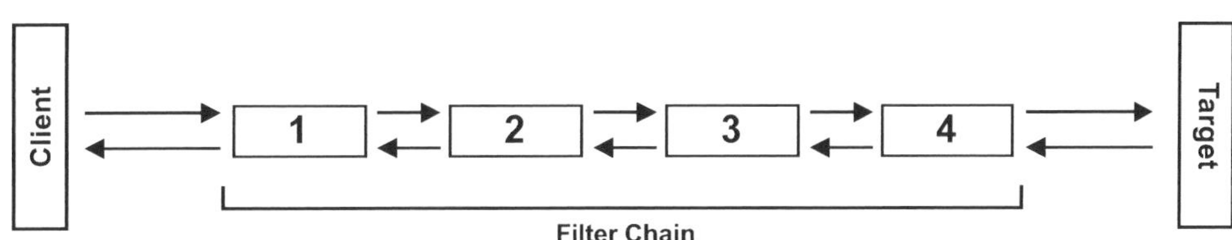

Figure 7.5

Example Filter Chain (completed)

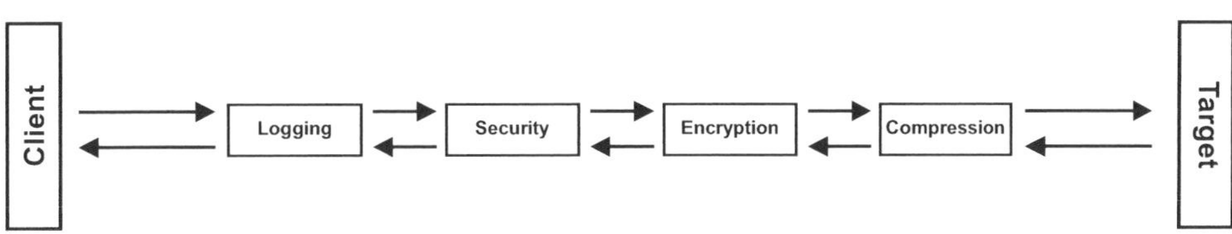

Filter vs. RequestDispatcher Mechanisms

It is sometimes tempting to compare filters with the `RequestDispatcher` mechanism, which we looked at in the last chapter, because they both edit the request and forward it to the next resource.

However, this is a misleading comparison to make, and the exam mandates that candidates must know the difference between the two, and the appropriate uses of both. There are a number of differences to ponder over; the more you can think of yourself, the better understanding of the topic you have. Here are a few to get you started:

1. The request dispatcher mechanism is designed to delegate processing between application components – physical resources which can be accessed by the client. The filter mechanism takes part in the provision of requests to these components, but does not constitute an accessible resource.
2. Filters are 'pluggable' components; removing a filter requires only the removal of a small section of deployment descriptor code. The removal of a servlet acting to parse requests/responses may require not only the removal of descriptor code, but also the modification of request-component mappings and at worst the change of other servlet code.
3. Filters are called in series, one after the other down the chain during a request, and the response is automatically 'bubbled up' back through that chain in precisely the reverse order. This is not the same behaviour as shown by the dispatcher's `forward` method, using which the caller forwards the request but then relinquishes all processing responsibility and may not make subsequent changes to the response. In contrast, the filter is always executed again when control is passed back from the next filter, and provided the response is not committed, the filter may make any changes it wishes to the response.
4. The `include` method is also not a replacement for filters because, despite halting (blocking) the caller's execution until the called component has completed its inclusion code, removal of one servlet from the chain would require other servlet inclusion code to be modified to compensate. This can be a costly business. In addition, resources invoked using `include()` cannot modify the headers of the response, unlike those resources invoked at the end of a filter chain.

In summary: use servlets and JSP components to represent resources, when either data need to be returned to the client or incoming data requires processing (e.g. from a Web form). Use filters when a request or response needs to be altered or examined *before* it reaches either application components (in the case of a request) or the client (in the case of a response).

RequestDispatcher Interception

As of the Servlet 2.4 specification, filters can be configured in the deployment descriptor to not only intercept communications between the client and application, but *between components* within the application as well. To achieve this, a filter can be inserted between communications which use a `RequestDispatcher`. This helps to resolve some issues between filters and request dispatchers, combining the power of both 'worlds'. The filter class requires no modification of code to achieve this, but instead the responsibility is placed declaratively on the deployment descriptor (Chapter 10) or `@WebFilter` annotation (Chapter 11). The deployment descriptor syntax for this uses `<dispatcher>` within the `<filter-mapping>` element.

One idea for such a configuration is the authentication filter which we exemplified earlier. Instead of just checking to see if a client is authorised to view the *initial* target resource, *all* requests made inside the application will be checked as well. This means that if one resource has to include another, an authorisation check will have to take place to ensure that the client is permitted to view the included resource as well. If not, the entire request could then be rejected using an error code as appropriate. This allows for a fine-grained approach to programmatic security, and just think how this would improve logging and fault finding as well!

The Filter Life Cycle

A filter goes through a number of stages which are very similar to those of a `Servlet` object:

1. The `Filter` implementation class is **loaded** from the `WEB-INF/classes` or `WEB-INF/lib` directories into the application by the class loader.
2. The filter is **instantiated** using a default, no argument, constructor.
3. The `init` method is called on the filter to **initialise** it.
4. The `doFilter` method is the `Filter` interface's **service** method. All requests and responses in the chain pass through this method. This filter may choose either to continue with passing the request along the chain, or block that particular request from proceeding and return a response immediately.
5. The filter is **destroyed** by the container by a call to the `destroy` method.

This life cycle is broadly identical to that of servlets, except in details such as method and interface names.

The Interfaces

There are three interfaces which we must look at in this chapter. The `Filter` interface is the filter-equivalent of the `Servlet` interface, supplying the framework upon which a filter is built; the `FilterConfig` interface is analogous to the `ServletConfig` interface, providing a way to initialise a filter with default configuration information; the `FilterChain` interface supplies the channel between filters through which a request/response must travel.

Filter

7

The `Filter` interface defines only three methods, the first two of which bear a striking resemblance to their `Servlet` counterparts:

- **`void init(FilterConfig)`**
  Initialises the filter using the given `FilterConfig` instance. See the next section for initialisation exceptions.
- **`void destroy()`**
  This is called when the filter is being permanently removed from service, and not when the garbage collector is actually releasing its memory allocation. This method allows the filter to clean up any resources (such as database connections or data streams) it may be holding open from initialisation.
- **`void doFilter(ServletRequest, ServletResponse, FilterChain)`**
  This is the filter's service method. Further discussion of this follows.

Initialisation Exceptions

The `init` method can throw a `ServletException` during the initialisation process. If this occurs, the container guarantees that, like servlets, filters will not be put into service. Alternatively, if the exception is of type `UnavailableException`, a subclass of `ServletException`, then the container will either try to reinitialise the filter later (in the case of a temporary error), or for permanent errors, the filter will be removed from the filter chain altogether for the lifetime of the deployed application.

Filter Servicing

The `doFilter` method is used to service both the requests and the responses between the client and target resource. While both the request and response objects passed can be accessed at any time during the method call, it is normal for the

ServletRequest object to be operated on first (during the request to the target resource), and the ServletResponse object to be examined later in the method, just before passing the response to the client (or previous filter in the chain).

Normally doFilter is implemented with semantics similar to this:

1. The method examines the request's headers.
2. The ServletRequest object can be configured (for example, changing attributes or wrapping the original request in a new ServletRequestWrapper implementation).
3. The ServletResponse object can be configured.
4. The next filter in the chain is called using the FilterChain.doFilter method. This is a blocking operation: i.e. the rest of the doFilter method will not proceed to be executed until this method returns.
5. Alternatively, this filter can block the request by not calling the next filter in the chain, and instead returning a response itself (such as an error code for unauthorised access);
6. Once the FilterChain.doFilter method returns, the execution of the filter's service method continues. Therefore the response *from the target resource* can now be manipulated, and returned to the next filter in the chain.
7. If at any time the filter throws an exception, the container must not call any filters further down the chain. It may either return an error status to the client, or attempt to make the request through the chain again; the action taken is dependent upon the type of exception thrown, for example, temporary or permanent.

Let's look at a sketch of a typical filter's implementation:

```
import javax.servlet.*;
import javax.servlet.http.*;

public class MyFilter implements Filter {

  public void init(FilterConfig config) {
    // Perform initialisation
  }

  public void doFilter(ServletRequest req, ServletResponse res,
                       FilterChain chain) {
    // Analyse request
    boolean goToNextFilter = true; // some condition
    if(goToNextFilter) {
      chain.doFilter(req, resp);
    } else {
      // return a response now and abort processing - e.g.:
```

```
            HttpServletResp r = (HttpServletResponse)resp;
            r.sendError(HttpServletResponse.SC_FORBIDDEN);
            return;
        }
        // Analyse response
    }
}
```

FilterChain

This declares only one method:

- **`void doFilter(ServletRequest, ServletResponse)`**
  Invoking this method calls the next filter in the current chain. This method blocks until the next filter's `doFilter` method has returned. This allows for the same service method on a `Filter` instance to be used for both requests and responses.

The container creates its own instances of an implementation class of this interface when required. Each instance is passed to the `doFilter` method on the appropriate filter when required. You will not find any situations where you need to, or should, create an instance of the implementation class directly. *Always* use the instance provided in the filter's service method, and use the `FilterChain` interface as the data type.

FilterConfig

Like with servlets, filters may need to be configured at initialisation time. The container provides an instance of a `FilterConfig` implementation during the initialisation stage of each filter's life. This is passed to the filter in its `init` method.

The `FilterConfig` interface is extremely similar to the `ServletConfig` interface in both semantics and method signatures. We begin with those three which should already look familiar:

- **`ServletContext getServletContext()`**
  Returns the application context within which the filter is executing.

- **`String getInitParameter(String name)`**
  Returns the value of an initialisation parameter called `name`, as declared in the deployment descriptor, or `null` if that initialisation parameter does not exist.

- **`Enumeration getInitParameterNames()`**
  Returns a `java.util.Enumeration` of all initialisation parameter names

which exist for the filter being initialised in the deployment descriptor.

- **`String getFilterName()`**
  Returns the logical name of this filter, as declared in the deployment descriptor.

NOTE: Filter initialisation parameters are different from servlet initialisation parameters which are different from context initialisation parameters. Don't get these confused. The syntax for the declaration of each in the deployment descriptor is in Chapter 10, or Chapter 11 for annotations.

Filters and Wrappers

In the last chapter we saw how to use the `RequestDispatcher` mechanism in conjunction with the `ServletRequestWrapper` and `ServletResponseWrapper` classes. Indeed, we can do exactly the same thing with filters: each time a filter receives a request/response object, instead of passing the original on to the next filter in the chain, it can encapsulate the object into one of the wrapper classes. This is useful when we want to add additional services onto the normal request and response objects–for example, to provide a second response `Writer` as a form of buffering, or when target components need to write to a Document Object Model (DOM) rather than to the normal `Writer`.

We'll look at one example here: this example is used to control buffering. Recall that a response is automatically committed by the container after the internal data buffer is flushed for the first time to the client, and that after commitment the response cannot be modified further. The internal buffer is only flushed when it becomes full.

Now, consider this scenario: we develop a filter which allows any component in the application to signal an error at any time (even after data has been written to the output) without raising an `IllegalStateException` as a result of commitment.

We can achieve this by creating a custom `ServletResponseWrapper` implementation and overriding certain methods which we don't want to delegate to the response. Those methods are:

- `void flushBuffer()`
  We do not provide an implementation for this method, since we don't want the component to write any data to the client. Only our filter will write content to the client.

- `PrintWriter getWriter()`
  We will provide a `Writer` inside the wrapper–this prevents data being written directly to the response stream, and hence the official response will not be committed by the container.

- `OutputStream getOutputStream()`
  As with `getWriter()`, we provide our own `OutputStream`.

We'll leave all the other methods to delegate to the container's original `HttpServletResponse` object for now. Note that we've chosen to use an `HttpServletResponseWrapper` so that methods such as `sendError()` are available in our wrapper for target components to utilise.

7

So, our wrapper looks like this:

```
public class NoCommitResponseWrapper extends

HttpServletResponseWrapper {
  /* Storage for our writers. We use 'out' as the main output
     stream for both types of stream*/
  private ByteArrayOutputStream out;

  private ServletOutputStream outBytes;
  private PrintWriter outWriter;

  /* ServletOutputStream is abstract; we need our own class */
  private class MyServletOutputStream extends
                                          ServletOutputStream {
    /* In order to provide an output stream, we require that
       'out' is already initialised */
    public void write(int b) {
        /* Use NoCommitResponseWrapper's 'out' */
        out.write(b);
    }
  } // end MyServletOutputStream class

  public NoCommitResponseWrapper(HttpServletResponse wrap) {
    super(wrap);
  }

  public void flushBuffer() {
    // Do nothing
  }

  public PrintWriter getWriter() {
    if(outWriter != null) {
      return outWriter;
    }

    /* If 'outBytes' is non-null, then
       getOutputStream() was already called */
    if(outBytes != null) {
      throw new IllegalStateException("getOut already invoked");
```

```
      } // end if(outBytes != null)

      /* Otherwise create and return a new PrintWriter */
      out = new ByteArrayOutputStream();
      outWriter = new PrintWriter(out);
      return outWriter;
    } // end getWriter()

    public ServletOutputStream getOutputStream() {
      if(outBytes != null) {
        return outBytes;
      }

      /* If 'outWriter' is non-null,
         then getWriter() was already called */
      if(outWriter != null) {
        throw new IllegalStateException("getWriter was invoked");
      }

      /* Otherwise create and return a new ServletOutputStream */
      out = new ByteArrayOutputStream();
      /* Note that MyServletOutputStream is an instance inner-
         class; it is backed by 'out' which must be non-null
         at this point */
      outBytes = new MyServletOutputStream();
      return outBytes;
    }

    /**
     * This custom method returns the enclosed output stream,
     * which is written to by either of the
     * Writer or ServletOutputStream streams.
     */
    public ByteArrayOutputStream getOut () {
      return out;
    }
  }
```

That wasn't too much work–but now how to do we use the wrapper? For that, we need a filter:

```
public class NoCommitFilter implements Filter {

  /* We'll store this anyway, but we don't use it */
  private FilterConfig config;

  public void init(FilterConfig conf) {
    this.config = conf;
  }
  public void destroy() {}

  public void doFilter(ServletRequest req, ServletResponse resp,
                       FilterChain chain) {
    /* Create a new wrapper for the response */
```

7

```
      HttpServletResponse r = (HttpServletResponse) resp;
      NoCommitResponseWrapper wrap= new NoCommitResponseWrapper(r);
      /* Pass wrapper to the next filter in the chain */
         chain.doFilter(req, wrap);

      /* Once chain.doFilter() returns, we'll be here. Either
         the components will have forced the response to be
         committed(e.g. by calling the HTTP sendError()), or the
         output stream will be full - so buffer to the client*/
      if(wrap.isCommitted()) {
        /* Then the original response has been committed
           (e.g. by sendError()). We don't need to do anything
           if commitment has already occurred */
        return;
      }

      /* Otherwise we need to copy the wrapper's buffer
         to the actual response */
      if(wrap.getOut() != null) {
        wrap.getOut().writeTo(resp.getOutputStream());
      }
    } // end doFilter()
  } // end NoCommitFilter class
```

We would then plug this filter implementation into the application using the deployment descriptor. Let's now review what this achieves:

1. Any components after the filter has been invoked will write only to an internal buffer and not the actual output stream. This prevents the response being committed until we are ready.
2. Calling `HttpServletResponse.sendError()` will commit the original response, since we didn't override this method in the wrapper, and send the error to the client as expected. It doesn't matter when this method is called, since the official response is not committed by just writing to our wrapper.
3. Any headers set by the target components are set on the original response object.
4. Once all target components have returned processing, the container invokes the filter chain. Eventually control will return to the `doFilter` method in the `NoCommitFilter` instance.
5. We use the `wrap` instance which was passed to the target components. If already committed, we assume that `sendError()` or similar was invoked, and we don't want to (and can't legally) write anything to the output stream.
6. Otherwise, we can copy all the contents of our wrapper's buffers to the real response stream.

Revision Questions

1 **A filter must implement which interface?** **(choose one)**

- A javax.enterprise.ServletFilter
- B javax.servlet.filter.Filter
- C javax.servlet.filter.ServletFilter
- D javax.servlet.Filter
- E javax.servlet.ServletFilter

2 **Which of the following methods must a filter implement?** **(choose two)**

- A void init(ServletConfig config)
- B void destroy()
- C void service(ServletRequest req, ServletResponse resp)
- D void doFilter(ServletRequest req, ServletResponse resp, FilterChain chain)
- E void doFilter(ServletRequest req, ServletResponse resp)

3 **Which package does FilterChain reside in?** **(choose one)**

- A javax.enterprise
- B javax.servlet
- C javax.servlet.filter
- D javax.servlet.http
- E javax.servlet.http.filter

4 **Which method is declared in FilterChain?** **(choose one)**

- A void doNext(ServletRequest, ServletResponse)
- B Filter getNext()
- C void next(ServletRequest, ServletResponse)
- D void doNextFilter(ServletRequest, ServletResponse)
- E void doFilter(ServletRequest, ServletResponse)

5 **Place the following life cycle for a filter in order:**

Initialised	Invoked	Loaded
Destroyed	Instantiated	

6 **Which of the following exceptions may be thrown by Filter's init(FilterConfig)?** **(choose two)**

- A java.lang.Exception
- B java.lang.RuntimeException
- C java.io.IOException
- D javax.servlet.Exception
- E javax.servlet.ServletException

7 **Which class can be extended to create a filter?** **(choose one)**

- A javax.servlet.Filter
- B javax.servlet.GenericFilter
- C javax.servlet.AbstractFilter
- D javax.servlet.filter.FilterAdapter
- E None of the above

8 **Which of the following are methods on FilterConfig used to obtain a filter initialisation parameter?** **(choose two)**

- A Map getParameters()
- B String getParameter(String)
- C String getInitParameter(String)
- D Enumeration getInitParameters()
- E Enumeration getInitParameterNames()

9 **Study the exhibit. What line of code should be inserted on line 10 to invoke the next filter in the chain?** **(choose one)**

EXHIBIT

- A next();
- B config.getServletContext().nextFilter();
- C chain.doFilter(req, resp);
- D chain.doFilter(req, resp, chain);
- E No further lines are required.

10 **Study the exhibit. Assuming the email filter initialisation parameter is configured in the deployment descriptor, what is the effect of invoking this filter?** **(choose two)**

EXHIBIT

A The filter invokes the next filter in the chain, then returns from doFilter().

B The filter invokes the next filter in the chain, sets the emailed request-scoped attribute, then returns from doFilter().

C The filter sets the emailed request-scoped attribute, then returns from doFilter().

D An exception occurs on line 9.

E A compilation error occurs.

11 **Study the exhibited wrapper. This wrapper is used in a filter inside a chain whose target resource is a JSP component. Assuming no exceptions are raised by any other resources or filters, what will be the result of using this wrapper in the filter?** **(choose two)**

EXHIBIT

A The filter uses the wrapper, all subsequent components interact with the wrapper, and the filter then writes all content from the wrapper's internal StringWriter to the response. To the client, this is transparent.

B The filter uses the wrapper, all subsequent components interact with the wrapper, but the filter doesn't write the contents to the response. The response to the client is empty.

C Components after the filter can no longer set headers or send response body.

D Components after the filter cannot use a PrintWriter for writing to the response.

E Components after the filter can set headers but cannot send response body

12 **Three filters are invoked in the order FilterA, then FilterB, then FilterC. FilterB uses a custom response wrapper called MyResponseWrapper, and FilterC uses a wrapper called HerResponseWrapper. FilterB's and FilterC's doFilter methods are implemented in the exhibit. What happens as a result of using this wrapper?** **(choose two)**

EXHIBIT

A The target resource and all other resources used by that target interact with the MyResponseWrapper object.

B The target resource and all other resources used by that target interact with the HerResponseWrapper object.

C The target resource, all its associated resources, and FilterA now see the MyResponseWrapper object.

D The container extracts the original object from its wrapper and all targets interact with the original wrapper.

E FilterA interacts with the MyResponseWrapper object.

F FilterA interacts with the original response object.

Exhibits

Q.9

```
public class MyFilter implements Filter {
    private FilterConfig config;

    public void init(FilterConfig config) {
        this.config = config;
    }
    public void doFilter(ServletRequest req, ServletResponse resp,
                         FilterChain chain)
                         throws IOException, ServletException {
        // insert here
        return;
    }
    public void destroy() {}
}
```

Q.10

```
public class MyFilter implements Filter {
  private FilterConfig config;
  public void init(FilterConfig config) {
    this.config = config;
  }
  public void doFilter(ServletRequest req, ServletResponse resp,
                       FilterChain chain) {
    String param = config.getServletContext().getInitParameter("email");
    if(param != null) {
      try {
        chain.doFilter(req,resp);
      } catch(Exception e) {}
    }
    req.setAttribute("emailed", Boolean.TRUE);
  }
  public void destroy() {}
}
```

Q.11

```
public class MyResponseWrapper extends HttpServletResponseWrapper {
  private PrintWriter pw;
  private StringWriter sw;
  public MyResponseWrapper(HttpServletResponse wrap) {
    super(wrap);
  }
  public PrintWriter getWriter() throws IOException {
    if(pw == null) {
      sw = new StringWriter();
      pw = new PrintWriter(sw);
    }
    return pw;
  }
  public ServletOutputStream getOutputStream() throws IOException {
    throw new IllegalStateException();
  }
}
```


Q.12

FilterB method:

```
public void doFilter(ServletRequest req, ServletResponse resp,
                     FilterChain chain)
                     throws IOException, ServletException {
    chain.doFilter(req, new MyResponseWrapper(resp));
}
```

FilterC method:

```
public void doFilter(ServletRequest req, ServletResponse resp,
                     FilterChain chain)
                     throws IOException, ServletException {
    chain.doFilter(req, new HerResponseWrapper(resp));
}
```

7

Answers to Revision Questions

1 **Correct answer: D**

D is correct; all others are nonexistent.

2 **Correct answers: B, D**

A and C are for servlets and not filters, which expose a completely different API. Method E doesn't exist on the Filter interface. The other method we haven't mentioned here, which must also be implemented, is init(FilterConfig).

3 **Correct answer: B**

4 **Correct answer: E**

5 **Correct answer:** Loaded, Instantiated, Initialised, Invoked, Destroyed.

6 **Correct answers: B, E**

A is wrong – this method isn't declared to throw all checked exceptions. D is wrong: the class doesn't exist. E is the 'obvious' answer (it is checked and declared as thrown), but of course any method may also throw an unchecked RuntimeException (B).

7 **Correct answer: E**

Since A is an interface and none of the others exist. Unlike servlets, there are no abstract classes which implement the base interface.

8 **Correct answers: C,E**

None of the others exist.

9 **Correct answer: C**

10 **Correct answers: B,C**

Note that we are told the filter initialisation parameter called email is set, but we know nothing about the context parameter, which is the one accessed on line 9. This example highlights the difference between filter and context parameters. Now, if the context parameter does exist, then B will happen, but otherwise C will occur, as the param variable will be null. Line 9 cannot throw any exceptions, so D is incorrect.

11 **Correct answers: B,E**

This serves as a warning of a notoriously bad filter/wrapper design! The wrapper incorporates an internal buffer, but provides no way to access that buffer after the response has been completed! However, since the wrapper doesn't alter the header methods, these can still be set by the components (and the response committed by invoking, for instance, sendError()), so C is wrong. Similarly, all components can obtain a PrintWriter, so D is wrong (it's a binary ServletOutputStream which can't be obtained from the wrapper). Also A is wrong because the filter can't get the internal buffer, so it can't write its contents to the response. B is true, because the wrapper provides no way to access the internal buffer, and E is correct as the wrapper leaves the header methods to delegate to the wrapped response object.

12 **Correct answers: B,F**

This tests your knowledge of container contracts; the contract states that the same response object/wrapper which leaves a filter must be the one which re-enters it on the return trip, and it is the container's responsibility to ensure this is the case. In other words, if the original object leaves FilterA on its way to FilterB, the original object (not a wrapper) must return on the journey back from FilterB to FilterA. Similarly, the wrapper MyResponseWrapper from FilterB to FilterC must be returned to FilterB on the way back, and the same for HerResponseWrapper passed from FilterC to the target resource – this must be passed back to FilterC after the target finishes executing. Hence A is incorrect since the target sees HerResponseWrapper, C is wrong since FilterA sees the original object, D is incorrect because the container only extracts the original object on its journey back to FilterA from FilterB. E is incorrect as FilterA always interacts with the original object.

In this chapter you'll:

- Understand how Web servers process concurrent requests using HTTP 1.0 connections, HTTP 1.1 persistent connections and Java's non-blocking IO
- Appreciate the motivations for improving efficiency, particularly with regards to AJAX "rich" client-side browser-based applications
- Learn about the Asynchronous Request model and its Servlet API
- Work through an example using the APIs

8 Asynchronous Requests

Web servers can only handle a finite number of concurrent requests. Traditionally, in HTTP 1.0, Web servers allocated each new connection either to a child process or a thread, taking those from a pool. The process or thread is then reserved exclusively for the client connection, and once the request is over, the client closes the connection so the process or thread is freed for another incoming request.

This was grossly inefficient for clients as each HTTP 1.0 request had to establish and tear-down a new TCP connection. As Web pages became more content rich – full of images and external files like stylesheets and scripts – each element of the page which had to be loaded incurred the same TCP setup overheads.

Improving HTTP Efficiency

HTTP 1.1 introduced the concept of a **persistent connection**, so the client can leave a TCP connection open and make new requests over that pipeline without having to establish and tear-down the connection each time. Once the client has finished with the connection (which is at its discretion – it could be when it has completed loading all the resources for an entire web page, after several pages, or after an inactivity timeout), it will then close its persistent connection which frees the server-side thread to handle another incoming connection.

Persistent connections improves performance considerably for clients, but leaves servers with a resource issue – each thread will reserve memory for itself even when it is sitting idle between client requests. This limits the scalability of this approach considerably, and typically a Web server will be configured with a maximum limit on thread count to prevent a runaway number of connections from destabilising the server. Once that limit is reached, no more connections can be processed until existing connections are closed by the clients.

Java SE 1.4 introduced Non-Blocking IO in the NIO libraries. These libraries use low-level operating system constructs to allow highly optimised code in the operating system, and hardware offloads in high-end systems, to manage TCP connections, each called a **channel**. Each channel is non-blocking in Java code, so a single thread can be used to wait on all those channels until data arrives, and only then execute processing code. By allowing the low-level routines to handle the waiting, and only using Java threads for the (relatively expensive) processing of that data, far fewer threads are needed in the system than when allocating one thread per connection. As with the HTTP 1.0 model, individual channels now become allocated for each independent request – allowing servers to support HTTP 1.1 persistent connections with far fewer (idle but resource-consuming) threads. Some high-performance Web servers tuned to deliver static resources (plain HTML, images, client-side scripts and binary files) only use a single thread with NIO and have been proven to scale extremely well.

As it offers significant performance benefits, most modern Java Web containers use NIO behind the scenes when handling such HTTP requests. They have been using this approach for years to internally optimise their engines, completely transparently to Web applications.

Until now in the discussion, we've been concerned with long idle times coming from clients holding open persistent connections but not making requests – leaving threads "in service" but underutilised. Use of NIO rather than connection threads solves that. But it doesn't solve delays incurred on the server-side when running time- or wait-intensive routines. Increasingly Web applications are becoming richer replacements for desktop software – for example online word processing, spreadsheets, calculations and realtime corporate reporting. They obtain their data from databases and other integrations with external systems and APIs, and these can incur delays whilst those requests or queries are made, processing occurs, and the response is returned to the server-side application before it can be handed back to the client. This again can leave threads "in service" but idle whilst they are waiting on third party service-side resources to respond. Whilst the thread is sitting idle consuming memory, it could have been temporarily re-tasked to process another HTTP request; once the data for the original request is available, the same (or another) thread can then respond to the original client request. In a busy Web application where thousands of requests may be made every second, being able to re-task otherwise idle threads until they are required allows a single server to be more efficient and scale significantly better for the same cost.

The **asynchronous request** processing model in Java EE 6 has been introduced to address this concern for server-side request processing comprised of (at least potentially) slow-running tasks.

AJAX

One of the more recent motivating factors to improve HTTP connection performance is the **Asynchronous JavaScript API for XML**, or **AJAX**. JavaScript (which has nothing to do with Java except the shared name part) has been one of the key driving forces for "feature rich" dynamic client-side applications in Web browsers. AJAX is a technique for Web browsers to make background HTTP requests without the user having to leave the page they are on, and without the use of HTML frames; it allows content within a single Web page to be updated in (relatively) realtime, without the entire page having to be refreshed. This means small widgets of content – for example the Outlook Web Access inbox, Twitter timelines and Facebook chat – to update themselves seamlessly without destroying the overall user experience.

AJAX was first introduced by Microsoft in 1999, and became so popular it has since been deployed throughout all other common browsers. Since 2000, AJAX technology has found its way into Microsoft Web applications, Google Apps, Facebook and Twitter to name just a few of the largest notable examples.

As all Web content has to be originated by the client with a request to the server, and a server cannot push data towards the client without such a corresponding request, AJAX fundamentally works by regularly **polling** the server to request if data has changed (such as a new message becoming available in your inbox or chat session). As this may happen many times each minute, this increases the demand on Web applications to handle more requests for each client connection. This in turn increases the processing load on the number of threads required. It is therefore an increasing concern that those threads be used as efficiently as possible, and again the Asynchronous Request processing model helps us to achieve this, in the event that we are using server-side slow-running tasks, such as checking a remote POP or IMAP mailbox for messages.

Server Push with Comet

It would be ideal if sometimes a server could **push** data towards the client when events are generated or data changes – rather than having to wait for the client to poll the server with a new request.

There are some techniques which can be used to emulate this approach for clients obtaining realtime data. These are most commonly grouped under the name of **Comet**, also known as **AJAX Push** and **Reverse AJAX**. Whilst outside the scope of this book, the general principle is that the server is able to send data to the client immediately as it becomes available. This is currently implemented in one of two ways:

- **Streaming**
  The server holds a single persistent connection open with a single request, and the server regularly sends back fragments of a response as they become available. This means the request never actually finishes and is just kept open. This is difficult to universally implement on all browsers.

- **Long polling**
  With this approach, the client sends a request to the server and the server keeps this open until an event is raised so the server can generate the response. This is identical to the typical polling model, except rather than the server keep returning a "no updates" response on almost every poll (at whatever polling rate the client is using), it is now able to return a single response as soon as data becomes available to update the client.

As this is very much a workaround for a non-existent feature of HTTP, the client-side scripting and server-side code has to be specially crafted to work with pushed data. Some common JavaScript libraries like jQuery and Dojo have client-side facilities for working with this kind of approach. Similarly, some container-specific libraries like CometProcessor (in Tomcat), Continuations (Jetty) and CometEngine (Grizzly) can be used on the server-side. The details of this are outside of the scope of this book and, as they are non-standard, will not be tested directly in the Web Component Developer exams. They are however topics of interest and you may wish to read around them separately.

What is particularly relevant with Comet AJAX is that it will hold requests open until the server is ready to send a response – triggered by a server-side event (such as a new message arriving on the server). Without the Asynchronous Request model, a thread would have to be assigned (sitting idle) to each of these Comet requests – again consuming resources for no reason. This is a second major driving factor for implementing Asynchronous Requests in Java EE Web applications.

The Asynchronous Request API

The first step to using asynchronous dispatching inside either Servlet or Filter components is to ensure they are explicitly enabled to support the technology. This is achieved through configuration, either with the deployment descriptor or by using annotations (these are discussed in detail in Chapter 11), like this:

- **Servlets**
  Deployment descriptor: <async-supported>true</async-supported>
  Annotation: @WebServlet(asyncSupported=true)

- **Filters**
  Deployment descriptor: <async-supported>true</async-supported>
  Annotation: @WebFilter(asyncSupported=true)

Once enabled, the container will be ready to handle any asynchronous requests made by our components; note that just because the capability has been enabled for a given component, that component doesn't have to start an asynchronous request cycle – it can execute a traditional synchronous request/response cycle, for example if a resource to serve the request is available immediately.

NOTE: Performing a request dispatch from a synchronous Servlet (`asyncSupported` is false, the default if the annotation or descriptor element are omitted) to an asynchronous Servlet is illegal, but only if the second Servlet actually operates in asynchronous mode at runtime. Doing this will cause an `IllegalStateException` to be thrown at runtime by the `startAsync()` method on `ServletRequest`. This method is discussed in detail next. Dispatching from an asynchronous component to a synchronous one is always allowed – the `dispatch()` mechanism is also discussed later.

Asynchronous Request/Response Cycle

In the traditional synchronous mode, the flow of events through a Servlet is:

1. Container receives request
2. The `service()` method of a mapped Servlet is invoked to handle the request
3. The `service()` method may delegate to other methods (e.g. `doGet()`) and the method implementations may call other helper classes or include/forward dispatch requests to other components managed by the container.
4. Eventually the `service()` method will return, and the response will be committed and written to the client, ending the request/response cycle.

This applies equally for Filters, by exchanging `service()` with `doFilter()`.

Under the *asynchronous* model, the flow of the incoming request thread for a Servlet instead looks like this:

1. Container receives request
2. The `service()` method of the appropriate Servlet is invoked
3. The `service()` method may be implemented to delegate/dispatch as normal
4. At some point in the execution, your code will call one of the `startAsync()` methods on the `ServletRequest`. This begins the asynchronous cycle, and returns an `AsyncContext` which is the environment which the asynchronous execution code will have access to – it provides the means for the execution code (which remember is likely not running in the same request thread) to get `ServletRequest` and `ServletResponse` objects, as well as re-dispatch

requests within the application and interact with the container to complete the asynchronous cycle and commit and return the response to the client.

5. The `service()` method returns, having left the asynchronous request to be executed in a parallel context. Unlike in the synchronous model, the container will not commit and close the response automatically at this point – the whole concept of the asynchronous request cycle is to defer the response to be processed and sent at a later time.

In parallel to this we therefore have another task running, or queued waiting to be run. Supplied with the `AsyncContext` we obtained in step 4 above, you would implement this task to follow this basic procedure running in its own thread:

1. Execute its task immediately, or block on some other queue or process until it can execute.
2. The task may use the `AsyncContext getRequest()` and `getResponse()` methods to obtain request information and make changes (including setting headers and writing data) to the response in the usual manner.
3. The task may then proceed in one of two ways (you cannot use both, else an `IllegalStateException` will be thrown when invoking the later method):

▷ **Complete the response itself**
It invokes the `complete()` method of the `AsyncContext` to signal to the container that it has fulfilled the original request and the response to the client should now be committed and closed;

▷ **Delegate processing by dispatching**
It may call the `dispatch()` method on `AsyncContext` to delegate the start processing of a new request/response cycle. The `dispatch()` returns immediately but the response is not committed until the target of the dispatch completes its execution – unless it too starts an asynchronous cycle of it own, in which case the current context will be waiting on the target `AsyncContext complete()` to be invoked. Dispatching to a component which does not support asynchronous processing (including to JSPs) is allowed; the response is committed when the target completes execution.

Asynchronous Dispatching

The `dispatch()` mechanism is similar to a regular `RequestDispatcher forward()` but with the following three differences:

1. The dispatcher type is set to `ASYNC` rather than `FORWARD` (affecting container authorisation mechanisms and filters to be applied to the request);
2. The response buffer and headers will not be reset, allowing content to be

carried over;

3. It is legal to `dispatch()` even if the response has already been committed, which allows for dispatching to other executing code provided it does not modify response headers.

For more details of the available `dispatch()` methods, including exception handling, see *The AsyncContext Interface* section later in this chapter.

If your task does not call `complete()` or `dispatch()` within a configurable timeout, the container will abort the original request, ensuring that the client gets some kind of response (even if it's just an error) returned in a reasonable timeframe and reducing the number of asynchronous requests being managed on the server. If the timeout is reached, the following steps occur:

1. The `onTimeout()` methods of all registered `AsyncListeners` are called.
2. If none of those listeners called `complete()` or any of the `dispatch()` methods on the `AsyncContext`, perform an error dispatch with a status code equal to `HttpServletResponse.SC_INTERNAL_SERVER_ERROR`.
3. If no matching error page was found, or the error page did not call `complete()` or any of the `dispatch()` methods, call `complete()`.

This ensures that eventually the original request/response cycle will be finished as `complete()` will be invoked, whether that is by a request Servlet or Filter, a listener, an error page or (as a last resort) by the container itself.

Running Asynchronous Tasks

The container doesn't implicitly run the background task for you, so you will need to start this up in a parallel thread yourself. To utilise a container-managed thread pool, the `AsyncContext` does provide a useful `start()` method which takes a `Runnable` task to start the asynchronous task. Let's use this in a very brief example. We'll first create a `Runnable` task called `MyAsyncTask` which does nothing but pause for a 3 seconds and then write the ubiqitous "Hello World" to the response:

```
public class MyAsyncTask implements Runnable {
  private javax.servlet.AsyncContext context;

  public MyAsyncTask(javax.servlet.AsyncContext actxt) {
    this.context = actxt;
  }
```

```
  public void run() {
    Thread.sleep(3000);
    javax.servlet.ServletResponse resp = context.getResponse();
    resp.getWriter().write("Hello World");
    resp.flushBuffer();
    context.complete();
  }
}
```

We'll then construct the Servlet and it's `service()` method to use the `AsyncContext start()` method to run our task in a new parallel thread:

```
@WebServlet(asyncSupported=true)
public class MyServlet extends GenericServlet {

  public void service(ServletRequest req, ServletResponse res) {
    /* Start the asynchronous process and get the context */
    AsyncContext ac = req.startAsync();

    /* Create an instance of our task implementing Runnable */
    MyAsyncTask t = new MyAsyncTask(ac);

    /* Start the task running in a container-managed thread */
    ac.start(t);
  }

}
```

Once the `service()` method returns, the response won't be committed but `MyAsyncTask` will be left running in the background. After its `sleep()` timeout expires it will write "Hello World" to the response and then calls the `complete()` method on `AsyncContext`. This signals that the container should then commit and close the response.

This simple example demonstrates all the fundamentals of the new asynchronous processing architecture. We will now elaborate on the details of the API so you are able to make full use of all its features.

The ServletRequest API

The following methods have been added to the `javax.servlet.ServletRequest` interface in order to support asynchronous request processing:

- **boolean isAsyncSupported()**
  Returns true if the request is in the scope of a filter or servlet for which `asyncSupported` is set to `true` in either the deployment descriptor or in an annotation.

- **boolean isAsyncStarted()**
  Returns true if the current request is operating in asynchronous mode – which is the case if either of the `startAsync()` methods have already been invoked successfully.

- **AsyncContext startAsync(ServletRequest, ServletResponse)**
  Puts the request into asynchronous mode and initialises the `AsyncContext` with the request and response objects – these must either be the same objects passed to the `service()` (Servlet) or `doFilter()` (Filter) methods or wrappers of those.

- **AsyncContext startAsync()**
  The same as `startAsync(ServletRequest,ServletResponse)` but with arguments of the original (unwrapped) `ServletRequest` and `ServletResponse` objects. Unless you are wrapping the request and/or response objects, use this method to start a new asynchronous request cycle.

- **AsyncContext getAsyncContext()**
  Returns the `AsyncContext` which was created by the most recent invocation of one of the `startAsync()` methods – or throws an `IllegalStateException` if these have not been invoked.

These methods simply allow the request to be put into asynchronous mode and for the corresponding `javax.servlet.AsyncContext` to be obtained. The effects of calling the `startAsync()` methods are:

1. The request is put into asynchronous mode, so the response will not be committed until the `complete()` method is invoked on the returned `AsyncContext`, or the asynchronous cycle times out.

2. The `hasOriginalRequestAndResponse()` method of the `AsyncContext` will return `true` only if the arguments supplied to the `startAsync(ServletRequest,ServletResponse)` are the original unwrapped request and response objects (this is implicit for the no arguments method). For details about why this is useful, see the description for this method in the later section.

3. The `AsyncContext` object returned is reset to its initial state; in particular, the list of `AsyncListener`s registered with the `AsyncContext` is emptied. Calling the no argument `startAsync()` will preserve the previous (possibly wrapped) request and response objects.

The AsyncContext Interface

Objects of this interface type are created by the container and passed as responses from the `ServletRequest startAsync()` method when it is invoked. The intention is that this object will be passed to the asynchronous code and used to obtain request data, populate the response, possibly dispatch the request onwards to other components and finally to `complete()` the cycle, committing the response.

Asynchronous processing code is most likely going to need to get the request and response objects, so `AsyncContext` provides these methods:

- **`ServletRequest getRequest()`**
  Returns the request object used to initialise this context, used by the asynchronous processes to examine request data.

- **`ServletResponse getResponse()`**
  Returns the response object used to initialise this context, used by the asynchronous processes to alter headers, send data and commit the response.
- **`boolean hasOriginalRequestAndResponse()`**
  This can be used by filters and servlets on the initial request/response cycle completion to determine whether they need to preserve any wrappers they created. If this returns true, then the filters or servlets can destroy any wrapper objects they may have passed down the request invocation chain, as only the original objects are being used in the asynchronous components. If this returns false, the wrapper objects are being stored in the asynchronous context and therefore will be required to persist the completion of the initial request/response cycle until the asynchronous cycle completes.

A timeout can be set on the entire asynchronous cycle to ensure the client does not wait indefinitely (the default is container-dependent, typically 5-10 seconds):

- **`void setTimeout(long milliseconds)`**
  Sets the timeout (in milliseconds) for this asychronous request cycle. This timeout is relative to the time when the container-initiated dispatch (during which one of the `startAsync()` methods on the `ServletRequest` was called) has returned to the container. If this timeout expires before either the `complete()` or any of the `dispatch()` methods are invoked, the container will abort the request following the approach outlined in the earlier Asynchronous Request/Response Cycle section. Use a negative value or 0 to disable the timeout.
- **`long getTimeout()`**
  Return the current setting for the context, negative or 0 if timeout is disabled.

To run an asynchronous task, you can manage the threading and execution of that task yourself; alternatively, `AsyncContext` provides a convenience method:

- **`void start(Runnable task)`**
  Causes the container to dispatch a thread, possibly from a managed thread pool, to run the specified `Runnable`.

The asynchronous tasks may need to re-dispatch the request to another container managed resource – in a similar way that RequestDispatchers are used to forward and include non-asynchronous resources – by invoking one of:

- **`void dispatch(String path)`**
  Dispatches the request and response to the given path, which must reside in the same `ServletContext` (application) in the container.
- **`void dispatch(ServletContext, String)`**
  Dispatches the request and response to the given `String` path in the supplied `ServletContext` (another application) in the same container.
- **`void dispatch()`**
  Dispatches the request and response back to the same resource – specifically if the request passed to `startAsync()` is an `HttpServletRequest` then this path is determined by `getRequestURI()` on that object; otherwise it is to the URI of the request when it was last dispatched by the container.

Control over the request and response is delegated to the dispatch target, and the response will be closed when the dispatch target has completed execution – this may also be asynchronous if one of the `startAsync()` methods is called within the target resource.

To prevent a dispatching loop (particularly when the no-argument `dispatch()` is used), any one of the `dispatch` methods can only be called once in the same asynchronous cycle (started by the `startAsync()` invocation on `ServletRequest`). Any additional dispatch invocation, within the same cycle, will cause an `IllegalStateException` to be thrown on the second or subsequent attempts.

An `IllegalStateException` will also be thrown if any `dispatch()` method is called after `complete()` or vice-versa. If `startAsync()` is subsequently called on the dispatched request, then any of the `dispatch()` or `complete()` methods may then be invoked without error.

Whenever a dispatch occurs, just as with a `RequestDispatcher`, it stores the original request path information in request-scoped attributes. These are stored in request attributes with names found in the following `AsyncContext` constants:

- **`ASYNC_REQUEST_URI`**
  The original complete request URI, composed (in order) of the parts below

8

- **ASYNC_CONTEXT_PATH**
  The context path of the original request URI
- **ASYNC_SERVLET_PATH**
  The path mapped to the servlet resource which handled the original request
- **ASYNC_PATH_INFO**
  The original path info (after the servlet mapped path, before the query string)
- **ASYNC_QUERY_STRING**
  The original query string

Any errors or exceptions occurring during the execution of a dispatch cause:

1. The `onError()` methods of all registered `AsyncListener` instances to be invoked; each listener can obtain the caught `Throwable` via `getThrowable()` on the `AsyncEvent`.
2. If none of the listeners called `complete()` or any of the `dispatch()` methods, perform an error dispatch with a status code 500 (Internal Server Error) and make the above `Throwable` available as the value of the `RequestDispatcher.ERROR_EXCEPTION` request attribute.
3. If no matching error page was found, or the error page did not call `complete()` or any of the `dispatch()` methods, call `complete()`.

An asynchronous task completing successfully without re-dispatching will invoke:

- **void complete()**
  Informs the container that asynchronous processing has completed successfully; the response is closed and sent to the client. Any registered `AsyncListeners` have their `onComplete()` methods invoked,

If the request was already dispatched, an `IllegalStateException` is thrown.

The last few methods on `AsyncContext` create and register listeners which will have their methods invoked during the lifecycle of the asynchronous processing:

- **<T extends AsyncListener> T createListener(Class<T>)**
  Instantiates a new `AsyncListener` of the given class and initialises it, providing support for annotation configuration and resource injection.
- **void addListener(AsyncListener l)**
  Registers the supplied listener with this context, to receive notification of events occurring on the most recently started asynchronous cycle.
- **void addListener(AsyncListener,ServletRequest,ServletResponse)**
  Registers the supplied listener with this context, to receive notification of events occurring on the most recently started asynchronous cycle. The request

and response objects supplied will be made available to the `AsyncListener` using the `getSuppliedRequest()` and `getSuppliedResponse()` methods on the `AsyncEvent` passed to each of the listener's methods. This makes them available to the listener so it may release resources they consume (particularly if they are wrappers) at various points in the asynchronous lifecycle.

AsyncListener

Listeners of this type may be registered for a specific asynchronous request/response cycle on its `AsyncContext` using `addListener()` methods covered previously.

Each listener has four methods following the lifecycle of an asynchronous request:

- **`void onStartAsync(AsyncEvent)`**
  Within the current asynchronous context, `startAsync()` has been invoked.
- **`void onComplete(AsyncEvent)`**
  The `AsyncContext`'s `complete()` has been called in the current cycle.
- **`void onTimeout(AsyncEvent)`**
  Notification that the current asynchronous cycle has timed out. This method can handle the timeout and call `complete()` or `dispatch()`, or do nothing in which case the container's default error handling is used (status code 500).
- **`void onError(AsyncEvent)`**
  Notification that an exception, or some other error, occurred during the asynchronous processing. This method can handle the error and then call `complete()` or `dispatch()`, or can do nothing in which case the container's default error handling is triggered (500 Internal Server Error on HTTP).

The `javax.servlet.AsyncEvent` has four methods of interest:

- **`AsyncContext getAsyncContext()`**
  Returns the context for the asynchronous cycle in which the event occurred
- **`Throwable getThrowable()`**
  This will be non-`null` if the `onError()` method is being invoked on the listener, and contains the original `Throwable` caught by the container.
- **`ServletRequest getSuppliedRequest()`**
  If this listener was added via `AsyncContext`'s 3-argument `addListener()` method, this is the request provided to that method. It is `null` otherwise.
- **`ServletResponse getSuppliedResponse()`**
  If this listener was added via `AsyncContext`'s 3-argument `addListener()` method, this is the response provided to that method. It is `null` otherwise.

An Example Application

In this section we will look at the key parts of a demonstration Web application employing the techniques discussed in this chapter: an online auction where registered users can check the highest bids for items and make their own higher offers. We use asynchronous technology to allow client-side techniques - namely AJAX - to use streaming or long-polling to wait on an update. Our server-side code will keep those requests pending as asynchronous until a new bid is made by a user, and then send the details of the latest high bid to all those pending requests. The client-side JavaScript, or similar, required to integrate this with the front-end is out of the scope of this book and the exam, and therefore is omitted.

The code in this section is designed to be a quick and functional example, with emphasis on the asynchronous code. It is therefore not suitable for deployment as the next eBay - it certainly won't scale as-is. We are also not building any extravagant HTML for this. The classes will be:

- **`AuctionItem`**
  Objects of this type represent a single auctioned item including its unique reference code, current highest bid and details of the registered user who bid.
- **`AuctionSystem`**
  There will be only one instance of this class within the Web application; it's purpose is to act as a factory for `AuctionItem`s, to enable us to look-up individual items by their unique reference code. This object will reside as a context-scoped attribute so it is accessible across the application.
- **`AuctionContextListener`**
  This will create the singleton `AuctionSystem` object when the container initialises the application, and bind it into the `Items` context attribute.
- **`BidServlet`**
  This servlet shows the form where new bids can be submitted, and accepts the POST data from that form to action a new (higher) bid.
- **`AsyncBidServlet`**
  This servlet component can be called by the client - notably through AJAX techniques - to obtain notification when a change occurs to the current highest bid. It will wait in the background as an asynchronous request until it can notify the client of a change.

The AuctionSystem

We'll begin with the least interesting components, which are really only being used in this application to act as our makeshift data store. In a real life scenario these would be replaced by databases and a more detailed object model.

The `AuctionSystem` is a factory with a `findItem()` method so servlet components can look up `AuctionItems` based on a reference code:

```
public class AuctionSystem {
  private Hashtable<String,AuctionItem> items;

  public AuctionSystem() {
    items = new Hashtable<String,AuctionItem>();
    // Initialise the list of items here - here's two examples:
    String[] itemCodes = { "ABC001", "XYZ987" };
    for(String c : itemCodes) {
      AuctionItem item = new AuctionItem(c);
      items.put("ABC001",item);
      new Thread(item).start();
    }
  }

  public AuctionItem findItem(String ref) {
    return items.get(ref);
  }
}
```

Most of this should be straightforward, none of it depends on Java EE techology. The reason for the `Thread.start()` will become clearer shortly.

In order for this singleton to be accessible by servlets, we use some "bootstrap" code in a `ServletContextListener` to create and register it in the context:

```
@WebListener
public class AuctionBootstrap implements ServletContextListener{

  public void contextInitialized(ServletContextEvent e) {
    /* Add the memory-based AuctionSystem storage */
    AuctionSystem sys = new AuctionSystem();
    ServletContext ctx = e.getServletContext();
    ctx.setAttribute("Items", sys);
  }

  public void contextDestroyed(ServletContextEvent e) {}
}
```

Hence when our application loads for the first time, the `Items` context-scoped attribute will contain the singleton `AuctionSystem` instance, pre-populated with a couple of example `AuctionItems`.

8

The AuctionItem

This class is the "meat" of the back-end processing; it represents a single item on the auction site, but also allows asynchronous requests to be registered to receive updates, and coordinates the updates when new bids are placed.

The class implements `Runnable` so it can be executed as a background thread, making the process of receiving updates independent from the process of updating (potentially thousands of) waiting asynchronous requests. In this code we use low-level `wait()` and `notify()` thread signals; in practice you would probably want to replace this with higher level objects from the `java.util.concurrent` package.

8

Here's the code:

```
public class AuctionItem implements Runnable {

  private String itemRef;
  // other fields omitted; e.g. description, condition, delivery
  private int highestBid; // e.g. in cents
  private User bidder; // some User object
  private List<AsyncContext> pendingRequests;

  public AuctionItem(String ref) {
    this.itemRef = ref;
    this.pendingRequests = new ArrayList<AsyncContext>();
  }

  public int getHighestBid() {
    return highestBid;
  }
  public User getHighestBidder() {
    return bidder;
  }

  public void addPendingRequest(AsyncContext ac) {
    synchronized(pendingRequests) {
      pendingRequests.add(ac);
    }
  }

  /**
   * Call this method with any new bid updates
   */
  public void updateBid(User bidder, int bid) {
    if(bid>highestBid) {
      synchronized(pendingRequests) {
        this.highestBid = bid;
        this.bidder = bidder;
      }
      pendingRequests.notify();
    }
  }
```

```
  /**
   * This method handles the background processing of
   * bid updates for this item, sending each update to
   * every pending request and completing them
   */
  public void run() {
    synchronized(pendingRequests) {
      int lastBid = 0;
      while(true) {
        /* If amount has changed, process pending requests */
        if(highestBid>lastBid) {
          while(!pendingRequests.isEmpty()) {
            AsyncContext ctx = pendingRequests.get(0);
            /* In the try we suppress any exceptions resulting
               from timed out async requests, for example */
            try {
              ServletResponse resp = ctx.getResponse();
              PrintWriter output = resp.getWriter();
              /* Print two lines: first is the bid amount,
                 second is the details of the bidder */
              output.println(highestBid);
              output.println(bidder);
              /* Now commit the asynchronous request */
              ctx.complete();
            } catch(Exception e) {}
            /* Remove the pending request from the queue */
            pendingRequests.remove(0);
          }
          lastBid = highestBid;
        } // ends if(highestBid>lastBid)
        pendingRequests.wait(); // wait of notify() in updateBid
      } // ends while(true)
    } // ends synchronized(pendingRequests)
  } // ends run()
} // closes class
```

The methods of interest here are `updateBid()` and `run()`. The former takes an update, and provided it is the highest bid to date, changes the latest high bid and the `User` object (we don't define this explicitly here - make it whatever you like!) for the bidder. It then calls `notify()` on the `pendingRequests` object, the effect of which is for the `run()` method's `pendingRequests.wait()` to return from its blocked state and execute another iteration of the `while` loop. In this loop we go through each of the pending `AsyncContexts` (each representing a waiting asynchronous request) and tell each about the update to the bid price and bidder just received. Once one has been processed and its `complete()` invoked, it is removed from the registered queue. Once all have been processed, the `run()` once again returns to the `pendingRequests.wait()` to pause execution until another update is received (and indeed more `AsyncContexts` have been registered for new requests).

The BidServlet

The AuctionSystem gives us a way to obtain AuctionItems which allow us to update the highest bid offer. We now provided the servlet HTTP interface which makes this happen for the user:

```
@WebServlet("/bids")
public class BidServlet extends HttpServlet {

  public void doGet(HttpServletRequest req, HttpServletResponse resp) {
    /* The itemRef is the code of item to display */
    String itemRef = req.getParameter("ref");

    /* Display the bid page; minimal incomplete HTML example: */
    Writer out = resp.getWriter();
    out.write("<form method=\"post\" action=\"\">");
    out.write("<p><strong>Bid amount:</strong> " +
              "<input type=\"text\" name=\"bid\" /></p>");
    out.write("<p><input type=\"hidden\" name=\"ref\" " +
              "value=\"" + itemRef + "\" />"+
              "<input type=\"submit\" /></p></form>");
  }

  public void doPost(HttpServletRequest req, HttpServletResponse resp) {
    /* Assume there is a User object in session from a login */
    User user = req.getSession().getAttribute("User");

    AuctionSystem s = getServletContext().getAttribute("Items");

    /* Expect an item reference ("ref") and amount ("bid") */
    String ref = req.getParameter("ref");
    int amount = Integer.parseInt(req.getParameter("bid"));

    AuctionItem item = s.findItem(ref);
    item.updateBid(user,amount);

    /* Redirect the user to the GET method display */
    resp.sendRedirect("/bids?ref=" + ref); // GET to self
  }
}
```

HTML forms and processing POST data aside, the code of interest here is:

```
AuctionSystem s = getServletContext().getAttribute("Items");
AuctionItem item = s.findItem(ref);
item.updateBid(user,amount);
```

which first obtains the singleton from the Items context-scoped attribute, then looks-up an AuctionItem based on the item reference supplied, and finally calls the updateBid() method on that item. This method should return quickly even though many other asynchronous requests may be updated, as we were using a background thread to do the updates in the AuctionItem class.

The AsyncBidServlet

Finally, we will implement a mechanism for client-side scripting (outside the scope of this book) to obtain almost instant updates when a new bid is made. This requires that the client scripting makes a long-polling or streaming request and leave the HTTP connection open. We in turn make this request asynchronous and add it to the appropriate `AuctionItem` queue, so that a future update will causes the item's background thread to notify the waiting request. Here's the code:

```
@WebServlet(asyncSupported=true,urlPatterns="/bidasync")
public class AsyncBidServlet extends GenericServlet {

  public void service(ServletRequest req, ServletResponse res) {

    /* The request must contain the "ref" parameter
       identifying the item to monitor */
    String ref = req.getParameter("ref");

    /* Start this as an asynchronous request */
    AsyncContext ac = req.startAsync();

    /* Add the context as "pending" to the AuctionItem */
    AuctionSystem s = getServletContext().getAttribute("Items");
    AuctionItem item = s.findItem(ref);
    item.addPendingRequest(ac);
  }
}
```

The interesting code here takes two steps; the first is to start a new asynchronous request/response cycle using:

```
AsyncContext ac = req.startAsync();
```

and the second is to register that `AsyncContext` with the `AuctionItem` so its thread will update the asynchronous request when a bid update is next available:

```
AuctionSystem s = getServletContext().getAttribute("Items");
AuctionItem item = s.findItem(ref);
item.addPendingRequest(ac);
```

Those are the key pieces of code: actual servlet code is minimal - most of the effort in developing scalable AJAX applications comes in the backend processing and thread handling, and the client-side cross-platform JavaScript.

NOTE: This example does not scale past a few dozen auction items, as creating a new thread for each item is resource-consuming. There are many better approaches to take, utilising thread pools to reduce idle thread counts, and only allocating a thread from the pool for processing once an update occurs to an item. These enhancements are not directly related to asynchronous request processing, and therefore are left as an exercise.

Revision Questions

8

1 **Which of the following configurations allow a Servlet implementation to start an asynchronous request cycle?** **(choose two)**

- A The @Asynchronous annotation applied to the class
- B <asynchronous>true</asynchronous> deployment descriptor declaration
- C <async-supported>true</async-supported> deployment descriptor declaration
- D asyncSupported="true" element of the @WebServlet annotation
- E Nothing required – servlets are asynchronous by default

2 **An object implementing which interface is used to interact with asynchronous requests?** **(choose one)**

- A javax.servlet.AsyncServletRequest
- B javax.servlet.AsyncRequest
- C javax.servlet.AsyncCycle
- D javax.servlet.AsyncServletContext
- E javax.servlet.AsyncContext

3 **Which method is used to start a new asynchronous request/ response cycle?** **(choose one)**

- A ServletContext.newAsync()
- B ServletContext.startAsync()
- C ServletRequest.newAsync()
- D ServletRequest.runAsync()
- E ServletRequest.getAsyncContext()

4 **When starting a new asynchronous request, under what conditions will an exception always be thrown?** **(choose three)**

- A Any attempt to start a second asynchronous cycle in the same client request
- B If a new asynchronous cycle is started in the scope of the same dispatch
- C If the response has already been closed
- D If the asynchronous cycle is started within a Filter component
- E If the Servlet where the cycle is started has not been configured to support asynchronous requests

5 **Which method should be invoked when an asynchronous request cycle is done processing its response to the client?** **(choose one)**

- A AsyncContext.complete()
- B AsyncContext.close()
- C ServletResponse.endAsync()
- D ServletRequest.endAsync()
- E ServletContext.endAsync()

6 **Which of these are always true about asynchronous timeouts?** **(choose two)**

- A The timeout facility can be removed by calling AsyncContext.setTimeout(0)
- B The timeout can be set to 30 seconds by calling AsyncContext.setTimeout(30)
- C The timeout can be set to 30 seconds by using the <async-timeout>30</async-timeout> deployment descriptor element
- D If not set explicitly, the default is to never timeout
- E If not set explicitly, the default timeout is container-dependent

7 **Which of these are always true about asynchronous dispatches?** **(choose two)**

- A A dispatch causes the response to be committed prior to processing the second (dispatched) resource.
- B When a dispatch is used, the second resource can always re-dispatch the asynchronous request elsewhere as it requires.
- C When a dispatch operation completes, the response will be closed.
- D The dispatch is executed in the same thread as the calling resource, so the dispatch operation blocks until the called resource returns from execution.
- E A dispatch can be invoked even if the response has already been committed.

8 **Which methods can be used to start an asynchronous dispatch?** **(choose two)**

- A RequestDispatcher.forward(ServletRequest, ServletResponse)
- B ServletRequest.dispatch(String)
- C ServletRequest.dispatch(ServletContext,String)
- D AsyncContext.dispatch(String)
- E AsyncContext.dispatch(ServletContext,String)

9 **Choose the best option to describe the effect of writing code including a no-argument dispatch() method within a servlet?** **(choose one)**

- A A new asynchronous cycle is started for the servlet in which the method is invoked
- B A new asynchronous cycle is started for the same request URI
- C A new async cycle is started for the ASYNC_SERVLET_PATH mapped resource
- D A runtime error occurs
- E A compilation error occurs

10 **Which of these describe how asynchronous requests execute?** **(choose three)**

- A When a new asynchronous cycle is started, the container puts the main request processing thread into a background state and continues running the code in the Servlet's service() method in the background.
- B When a new asynchronous cycle is started, the Servlet service() or Filter doFilter() code is completed as normal but the response is left open for further modification.
- C When a new asynchronous cycle is started, it must be passed a Runnable job to start processing in the background.
- D It is the application developer's responsibility to maintain all threading and background jobs relating to asynchronous request processing.
- E The container provides the ability to run a new background job in its own thread using the AsyncContext.start(Runnable) method.

11 **What type of exception is thrown by AsyncContext methods when a dispatch or completion problem occurs?** **(choose one)**

- A ServletException
- B AsynchronousException
- C AsynchronousServletException
- D IllegalStateException
- E IOException

12 **Which of these are methods in the AsyncListener interface?** **(choose two)**

- A onInterrupt(AsyncEvent)
- B onTimeout(AsyncEvent)
- C onComplete(AsyncEvent)
- D onStart(AsyncEvent)
- E onDispatch(AsyncEvent)

Answers to Revision Questions

1 **Correct answers: C,D**

2 **Correct answer: E**

3 **Correct answer: C**

Note that the method returns an AsyncContext but is executed on ServletRequest (not ServletContext). Whilst E also exists, it only obtains an existing context and does not start a new one. The other methods do not exist.

4 **Correct answers: B,C,E**

A is incorrect because a second cycle can be started in another dispatch context but still in the same overall client request. D is wrong because Filters can also be configured to support asynchronous requests in the same way as Servlets (as in E).

5 **Correct answer: A**

6 **Correct answers: A,E**

B is incorrect as the setTimeout() method uses milliseconds, so the argument should be 30000 for 30 seconds. For C, there is no such setting in the deployment descriptor. D is incorrect as E is correct.

7 **Correct answers: C,E**

A is wrong as the response is not altered prior to dispatching, which can be thought of more as an "include" than a "forward" operation; along these lines, E is correct. B is incorrect: a re-dispatch in a second component can be made only if that component also calls startAsync() - it is illegal to do two dispatches in the same asynchronous context. D is wrong: the dispatch is executed in its own thread and the dispatch() method returns immediately. C is correct: the dispatch completes in its own thread.

8 **Correct answers: D,E**

9 **Correct answer: B**

Whilst A could be correct (if the original request URI is mapped to the servlet) in general it will not be correct if the current servlet was included/forwarded to.

10 **Correct answers: B,D,E**

11 **Correct answer: D**

12 **Correct answers: B,C**

D is almost correct, but should be onStartAsync(AsyncEvent). The other method omitted is onError(AsyncEvent).

In this chapter you'll:

- Discover what sessions are, and how they help overcome problems with stateless protocols like provide HTTP.
- Learn how sessions are tracked across independent requests from clients.
- Understand the typical session lifecycle in the Java EE Web container.
- Utilise the Session API (HttpSession interface).
- Implement listeners to respond to events corresponding to changes in the session or session-scoped attributes.

9 Session Management

HTTP is a **stateless** protocol (unlike FTP for example); this means that it doesn't maintain a persistent connection with the client. Instead, connections are formed on an ad-hoc basis, only for the duration of the request-response cycle. On the contrary, a **stateful** protocol maintains a constant (e.g. TCP or FTP) connection with the client until either party chooses to close that connection, at which point the other party is notified of the closure.

The advantage of HTTP is that it doesn't depend on such permanent connections, which ensures resources are released quickly for use by another client. The disadvantage is that because each request-response cycle is treated separately, it is not possible to maintain a conversational state between the client and server over multiple requests.

Operating with Sessions

Sessions provide a way for the server (in our case, the Web container particularly) to keep track of all the requests made by a single client during its interaction with the server. Nearly all data about the session is maintained on the server: all the client does is to identify the session it belongs to during every request to the server. Every client will belong to a different session. Hence, the server can maintain information about the client across all of the client's interactions. Sessions therefore provide a way for all requests, made from the same client, to be associated with each other.

Consider a shopping basket: during several independent requests, the client might add items to that basket, and eventually, the client will probably want to get a list of all the items in the basket (and possibly remove some). In order that the basket's contents are available for the client's inspection across multiple requests, the server must be able to store data explicitly for that client, across many requests. If we added the basket's contents to the `ServletContext` (application-scoped) attributes, then all clients would have the same basket contents, which would be far from desirable. If we added the basket's contents to the request scope, the contents would be lost since the attributes are cleared for every new request. Hence, a third scope is needed, one which remains consistent across multiple requests from the client but is different for each client: this is the **session scope**, the subject of this chapter.

Session Tracking

Evidently, a client needs to be able to uniquely identify to the server which session it belongs to during a request, and it does so using a session ID variable (maintained by the container) called **`jsessionid`**, which is like a unique serial number for every different session being handled by the server. When a client first contacts the server, it is said to **join** a new session. At this point, the server (Web container) will establish a new session, with a unique `jsessionid`, for communication with that client. The server will send the new `jsessionid` back to the client, which stores it for use in all future requests. When the next request is made, the client includes the value of its `jsessionid` in its request data, and the server knows it should pick up that session where it last left off.

Most of the burden of session management therefore lies on the server. However, it is equally as important that the client is able to store and transmit its value of `jsessionid`. There are three main ways to achieve client storage, which are discussed in the subsequent sections. Sometimes all of these approaches will fail, in which case it is not possible for a client to join a session, and each request will be completely independent from the next. There is no compulsion for a client to have to participate in sessions, and indeed browsers may provide a feature for disabling interactions with sessions for security reasons. Bear this in mind, although you'll find that nearly all clients do use sessions anyway. There are some security considerations with sessions implemented in this way – for example, what if an unauthorised client were able to obtain (or guess) the `jsessionid` of an authorised client? However, we will not look at these in any detail.

Cookies

We first saw cookies in Chapter 1; the primary use of a cookie is to store small amounts of temporary data on the client machine across multiple requests and browser interactions. This makes cookies perfect for the storage of the `jsessionid` (a unique combination of letters and numbers). This is the most common mechanism, since it is the tidiest, by which I mean it avoids having to include ugly parameters in the request URL (see the next section). However, many clients do still have cookies disabled, so don't rely fully on this mechanism.

The cookie required for storage of the `jsessionid` is automatically created by the container during the first request made by the client in which a session is requested by the Web application. Figure 9.1 summarises session tracking using cookies.

Figure 9.1

Cookie-Managed Sessions

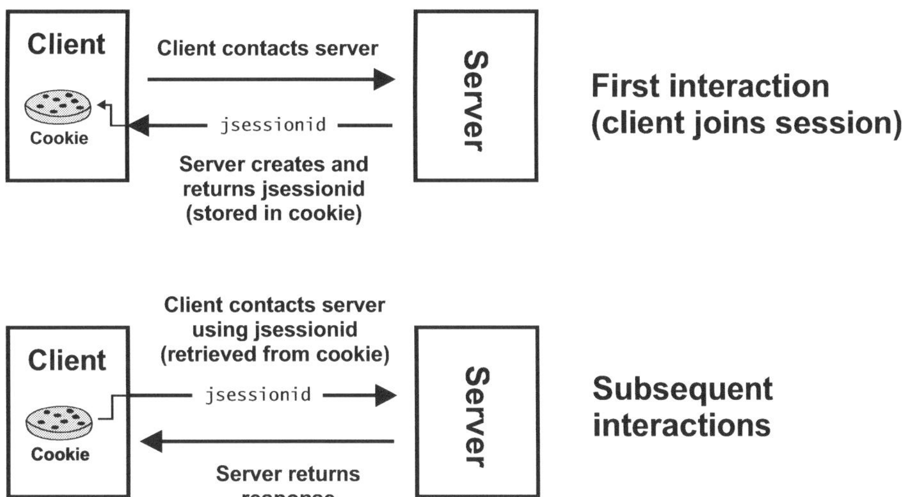

9

URL Rewriting

If nothing else works, always turn to URL rewriting. This mechanism puts the `jsessionid` parameter in the request URI. For example:

```
http://www.domain.ext/shop/catalogue;jsessionid=A1234Z
```

This mechanism does not rely on the client remembering its session ID (unlike cookies). Instead, the session ID is inserted by the container into every encoded URL in the pages and forms of the deployed applications we create. Then, when the user clicks on a link or submits a form (the usual ways of travelling between pages on a website), the client's `jsessionid` will automatically be included in the new request. Hence, each request is maintained from the last in a chain, as shown in Figure 9.2. Step 1 is the initial request; steps 2-4 repeat for every subsequent request-response cycle.

The main problem with URL rewriting on its own (as opposed to in conjunction with cookies) is that if one link in the chain breaks, such as a single hyperlink not including the client's current `jsessionid`, then the whole chain collapses. The new request, without a previous session ID, will be interpreted as a totally new request and the client will be forced to join a new session–all the data from the previous session will be lost. It is therefore extremely important that all URL encoding guidelines are followed, or you'll end up with a lot of disjointed sessions, and a lot of unhappy customers.

Additionally, if a user manually types in an address and omits the `jsessionid` (which they are pretty likely to, especially if they don't know what it's for), then all the old session data is lost and they will join a new session. This does not happen with cookies, since a cookie should exist across all browser windows for a given website, and is not dependent on parametric data written into the URL for a specific request.

The container can automatically encode URLs to contain the `jsessionid` (yet again saving us the trouble). In order for this automatic 'rewriting' process to work, all URLs used in the document must be passed through the `HttpServletResponse.encodeURL(String)` method; for example:

```
System.out.print("<a href=\"");
System.out.print(response.encodeURL("catalogue/basket"));
System.out.print("\">View basket</a>");
```


This will result in something like this at run time, where `A1234Z` is the actual session identifier:

```
<a href="catalogue/basket;jsessionid=A1234Z">View basket</a>
```

NOTE: The JSTL tag `<c:url />` can be used to encode URLs in JSPs where scripting elements are disabled (or the author chooses not to use them). This tag also provides other useful features, such as resolving paths relative to the context root into absolute URLs.

Figure 9.2

URL Rewriting Session Management

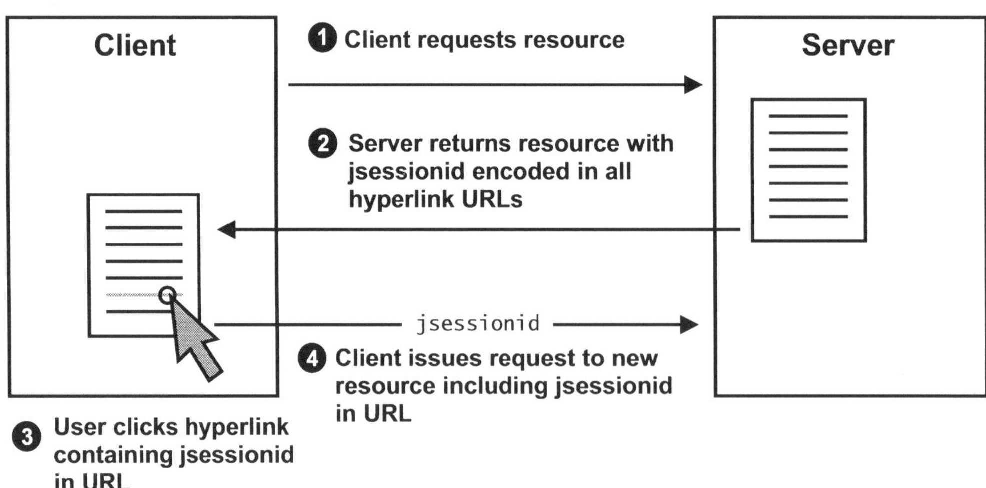

SSL Sessions

SSL (Secure Sockets Layer) provides an inherent session tracking mechanism in its connection between the client and server. The container can use this mechanism to track the client when the client is using an SSL-based protocol such as Secure HTTP (HTTPS).

Session Life Cycles

There are three stages in the life of a session:

1. A session is said to be **new** when the client does not yet know about it – i.e. it remains 'new' until it has actually been established with the client.
2. A client **joins** a session when it returns tracking data to the server indicating that the session has been correctly established. A client may not be able, or may choose not, to join a session, in which case the session will always be new (since it can never be correctly established).
3. The session is explicitly invalidated or the session timeout period expires, causing the session to be **destroyed**.

Stateful protocols (e.g. FTP) typically have a `CLOSE` command which is used to indicate that the connection is being terminated. However, being stateless, HTTP has no such commands, so it is impossible for the server to know from the client's connection when the client has finally had enough and left the session. For this reason, a session can never be terminated, but it can time out. The timeout is a fixed duration for which the session will be kept 'alive'; if there are no client requests in a session for the entire duration of the timeout, the session will be destroyed by the container. This helps to conserve memory resources for sessions which are no longer being used; it also improves security by closing unused sessions down. Usually a timeout value of around 30 minutes is chosen: this gives the client plenty of time to casually browse and read pages on a site, but represents a time after which a client is likely to have left the site altogether. The timeout for security-critical applications (such as online banks) may be closer to 5 minutes or less. Note that, because it will take the entire timeout period for a session to expire, it is not possible to know exactly how many users are online at any one time, and it is possible that any 'total users online' counters (like those in forums) will be 30 minutes or so out of date.

A client can ask for a session to be **invalidated** (i.e. removed from service), but this is not the same as closing a stateful protocol's connection. The manner in which a client invalidates a session will be dependent on the Web application itself, which will have to provide an explicit method for achieving this. On the contrary, closing a stateful connection is an implicit action which occurs when a client simply chooses not to continue with the communication – it doesn't require another request to the server to order invalidation, and this operation is dependent on the protocol, and not the application.

There are container-wide listeners designed specifically for the purposes of monitoring the session life cycle. These are discussed later in the chapter.

Passivation

A session can stay 'alive' for either a finite or an infinite amount of time, depending on its timeout configuration. For sessions with short timeout periods, this is fine since there are unlikely to be many session objects existing concurrently in the container. However, when sessions are configured with longer timeouts, more and more objects will be accumulated on the container's heap, increasing the memory usage of the application. If hundreds or thousands of session objects had to run concurrently in the container, each with a long timeout, the server's physical resources (its RAM) would soon become overwhelmed and the server would crash.

To limit the number of session objects which are consuming precious memory, the container undertakes **passivation**, whereby it serialises inactive objects to persistent storage (such as files in a temporary directory of the hard disk). The term **inactive** means sessions within which no requests have been made for a substantial time, but the session has not yet been invalidated or timed out. The typical method for passivation is to serialise the objects to disk using Java's standard serialisation mechanism.

When a request is made in an already passivated session, the session must be **activated**, which involves reading the object back into memory from its serialised form. Only once an object has been activated is it free to undergo further interactions with the container and client requests. This is important: the container can only interact with active object forms of a session, not passive serialised data.

Passivation is a similar idea to virtual memory, which operating systems use to provide an overflow mechanism for RAM consumption: when the memory becomes too full, older memory content is written to the hard disk (so-called 'virtual memory') so that the high-speed RAM is available for more recent operations. Hard disk write-cycle times (about 50MBps data transfer) are very slow in comparison to memory speeds (over 1000MBps for DDR 133MHz RAM).

Passivation is also used in distributed applications, where sessions are passed between containers running on different JVMs on independent server machines.

Sessions in Distributed Applications

For critical enterprise applications, it is common for the application to be deployed on several servers simultaneously; each server contains an identical but independent copy of the application. When a request is subsequently received for a component in that application, the request is delegated to one of those servers. Having multiple servers available enables concurrent requests from clients to be farmed to whichever server is currently working the least, thus the application becomes **load-balanced**. Load balancing is about sharing the processing duties between a cluster of networked machines (servers), and not relying on a single machine to do all of the work. This is a common requirement in big networks which consistently have large amounts of traffic.

Load-balancing is simple for basic applications which do not make use of sessions: the same application is deployed across each server, and each request is handled by an independent servlet or JSP component; none of the servers actually needs to know what the others are doing, because servlets are atomic components – i.e. they are stand-alone, not necessarily requiring communication with other components.

However, since the client's request may go to any one of the available servers, each server needs to know about the client's *session data*. This is achieved through **session migration** – a single session object is transferred from one Web container to another via serialisation. In order for migration (and indeed passivation) to occur correctly, all `Object`s added to an `HttpSession` as attributes need to implement `Serializable`.

The HttpSession Interface

Sessions are an HTTP concept; for this reason, it is an object of the `javax.servlet.http.HttpSession` interface which is used to represent a session attached to the HTTP protocol in code. On the plus side, it does mean that this is the only session API definition you need to learn for the exam! The methods have been grouped by function for ease of reference.

Session-Scoped Attributes

Attributes in the session scope are stored in the `HttpSession` instance. The related methods are:

9

- **`Object getAttribute(String name)`**
  Returns the `Object` bound in the attribute called `name`, or `null` if no attribute with this name exists.
- **`Enumeration getAttributeNames()`**
  Returns a `java.util.Enumeration` of all the attribute names bound into this session.
- **`void setAttribute(String name, Object value)`**
  Binds the `Object` into the session attribute called `name`. If an attribute with this name already exists, its value is replaced by the new `Object` parameter.
- **`void removeAttribute(String name)`**
  Removes (unbinds) the attribute called `name` from this session. If an attribute with this name does not already exist, then the method simply does nothing and returns.

Life Cycle

There are several methods which are used to access information about the session during its life cycle:

- **`long getCreationTime()`**
  Returns the time, in UTC format (see below), when the client joined this session.
- **`String getId()`**
  Returns a `String` containing the session ID; this is the same as the `jsessionid` value.

- **`long getLastAccessedTime()`**
  Returns the time, in UTC, when the client last made a request in this session. This is used by the container to decide when a session should be timed out.

- **`int getMaxInactiveInterval()`**
  Returns the maximum time, in seconds, between requests before the container will invalidate (time out) the session. This is configured in the deployment descriptor for the application.

- **`void invalidate()`**
  Invoking this method explicitly invalidates the current session. Once invalidated, a session cannot be rejoined by a client.

- **`boolean isNew()`**
  Returns `true` if the session is new–i.e. the client has not yet joined it, or if the client refuses to participate in the session.

- **`void setMaxInactiveInterval(int timeoutSeconds)`**
  Used by developers (or the container when a session is initialised) to set the maximum period, in seconds, between client requests before the session times out. This method can be used to override the default timeout period for sessions configured in the deployment descriptor. If the `int` parameter is negative, the timeout is infinite (i.e. the session will never time out). Calling `setMaxInactiveInterval(0)` times out the session at the end of the current request-response cycle. In contrast, `invalidate()` does this immediately where it is invoked.

9

By **UTC** (**coordinated universal time**) format, we mean the number of milliseconds since the official 'epoch' which was at 00:00:00 on the 1st January 1970 GMT (timestamps these days are pretty large numbers, for obvious reasons!).

Note also that although a session can be configured to never time out, this is generally inadvisable due to the load this would place on the server's precious resources (like RAM and disk space).

In addition, this method can be used to access the application context:

- **`ServletContext getServletContext()`**
  Returns the application's `ServletContext`.

Session Listeners

We looked at all the `HttpSession` API details in the last section; however, don't think you've gotten away from coding sessions just yet! Those lovely examiners have got us learning the event and listener models for sessions as well; still, it could be worse (any suggestions as to how should be sent on a postcard!).

HttpSessionListener

This interface is designed to be implemented by container-level listener classes which need to be informed about the life of active session objects. It has only two methods:

9

- **`void sessionCreated(HttpSessionEvent)`**
  Called by the container when a session is first created. Interrogate the `HttpSessionEvent` parameter to obtain a handle on the actual session object being created.
- **`void sessionDestroyed(HttpSessionEvent)`**
  Called by the container when a session is about to be (i.e. before it is) destroyed. The `HttpSessionEvent` can be examined to get a handle on the actual session object.

Like the servlet and context listeners, any classes implementing this interface must be declared in the deployment descriptor if they are to be initialised and invoked by the container.

The HttpSessionEvent Class

This class represents events related to the life cycle of an `HttpSession` object as a whole (i.e. creation, destruction and passivation). It defines only one method:

- **`HttpSession getSession()`**
  Used to obtain the session which changed, causing this event.

HttpSessionActivationListener

This interface is designed to be implemented by classes which may be bound into sessions *as attributes*. Its methods are:

- **`void sessionDidActivate(HttpSessionEvent)`**
  Called by the container when a session has just been activated (i.e. brought

out of passivation). The event parameter can be used to get a handle on the actual session object. Only attributes of the relevant session and implementing this interface will be notified that the session is being activated.

- **`void sessionWillPassivate(HttpSessionEvent)`**
  The container will call this method on each implementing session attribute before the session object containing that attribute is passivated. This allows attributes to provide special procedures for their serialisation.

Since this interface is implemented by attributes being added to the sessions themselves, classes which provide an implementation should not be configured in the deployment descriptor.

It is important that attributes bound to a session will receive passivation notifications only about *that* session; an object bound into one session will not receive event notifications from other sessions.

HttpSessionAttributeListener

This interface is designed to be implemented by container-level listener classes which need notification of changes to attributes in all sessions in the container. It defines:

- **`void attributeAdded(HttpSessionBindingEvent)`**
  Called to provide notification that a new attribute has just been added to a session in the container. The event parameter can be interrogated to find the session object modified, the name of the new attribute, or the new attribute's `Object` value.

- **`void attributeRemoved(HttpSessionBindingEvent)`**
  Invoked by the container to provide notification that an attribute has been removed from a session in the container. The event parameter provides access to the session object which has changed, the name of the old attribute and the value of the old attribute.

- **`void attributeReplaced(HttpSessionBindingEvent)`**
  Called to provide notification that an existing attribute has been overridden with a new value. This method is called after the replacement has taken place. The event parameter provides access to the modified session object, the name of the attribute, and the old value of the attribute.

Since this interface provides a generic way to receive notification of changes to any session objects, any implementing classes must be declared in the deployment descriptor if they are to be called by the container at run time.

The HttpSessionBindingEvent Class

This extends `HttpSessionEvent` and provides two extra methods in addition to `getSession()`:

- **`String getName()`**
  Returns the name of the attribute (being modified) which caused this event.

- **`Object getValue()`**
  Returns the value of the attribute being modified. If the attribute is being added, this will be the new value; if the attribute is being removed, this will be the old value, prior to removal; if the attribute is being replaced, this will be the old value (the new value can be obtained by retrieving the attribute from the session object directly).

The HttpSessionBindingListener Interface

This interface should be implemented by classes which may be bound into sessions as attributes. It provides notification that an object is being added/removed from session scope. Its methods are:

- **`void valueBound(HttpSessionBindingEvent)`**
  Notifies the implementing object that it is being bound into a session. The session object can be retrieved using the event parameter, which also provides access to the name of the attribute being added, as well as its new value.

- **`void valueUnbound(HttpSessionBindingEvent)`**
  Notifies the implementing object that it is being unbound (removed) from a session. Use the event parameter to identify the session involved, as well as the name and old value of the attribute being removed.

Since this interface is implemented by attributes being added to the sessions themselves, classes which provide an implementation should not be configured in the deployment descriptor – instead they are automatically called by the session object which is being modified at the appropriate time.

Revision Questions

1 **Which class or interface models a session?** **(choose one)**

- A javax.servlet.Session (interface)
- B javax.servlet.Session (class)
- C javax.servlet.http.Session (class)
- D javax.servlet.http.HttpSession (interface)
- E javax.servlet.http.HttpSession (class)

2 **Which of the following methods can be used to perform URL rewriting?** **(choose one)**

- A rewriteURL(String) in javax.servlet.ServletRequest
- B encodeURL(String) in javax.servlet.http.HttpSession
- C rewriteURL(String) in javax.servlet.http.HttpSession
- D encodeURL(String) in javax.servlet.http.HttpServletRequest
- E encodeURL(String) in javax.servlet.http.HttpServletResponse

3 **In what ways can a session be invalidated?** **(choose three)**

- A Invoking destroy() on HttpSession
- B Invoking invalidate() on HttpSession
- C Invoking sendError() on HttpServletResponse
- D Invoking setMaxInactiveInterval(0) on HttpSession
- E When the session exceeds its timeout period.

4 **Study the exhibit. What line(s) of code inserted on line 7 provide(s) an error-free way to always create a new session, provided the current response has not yet been committed?** **(choose one)**

EXHIBIT

- A
```
session = req.getSession();
```
- B
```
session = req.getSession(true);
```
- C
```
session = req.getSession();
session.invalidate();
session = req.getSession();
```
- D
```
session = req.newSession();
```
- E
```
session = req.getSession(false);
session.invalidate();
session = req.getSession();
```

5 **What methods can be used to access and modify session-scoped attributes?** **(choose two)**

- A Object getAttribute(String) in ServletContext
- B String getAttribute(String) in HttpSession
- C Object removeAttribute(String) in HttpSession
- D Object getAttribute(String) in HttpSession
- E void unbindAttribute(String) in HttpSession
- F void setAttribute(String,Object) in HttpSession

6 **How can a session be configured never to time out?** **(choose two)**

- A In the deployment descriptor
- B Invoke setTimeout(-1) on the HttpSession instance
- C Invoke setMaxInactiveInterval(0) on the HttpSession instance
- D Invoke setMaxInactiveInterval(-1) on the HttpSession instance
- E Invoke setMaxInactiveInterval(HttpSession.NEVER) on the HttpSession instance.

7 **In what situations may session tracking fail?** **(choose three)**

- A When the client has disabled cookies.
- B When the client has disabled cookies and a component developer hasn't used encodeURL() on all her URLs.
- C When the client disables sessions.
- D When a response is committed before getSession() is invoked for the first time on the HttpServletRequest instance.
- E When a user manually types a URL to a resource directly into their browser.

8 **What is the result of compiling, deploying and issuing a request to the servlet shown in the exhibit?** **(choose one)**

EXHIBIT

- A The user context attribute is set to the value 'joe'
- B The user session-scoped attribute is removed from scope.
- C The user session-scoped attribute is set to 'joe' only if it doesn't already exist.
- D The user session-scoped attribute is set to 'joe', replacing any old value.
- E A compilation error occurs.

9 **Study the exhibit. What are the possible outcomes of compiling, deploying and issuing a request to this servlet?** **(choose three)**

EXHIBIT

- A The session-scoped attribute user is set to 'janet' and the servlet forwards to the resource given by the session-scoped url attribute.
- B The request-scoped attribute user is set to 'janet' and the servlet forwards to the resource given by the session-scoped url attribute.
- C NullPointerException thrown on line 7.
- D NullPointerException thrown on line 8
- E NullPointerException thrown on line 9.
- F Compilation error occurs.

10 **Study the exhibit. What is the result of compiling, deploying and issuing a request to this servlet?** **(choose one)**

EXHIBIT

- A The session is invalidated, the userid attribute removed from session-scope and the request returns.
- B A NullPointerException is thrown on line 8.
- C An exception is thrown on line 9.
- D An exception is thrown on line 10.
- E A compilation error occurs

11 **Study the exhibit. What are the possible results of compiling, deploying and issuing a request to this servlet?** **(choose three)**

EXHIBIT

- A The request is forwarded to the other.jsp resource, and upon return the orderid session-scoped attribute is set to '1234'.
- B Exception thrown on line 7.
- C Exception thrown on line 8.
- D Exception thrown on line 9.
- E Compilation error occurs.

12 **Which interface can be implemented to receive event notification about a session's life cycle?** **(choose one)**

- A javax.servlet.SessionLifecycleListener
- B javax.servlet.SessionListener
- C javax.servlet.http.SessionListener
- D javax.servlet.http.HttpSessionListener
- E None of the above

13 **Subclasses of the HttpSessionActivationListener interface need to implement which methods?** **(choose two)**

- A void sessionActivated(HttpSessionEvent)
- B void sessionIsActivated(HttpSessionEvent)
- C void sessionDidActivate(HttpSessionEvent)
- D void sessionPassivated(HttpSessionEvent)
- E void sessionWillPassivate(HttpSessionEvent)

14 **Which interface should be implemented by a listener installed in the container to receive event notifications about session-scoped attributes?** **(choose one)**

- A javax.servlet.SessionListener
- B javax.servlet.SessionAttributeListener
- C javax.servlet.HttpSessionAttributeListener
- D javax.servlet.http.SessionAttributeListener
- E javax.servlet.http.HttpSessionAttributeListener

15 **Which interface should be implemented by an object which needs to be notified when it is used as the value of a session-scoped attribute?** **(choose one)**

- A javax.servlet.SessionAttributeListener
- B javax.servlet.SessionBindingListener
- C javax.servlet.HttpSessionAttributeListener
- D javax.servlet.http.HttpSessionBindingListener
- E javax.servlet.http.HttpSessionBoundAttributeListener

16 **Which method on an implementation of HttpSessionAttributeListener is invoked when a new value is assigned to an existing attribute?** **(choose one)**

- A void attributeModified(HttpSessionBindingEvent)
- B void attributeAdded(HttpSessionBindingEvent)
- C First void attributeAdded(HttpSessionBindingEvent) then void attributeRemoved(HttpSessionBindingEvent)
- D void attributeReplaced(HttpSessionBindingEvent)
- E void attributeUpdated(HttpSessionBindingEvent)

17 **What pair of methods exists in the HttpSessionBindingListener interface?** **(choose one)**

- A attributeSet(HttpSessionBindingEvent), attributeRemoved(HttpSessionBindingEvent)
- B attributeAdded(HttpSessionBindingEvent), attributeRemoved(HttpSessionBindingEvent)
- C valueBound(HttpSessionBindingEvent), valueUnbound(HttpSessionBindingEvent)
- D valueSet(HttpSessionBindingEvent), valueUnset(HttpSessionBindingEvent)
- E valueSet(HttpSessionBindingEvent), valueRemoved(HttpSessionBindingEvent).

9

18 **The exhibit shows a listener class implementing HttpSessionAttributeListener. This listener is compiled and installed in the container. At run time, the session-scoped attribute username is removed from scope. What will be the state of the name and value variables after the listener has been invoked?** **(choose one)**

EXHIBIT

- A name is null, value is null
- B name is 'username', value is null.
- C name is 'username', value is the old value before the attribute was removed.
- D name is null, value is the old value before the attribute was removed.
- E Compilation error occurs.

Exhibits

Q.4

```
import javax.servlet.*;
import javax.servlet.http.*;

public class MyServlet extends HttpServlet {
  public void doGet(HttpServletRequest req,HttpServletResponse resp) {
    HttpSession session;
    // insert here
  }
}
```

Q.8


```
import javax.servlet.*;
import javax.servlet.http.*;

public class MyServlet extends GenericServlet {

    public void service(ServletRequest req, ServletResponse resp) {
        req.getSession().setAttribute("user", "joe");
    }
}
```

Q.9

```
public class MyServlet extends HttpServlet {

  public void doGet(HttpServletRequest req,HttpServletResponse resp)
                     throws ServletException, IOException {
    HttpSession s = req.getSession(false);
    req.setAttribute("user", "janet");
    RequestDispatcher rd = getServletContext().getNamedDispatcher(
                                              (String) s.getAttribute("url"));
      rd.forward(req, resp);
  }
}
```

Q.10

```
public class InvalidationServlet extends HttpServlet {
  protected void doGet(HttpServletRequest req,
                        HttpServletResponse resp) {
    HttpSession s = req.getSession();
    s.invalidate();
    String userid = s.getAttribute("userid");
    s.removeAttribute("userid");
  }
}
```

Q.11


```
public class MyServlet extends HttpServlet {

  protected void doGet(HttpServletRequest req,
                        HttpServletResponse resp)
                        throws ServletException, IOException {
    RequestDispatcher rd = req.getRequestDispatcher("/other.jsp");
    rd.forward(req, resp);
    HttpSession s = req.getSession();
    s.setAttribute("orderid", "1234");
  }

}
```

Q.18

```
import javax.servlet.*;
import javax.servlet.http.*;

public class MySessionAttributeListener
       implements HttpSessionAttributeListener {

    public void attributeAdded(HttpSessionBindingEvent event) {}
    public void attributeReplaced(HttpSessionBindingEvent event) {}

    public void attributeRemoved(HttpSessionBindingEvent event) {
        String name = event.getName();
        Object value = event.getValue();
    }

}
```

Answers to Revision Questions

1 **Correct answer: D**

2 **Correct answer: E**

3 **Correct answers: B,D,E**

A is an invalid method. C doesn't affect the state of a session. B will explicitly invalidate a session programmatically. E is the standard mechanism for invalidating sessions, when they exceed their established timeout. D sets the timeout to 0 seconds, causing the session to expire at the end of the current request-response cycle.

4 **Correct answer: C**

A and B will only create a new session if there is no existing one; they therefore won't always create a fresh one. D invokes a nonexistent method. E almost works except for the fact that session could be null as a result of invoking getSession(false), and so this could cause a NullPointerException on its second line. This leaves only C to be the correct answer, which first obtains a session (which may or may not be new), then explicitly invalidates it, then creates a guaranteed new one. Note the requirement that the response not yet be committed: if it were, and the client is using cookies for session tracking, getSession() or getSession(true) would throw an IllegalStateException.

5 **Correct answers: D,F**

A is obviously incorrect, as this refers to the context and the application-scoped attributes. B is incorrect; the return type should be Object, as in D. C is incorrect; the return type should be void. E is incorrect – there is no such method. F is correct. The only methods omitted from the list are: the correct void removeAttribute(String) and the Enumeration getAttributeNames(), both in HttpSession.

6 **Correct answers: A,D**

B is incorrect – the method doesn't exist; E uses a constant, NEVER, which doesn't exist. C is incorrect: it causes session invalidation at the end of the request-response cycle.

7 **Correct answers: B,D,E**

A alone should lead immediately to the container using URL rewriting, so session-tracking is no longer dependent on cookies; if the page author hasn't used encodeURL() (or an equivalent JSP action) on their links, this also prevents URL rewriting from happening, and therefore session tracking would fail – making B correct. C is wrong as it isn't possible for a client to 'disable sessions'; sessions are maintained on the server. It is, however, possible for a client to refuse cookies or to (deliberately, but perhaps improbably) remove the jsessionid from all its URLs. D is correct, and will typically result in an IllegalStateException being thrown on the invocation of getSession(). E is correct: users don't bother to insert the jsessionid into typed URLs unless they're copying and pasting.

8 **Correct answer: E**

This answer is correct because there is no getSession method on ServletRequest – sessions are only available in HTTP, and therefore getSession() is found on HttpServletRequest. If a cast were provided, the correct answer would have been D.

9 **Correct answers: B,D,E**

A is incorrect as line 7 sets a request-scoped, not session-scoped, attribute. C is incorrect as no exceptions are ever raised by setting attributes (the only possibility is if req is null, but this is guaranteed by the container not be the case). B is correct if nothing is null; D will happen if s is null, caused by there being no session currently in existence with the client – if we had used getSession(true) or getSession() on line 6, s would never be null, as a new session would be created if necessary. E is correct if a RequestDispatcher cannot be obtained, as rd will then be null. There are no errors in code, so F is incorrect.

10 **Correct answer: C**

C is the correct answer, as all the methods (including invalidate()) in HttpSession throw an IllegalStateException if the session has already been invalidated. This would also mean that D is true, but this line is never reached, so it isn't the correct answer. A is incorrect as lines 9 and 10 are never executed; B is incorrect as getSession() always returns a valid session, creating a new one if necessary. It never returns null.

11 **Correct answers: A,B,C**

B happens if rd is null – we get a NullPointerException. C happens if the response has already been committed, the container is using cookie-based tracking, and the session must be created newly; in this case, the container cannot declare the new session with the client, as this involves setting a cookie in the response headers, which cannot happen as the response has been committed. D won't ever happen; either an exception occurred on the previous line, or this is a new session (in which case it isn't invalid, so there is no reason to stop an attribute being set). A will be the result if no exceptions are raised. There are no errors in code, so E is incorrect.

12 **Correct answer: D**

13 **Correct answers: C,E**

14 **Correct answer: E**

15 **Correct answer: D**

16 **Correct answer: D**

17 **Correct answer: C**

18 **Correct answer: C**

In this chapter you'll:

- Discover the roles involved in deploying a Java EE Web application into a container.
- Review the basic XML syntax for the Servlet 2.4 deployment descriptor.
- Learn the important elements which appear in the deployment descriptor.
- Study what happens in the container when an application is newly deployed or re-deployed.
- Be introduced to how in Java EE 6 the deployment descriptor will be replaced by more favourable annotations (this is a very brief note)!

10 Application Deployment

Once all the components of an application have been created, and in the case of servlets, compiled, the application must be assembled and deployed to the application server in order to be available for the servicing of client requests. In fact, this process constitutes three main roles as defined in the Java EE specification:

1. **The Application Assembler**
   This person is responsible for preparing the application components for deployment; in the case of a Web application, this is normally performed by packaging them correctly within a WAR.
2. **The Deployer**
   This person is responsible for deploying all enterprise and client applications to their appropriate locations, and to ensure that the application is correctly configured to run inside the given server's containers. Ultimately the Deployer must install and start the application on the server.
3. **System Administrator**
   This role departs a little from the developer roles listed above, but it is nonetheless as important. The System Administrator is responsible for the well-being of the application and server–and who said people couldn't care about computers and programs? The Administrator effectively maintains the server and any network connections necessary for the day-to-day running of the service offered by the application.

More often than not, the first two roles are combined into that of a single person since they bear resemblances to each other. Anyone really overworked (and probably underpaid) might just find themselves doing all three!

The Application Assembler's role for a Web application is primarily the packaging of files into their correct locations in a WAR. We covered all the exam objectives for this in Chapter 2. When considering the certification objectives for application deployment and the Deployer's role, we need to look at the deployment descriptor and its structure, and you need to *learn* (that gruelling word again) all the syntax unless otherwise noted. This chapter does not introduce XML itself since it assumes you have a working and sufficient knowledge of the basics from previous descriptor encounters (of the third kind?). For the exam, you only need to be aware of the syntax for elements and attributes, and how to create well-formed XML documents.

The Deployment Descriptor

The deployment descriptor is an XML document, which is created by the application's Deployer and stored in the /WEB-INF/web.xml file in a Web application archive. It is used to tell the Web container about the deployed components, decoupling the resources and components in the application from their installation and configuration.

The deployment descriptor is used most frequently to declare servlets and initialisation parameters, and specify mappings between URLs and target components. Other uses include declarative security, specifying MIME types and configuring JSP pages and documents.

Basic Syntax

10

Most formalised XML documents are described by a DTD or XML Schema, which provide a set of rules that the document must conform to. The declaration of a DTD or Schema is found at the beginning of an XML file, after the XML declaration itself. Thus, a descriptor begins with:

```
<?xml version="1.0" ?>
<!DOCTYPE web-app
 PUBLIC "-//Sun Microsystems, Inc.//DTD Web Application 2.4//EN"
 "http://java.sun.com/dtd/web-app_2_4.dtd">
```

While you do not need to learn the above syntax for the exam, it is useful to have it here for reference. This declaration is for the v2.4 DTD. The XML Schema declaration for v2.4 occurs on the <web-app> root element (admittedly, it looks forbidding, but then so do all Schema declarations):

```
<?xml version="1.0" ?>
<web-app xmlns="http://java.sun.com/xml/ns/j2ee"
         xmlns:xsi="http://www.w3.org/2001/XMLSchema-instance"
         xsi:schemaLocation="http://java.sun.com/xml/ns/j2ee
            http://java.sun.com/xml/ns/j2ee/web-app_2_4.xsd"
         version="2.4">
```

The <web-app> Elements

All deployment descriptors have the <web-app> element as the document root:

```
<!-- XML+DTD Declarations -->
<web-app version="2.4">
  <!-- nested elements (Fig. 10.1) here -->
</web-app>
```

The <web-app> element may contain the elements shown in Figure 10.1. A tree similar to this one is depicted in the servlet specification, and I thought that it was far more useful, for both revision and reference, than a Schema definition so I've put my own version in here. The boxes represent elements; the text in the boxes are the element names. Figure 10.2 shows the meaning of the multiplicity symbols displayed on the right corner of the elements. Those elements shown shaded in grey in Figure 10.1 are not covered in this book and will certainly not appear on the exam.

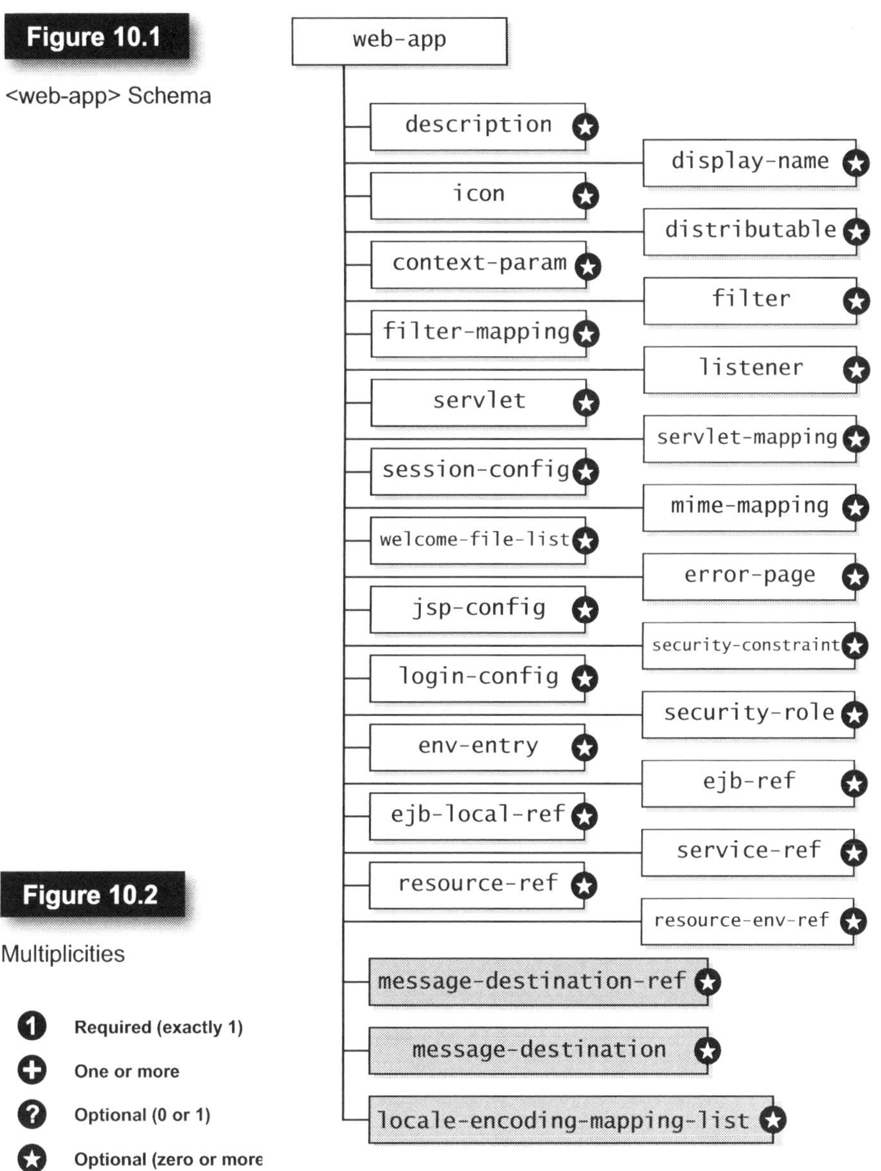

Figure 10.1

<web-app> Schema

Figure 10.2

Multiplicities

10

Web Application Metadata

The optional `<description>` element is used to provide a textual explanation of the parent element. This element can appear *in many places* throughout the descriptor and isn't limited to being a direct child of the `<web-app>` element. However, when contained directly inside the `<web-app>` element, it is used to describe the Web application as a whole. Other uses include providing descriptions for servlets and filters inside the `<servlet>` and `<filter>` elements respectively. The `<description>` element will be shown on other descriptor element diagrams where appropriate, but is not further explained.

The `<display-name>` element is used to provide a user-friendly name, often displayed in tools and error reports, for an application or component. Like `<description>`, it can be used throughout the descriptor, in servlet and filter configurations for instance. When used as a direct child of the `<web-app>` element, it names the application; as a child of `<servlet>` or `<filter>`, it provides a friendly name for that component.

10

The `<icon>` element is used to reference an image which can be loaded by GUI tools and displayed to the user (for example, an online shopping basket application might have an icon of a basket or trolley, while a bookstore catalogue may have a picture of a book as its symbol). Like `<description>` and `<display-name>`, there are many components which can have icons, as well as the application as a whole. There are two optional subelements of `<icon>`: `<small-icon>` and `<large-icon>`. Generally icon images should be in either GIF or JPEG format, since processing of these formats is embedded in Java's Image IO API as standard.

Finally, the `<distributable>` element, if present in the descriptor, marks the Web application as being suitable for deployment across a distributed network, such as a cluster of (load-balancing) servers. If your application is not distributable, omit this element completely. The element is declared as being empty in the DTD, which means that if declared at all, it should have syntax of either:

`<distributable></distributable>` or `<distributable />` (preferred).

Context Parameters

Recall that the Assembler and/or Deployer can establish application-scoped initialisation parameters which are read-only to components, but can be used to configure the application at deployment time. We do this using one or more `<context-param>` elements in the descriptor. Each `<context-param>` element has two mandatory child elements, as well as the optional `<description>` element, as shown in Figure 10.3.

The `<param-name>` element is used to declare the name of the context parameter which will be called by components in the application, while `<param-value>` is used to give the value of the parameter. Both are parsed as `String` objects.

For example, to declare the `admin_email` parameter with the value `me@dom.ext`, you would use this snippet in the descriptor:

```
<web-app>
...
 <context-param>
  <param-name>admin_email</param-name>
  <param-value>me@dom.ext</param-value>
 </context-param>
...
</web-app>
```

Figure 10.3

<context-param> Schema

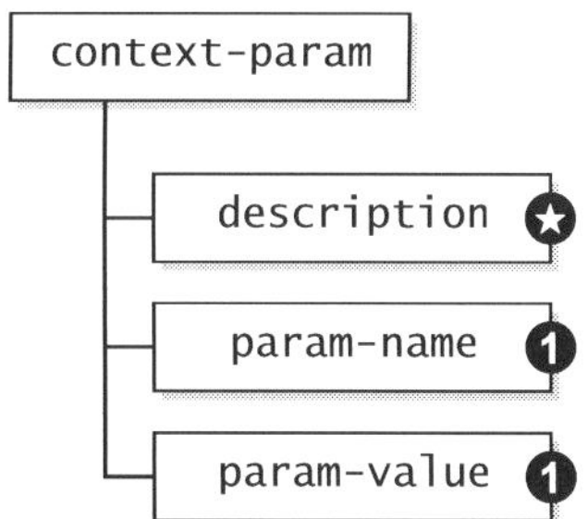

Filter Configuration

Each filter is configured with its own `<filter>` element, as shown in Figure 10.4.

`<filter-name>` is used to declare the *logical* name of the filter. This is not the class name of the filter, but instead a convenient and unique textual identifier for the component (chosen by the author or deployer), which can be referenced by other components.

`<filter-class>` is used to specify the fully-qualified class name of the filter inside the application.

Figure 10.4

<filter> Schema

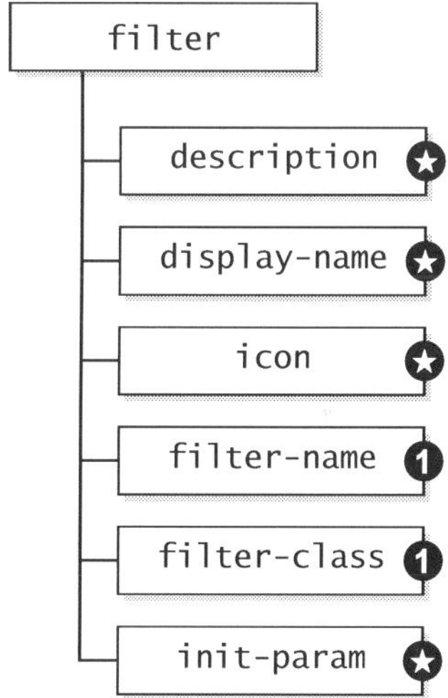

10

The optional `<init-param>` elements, as shown in Figure 10.5, work much like the `<context-param>` elements above. Each `<init-param>` is used to initialise this *specific filter only*. It has two mandatory child elements, `<param-name>` and `<param-value>` as well as the optional `<description>` element (which can appear just about everywhere anyway!).

The `<param-name>` element is used to declare the name of the initialisation parameter, and the `<param-value>` element its value.

Figure 10.5

<init-param> Schema

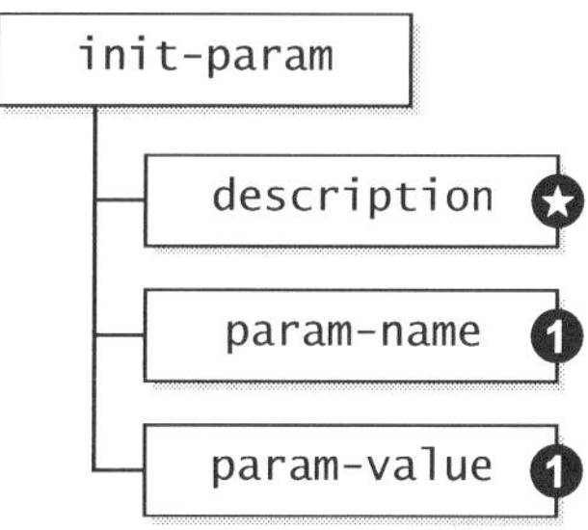

Filter Mappings

Although we have now made the application aware of a filter implementation class inside the archive, it doesn't know when to use it—what requests and URLs does the filter need to interpose its services upon?

The definition of relationships between components and the requests they serve are referred to technically as **mappings.** For example, a filter can be mapped against a URL, which then causes the filter to be invoked when a request for that URL is received by the container.

We achieve this for filters using the `<filter-mapping>` element, as shown in Figure 10.6.

Figure 10.6

<filter-mapping> Schema

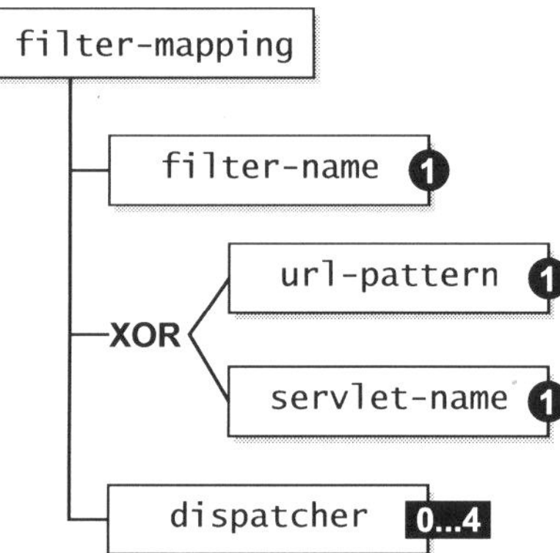

10

The `<filter-name>` element is used to reference a filter implementation, and for a particular mapping, should be the same as the `<filter-name>` inside the `<filter>` element for that implementation class.

Secondly, *either* the `<url-pattern>` *or* `<servlet-name>` elements must be declared. The former is used to map the filter invocation against a particular URL or a URL pattern; the second causes the filter to be invoked when the given servlet (identified by the servlet's logical name) is executed.

Finally, the `<dispatcher>` element can be optionally declared, up to four times. Possible values for this element's content are:

- **FORWARD**
  Causes the filter to be invoked as a result of a `RequestDispatcher.forward()` call.
- **INCLUDE**
  Causes the filter to be invoked as a result of a `RequestDispatcher.include()` call.
- **REQUEST**
  The filter will impose its services only during a normal client call to the given path or servlet.
- **ERROR**
  The filter is applied only in an error situation. This is useful for fault-finding and error logging.

If no <dispatcher> elements are declared, the container will default to applying the filter during REQUESTs only.

For example, the following snippet might be used to map the mypkg.AuthenticationFilter filter implementation class against the /accounts/ path under the context root of our application. This filter is invoked only when either a client request is received or the forwarding mechanism is used:

```
<web-app>
...
  <filter>
    <filter-name>UserAuthFilter</filter-name>
    <filter-class>mypkg.AuthenticationFilter</filter-class>
  </filter>

  <filter-mapping>
    <filter-name>UserAuthFilter</filter-name>
    <url-pattern>/accounts/*</url-pattern>
    <dispatcher>REQUEST</dispatcher>
    <dispatcher>FORWARD</dispatcher>
  </filter-mapping>
...
</web-app>
```


Listener Configuration

Listener classes must be declared in the deployment descriptor if the application is to instantiate and call them during the application's life. Each listener requires its own instance of <listener>, shown in Figure 10.7.

There is only one mandatory child element, <listener-class> which specifies the fully-qualified class name of the listener. The Web container must be able to instantiate an instance of this class at run time, so its class file needs to be placed either in /WEB-INF/classes/, or inside a JAR in /WEB-INF/lib/.

Figure 10.7

<listener> Schema

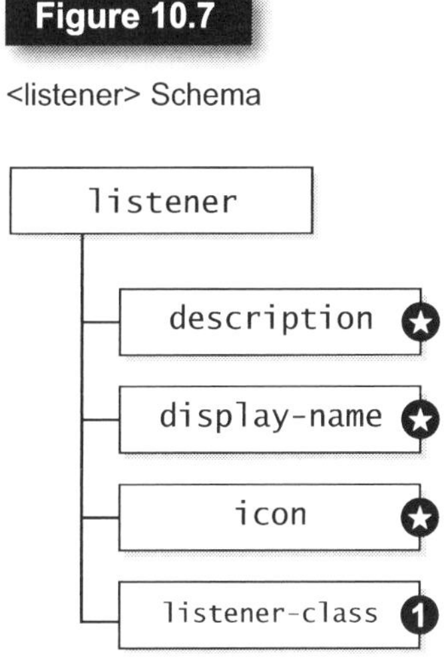

Servlet Configuration

The descriptor definitions for servlets are similar to those for filters – in fact many of the child elements are named identically. Similarly, mappings between servlets and request URLs are declared in a *separate* mapping element. This section examines the `<servlet>` element only, as shown in Figure 10.8.

Figure 10.8

<servlet> Schema

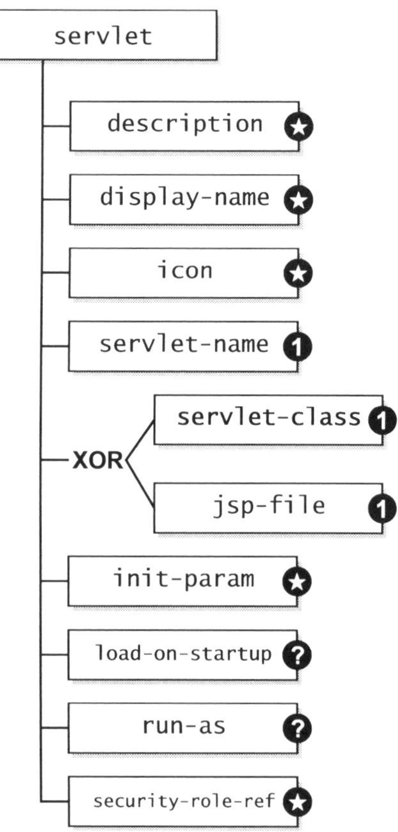

The `<servlet>` element is complicated slightly by its nature, as a way of describing both servlet classes and compiled *JSPs* as well. Additionally, there are elements describing security which help to pad it out (as if candidates need that!).

The mandatory `<servlet-name>` element is used to declare the logical name for the servlet. This is similar to the logical name for a filter, but it has more uses. For example, this name can be used when obtaining a `RequestDispatcher`, by calling the `ServletContext.getNamedDispatcher` method with the logical name of the servlet or JSP as the parameter.

Next, we must either specify the fully qualified name of the compiled servlet class, or the context-relative location of the JSP. It is illegal to declare both. For example, to specify the `ext.domain.web.FormServlet` class as the servlet implementation would use this:

```
<web-app>
...
  <servlet>
    <servlet-name>FormProcessor</servlet-name>
    <servlet-class>ext.domain.web.FormServlet</servlet-class>
  </servlet>
...
</web-app>
```

To declare the `/registration/form.jsp` page as the servlet, we use:

```
<web-app>
...
  <servlet>
    <servlet-name>FormTemplate</servlet-name>
    <jsp-file>/registration/form.jsp</jsp-file>
  </servlet>
...
</web-app>
```

The container uses the <jsp-file> element to determine the location of the JSP before compilation, and then using an internal mapping, the generated servlet class. This enables the <servlet> element to be used to declare *both* servlets and compiled JSPs, which are of course servlets as well. Don't be fooled by the name of the element: it can be used to configure some aspects of JSPs as well. Also, remember that the location of the JSP file is *context-relative*.

The <init-param> element here has exactly the same syntax as the <init-param> for the <filter> element, as shown in Figure 10.5. Its semantics are the same, except that the parameters declared here are accessed using the servlet's ServletConfig object, and not using the filter's FilterConfig object.

The <load-on-startup> element is used by the Deployer (the person, not the application) to specify when the servlet is instantiated and initialised during the application's lifetime. The value must be a positive integer or 0 to have any effect; in this case, servlets declared with lower values are loaded before servlets with higher values. For example, a servlet with <load-on-startup>12</load-on-startup> will be loaded *after* a servlet with <load-on-startup>2</load-on-startup>. If the value is negative, or the element is omitted completely, or two values are the same for two different servlets, the container will load the servlet(s) whenever it pleases (which serves you right if you used an illegal negative value!).

10

The <run-as> and <security-role-ref> elements are used for security purposes. Since we have not yet covered security in any detail, descriptions of these elements are left until Chapter 21, which deals with security in its entirety.

Servlet Mappings

As shown in Figure 10.9, this is a simple element, consisting of two mandatory elements, <servlet-name> and <url-pattern>. These reflect closely those in the <filter-mapping> element.

The <servlet-name> is used to specify the logical name of the servlet to which this mapping applies.

The <url-pattern> is used to declare a request URL pattern which will cause this servlet to be invoked.

Figure 10.9

<servlet-mapping> Schema

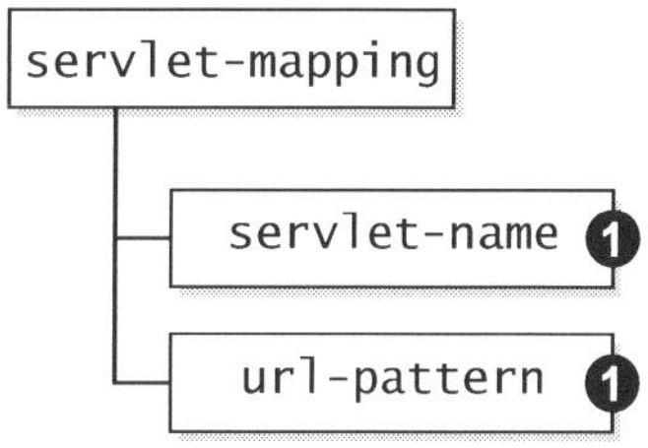

Session Configuration

We looked at sessions back in the last chapter. The only configuration that can take place for sessions in an application is to set their timeout, which as you'll recall, is the period after which a client is to be considered inactive in their interaction with the application. We do this using the `<session-timeout>` child element, as shown in Figure 10.10.

Figure 10.10

<session-config> Schema

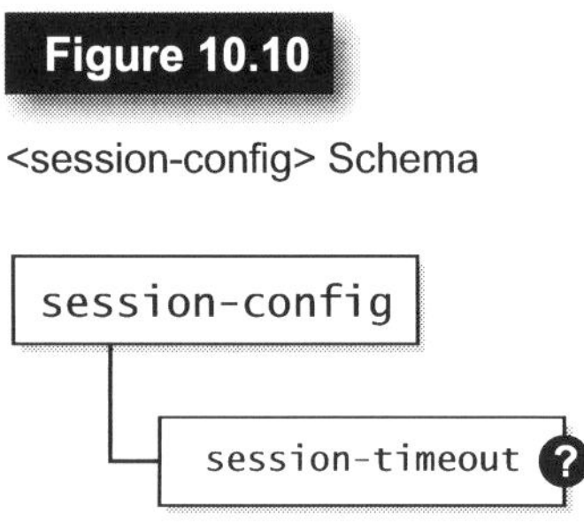

The `<session-timeout>` element must have a value which is a positive integer, expressing the timeout interval in minutes. If the value is 0 or negative, sessions will never timeout. If this element is omitted, the Java EE server will use its own default value for the timeout; while this varies from server-to-server, it averages around 30 minutes.

MIME Mappings

The **Multipurpose Internet Mail Extension**s (**MIME**) system was developed to succinctly describe the type and format of a file. For example, a plain text file has the MIME type `text/plain`. MIME types always consist of two parts: a major category (here, a `text` file) and a subcategory (the type of text is `plain`). Other (non-plain) text files include `text/rtf` for Rich Text File and `text/html` for HTML web pages. Similarly, other major categories include images, music and video; for example, `image/jpeg` and `video/mpeg`. In general, the MIME type of a file is referenced against the extension of that file. Thus, the `gif` extension is associated with the `image/gif` MIME type by default. HTTP can optionally use the `Content-Type` response header to notify the client of the MIME type of the data being transmitted, in case the client is either not aware of the file extension being used, or the file format differs from the MIME type normally associated with that extension.

You do not need to be able to match MIME types against file formats for the exam, but you do need to be able to configure a given MIME type against a given file extension for a Web application. You may well be asked to do this in the exam.

The matching of MIME types against file extensions is achieved using the deployment descriptor (after all, why else would we be talking about it here?) using the `<mime-mapping>` element and its subelements, as shown in Figure 10.11.

The `<extension>` element specifies the file extension of the group of files to which we are applying the mapping. The `<mime-type>` element declares the actual

MIME type associated with that extension. For example, an extension might be `txt`, associated with the MIME type `text/plain`. Don't panic, however, since Java EE servers typically provide default mappings for all the common file formats (and many more you haven't heard of as well) so you don't have to. Sun's Application Server 8 ships with 127 default mappings. Practically the only situation to override the mappings is when you use an extension for a file which normally does not map to that extension. For example, associating the `txt` extension with `text/html` and not plain text. This is obviously not a wise decision, but nonetheless can be done.

Figure 10.11

<mime-mapping> Schema

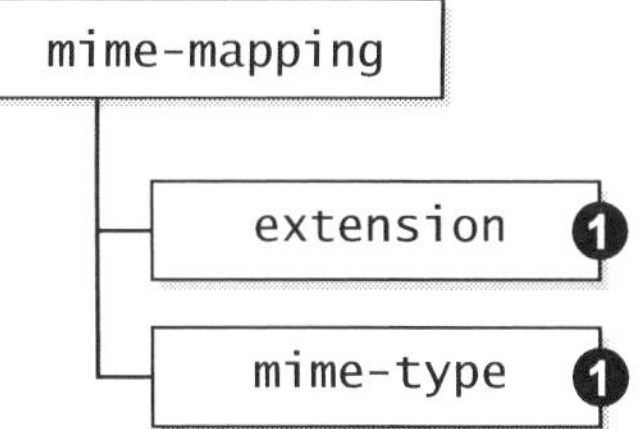

Welcome Files

Most servers have a method for configuring a set of default filenames to be loaded when a request is made to a directory path, but not to an actual resource residing in that directory. The server will search in the directory for any file matching the default name and load it. If no default file for that directory can be found, a 404 ('Not Found') error is returned, or in a security unconscious environment, a directory listing is displayed. Usually these files are named `index.html` or `default.html`, or any other extension variant. For this reason, they are often known as directory indices or default files. Java EE on the other hand calls them **welcome files**, and a list of each welcome file name is configured inside the deployment descriptor's `<welcome-file-list>` element.

There should ideally only be one `<welcome-file-list>` element in the deployment descriptor, which lists the welcome files to be searched in order (see Figure 10.12). The actual filenames are configured using the `<welcome-file>` child element. A typical configuration looks like this:

```
<welcome-file-list>
  <welcome-file>index.html</welcome-file>
  <welcome-file>index.jsp</welcome-file>
  <welcome-file>default.html</welcome-file>
  <welcome-file>default.jsp</welcome-file>
</welcome-file-list>
```

Figure 10.12

<welcome-file-list> Schema

welcome-file-list

welcome-file

For example, if a request was received to the path `/catalogue` in an application, this path would first be checked against servlet or resource mappings. Next, if no mappings are configured for this URL, the path will be transformed into the directory `/catalogue/`, and then each welcome file in the above list would be tried in order. If any of the files in the list point to a valid resource in that directory, e.g. `/catalogue/default.html`, then that resource will be returned. Otherwise the server will return its default (404 or directory listing) message.

Many Java EE server implementations already ship with a default set of welcome files configured so you don't need to type the same things for every application. Sun's Application Server 8 (the Java EE 1.4 Reference Implementation) is preconfigured for `index.html`, `index.htm` and `index.jsp`.

Error Pages

10

The `<error-page>` element, as shown in Figure 10.13, provides a mapping between an error code or Java exception type and the path to a resource in the Web application which is to be displayed. There are three child elements: `<location>` and *either* `<error-code>` *or* `<exception-type>` must be declared.

Figure 10.13

<error-page> Schema

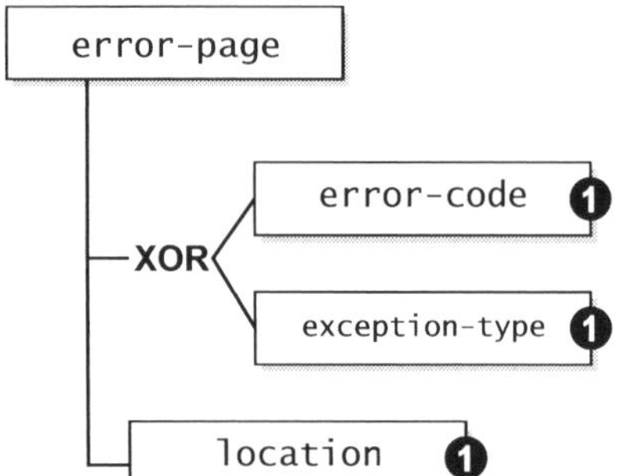

It is mandatory for one (only) of the `<error-code>`, used to specify the HTTP status code which will invoke the page to be called, or the `<exception-type>`, specifying the fully-qualified name of an exception class which caused the error, elements to be declared. Additionally, the `<location>` element is used to specify the context-relative URL to the error page or servlet.

At its most basic, this element is used to configure a redirect to a static custom HTML page when an error is encountered. A more complex implementation might, in the case of a 404 ('Not Found'), interpret the user's requested URL and display a list of other suggested and similar valid URLs, or present a search page. Alternatively, a servlet can be configured to receive errors and alert an administrator to a server fault in the case of a permanent '5xx' status code.

Note that when the container forwards to an error page, it sets the following request-scoped attributes:

- **`javax.servlet.error.status_code`** (`Integer`)
  The status code of the servlet which generated the error.

- **javax.servlet.error.exception_type** (Class)
  The Class of the exception which caused the error, if any.
- **javax.servlet.error.message** (String)
  The error message supplied by the servlet/JSP author or a default container-generated message, if any.
- **javax.servlet.error.exception** (Throwable)
  The actual exception instance which caused the error, if any.
- **javax.servlet.error.request_uri** (String)
  The original URI of the resource which caused the error, before forwarding to the error page.
- **javax.servlet.error.servlet_name** (String)
  The logical name (as configured in the deployment descriptor) of the servlet which caused the error.

In addition, the request attributes found in the *Additional Request Attributes* section of Chapter 6 are set as though we are forwarding to the error page.

JSP Configuration

Although we haven't looked at JSPs or tag libraries in any detail yet, I'll assume that your background knowledge is sufficient to look at their configuration here. It is the <jsp-config> element which is used for this purpose. There is normally only one instance of a <jsp-config> element in the descriptor. This element has two child elements, which in turn have other subelements, as shown in Figure 10.14.

The <taglib> element is used to specify the location of a tag library which is used by any JSPs in the application. There is usually one instance of this element for each tag library which requires importation. Additionally libraries can be loaded within the JSPs themselves if required. The mappings defined here are globally applied to all pages and documents. It has two child elements. The first is used to define a URI for the library being referenced, and the second specifies the context-relative location of the Tag Library Description (TLD) file for that library. The content of the <taglib-uri> element must be *unique* for every <taglib> declaration in the document (otherwise one library couldn't be differentiated from another), and this URI may be absolute or relative. The <taglib-location> element is used to specify the context-relative location of the TLD file or the JAR file containing the TLD for the referenced library. Using <taglib> is only one of many ways to reference a tag library: see Chapter 20 for more details on deployment.

JSPs are configured in groups; properties are applied to each of the group of JSPs separately from any other group. To describe this grouping, and the properties of the group, the `<jsp-config>` element may contain zero or more `<jsp-property-group>` elements. Any individual JSP in a group may override the general properties defined in that group, for itself only, by including configuration information in one of its `page` directives (we will look at this when we look at JSPs in full). Now we'll look more closely at how to configure groups of pages or documents.

The `<url-pattern>` element declares the request URL pattern to which all JSPs in the group conform. It is used to select those JSPs which are to be modified by the properties in the group. For example, if all the JSPs in the group are found in the `/archives` directory, then the URL pattern would be `/archives/*` to specify all resources in the `/archives` directory. There may be multiple `<url-pattern>` elements per group; this enables the mapping of JSPs from totally different URLs to the same group.

The `<page-encoding>` element is used to inform the container about the character encoding being used in the JSP. This is not necessarily the character set which will be returned to the client, but instead that used to encode the JSP which is to be parsed.

The `<el-ignored>` element is used to disable expression language (EL) parsing; its value must either be `true` or `false` . By default EL parsing is enabled for applications using a deployment descriptor conforming to the Servlet 2.4 specification or later, and disabled otherwise. This provides backwards compatibility. Configuration of EL is discussed further in Chapter 15 (see *Evaluation of EL Expressions in JSPs*).

`<scripting-invalid>` is used to disable Java-

Figure 10.14

<jsp-config> Schema

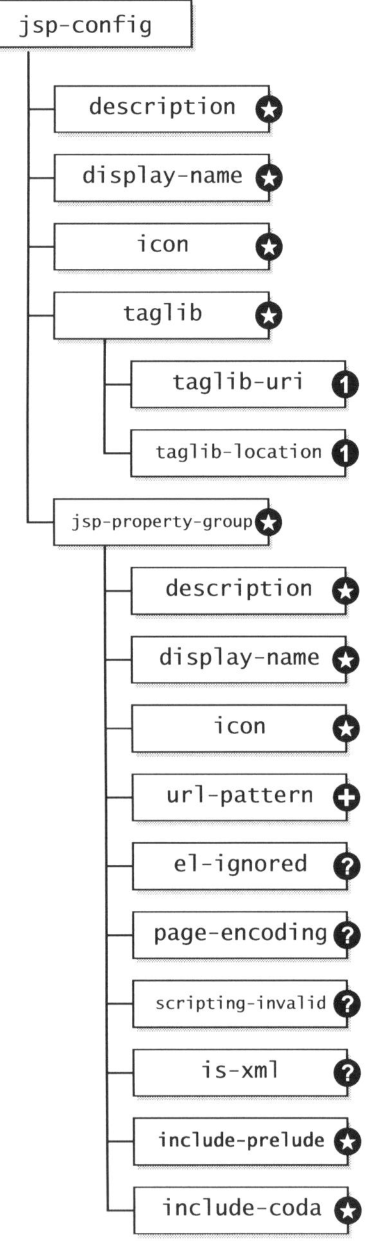

based coding in JSPs. Valid values are `true` or `false` . By default, in all versions of the specification, scripting is enabled.

When it is necessary to denote a group of JSPs as being XML-formatted *documents* and not JSP *pages*, the `<is-xml>` element can be used with the value `true` . If the value is `false`, or the element is omitted, the group is assumed to be a set of traditional JSP pages. The container uses other mechanisms to detect documents against pages as well.

It is also possible to include standard headers and footers in the responses from JSPs. This can be performed in one of two ways: either the inclusion must be coded for programmatically in the JSP itself, or declaratively in the deployment descriptor. We will look at two ways to achieve the first method in Chapters 13 and 16. The second method is less flexible but much more elegant, providing a more scalable application–it is however only applicable if the same headers/footers need to be included across an entire batch of JSPs. It uses two elements from the property group: `<include-prelude>` for headers and `<include-coda>` for footers. The semantics of both of these elements is identical: they both take a context-relative path as their value, and include the resource located there in the output. There may be zero or more of each of these elements, in which case the inclusion is performed in the order that the elements are found in the document. For example, to include `header.html` followed by `banner.jsp` at the top of the web page, and `modified.jsp` at the bottom:

```
<include-prelude>/WEB-INF/header.html</include-prelude>
<include-prelude>/WEB-INF/banner.jsp</include-prelude>
<include-coda>/WEB-INF/modified.jsp</include-coda>
```

Note the use of the `/WEB-INF` application-private directory here, since we assume that the JSPs are only fragments of a response and should not be accessed by the client directly.

Security Configuration

We defer all discussions of declarative security to Chapter 21, which concentrates on security issues as well as the deployment descriptor syntax.

Application Deployment

To round off the chapter, we'll look at exactly what happens from the moment after the application has been uploaded and deployed to the server, to just before the first resource from the application is requested.

There are four steps which must be completed by the container before request servicing can begin:

1. **Listener instantiation**
   Each listener class identified by a `<listener>` element in the deployment descriptor is instantiated and registered with the container. This enables all events, including those at the container and context levels, to be reported to their relevant listeners.
2. **Context instantiation**
   Before the loading procedure for filters or servlets can be started, the `ServletContext` object for the application must be instantiated.
3. **Filter initialisation**
   Filters are started before servlets so that all filters are ready to intercept requests even if the target servlet has not been loaded yet. Each filter is instantiated from its declaration in the `<filter>` deployment descriptor element, and then the `init` method is invoked.
4. **Servlet initialisation**
   Finally, the target servlet and JSP components are instantiated and initialised, according to the order specified by the `<load-on-startup>` elements in the deployment descriptor. If a value is not specified for a servlet, the container may wait until a request is actually made to the servlet before it is loaded, instantiated and initialised. The `init` method is called on each servlet to initialise it after its instantiation. JSPs may either be translated on start-up, or translated the first time they are requested by a client (depending on the configuration in the deployment descriptor, or the container's own preference if no configuration data is supplied).

With that under your belt it should just about be time to try some questions.

NOTE: As an aside, in Servlet 3.0 to be incorporated in Java EE 6, the deployment descriptor is likely to be removed in favour of annotations. For example, using `@Servlet` on a class will tell the container the class is a servlet and to what URLs it should be mapped. Eliminating the deployment descriptor makes developing modular components far easier.

10

Revision Questions

1 **Which of the following is the root element for a deployment descriptor?** **(choose one)**

- A <deployment>
- B <web-application>
- C <web-app>
- D <WAR-app>
- E <descriptor>

2 **What is the result of declaring the exhibited code in the deployment descriptor?** **(choose one)**

EXHIBIT

- A Declares a servlet initialisation parameter with name 'title'.
- B Declares an application configuration property.
- C Declares a default value for the session-scoped attribute with name 'title'.
- D Declares an application initialisation parameter with name 'title'.
- E Declares the context root for the application called 'title'.

3 **Which of the following declarations sets the default session timeout to 1 minute?** **(choose one)**

A
```
<session-timeout>60</session-timeout>
```

B
```
<session-config>
  <session-timeout>1</session-timeout>
</session-config>
```

C
```
<session-config>
  <timeout>1</timeout>
</session-config>
```

D
```
<session-config>
  <session-timeout>60</session-timeout>
</session-config>
```

E
```
<sessions>
  <timeout>1</timeout>
</sessions>
```

4 **What pair of declarations must appear in the deployment descriptor to configure the MyAuthenticationFilter filter to intercept all client requests to all contents of the /secure directory?** **(choose two)**

A
```
<filter>
  <class>MyAuthenticationFilter</class>
  <name>Auth Filter</name>
</filter>
```

B
```
<filter>
  <filter-name>Auth Filter</filter-name>
  <filter-class>MyAuthenticationFilter</filter-class>
</filter>
```

C
```
<filter>
  <filter-name>Auth Filter</filter-name>
  <filter-class>MyAuthenticationFilter</filter-class>
  <url-pattern>/secure/*</url-pattern>
</filter>
```


D
```
<filter-url class="MyAuthenticationFilter">/secure/*</filter-url>
```

E
```
<filter-mapping>
  <filter-class>MyAuthenticationFilter</filter-class>
  <url-pattern>/secure/*</url-pattern>
</filter-mapping>
```

F
```
<filter-mapping>
  <filter-name>Auth Filter</filter-name>
  <url-pattern>/secure/*</url-pattern>
</filter-mapping>
```

5 **Which of the following elements is used to declare a mapping between MIME types and file extensions?** **(choose one)**

A <mime-types>

B <file-extension>

C <mime-extension>

D <mime-mapping>

E <file-mapping>

6 **Which elements in the deployment descriptor can be used to configure JSPs?** **(choose two)**

A <filter>

B <servlet>

C <jsp>

D <jsp-page>

E <jsp-config>

7 **Which of the following declarations causes a filter with logical name Logger to be invoked for all invocations of all resources?** **(choose one)**

A
```
<filter-mapping>
  <filter-name>Logger</filter-name>
  <servlet-name>*</servlet-name>
</filter-mapping>
```

B
```
<filter-mapping>
  <filter-name>Logger</filter-name>
  <url-pattern>/*</url-pattern>
</filter-mapping>
```

C
```
<filter-mapping>
  <filter-name>Logger</filter-name>
  <url-pattern>/*</url-pattern>
  <dispatcher>ALL</dispatcher>
</filter-mapping>
```

D
```
<filter-mapping>
  <filter-name>Logger</filter-name>
  <url-pattern>/*</url-pattern>
  <dispatcher>*</dispatcher>
</filter-mapping>
```

E
```
<filter-mapping>
  <filter-name>Logger</filter-name>
  <url-pattern>/*</url-pattern>
  <dispatcher>REQUEST</dispatcher>
  <dispatcher>FORWARD</dispatcher>
  <dispatcher>INCLUDE</dispatcher>
  <dispatcher>ERROR</dispatcher>
</filter-mapping>
```

8 **What is the guaranteed action of the declaration in the exhibit when used in the deployment descriptor?** **(choose one)**

EXHIBIT

A The JSP /WEB-INF/order.jsp is never translated or put into service.

B The JSP /WEB-INF/order.jsp is assigned the Order Form logical name.

C The JSP /WEB-INF/order.jsp is set as the welcome page for the application.

D The JSP /WEB-INF/order.jsp is translated at deployment time.

E The declared syntax is illegal and causes a deployment error.

10

9 **Study the exhibit. What line(s) need to be inserted to specify an initialisation parameter with name file and value '/WEB-INF/log.txt'?** **(choose one)**

EXHIBIT

A
```
<context-param>
  <param-name>file</param-name>
  <param-value>/WEB-INF/log.txt</param-value>
</context-param>
```

B
```
<param name="file" value="/WEB-INF/log.txt" />
```

C
```
<param>
  <name>file</name>
  <value>/WEB-INF/log.txt</value>
</param>
```

D
```
<init-param>
  <param-name>file</param-name>
  <param-value>/WEB-INF/log.txt</param-value>
</ init-param>
```


E
```
<init-param>
  <name>file</name>
  <value>/WEB-INF/log.txt</value>
</init-param>
```

10 **Which of the following configures the MyServletContextListenerImpl to be instantiated and invoked by the container?** **(choose one)**

A
```
<context-listener>
  <class>MyServletContextListenerImpl</class>
</context-listener>
```

B
```
<listener>
  <class>MyServletContextListenerImpl</class>
</listener>
```

C
```
<listener class="MyServletContextListenerImpl" />
```

D
```
<listener>
  <listener-class>MyServletContextListenerImpl</listener-class>
</listener>
```

E
```
<listener type="context">
  <listener-class> MyServletContextListenerImpl</listener-class>
</listener>
```

11 **Which of the following declares the default.jsp page to be used as a welcome page?** **(choose one)**

A <welcome-file-list>
<welcome-file>default.jsp</welcome-file>
</welcome-file-list>

B <welcome-file-list>
<welcome-file name="default.jsp" />
</welcome-file-list>

C <welcome-files>
<file>default.jsp</file>
</welcome-files>

D <welcome-files>
<welcome-file>default.jsp</welcome-file>
</welcome-files>

E <welcome-file name="default.jsp" />

12 **Place the following declarations in the order they should appear in a servlet declaration:**

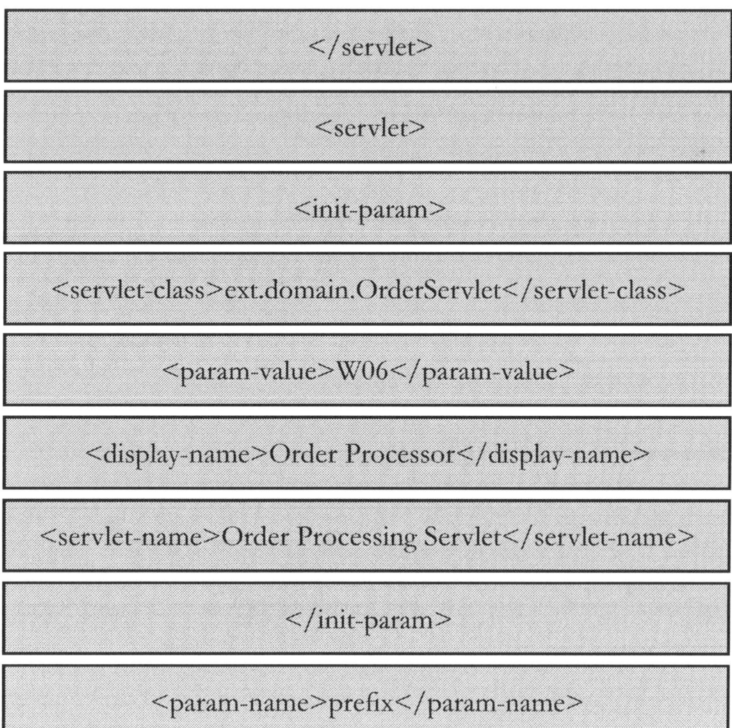
</servlet>
<servlet>
<init-param>
<servlet-class>ext.domain.OrderServlet</servlet-class>
<param-value>W06</param-value>
<display-name>Order Processor</display-name>
<servlet-name>Order Processing Servlet</servlet-name>
</init-param>
<param-name>prefix</param-name>

13 **Which of the following declarations configures the /500.html error page to be invoked when either a 500 error occurs, or a RuntimeException is raised?** **(choose one)**

A
```
<error-page>
  <url>/500.html</url>
  <status-code>500</status-code>
  <exception>java.lang.RuntimeException</exception>
</error-page>
```

B
```
<error-page>
  <error-code>500</error-code>
  <location>/500.html</location>
</error-page>
<error-page>
  <exception>java.lang.RuntimeException</exception>
  <location>/500.html</location>
</error-page>
```


C
```
<error-page>
  <error-code>500</error-code>
  <location>/500.html</location>
</error-page>
<error-page>
  <exception-type>java.lang.RuntimeException</exception-type>
  <location>/500.html</location>
</error-page>
```

D
```
<error-page>
  <error-code>500</error-code>
  <exception>java.lang.RuntimeException</exception>
  <location>/500.html</location>
</error-page>
```

E
```
<error-page>
  <error-code>500</error-code>
  <exception-type>java.lang.RuntimeException</exception-type>
  <location>/500.html</location>
</error-page>
```

14 **Which of the following are direct subelements of <jsp-config>?** **(choose three)**

A <display-name>

B <taglib>

C <page-encoding>

D <include-coda>

E <url-pattern>

F <jsp-property-group>

15 **Which of the following declarations as a direct child of <web-app> associates the TLD located at /WEB-INF/mytags.tld with the URI http://mytags.com?** **(choose one)**

A
```
<taglib>
  <uri>http://mytags.com</uri>
  <tld>/WEB-INF/mytags.tld</tld>
</taglib>
```

B
```
<jsp-config>
  <taglib>
    <uri>http://mytags.com</uri>
    <location>/WEB-INF/mytags.tld</location>
  </taglib>
</jsp-config>
```

C
```
<jsp-config>
  <taglib>
    <taglib-uri>http://mytags.com</taglib-uri>
    <taglib-location>/WEB-INF/mytags.tld</taglib-location>
  </taglib>
</jsp-config>
```

D
```
<jsp-config>
  <jsp-property-group>
    <url-pattern>/*</url-pattern>
    <taglib>
      <uri>http://mytags.com</uri>
      <location>/WEB-INF/mytags.tld</location>
    </taglib>
  </jsp-property-group>
</jsp-config>
```

E
```
<jsp-config>
  <jsp-property-group>
    <url-pattern>/*</url-pattern>
    <taglib>
      <taglib-uri>http://mytags.com</taglib-uri>
      < taglib-location>/WEB-INF/mytags.tld</taglib-location>
    </taglib>
  </jsp-property-group>
</jsp-config>
```

16 **How many <jsp-config> elements can and are typically declared in a deployment descriptor?** **(choose one)**

- A There must be only one <jsp-config> per document.
- B There may be any number of <jsp-config> elements, but typically only one is used.
- C There may be any number of <jsp-config> elements, and typically each is configured for a new JSP component.
- D There should be one <jsp-config> element per JSP to be configured.

17 **Which of the following declarations causes the /WEB-INF/footer.jsp to be inserted at the end of every JSP page in the application?** **(choose one)**

A
```
<jsp-config>
  <jsp-property-group>
    <footer>/WEB-INF/footer.jsp</footer>
  </jsp-property-group>
</jsp-config>
```


B
```
<jsp-config>
  <jsp-property-group>
    <url-pattern>/*</url-pattern>
    <footer>/WEB-INF/footer.jsp</footer>
  </jsp-property-group>
</jsp-config>
```

C
```
<jsp-config>
  <jsp-property-group>
    <url-pattern>/*</url-pattern>
    <include-code>/WEB-INF/footer.jsp</include-code>
  </jsp-property-group>
</jsp-config>
```

D
```
<jsp-config>
  <jsp-property-group>
    <url-pattern>/*</url-pattern>
    <include-coda>/WEB-INF/footer.jsp</include-coda>
  </jsp-property-group>
</jsp-config>
```

E
```
<jsp-config>
  <jsp-property-group>
    <url-pattern>/*</url-pattern>
    <include-prelude>/WEB-INF/footer.jsp</include-prelude>
  </jsp-property-group>
</jsp-config>
```

Exhibits

Q.2

```
<context-param>
  <param-name>title</param-name>
  <param-value>Website for Widgets.com</param-value>
</context-param>
```

Q.8

```
<servlet>
  <servlet-name>Order Form</servlet-name>
  <jsp-file>/WEB-INF/order.jsp</jsp-file>
  <load-on-startup>-1</load-on-startup>
</servlet>
```

Q.9

```
<filter>
  <filter-name>Logger</filter-name>
  <filter-class>LoggingFilter</filter-class>
  <!-- Insert here -->
</filter>
```

Answers to Revision Questions

1 **Correct answer: C**

Note that no deployment descriptor elements contain capital letters, so this discounts option C as being correct immediately.

2 **Correct answer: D**

An alternative, more correct, name is context initialisation parameter, but they are configured for application-wide usage.

3 **Correct answer: B**

A is invalid – it needs to be contained within a <session-config> element. It is also incorrect as it declares the time as 60, but the value of the timeout is in minutes not seconds, so this time should be 1. C and E are incorrect as they make use of the nonexistent <timeout> element. D is incorrect as it declares 60 minutes as the time.

4 **Correct answers: B,F**

A is incorrect; there are no <class> and <name> elements (note also that the correct declaration order is <filter-name> then <filter-class>). C is incorrect as filters are mapped to URLs using the separate <filter-mapping> element and not within the <filter> element. D is just plain wrong altogether! E is incorrect, as mappings use logical names to refer to components and not class types.

5 **Correct answer: D**

6 **Correct answers: B,E**

<servlet> can be used to configure a few select properties of the servlet resulting from translating and compiling the JSP. For this we use the <jsp-file> subelement (rather than <servlet-class>) of <servlet>.

7 **Correct answer: E**

Under Servlet 2.4, A would have been invalid as no wildcards for servlets existed; under Servlet 2.5, however, this is valid. Regardless, it is incorrect in both cases because it will only map client requests to all servlets, as the <dispatcher> element is missing (and therefore defaults to only REQUEST). Furthermore, A does not log request to non-servlet components (namely static resources). B is incorrect as although it maps to all component paths in the application, it omits the <dispatcher> element. C and D have illegal values (ALL and *) for <dispatcher>. Finally, E is correct as it declares all the <dispatcher> elements for all possible types, including those invoked by RequestDispatchers and the container. Note further that the URL pattern /* is valid, but * would not be.

8 **Correct answer: B**

The only catch here is the value -1 for <load-on-startup>. If the value is negative, the container may initialise the servlet/JSP whenever it pleases, which may be upon the first invocation of the page or any other time. This makes A wrong since it will be translated at some point in time, provided it is accessed at least once, and D is incorrect as we can't guarantee that it will be translated when deployed. This syntax is valid, making E incorrect, and C is wrong as we declare this elsewhere. In fact, this tag declares a JSP stored in the private /WEB-INF directory and assigns it the Order Form logical name. This allows us to use a <servlet-mapping> to assign it to a public URL; it also allows us to use a <filter-mapping> with an appropriate <servlet-name> to target just this JSP.

9 **Correct answer: D**

A is incorrect, as it initialises a context (application) initialisation parameter, and should be declared under <web-app> only. B is incorrect; note that very few if any elements in the deployment descriptor actually use attributes for declarations – most use elements. There are no elements called <param>, <name> nor <value>, so C and E are invalid.

10 **Correct answer: D**

A is incorrect as no <context-listener> element exists; all listeners are configured uniformly using the <listener> interface. The container infers which listener interfaces the class implements using reflection when the application is deployed. This also makes E an incorrect option, as a type attribute is neither valid nor required. There is no <class> element; in general, these are all preceded by the name of the type of component (<filter-class>, <servlet-class> and <listener-class>), hence A and B are incorrect. C is wrong as elements rarely take attributes, but instead have sub-elements.

11 **Correct answer: A**

Note that E and B are incorrect – always be doubtful about using attributes in the deployment descriptor; it's nearly always wrong. C makes use of the nonexistent <file> element, and D uses <welcome-files> which doesn't exist.

12 **Correct answer:**

```
<servlet>
<display-name>My Servlet</display-name>
<servlet-name>Order Processing Servlet</servlet-name>
<servlet-class>ext.domain.OrderServlet</servlet-class>
<init-param>
<param-name>prefix</param-name>
<param-value>W06</param-value>
</init-param>
</servlet>
```

13 **Correct answer: C**

Note that it is legal to declare only one of <error-code> or <exception-type>; so if you need the same page to be invoked if several different errors or exceptions occur, you need to use two separate <error-page> elements. Since the only valid subelements are <error-code>, <exception-type> and <location>, this leaves C as the only correct option.

14 **Correct answers: A,B,F**

The others are subelements of <jsp-property-group>, which is where most of the fun happens!

15 **Correct answer: C**

Remember here that <taglib> is a direct child of <jsp-config> (it is the only important property not found in <jsp-property-group>), and that it has the children <taglib-uri> and <taglib-location>.

16 **Correct answer: B**

Note that it is valid in the Schema to declare any number of <jsp-config> elements (making (a) incorrect); but since all configuration is done inside a <jsp-property-group> for the appropriate <url-pattern>, it is unnecessary to have multiple <jsp-config>s (hence C and D are wrong). When this is the case, the container effectively merges the settings from each <jsp-config> declaration to form a single element. The important things to remember for <jsp-config> are <taglib> and <jsp-property-group>, and the latter's subelements.

17 **Correct answer: D**

A is illegal as it omits the mandatory <url-pattern> element (which makes no sense as a property group is useless without being assigned to a group!); B and C make use of the illegal <footer> and <include-code> elements respectively. E uses <include-prelude>, but this inserts the resource at the start of the JSP, so that isn't appropriate.

In this chapter you'll:

- Understand why building modular Web components is ideal.
- Learn how to write and deploy individual Deployment Descriptor "snippets" called Web Fragments.
- Use annotations to write Web components which do not require a separate Deployment Descriptor, promoting ease of re-use and "pluggability".
- Programmatically deploy and configure Servlets, Filters and Listeners, permitting runtime conditional deployment of Web components.

11 Modular Deployment

In the previous chapter we looked at the Deployment Descriptor, an XML document used to configure the various components (e.g. servlets, filters, listeners, JSPs, security, external resources) in the Web application prior to deployment. This has always been the traditional way to configure applications for deployment. However, it places a great burden on the Application Assembler person outlined at the beginning of that chapter – they need to combine components which may have been written by different developers (or even worse, many external open source projects or other software houses) and write the Deployment Descriptor to ensure all components are configured correctly. That means including all the programmatic components (like servlet, filters and listeners), URL mappings, context and initialisation parameters, security roles, resource injections and "tweaking" the JSP container settings. To bring together all of those settings for a given application requires the Application Assembler to work with all the associated developers and documentation. That could be a lot of extra overhead!

To make applications easier to assemble and deploy, we'd ideally like to build fully modular components and libraries which can be reused easily in our applications – a goal the specifications calls **pluggability**. For example, our in-house developers might be programming up the application controller servlets and filters, also mapping those servlets to URLs and using resource injection to get handles on database connections managed by the Web container. We might "borrow" a few basic filter implementations from the Apache Tomcat project which our programmers will extend and enhance ready for deployment in our application. The JSP coding team will need to set their environment. The security team require that our Servlet developers code specific roles against their certain functionality exposed by their servlets. Once all the individual parts are built, at any time we can then "plug" any or all them together to form a new application, promoting reuse of those specialised components without any need for explicit duplication of configuration information.

In many ways JSPs already do this using per-JSP page directives and with JSTL tag libraries having their own per-library configuration created by the tag library developer. It makes a lot of sense to shift configuration away from the Application Assembler at deployment time, and onto the programmers during development; for that reason there are three tools available since the Servlet 3.0 specification which do this:

- **Annotations**
  Using the annotations framework first introduced in Java SE 5. This allows

developers to specify, for example, that a given class is a servlet and at the same time tell everyone (ultimately the container) what URL path it should be mapped to, what initialisation parameters it has, and what security roles it is owned by. This eliminates the entire <servlet> tag from the deployment descriptor – powerful stuff!

- **Web fragments**
  These are "sections" of a web.xml deployment descriptor which can be used to define individual deployment descriptor elements (for example a single servlet, or a filter and a listener combination). When deployed, the container will combine all the fragments and treat the collective result like a single web.xml deployment descriptor. That means our various different parties can each write their essential deployment descriptor information separately, so our Application Assembler person needs to know nothing about those components to deploy them.
- **Programmatic configuration**
  Servlets, filters and listeners can now be added to the container runtime environment dynamically, by code run inside the application itself.

We'll examine each of these in turn, and finally look at how the various deployment techniques are combined by the container when deploying an application.

Annotations

J2SE 5.0 introduced the concept of an **annotation**, which is essentially a note attached to a Java construct such as a class, interface, method/constructor, method parameter, field (a class-scoped instance or static variable) or method-local variable. In fact, we've seen this sort of thing for a long time – the use of Javadoc taglets to declare a deprecated method became commonplace:

```
/**
 * @deprecated
 */
public abstract void myMethod();
```

Normally the compiler neglects all comments, but it did look specifically for the `@deprecated` taglet. However, since this was only available at compilation time and there were very few recognised annotations, this was deemed insufficient. So, J2SE 5.0 introduces a generic model for annotations which can be included in compiled bytecode as well as source code. These use the same syntax as Javadoc taglets, but are no longer placed inside comments. So, for example, the above annotation becomes:

```
@Deprecated public abstract void myOldMethod();
```

This could equally well be declared as:

```
@Deprecated
public abstract void myOldMethod();
```

as the whitespace is ignored (annotations are applied to the next construct encountered in the source code, after skipping ignorable source text like comments and whitespace).

A slightly less obvious example of annotations is the use of marker interfaces like `java.lang.Cloneable`, `java.io.Serializable` and `java.util.RandomAccess`. Classes simply implemented the interface, which added no direct behaviour or methods, to mark themselves as having certain properties. It was then up to the application or JVM to determine if those properties were significant. The need for such interfaces can be replaced with annotations.

NOTE: Although comments are ignored when processing annotations during compilation, the J2SE 5.0 Javadoc tool fails to document the comment in this code:

```
@Deprecated
/**
 * My old method
 */
public abstract void myOldMethod();
```

whereas the following works correctly in all respects, and therefore should be used instead:

```
/**
 * My old method
 */
@Deprecated
public abstract void myOldMethod();
```

The Java Metadata specification (JSR-175) itself actually defines very few annotations: the common ones are `@Deprecated`, `@Override`, `@Target` and `@Retention`, with these last two being used solely in defining new annotation types. However, the model is extensible—we are free to add new annotations as we require (exactly how to do this is out of the scope of this book). Several parties recognised the need for a set of standard annotations, and therefore the following

JSRs applicable to us have come into being:

- JSR-250: Common Annotations for the Java Platform
- JSR-220: Enterprise JavaBeans 3.0
- JSR-224: Java API for XML-Based Web Services (JAX-WS) 2.0
- JSR-181: Web Services Metadata for the Java Platform

Unless otherwise noted, annotations may only be applied to the following Web-oriented classes (and any subclasses):

- `javax.servlet.Servlet`
- `javax.servlet.Filter`
- `javax.servlet.ServletContextListener`
- `javax.servlet.ServletContextAttributeListener`
- `javax.servlet.ServletRequestListener`
- `javax.servlet.ServletRequestAttributeListener`
- `javax.servlet.HttpSessionListener`
- `javax.servlet.HttpSessionAttributeListener`

In this book, we will only concern ourselves with the annotations which are readily applicable to Web applications–unless necessary for context, we do not discuss those relating to EJBs and Web services. For more detailed information on those, consult the relevant specifications and JSR documents.

When Java Web applications are deployed into a container, the container looks at the annotations attached to each class (for example, specifying that class is a servlet and what URL path it should be mapped to) and uses the information obtained from these annotations to configure the environment.

All Servlet specific annotations are found in the `javax.servlet.annotation` package; Java EE security annotations are in the `javax.annotation.security` package and are discussed together fully in Chapter 21.

Annotations and the Deployment Descriptor

The deployment descriptor hasn't gone away, and to preserve compatibility, all deployment descriptors still function as expected. However, due to the truly modular nature of the resulting components, it is preferred that annotations are used–a servlet which uses annotations is less coupled to the deployment descriptor, and hence to that particular deployed application, which makes it a more portable component. However, there are additional container overheads when using annotations: in order to support annotations correctly, the container must use reflection to examine each class in the application when first deployed. It has to load all classes from /WEB-INF/classes/ and /WEB-INF/lib/ and look for annotations. This has a performance overhead both at startup (since the container must now load and examine all available classes), but also there is a small memory overhead for the duration of the run time since the container can no longer participate in lazy class loading (i.e. loading classes only when required).

If these performance issues are a problem, then the use of the deployment descriptor is recommended. Further, you should set the metadata-complete attribute of <web-app> to the value true (the default is false) so that no other annotation processing is attempted by the container:

```
<web-app ... version="2.5" metadata-complete="true">
  ...
</web-app>
```

NOTE: Early drafts of the specification called the attribute full instead of metadata-complete, but the name has officially been changed, and the above is now correct. Resources referring to full are in error.

Servlet Annotations

Let's begin with an example of a deployment descriptor excerpt for a servlet whose purpose is to allow searching a book catalogue on a website. This is based on the deployment descriptor syntax from the previous chapter:

```
<servlet>
  <description>Book Catalogue Search Controller</description>
  <servlet-name>BookCatalogueSearch</servlet-name>
  <servlet-class>ext.domain.books.CatalogueSearch</servlet-class>
  <async-supported>true</async-supported>
  <init-param>
    <param-name>Warehouses</param-name>
    <param-value>All</param-value>
  </init-param>
</servlet>
<servlet-mapping>
  <servlet-name>CatalogueSearch</servlet-name>
  <url-pattern>/catalogue/search</url-pattern>
</servlet-mapping>
```

The initialisation parameter (fictitiously) allows us to configure which warehouses or book distributors we will search for catalogue information (here simply "All"), and I have included an example URL mapping. Our servlet looks something like:

```
package ext.domain.books;

import javax.servlet.http.*;

public class CatalogueSearch extends HTTPServlet {

  protected void doGet(HttpServletRequest req,
                       HttpServletResponse resp) {
    // implementation
  }
}
```

We can now replace all the earlier deployment descriptor configuration by attaching annotations directly to the class (note the extra `import` as the annotations are in `javax.servlet.annotation`):

```
package ext.domain.books;

import javax.servlet.http.*;
import javax.servlet.annotation.*;

@WebServlet(
  description="Book Catalogue Search",
  name="BookCatalogueSearch", asyncSupported=true,
  initParams={@WebInitParam(name="Warehouses",value="All")},
  urlPatterns={"/catalogue/search"}
)
public class CatalogueSearch extends HTTPServlet {

  protected void doGet(HttpServletRequest req,
                       HttpServletResponse resp) {
    // implementation
  }
}
```

This configures everything we configured in the previous deployment descriptor excerpt, but can be coded by the programmer and no longer requires the (longer) deployment descriptor syntax.

Every element of the `@WebServlet` annotation is optional – enabling us to deploy a servlet with an absolute minimum of information. For example, if we didn't want asynchronous support (the default of this element is `false`) and didn't need to declare the initialisation parameter, we could deploy the above with an annotation as simple as:

```
@WebServlet(urlPatterns={"/catalogue/search"})
public class CatalogueSearch extends HTTPServlet
```

or go one step further, as if no other annotation elements are supplied, the value of the annotation is the list of URL patterns:

```
@WebServlet({"/catalogue/search"})
public class CatalogueSearch extends HTTPServlet
```

and we can go another step, since annotations allow that we can omit the curly brackets {} for an array with only a single element:

```
@WebServlet("/catalogue/search")
public class CatalogueSearch extends HTTPServlet
```

Just those 32 characters on the first line are sufficient to deploy this servlet into the Web application at the `/catalogue/search` URL path. I think you'll agree that's significantly less code than using the deployment descriptor `<servlet>` and `<servlet-mapping>` combination, and takes all need for servlet configuration away from the Application Assembler person.

11

To list the format of annotations in this book, I'm going to use a pseudo-annotation syntax which encloses each annotation in a `@AnnotationName(...)` block, and then gives each element definition on a new line terminated with a comma (as you would declare if you were actually declaring it). Each element definition contains the type and name of that element, and if it is optional, then an equals sign followed by the default value; required elements do not have the equals sign/ default value. My intention is that you will find this concise syntax useful to copy to flash cards or similar, in preparation for the exam.

The definitions for this group of annotations are (the final four are the most commonly used):

```
@WebServlet (
  boolean asyncSupported=false,
  String description="",
  String displayName="",
  String largeIcon="",
  String smallIcon="",
  int loadOnStartup=-1,
```

```
  String name="",
  String[] urlPatterns={},
  String[] value={},
  @WebInitParam[] initParams={}
)
```

and then each initParam array entry is one of:

```
@WebInitParam (
  String name,
  String value,
  String description=""
)
```

The meanings of each of the elements correlate directly with the equivalents in the deployment descriptor, as discussed in the previous chapter. The one exception is the value element for the @WebServlet. The value is the default element if no others are supplied, and for convenience takes on the same role as urlPatterns. This was what allowed us to configure the servlet so easily in just 32 characters in the earlier code example.

The annotation needn't be declared at all of course, if you want to use the deployment descriptor to configure your servlet instead. However, if it is declared on a class, two points to note are:

- The annotation *must specify at least one URL pattern mapping*, either using the urlPatterns or the value elements (the latter can be used without the value= identifier if it is the only element present). It would be confusing to use both urlPatterns and value in the same annotation, so this is also illegal – *you must specify only one* of urlPatterns or value. This does make annotations impossible to use for unmapped servlets – that is those that you can call with a RequestDispatcher obtained by servlet name but where the servlet is not actually mapped to a URL. You can of course still do this in the web.xml descriptor, or via the programmatic ServletContainerInitializer method explained later in this chapter.
- You may recall that the <servlet-name> is mandatory in the deployment descriptor, but it is an optional element of @WebServlet. If it is omitted from the annotation, then the container will use the *fully qualified class name* for the annotation's name element. This can then be referenced in the deployment descriptor as though it had been declared using a <servlet-name> element therein.

If you do declare another occurrence of this servlet in the deployment descriptor with a different name, then the container will create two instances of the servlet – one for each distinct name. If you declare a servlet of the same name in the deployment descriptor, then the values for overriding properties given in the deployment descriptor override those of the annotations – which makes sense as it allows us to still make application-specific configuration changes before final deployment, without having to recompile the servlet code.

Multi-Part Form Uploads

For completeness, one new feature introduced in Servlet 3.0 is handling of multipart MIME file uploads. Enabling this functionality on a servlet makes the container examine the HTTP request and make the following methods available on an `HttpServletRequest`:

- **`public Collection<Part> getParts()`**
  Retrieves all the Parts available on this request
- **`public Part getPart(String name)`**
  Retrieves a named part – typically a single file.

Each `javax.servlet.http.Part` object has the following public methods, most of which have the same return types and purposes as those on `HttpServletRequest` for an entire request:

- **`String getName()`**
  Returns the name of the part
- **`long getSize()`**
  The size of the part in bytes
- **`String getContentType()`**
  The MIME type of this part
- **`String getHeader(String name)`**
  Returns the named header, the value of the first declaration if multiple headers were given of the same name, or `null` if no matching header is found
- **`Collection<String> getHeaders(String name)`**
  Returns all values for the named header, or an empty `Collection`.
- **`Collection<String> getHeaderNames()`**
  A list of all header names, empty if none were supplied, or null if the container denied access to this functionality.

and finally some methods which are used to get the uploaded data:

- **`java.io.InputStream getInputStream()`**
  Gets the data in this part as an `InputStream` for reading

- **void write(String filePath)**
  Writes the data in this part to the filePath on disk. If the uploaded file has been cached to the filesystem (rather than held in RAM), then this typically allows the container to simply rename that temporary file to the location specified, rather than open InputStreams and OutputStreams to do byte copying. This is significantly more efficient. However, invoking this method twice gives undefined behaviour – as the file may have been permanently moved and the temporary file no longer exist. So only call it once!

- **void delete()**
  Removes the (temporary) file from any underlying storage. This should happen anyway as part of container cleanup, but if you are handling large files you may wish to do this as soon as possible to reduce clutter!

NOTE: One point worth noting about multipart uploads generated from HTML forms is that there will be one or more Parts which have a Content-Disposition header set to form-data but do not represent file uploads (an example of this later). These will contain the other non-file variables supplied by an HTML form – for example, free form text boxes, sets of checkboxes or radio buttons, or drop-down <select> combo boxes. As with non-multipart forms (those not including any file uploads), these form variables and their values are all available via the standard ServletRequest getParameter() and getParameterValues() methods. It is far more convenient to access those in that traditional way, and only use the getParts() and getPart() methods on HttpServletRequest to access uploaded file data.

One other interesting point is the omission of a convenience method to get the original filename used when uploading. Later I'll demonstrate how to get this.

This functionality largely brings to Java EE what Web servers based on PHP and ASP/.NET have provided for quite a while, and is a welcome addition to the core platform, saving having to use other third party libraries for the multipart "heavy lifting". It does of course carry a performance overhead for the container to parse the request however, and so it is an optional extension enabled on a servlet-by-servlet basis using the @MultipartConfig annotation:

```
@MultipartConfig (
  int fileSizeThreshold=0,
  long maxFileSize=-1L,
  long maxRequestSize=-1L,
  String location=""
)
```

The `maxFileSize` and `maxRequestSize` supply the maximum permitted upload size for each file and for the entire request, respectively. The defaults are `-1` which means "no limit". If an upload exceeds either of these limits, then it is aborted and an `IllegalStateException` exception is thrown when `getParts()` or `getPart(name)` are invoked.

The `fileSizeThreshold` is a byte limit above which the file will be saved to a temporary file on the hard drive, rather than cached in RAM. This helps to reduce your application's RAM footprint for large file uploads; unless you intend to save all the uploads to the hard drive, you may wish to set this larger than the `0` default to avoid using slower disk-based access when reading the file contents. Files with byte sizes above this value will be cached in the directory given by the location element – or the value of the `javax.servlet.context.tempdir` environment variable in the container if omitted. If the location is given as a relative path, it will be relative to that `tempdir` set in the container.

Let's look at an example (I've omitted the package declaration and imports for brevity):

```
@WebServlet("/myfiles/upload")
@MultipartConfig(
  fileSizeThreshold=1000000, maxRequestSize=10000000L
)
public class MyUploadServlet extends HttpServlet {
  public static String getFilename(Part p) {
    String h = p.getHeader("content-disposition");
    /* This header usually looks like (all on one line):
     * Content-Disposition: form-data; name="partname";
     *   filename="name.ext"
     */
    String[] sections = h.split("\\s*;\\s*");
    for(String s : sections) {
      if(s.startsWith("filename=")) {
        return s.substring(9).replace("\"", "");
      }
    }
    return null;
  }

  protected void doPost(HttpServletRequest req,
                HttpServletResponse resp) throws IOException {
    Part p = null;
    try {
      p = req.getPart("file1");
    } catch(IllegalStateException ise) {
      /* Size limit */
      resp.sendError(HttpServletResponse.SC_REQUEST_ENTITY_TOO_LARGE);
      return;
    }
    if(p==null) {
      /* The named part did not exist */
```

11

```
      resp.sendError(HttpServletResponse.SC_BAD_REQUEST,
                     "Expected file1 part");
      return;
    }
    String mimeType = p.getContentType();
    long fileSize = p.getSize();
    String originalFileName = MyUploadServlet.getFilename(p);
    if("yes".equals(req.getParameter("inspect")) {
      java.io.InputStream is = p.getInputStream();
      // we can now read and manipulate the file content
      is.close();
    } else {
      /* Discard the upload immediately to
       * conserve RAM/filesystem space */
      p.delete();
    }
    /* Send user to an upload successful page */
    resp.sendRedirect("/uploadok.html");
  }
}
```

11

With the `@MultipartConfig` configured above, we limit the request size to a maximum of 10MB (counting by powers of 10) and will save any file uploads to temporary disk storage if they exceed 1MB. That will allow us to manipulate the file quickly and more efficiently in RAM, unless it's simply too big for our application to store in RAM and will use disk space instead. Our Servlet then goes on to check the file size hasn't been exceeded, presenting an HTTP 413 Request Entity Too Large response error, check that the file1 part has been supplied in the upload, and then get a handle on the InputStream of the data for analysis.

If you were coding an HTML form to support this upload, you might use something like:

```
<form action="/myfiles/upload" enctype="multipart/form-data"
      method="post">
<p>Upload File: <input type="file" name="file1" /></p>
<p><input type="checkbox" name="inspect" value="yes" /> Should
we analyse this file?</p>
<p><input type="submit" value="Upload Now" /></p>
</form>
```

This is just a regular HTML form with one point worthy of emphasis: the enctype attribute must be supplied and set to `multipart/form-data`. This is true for any HTML form where a file upload is occurring, in order to properly separate that binary data from the other "plain text" variables submitted by the form.

If you're wondering how I arrived at the implementation of `getFilename()` in the example above, this is because a multipart request is sent in the following format by a browser (or any other user agent):

```
Content-Type: multipart/form-data; boundary=AzFLJ081x
--AzFLJ081x
```

```
Content-Disposition: form-data; name="inspect"
yes
--AzFLJ081x
Content-Disposition: form-data; name="file1"; filename="name.ext"
Content-Type: text/plain
[contents of thename.ext file are here]
--AzFLJ081x--
```

The precise details of this are outside the scope of this book, and totally unnecessary for the exam. Suffice to say that each Part starts with a boundary delimiter (in the example above this was `--AzFLJ081x`) and the `Content-Disposition` header for the relevant `Part` is what contains the filename for the upload. So in the `getFilename()` implementation, we simply extract the the value of the filename part of the `Content-Disposition` header and discard the rest. It is surprising that this hasn't been implemented directly on the `Part` class; I suppose we may see this addition in a future Servlet specification.

Security Annotations

There are a number of security-related annotations which can be attached to Web application components, for example to set the security roles required by a servlet. These are discussed in Chapter 21 with a thorough treatment of the container's declarative security features. These annotations are packaged separately from those discussed in this chapter, found in the `javax.annotation.security` package. These annotations - for example `@RunAs`, `@ServletSecurity` and `@DeclareRoles` - can of course be used to augment or replace deployment descriptor security.

11

Filter Annotations

Filters are configured fundamentally with this annotation:

```
@WebFilter (
  boolean asyncSupported=false,
  String description="",
  String displayName="",
  String largeIcon="",
  String smallIcon="",

  String filterName="",
  String[] urlPatterns={},
  String[] value={},
  @WebInitParam[] initParams={},
  String[] servletNames={},
  DispatcherType[] dispatcherTypes={DispatcherType.REQUEST}
)
```

Notice that this is almost identical to `@WebServlet` except that name is replaced by filterName, and these two elements are added:

- **`String[] servletNames`**
  A list of servlets to which this filter will apply. The filter will be invoked for any URL mappings applied to those servlets.
- **`DispatcherType[] dispatcherTypes`**
  An array of conditions under which this filter will be invoked. The `DispatcherType` enumeration has the following possible values: `REQUEST` (the sole default if the `dispatcherTypes` element is omitted), `INCLUDE`, `FORWARD`, `ERROR`, `ASYNC`.

As with `@WebServlet`, the `@WebInitParam` annotations can be given to supply initialisation parameters for the filter and the default name is the fully-qualified class name. The requirements are modified slightly: although `urlPatterns` and value are mutually exclusive (cannot both be specified together), it is now the case that exactly one of `urlPatterns`, `servletNames` or `value` must be supplied. You can specify arrays for *both* `servletNames` and `urlPatterns` (or via the `value` element), so the filter will be applied to all matching servlets and URL paths.

11

That's really all there is to filters. We can now simplify filter deployment considerably. For example, here is a simple IP address blocking filter, applied to the `ext.domain.books.CatalogueSearch` (named `BookCatalogueSearch` and mapped to `/myfiles/upload`) and `ext.domain.MyUploader` (mapped to `/catalogue/search`) servlets from earlier in the chapter (again, I've omitted `package` and `import` declarations for brevity):

```
@WebFilter({"/myfiles/upload","/catalogue/search"})
public class IPBlockFilter implements Filter {
  public void destroy() {}
  public void init(FilterConfig c) {}

  public void doFilter(ServletRequest req, ServletResponse resp,
FilterChain chain) {
    String[] blocked = { "10.1.102.2", "172.18.0.54" };
    for(String b : blocked) {
      if(b.equals(req.getRemoteAddr())) {
        /* Abort this request */
        HttpServletResponse hresp = (HttpServletResponse) resp;
        hresp.sendError(HttpServletResponse.SC_FORBIDDEN);
        return;
      }
    }
    /* Success, so continue along the chain */
    chain.doFilter(req,resp);
  }
}
```

In the example, any of the following would have been totally equivalent (due to the servlet names set up previously, and the default values of the other options):

```
@WebFilter(urlPatterns={"/myfiles/upload","/catalogue/search"})

@WebFilter(value={"/myfiles/upload"},
    servletNames="BookCatalogueSearch")

@WebFilter(value="/catalogue/search",
    servletNames="ext.domain.MyUploadServlet")

@WebFilter(urlPatterns={"/catalogue/search"},
    servletNames="ext.domain.MyUploadServlet",
    dispatcherType=DispatcherType.REQUEST)
```

Once you are confident that, in this example, each of those are equivalent to the "short version" declared in the full example above, you can move on!

Listener Annotations

Our final simple configuration annotation is to tell the container about listeners – i.e. classes implementing any of these interfaces:

- `javax.servlet.ServletContextListener`
- `javax.servlet.ServletContextAttributeListener`
- `javax.servlet.ServletRequestListener`
- `javax.servlet.ServletRequestAttributeListener`
- `javax.servlet.http.HttpSessionListener`
- `javax.servlet.http.HttpSessionAttributeListener`

11

NOTE: Section 11.3.2 of the Servlet 3.0 specification states explicitly that "unlike other listeners, listeners of type `javax.servlet.AsyncListener` may only be registered (with a `ServletRequest`) programmatically". That is, they cannot be registered in the deployment descriptor or by annotations. However, confusingly, section 15.5 treats `AsyncListeners` identically to all of the above for the purposes of resource injection.

The `@WebListener` annotation tells the container to treat any implementation of the above as a listener, and instantiate it at deployment time. It doesn't have any elements except an optional `value` which is the description for the listener:

```
package ext.domain;

import javax.servlet.*;
import javax.servlet.annotation.WebListener;
```

```
@WebListener
public class MyCtxtInitListener
             implements ServletContextListener {

  public void contextDestroyed(ServletContextEvent sce) {}
  public void contextInitialized(ServletContextEvent sce) {
    // Here we will implement programmatic configuration later!
  }
}
```

The equivalent deployment descriptor syntax for `@WebListener` would be:

```
<listener>
<listener-class>ext.domain.MyCtxtInitListener</listener-class>
</listener>
```

so our new approach decouples responsibility from the Application Assembler, and reduces the overall code by 85%. Over a large scale project this increased efficiency will be most welcomed.

Web Fragment Deployment

The modularity design goals in Servlet 3.0 target being able to separate specialist, potentially complex, configuration of individual components from assembly of the application as a whole. So far in this chapter, we've covered how to use annotations to configure individual Web components like servlets, filters and listeners. These are all considered by the Web container during application deployment.

However, not everything can be configured by an annotation – for example, JSP `welcome-lists` (a list of page names which will be displayed as the "default" page when a URL path to a directory is requested) cannot be configured with annotations. JSP configuration in general cannot be performed using annotations.

It may also be desirable to override some of the default annotation configuration from time-to-time. As the deployment descriptor takes precedence over annotations, this is the place to make those overrides. But again, we want to decouple as much of the descriptor writing as possible from the Application Assembler and onto our developers who really understand the configuration required for their code.

Servlet 3.0 introduces the concept of web fragments – which perhaps should more accurately be called deployment descriptor fragments. These allow you to write modular "chunks" of `web.xml` configuration which will then be combined by the container during deployment to form the entire application. For example, this allows front controller developers to configure their servlets, a security expert to work on filters and declarative security, and our JSP designers to tweak their environments – all working separately and without needing to explicitly converge their work into a single `web.xml` file.

In order that fragments can be found by the container, and do not clash or become overwritten by one another, there are two requirements:

1. Each fragment must reside in its own JAR (typically along side the classes being configured that make up the application) inside the `META-INF/web-fragment.xml` file;
2. The JAR must be deployed to the `/WEB-INF/lib/` directory of the Web application.

The container will then scan each JAR to find its `web-fragment.xml` file (if it exists), and follow the rules explained in the *Container Deployment* section later to combine all fragments alongside the main `web.xml` into a working deployment descriptor unit.

Any annotations on classes inside JARs inside `/WEB-INF/lib/` will also be treated as configuration data, whether or not the JAR contains a `web-fragment.xml`.

A `web-fragment.xml` file is composed of a root `<web-fragment>` element (in place of `<web-app>`) and then any of the regular sub elements of `<web-app>` as discussed in the previous chapter. The full form of the root element is:


```
<web-fragment xmlns="http://java.sun.com/xml/ns/javaee"
   xmlns:xsi="http://www.w3.org/2001/XMLSchema-instance"
   xsi:schemaLocation="http://java.sun.com/xml/ns/javaee/web-fragment_3_0.xsd"
   version="3.0">
```

however this can be abbreviated to simply:

```
<web-fragment>
```

and the container will infer the rest (at least until there are multiple versions of the specification).

NOTE: In general `<web-app>` and `<web-fragment>` sub-elements can appear any number of times and in any order. The exceptions are `<session-config>`, `<jsp-config>` and `<login-config>` which may appear at most once per application deployment. The elements `<welcome-file-list>` and `<locale-encoding-mapping-list>` will simply have their values merged by the container during deployment so the result is the union of all supplied values across the deployment descriptor and all fragments.

This is an example of a `web-fragment.xml` file which configures a context parameter and the container managed authentication method:

```
<web-fragment>
  <context-param>
    <param-name>BookCatalogueURLPrefix</param-name>
    <param-value>http://www.garnerpress.com/catalogue/</param-value>
  </context-param>
  <login-config>
    <auth-method>FORM</auth-method>
    <form-login-config>
      <form-login-page>/login.html</form-login-page>
      <form-error-page>/errors/403.html</form-error-page>
    </form-login-config>
  </login-config>
</web-fragment>
```

By the rules of deployment descriptor uniqueness, we could not now declare the `<login-config>` again anywhere else in our deployment unit (not in the main `web.xml` nor in any other `web-fragment.xml`).

Deployment Sequence

11

During deployment of the application, the container will load each component it encounters as it encounters its deployment configuration. This has these important consequences:

- The ordering of components configured using annotations is not defined and may not be consistent across different deployments of the same application;
- The `web.xml` deployment descriptor is always examined first to give us chance to configure an `<absolute-ordering>` for other fragments;
- For `web.xml` or each fragment, components defined therein will be loaded in the order declared;
- Annotations for a given component are processed after the corresponding web fragment (if deployed in a library JAR) or `web.xml` (deployed into the application) is examined, and any metadata not already declared (in the fragment or descriptor) is set from the annotation;
- For `Servlet` and `Filter` components, initialisation parameters supplied in annotations but not declared in the deployment descriptor or fragments will use the annotation value, but the descriptor/fragments will override the values of any duplicate named parameters. On the contrary, the `url-patterns` and `DispatcherTypes` (for `Filters`) supplied to the annotations are strictly overridden by the descriptor/fragments and will not be merged by union;
- Web fragments are merged into the main application configuration only after completing processing of their configuration and all annotations for the JAR;

- The order of loading of web-fragment.xml files is not defined or guaranteed by default;
- If the loading order of fragments is important, the process can be controlled in web.xml using <absolute-ordering>, or in web fragments themselves using <ordering> elements;
- If the metadata-complete attribute of <web-app> is set to true, then all annotations and all fragments are ignored (hence any declared loading order is irrelevant and also ignored);
- If the metadata-complete attribute of <web-app> is omitted or false, but metadata-complete attribute of a <web-fragment> is set to true, then only the annotations for components packaged in that fragment's JAR are ignored;
- Configuration from multiple descriptors will be merged. Where elements can take multiple values (e.g. <context-param> which can be declared multiple times, each for a named parameter), the result of merging will be the union of all values. However, should a conflict occur between a fragment and the main descriptor, then the web.xml value takes precedence. If the conflict occurs between two fragments, an error will be raised by the container. <init-param>s and <mime-mapping>s may only be declared once for the same <param-name> or <extension> respectively – if found in multiple fragments or web.xml an error is raised;
- The application is considered <distributable> only if all web fragments are also marked as <distributable>.

Most of this is common sense – generally web.xml takes precedence, but if you can't figure out how to inherit or override a configuration property, then it's likely that an error will occur.

In order to assist referencing multiple web-fragment.xml files, it is usual to give each a unique name. This is supplied with a top-level <name> element – for example:

```
<web-fragment>
  <name>SecurityLibrary1</name>
  <!-- rest of configuration -->
</web-fragment>
```

<ordering> and <absolute-ordering>

Let's start by looking at how to control the loading order of individual web-fragment.xml files, for example in libraries which co-operate with each other during application deployment. It is natural to require that you need all components to be registered and configured, for example, in libraries providing ancillary services, security, connectivity and storage helpers, before loading front controllers, in turn before loading (JSP) display pages or (e.g. JSF) framework.

Let's assume that we have the following named `web-fragment.xml` files in JAR libraries:

- CommonLib – a library of common components we use;
- StorageLib – a library which abstracts some storage requirements for our application;
- SecurityLib – a library of security filters and declarative login configuration;
- ServletsLib – a library of controller servlets;
- ContentLib – a library of content producers (e.g. a display framework like Struts or JSF)

We want those library to be loaded in the order specified, although (in our fictitious scenario), we'll allow StorageLib and SecurityLib to be reversed – whilst both use CommonLib, and both are used by ServletLib, they don't depend on each other, and hence could be loaded in either order.

To accomplish this ordering requirement, we will initially set up cross-library dependencies by using the `<ordering>` element in each library's `web-fragment.xml` file. This allows us to say "load this library before all others", "load this library after library X" etc. It is accomplished by using two sub-elements of `<ordering>` which are:

- **`<before>`**
  The web fragments listed here must be loaded strictly before this fragment
- **`<after>`**
  The web fragments listed here must be loaded strictly after this fragment

Each of these may then have one or more `<name>` elements, where the contents of each is the name of another `web-fragment.xml`, as declared using the `<name>` top-level element in that fragment, and an optional `<others />` element which refers to all (other) fragments not explicitly named. This all makes more sense with a worked example.

We want components and configuration in our CommonLib to always be loaded first – everything else might depend on something from this library. We can therefore force it to become top of the loading list by "ordering it before all others" - in our CommonLib's `web-fragment.xml` we'll therefore use:

```
<web-fragment>
  <name>CommonLib</name>
  <ordering>
    <before><others /></before>
```

```
  </ordering>
  <!-- Other configuration -->
</web-fragment>
```

Next on the task list is our ContentLib – as the user's view of the application, this should always be the very last component to be loaded. We'll therefore use:

```
<web-fragment>
  <name>ContentLib</name>
  <ordering>
    <after><others /></after>
  </ordering>
  <!-- Other configuration -->
</web-fragment>
```

That sorts the two extremes. Recall we don't care about the order of StorageLib and SecurityLib, and based on the fact that CommonLib is always going to be first, then all we need to do is configure ServletsLib to come after all of those. This just needs:

```
<web-fragment>
  <name>ServletsLib</name>
  <ordering>
    <after>
      <name>StorageLib</name>
      <name>SecurityLib</name>
    </after>
  </ordering>
  <!-- Other configuration -->
</web-fragment>
```

NOTE: There is a strict requirement that, to avoid confusion, `<name>` elements only appear once, uniquely, in the entire deployment context. If any duplicate names are encountered, or any circular references or loops are discovered (such as two libraries both declaring each other as being after themselves), the container is required to abort the application deployment and write a helpful error message to the container's log. It is critical that you ensure fragments declared with individual `<ordering>` elements follow a sensible order – otherwise you can use `<absolute-ordering>` in a `web.xml`.

If you need to override the configuration order of all libraries on an application basis, you can use the `<absolute-ordering>` element in the application's main `web.xml` file – there must be at most one occurrence of this element in the application's `web.xml`, and if present then it will be processed before any `web-fragment.xml` files; any relative `<ordering>` elements in the fragments will be ignored. This is an example of the element which would be suitable for the example given previously:

```
<web-app>
  <!-- Other configuration here -->
  <absolute-ordering>
    <name>CommonLib</name>
    <others />
    <name>ServletsLib</name>
    <name>ContentLib</name>
  </absolute-ordering>
</web-app>
```

This should be fairly clear: it tells the container that we need CommonLib loaded first, and finally need ServletsLib and ContentLib loaded (in that order). The `<others />` signals that any fragments not explicitly loaded should be loaded at that point – the exact default order in which those fragments are examined appears to be undefined. If an `<others />` is not present and a fragment is not explicitly named, then that fragment will be completely ignored and not considered at all as part of the application initialisation process.

Application Component Ordering

11

We've covered the basic ways to control ordering: use web-fragment.xml files and either relative `<ordering>` in those fragments, or `<absolute-ordering>` in the `web.xml`. This can be used to control most ordering requirements. In all cases, `web.xml` has precedence over annotations and fragments.

When a given fragment or the `web.xml` itself are processed, the container then applies this basic ordering:

- **Filters**
  Chained in the order they are declared in the assembled descriptor.
- **Servlets**
  Usually loaded lazily when they are required for the first time by a request, unless their `<load-on-startup>` elements or `loadOnStartup` annotation element are set, in which case they are loaded at deployment time in the determined order. If the servlet is disabled using the enabled deployment descriptor element, then it will not be loaded at all.
- **ServletContextListeners**
  The `contextInitialized` methods are invoked in the order in which the listeners were declared, and the `contextDestroyed` methods in reverse order.
- **ServletRequestListeners**
  The `requestInitialized` methods are invoked in the order in which the listeners were declared, and the `requestDestroyed` methods in reverse order.

- **HttpSessionListeners**
  The `sessionCreated` methods are invoked in the order in which the listeners were declared, and the `sessionDestroyed` methods in reverse order.
- All other listeners have an undefined invocation order.

NOTE: To avoid clutter, I've omitted the less pertinent sequences. Should you have a need, or are inclined to be especially thorough, you can find the complete sequence in section 8.2.3 of the Servlet 3.0 specification.

Programmatic Registration and Configuration

Along with the other major changes to deployment in Servlet 3.0, this specification version adds the ability to insert new components into the application dynamically, at runtime and after the usual container deployment sequence. This is all made possible with new methods in the `javax.servlet.ServletContext` interfaces.

11

Programmatic Registration

Servlets, filter and listeners can all be registered via code as well as in descriptors and by using annotations.

Servlets and Filters

Adding both Servlets and Filters programmatically to the application follows the same approach. There are three basic ways to achieve this on `ServletContext`:

1. By specifying the fully-qualified class name (as in the deployment descriptor)
2. By specifying the Class object for the servlet or filter
3. By creating an instance of the Servlet or Filter and then registering it

The first approach uses one of these methods (for servlets and filters respectively):

```
ServletRegistration.Dynamic addServlet(String name, String servletClass)
FilterRegistration.Dynamic addFilter(String name, String filterClass)
```

The second approach uses these (essentially equivalent to the previous two):

```
ServletRegistration.Dynamic addServlet(String servletName,
    Class<? extends Servlet> servletClass)

FilterRegistration.Dynamic addFilter(String filterName,
    Class<? extends Filter> filterClass)
```

The third approach is more complex – you must first use a `createXxx()` method to instantiate a `Servlet` or `Filter` instance, and then register it with the container. You should not instantiate it directly – if you were to do so, none of the annotations on the class would be processed. Using the createXxx() method ensures correct processes are followed for instantiating the component. These are the methods on `ServletContext`:

```
<T extends Servlet> T createServlet(Class<T> servletClass)
<T extends Filter> T createFilter(Class<T> filterClass)

ServletRegistration.Dynamic addServlet(String name, Servlet s)
FilterRegistration.Dynamic addFilter(String filterName, Filter f)
```

The following is an example of programmatic servlet registration using the third approach:

```
addServlet("MyServlet",
  createServlet(Class.forName("ext.domain.MyServlet")) );
```

Listeners

In the same way as servlets and filters can be registered using new methods added on `ServletContext`, so can listeners by using either of these methods:

- **`void addListener(Class<? extends java.util.EventListener> listenerImplementationClass)`**
- **`void addListener(String listenerImplementationClassName)`**

Alternatively you can create an explicit listener instance (which will also fire resource injection annotations, if the listener is a Managed Bean) and then add the instance to the application container using:

- **`<T extends java.util.EventListener> T createListener(Class<T> c)`**
- **`<T extends java.util.EventListener> void addListener(T t)`**

Unlike servlets and filters, listeners cannot be configured in any other way, and therefore there do not need to be any `Registration` methods or implementations for listeners.

NOTE: I mention above that the listener has to be a Managed Bean for resource injection to occur. For reasons of higher performance, normally the container will not scan "plain old Java objects" (POJOs – of which listeners are) for resource injection. In order for this to occur, you need to tell the container that the object should be treated as a "Managed Bean" (see JSR-299 for more details). The simplest way is to add the @ ManagedBean annotation on the class.

Programmatic Configuration

When registering servlets and filters programmatically, those methods provide access to objects of interface types `XxxRegistration.Dynamic` to allow configuration of those resources. In addition, methods have been added to `ServletContext` to allow some programmatic configuration of the application as a whole.

Registered Servlet and Filters

You'll notice that the earlier servlet and filter registration methods return a `XxxRegistration.Dynamic` object; like most container-managed objects, these are interfaces. They provide functionality for modifying the configuration of servlet and filter components after they have been registered in the container – whether this be programmatic ("dynamic") registration, or during the usual deployment process using annotations, `web.xml` or Web Fragments. The following `ServletContext` methods also allow `Registration` implementations to be obtained for components already installed in the application through annotations, `web.xml` or web fragments:

11

- **`FilterRegistration getFilterRegistration(String filterName)`**
  Gets the `FilterRegistration` for the filter with the supplied `<filter-name>`
- **`Map<String,? extends FilterRegistration> getFilterRegistrations()`**
  Retrieves a `Map` of `<filter-name>` keys against the `FilterRegistration` objects for those filters
- **`ServletRegistration getServletRegistration(String servletName)`**
  Gets the `ServletRegistration` for the servlet with the `<servlet-name>`
- **`Map<String,? extends ServletRegistration> getServletRegistrations()`**
  Retrieves a `Map` of `<servlet-name>` keys against the `ServletRegistration` objects for those servlets.

Figure 11.1 shows the hierachy of `Registration` interfaces.

The `javax.servlet.Registration` interface at the root of the hierarchy covers the settings common to both servlets and filters:

- **`String getClassName()`**
  Returns the fully-qualified class name of the registered servlet or filter
- **`String getName()`**
  Returns the unique `<servlet-name>` or `<filter-name>` for the component
- **`String getInitParameter(String name)`**
  Retrieves the value of the `<init-param>` called `name` configured.

Figure 11.1

Registration Interfaces

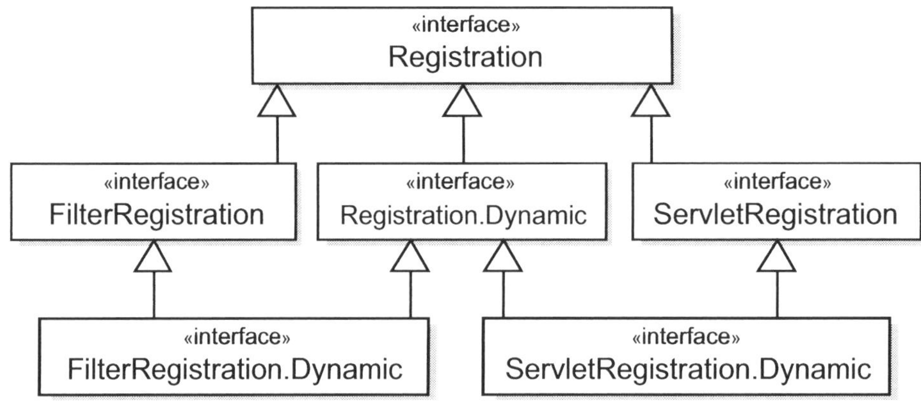

11

- **`Map<String,String> getInitParameters()`**
  Returns a `Map` of names (keys) against values for all initialisation parameters configured for the component

- **`boolean setInitParameter(String name, String value)`**
  Adds the named `<init-param>` with the supplied value. The value must not be null (or an `IllegalArgumentException` is thrown). This method does nothing and returns `false` if `name` matches an existing parameter. A successful update returns `true`.

- **`Set<String> setInitParameters(Map<String,String> initParams)`**
  Sets all `<init-param>` parameters to those in the supplied `Map`. Each name and value must be non-`null` (or an `IllegalArgumentException` is thrown). Each parameter is processed separately, but if any fail to be inserted (because those named parameters are already present for this component), then the returned `Set` contains the name of the failed parameter and the operation is aborted with no parameters being updated.

The `Registration.Dynamic` interface extends `Registration` and adds a method for `asyncSupported` (assuming it has not been set by annotation on the class):

- **`void setAsyncSupported(boolean isAsyncSupported)`**
  Configures the `Servlet` or `Filter` represented by this dynamic `Registration` as supporting asynchronous operations or not.

The `ServletRegistration` interface extends `Registration` to add support for URL mappings and one security accessor method:

- **`Set<String> addMapping(String... urlPatterns)`**
  Adds one or more URL patterns against this `ServletRegistration`'s servlet.

- **Collection<String> getMappings()**
  Gets the current URL mappings set for this `ServletRegistration`'s servlet.

- **String getRunAsRole()**
  Gets the name of the `runAs` role of this `ServletRegistration`'s servlet.

Similarly, the `FilterRegistration` interface extends `Registration` to add support for mappings:

- **void addMappingForServletNames(EnumSet<DispatcherType> dispatcherTypes, boolean isMatchAfter, String... servletNames)**
  Adds a mapping for the `Filter` represented by this `FilterRegistration` against the servlet names and dispatcher types. The `isMatchAfter` parameter should be `true` if the given filter mapping should be matched after any declared filter mappings, and `false` if it is supposed to be matched before any declared filter mappings in the application.

- **void addMappingForUrlPatterns(EnumSet<DispatcherType> dispatcherTypes, boolean isMatchAfter, String... urlPatterns)**
  Adds a mapping for the `Filter` represented by this `FilterRegistration` against the given URL patterns and dispatcher types. See the previous method for the meaning of `isMatchAfter`.

- **Collection<String> getServletNameMappings()**
  Gets the servlet names mapped against the `Filter` represented by this `FilterRegistration`.

- **Collection<String> getUrlPatternMappings()**
  Gets the URL patterns mapped against the `Filter` represented by this `FilterRegistration`.

The `FilterRegistration.Dynamic` interface extends both `FilterRegistration` and `Registration.Dynamic` but does not declare any additional methods, unlike `ServletRegistration.Dynamic` which extends `ServletRegistration` and `Registration.Dynamic`, and then adds:

- **void setRunAsRole(String roleName)**
  Sets the name of the `runAs` role for this `ServletRegistration` – this is the counterpart of `ServletRegistration.getRunAsRole()`.

- **void setLoadOnStartup(int loadOnStartup)**
  Sets the `loadOnStartup` priority for the servlet

- **void setMultipartConfig(MultipartConfigElement multipartConfig)**
  Sets the `javax.servlet.MultipartConfigElement` to be applied to the mappings defined for this `ServletRegistration`. This class has a constructor you can use to set the multipart upload parameters:

11

`MultipartConfigElement(String location, long maxFileSize, long maxRequestSize, int fileSizeThreshold)`

- **`Set<String> setServletSecurity(ServletSecurityElement sse)`**
  Sets the `javax.servlet.ServletSecurityElement` to be applied to the mappings defined for this `ServletRegistration`. This has a constructor which takes a `javax.servlet.HttpConstraintElement` object, or a collection of `HttpMethodConstraintElement` objects. This process is quite involved from an API perspective: check the public JavaDoc documentation for more details of the objects.

Application Configuration using ServletContext

There are some methods on `ServletContext` which are used simply to configure the application's container:

- **`boolean setInitParameter(String name, String value)`**
  Adds the context initialization parameter with the given name and value. If the named parameter already exists, this method does nothing but return false. Otherwise it adds the parameter and returns true.

- **`void declareRoles(String... roleNames)`**
  Declares additional role names that can then be tested, for example in `HttpServletRequest.isUserInRole()`.
- **`JspConfigDescriptor getJspConfigDescriptor()`**
  Retrieves an object encapsulating the `<jsp-config>` related configuration that was aggregated from the `web.xml` and `web-fragment.xml` deployment descriptor files. This is all immutable.
- **`SessionCookieConfig getSessionCookieConfig()`**
  Gets a `javax.servlet.SessionCookieConfig` object through which properties of the session tracking cookies created on behalf of this `ServletContext` may be configured. Common properties used on the object are: `setDomain(String)`, `setName(String)`, `setMaxAge(int)` and `setPath(String)`. Check the JavaDoc API documentation for more details.

The following three methods are used in configuring the way sessions are tracked – if you'll recall, this requires a session ID (`jsessionid`) to be communicated from the client to our application during each HTTP request. The most common way to do this is via cookies, but should that fail, the jsessionid can be written into the URL. The least common way (which is not implemented in all containers) is to use the SSL session ID if your application is using HTTPS (this obviously doesn't work if you are not running with SSL encryption). The following configure this:

- **`Set<SessionTrackingMode> getDefaultSessionTrackingModes()`**
  Gets the session tracking modes supported by default for the application.
- **`Set<SessionTrackingMode> getEffectiveSessionTrackingModes()`**
  Gets the session tracking modes that are in effect for the application.
- **`void setSessionTrackingModes(Set<SessionTrackingMode> modes)`**
  Sets the session tracking modes that should be effective for the application.

The `javax.servlet.SessionTrackingMode` is an enum with constants `COOKIE`, `URL` and `SSL` for each of the three possibilities mentioned above.

Conditional Configuration by Versioning

The primary reason for using any of the conditional configuration discussed in this section is that you will need to make runtime decisions about whether to enable certain components or configuration features. Of course, you can't go much lower than a Servlet 3.0 compliant container – as the functionality didn't exist before this version – but as time progresses and more platform revisions are released, it may be helpful to determine the version of the specification an application supports (which may be less than Servlet 3.0) and the latest supported by the container.

These methods on `ServletContext` allow for this conditional checking:

- **`int getEffectiveMajorVersion()`**
  The major version of the Servlet specification that the application is for.
- **`int getEffectiveMinorVersion()`**
  The minor version of the Servlet specification of application compatibility.
- **`int getMajorVersion()`**
  The major version of the Servlet API that this servlet container supports.
- **`int getMinorVersion()`**
  The minor version of the Servlet API that this servlet container supports.
- **`String getServerInfo()`**
  Returns the name and version of the servlet container on which the servlet is running.

Implementing Programmatic Registration

Until now we've seen what methods are available on `ServletContext` for performing dynamic registration and configuration of the application, but without regard to exactly when or how these methods can be invoked. There are in fact only two conditions under which the dynamic registration and configuration methods of `ContextServlet` may be invoked:

- From code (directly or indirectly) inside the `contextInitialized()` method of a registered `ServletContextListener`
- By an implementation of `javax.servlet.ServletContainerInitializer` interface which is declared with fully-qualified class name as a line inside the `/META-INF/services/javax.servlet.ServletContainerInitializer` file in an application library JAR

The first method is used for an application-specific initialisation process, whilst the latter provides modularity to allow a single JAR library to inject its own dynamic initialisation into any application in which it is used.

NOTE: The state of the application's container is frozen once all normal and (the above two) dynamic deployment sequences have been completed. If any of the registration/configuration methods are called on a `ServletContext` when it has already been fully initialized, it will throw an `IllegalStateException`. In addition, if you attempt to call any of the `ServletContext` registration/configuration methods from a `ServletContextListener` which has not been declared in `web.xml`, `web-fragment.xml` or using an annotation, an `UnsupportedOperationException` is thrown; this means that you cannot dynamically add a `ServletContextListener` which then attempts dynamic configuration or registration of other components.

Implementing the first method is simple, using our experience of the `ServletContextListener` implementation and listener configuration in the deployment descriptor or using annotations. This is an example using the `MyCtxtInitListener` I sketched out earlier, now implemented more completely:

```
package ext.domain;


import javax.servlet.*;
import java.util.*;
import javax.servlet.annotation.WebListener;

@WebListener
public class MyCtxtInitListener implements ServletContextListener {
  public void contextDestroyed(ServletContextEvent sce) {}
  public void contextInitialized(ServletContextEvent sce) {
    ServletContext sc = sce.getServletContext();
    /* Register a new filter */
    FilterRegistration.Dynamic r =
        sc.addFilter("AuthFilter","ext.domain.MyAuthFilter");

    /* Configure the filter - here with its mappings */
```

```
      EnumSet<DispatcherType> types = new EnumSet<DispatcherTypes>();
      types.add(DispatcherType.REQUEST);
      types.add(DispatcherType.FORWARD);
      r.addMappingForUrlPatterns(types,false,"*");
    }
  }
```

Using the second (JAR library) method requires that we create a class implementing `javax.servlet.ServletContainerInitializer` and its `onStartup()` method:

```
package ext.domain.startup;

import javax.servlet.*;
import java.util.*;

import javax.servlet.annotation.HandlesTypes;

public class MyLibraryInitializer
        implements ServletContainerInitializer {

  public void onStartup(java.util.Set<Class<?>> c, ServletContext sc) {
    /* Register a new filter */
    FilterRegistration.Dynamic r =
         sc.addFilter("AuthFilter","ext.domain.MyAuthFilter");

    /* Configure the filter - here with its mappings */
    EnumSet<DispatcherType> types = new EnumSet<DispatcherTypes>();
    types.add(DispatcherType.REQUEST);
    types.add(DispatcherType.FORWARD);
    r.addMappingForUrlPatterns(types,false,"*");
  }
}
```

This will then be configured in the JAR with the line:

```
ext.domain.startup.MyLibraryInitializer
```

in the following file in the JAR:

```
/META-INF/services/javax.servlet.ServletContainerInitializer
```

In the above example, we haven't used the first parameter of the `onStartup()` method at all. This is used in conjunction with the `@HandlesTypes` annotation to ask the container to pass us all `Class` types deployed into the application which match, implement or extend the classes supplied in the `@HandlesTypes` annotation. An example will make this easier to understand.

Let's suppose we want to dynamically register some `Filters` and `Servlets`, but don't want to hard code all their classes into either a `ServletContextListener` or a `ServletContainerInitializer`. One place to start is to create an interface which they can use to be dynamically inserted – let's create one for `Filters` and one for `Servlets` (assume these are in separate class files in the same package):

```
package ext.domain.dynamics;

public interface DynamicFilterInit {}
public interface DynamicServletInit {}
```

and then we'll make any of our dynamic components implement these interfaces:

```
package ext.domain;

import ext.domain.dynamics.DynamicFilterInit;
import javax.servlet.*;

public class MyAuthFilter implements Filter, DynamicFilterInit {
  // implement here
}
```

Then we can create a `ServletContainerInitializer` which dynamically registers this component. Except at the moment it doesn't know where to find all the implementing classes. But if we add the `DynamicFilterInit` interface class type with a `@HandlesTypes` annotation, the container will return all classes implementing this interface:

```
package ext.domain;

import ext.domain.dynamics.*;
import javax.servlet.*;
import javax.servlet.annotation.HandlesTypes;


@HandlesTypes({DynamicFilterInit,ServletFilterInit})
public class MyLibraryInitializer
    implements ServletContainerInitializer {

  public void onStartup(java.util.Set<Class<?>> c, ServletContext sc) {
    /* c is the Set of all classes found matching
     * the @HandlesTypes */
    int fcount=0; // counts number of dynamic filters added
    int scount=0; // counts number of dynamic servlets added
    for(Class k : c) {
      if(DynamicFilterInit.class.isAssignableFrom(k)) {
        /* This is a dynamic filter, register it */
        FilterRegistration.Dynamic r =
            sc.addFilter("DynFilter" + fcount,k);
        fcount++;
        // Can now use r to configure here
      } else if(ServletFilterInit.class.isAssignableFrom(k)) {
        /* This is a dynamic servlet, register it */
        ServletRegistration.Dynamic r =
            sc.addServlet("DynServlet" + scount,k);
        scount++;
        // Can now use r to configure
      }
    }
  }
}
```

The `@HandlesTypes` technique can be used with classes, interfaces or annotations which can be extended, implemented or used to annotated the actual implementation classes of interest. I'll leave it as an exercise to apply the above with an annotation! (Hint: use the `Class.getAnnotation()` method in the loop, and possible use the same general technique but with `Filter.class` and `Servlet.class` checks)

NOTE: The order in which classes are discovered is mandated by the order of the Web container's application `ClassLoader`. When examining the classes of an application to see if they match any of the criteria specified by the `HandlesTypes` annotation, the container may run into classloading problems if any of the application's optional JAR files are missing.

Revision Questions

1 **Which package contains the Java EE Web annotations?** **(choose one)**

- A javax.servlet
- B javax.annotations
- C javax.servlet.annotation
- D javax.servlet.annotations
- E javax.annotations.servlet

2 **In what way can an application deployer disable processing of annotations?** **(choose one)**

- A By adding the line "disable" to the file /META-INF/annotations to the application WAR.
- B By adding the element <annotations>false</annotations> in the <web-app> in the deployment descriptor.
- C By adding the attribute annotations="false" to the <web-app> element of the deployment descriptor.
- D By adding the attribute metadata-complete="true" to the <web-app> element of the deployment descriptor.
- E Do nothing – annotations are disabled by default.

3 **Which of the following are Java EE Web annotations?** **(choose two)**

- A @Servlet
- B @WebServlet
- C @WebListener
- D @Filter
- E @Asynchronous

4 **Which of these are true regarding annotations?** **(choose one)**

- A Annotations provide a more modular deployment model compared with the previous XML descriptor
- B Annotations require increased runtime processing
- C Annotations require additional time during application startup to process
- D Annotations take precedence over XML descriptor elements
- E The deployment descriptor has been completely replaced by annotations

5 **Which of these are valid ways to configure the URL mappings "/myservlet" and "/aservlet" to a single Servlet component?** **(choose one)**

- A @WebServlet("/myservlet","/aservlet")
- B @WebServlet(value={"/myservlet","/aservlet"})
- C @WebServlet(mappings={"/myservlet","/aservlet"})
- D @WebServlet(urlPatterns={"/myservlet","/aservlet"})
- E @WebServlet({"/myservlet","/aservlet"})

6 **Which of these configure two Servlet initialisation parameters param1 and param2 on the servlet mapped to URL /myservlet?** **(choose two)**

- A @WebServlet(urlPatterns="/myservlet",param1="value1",param2="value2")
- B @WebServlet(urlPatterns="/myservlet",
  params={param1="value1",param2="value2"})
- C @WebServlet(urlPatterns="/myservlet",
  initParams={param1="value1",param2="value2"})
- D @WebServlet(urlPatterns="/myservlet",initParams={
  @WebInitParam(param1="value1"),@WebInitParam(param2="value2")})
- E @WebServlet(urlPatterns="/myservlet",initParams={
  @WebInitParam(name="param1",value="value1"),
  @WebInitParam(name="param2",value="value2")})

7 **Which of these applied to a Filter will configure it to apply to the "/items/*" mapping for all incoming client requests only?** **(choose one)**

- A @WebFilter("/items/*")
- B @WebFilter("/items/*", dispatcherTypes=DispatcherType.REQUEST)
- C @WebFilter(urlPatterns="/items/*", dispatcherTypes=DispatcherType.REQUEST)
- D @WebFilter(urlPatterns="/items/*", type=DispatcherType.REQUEST)
- E @WebFilter("/items/*", DispatcherType.REQUEST)

8 **Which of the following are true regarding Web fragments?** **(choose one)**

- A All Web fragment XML files should be placed in the /WEB-INF/fragments/ directory in the application WAR
- B Web fragments are located in /META-INF/fragments/ directory in JARs
- C Web fragments override the application web.xml deployment descriptor
- D At most one fragment file can be deployed in the /META-INF/web-fragment.xml file inside a library JAR
- E Web fragments override configuration declared by annotations

11

9 **Examine the exhibit, which shows two web fragments and a section from a web.xml deployment descriptor. What is the result of deploying this descriptor along with the fragments?** **(choose one)**

EXHIBIT

- A The application successfully deploys and the context parameter AppName is set to "Third Party Application"
- B The application successfully deploys and the context parameter AppName is set to "My Application"
- C The application fails to deploy due to a circular fragment ordering reference
- D The application fails to deploy due to a conflicting <context-param> declaration
- E The application fails to deploy due to a syntax error in the fragment file(s).

10 **When the deployment descriptor (including any fragments) is inspected by the container, in what order are components configured (starting with the first group to be configured)?**

- A ServletContextListeners
- B HttpSessionListeners
- C ServletRequestListeners
- D Servlets
- E Filters
- F All other listeners

11

11 **Which class in the javax.servlet package provides methods for programmatic registration of servlets, filters and listeners?** **(choose one)**

- A ServletContext
- B ServletRequest
- C ServletRegistration
- D WebAppRegistration
- E ServletConfig

12 **Which of the following are methods used to programatically register a servlet named "MyServlet1" of class mypkg.MyServlet?** **(choose two)**

- A addServlet("MyServlet1","mypkg.MyServlet")
- B addServlet("mypkg.MyServlet","MyServlet1")
- C registerServlet("MyServlet1","mypkg.MyServlet")
- D registerServlet("MyServlet1",Class.forName("mypkg.MyServlet"))
- E addServlet("MyServlet1",Class.forName("mypkg.MyServlet"))
- F registerServlet(Class.forName("mypkg.MyServlet"),"MyServlet1")

13 **Which of these are correct ways to programmatically register a filter named "AuthFilter" of class mypkg.MyAuthFilter?** **(choose three)**

A addFilter("AuthFilter","mypkg.MyAuthFilter")

B addFilter("AuthFilter", new mypkg.MyAuthFilter())

C addFilter("AuthFilter", mypkg.MyAuthFilter.class)

D addFilter("AuthFilter", createFilter(mypkg.MyAuthFilter.class))

E addFilter("AuthFilter", createFilter("mypkg.MyAuthFilter"))

14 **Which of these are true regarding programmatic configuration?** **(choose two)**

A Only components registered programmatically can be configured programmatically.

B Servlets, Filters and Listeners can all be configured programmatically

C Only Servlets and Filters can be configured programmatically

D Regardless of whether components are registered declaratively or programmatically, all the same properties can be configured programmatically

E More properties can be configured programatically on components which are registered programmatically, than on components registered declaratively.

15 **Which of the following methods for servlet configuration are available on a ServletRegistration implementation?** **(choose two)**

A setInitParam(String name, String value)

B setInitParameter(String name, String value)

C addServletMapping(String pattern)

D addMappings(String... pattern)

E addMapping(String... patterns)

16 **Which of the following are methods on ServletContext?** **(choose one)**

A setDistributable(boolean)

B setContextParam(String,String)

C setInitParam(String,String)

D addRole(String)

E declareRoles(String...)

17 **Which of these method names (parameters omitted) for filter configuration are available on a FilterRegistration implementation?** **(choose one)**

- A addMapping
- B addUrlPatterns
- C addMappingForServletName
- D addMappingForUrlPatterns
- E removeMapping

Exhibits

Q.9

web.xml:

```
<absolute-ordering>
  <name>Fragment1</name>
</absolute-ordering>
```


web-fragment.xml in first JAR:

```
<web-fragment>
  <name>Fragment1</name>
  <ordering>
    <before>Fragment2</before>
  </ordering>
  <context-param>
    <param-name>AppName</param-name>
    <param-value>Third Party Application</param-value>
  </context-param>
</web-fragment>
```

web-fragment.xml in second JAR:

```
<web-fragment>
  <name>Fragment2</name>
  <context-param>
    <param-name>AppName</param-name>
    <param-value>My Application</param-value>
  </context-param>
</web-fragment>
```

Answers to Revision Questions

1 **Correct answer: C**

2 **Correct answer: D**

3 **Correct answers: B,D**

General rule: all component annotations start with @Web

4 **Correct answers: A,C**

Whilst using annotations requires more processing of classes during application startup, it doesn't impact on runtime CPU utilisation, so B is incorrect. D is incorrect as the deployment descriptor always takes precedence over annotations, and E is incorrect as there are many application properties (e.g. application ServletContext init-params) which can only be configured in the descriptor and not using annotations.

5 **Correct answers: B,D,E**

A is illegal annotation syntax (no array braces), and C uses a non-existent "mappings" element. E is a shortcut syntax for B when there are no other elements to be declared.

6 **Correct answer: E**

7 **Correct answers: A, C**

E and B are illegal annotation syntax, D uses an element "type" which doesn't exist.

8 **Correct answers: D,E**

A and B are incorrect as fragments are declared only (at most once) in library JARs, and must be in the /META-INF/web-fragment.xml file in the JAR. C is incorrect as the main application web.xml deployment descriptor always overrides both fragments and annotations; as the fragments are collectively merged to form the application descriptor, they will override annotations.

9 **Correct answer: A**

The <absolute-ordering> element in the web.xml takes precedence over any relative <ordering> in any of the fragments, and it also does not declare an <others /> element – therefore only Fragment1 will ever be examined. This sets the AppName context parameter to the "Third Party Application" value. If Fragment2 were also examined at any time, this would cause an error because a duplicate context param exists with a different value – in that case, D would have been the correct answer.

10 **Correct order: E,D,A,C,B,F**

11 **Correct answer: A**

D does not exist and whilst C does exist, this is actually used to configure a component already registered programmatically.

12 **Correct answers: A,E**

There are no registerServlet methods on the standard classes, and the class name or Class object is always the second argument, after the servlet's logical name.

13 **Correct answers: A,C,D**

B is syntactically correct (it would compile), but it is a wrong practise to instantiate a new instance of a container-managed implementation class directly – this will prevent the container from handling the class correctly, for example by processing resource injections . E is incorrect as the createFilter(), and createServlet(), methods only accept Class arguments and not qualified class name strings.

14 **Correct answers: C,E**

See Figure 11.1 – this shows that only Servlets and Filters can be configured; it also shows that "Dynamic" components (i.e. those registered programmatically) have sub-interfaces which expose further methods than the standard Registration interfaces – for example, the ability to set asynchronous behaviour and servlet security.

15 **Correct answers: B,E**

16 **Correct answers: C,E**

17 **Correct answer: D**

There are no methods to remove or override mappings for any servlet or filter components – once set, a mapping is read-only. This makes E immediately incorrect. Whilst A exists for servlets, it does not exist for filters. C looks like it should exist, but the actual method is pluralised – it is addMappingForServletNames (annoyingly, the ServletRegistration has the singular method addMapping despite taking multiple mapping arguments, but the FilterRegistration mapping methods which take multiple servlet names or URL patterns are of the form addMappingForXxxs ending with a plural!)

In this chapter you'll:

- Learn the fundamentals of resource injection and why it is useful
- Use injection to obtain database connections using Java Database Connectivity (JDBC) references
- Use injection to work with Enterprise JavaBeans (EJBs)
- Briefly use the Java Persistence Architecture (JPA) in example code

12 Resource Injection

At some point whilst working with Web applications you have probably needed to utilise resources like backend databases, an interface with Enterprise JavaBeans in a business logic tier, or a persistence framework as the middleware between your application and its storage.

In order to decouple the application code from the environment, this has always been achieved using the container's managed services – for example, rather than open an SQL database connection directly in the application by specifying the hostname, port, username, password and schema, the connection parameters will be configured by the System Administrator when creating the Java Web container. The container will then allow new connections based on these parameters to be obtained by applications using the Java Naming and Directory Interface (JNDI). The configuration of the resource in the environment is container-specific, but obtaining a handle on a resource available in the container always uses the same basic steps:

1. Create a new `javax.naming.InitialContext` object (it has a default constructor, or you can pass the constructor arguments to set up the context environment);
2. Call the `lookup()` method on the `InitialContext`, supplying the JNDI name of the resource to obtain a handle for;
3. For databases, the `lookup()` would return a `DataSource` object for the configured database, whilst when using EJBs it would return your bean reference.

Here is a code example showing the traditional "boilerplate" code required to get a `DataSource` for a Java Database Connectivity (JDBC) session:

```
public class MyCatalogueServlet extends HttpServlet {

  private javax.sql.DataSource bookdb;

  public void init() throws ServletException {
    /* To setup the DataSource, first get an InitialContext */
    InitialContext ctx = new javax.naming.InitialContext();

    /* Then lookup the connection we require. All Java EE container
     * JNDI names start with java:comp/env/ and then jdbc for JDBC.
     * Our JDBC data source is called bookdb, so...
     */
    bookdb = (javax.sql.DataSource) ctx.lookup("java:comp/env/jdbc/bookdb");
```

```
    }

    public void doCatalogueSearch(String query) {
      /* Open database connection using the DataSource */
      java.sql.Connection conn = bookdb.getConnection();
      try {
        // now execute a query on the conn
      } catch(java.io.IOException ioe) {
        // handle the exception
      } finally {
        /* Clean up */
        try {
          conn.close();
        } catch(Exception e) {}
      }
    }
  }
```

For this to work it also requires a resource mapping to be set in the deployment descriptor:

```
<resource-ref>
    <description>Book Catalogue DataSource</description>
    <res-ref-name>jdbc/bookdb</res-ref-name>
    <res-type>javax.sql.DataSource</res-type>
    <res-auth>Container</res-auth>
</resource-ref>
```

12

A similar technique is used to inject Enterprise JavaBean (EJB) components – for example a session bean:

```
<ejb-ref>
  <ejb-ref-name>ejb/catalogueBean</ejb-ref-name>
  <ejb-ref-type>Session</ejb-ref-type>
  <ejb-ref-home>ext.domain.ejbs.HomeInterface</ejb-ref-home>
  <ejb-ref-remote>ext.domain.ejbs.RemoteInterface</ejb-ref-
remote>
</ejb-ref>
```

and then a `ctx.lookup("java:comp/env/ejb/catalogueBean")` will return the bean reference.

The "boilerplate" code in the `lookupDatasource()` method and in the deployment descriptor are required for each application/library and data resource, respectively, in order for the application to obtain access to those resources. Using annotations, we can replace all of that with just one line of code! This resource injection can be used on `javax.servlet.Servlet` classes, `javax.servlet.Filter` implementations, `javax.servlet.jsp.tagext.JspTag` implementations, or any classes implementing the listeners declared in the *Listener Annotations* section earlier in this chapter (including `AsyncListener`).

Let's find out how...

Resource Annotations

After such a build up, the actual use of resource injection is as simple as just adding the `@Resource` annotation (an import of `javax.annotation.Resource` or the entire package is required) :

```
@Resource(name="jdbc/bookdb")
private javax.sql.DataSource bookdb;
```

The container then has everything it needs by default:

- We've specified that the JNDI name to use for the lookup is "jdbc/bookdb". This is appended to the `java:comp/env/` namespace to give the full `java:comp/env/jdbc/bookdb`.
- The type of the variable is `javax.sql.DataSource` – this tells the container the type of injected object required, here that we're expecting an SQL database. The container will coerce the object obtained from JNDI to the `DataSource` type.
- The default behaviour for the authentication (`<res-auth>`) is `container`, so we don't need to change this.

So in our earlier `MyCatalogueServlet` class, we can do away with the `init()` implementation and just have:

12

```
package ext.domain;

import javax.servlet.http.HttpServlet;
import javax.annotation.Resource;

public class MyCatalogueServlet extends HttpServlet {

  @Resource(name="jdbc/bookdb")
  private javax.sql.DataSource bookdb;

  public void doCatalogueSearch(String query) {
    /* Open database connection using the DataSource */
    java.sql.Connection conn = bookdb.getConnection();
    try {
      // now execute a query on the conn
    } catch(java.io.IOException ioe) {
      // handle the exception
    } finally {
      /* Clean up */
      try {
        conn.close();
      } catch(Exception e) {}
    }
  }
}
```

and there is no need for any deployment descriptor configuration either! Should you need to configure any explicit parameters, these can be done directly using the annotation's elements:

```
@Resource (
  String description="",
  String name="",
  String mappedName="",
  Class type=Object.class,
  Resource.AuthenticationType authentication=CONTAINER,
  boolean shareable=true
)
```

The description is just for informational purposes – and is usually omitted. The other parameters are:

- **`String name`**
  The JNDI name of the resource being injected, appended to `java:comp/env/` so you should not include that. The default is the fully-qualified class name followed by a `/` followed by the variable name or JavaBeans property name (if the annotation is on a method). For example, if we omitted the name from the previous example, it would have defaulted to `ext.domain.MyCatalogueServlet/bookdb` - so the full JNDI name would be `java:comp/env/ext.domain.MyCatalogueServlet/bookdb`. If the annotation is supplied on a class, this element must be supplied as there is no sensible default available in that case.

12

- **`Class type`**
  The class type of resource being injected. For variables and methods, this defaults to the type and first (and only) parameter type respectively. For an annotation on a class, this must be supplied as there is no sensible default in that case.

- **`Resource.AuthenticationType authentication`**
  This establishing the authentication settings source for the resource. The `AuthenticationType` enumeration allows either `CONTAINER` (the default) or `APPLICATION`.

- **`boolean shareable`**
  The default is `true` – set this to `false` if the injected resource is a connection factory which you do not want to share between different components in the same application.

- **`String mappedName`**
  If your container uses a different JNDI name for the resource, this is the name as assigned in the container. For example, the default database in the Glassfish server is called `jdbc/__default` – so you could use that as the `mappedName`

but still use jdbc/bookdb as the application's JNDI name.

Whilst the mappedName allows for some decoupling of application from deployment environment, it is not practical to code that into your application's bytecode (other than as a default value for a single server type you'll be deploying into). For that reason, it is more common to omit the mappedName element and instead create a deployment descriptor fragment like:

```
<resource-ref>
   <res-ref-name>jdbc/bookdb</res-ref-name>
   <jndi-name>jdbc/__default</jndi-name>
</resource-ref>
```

which is then deployed along with the application on a container-specific basis. You could have several versions of the fragment which can be included for different target vendor's containers, all without modifying the application's codebase.

In our example above we have used JDBC database (pool) injection. However, using @Resource we can reference any of the following types of resources (with their equivalent deployment descriptor elements shown):

- A data source (<resource-ref>)
- A Java Messaging Service (JMS) destination (<message-destination-ref> or <env-ref>)
- An environment entry (<resource-env-ref>)

12

The annotation can be specified on a class, method or (most commonly, as above) field. The injection will always be completed before the class is instantiated for the first time; moreover the visibility of the method or field is irrelevant – it can be private and the container can still successfully inject the resource.

The @Resource annotation can be used on a field (class scoped variable), method or on the class itself. We've seen what happens when applying to a field already. If applied to a method, that method must follow the JavaBean setter convention (named setXxx, with a single argument and a void return type) but can have any visibility. For example, we could have declared the following in the MyCatalogueServlet class above:

```
package ext.domain;

public class MyCatalogueServlet {
  // No annotation here
  private DataSource bookdb;

  // Instead we've put it on the setter:
  @Resource(name="jdbc/bookdb")
  private void setBookdb(DataSource ds) {
    this.bookdb = ds;
  }
```

```
    // rest of class
}
```

Again, all elements of the `@Resource` annotation are optional, as the container can infer them from the structure of the setter method. The default JNDI name is the fully-qualified class name followed by a `/` and then the JavaBean name derived from the setter method following standard conventions (drop the `set` and then make the first letter lower case unless the second letter is also upper case in which instance the case of all letters is preserved – for example `setMyProperty()` has JavaBean name `myProperty` but `setURL()` has name `URL`). For example, if we were to omit the `name` element in the above, the element would default to name `ext.domain.MyCatalogueServlet/bookdb` and so the full JNDI name to lookup would be:

```
java:comp/env/ext.domain.MyCatalogueServlet/bookdb
```

NOTE: The JavaDoc API for the `@Resource` annotation actually states about the name element: *"For field annotations, the default is the field name. For method annotations, the default is the JavaBeans property name corresponding to the method."* This is misleading, as JSR-250 is the original specification for the resource annotations, and section 2.3 states that *"the default value of the name element is the field name qualified by the class name. When applied on a method, the default is the JavaBeans property name corresponding to the method qualified by the class name."* Unfortunately this has led to some confusion with a select few containers following the misleading JavaDoc API and dropping the default fully-qualified class name, whilst others implement JSR-250 as intended. For reasons of consistency, I strongly recommend including the name element at all opportunities in your `@Resource` annotations, to ensure you get consistent and obvious results across all platforms.

12

Finally, you can declare `@Resource` on a class itself. In this case it is used to flag what dependencies your class has on external resources, but the actual lookup of those resources must be performed by your class implementation at runtime – using the `InitialContext` and JNDI lookup mechanisms we discussed earlier. Whilst this removes the need for the deployment descriptor elements, it still leaves us with the "boilerplate" code required to do the lookup, and therefore is less popular than the field or method injections, except if you require special handling of the JNDI lookup (for example, assigning one of several injection possibilities to a class field, depending on runtime conditions). You may therefore want to declare several dependencies at the class level – since annotations can only be applied once per class/field/method, the `@Resources` annotation is a special wrapper used at the class level to contain an array of `@Resource` annotations. Here's an example:

```
@Resources ({
  @Resource(name="myMessageQueue" type=javax.jms.ConnectionFactory),
  @Resource(name="myMailSession", type=javax.mail.Session)
})
public class MyServlet extends HttpServlet {
  // implementation
}
```

In line with common sense, `@Resources` can only be declared on a class and not a field or method.

Lifecycle Callbacks

As mentioned earlier, resource injection of dependencies occurs before a new object of the class is instantiated. However, you may want to be able to run initialisation code after a resource is injected and then run destruction code before an injection is removed from the object (which only happens when the object itself is being garbage collected).

One way to do this at initialisation is to use a JavaBean setter method and implement the initialisation code for each injection there; for example:


```
@Resource(name="jdbc/bookdb")
private void setBookdb(DataSource ds) {
  this.bookdb = ds;
  // initialisation of this.bookdb goes here
}
```

However, there is no way to clean up during destruction – the basic `Object finalize()` method may be too late in the lifecycle to be useful before injected resources are removed.

An alternative approach exists in the form of `@PostConstruct` and `@PreDestroy` annotations which can be attached to any method following these rules:

- **Return type:** void
- **Thrown checked exceptions:** none
- **Visibility:** any
- **Static:** not permitted (except for an application client)
- **Final:** permitted (optional)
- **Parameters:** none (except for an EJB interceptor, which can take an optional `InvocationContext` argument)

If an unchecked exception is thrown by the method, then the object must not be placed into service (with the exception of an EJB which can handle and recover from exceptions).

Applying these is simple – create your method(s) and apply the annotations. For example:

```
@PostConstruct
private void initInjection() {
  // implement initialisation
}

@PreDestroy
private void removeInjection() {
  // implement destruction
}
```

Simple!

Specific Resource Annotations

In addition to the JDBC and JMS examples used earlier, there are two specific cases of resource injection the newer exams require studying: that of integration with Enterprise JavaBeans (EJBs) and use of the Java Persistence Architecture (JPA).

EJB Annotations

If you are programming in a full Java EE Web server such as Glassfish (as opposed to Tomcat which is just a Web container) then you may be implementing your business logic in Enterprise JavaBeans (EJBs). Like the Web container, the EJB container provides a managed services framework which can help us deploy complex server-side functionality faster. EJBs can be invoked directly in client-side desktop applications and/or you can provide a Web interface by utilising servlets and JSPs in the Web container.

A more detailed discussion of EJBs is outside the scope of this book and exam. However, the annotations required to get a handle on EJB components and use these in your Web applications is of importance. Let's suppose you have an EJB called `ext.domain.ejb.BookCatalogueBean` with a business interface `ext.domain.ejb.BookCatalogue`. The code required to access this bean in your Web components is (also required is an import of the `javax.ejb.EJB` annotation):

```
@EJB
private ext.domain.ejb.BookCatalogue catalogue;
```

This will then inject a reference to the `BookCatalogueBean` component in the remote EJB container, assuming that the EJB is exported with the name `catalogue` (under the standard `java:comp/env/` JNDI namespace). The configuration is:

```
@EJB (
  String description="",
  Class beanInterface=Object.class,
  String name="",
  String beanName="",
  String mappedName="",
)
```

The final four are the most important. The `beanInterface` is simply the business interface type for the EJB component – unless you are declaring `@EJB` on a class, you will never need to use this as it is inferred from the field type or setter method parameter. The three naming elements are:

- **`String name`**
  The logical name of the EJB reference to use within the component's JNDI environment (the value of this name is appended to `java:comp/env/`). This is the equivalent of the `<ejb-ref-name>` in the `web.xml` deployment descriptor. The default value is the fully-qualified class name along with the field or method name.

- **`String beanName`**
  The EJB name of the bean being referenced. This is configured in EJB either using the `<ejb-name>` EJB deployment descriptor element, or by using the `name` elements of the `@Stateless` or `@Stateful` annotations on those beans – for example, if you deployed a stateless bean using `@Stateless(name="myBean")` then you would use `myBean` as the `beanName` element value too. This is the equivalent of the `web.xml` `<ejb-link>` element.

- **`String mappedName`**
  This is a container vendor/product specific mapping and therefore is usually omitted.

As `@Resource` has `@Resources`, so multiple `@EJB` annotations at the class level can be injected using an `@EJBs` wrapper annotation:

```
@EJBs ({
  @EJB(name="ejb/catalogue",
       beanInterface=ext.domain.ejb.BookCatalogue),
  @EJB(name="ejb/warehouse",
       beanInterface=ext.domain.ejb.DistributorWarehouses)
})
public class MyServlet extends HttpServlet {
  // implementation
}
```

As with dependent resources, when applied to a class the EJBs will still need to be looked up using JNDI (at `java:comp/env/ejb/catalogue` and `java:comp/`

12

`env/ejb/warehouse`) in the servlet implementation code, but they will not need to be declared in the deployment descriptor.

Persistence (JPA) Annotations

In the common three tier model-view-controller (MVC) application design, the model is usually composed of two parts: the object code which represents the structure, and the data storage component which makes that data persistent between requests and reloads of the Web container. One such way to build this is using Enterprise JavaBeans in the EJB container – and to use the annotations previously discussed to inject these beans into your Web application.

For simpler Web applications, use of EJBs may be adding unnecessary complexity, and you may prefer to deploy an application which requires only a Web container (such as Tomcat or Jetty) without the overheads of a full EE application server.

The **Java Persistence Architecture** (**JPA**) is an API which allows you to easily load and save object models into persistent storage – typically an SQL database – without writing SQL statements and maintaining SQL-object property mappings. The JPA is an involved API in itself, to the extent that it has a study path and exam of its own: Oracle Certified Expert Java EE 6 Java Persistence API Developer. We will therefore not look at JPA in any depth, but the exam does require us to "understand the fundamentals of JPA". We'll do this by writing a very simple persistent object (called a JPA **Entity**) and writing the Servlet code to load, manipulate and store that object.

12

We shall build a very simple food shopping catalogue model and a `Servlet` which does a lookup for a given barcode (as though it had been scanned at the checkout), returns the total price of the item, modifies the unit price and stores the modified object back into the SQL database.

```
import javax.persistence.*;

// this annotation sets up the Entity name to reference later
@Entity(name="FoodItem")
// this annotation sets the SQL table name and a unique key
@Table(name="food_items",
   uniqueConstraints=@UniqueConstraint(columnNames={"barcode"})
)
public class FoodItem {
  @Id // signifies this class property is the primary key
  @Column(name="uid") // set SQL field (default is variable name)
  // set method for auto key generation for inserts
  @GeneratedValue(strategy = GenerationType.AUTO)
  private long id;
  @Column(name="unit_weight")
  private float unitWeight;
```

Table 12.1 Example SQL Table Structure

Field Name	Field Type	Notes
uid	BIGINT UNSIGNED	Auto-incrementing primary key
barcode	CHAR(12)	12-digit UPC barcode number; unique
category	VARCHAR(32)	E.g. "vegetables" or "pet food"
name	VARCHAR(128)	
unit_weight	DECIMAL(9,4)	In kg (to four decimal places)
unit_price	DECIMAL(9,4)	In GBP per unit_weight (to four decimal places)

```
    @Column(name="unit_price")
    private float unitPrice;

    // All of these will be persisted with column names
    // matching their variable names:
    private String barcode;
    private String category;
    private String name;

    // Standard getters and setters
    /* This method calculates the price for a given weight */
    public float calculatePrice(float weight) {
      return (unit_price * weight / unit_weight);
    }
}
```


Based on this we also need an SQL table called `food_items` in a database, and it needs a structure similar to that in Table 12.1.

Some container configuration then needs to be done, in the form of configuration of a JPA `persistence.xml` file. This is quite involved, and depends on the JPA implementation you are using (for example, OpenJPA or Hibernate), and therefore the specifics are beyond the scope of this book. Through this configuration you would aim to:

- Create a persistence unit and give it a name – this unit is used to manage all persistence requirements, and the name is used to inject the management functionality into our Web application code, just like a `@Resource` can inject a `DataSource`. In this example we'll name this `FoodPersistenceUnit`.
- Choose a provider implementation, for example OpenJPA, by specifying the

fully-qualified provider class name.

- List provider-specific properties such as SQL driver class, database server hostname, username, password and the schema name into which tables and data will be populated.
- List all classes which you want the persistence unit to manage – these classes should be annotated with `@Entity` as we have done in our example.

With that configured, we can then write our `Servlet` component. The steps are:

1. Get hold of the persistence unit configured above – this will be injected as an `EntityManagerFactory` into our `Servlet` by the container using the `@PersistenceUnit` annotation.
2. Use the injected factory to obtain an `EntityManager` on a per-request basis – this will allow us to load/store our `Entity` from/to persistent storage.
3. Issue a query on the `EntityManager` to lookup the actual `Entity` object we want to find.
4. Perform a calculation to get the total price of the item.
5. Update the item's `unit_price` and submit it back to the database.
6. Close the `EntityManager` to clean-up open database connections etc.

12

Using these steps as a guide, this is the code:

```
import javax.servlet.*;
import javax.persistence.*;

@WebServlet(name="TestItemServlet", urlPatterns={"/items/food"})
public class MyItemServlet extends GenericServlet {

  // This annotation causes container to inject the
  // correct object into emf
  @PersistenceUnit(unitName="FoodPersistenceUnit")
  private EntityManagerFactory emf;

  public void service(ServletRequest req, ServletResponse resp)
             throws IOException {
    // Create the EntityManager for this request
    EntityManager em = emf.createEntityManager();

    // The query string parameter "s" contains a search term
    String searchString = req.getParameter("s");

    // Lookup the Entity we require using the JPA query
    // syntax (similar to SQL). This does a search for a
    // matching unique ID or barcode number. Note we use
    // parameter substitution which eliminates need to escape
    // the query string
    Query q =
```

```
      em.query("SELECT x FROM FoodItem x WHERE x.id=?1 OR x.barcode=?1");
    q.setParameter(1,searchString);

    // Execute the query
    List<FoodItem> items = (List<FoodItem>) q.getResultList();
    if(items.size()>0) {
      FoodItem item = items.get(0);
      Writer w = resp.getWriter();
      w.print("Pricing for " . item.getName() . " is currently: ");
      // prints current price for 4.5kg of this item
      resp.getWriter().println(item.calculatePrice(4.5));
      // prints current price for 4.5kg of this item

      // Update the item in the usual way, using a
      // setter method to add 10%
      item.setUnitPrice(item.getUnitPrice()*1.1);
      // Save the object with the change back into its storage
      em.persist(item);
    }

    // Clean-up the EntityManager
    em.flush(); // ensure changes are synchronised with database
    em.close(); // close open SQL connections
  }
}
```

Once deployed, assuming there is an object in your database with the ID 12345, then you can call this `Servlet` like `/items/food?s=12345` to query, load, update and persist the JPA managed object.

12

In this example we've used a `@PersistenceUnit` annotation to resource-inject an `EntityManagerFactory` into the servlet. There are other ways to achieve the same goal – for example, this annotation won't inject the factory instance directly, but it will make it available via JNDI lookup:

```
// The name element is the JNDI context lookup name
@PersistenceUnit(name="persistence/FoodUnit",
                 unitName="FoodPersistenceUnit")
public class TestServlet extends GenericServlet {

  private EntityManagerFactory emf;

  public void init() {
    Context ctx = InitialContext().lookup("java:comp/env");
    // The JNDI lookup name must match the name element
    // of @ PersistenceUnit
    emf = (EntityManagerFactory) ctx.lookup("persistence/FoodUnit");
  }

  public void service(HttpServletRequest req, HttpServletResponse resp)
            throws IOException {
    // Implementation as before
  }
}
```

When declared in this fashion, the `@PersistenceUnits` annotation can be used to specify multiple `@PersistenceUnit` annotations on the same class.

There is also a `@PersistenceContext` annotation which can be used to inject a new `EntityManager` directly, without the requirement to obtain it from an `EntityManagerFactory`. Sounds easy? Sure... except there's a huge "gotcha"! Suppose you used the annotation like this:

```
public class MyServlet extends GenericServlet {
  @PersistenceContext(unitName="FoodPersistenceUnit")
  private EntityManager em;

  public void service(ServletRequest req, ServletResponser resp)
              throws IOException {
    FoodItem item = new FoodItem();
    item.setName("New product");
    em.persist(item);
  }
}
```

On the surface this looks great – much reduced code and it gets the job done. The "gotcha" is when you start to get significant traffic and concurrent requests. Because servlets aren't thread safe, multiple threads can be executing the `service()` method at the same time. In this case, this means sharing the single `em` `EntityManager` reference between all of those concurrent request threads. But the JPA specifications also state that `EntityManager` aren't guaranteed to be thread safe, so multiple threads all acting on the same `em` object is a recipe for trouble.

In short, you should *never* use this design in your multi-threaded applications. You can however, use JNDI injection to get hold of an `EntityManager` within a single request thread – usually in the `service()` method or any delegate like the `doXxx()` methods – like this:

```
@PersistenceContext(name="persistence/FoodManager",
                    unitName="FoodPersistenceUnit")
public class MyServlet extends GenericServlet {

  public void service(ServletRequest req, ServletResponser resp)
              throws IOException {
    Context envCtx = InitialContext().lookup("java:comp/env");
    // This is now safe as the same instance isn't
    // shared between request threads
    EntityManager em =
        (EntityManager) envCtx.lookup("persistence/FoodManager");
    FoodItem item = new FoodItem();
    item.setName("New product");
    em.persist(item);
  }
}
```

Finally, multiple `@PersistenceContext` annotations can be added to the class by wrapping them in a `@PersistenceContexts` annotation.

This was a brief introduction into the power of the Java Persistence Architecture from the perspective of Web applications, demonstrating how to set up a basic model and then obtain references to the persistence environment to query, load and save that model.

Revision Questions

1 **Which annotation can be used to inject a JDBC database connection into a Web application component?** **(choose one)**

- A javax.servlet.DatabaseConnection
- B java.sql.Connection
- C javax.sql.DataSource
- D javax.annotation.Resource
- E javax.servlet.InjectedResource

2 **A JDBC resource is injected with name "jdbc/MyConnection". What is the full name used in the JNDI lookup for that resource?** **(choose one)**

- A java:jdbc/MyConnection
- B java:comp/jdbc/MyConnection
- C java:env/jdbc/MyConnection
- D java:comp/env/jdbc/MyConnection
- E java:jndi/env/jdbc/MyConnection

12

3 **Study the exhibit. Which of the following statements is true?** **(choose one)**

EXHIBIT

- A The JDBC DataSource at JNDI path java:comp/env/ext.domain.web.MyServlet/dbConn is injected
- B The JDBC DataSource at JNDI path java:comp/env/jdbc/dbConn is injected
- C A compilation error occurs as @Resource is missing the name attribute
- D A deployment error occurs as @Resource is missing the name attribute
- E A compilation error occurs within the service() method

4 **Study the exhibit. Which of the statements are true?** **(choose two)**

EXHIBIT

- A The JDBC DataSource at JNDI path java:comp/env/jdbc/GroupDB is injected
- B The JDBC DataSource at JNDI path java:comp/env/GroupDB is injected
- C A deployment error occurs as @Resource is missing the name attribute
- D A deployment descriptor <resource-ref> must be supplied to map the "GroupDB" name against an existing container JNDI reference
- E A deployment descriptor <resource-ref> should be used in preference to mappedName

5 Study the exhibit. You should assume the remainder of the deployment descriptor is configured correctly so the component will be loaded and made available within the Web application, and that only the JDBC resource jdbc/containerDB is configured. Which is true when deploying and running the component? **(choose one)**

EXHIBIT

- A The JDBC DataSource at JNDI path java:comp/env/jdbc/appDB is injected
- B The JDBC DataSource at JNDI path java:comp/env/jdbc/containerDB is injected
- C A deployment error occurs as @Resource is missing the name attribute
- D A deployment error occurs as jdbc/containerDB is not declared using the mappedName element of the @Resource annotation
- E None of the above

6 Study the exhibit. Which of the following statements is true? **(choose one)**

EXHIBIT

- A The JDBC DataSource at JNDI path java:comp/env/jdbc/dbConn is injected into the dbConn class property
- B The JDBC DataSource at JNDI path java:comp/env/jdbc/Database is injected into the dbConn class property
- C The JDBC DataSource at JNDI path java:comp/env/mypkg.MyServlet/dbConn is injected into the dbConn class property
- D The JDBC DataSource at JNDI path java:comp/env/mypkg.MyServlet/Database is injected into the dbConn class property
- E A deployment error occurs because the setDatabase method doesn't have public visibility
- F None of the above

7 The @PostConstruct and @PreDestroy annotations can be used to perform processing after injection and before releasing of resources, respectively. Which of the following are true about the methods to which these annotations can be attached? **(choose three)**

- A The methods will be executed once for each resource injection annotation declared on the class (e.g. for 3 injections, the methods are invoked 3 times).
- B The @PostConstruct and @PreDestroy methods will be executed only once, at the point all injection has completed or when de-injection occurs respectively.
- C The methods must be declared public
- D The methods must be declared final
- E The methods must not throw any exceptions
- F The methods must return void

8 **Which annotation is used to inject references to Enterprise JavaBean components?** **(choose one)**

A javax.annotation.JavaBean

B javax.annotation.EJB

C javax.entity.EJB

D javax.ejb.EJB

E javax.ejb.JavaBean

9 **When constructing a class for which the storage is to be managed by the Java Persistence API (JPA), what annotation should be applied to the class?** **(choose two)**

A javax.annotation.JPABean

B javax.entity.PersistentBean

C javax.persistence.Entity

D javax.jpa.PersistentEntity

E javax.jpa.PersistentBean

10 **When injecting Java Persistence into a container-managed component such as a servlet or filter, which of the following annotations applied to a class, method or class field can be used for the injection (you should assume the appropriate package has been imported in each case)?** **(choose one)**

A @PersistenceContext

B @EntityManager

C @PersistentUnit

D @PersistenceUnits

E @EntityManagerFactory

11 **Which of the following statements are true about JPA resource injection when the annotation is applied to a class field in a servlet or filter?** **(choose one)**

A @PersistenceContext injects an EntityManagerFactory

B @PersistenceContext injects an EntityManager

C @PersistenceUnit injects an EntityManagerFactory

D @PersistenceUnit injects an EntityManager

E An EntityManagerFactory provides for thread-safety when using JPA queries (load) and persistence (save) across multiple requests.

F An EntityManager provides for thread-safety when using JPA queries (load) and persistence (save) across multiple requests.

12 **Which of the following are annotations used with JPA persistent objects?** **(choose one)**

- A @Entity
- B @Key
- C @Field
- D @Column
- E @Table

Exhibits

Q.3

```
package ext.domain.web;
import javax.servlet.*;

public class MyServlet extends GenericServlet {
  @Resource
  javax.sql.DataSource dbConn;

  public void service(ServletRequest req, ServletResponse resp)
    throws ServletException {
     try {
       java.sql.Connection c = dbConn.getConnection();
    } catch(SQLException sqle) {
       throw new ServletException(sqle);
    }
  }
}
```

Q.4

```
package ext.domain.web;
import javax.servlet.*;

public class MyServlet extends GenericServlet {
  @Resource(mappedName="GroupDB")
  javax.sql.DataSource dbConn;

  public void service(ServletRequest req, ServletResponse resp) {}
}
```

Q.5

Servlet:

```
package ext.domain.web;
import javax.servlet.*;

public class MyServlet extends GenericServlet {
  @Resource
  javax.sql.DataSource appDB;

  public void service(ServletRequest req, ServletResponse resp) {}
}
```

Deployment Descriptor:

```
<resource-ref>
  <res-ref-name>jdbc/appDB</res-ref-name>
  <jndi-name>jdbc/containerDB</jndi-name>
</resource-ref>
```

Q.6

```
package ext.domain.web;
import javax.servlet.*;

public class MyServlet extends GenericServlet {
  javax.sql.DataSource dbConn;

  @Resource
  protected void setDatabase(DataSource dbConn) {
    this.dbConn = dbConn;
  }

  public void service(ServletRequest req, ServletResponse resp) {}
}
```

Answers to Revision Questions

1 **Correct answer: D**

The @Resource annotation is used as a generic annotation to inject a variety of external connections. Note that C is the class of object injected for a JDBC database, but is not the annotation itself.

2 **Correct answer: D**

This path is standard across Java EE and is constructed from the parts: "java:" being the basic URL scheme, "comp" meaning "[Java EE] component", "env" meaning "environment-related binding" and then "jdbc" referring to the JDBC API. The "java:comp/env/" prefix is standard across Java EE; other recommended sub-contexts include "ejb" for EJBs, "jms" for JMS, "persistence" for Java Persistence API (JPA), "mail" and "url" for the connection factories of JavaMail and URLs respectively. These sub-contexts are conventional but not enforced.

3 **Correct answer: A**

If the name and mappedName attributes of @Resource are omitted, the default JNDI lookup path is the fully-qualified class name, then / followed by the variable name.

4 **Correct answers: B,E**

The effect of mappedName is to reference container-native JNDI bindings. In general this makes the application component tightly bound to the container in which it is deployed, and making a change to the JNDI name means re-writing and re-compiling code. The better solution is to use an application logical name (the name element of @Resource) and then to map the container's JNDI binding declaratively using a deployment descriptor/fragment.

5 **Correct answer: E**

The @Resource doesn't include the "name" attribute; this means it's default name is the fully-qualified class name, then /, then the variable name – i.e. "ext.domain.web.MyServlet/appDB". So this immediately makes options A and C incorrect. Likewise, mappedName is not a required element of @Resource and the deployment descriptor syntax shown in the exhibit is used instead of mappedName – so D is incorrect. If we had specified @Resource(name="jdbc/appDB") - which would be the usual approach - then B would be correct, as the deployment descriptor maps the application's logical name jdbc/appDB to the jdbc/containerDB JNDI name which we know exists (we are told in the question). However, as the default name of "ext.domain.web.MyServlet/appDB" neither exists in the JNDI context nor is mapped to another JNDI name in the deployment descriptor, an injection failure will result, usually in the way of a javax.naming.NamingException during deployment.

6 **Correct answer: F**

E is incorrect as the setter method can have any visibility. When @Resource doesn't have the name element, the default value is constructed from the fully-qualified class name, then /, then the JavaBean property name of the method – in this case, "database" with a lower-case first letter. This would make the injected JNDI name "java:comp/env/ mypkg.MyServlet/database". So the closest (almost correct) answer is D, but as JNDI names are case-sensitive, it is incorrect.

7 **Correct answers: B,E,F**

Note that C is incorrect: the methods can be any visibility, and D is incorrect as the methods may be declared final but this is not a requirement (as implied by "must"). Other rules: methods must not be declared static, and they must not take any parameters (except for an EJB interceptor).

8 **Correct answer: D**

9 **Correct answer: C**

10 **Correct answer: A**

B and E are the names of interfaces, of which implementations are the objects being injected into the managed components. C is nearly correct – it should be PersistenceUnit. D is an existing annotation, but it can only be applied to a class, and not to a method or field (it makes no sense to inject multiple resources in those cases).

11 **Correct answers: B,C,E**

Note in particular the discussion at the end of the chapter about how EntityManager is not thread-safe when making queries/persists on multiple objects in different threads (as requests are executed in separate threads, this applies to servlets and filters).

12 **Correct answers: A,D,E**

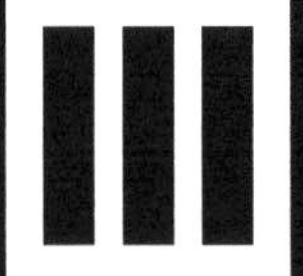

PART 3

JavaServer Pages

Chapter Overview

In this chapter you'll:

- Learn what JavaServer Pages are and how they fit into a Web application.
- Understand the JSP lifecycle.
- Use the four key scripting elements: directives, declarations, expressions and scriptlets.
- Memorise the implicit objects used in expressions and scriptlets.
- Use the PageContext API to obtain information about the environment in which a JSP is deployed.

13 JSP Basics

The Java EE Servlet technology, which we've looked at up to this point, gives us the ability to program any Web-based application we could possibly ever require. Using the Servlet API, we can interpret requests, perform processing and request servicing by connecting to databases and making business logic decisions, and ultimately return the requested information via the API's response mechanisms. Servlet technology also allows us to communicate between applications, make effective use of HTTP sessions, and implement security in a declarative manner. So what's missing from this seemingly complete platform?

Nothing is so much missing, as we've been given *too much* power and flexibility that most applications do not require. Servlets allow all types of data, including images and proprietary bytecode file formats to be returned as well as the more common textual data types such as plain text, HTML and XML. For the majority of applications, where it is a textual format that is to be returned, servlets are overkill. Consider how each line of returned data would have to be written in a servlet for a dynamic HTML page:

```
Writer out = response.getWriter();
out.write("<html>\n<head>\n<title>");
out.write(title);
out.write("</title>\n<body>");
out.write(someBodyString);
out.write("</body>\n</html>");
```

For a page which actually outputs very little content, this amount of code is certainly excessive. It isn't easy to see what's going on with the returned data, and would make code modification very difficult indeed. If you're working in a development team, where the division of labour is such that page authoring and server-side programming are handled separately, then those working with HTML code are not likely to understand all of the above Java syntax; if servlets had to be used for every component in a Web application, there would be few extensible applications, and everyone on the team would have to understand both Java and HTML to work together.

Introduction

There is a saviour: the creators of the Java EE platform realised that having servlets as the only technology presented serious disadvantages, least of all those listed above.

They therefore created **JavaServer Pages™** (**JSP**) technology, which allows for components to be written as though they are HTML pages, XML documents or plain text files, but with embedded Java code at relevant points in the page. This complements the servlet model, whereby everything is written in Java code with only some embedded HTML/XML.

The servlet technology interoperates completely with JSPs (and vice versa), so you should always use the more appropriate of the two for each component in an application. The decision is thus: does a component require a lot of Java processing code with very little returned text, or is that component concentrated largely on the textual return, with some inherent logic? If the former is true, then you should use servlets; if the latter describes your situation better, then use JSPs.

Codeless JSP Pages

The most basic JSP page is one which contains no Java code whatsoever! In fact, this is just a normal document returned as a response without any further processing. For example:

```
<html>
  <head>
    <title>A Codeless JSP Page</title>
  </head>
  <body>
    This page contains no Java code!
  </body>
</html>
```


Alternatively, an XML document might be returned:

```
<?xml version="1.0" ?>
<catalogue>
  <item>
    <name>SCWCD Study Companion</name>
    <author>Charles Lyons</author>
  </item>
</catalogue>
```

You may be asking what use a JSP page without any Java code is, when a static document could be used instead. Of course, the power of JSPs does not lie in their ability to return static content, but these examples merely illustrate that they can, and most often do, consist of largely non-Java code.

The text which makes up the returned content, such as that in the above examples, is known as **template text**. The derivation of the qualifier 'template' is that the documents like those above provide a layout into which Java code fragments can be placed.

The JSP Life Cycle

JSPs, like all other dynamic components, have an associated life cycle. What some beginners do not realise is that JSPs are in fact servlets underneath, just like every other dynamic Java EE component. JSPs only provide an easy way to *create* components containing non-Java code; they do not replace servlets.

Once written and deployed, JSPs are actually translated into servlet classes, with all the laborious output writing code being handled for us by the container. Now that the JSP is in servlet form, the code can be compiled into Java bytecode representing that class, and executed just like any other servlet or Java class. As you can see, we can't do away with the underlying servlet technology, but we can make developers' lives easier (which is always a good thing!).

The actual life cycle of a JSP is therefore:

1. **JSP Creation**
   The JSP author creates a JSP page or document (see the next chapter for a discussion of JSP documents).
2. **Deployment**
   The JSP author deploys the JSP to the container, which automatically invokes the next stage, or the author may choose to invoke the next stage manually.
3. **Validation**
   All references to tag libraries, actions and EL functions made in the JSP are verified to ensure that they exist and are accessible to the page. If not, an error occurs which prevents the translation process from continuing.
4. **Translation**
   The JSP is translated into (human readable) servlet source code. Many containers provide access to the generated servlets – for example, the Glassfish Java EE 5 server stores translated JSPs in the `generated/jsp/` directory (and its subdirectories) underneath the current domain's directory (e.g. the domain `domain1` would store its JSPs in `{Server}/domains/domain1/generated/jsp/` where `{Server}` is the path to your Glassfish installation).
5. **Compilation**
   The servlet source code is compiled into Java bytecode (a `.class` file). In the reference implementation, this is stored alongside the translated JSP files in `generated/jsp/` under the current domain's directory. These first five steps are summarised in Figure 13.1.
6. **Load class**
   The servlet class is loaded into memory using the application's `ClassLoader`.

13

7. **Instantiate**
   The application instantiates an instance of the servlet class for each JSP in the application; depending on the container, one or more instances may be created.

8. **Initialise**
   The `jspInit` method is called on the instance to initialise it. This is similar to invoking `init()` on a `Servlet` object. You can override `jspInit()` using a declaration (see later).

9. **Service**
   The `_jspService` method is invoked for each request received for the JSP. Note that the parameters of this method depend on the protocol supported by the JSP. For example, in most containers HTTP is the default protocol, so the method signature is actually `_jspService(HttpServletRequest request, HttpServletResponse response)`. This allows JSP authors to make use of the HTTP parameters without having to cast them.

10. **Destruction**
    When the container is shut down, or the servlet instance is otherwise taken out of service, the `jspDestroy` method is called. You can override `jspDestroy()` using a declaration.

13

NOTE: The above life cycle is slightly simplified. In reality, before Validation can occur the JSP page is first converted into an 'XML View' of the JSP; it is the XML View which is then validated and translated. The XML View simplifies the translation process, since JSPs may be authored as both pages and documents. See the next chapter for more details.

Figure 13.1

Simplified Translation Process

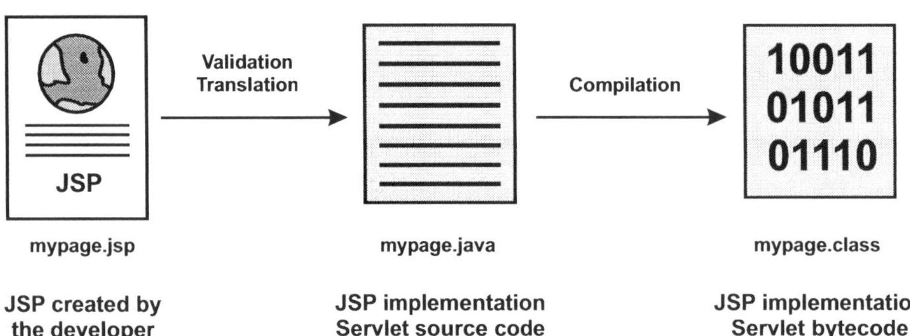

The most common way for JSPs to be deployed is simply to include the JSP source file (e.g. `mypage.jsp`) in a directory (e.g. `/path/`) in the WAR and upload this as an application to the server. When a request for `/path/mypage.jsp` is received by the container for the first time, it will automatically translate and compile the JSP into the servlet class, then execute this new servlet. This initial translation causes a delay when the page is served for the first time. On all subsequent requests, the container will just execute the servlet class which already exists and there will be no further delay. A second way is for the developer to *precompile* the JSPs into servlets before adding them to the WAR; deployment for this method is the same as the deployment for servlets, and hence appropriate deployment descriptor mappings must be provided. Java EE servers often provide tools for translating JSPs into Java source files; consult your server's documentation for more information (the reference implementation provides a utility called `jspc` for example). You may wish to precompile JSPs if you want to avoid the one-off time delay normally associated with serving the page for the first time. Figure 13.2 summarises the two possible deployment methods.

Make sure you memorise the stages in the life cycle; once you've got a solid understanding that JSPs are just servlets 'made easy for developers', you're halfway towards knowing the entire cycle. The rest can be deduced, although I recommend learning it. Any questions relating to this life cycle on your exam will be easy marks: don't let yourself down!

Figure 13.2

JSP Deployment
(1) Directly into the container
(2) Precompiled

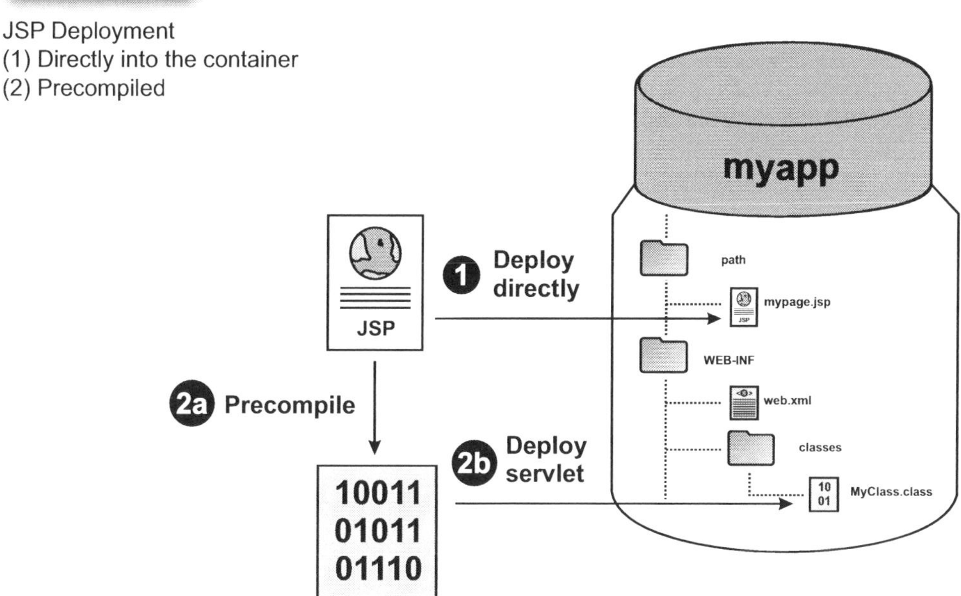

Scripting Elements

Java code is embedded into JSP pages using **scripting elements**, which demarcate their contents as being code to be processed and not directly rendered to the output. There are four main scripting elements:

1. **Directives**
2. **Declarations**
3. **Scriptlets**
4. **Expressions**

Each of these is discussed separately in the sections below. There is also a mechanism for commenting using scripting elements; a discussion of this follows.

Directives

These scripting elements are used to provide the JSP translator with instructions (**directives**) about how it should treat the JSP page being translated. For example, setting the MIME type of the page, declaring whether the page represents an error page, and notifying the translator about a page's interaction with sessions are all uses of directives.

13

There are three directives which are of importance: `page` controls the translator's processing of the JSP page, `taglib` specifies the locations of tag libraries used in the page, and `include` provides a static importation method.

In general, directive elements begin with a `<%@` delimiter, and close with a `%>` delimiter. Immediately after the opening tag, with any amount of optional white space, the name of the directive is placed. This must be one of the `page`, `taglib` or `include` names already mentioned. Following this, but still inside the directive, are a set of attribute and value pairs which set the properties of the page such as MIME type and the output buffer size. The available attribute/value pairs depend upon which directive is being used. We discuss these separately below.

The page Directive

The purpose of the `page` directive is to provide information about the page to the translator. This directive therefore contains some important properties which describe the page as a whole. This is a complete list of the available attributes for this directive:

- **`language`**
  Declares the scripting language to be used in scripting expressions in the page; in JSP 2.0, the only defined value is `java` (note the lowercase `j`).

- **`extends`**
  A fully-qualified Java class name which names the superclass of the class to which this JSP should be translated. Omitting this attribute allows the container to use its own optimised superclass, which is generally preferred.

- **`import *`**
  A comma-separated list of packages and classes to import into the translated servlet class. See below for an example.

- **`session *`**
  Declares whether this JSP requires participation in HTTP sessions. If `true` (the default), the `session` implicit object is made available and will contain either the existing session, or if that doesn't exist, a new session. This is equivalent to declaring `HttpSession session = request.getSession()` in the `service` method of an HTTP servlet. If `false`, the `session` implicit object is not available; attempts to reference it in the page will raise a translation exception.

- **`buffer`**
  Specifies the buffer size for the `JspWriter out` implicit object. If `none` is used as the value, then no buffering is used. Otherwise, the value must be a non-negative size in kilobytes, including the mandatory suffix `kb`. For example, a value of `16kb` specifies a 16 kilobyte buffer size. The default value is a buffer size greater than or equal to `8kb`.

- **`autoFlush`**
  Specifies whether buffered text in the `JspWriter out` object should be flushed automatically to the output stream when the buffer becomes full (value of `true`, the default), or whether an exception should be raised to indicate buffer overflow (value of `false`). A translation error will occur if the illegal combination `buffer="none"` and `autoFlush="false"` appears (since under this condition, it would be impossible to add *any* text to the buffer without raising an exception!).

- **`info`**
  Used to declare an arbitrary string which can be obtained via the `getServletInfo` method of the `ServletConfig` for this JSP's translated servlet class.

- **`isErrorPage`**
  Indicates if this JSP is intended to be the target of another page's `errorPage`;

if set to `true`, the `exception` implicit object is available and reflects the exception thrown during execution of the other page. If the value is `false` (the default), the `exception` object is unavailable; any attempt to reference it in the page will raise a translation error. However, just because `false` is used as the value, this does not indicate that this page *cannot* be used as an error page–it just means that the `exception` implicit object will be unavailable!

- **`errorPage`**
  Declares the URL to the JSP to which any exceptions not caught and handled in this page should be forwarded. Declaring the error here, however, is inadvisable; a much more flexible way to declare an error page is to use the deployment descriptor to configure error pages. Note that the `Throwable` cause is made available to the error JSP through the `exception` implicit object (if the error JSP uses the `isErrorPage` attribute above), but also through the request-scoped attributes `javax.servlet.jsp.jspException` (for backwards compatibility) and `javax.servlet.error.exception` (for compatibility with the servlet error model–see *Error Pages* in Chapter 10).

- **`contentType *`**
  The value should be the MIME type and character-set encoding used for the response, which should also be the encoding used in the JSP page itself. The format of this value has the same as for the `setContentType` method of the `ServletResponse` class: either *`TYPE`* or *`TYPE`*`;charset=`*`CHARSET`*. For example, `text/html` or `text/html;charset=UTF-8`. The default values are `text/html` for a JSP page and `text/xml` for a JSP document.

- **`pageEncoding`**
  Describes the character encoding used in the JSP page. The encoding is first derived from the value of this attribute, and next from the `contentType` attribute's `charset` definition if it exists. Otherwise, the default encoding is `ISO-8859-1`.

- **`isELIgnored *`**
  Use `true` if expression language statements in the page are to be ignored, or `false` if they are to be parsed. The default parsing rules for EL are given in Chapter 15 (*Evaluation of EL Expressions in JSPs*).

NOTE: The only `page` directive attributes which need to be known *for the exam* are the four marked with a `*` above.

Let's look at an example (you can also use *single quotes* around attribute values, but this is uncommon):

```
<%@ page import="java.io.*, java.math.BigDecimal" buffer="16kb"
```

```
session="true" contentType="text/html" %>
```

This tells the translator that the servlet class, in order to be compiled correctly, will have to import all classes from the `java.io` package, as well as the `BigDecimal` class. It also sets the response buffer to 16KB, the returned MIME type to `text/html`, and indicates that the page will participate in the current user's session.

Ideally, `page` directives should appear at the beginning of a page, but in general their position in the page is irrelevant. If statically including another page into the current one using the `include` directive (discussed below), you have no choice that any `page` directives in the imported page will be included amongst the template text in the middle of the page. It is acceptable for `page` directives to appear in the middle of a page, except when they contain the `pageEncoding` and `contentType` attributes, whose declaration *must always appear at the beginning* of the document since their values must be set on the response object before any content is written back to the client stream. A `pageEncoding` attribute can be present at most once in a page, or a fatal translation error will occur.

There should also be only one occurrence of any one name/value attribute pair in the page, except where the value of a duplicate attribute is the same. This prevents conflicts occurring, and a fatal translation error will occur if non-identical redefinitions appear. The exception to this rule is the `import` attribute, which accepts a *comma-separated list* of values. In this case, it is legal to have many in the page, in which case the values are compounded together to form the complete list. For example, the following have the same meaning: 13

```
<%@ page import="java.io.File" %>
<p>
  <strong>Test:</strong>
  <%@ page import="java.util.*" %>
  Some page
</p>
```

is the same as:

```
<%@ page import="java.io.File, java.util.*" %>
<p>
  <strong>Test:</strong>
  Some page
</p>
```

With the exception of the `import` attribute, care must be taken with statically included pages to ensure that conflicting redefinitions of `page` directive attributes do not appear, and that the `contentType` and `pageEncoding` attributes are not used in the imported page (otherwise they will no doubt appear in the middle of template text and a translation error will occur). Unrecognised attributes or values will, not surprisingly, result in a fatal translation error.

The taglib Directive

Basic tag libraries are the subject of Chapter 17, and Chapter 20 is devoted to tag library deployment, so we will discuss the purpose and semantics of these attributes there; for completeness, these are the attributes and their syntax for this directive:

- **uri**
  Either an absolute or relative URI used to uniquely identify the tag library.
- **tagdir**
  Specifies the directory within the WAR of the library of tag files which this page references.
- **prefix**
  Defines the prefix to be associated with this tag library in this JSP.

A translation error will occur if both the `uri` and `tagdir` attributes are declared; only one may be specified.

The include Directive

It is a common requirement to be able to import the content of another file into a page – for example, a common banner or menu bar on each page. The `include` directive performs static inclusion; the page to be included is added at *translation time*, not at request time. Even if the included resource changes at a later date, the page including it will not necessarily change. Some containers do have support for recompiling pages which have an include file that has changed, but this is not guaranteed. For example, if including another JSP page into the current one, the code of the other JSP page will be inserted into the current page at translation time, and the entire combined JSP will be translated and compiled. The container will always parse the statically included document before it goes to translate it, so any translation errors which appear in the included document will cause the translation of *both* documents to fail.

13

The syntax for the include directive is:

```
<%@ include file="..." %>
```

where the value of the `file` attribute is a URL to the resource, relative to the context root if starting with a forward-slash (/), or relative to the current page otherwise.

Let's look at a quick example to see how static inclusion works. This is the `banner.jsp` page:

```
<%@ page import="java.util.Random" %>
<p>
<em>Banner with random #<%= new Random().nextInt(20) %></em>
</p>
```

Let's assume this is included in the `index.jsp` page, at the same path, as follows:

```
<html>
  <head>
    <title>A simple test</title>
  </head>
  <body>
    <%@ include file="banner.jsp" %>
    <p>Body text</p>
  </body>
</html>
```

The result of translating `index.jsp` will be a JSP page, ready to be converted to servlet code, which looks like this:

```
<html>
  <head>
    <title>A simple test</title>
  </head>
  <body>
    <%@ page import="java.util.Random" %>
    <p>
      <em>
        Banner with random #<%= new Random().nextInt(20) %>
      </em>
    </p>
    <p>Body text</p>
  </body>
</html>
```


Regardless of any changes made to `banner.jsp`, the translated and compiled servlet for this page will always remain the same: it will always output the text 'Banner with random #' followed by a random number. The exception here is if you have an intelligent container which senses when `banner.jsp` has changed and has been redeployed, retranslating and compiling all affected pages, such as `index.jsp`, automatically. However, you should never rely on this functionality, since an application could be deployed to many different containers which each offer different 'features'.

The alternative to static inclusion is dynamic inclusion mechanisms, which instead of including code at translation time, include the results of using a `RequestDispatcher` to include the request to the other resource *at run time*. We will look at this approach, and contrast it against this static inclusion directive, in Chapter 16 when we look at standard actions. In general, use the static `include` directive *only* when the result of a request to a resource is not likely to change much; static inclusion doesn't require any processing at run time, since all the work is done once only at translation time. Using the `RequestDispatcher` to include a component dynamically is more resource intensive, since it's invoked during every request. There is often a trade-off to make here; understanding the alternatives is therefore of key importance (and be sure this will be tested on the exam!).

Declarations

Directives, with the exception of `include`, are generally placed at the top of a JSP page and give instructions to the container at translation time. **Declarations** provide a way to insert content directly into the servlet class during translation. Declarations describe the basic layout of a servlet, such as specifying variables at the class or object scopes (i.e. static and instance attributes) and adding to the structure of, or overriding methods from, the compiled servlet.

The template text of a JSP is inserted into the `_jspService` method by default when the JSP's translated servlet is compiled. Any other method modifications are made using a declaration.

Declarations begin with a `<%!` delimiter and end with a `%>` delimiter. For example, to insert an instance attribute into the compiled servlet, we can write:

```
<%! int randomNumber; %>
```

From your Programmer exam knowledge, you should recall that instance variables not explicitly initialised are initialised to their default value, which here is 0 (for objects it is `null`). To initialise the variable explicitly, we can write:

```
<%! java.util.Random randomObj = new java.util.Random(); %>
```

13

NOTE: The line-terminating semicolon must be present here, just as in regular class code. As we shall see momentarily, this is because declaration code is inserted *verbatim* into the generated servlet code.

To declare a method for the class, we write:

```
<%!
    private int generateNextNumber() {
        return randomObj.nextInt();
    }
%>
```

This method can then be accessed by code in the template text and used as any other method in a class would be. Another use of a declaration is to override JSP default methods, such as `jspInit()` which is equivalent to the servlet's `init` method, but is designed to be overridden by JSP page authors. Taking the random number generator example from above, we can best write:

```
<%@ page import="java.util.Random" %>
<%! Random randomObj; %>
<%! public void jspInit() { randomObj = new Random(); } %>
<%! private int generateNextNumber() {
        return randomObj.nextInt();
} %>
```

The `page` directive imports the `Random` class which this JSP page uses. For clarity I have split the above into several declarations, each doing a specific function, but these can just as easily have been put into one single declaration:

```
<%@ page import="java.util.Random" %>
<%!
    Random randomObj;
    public void jspInit() {
        randomObj = new Random();
    }
    private int generateNextNumber() {
        return randomObj.nextInt();
    }
%>
```

This is equally as acceptable to the container and compiler. The results of this would be inserted *directly* into the translated servlet class. Declarations should be used to make page-global definitions of methods and variables which will be used by the content of the page during its processing. Declarations are inserted into servlet code as direct members of the class as shown in Figure 13.3.

NOTE: If you want to perform lifecycle operations, you should supply implementations of `jspInit()` and `jspDestroy()`. However, you should *never* override `_jspService()`.

Figure 13.3

Scripting Expression Insertion Points in Translated JSP

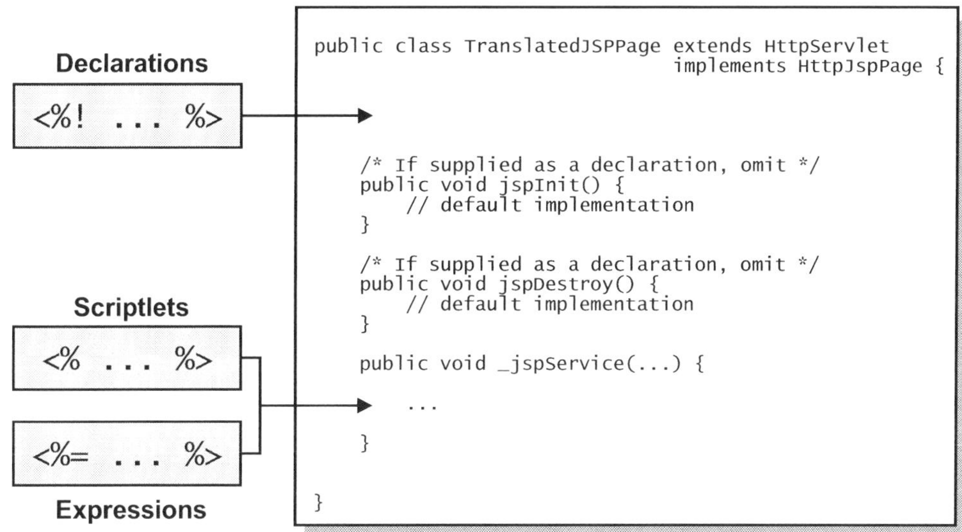

Scriptlets

Scriptlet scripting elements are arguably the most important of the lot, since they contain *any* Java processing code for the body of a JSP. They provide the logic functions for the processing in the `_jspService` method. The content of a scriptlet must be valid, well-formed, Java code. This code is inserted directly into the `_jspService` servlet class method at the relevant point amongst the other template text. As well as performing processing code, scriptlets can write output to the response stream, making them powerful tools for conditional output and iterations through a list or database records.

A scriptlet is denoted by an opening `<%` delimiter, and a closing `%>` delimiter. Note that all scripting elements end with `%>`, and all begin with `<%` along with another special character, such as `@`, `!`, `=` and `--`. Scriptlets do not have a special character following the `<%`.

NOTE: Variables declared in a scriptlet are *method-local* to the JSP's service method. Their values will be different between requests and will not be available between pages. This contrasts with the use of the declarations, which place variables at class scope, available across all requests to a JSP.

An example of a page containing scriptlets might be:

```
<%@ page import="java.util.*, java.text.DateFormat" %>
<%
    Calendar cal = Calendar.getInstance();
    boolean morning = (cal.get(Calendar.AM_PM)==Calendar.AM);
%>
<p>
Good
  <% if(morning) { %>
    morning.
  <% } else { %>
    afternoon.
  <% } %>
The date is <% out.write( DateFormat.getDateInstance().format(
               cal.getTime()) ); %> and the time now is
<% out.write( DateFormat.getTimeInstance().format(cal.getTime())
); %>
</p>
```

The `page` directive imports classes from the core utilities package and the `DateFormat` class. The first scriptlet creates a method-local `Calendar` instance and determines if the current time is before or after noon using the `Calendar` class's `get` method, storing the result in the `boolean` variable. The second scriptlet then outputs 'morning' or 'afternoon' depending upon the state of the `boolean` variable we created in the first scriptlet block. Notice how we've broken the scriptlet up and put template text between the conditional scriptlet blocks. This is perfectly valid; when translated, all template text becomes Java code anyway, just wrapped in a call to the response stream's `Writer`. Thus, after translation, the second scriptlet block becomes:

```
if(morning) {
  out.write("morning.");
} else {
  out.write("afternoon.");
}
```

This clearly is legal code. It is a fairly common practise to break apart scriptlet blocks and insert template text between them in order to achieve conditional and iterative effects. If you're not sure whether breaking blocks into two fragments will work, think about what translation will do to the page and you'll probably be able to see through any difficulties. A common source of error is to omit the curly braces, `{` and `}`, where there are multiple lines of template text, since then only the first line will be conditional or iterative, which is not normally the desired effect. My advice: *always* use curly braces when breaking apart blocks into fragments and you shouldn't go far wrong.

The final two scriptlet blocks format the current timestamp using the `DateFormat` class and output the current date and time respectively. The variable `out` in the example is called an **implicit object**; we discuss these later, but for now you may assume that `out` represents the `Writer` object for the response stream.

Expressions

In the code example in the previous section, there were a large number of `out.write()` invocations, which cause the contents to be written to the response stream. You can see that using `out.write()` increased the amount of code slightly in the last two scriptlet blocks; this only gets worse when multiple lines of output are required! To save us the trouble of coding the `out.write()` procedure every time output is required (which, given that this is a JSP, is quite often), the **expression** scripting element was created. An expression element evaluates its contents, converts the result to a `String` and outputs it to `out` (usually the response stream). If the contents cannot be cast to a `String` (including via `toString()` on objects), either a translation error will occur if the container detected the problem at translation time, or a `ClassCastException` will be thrown at request time. You do not need to know about these errors for the exam.

The expression to be written must be contained between `<%=` and `%>` delimiters. Taking the previous example, we could simplify the last two scriptlet blocks using expressions:

```
The date is <%= DateFormat.getDateInstance().format(cal.getTime())
%> and the time now is <%= DateFormat.getTimeInstance().format(cal.
getTime()) %>
```

If nothing else, this is slightly clearer to read. Notice how there is no longer any line-terminating semicolon as there would normally be in a line of code, or as there was in the scriptlet version. This is because, during translation, the content of an expression is inserted as the parameter to the response stream's `write()` method. It is illegal to terminate a parameter definition with a semi-colon. The above, translated, becomes:

```
out.write("The date is ");
out.write(DateFormat.getDateInstance().format(cal.getTime()));
out.write(" and the time now is ");
out.write(DateFormat.getTimeInstance().format(cal.getTime()));
```

It would be illegal to use the semicolon for any expression, since this would result in a translation of, for example:

```
out.write(DateFormat.getTimeInstance().format(cal.getTime()););
```

The semi-colon inside the method call will cause the compiler to complain about bad syntax, and hence a fatal translation error would occur.

13 Comments

In addition to the four main scripting elements above, one element is reserved for placing Java code comments in the page. A clear distinction must first be drawn between returned (non-Java) comments and Java comments.

A comment of the form:

```
<!-- comment text here -->
```

is a standard XML/HTML comment, which could just as easily appear in a static document, and will be returned to the client during a request. XML comments are not typically rendered visibly by an XML-compliant browser however. This type of comment is treated as template text and written to the response as normal.

When you don't want to make the comment public knowledge, you need to use a Java-style, JSP-specific comment. These take the form:

```
<%-- JSP comment here --%>
```

Anything inside the opening `<%--` delimiter and the closing `--%>` delimiter will be ignored by the JSP translation engine, and will not appear in the translated servlet code. This allows for portions of JSP code to be 'commented out' during development and testing of a component.

There may also be some situations where you wish for the comment to be included in the translated servlet source code, but not in the response to the client; bear in mind however that when compiled into Java bytecode, all comments are ignored by the compiler anyway. If source-code comments are what you require, then you can use a scriptlet containing Java commenting syntax:

```
<% /** Java commenting here */ %>
```

This particular comment is a documentation comment, with two opening asterisks; this method of commenting can be used for the documentation of compiled JSP servlets if at all necessary.

Each of these three methods for supplying comments differs in where the comments eventually end up. Make sure you understand what each method achieves and the syntax for declaring it.

Implicit Objects

Because a JSP page has no exposed methods or variables, and is in fact a plain text file in an arbitrary format, there would appear to be no ways to directly access any of the objects available to a servlet, such as the request, response and session objects, the `ServletContext` of the application and the `Writer` for the response stream. This is obviously a major inconvenience since we may need to make decisions about included template text depending upon the state of the request and session objects, and we need some way to write to the response body or modify headers.

Underneath, a JSP is just a servlet, and a servlet has all these objects available to it–so why should they also not be accessible to JSP authors? In fact they are, through the use of the **implicit objects** of a JSP page. These are a set of variables which expose commonly used objects from the API to the JSP developer. They are created by the container when the JSP page is translated, and are added to the servlet class at compilation time. Before we see how to use them and how the container treats them, let's see what they are:

- **`request`** (interface `javax.servlet.ServletRequest` implementation)
  The request which caused this page to be invoked. The type of object is a protocol-dependent subclass of `ServletRequest`–e.g. `HttpServletRequest` under the HTTP protocol.
- **`response`** (interface `javax.servlet.ServletResponse` implementation)
  The response to the client. The type of object is a protocol-dependent subclass of `ServletResponse`–e.g. `HttpServletResponse` under the HTTP protocol.

- **pageContext** (class `javax.servlet.jsp.PageContext` subclass)
  The page context for this JSP. See the section on *The PageContext API* next.

- **session** (interface `javax.servlet.http.HttpSession` implementation)
  The session object for the client which invoked the request, if one exists. If either HTTP is not being used as the protocol, or if the `page` directive contains the attribute
  `session="false"`, this object will not exist (and a translation error will occur if you attempt to use it in the page).

- **application** (interface `javax.servlet.ServletContext` implementation)
  The context for this application.

- **out** (class `javax.servlet.jsp.JspWriter` subclass)
  An output stream which buffers between the page and the response stream. Its properties (such as buffer size and flush control) can be configured in the `page` directive. Your JSP scripting elements should always write to the `out` implicit object and not directly to the response stream.

- **config** (interface `javax.servlet.ServletConfig` implementation)
  The configuration object used to initialise the servlet created by translating this JSP.

- **page** (`Object` subclass)
  The instance of this page's implementation class. If the scripting language is `java` (i.e. the `page` directive has `language="java"`), using `this` in scripting expressions is equivalent.

- **exception** (class `java.lang.Throwable`)
  The exception thrown by another page. Only available when this JSP declares the `page` directive `isErrorPage="true"`.

We make use of these variables simply by using their names in any scripting element code. For example, we've already seen how to buffer text to the response stream using `out.write()`. To access the request and examine the currently authenticated user in the session we can write the following in a scriptlet:

```
<% String username = request.getRemoteUser(); %>
```

This makes use of the implicit `request` object, which under an HTTP protocol, is of class `HttpServletRequest`.

Each implicit object is also associated with a scope. This scope determines the life cycle for that implicit object. Nearly all the objects have **page scope**, which means that the instances will exist only during execution of the current page and will be nonexistent (with `null` references) elsewhere. The exceptions are:

- `request` is in the **request scope**, which means that the instance is valid only during the current client's request and has `null` references elsewhere.

- `session` is in the **session scope**, which means that the instance exists only for the current session and has `null` references elsewhere.
- `application` is in the **application scope**, which means that the instance exists for the entire time the application is deployed.

Unless you attempt to store the implicit objects in some other location (for example, store the `pageContext` object in the `session` object), the scopes of each of the implicit objects is largely irrelevant. If you did try to store the `pageContext` in the `session`, you might find that once the page has finished executing, the container modifies the `pageContext` instance and it is no longer consistent with the previous state. To avoid such volatile code, only ever make use of the implicit objects *within the page* and never store them anywhere else over long periods.

The important thing is to learn the implicit objects' names and their class types; an indication of what scope they are might help a little, but it's not as important. An in-depth exam question will expect you to analyse a piece of code which makes use of an implicit object and make comments about its validity.

The PageContext API

We mentioned the `pageContext` implicit object in the last section. It is the only object whose purpose is not obvious from our previous knowledge of the Servlet model. In fact, page contexts are a JSP-specific API, and the exam mandates an understanding of at least some of the API's features.

The PageContext API actually consists of two abstract classes: `JspContext` abstracts all data about a JSP page that does not depend on servlets to work, and the `PageContext` subclass used by JSPs operating in a servlet environment. These are implemented by Java EE server- and container-specific concrete classes, which are of little interest to us.

You may ask why there are two classes in this API, and not just one; surely a JSP can only be represented by one type of context? Because JSP technology focuses on being an HTML or XML template, the script code doesn't have to be written in the Java language; we'll be looking at a new alternative called the Expression Language in Chapter 15. This means that, technically, JSPs are not bound to the Java environment and to the Java EE platform – in theory, therefore, a JSP does not have to be used on a Java platform. In the Java platform, contexts can make use of the powerful Servlet models, which we covered in Part I of this book, to interrogate requests and handle exceptions. On other platforms, however, servlets (or an equivalent) may not be available, and this platform may not even know what an exception is! In order that JSPs can be portable, without being bound necessarily to the servlet model, there are two versions of the context: a `JspContext` represents everything that is essential about a JSP (such as the management of attributes in different scopes, and obtaining an output stream for the response). In order to make practical use of JSPs for the Java EE platform, we must use an instance of `PageContext`.

If you find it hard to remember which class is the superclass, think that, from its name, `JspContext` is the context given to *any JSP*, regardless of what platform it's implemented on. Therefore, `JspContext` must be the most generic and is therefore the parent of `PageContext`.

The JspContext Abstract Class

The most important use of this class is to access all of the attributes (i.e. those in the request, session, application and page scopes) available to a JSP component. We know already that it is much quicker for a page author to use the JSP's implicit objects to access the attributes, so this class is really used 'behind the scenes'. Inside the container provided with a Java EE server, each JSP is represented by its servlet class and a per-JSP instance of the `JspContext` class. The former provides the actual processing code, while the latter provides information about, and gives supplementary data to, the JSP component. You may ask again why contexts are necessary when the compiled servlet already has access to all the attributes in an application, but remember that JSPs do not have to be compiled into servlets on every (non-Java) platform. The context therefore provides a uniform way for JSPs to gather information about their environment, regardless of the type of platform on which they are executing.

The methods relating to attributes are:

- **`Object findAttribute(String name)`**
  Searches for the attribute called `name` in the page, request, session and application scopes in that order, and returns the value of the first occurrence found. Note that these scopes are searched starting with the most specific and working outwards to the least restrictive storage locations. If no attribute with this name can be found in any of the scopes, `null` is returned. This is a useful method used widely by EL expressions when locating scripting variables which may reside in any scope.

- **`Object getAttribute(String name)`**
  Returns the page-scoped attribute called `name`. This method is synonymous with the `getAttribute` methods found in `ServletContext`, `HttpSession`

and ServletRequest, but here represents the page scope (rather than the application, session and request scopes, respectively).

- **Object getAttribute(String name, int scope)**
  Returns the attribute called name which resides in the specified scope—which must be one of the constants PageContext.PAGE_SCOPE, PageContext.REQUEST_SCOPE, PageContext.SESSION_SCOPE or PageContext.APPLICATION_SCOPE. This method provides a common gateway for accessing the page-scoped attributes found in this JspContext, the request-scoped attributes in the current ServletRequest, the session-scoped attributes in the client's HttpSession and the application-scoped attributes in ServletContext. It is used as part of the findAttribute method's operation.

- **Enumeration getAttributeNamesInScope(int scope)**
  Returns a java.util.Enumeration of all the attribute names which exist in the specified scope—which must be one of the constants PageContext.PAGE_SCOPE, PageContext.REQUEST_SCOPE, PageContext.SESSION_SCOPE or PageContext.APPLICATION_SCOPE.

- **int getAttributesScope(String name)**
  Returns the first scope in which the attribute called name resides. The scopes are searched in order, and the returned value will be the first one of the scopes which contains the named attribute. The returned value will be one of the constants: PageContext.PAGE_SCOPE, PageContext.REQUEST_SCOPE, PageContext.SESSION_SCOPE or PageContext.APPLICATION_SCOPE.

13

- **void removeAttribute(String name)**
  Removes the attribute with the supplied name from all scopes in which it occurs.

- **void removeAttribute(String name, int scope)**
  Removes the attribute called name from the supplied scope. scope must be one of the constants PageContext.PAGE_SCOPE, PageContext.REQUEST_SCOPE, PageContext.SESSION_SCOPE or PageContext.APPLICATION_SCOPE.

- **void setAttribute(String name, Object value)**
  Sets the page-scoped attribute called name to value. A value of null removes the attribute from the page scope.

- **void setAttribute(String name, Object value, int scope)**
  Sets the attribute called name within the specified scope to value. Using a value of null removes the attribute from the scope. scope must be one of the constants PageContext.PAGE_SCOPE, PageContext.REQUEST_SCOPE, PageContext.SESSION_SCOPE or PageContext.APPLICATION_SCOPE.

NOTE: The `JspContext` or `PageContext` objects are used *as the* storage location for page-scoped attributes, just like `ServletContext` is used to store attributes at the application scope. However, the `JspContext` and `PageContext` objects also provide methods for conveniently accessing the other scopes as well—it is important to be certain about which methods are used to access just the page-scoped attributes *stored in* the `JspContext`, and which methods are used for accessing the other objects and scopes.

Additionally, every JSP component, regardless of which platform it is executing on, must have a way to send response data back to the client. This is accomplished using the `out` implicit object, which for convenience is available through these:

- **`public JspWriter getOut()`**
  Returns the current output `Writer` being used for this page.
- **`public JspWriter pushBody(Writer writer)`**
  Creates a new, unbuffered, `JspWriter` and sets the `out` implicit object to the new writer instance. The output of the `JspWriter` will be directed to the supplied `writer`. This method saves the current `out` implicit object (which will be restored on calling `popBody()`) before replacing it. Using this method allows nested `JspWriter` streams to be created; these are used widely in Simple Tag Extensions (see Chapter 18) to provide conditional output.

13

- **`public JspWriter popBody()`**
  Restores the previous `JspWriter` to the `out` implicit object. This `JspWriter` was initially saved during the previous invocation of `pushBody(Writer)`.

The last two relate to the Expression Language, and are used to retrieve parsers:

- **`public ExpressionEvaluator getExpressionEvaluator()`**
  This method returns an EL parser for the current page. This object is used to examine and compute EL statements, and is primarily of concern to Java EE implementors. The exam will not expect you to recall this method or the use of the `ExpressionEvaluator` class.
- **`public VariableResolver getVariableResolver()`**
  Returns an instance of the `VariableResolver` interface. This interface allows custom variable recognition systems to be implemented by a container vendor; for example, for the Java EE platform, it defines the order of precedence for attribute look-up for variables declared in EL script. In general, implicit objects are returned as a priority, followed by page-, request-, session- and finally application-scoped attributes in that order. We will look at this more closely in Chapter 15.

The PageContext Abstract Class

This is designed to be implemented by Java EE containers which incorporate servlet technology. It inherits all the generic JSP context methods from `JspContext`, and then adds its own servlet-specific methods.

Many of these methods are used for convenient access to the implicit objects defined in a servlet-based JSP:

- **`public Exception getException()`**
- **`public Object getPage()`**
- **`public ServletRequest getRequest()`**
- **`public ServletResponse getResponse()`**
- **`public ServletConfig getServletConfig()`**
- **`public ServletContext getServletContext()`**
- **`public HttpSession getSession()`**
- **`public JspWriter getOut()`**

Most of these follow the pattern `getXxx()` where `Xxx` is the name of one of the standard implicit objects we've already looked at. The deviations from this pattern are: `getServletConfig()`, whose implicit object is just `config`, and `getServletContext()`, whose implicit object is `application`. Additionally, note the absence of a method for obtaining the current `pageContext`. This isn't an oversight: the returned value of a `getPageContext` method would always refer to the same `PageContext` object on which the method is being invoked – pointless!

13

The following are used for inclusion/forwarding:

- **`public void forward(String relativeURL)`**
- **`public void include(String relativeURL)`**
- **`public void include(String relativeURL, boolean flush)`**

These are particularly important because they send content to the current `out` writer, and not directly to the response stream (which is the result of using a `RequestDispatcher`). `out` acts as a buffer, and therefore will be flushed to the response stream sometime during processing the JSP. If you use a `RequestDispatcher` in a JSP to include content, you'll likely find that the included content is not positioned in the correct place inline, but instead is found at the start of the response because the `RequestDispatcher` writes to the response stream before `out` has flushed. This is therefore an error, so any JSP code which writes content to the response stream should use the methods above, or use one of the standard or JSTL actions (see Chapters 16 and 17).

These are related to errors and exceptions which this page might have to handle:

- **`public ErrorData getErrorData()`**
  If this page is an error page, i.e. if the `page` directive's attribute `isErrorPage="true"`, then use this method to retrieve data about the exception that caused the page to be called. Otherwise this data is useless.
- **`public void handlePageException(Exception e)`**
  Processes all uncaught exceptions at the page level. Its implementation should forward the exception to the error page for this JSP (see the `page` directive's `errorPage` attributes).
- **`public void handlePageException(Throwable t)`**
  Same functionality as `handlePageException(Exception)`.

Practical Uses of the PageContext API

13

That's about all that's useful here, although of course its use depends upon what you want to do with it! So far I've said that everything can be done better with JSP syntax than having to involve `PageContext` objects in the picture, so you might think they're pretty useless. However, I hope that I have shown you that JSPs have the potential to be cross-platform compatible, and for this reason we need a platform-neutral context for accessing data about pages – and that comes in the form of `JspContext`. Additionally, when we come to look at the Expression Language in Chapter 15, and custom tag libraries in Chapter 18, an understanding of the PageContext API should help you understand what's going on behind the scenes.

Revision Questions

1 **Arrange the following life-cycle stages in the correct order.**

Compilation | Instantiation | Destruction | Loading

Translation | Service | Initialisation

2 **Place the scripting element syntax over its correct name.**

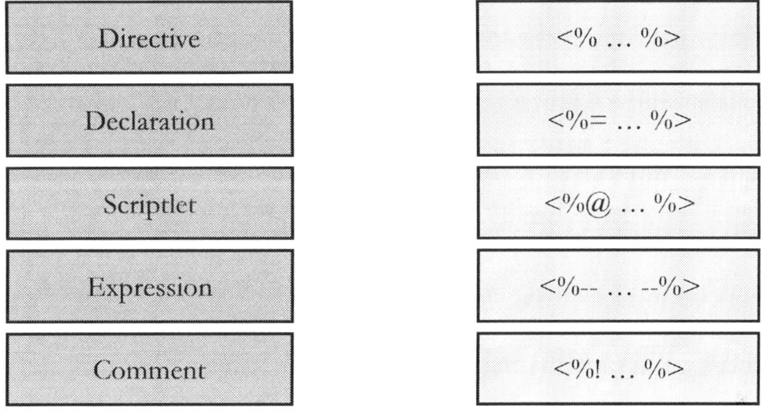

3 **Which of the following declares a comment in a JSP page?** **(choose three)**

A <% comment %>

B <%-- comment %>

C <%-- comment --%>

D <% // comment %>

E <%! /* comment */ %>

F <%= /* comment */ %>

4 **What is the result of compiling and deploying the exhibited JSP?** **(choose one)**

EXHIBIT

A The application-scoped attribute called prefix is set to the value 'W06'.

B The page does nothing and returns a blank response.

C A runtime exception occurs.

D A translation error occurs.

E A compilation error occurs.

5 **What is the result of compiling and executing the following JSP?** **(choose one)**

```
<%= new Date() %>
```

- A The current date and time is written to the response.
- B The response is empty.
- C A runtime exception occurs.
- D A translation error occurs.
- E A compilation error occurs.

6 **Which of the following is a correct way to write the value of the concatenation of a string and the current date to the response?** **(choose two)**

- A <% "Current time: " + new java.util.Date() %>
- B <%="Current time: " + new java.util.Date() %>
- C <%="Current time: " + new java.util.Date(); %>
- D <% out.write("Current time: " + new java.util.Date()); %>
- E <% out.write("Current time: " + new java.util.Date()) %>
- F <%= out.write("Current time: " + new java.util.Date()) %>

7 **Which of the following imports the java.util and java.io packages into the current JSP?** **(choose one)**

- A <%@ import packages="java.util, java.io" %>
- B <%@ import="java.util, java.io" %>
- C <%@ page import="java.util, java.io" %>
- D <%@ page import="java.util.*, java.io.*" %>
- E <%@ page import="java.util.*; java.io.*" %>

8 **What is the result of compiling and executing the following page?** **(choose one)**

```
1. <%@ page session="false" %>
2. <%= session.getAttribute("userid") %>
```

- A The value of the userid session-scoped attribute is written to the response.
- B A NullPointerException is thrown on line 2.
- C A translation error occurs on line 1.
- D A translation error occurs on line 2.
- E A compilation error occurs

9 **What is the result of compiling and executing the following page?** **(choose one)**

```
1. <%@ page import="java.io.*" %>
2. <% request.setAttribute("list", new ArrayList()); %>
3. <%@ page import="java.util.*" %>
```

A A new ArrayList variable is created in the request-scoped list attribute.

B A NullPointerException is thrown on line 2.

C A translation error occurs on line 2.

D A translation error occurs on line 3.

E A compilation error occurs.

10 **Which of the following statements is used to associate the tag library identified by the http://java.sun.com/jsp/jstl/core URI with the namespace prefix c?** **(choose one)**

A <%@ page tag-uri="http://java.sun.com/jsp/jstl/core" tag-prefix="c" %>

B <%@ tags uri="http://java.sun.com/jsp/jstl/core" prefix="c" %>

C <%@ tags location="http://java.sun.com/jsp/jstl/core" tag-prefix="c" %>

D <%@ taglib uri="http://java.sun.com/jsp/jstl/core" prefix="c" %>

E <%@ taglib location="http://java.sun.com/jsp/jstl/core" prefix="c" %>

11 **Which of the following statements performs static inclusion of the banner.html resource, located at the context root?** **(choose one)**

A <%@ page include="banner.html" %>

B <%@ include="banner.html" %>

C <%@ include url="/banner.html" %>

D <%@ include file="/banner.html" %>

E <%@ include page="/banner.html" %>

12 **What is the result of compiling and executing the exhibit?** **(choose one)**

EXHIBIT

A The output to the response is '18'.

B The output to the response is '6'.

C The output to the response is '06'.

D A translation error occurs.

E A compilation error occurs.

13 **Which of the following methods should you not declare in a JSP, using a declaration?** **(choose two)**

- A jspInit()
- B service(ServletRequest, ServletResponse)
- C jspService(HttpServletRequest, HttpServletResponse)
- D _jspService(HttpServletRequest, HttpServletResponse)
- E jspDestroy()

14 **Which of the following cause the value 'yes' to be written to the response if the state scripting variable is true, and 'no' otherwise?** **(choose two)**

A
```
<%=
 if(state) {
   "yes";
 } else {
   "false";
 }
%>
```

B
```
<%= state ? "yes" : "no" %>
```

C
```
<% if(state) %>yes<% else %>no
```

D
```
<% if(state) out.write("yes");
   else out.write("no"); %>
```

E
```
<% state ? out.write("yes") : out.write("no"); %>
```


15 **Which of the following copies the value of the item session-scoped attribute to the request-scoped attribute of the same name?** **(choose three)**

A
```
<% request.setAttribute("item", session.getAttribute("item")); %>
```

B
```
<% request.setAttribute("item", pageContext.getSession().getAttribute("item")); %>
```

C
```
<% pageContext.setAttribute("item", session.getAttribute("item")); %>
```

D
```
<% pageContext.getRequest().setAttribute("item", session.getAttribute("item")) %>
```

E
```
<% request.setAttribute("item", request.getSession().getAttribute("item")); %>
```

16 **Which of the following are not methods in PageContext?** **(choose two)**

- A ServletRequest getRequest()
- B ServletConfig getConfig()
- C HttpSession getSession()

D PageContext getPageContext()

E Object getPage()

F JspWriter getOut()

17 **Which of the following statements retrieve the value of the page-scoped attribute called counter?** **(choose two)**

A <% Object counter = page.getAttribute("counter"); %>

B <% Object counter = pageContext.getAttribute("counter"); %>

C <% Object counter = pageContext.findAttribute("counter"); %>

D <% Object counter = getAttribute("counter"); %>

E <% Object counter = pageContext.getPage().getAttribute("counter"); %>

18 **Which of the following scriptlets used as the only line in a JSP places the value of the servlet initialisation parameter called file for this JSP in the value variable?** **(choose one)**

A <% String value = context.getInitParam("file"); %>

B <% String value = application.getInitParameter("file"); %>

C <% String value = getInitParameter("file"); %>

D <% String value = config.getInitParameter("file"); %>

E <% String value = initParams.get("file"); %>

19 **The exhibit shows the contents of /item.jsp. What is the result of including this in the following page?** **(choose one)**

EXHIBIT

```
<%@ page import="java.util.*" session="true" contentType="text/html" %>
<p>Item code <%@ include file="/item.jsp" %></p>
```

A The text '<p>Item code: </p>' followed by the contents of the request-scoped itemid attribute is returned.

B The text '<p>Item code: null</p>' is returned.

C The text '<p>Item code: </p>' is returned.

D A translation error occurs.

E A compilation error occurs.

Exhibits

Q.4

```
<%
  public void jspInit() {
    application.setAttribute("prefix", "W06");
  }
%>
```

Q.12

```
<%! int num; %>
<%!
  public void jspInit() {
    num = 12;
  }
%>
<%= num + 6 %>
```

Q.19

13

```
<%@ page contentType="text/plain" %>
<%= request.getAttribute("itemid") %>
```

Answers to Revision Questions

1 **Correct answer:** Translation, Compilation, Loading, Instantiation, Initialisation, Service, Destruction.

Note that often 'translation' includes validation implicitly; however, technically, translation is the process of converting the JSP into servlet source code, while validation is ensuring the JSP is valid. The term 'translation' is often (including in the JSP specification) used to mean 'validation' followed by 'source code translation' as a whole.

2 **Correct answer:**

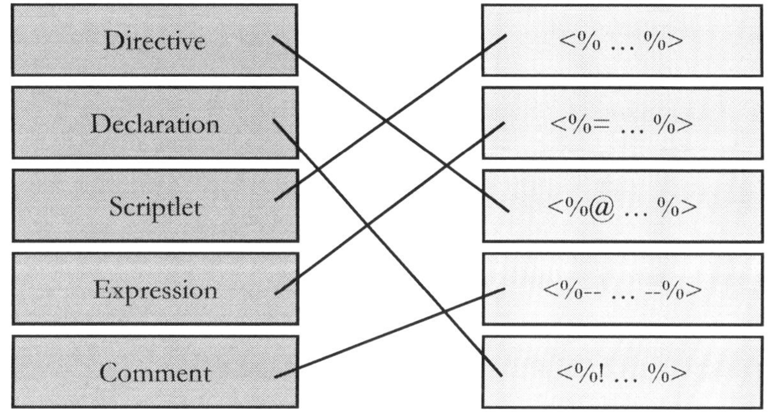

3 **Correct answers: C, D, E**

C is the standard JSP comment; note that unlike all the other scripting elements, the closing delimiter *must* be a --%> and not just a %>, making B incorrect (this ensures that this type of comment can be used to 'comment out' other scripting elements). D is just a single line comment in a scriptlet. E inserts a comment at the class level. F is invalid; it would cause a Java statement like out.write(/* comment */) to be created in the servlet, which will clearly cause a compilation error. A is a scriptlet and is therefore incorrect (it in fact references a JSP scripting variable called comment).

4 **Correct answer: E**

A couple of things are wrong here: firstly, we've declared a method in a scriptlet and not in a declaration, which would cause a compilation error as we're trying to nest one method inside another. Secondly, the application implicit object is only available in the _jspService method, not in jspInit(), so this would also cause a compilation error.

5 **Correct answer: E**

Note that we have declared no import of the java.util package, and we haven't given a fully-qualified class name; therefore a symbol error will ensue. We should have written 'new java.util.Date()' or used an import in the page directive.

6 **Correct answers: B, D**

A is wrong as it doesn't automatically write the value to the response; C is invalid because of the closing ';' – this would be translated into out.write(…;); which is clearly illegal. Similarly, F is wrong as this would be translated into out.write(out.write(…)). But out.write() returns void, so passing one void method into one expecting a String is seeking disaster! D is correct, and directly writes the string to the out implicit object. Note that E is incorrect as it omits the line-terminating ';' (which is mandatory for declarations and scriptlets, but illegal in expressions).

7 **Correct answer: D**

The *comma*-separated list of fully-qualified classes, or packages ending with '.*', inside the import attribute's value for the page directive is correct.

8 **Correct answer: D**

A translation error occurs because you try to use the session implicit object, which doesn't exist on account of the session="false" in line 1.

9 **Correct answer: A**

The 'trick' with this question is to know that it doesn't matter where (in general) page directives are located in the page. These directives are the first things to be parsed out of the entire document before translation occurs. Hence all the import statements will be inserted at the top of the servlet's source code before compilation occurs. Therefore line 2 won't raise a translation or compilation error because the compiler will see ArrayList as being declared in the package java.util as required. It also won't raise a NullPointerException since request is guaranteed not to be null. Hence A is the only viable correct answer.

13

10 **Correct answer: D**

11 **Correct answer: D**

The only tricky thing is remembering the attribute is called *file* and not page!

12 **Correct answer: B**

Note that the initialisation method for a JSP is jspInit() *not* _jspInit(), which isn't invoked at all. Hence num is initialised to 0. Also, the integers will be added together before being converted to a string (numerical addition takes precedence over string concatenation unless the first object is a String). Hence the answer is B.

13 **Correct answers: B, D**

A and E are designed to be overridden. C doesn't exist, at least in the standard API, so it is perfectly legal to declare (just don't expect anything to happen by default!). You should never override B or D because they will both be provided by the container automatically (note that some containers such as Tomcat actually make these methods final in their HttpJspPage implementation to prevent overriding and instead to raise a translation or compilation error.

14 Correct answers: B, D

B simply uses the one-line conditional operator, returning a String. C is incorrect because when translated it becomes:

```
if(state)
// some expression for output 'yes'
else
// some expression for output 'no'
```

where the comments are replaced with the container's invocation of the template text. But this invocation won't necessarily be a one-liner. For instance, the AppServer 8 container converts this to:

```
if(state)
  out.write('y');
  out.write('e');
  out.write('s');
else
  out.write("no");
```

Quite why it does this is unknown to me, but the net effect is that the compiler complains about 'else without if' because the else is separated from the if by more than one statement. To avoid any such issues, the valid adaptation of C uses braces:


```
<% if(state) { %>yes<% } else { %>no<% } %>
```

D is correct; it writes the output directly. Finally, E is wrong as the conditional operator must *return a value* and therefore cannot be used to invoke void methods; this results in a 'not a statement' compilation error.

15 Correct answers: A, B, E

D is syntactically incorrect as it omits the line-terminating semicolon. C is incorrect as it sets the page-scoped rather than request-scoped attribute item. Note that we've used a mixture of implicit objects and the PageContext API.

16 Correct answers: B, D

All of these reflect JSP implicit objects, but B is incorrectly named, it should be getServletConfig() even though the implicit object is config, and D doesn't exist because the pageContext implicit object is the one on which these methods are being invoked!

17 **Correct answers: B, C**

Note that page-scoped attributes are *stored in the PageContext* (and this object can also be used to conveniently search all other scopes). The page object, also obtained by pageContext.getPage(), is the Object representing the current JSP – and this doesn't store any attributes. Hence A, D and E all point to this JSP and are wrong (also note that A and E reference an Object type, and therefore would raise a compilation error since getAttribute(String) cannot be found on Object).

18 **Correct answer: D**

A is incorrect as the context implicit object doesn't exist (and it can't reference anything else, as we are told this is the *only* line in the JSP); B will get you the context parameters; C implies there is a getInitParameter method on this servlet, which isn't true (we are told this will be the *only* line in the JSP); E is wrong as there is no initParams implicit object.

19 **Correct answer: D**

Note that the contentType attribute has been duplicated in two places in the same 'translation unit' (a JSP source file and any files included using the include directive). Since it doesn't have the same value both times, a translation error occurs. This is true for all attributes except import and pageEncoding which may appear multiple times in a translation unit with different values (pageEncoding may only appear *once at the start* of each JSP file).

In this chapter you'll:

- Learn what an XML view is, and how the container utilises it.
- Structure a JSP document.
- Use scripting elements in JSP documents, and ensure the resulting XML is well-formed.

14 JSP Documents

In the last chapter we looked at the traditional way to write JSP pages, using template text, directives and Java-based scripting code. On the whole, these pages are pretty unstructured: they can contain any template text, with scripting code embedded *anywhere*. This makes parsing these documents a little harder, because the parser doesn't know what to expect, or where to find it before loading the file.

The alternative to JSP *pages* are JSP *documents*, which are written in XML. Make this distinction clear: *documents* are XML-formatted. The documents automatically incorporate the well-defined structure that XML provides, making the parsing of these documents easy for computer software, including the Java EE Web container at run time when the JSP is first requested. It is becoming increasingly common for any JSP-authoring tools to output the final JSP as an XML document, as well as import existing XML documents to be edited; XML is much easier for tools to work with.

NOTE: Throughout, I use the common (but not official) convention that 'JSP page' is the traditional JSP component discussed in the last chapter, 'JSP document' is the XML-formatted JSP component which forms the subject of this chapter, and the term 'JSP' refers to both types of component when the distinction is unnecessary.

Document Structure

So far, we've seen that JSPs are converted into servlet classes in order to be executed: JSPs are servlets. But now we are faced with another problem: how can pages written using the traditional JSP page syntax be interoperable with JSPs written using the XML syntax? How can an efficient translation engine be designed such that both types of JSPs can be translated with maximum code reuse and no redundancy?

The answer lies in what the container does with both types of JSP when it comes to translate them. Regardless of which type of JSP you have programmed, page or document, the container creates what is termed an **XML view**. This is an internal XML representation of either the page or the document. Once this document has been correctly assembled and parsed, the container will be in a position to perform

Figure 14.1

JSP Translation including XML View

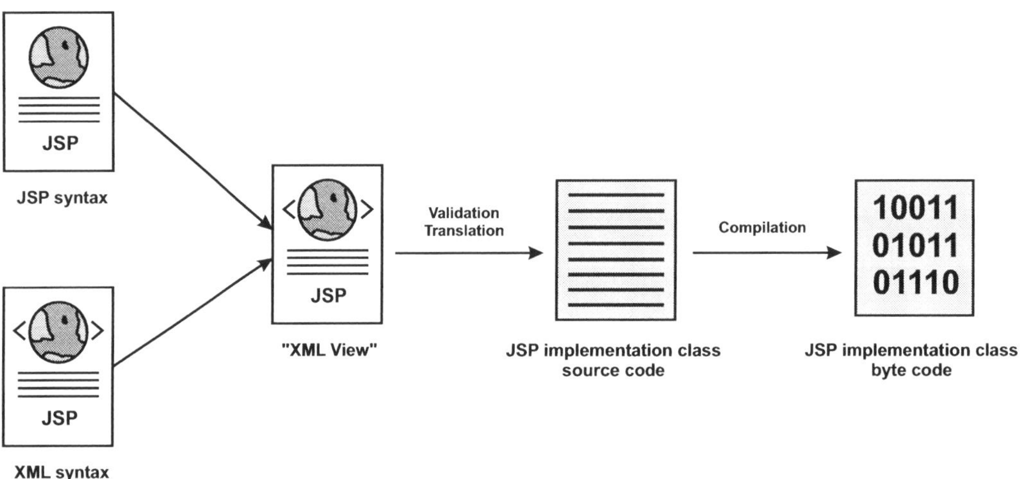

additional associations and tasks before compilation can occur. These tasks might include associating a JSP with its tag libraries, and performing validation on language syntax. Once all pre-compilation checks have been made on the XML view, the view is translated into a servlet class and then compiled in the same way as before. The XML view represents an extra step in the translation process which we did not consider before; all other stages of the JSP life cycle remain the same. An XML view is practically identical to a JSP document in syntax.

In order to be well-formed XML, JSP documents must contain correct XML tag and attribute syntax and element nesting. They all follow the same basic rules. JSP documents must not contain the JSP directives or scripting elements presented in the last chapter; instead there are XML-based equivalents.

XML Namespaces

XML documents often use many different elements, each with its own defined semantics. Each formal document type is associated with either a Document Type Definition (DTD) or an XML Schema. Sometimes it is necessary to use elements from *different* DTDs or Schemas in the *same* document (we will see examples of this later on). In order to separate elements which come from different sources, we use **namespaces**. Elements are said to belong to namespaces: they 'live' inside one. Namespaces themselves must be valid and unique URIs for each source of elements, usually in the form of URLs. Elements are bound to namespaces using simple strings which relate the element to a namespace. These **prefix** the name of an element, in both the start and end tags, separated by a colon:

```
<namespace:element attributes...>content</namespace:element>
```

For example, some elements in a document inevitably belong to the JSP namespace. These elements are used by the container to do JSP-specific processing (e.g. the execution of scripting code). The JSP namespace is mapped to the `http://java.sun.com/JSP/Page` URI. In turn, this namespace is normally mapped to the `jsp` prefix string. The scriptlet scripting element is therefore written as:

```
<jsp:scriptlet> scriplet code </jsp:scriptlet>
```

The name of the element (`scriptlet`) is prefixed by the namespace prefix, here `jsp`. Note that it is the *URI of the namespace* which is important, not the prefix used by elements. The prefix is established typically in the root element of a document, using the `xmlns` (**XML n**ame**s**pace) attribute.

The Root Element

All valid XML documents must have a root element, which is the containing element for the entire document. In the case of a Web application deployment descriptor, this is the `<web-app>` element. For JSP documents, it was traditionally the `<jsp:root>` element. This element is used as follows:

```
<jsp:root xmlns:jsp="http://java.sun.com/JSP/Page" version="2.0">
  <!-- other document syntax, e.g.: -->
  <jsp:expression>request.getRemoteUser()</jsp:expression>
</jsp:root>
```

14

The root element usually declares the JSP namespace which is used throughout the document, along with its prefix, which by convention is `jsp`, but could be any valid XML prefix, for example:

```
<blog:root xmlns:blog="http://java.sun.com/JSP/Page"
version="2.0">
  <!-- other document syntax, e.g.: -->
  <blog:expression>request.getRemoteUser()</blog:expression>
</blog:root>
```

As long as the URI of the namespace remains the same, the prefix assigned to the elements is so unimportant that it could be called `blog`; for uniformness, and to avoid having to declare the namespace-prefix mapping all the time, the specification and exam stick to using the `jsp` prefix to represent all JSP standard syntax. We will look at using more prefixes for tag libraries when we get to Chapter 17.

The `version` attribute is mandatory, and must be set either to `1.2` or `2.0` for the current JSP specifications.

In JSP 1.2, the `<jsp:root>` element was mandatory. As of JSP 2.0, it is not necessary to have the `<jsp:root>` element as the root of the document, as long as a valid root element does exist. The practicalities of this lie in template text.

Template Text

With a JSP page, template text could go just about anywhere. This is almost the case in documents as well, so long as XML's 'well-formed' rules are followed.

By taking advantage of XML namespaces, it is possible to include different types of elements in the same document. To us, this really means that a JSP can not only contain the core JSP syntax, which is parsed by the container and removed before the final response output to the client, but also tag extensions (the subject of Chapters 18 and 19) and HTML or other XML elements. Each of these elements is distinguished by its namespace. One set of elements only is permitted to have the default namespace, whereby each element in that namespace is not prefixed. This saves on typing, and more often than not, is used for the HTML or XML template text since this likely comprises the bulk of the document.

This is easiest seen through an example HTML document which has some embedded scriptlet code:

```
<jsp:root xmlns:jsp="http://java.sun.com/JSP/Page" version="2.0">
<html xmlns="http://www.w3.org/1999/xhtml">
  <head>
    <title>Test JSP Page</title>
  </head>
  <body>
    <jsp:expression>request.getRemoteUser()</jsp:expression>
  </body>
</html>
</jsp:root>
```

14

All of the elements in the JSP namespace are processed at the translation stage, so the result from a request to this document will only contain the HTML syntax.

NOTE: To be useful XML, every element in the document must be associated with some namespace. In the case of XHTML, this is `http://www.w3.org/1999/xhtml` as used above. When no prefix is associated with an element, it is assumed to have come from the default namespace which is declared using the `xmlns` attribute with no qualifier. Since most of my document above is XHTML and not JSP, I've assigned the XHTML namespace as the default one to reduce the number of prefixes I had to type! This also provides some backward compatibility for older browsers supporting only HTML and not XML namespaces.

The developers of JSP 2.0 realised that, since the template text itself must also always include a root element for the returned data to be valid XML, the `<jsp:root>` element was redundant. For example, in the above code, `<html>` also has the potential to act as a document root (and in HTML, this is the case).

Thus, the above code can be condensed slightly into:

```
<html xmlns="http://www.w3.org/1999/xhtml"
      xmlns:jsp="http://java.sun.com/JSP/Page">
  <head>
    <title>Test JSP Page</title>
  </head>
  <body>
    <jsp:expression>request.getRemoteUser()</jsp:expression>
  </body>
</html>
```

You might think that the removal of the `<jsp:root>` element makes the document less well structured, since now the parser doesn't know what to expect as the root element. However, when JSP documents are translated into their XML views, the `<jsp:root>` element is reinstated if it is not already present anyway: the omission of it just helps to increase the clarity of the author's code and to reduce the amount of typing. Legally omitting the `<jsp:root>` element in a document implies that version 2.0 or later of the JSP specification is being used, so the XML view's `<jsp:root>` element will have the `version="2.0"` attribute set, not that you need to know that for the exam!

Directives and Scripting Elements

14

It is illegal to use JSP-style scripting elements in XML-formatted documents because XML has no idea what Java's scripting elements are. Instead, an alternative XML syntax has been developed; this is pretty intuitive:

- `<%@ page` *`attribute_list`* `%>`
  becomes `<jsp:directive.page` *`attribute_list`* `/>`
- `<%@ include` *`attribute_list`* `%>`
  becomes `<jsp:directive.include` *`attribute_list`* `/>`

Each of the attribute lists in the above directives remains unchanged from their JSP counterparts: i.e. the typical document's `include` action becomes:

```
<jsp:directive.include file="URL" />
```

Note that all of the above are defined as *empty elements*, since they need no content; all the information that directives provide is contained in the element's attributes.

Note however that there is no `<jsp:directive.taglib />`; this is because namespaces, and therefore `taglib` URIs, are configured using standard XML namespace techniques. For example, to import the core JSTL library (see Chapter 14), we could use an `xmlns` declaration on `<jsp:root>`:

```
<jsp:root xmlns:jsp="http://java.sun.com/JSP/Page"
          xmlns:c="http://java.sun.com/jsp/jstl/core"
version="2.0">
  <c:forEach var="counter" begin="1" end="5">
    ${ counter }
  </c:forEach>
</jsp:root>
```

which binds the `c` prefix to the JSTL core URI `http://java.sun.com/jsp/jstl/core`. Note also that we could have bound the URI directly to the action by redefining the default namespace on that tag (see also Chapter 20):

```
<forEach xmlns="http://java.sun.com/jsp/jstl/core"
         var="counter" begin="1" end="5">
  ${ counter }
</forEach>
```

Now note that declarations, scriptlets and expressions are defined thus:

```
<jsp:declaration> legal Java code </jsp:declaration>
<jsp:scriptlet> legal Java code </jsp:scriptlet>
<jsp:expression> argument to print(String) </jsp:expression>
```

The body content in each of these elements should be valid Java code, as would appear in the JSP scripting elements, except to ensure the document is well-formed XML you should use a CDATA section or replace `&` and `<` characters with the entity references `&` and `<` respectively.

14

As you can see, the transition from traditional JSP pages to XML documents is pretty intuitive and easy to implement. It's also easy to remember, and since you may get several questions on valid JSP documents, *learn the syntax*!

Advanced Template Text and CDATA Sections

As well as inserting XML syntax as template text, we can use the `<jsp:text>` element. The body contents of this element can be virtually any well-formed XML; the value will be written directly to the response stream. The body may *not* contain any of Java's scripting elements, like `<jsp:expression>`, or any other standard actions. An example of this is:

```
<jsp:text>
  <table>
    <tr>
      <th>Col 1</th>
      </th>Col 2</th>
```

```
    </tr>
  </table>
</jsp:text>
```

Here the <jsp:text> element contains valid XML in the form of some elements and plain character data.

This doesn't seem all that useful, since the document works just as well when the <jsp:text> and </jsp:text> tags are omitted. Now take the JSP page syntax:

```
<img src="<%= request.getAttribute("image_source") %>" />
```

This is designed to dynamically insert the URL of the source of an image into the HTML `img` element's `src` attribute at run time.

The equivalent document syntax isn't as straightforward: the use of the old JSP scripting elements is not allowed, and we can't insert elements directly inside the `src` attribute value since this violates the rules for XML 'well-formedness'. Instead, we need to use XML's CDATA section, which is arguably the ugliest, and yet most necessary, escaping mechanism that XML provides. XML escaping is necessary because we can only use well-formed tag data, and not fragments of HTML such as `<img src="` and `" />`. The use of the <jsp:text> element is also required to ensure the contents of our CDATA sections are written to the output, but the `<![CDATA[` and `]]>` syntax is stripped off.

The previous example written in XML therefore becomes:

```
<jsp:text><![CDATA[<img src="]]></jsp:text>
<jsp:expression>request.getAttribute("image_source")</
jsp:expression>
<jsp:text><![CDATA[" />]]></jsp:text>
```

This is extremely untidy in comparison with the traditional JSP page syntax. The content of the <jsp:text> elements will be parsed by the translation engine, the CDATA sections stripped and the contents added to the response stream. The <jsp:expression> contents will be added to the compiled servlet's code.

NOTE: Using CDATA sections isn't the only way to insert scripting elements in attribute values; a second way uses the <jsp:element> and <jsp:attribute> standard actions (see Chapter 16).

Thankfully there is an alternative to all this extra typing which comes in the form of the **Expression Language** (**EL**). Using EL, the code becomes:

```
<img src="${ requestScope['image_source'] }" />
```

which takes us practically back full-circle to our original page's code; the difference is that this snippet can be directly inserted into a JSP document, and it is perfectly valid! The Expression Language is the subject of the next chapter.

NOTE: The use of a double quote mark inside an attribute value represents malformed XML, since the quote would be interpreted as the closing quote for the attribute value. Hence, we couldn't have used `src="${ requestScope["image_scope"] }"` above, so we chose to use EL's alternative *single-quote* mechanism for strings: `src="${ requestScope['image_scope'] }"`. In EL, unlike in Java, the single quote syntax `'...'` can be used interchangeably with the double quote `"..."` syntax for enclosing string values – this is often very useful as we've just demonstrated above.

Revision Questions

1 **Which of the following is the correct JSP document syntax for declaring a page directive?** **(choose one)**

- A <jsp:page ... />
- B <jsp:page-directive ... />
- C <jsp:page.directive ... />
- D <jsp:directive.page ... />
- E <jsp:directive-page ... />

2 **Which of the following performs a static inclusion of /footer.html in a JSP document?** **(choose one)**

- A <jsp:scriptlet>pageContext.include("/footer.html");</jsp:scriptlet>
- B <jsp:include file="/footer.html" />
- C <jsp:include page="/footer.html" />
- D <jsp:directive.include file="/footer.html" />
- E <jsp:directive.include page="/footer.html" />

3 **What is the result of compiling and executing the following JSP document?** **(choose one)**

```
1. <jsp:directive.page import="java.io.*" />
2. <jsp:scriptlet>request.setAttribute("items", new ArrayList())
   </jsp:scriptlet>
3.<jsp:directive.page import="java.util.*" />
```

- A A new ArrayList is bound into the request-scoped attribute called items.
- B A NullPointerException is thrown on line 2.
- C A translation error occurs on line 2.
- D A translation error occurs on line 3.
- E A compilation error occurs.

4 **Which of the following are valid in a JSP document?** **(choose two)**

- A <%= request.getAttribute("item") %>
- B <%= request.getAttribute("item") %>
- C <jsp:expression>request.getAttribute("item")</jsp:expression>
- D <jsp:expression>request.getAttribute("item");</jsp:expression>
- E <jsp:text evaluate=“true”>request.getAttribute("item");</jsp:text>

5 **Which of the following appearing at an appropriate point in a JSP document associates the prefix c with the tag library with URI http://java.sun.com/jsp/jstl/core?** **(choose one)**

- A <jsp:taglib uri="http://java.sun.com/jsp/jstl/core" prefix="c" />
- B <jsp:directive.taglib uri="http://java.sun.com/jsp/jstl/core" prefix="c" />
- C <jsp:root xmlns:c="http://java.sun.com/jsp/jstl/core" prefix="c" ...>
- D <jsp:root taglib:c="http://java.sun.com/jsp/jstl/core" ...>
- E <jsp:root xmlns:c="http://java.sun.com/jsp/jstl/core" ...>

6 **Which of these are valid server-side comments in a JSP document?** **(choose two)**

- A <%-- comment --%>
- B <jsp:comment>comment</jsp:comment>
- C <jsp:scriptlet>/* comment */</jsp:scriptlet>
- D <!-- comment -->
- E <!-- comment --!>

7 **What are the possible outcomes after compiling and executing the following JSP document?** **(choose one)**

```
<jsp:text><jsp:directive.include file="/WEB-INF/menu.jsp" /></jsp:text>
```


- A The resource /WEB-INF/menu.jsp is included in the response
- B The text '<jsp:directive.include file="/WEB-INF/menu.jsp" />' is included verbatim in the response.
- C The response is empty.
- D A translation error occurs.
- E A compilation error occurs.

8 **What is the result of compiling and executing the following JSP document?** **(choose one)**

```
<a href="<jsp:expression>request.getContextPath()</jsp:expression>">
click here</a>
```

- A A hyperlink is created with the text 'click here', linking to the path at the root of the application.
- B The text '<a href="">click here</a>' is written verbatim to the response.
- C A validation error occurs.

D A translation error occurs.

E A compilation error occurs.

9 **What is the result of compiling and executing this JSP document? (choose one)**

```
<jsp:text>You are logged in as:
<jsp:expression>request.getRemoteUser()</jsp:expression></jsp:text>
```

A The text 'You are logged in as: ' followed by the client's username is returned to the response.

B The text 'You are logged in as: <jsp:expression>request.getRemoteUser()</jsp:expression>' is output verbatim to the response.

C The response is empty.

D A translation error occurs.

E A compilation error occurs.

10 **What is the result of compiling and executing this JSP document? (choose one)**

```
<jsp:text><![CDATA[You are logged in as:
<jsp:expression>request.getRemoteUser()</jsp:expression>]]></jsp:text>
```

A The text 'You are logged in as: ' followed by the client's username is returned to the response.

B The text 'You are logged in as: <jsp:expression>request.getRemoteUser()</jsp:expression>' is output verbatim to the response.

C The response is empty.

D A translation error occurs.

E A compilation error occurs.

14

11 **What is the result of compiling and executing this JSP document? (choose one)**

```
<jsp:scriptlet>
boolean b = application.getIntHeader("counter") < 100;
</jsp:scriptlet>
```

A The method-local variable b is set to the appropriate value.

B A runtime exception is thrown.

C A validation error occurs.

D A translation error occurs.

E A compilation error occurs.

Answers to Revision Questions

1 **Correct answer: D**

2 **Correct answer: D**

Note that static inclusion uses the file attribute, while the <jsp:include> action for dynamic inclusion uses the page attribute; hence B is totally invalid while C is valid but performs dynamic inclusion. A also performs dynamic inclusion by directly using a RequestDispatcher. E uses the page attribute which is incorrect (it should be file).

3 **Correct answer: E**

All would have worked well had we not missed the semicolon from the end of the scriptlet's contents! Remember that it largely doesn't matter where page directives are placed (all imports are merged before compilation), but that the contents of a scriptlet are inserted verbatim into the translated servlet source code. We must therefore write:

```
<jsp:scriptlet>request.setAttribute("items", new ArrayList());</jsp:scriptlet>
```

4 **Correct answers: B, C**

A is invalid XML syntax. B is valid syntax so is correct; it will however be written literally to the response. C is probably what we're expecting. D uses a closing semicolon, causing a translation error. E is wrong: there isn't an evaluate attribute on <jsp:text>.

5 **Correct answer: E**

14

Note that neither A nor B exist; it is tempting to think B is correct because the other directives follow the this <jsp:directive.xxx /> pattern. C is wrong, as the prefix attribute is neither declared on <jsp:root> nor required. D is incorrect, as there is no taglib attribute for <jsp:root>. E is the only correct way, as it declares the namespace prefix and URI for the XML document (note that it should also declare the jsp namespace, but we've omitted it for clarity).

6 **Correct answers: C, D**

A is invalid syntax in an XML document; B doesn't exist; E is invalid XML. This leaves C and D as the only valid options; note that XML comments used in JSP documents are stripped from the output. However, this has only been clarified in the Servlet 2.5 specification for Java EE 5, so the behaviour in some containers is not well-defined.

7 **Correct answer: D**

A translation error occurs, which in AppServer 8 has the message '<, when appears in the body of <jsp:text>, must be encapsulated within a CDATA'. This is because the <jsp:text> tag can only contain template text and EL expressions.

8 **Correct answer: C**

This is an invalid XML document, as it is illegal to put an XML element inside another element's attribute value. A validation error will occur when the document is first parsed by the container, before being converted into the XML View.

9 **Correct answer: D**

It is illegal to use any other elements of any type inside a <jsp:text> without escaping; therefore a translation error occurs. We should write:

<jsp:text>You are logged in as:</jsp:text><jsp:expression>...</jsp:expression>

and could even omit the <jsp:text> element in this case (leaving just template text).

10 **Correct answer: B**

The container leaves the contents of any CDATA sections unevaluated when translating JSP documents. Hence the effect of the CDATA section is to pass the contents through literally to the response. The <jsp:text> element is in fact not required here, and the example would work just the same without it.

11 **Correct answer: C**

It is illegal to include '<' in an XML document when it doesn't denote the start of an element. Hence this symbol causes an XML validation error to occur when the container first parses the document. The valid alternatives are to use a CDATA section to enclose the content of the <jsp:scriptlet>, or to use the '<' entity reference.

In this chapter you'll:

- Discover what the Expression Language is.
- Use EL in template text to add dynamic content.
- Understand how different data types are output from EL expressions.
- Use EL in both attributes and body content of actions.
- Learn how EL variables are resolved.
- Memorise the names and types of EL implicit objects.
- Review the EL operators and their precedence.
- Learn about EL functions and how to invoke them.
- Write a custom EL function.
- Disable or enable EL expression evaluation in JSPs.

15 Expression Language

The problem with pure JSP is the reliance on the JSP author to know both HTML or XML and the Java programming language. At a commercial level, developers often find themselves working as part of a team of developers, each having their own expertise. Some will be brilliant with (X)HTML and XML, others with dynamic scripting languages like JavaScript, and others with fully-fledged programming languages like Java. If you're really lucky, everyone will be versed in all technologies, but individuals possessing such a diversity of skills is hard to find on a large scale.

The idea with enterprise teams is to be able to divide tasks between the team members: some HTML developers will work on the page and site layout and design, others will develop XML business-to-business interface specifications, Java EE programmers will develop front-end Web components like servlets and protocol interfaces, and finally a group of EJB programmers would work on the business logic. The division of these tasks is often essential to ensure a timely delivery of the project.

From what we've seen of JSPs so far, we would like to say that they enabled the HTML and XML authors in the list above to get on with their jobs, leaving the Java programmers to do all the hard work (just don't tell the web page authors I said that!). Given that all the JSPs we've looked at so far include some Java code, in the form of scripting elements (and to some degree require a prerequisite understanding of the way the Java EE platform works), it can be difficult for web page authors to write JSPs without either extensive training or a dedicated Java programmer for assistance. This fragments the team, melting the clear divisions which we would prefer to have in place (at least we would then know who to blame if it all goes wrong!).

The **expression language**, abbreviated to **EL**, is a new addition to JSP starting in version 2.0 (i.e. since J2EE 1.4). Its syntax closely resembles that of ECMAScript (the foundations of which form JavaScript, the popular dynamic scripting language for web pages) and XPath (a standard for navigating through XML documents). The former language, ECMAScript, is likely to be known by most HTML authors who work with Dynamic HTML (DHTML) to create interactive web pages. The latter language, XPath, is likely to be known by a professional XML author. Hence, EL acts as a gateway between Java EE and JSP authoring, allowing us to reinstate the division of labour in a team of Web experts.

Don't think that EL's uses lie just in providing equal shares of work in a team, however;

you're not let off the hook that easily. The expression language also has another important use for Java EE (in particular JSP document) developers: due to its carefully-chosen syntax, it enables data to be dynamically inserted *anywhere* in a JSP page or document, even in XML attributes within a document. We first discussed this problem at the end of the last chapter: if you need a refresher of the predicament, take a quick look back there. We will see exactly how to do this later in the chapter. EL also has applications with regards to standard actions and custom tags, which we will also examine.

The principle behind EL is to provide *script-less* JSP components – i.e. those which contain no Java-based syntax (like scripting elements and declarations). This decouples the creation of a JSP from a Java platform; one of the modern day aims of JSP is that it should be independent of a particular platform (unlike servlets, which require a Java EE-compliant server to work). JSP has evolved into being, at least potentially, completely cross-platform compatible (even if this isn't all that practical).

Having said that, the expression language is a replacement for JSP *expression* scripting elements; the EL is not a general-purpose programming language, and does not attempt to replace directives, scriptlets or declarations. In a good application, however, the functionality of these scripting elements would be replaced by tag libraries, servlets or helper classes.

The exam requires that its candidates understand all the syntax of the expression language, where and how EL is used, its operators and operator precedence, and how to write and declare functions to use in EL code. Since EL is new in only the latest version of both JSP and the exam, and most candidates will not have used the language before, we'll take the explanations at a slower pace than we have done so far. I hope this will instil confidence in you – the expression language syntax isn't any more difficult to master than Java's. Luckily, much of the syntax and operator precedence which you know from your Programmer exam studies will still apply.

Basic Syntax

Much like scriptlets have opening and closing tags, EL expressions are demarcated using opening and closing braces:

```
${ expression }
```

The curly braces which enclose the expression act like a code block in Java; anything outside the expression block created by the braces is not evaluated as EL. All EL expression blocks begin with the dollar sign, placed hard up against the opening brace as in the above syntax, which prevents confusion between template text contained in braces, and EL code blocks in the JSP. Any whitespace between the braces and the enclosed expression is ignored; the following are syntactically identical to the above:

```
${expression}
${     expression }
```

Each EL expression evaluates to one of the standard Java primitives or to an object type. For example, assume that the variable `title` is a string containing some text; the EL syntax for writing that text to the web page is simply:

```
${ title }
```

The expression language's primary use is to *retrieve objects from scoped attributes* (e.g. request, session and context). When used in template text, EL expressions *write the evaluation of variables or expressions* into the `out` (implicit object) output stream.

Expressions and Template Text

Suppose you have an expression embedded in the middle of some template text; for example, to create a dynamically-derived title for the web page. A typical JSP, with the EL code omitted, might look like this:

```
<html>
  <head>
    <title><!-- title here --></title>
  </head>
  <body>
    <h1><!-- title here --></h1>
  </body>
</html>
```

The simplest way to achieve this is to use two identical expressions which resolve to a string containing the desired title at run time:

```
<html>
  <head>
    <title>${ title_expression }</title>
  </head>
  <body>
    <h1>${ title_expression }</h1>
  </body>
</html>
```

When this JSP (the above syntax could be either page or document) is sent for translation, the JSP, regardless of whether it is a page or document, is first converted to an XML view. Since this view must be a well-formed JSP document, any EL syntax in the XML view needs to maintain the well-formedness of the view. The translation engine will complain if while parsing a JSP document, any

EL expressions contain characters which make the XML view malformed (most notably <, &, and " within attribute values). The requirements are more relaxed for JSP pages because the container first escapes all characters in the page which would otherwise lead to a malformed XML view.

It is important to realise that EL is not a processing language like Java; its only purpose in life is to retrieve data and perform automatic casting and comparisons. EL does not have the ability to directly instantiate objects or modify variables which exist in the container. All processing (instantiation and modification) must be done by Java code, either in scripting elements (if the JSP is not 'script-less') or in servlets or helper beans. Better still, all the processing could be indirectly delegated to Enterprise JavaBeans, but this is beyond the scope of this book and the exam. Also, tag libraries (the subject of the rest of Part III) are an excellent way to introduce processing behaviour into the JSP.

Therefore, assuming that a string variable called `title` already exists in the container somewhere (for example, in the current request object or at the application scope in the application's context), and it has been initialised, then this snippet will output its value amongst the template text:

```
<html>
  <head>
    <title>${ title }</title>
  </head>
  <body>
    <h1>${ title }</title>
  </body>
</html>
```


You might be asking if:

```
<b>${ "Here lies a quote" }</b>
```

will resolve to:

```
<b>Here lies a quote</b>
```

after the expression has been evaluated and the response committed to the client. The answer is yes: the previous syntax is perfectly valid; however, it would be pretty pointless to include a string literal in an EL expression, since the literal could just have easily been inserted directly into template text without the use of the expression language at all. In fact, this is highly preferred.

Now that we know EL parses literals on their own, you might be wondering about concatenation of strings–how can the value of a string variable be appended to another? Can we use syntax like this:

```
<b>${ "Here lies" + " a quote" }</b>
```

to achieve the same output as the previous example? The simple answer is that *concatenation is not supported*, but surely this is madness? The reason is that the + operator in EL is not overloaded for string concatenation, unlike in Java. In EL, + can only operate on numerals like integers and floating points, for the purpose of numerical addition.

As an alternative to concatenation, consider the following snippet:

```
<p>
  Some text of mine with a quote:
  "${ quote1 }${quote2}; therefore ${ conclusion }"
</p>
```

Note how two EL expressions have been placed back-to-back. The first resolves to the value of the `quote1` variable, and the second to the value of `quote2`. Each of these strings is then inserted into the document one after the other, which is in effect concatenation without the associated overheads (like the problems associated with the immutability of a `String` object). The last EL expression is inserted just to reinforce that these expressions can appear *anywhere*, as we already know. The end result is the effect of concatenation of `quote1` and `quote 2`:

```
<p>
  Some text of mine with a quote:
  "quote1quote2; therefore conclusion"
</p>
```

You may ask whether the two expressions need to be placed right up against each other, or if white space is permitted. It actually depends on what you want to do. For example:

```
${ "expr1" }${ "expr1" }
```

resolves to:

```
expr1expr2
```

with no space. Alternatively:

```
${ "expr1" }        ${ "expr2" }
```

resolves to:

```
expr1        expr2
```

with several spaces (or even a tab). In other words, all that matters to the EL parser is what is contained within the expression block. All other template text is passed 'as is' to the client.

15

Escaping

The EL opening syntax `${` was chosen so that it was both easy and quick to type, but so that the likelihood of it conflicting with existing JSP template text was small. However, it is feasible that you may still wish to write statements containing this text in a web page. For example, a JSP containing template text equations for exchange rate conversions between the GB Pound Sterling and the US Dollar might contain the literal text:

```
£{ x } = ${ rate * x } where rate = 1.5 approximately.
```

The expression here is not intended to be part of the Expression Language, but instead should be included literally in the response. One alternative, if the JSP contains no EL at all, is to disable the parsing of EL in the JSP altogether; this is particularly useful for old, pre-EL, JSPs which contain lots of the `${` character sequences. We will see how to disable EL at the end of the chapter–for now we'll assume we actually *want* to use EL!

Otherwise, there are no strict escaping mechanisms for EL expressions, so to escape just the `${` sequence it is best to write this as a literal:

`${ "${" }` (using double quotes) or `${ '${' }` (using single quotes)

which will output as

`${`

Another alternative is to use a back-slash preceding the dollar sign:

`\${`

which will output as:

`${`

to the client. This is useful particularly when entire EL expressions are being sent as output to the client (e.g. in an EL tutorial web page). Note that these escapes only work when EL is enabled for a JSP. If EL is disabled, they will be treated as literal output–i.e. as:

`${ "${" }` or `\${`

to the client, which is not what is desired. Escaping EL is, therefore, a fickle thing; the good news is that removing or escaping only the opening `${` causes the *entire* rest of the expression to be literal template text.

Expression Language Data Types

When expressions appear in template text, they nearly always output human-readable textual strings (displaying the hashcode of an `Object` wouldn't be that useful after all). However, EL is not just limited to being an alternative to JSP expressions; the result of evaluating an EL expression may be any of the following data types:

- Boolean, a `true` or `false` value [implementations typically use `java.lang.Boolean`].
- Integer, a whole number; may contain only digits 0 to 9 and an optional sign [implementations typically use `java.lang.Long`].
- Floating point, a *decimal* number; may be in the form `x`, `.y` or `x.y` where `x` and `y` are integers, and may be followed by an optional exponent, with a syntax identical to Java's [implementations typically use `java.lang.Double`].
- String, containing textual data. Strings may be demarcated in EL using either double quotes or single quotes. Backslashes may be used to escape quote marks as literals: for example `"\"text in quotes\""` escapes a double quote in a string demarcated using double quotes. Alternatively, alternating quote types may be used, in which case escapement is not necessary: `"'text in quotes'"` and `'"text in quotes"'` are both valid. Additionally, a backslash is escaped by another backslash, e.g.: `"\\home-dir\\mydocs\\"`. These are the same escape procedures as found in core Java (with the exception of a string being enclosed in single quotes).
- Object, any Java object.
- Null, indicated by the `null` keyword.

These types have the same semantics as in Java, but EL has only the notion of one type of integer and one type of floating point (unlike Java, which has `byte`, `short`, `int`, `long` and `float` and `double` types of different bit lengths). Additionally, EL treats strings as though they are *primitives*, whereas Java treats them as special *objects*.

The result of evaluating an EL expression depends on the context in which it is used. When an EL expression is evaluated, the container tells it what data type is expected from the expression, and the EL evaluation engine will try to coerce the evaluated expression to that type. If that coersion is not possible, an exception is thrown at run time. This allows the expression language to be used not only for inserting strings in the response stream (by coercing to a string data type), but also to be used as the arguments to tag library attributes which may require Boolean or integer types.

Thus the following in a JSP:

```
${ 1 < 2 }
```

is evaluated into the *string* `"true"` if included in the output, but the `boolean` primitive (or an instance of the `Boolean` wrapper object) with the value `true` if a

Boolean type is expected. The good news is that we don't have to worry about the internal coersion mechanism, provided we're careful and sensible about what data types are used where.

Putting EL to Use

Expressions as Template Attribute Values

EL expressions can be contained anywhere in the JSP, and they do not constitute malformed XML (unlike JSP's scripting elements). This makes EL perfect for use as the scripting language in a JSP document, in particular inside attribute values, where <jsp:expression> elements cannot be placed (since this would violate the rules for XML 'well-formedness'):

```
<jsp:root xmlns:jsp="http://java.sun.com/JSP/Page" version="2.0">
...
<body>
  <p style="font-size: ${ normalsize * parapercent }pt;">
    Some text
  </p>
</body>
...
</jsp:root>
```

In this example, the variable normalsize is assumed to contain an integer representing the default point size of text in the web page. parapercent is assumed to be a floating point percentage representing the relative size of paragraph font compared to normalsize. Assume that normalsize = 12 and parapercent = 0.85, just so we can follow through the processing of the above statement.

In order, this is what happens at run time:

1. The values of the normalsize and parapercent variables are retrieved from the container,
2. normalsize is multiplied by parapercent using EL's multiplication mechanism (the * operator syntax, as in Java),
3. The result is converted to a string and inserted dynamically into the returned web page.

The result of evaluating the JSP (with our assumed variable values) is:

```
...
<body>
  <p style="font-size: 10.2pt;">
```

```
    Some text
  </p>
</body>
...
```

The `10.2` shown in bold is the result of the entire `${ ... }` EL expression.

This is powerful stuff: not only can EL be used to insert data into normal template text (like JSP scripting elements can), but also its use is extended to the insertion of dynamic data into attribute values of a JSP document *where scripting elements cannot normally be used.*

Expressions in Actions

Standard and custom actions are the subject of the subsequent chapters, but in essence they provide encapsulation of specific processing to which the JSP can delegate control. This is easiest seen as a quick example using the `<c:if>` standard action which we cover fully in Chapter 17:

```
<jsp:root xmlns:jsp="..."
          xmlns:c="http://java.sun.com/jsp/jstl/core">
...
  Price of item:
  <c:if test="${ price > 0 }">
    ${ price }
  </c:if>
  <c:if test="${ price le 0 }">
    [not available]
  </c:if>
...
</jsp:root>
```


The idea behind this snippet is as follows:

- If the value of the `price` variable is greater than 0, it is written to the output stream amongst the template text.
- If, however, the value in the `price` variable is less than or equal to 0, then the variable does not contain a valid price, so `[not available]` is displayed instead.

Without going into too much detail about the `<c:if>` standard action at the moment (I wouldn't want to spoil the excitement for Chapter 17!), if the result of the expression contained in the action's `test` attribute is the Boolean value `true`, the body is processed. Otherwise, the body of the element is ignored. Since JSP scripting elements cannot be used in attributes in JSP documents, the expression language provides the ideal alternative: in the first instance, the expression `price > 0` is evaluated; if this returns `true`, then `price` is included in the response. If the EL expression `price le 0` (which is equivalent to `price <= 0`) returns `true`, then the alternative template text is used.

The way to look at the processing of these expressions is:

1. The variable `price` is retrieved from the container (see *Variable Resolution* next).
2. The expression in each case is evaluated; e.g. `price > 0` is evaluated to its `Boolean` result (note that even though a primitive `boolean` is the result of the expression, EL supports only `Object` types, so it boxes primitives up into their `java.lang` wrapper classes like `Integer`, `Double` and `Boolean`).
3. The resulting `Boolean` object is passed to the `<c:if>` action, which uses the `Boolean` to determine whether to write to the action's contents to the response stream (the action may *opt* to have the EL evaluator extract a `boolean` primitive from the `Boolean` wrapper if it finds the primitive easier to work with).
4. Should the EL expressions not resolve to a Boolean value (as expected by the action), an exception will be thrown at run time.

NOTE: The Expression Language was originally proposed by the JSTL (Java Standard Tag Library) expert group to provide a dynamic mechanism for the processing of expressions in standard actions and in particular in attribute values; this might explain its suitability for this purpose somewhat! EL was adopted fully for JSP 2.0 from JSTL draft proposals.

Variable Resolution

We've already seen the sorts of expressions which EL is capable of handling; these come in their most useful form when a variable is involved in the expression. For example, when the value of an integer is multiplied by another integer and the result written to the response stream. Alternatively, an expression is evaluated to either true or false, and an action is used to provide conditional page flow. You may however be wondering how exactly the expression language knows where to find the variables we declare. The answer lies in how EL expressions are parsed.

ExpressionEvaluator and VariableResolver

You won't be asked any of the technical details from this short section in the exam, but I hope you will find it useful to know fully how things work–I find it 'glues' together all the pieces and makes everything more memorable.

Each time an EL expression is encountered in a JSP at run time, the container invokes the JSP's instance of the `javax.servlet.jsp.el.ExpressionEvaluator` class, calling the `evaluate` method. This method first checks for syntactic errors in the expression. Then it performs variable resolution, by which we mean that it uses an implementation of the `javax.servlet.jsp.el.VariableResolver` interface to seek out variables with the same names used in the expression somewhere in the container. For example, if the variable `price` is used in an EL expression, and a variable with the name `price` also exists in the session scope (as an attribute in an instance of `HttpSession`), then the `VariableResolver` will return this value. If no variable of that name can be found, then `null` is returned. Finally, the `evaluate` method, using the resolved variables, examines the operators in the statement and evaluates the resulting expression in its entirety. The expression is coerced to the type expected by its context (e.g. a `boolean` value in the `test` attribute of `<c:if>` which we saw in the previous example). If coercion fails, an exception of type `javax.servlet.jsp.el.ELException` will be thrown at run time.

The default implementation of the `VariableResolver` uses the `findAttribute` method of the `JspContext` instance for the current JSP component. The PageContext API, to which `JspContext` belongs, was discussed in Chapter 13. This method works by looking in the following locations in order:

15

- The implicit object set (see next section). If any variable name used in an expression matches an implicit object, then this is returned as a priority.
- The page scope (`PageContext` object's attributes).
- The request scope (`ServletRequest` object's attributes).
- The session scope (`HttpSession` object's attributes).
- The application scope (`ServletContext` object's attributes).

Notice how the scopes become more generalised: the `VariableResolver` attempts to find a variable which is specific to the JSP, then inside the current request (which may contain many JSPs), inside a session (a collection of many requests) and finally an application (containing many sessions). Thus, an attribute declared in the page scope overrides an application-scoped attribute when resolved in an expression.

Functions are resolved in much the same way: the `ExpressionEvaluator` parses the EL expression, this time delegating the locating of functions to an implementation of the `javax.servlet.jsp.el.FunctionMapper` interface. The `resolveFunction` method is called on this object, passing in the name of a function. This method returns a `java.lang.reflect.Method` object (a member of the Java Reflection API) which can then be invoked. We will see how functions are both utilised and implemented (as Java methods) later in the chapter.

Implicit Objects

The set of implicit objects available in EL closely follows those available in JSPs. However, since EL is primarily focused on the retrieval of data, many of these variables are concentrated on locating data in scoped *attributes*, and not the actual request or context *objects* themselves. Each of the implicit variables, with the exception of `pageContext`, is a `Map`, connecting attribute names to their values:

- **`pageContext`**: the `PageContext` object for the current JSP.
- **`pageScope`**: a `Map` of the page-scoped attributes; attribute names are stored and retrieved as map keys. The values in the `Map` reflect the attribute values. Equivalent to `JspContext.getAttribute()`.
- **`requestScope`**: a `Map` of the request-scoped attributes; attribute names are map keys, while the values in the `Map` reflect the attribute values. Equivalent to `ServletRequest.getAttribute()`.
- **`sessionScope`**: a `Map` of the session-scoped attributes and their values. Equivalent to `HttpSession.getAttribute()`.
- **`applicationScope`**: a `Map` of the application-scoped attributes and their values. Equivalent to `ServletContext.getAttribute()`.
- **`param`**: a `Map` of request parameter names matched against a single `String` parameter value. Equivalent to a call to `ServletRequest.getParameter()`.
- **`paramValues`**: a `Map` of request parameters against an array (`String[]`) of all values for a given parameter name. Equivalent to a call to `ServletRequest.getParameterValues()`.
- **`header`**: a `Map` of request header names against a single `String` header value. Equivalent to the invocation of `ServletRequest.getHeader()`.
- **`headerValues`**: a `Map` of request header names against an array (`String[]`) of all values for a given header. Equivalent to a call to `ServletRequest.getHeaders()`.
- **`cookie`**: a `Map` of all the available cookie names against the single `Cookie` object which represents them. You could also, less easily, use

`HttpServletRequest.getCookies()`.

- **`initParam`**: a `Map` of the context initialisation parameter names against their `String` values. Same as `ServletContext.getInitParameter()`.

Operators

The operators in a language are just as important as the variables: without the former, we wouldn't be able to do anything useful with the latter! The expression language has a similar set of operators to those in ECMAScript (JavaScript) and in Java. This should make most of them pretty intuitive. We'll begin with the access operators that are less familiar to Java programmers.

Property and Collection Access

Many candidates of the exam who have not used EL before become very confused by the both of these operators: both resemble Java's syntax, but have subtle differences.

The EL parser assumes that all objects being used are solely providing data to the expression (recall that EL does not have the power to modify Java objects, only access them), and hence there is a requirement that all objects referenced must either be JavaBeans with `getXxx()` methods (where `xxx` is the name of a particular bean property), arrays (recall that arrays in Java are actually `Objects`), or `Collection` classes (i.e. `List`, `Map` and `Set` implementations).

15

The property access operator (`.` operator) has two parts to it: the first (preceding the dot) is the name of the variable containing the object being accessed (e.g. the implicit objects `param` or `requestScope`, or any other available variable), while the second part (following the dot) is the name of the property within that object. In the case of a `Map` collection type, this will be a string (without any quotation marks or whitespace) which represents the key of the object in the `Map` to be accessed. Otherwise, if the object is JavaBeans-compliant, the value following the dot is coerced into a string and used to call the accessor method for that property (i.e. if `xxx` follows the dot, then the `getXxx()` method will be called on the object). It is illegal to access *numerically-indexed* `Collections` like `List` and `Set`, or any arrays, using the `.` operator.

The alternative to the `.` operator is the collection access operator (`[]` operator), which is especially useful as it can access numerically-indexed `Collections`, which the `.` operator cannot. However, there is overlap: the `[]` operator isn't restricted to array-type `Collections`, but can also be used to access bean properties and values in `Maps`, just as the `.` operator can; for these applications, `.` and `[]` are simply alternatives offered to be compatible with ECMAScript's available syntax. The syntax is:

`object``["`*`property`*`"]` or *`object`*`[`*`number`*`]` for numerical indices

This accesses the property inside the supplied object; if *`object`* is a `Map`, then this expression retrieves the value whose key is *`property`*. If *`object`* is a `Set` or `List` or array, then the *`property`* string should resolve to an integer (*`number`*), which is used as the index for the `Collection`. Alternatively, if *`object`* is a JavaBean, *`property`* represents the accessor name: i.e. `get`*`Property`*`()` is invoked. The collection access operator is the only way to access numerically-indexed objects like `Sets`, `Lists` and arrays.

A typical exam-style question might ask you to pick out the valid ways of accessing various types of data. For this reason, and for your general all-round benefit, these are the syntaxes for using these operators:

- If the property name is *string-based* (i.e. either a `Map` key or a JavaBeans accessor name), the valid syntax is:

`object.string_property`	(without any quotation marks)
`object``["`*`string_property`*`"]`	(with quotation marks)

  The advantage of the second syntax is that the property name may contain whitespace (for keys in a `Map` for instance), while the first syntax must not.

  15

  You could of course omit quotes from the collection access operator, for example: `object[property]`. However, this now means 'find the property in the object which is indexed (either numerically or by string) by the value of the property variable'. This is clearly distinct from `object["property"]` and will therefore result in indeterminate behaviour if you don't use the quotes correctly!

- For *integer* (i.e. `List`, `Set` and array index) values:

`collection``["`*`number`*`"]`	(with quotation marks)
`collection``[`*`number`*`]`	(without quote marks, resembling Java arrays)

  It is not valid to attempt to access integer-indexed objects using the property access operator; i.e. *`collection.number`* is *illegal*, resulting in a compile-time error, and *`collection`*`."`*`number`*`"` always results in a compile-time error, regardless of whether *`number`* is an integer or a string.

As a mnemonic, you can often compare this EL syntax with Java's. For example, we never use quotation marks after a . operator, and arrays (which `Lists` and `Sets` resemble) are always accessed using the integer inside the square brackets. In EL, strings can automatically be converted (technically, **coerced**) to other data types like integers, floating points or Booleans, when required. Hence, using the collection access operator with a string value, but when an integer index is required, will cause the string to be coerced to an integer. For example, `myarr["3"]` is equivalent to `myarr[3]` after the EL evaluator has converted the string `"3"` to the integer `3`; array indexing then continues as normal.

NOTE: All string identifiers are *case-sensitive*, so using `mymap` in an expression is different from using `MyMap` etc.

Compounding Property and Collection Operators

Occasionally, you might need to access a value from a chain of objects. For example, suppose that a `List` in Java contains an `Object` (e.g. at index 0) whose `getClass()` method you need to call. In Java, you would code for:

```
list.get(0).getClass()
```

This is a chain of two methods calls; sometimes the chain is even longer. EL has facilities for just the same sorts of chain invocations. For example, suppose there is a JavaBean-compliant object located in the session scope with a method `getName()` that needed to be called. The object is bound into the session with the name `myobj`. This could be written as any one of the following lines:

- `sessionScope["myobj"]["name"]`
- `sessionScope["myobj"].name`
- `sessionScope.myobj.name`
- `sessionScope.myobj["name"]`
- `(sessionScope.myobj)["name"]`
- `(sessionScope.myobj).name`

These are several ways of writing the same thing, but this comes from there being a couple of different ways to write property and collection access operator statements. Note that brackets on the left side of a . are legal, but that the following are illegal:

- `sessionScope.(myobj["name"])`
- `sessionScope.(myobj.name)`

A . must always be *immediately followed* by either an alphabetic character, or _ or $ and nothing else (this is consistent with Java's variable naming convention for the first letter of a variable name). The following are legal but have different behaviour to the previous set of six statements:

- `sessionScope[myobj["name"]]`
- `sessionScope[myobj.name]`

When evaluating nested `[]` operators, the inner operators are evaluated first. So in these expressions, the value of the `name` property of `myobj` is first evaluated; then the container attempts to coerce this to either a string or an integer – if it fails, a runtime exception is raised. Otherwise, it uses this string/integer value to access that property/entry in `sessionScope` and returns the result. The collection access operator is more useful than the property access operator for exactly the reason that then property names can be determined dynamically from the values of other variables or properties.

Memorise the correct access expression syntaxes shown in the last section, and have an appreciation of chaining invocations and you'll be able to use one of the most revolutionary JSP technologies for several releases (and you'll be well on the way to getting 100% in the Expression Language section of the exam, but I'm sure you feel that's not as important!).

[] and . Operator Exceptions

15

On the whole, EL suppresses exceptions thrown during evaluation of an EL expression, choosing instead to return `null`. This includes suppressing situations where `NullPointerExceptions` would be raised. The situations in which EL does raise exceptions for an expression of the form:

`exprA.exprB` or `exprA[exprB]`

are:

- When `exprA` evaluates to a `List`, `Set` or array, and `exprB` does not evaluate to an `int`. In this case, coercion of `exprB` to `int` fails and an error is raised.
- If obtaining the value, either by evaluating `exprA` to a `List` or `Set` and invoking its `get` method, or evaluating `exprA` to an array and obtaining the entry at index given by `exprB`, throws an exception, this exception will be propagated (possibly wrapped in another exception). However, `IndexOutOfBoundsException` and its subclasses are always suppressed – the container instead returns `null`.
- If `exprA` evaluates to a JavaBean object, but `exprB` is not a valid property of that bean.

Standard Operators

These closely resemble Java's standard operators, so I don't propose to spend long discussing their functions.

The arithmetic operators are:

- Addition: +
- Subtraction: -
- Multiplication: *
- Division: / or div
- Remainder (modulo): % or mod

The remainder operator is used in modular arithmetic, having the same meaning as in Java's core syntax. Note that the last two operators, division and remainder, have alternative keywords as well as symbols, to be consistent with the ECMAScript.

Note that the - (subtraction) operator can either be *binary* where one term is subtracted from another, or *unary* where a single term is negated (multiplied by -1). Which function the operator is performing should be pretty clear from the code.

The relational operators are:

- Equality comparison: == or eq
- Inverted (not) equality: != or ne
- Strictly less than: < or lt
- Strictly greater than: > or gt
- Less than or equal to: <= or le
- Greater than or equal to: >= or ge

Again, all of the above operators have keywords as well as symbols. In particular, the keywords are useful in embedded script (including JavaScript and the EL) contained in an XML document, since placing < or & as textual content in an XML document is illegal–instead an entity reference would have to be used (e.g. >). The worded alternatives provide a more convenient syntax. If you look back to the section *Expressions in Actions* earlier, you will see we used le as the operator, instead of <=; if we wanted to use <= rather than le, we would have to write price <= 0, which I think is less instructive (and is more typing than just le!).

The logical operators are:

- Logical AND: `&&` or `and`
- Logical OR: `||` or `or`
- Logical NOT: `!` or `not`

The final operator is the conditional operator, which has the same syntax and function as in Java:

```
Boolean_condition ? true_result : false_result
```

If *`Boolean_condition`* resolves to `true`, then *`true_result`* will be evaluated; if not, then *`false_result`* is evaluated.

The Empty Operator

This is an EL-specific operator, not seen in Java. It is written simply as the keyword `empty`, followed by a space, then the expression or name of variable to test:

```
empty expr_or_variable_name
```

The result of evaluating this expression is a Boolean, either `true` if the variable is classed as being 'empty' (see below), or `false` otherwise.

A variable, or its resolved object, is said to be empty if:

- The variable resolves to `null`.
- It is a string which has no length–i.e. `""`.
- It is an array with no content (a length of 0).
- It is a `Collection` (`List`, `Set` or `Map`) with no entries (size is 0).

The empty operator is useful because it allows us to predict and allow for `null` object references, such as attributes not being bound into a scope as expected. We therefore avoid nasty `NullPointerExceptions` being thrown at run time.

Operator Precedence

Unfortunately, you can't get away with simply having an *understanding* of EL for long; oh no, those nice examiners make you *learn* it as well! This isn't a huge list of precedence, but you do need to memorise it so you can immediately parse a given script, and say in what sequence code fragments will be executed. A likely exam question will give you a single line of relatively complex code (especially code resolving to a Boolean) and ask what the result is. If you don't know this list, it's pretty hard to guess (even though you can probably see some logic behind the ordering of the list, somewhere):

- `[], .` (collection and property access operators)
- `()` (parentheses)
- `-` (unary), `not`, `!`, `empty` (negation, logical NOT, empty operator)
- `*`, `/`, `div`, `%`, `mod` (multiplication, division, modulo)
- `+`, `-` (binary) (addition, subtraction)
- `<`, `lt`, `>`, `gt`, `<=`, `le`, `>=`, `ge` (less than/greater than operators)
- `==`, `eq`, `!=`, `ne` (equality and negated equality)
- `&&`, `and` (logical AND)
- `||`, `or` (logical OR)
- `? :` (conditional operator)

Parentheses, as in Java, can be used to force or make explicit a particular execution order for a statement. Statements involving operators at the top of the list will be evaluated first, those at the bottom last. Expressions involving operators on the same line are executed from left-to-right as written in the expression (unless acted on by parentheses). Let's look at one example:

```
5>6 || 2<3 && !true==false ? "Evaluates true":"Evaluates false"
```

Firstly, the less than/greater than operators are evaluated: `5>6` to `false`, and `2<3` to `true`. Then the equality is evaluated: `!true==false`, resulting in `true`. Next, the logical AND is evaluated: `2<3` (which is `true`) `&& !true==false` (also `true`), resulting in an evaluation of `true`. Now, the logical OR is evaluated: `5>6 || 2<3 && !true==false` (which is collectively `true`). Hence, the result is still `true`. Finally, the conditional operator is executed, and since the Boolean expression resolves to `true`, the string `"Evaluates true"` is output.

If it helps when parsing these types of expressions, you can always insert your own parentheses; the logic section from the above expression becomes clearer if you do:

```
( (5 > 6) || ( (2 < 3) && ((!true) == false) )  )
```

Now working from the inside out will give the same evaluation result as before. Parentheses are first placed around operators which have the most precedence, then working outwards through those with less precedence.

Functions

The expression language has a simple facility for making calls to functions. However, as with all EL-related tasks, these functions should *not modify* data; instead they should be used to gather together data from several sources (such as several different objects in the application-scope) and combine them for a response. Alternatively, the function might get the latest exchange rate for a currency and return the result of a conversion. Normally, the purpose of an EL function is to provide a *convenient* mechanism for doing several things at once, or for doing a limited amount of programmatic work which the expression language itself cannot perform. Remember though: EL functions *should only be fetchers of simple data*, they should not handle business transactions (this task should be left to helper JavaBeans or EJBs) and should not provide large amounts of data back to the EL expression (if this is the case, consider a JSP custom tag). Functions may of course do simple operations on the variables they return – for example, if a function exists for calculating the value of one currency from another, the function would have to obtain the exchange rate (e.g. from an EJB mechanism) and then perform a multiplication before returning the final value.

Using EL Functions

All EL functions *must belong to a tag library namespace* in the JSP. This prevents conflicts if multiple functions share the same name in a document, but each function is implemented differently (e.g. from different component vendors). All functions are defined and implemented as part of tag libraries (see Chapter 20), which have an inherent namespace; logically, therefore, a function inherits the namespace of its associated tag library.

For example, assume we have a tag library associated with the namespace prefix `mytags` which contains the function `getName()`. In EL code, this function is invoked by writing:

```
mytags:getName()
```

NOTE: This is syntactically the same as XML's namespace mechanism, which we saw in the last chapter when we first looked at the `jsp` namespace for tags like `<jsp:scriptlet />`. The namespace prefix used must be configured either in the `taglib` directive (for a JSP page), or by declaring the appropriate `xmlns` attribute on the root element in a JSP document.

In general, EL functions are written as:

```
namespace:function(param1, param2, ... paramN)
```

If a namespace is not declared, the function is assumed to belong to tag library which has the default namespace for the JSP (if one exists).

The parameters of an EL function can either be literals, like `false`, `12342.34` or a string like `"mystring"`, or variables which resolve to valid values at run time. We will see what is meant by valid values in a minute. For example:

```
${ currency:exchange("USD", "GBP", 432.5) }
```

might be used to return the value for a currency conversion of 432.5 US dollars into the GB pound. In this example, `currency` is the namespace of the tab library, `exchange` is the name of the function, `"USD"` and `"GBP"` are string literal parameters and `432.5` is an integer literal parameter. Alternatively:

```
${ currency:exchange("USD", "GBP", amount) }
```

will do the same calculation, but on the value of the `amount` variable, which is assumed to exist in one of the scopes. It must resolve to a floating point number (or something which can be cast to a floating point number) at run time, or an error will occur.

Writing Custom EL Functions

Each EL function is actually a Java method behind the scenes. In fact, every EL function has an associated `public static` method in a compiled Java class.

Let's make this subtle point clear: EL has *functions*, Java has *methods*. When we write custom functions, we are mapping *functions to methods* (never the other way around). If we are talking about functions, we mean EL ones; if we're talking about methods, we mean those belonging to Java. This is a relatively minor issue, but it is easy to become confused if you don't appreciate the difference (many of the official specifications refer to just 'methods' and 'functions' without qualifying which language they belong to).

Assume we wish to implement the `exchange` function which we saw in use in the last section; this could be defined in a Java class as:

```
package mypackage;

public class MyExchangeClass {
    public static float exchangeConversion(String from,
                                           String to,
                                           float amount) {
        float calculatedAmount = 0.0f;
        // implementation code
        return calculatedAmount;
    }
}
```

Notice how the method must be `public` and `static`, and the parameter list must be the same as the EL function, but that the method name does *not have* to match the associated function. This is because a third force is involved in the picture; the following code snippet would be inserted into the Tag Library Descriptor (TLD):

```
<taglib>
...
 <function>
  <name>exchange</name>
  <function-class>mypackage.MyExchangeClass</function-class>
  <function-signature>
 float exchangeConversion(java.lang.String,java.lang.String,float)
  </function-signature>
 </function>
...
</tablib>
```

15

The TLD is the subject of Chapter 20, but we'll look at the EL-specific syntax here. The `<function>` element is used to declare an EL function in the tag library, the `<name>` is used to declare the function name as used in EL code, `<function-class>` specifies the fully-qualified name of the Java class in which the function is implemented, and `<function-signature>` supplies the name, return type and parameters of the method (in the specified `<function-class>`) which implements the function. Class names must be fully-qualified.

If a method is declared to return `void`, the EL function will return `null` (given the purpose of EL functions, as a convenient way to *return data*, a return type of `void` would usually indicate a bad design of function anyway).

Errors and Exceptions

Note that, unlike Java, a tag library can only contain uniquely-named functions: i.e. each function declared in a TLD must have a different `<name>` attribute value. Thus, overloading EL functions (having the same name, but different parameters) is not possible.

If you use a namespace prefix which does not map to a tag library, a translation error occurs. If a function (with a valid namespace) is used in a JSP, but the function cannot be mapped to a correct TLD element or Java implementation method, a translation error occurs.

If an argument to an EL function cannot be coerced to the parameter type required by the Java implementation method, then a runtime error will result.

Configuring EL and Scripting in JSPs

Evaluation of the expression language and traditional JSP scripting can be disabled using either the deployment descriptor or the `page` directive. In particular, the deployment descriptor can be used to assign general properties to *entire groups* of JSPs, while individual JSPs can override these to provide *page-specific* rules using the `page` directive.

Before JSP 2.0, the expression language was not an integral part of the JSP architecture, but scripting was. Increasingly now, developers should be striving to rid JSPs of complex scripting code, turning towards EL and standard and custom actions to solve their problems instead. For this reason, it is now possible to disable scripting from being evaluated. Additionally, for backward compatibility with JSPs containing the `${` syntax as template text or web page content, evaluation of EL can also be disabled.

Evaluation of Scripting Elements

15

By default, scripting elements are evaluated in all JSPs. However, they may be disabled as follows:

- **Through the deployment descriptor**
  Use the sequence `<scripting-invalid>true</scripting-invalid>` inside a `<jsp-property-group>` which targets the required JSP(s).

Attempting to translate a JSP which contains scripting elements while scripting is disabled will result in a translation error (and hence the JSP will not actually be compiled or available for servicing). Note that it is *not* possible to disable scripting through the `page` directive.

Evaluation of EL Expressions in JSPs

Parsing of the expression language can be disabled as follows:

- **Through the deployment descriptor**
  Use the sequence <el-ignored>true</el-ignored> in a <jsp-property-group> which targets the required JSP(s).
- **Using the page directive**
  Use the following attribute sequence in a page directive: isELIgnored="true". Use of this page directive attribute overrides the deployment descriptor rule for the JSP (if one exists).

The default semantics are a little more difficult for EL expressions than for traditional scripting (which is simply enabled by default). If the deployment descriptor being used is v2.3 or lower, EL is ignored (for backward compatibility); if the descriptor is more recent than v2.3, then EL is enabled (it is assumed that most developers using modern versions of the descriptor will be using EL, or at least make considerations for escaping sequences containing EL patterns in the JSP). This is summarised in Table 15.1.

Table 15.1 Configuring Evaluation of EL Expressions

Deployment Descriptor's <el-ignored>	page Directive's isELIgnored	Evaluation of EL expressions?
Not declared	Not declared	Enabled only if DD is newer than v2.3
false	Not declared	Enabled
true	Not declared	Disabled
Don't care	false	Enabled
Don't care	true	Disabled

What You Need to Know–Exam-wise!

We've covered a lot of ground in this chapter, discussing all of the intricacies of the language–something that potentially whole books could be written about. Now comes the all-important question: because this is an exam text, you'll be asking 'how much do I actually need to know for the exam?'. We've clearly gone into a lot of depth, but I would hope that this gives you a firm grasp of the language–not just the syntax and keywords, but the methodology which lies behind it. The expression language is powerful, but only if you know how to use it and what its limitations are.

For the exam, I recommend that you particularly review the following topics:

- Writing expressions, the `${` and `}`, and an appreciation of their use amongst template text and as tag attribute values.
- Variable declaration and the searching of scopes, including the order in which they are examined. You do not need, however, know the actual resolution mechanism and APIs.
- The implicit object names and their purposes.
- The property and collection access operators, the distinction between them, and valid declarations and expressions incorporating them.
- The operators and operator precedence.
- The basics of using and writing functions.

This is still a hefty list to learn, especially if you haven't encountered EL before, but it condenses the content in the chapter into a set of manageable learning outcomes–and hey, noone said passing the exam would (or should) be too easy!

As normal, the best way to learn something new is to try out examples. If you've got some JSPs lying around on your hard disk, my advice would be to convert some of those which use scripting elements (in particular expressions) into scriptless JSPs by rewriting them using only EL. Then you'll see just how powerful and quick it is to use.

Revision Questions

1 **Assuming the variable counter contains an Integer, which of the following are valid EL expressions which don't throw exceptions?** **(choose two)**

- A %{ counter + 5 }
- B ${ counter + 5 }
- C ${ "counter" + 5 }
- D ${ "25" + 6 }
- E ${ "john" + " smith" }

2 **Which of these ways can be used to escape an EL sequence?** **(choose three)**

- A Replace ${ with /${
- B Replace ${ with \${
- C Replace ${ with ${ "${" }
- D Configure the page directive's isELIgnored attribute to false.
- E Use configuration in the deployment descriptor.

3 **What is the result of compiling and executing this JSP page?** **(choose one)**

```
<% request.removeAttribute("counter"); %>
Hit count: ${ request['counter'] }
```


- A The text 'Hit count: ' is displayed.
- B The text 'Hit count: null' is displayed.
- C The text 'Hit count: 0' is displayed
- D A runtime exception is thrown.
- E A translation error occurs.
- F A compilation error occurs.

4 **What is the result of compiling and executing this JSP page?** **(choose one)**

```
<%@ page session="false" %>
${ sessionScope.basket }
```

- A Outputs the string value of the session-scoped attribute called basket.
- B Outputs the string 'null'.
- C Outputs the string ''.
- D A runtime exception is thrown.
- E A translation error occurs.

5 **Which of the following can be inserted into this JSP page to output the current counter value to the response?** **(choose three)**

```
<% application.setAttribute("hitcount", new Integer(10)); %>
// insert here
```

A <%= hitcount %>

B <%= application.getAttribute("hitcount"); %>

C <%= pageContext.getServletContext().getAttribute("hitcount") %>

D ${ application.hitcount }

E ${ applicationScope['hitcount'] }

F ${ applicationScope.hitcount }

6 **Which of the following statements set the page-scoped attribute called itemid to the value 'book1'?** **(choose one)**

A <% itemid = "book1"; %>

B <% pageContext.setAttribute("itemid", "book1"); %>

C ${ itemid = "book1" }

D ${ pageScope["itemid"] = "book1" }

E ${ page.itemid = "book1" }

7 **Which of the following statements are valid?** **(choose two)**

A ${ myArr[0] }

B ${ myArr['0'] }

C ${ myArr.0 }

D ${ myArr."0" }

E ${ Array.get(myArr, 0) }

8 **Which of the following retrieves the request URI used to invoke the current JSP page?** **(choose one)**

A ${ context["requestURI"] }

B ${ pageContext.requestURI }

C ${ pageContext.getRequest().getRequestURI() }

D ${ pageContext.request.requestURI }

E ${ pageContext["request"].getRequestURI() }

9 **Which of the following obtains the complete list of values for the options request parameter?** (choose one)

- A ${ requestParams["options"] }
- B ${ params['options'] }
- C ${ param.options }
- D ${ paramValues.options }
- E ${ param[options] }

10 **Which of the following expressions search each scope in turn until an attribute called properties is found?** (choose two)

- A ${ scopes["properties"] }
- B ${ scopes.properties }
- C ${ properties }
- D ${ pageContext.findAttribute("properties") }
- E <% pageContext.findAttribute("properties"); %>

11 **Arrange the following attribute scopes into the order they are examined when using the default EL resolution mechanism (the PageContext API):**

session	page	request	application

12 **Study the exhibited JSP page. What is the output?** (choose one)

EXHIBIT

- A Statement is true.
- B Statement is false.
- C A runtime exception is thrown.
- D A translation error occurs.
- E A compilation error occurs.

13 **Place the following EL operators in order of precedence:**

%	()	&&	? :	+
ne	empty	[]	or	ge

14 **What is the result of compiling and executing this JSP page?** **(choose one)**

```
1. <%@ page isELIgnored="true" %>
2. <% pageContext.setAttribute("user", "John"); %>
3. <jsp:text>
4.   Welcome ${ user }
5. </jsp:text>
```

- A The text 'Welcome John' is output.
- B The text 'Welcome ${ user }' is output.
- C A translation error occurs on line 1.
- D A translation error occurs on line 3.
- E A compilation error occurs.

15 **What is the result of compiling and executing this JSP document?** **(choose one)**

```
<jsp:root xmlns:jsp="http://java.sun.com/JSP/Page" version="2.0">
  <jsp:text>Statement is ${ 3 > 2 && 5 lt 6 }</jsp:text>
</jsp:root>
```

- A Statement is true.
- B Statement is false.
- C A runtime exception is thrown.
- D A translation error occurs.
- E A compilation error occurs.

16 **Which two of these operators have the same level of precedence?** **(choose two)**

- A and
- B lt
- C ==
- D !
- E >=

17 **Which of the following implicit objects contains a map of all servlet initialisation parameters for this JSP?** **(choose one)**

- A param
- B paramValues
- C initParams
- D initParam
- E None of the above

18 **What is the result of compiling and executing this JSP document? (choose one)**

```
<jsp:root xmlns:jsp="http://java.sun.com/JSP/Page" version="2.0">
<jsp:text><![CDATA[Application title: ${ context['title'] }]]></jsp:text>
</jsp:root>
```

A The text 'Application title: ' followed by the value of the context parameter title is written to the response.

B The text 'Application title: ${ context['title'] }' is written to the response.

C The text '<![CDATA[Application title: ${ context['title'] }]]>' is written to response.

D A translation error occurs.

19 **Which of the following obtains a String for the first value set for the request header called Accept-Language? (choose one)**

A ${ request.header("Accept-Language") }

B ${ pageContext.request.header["Accept-Language"] }

C ${ headerValues["Accept-Language"] }

D ${ header["Accept-Language"] }

E ${ header.Accept-Language }

20 **What is the result of executing the following in a JSP page? (choose one)**

```
<% java.util.HashMap map = new java.util.HashMap();
    map.put("Accept-Language", "en");
    pageContext.setAttribute("param", map); %>
${ param["Accept-Language"] }
```

15

A The text 'en'.

B The value of the Accept-Language request parameter.

C The response is empty.

D A translation error occurs.

E A compilation error occurs.

21 **The JSTL Functions tag library is associated with the fn prefix in a JSP page; the length EL function is defined in a class file by the method shown in the exhibit. Which of the following finds the length of the String contained in the description request parameter? (choose one)**

EXHIBIT

A ${ length(${ param['description'] }) }

B ${ length[param.description] }

C ${ fn:length(param["description"]); }

D ${ fn:length(param.description) }

E ${ fn:length[param.description] }

22 **The JSTL Functions tag library is associated with the fn prefix in a JSP page; the library contains the split EL function taking two arguments: the first is the string to be tokenised, and the second is the delimiter string. We implement this tag by the method in the exhibit. This can be invoked in code by ${fn:split(mylist, ",")} for instance, where mylist is the variable containing the string to be tokenised. What declaration must occur in the tag library descriptor for this function?** **(choose one)**

EXHIBIT

A
```
<function>
  <name>split</name>
  <class>mytags.functions.Functions</class>
  <function-signature>String[] splitStr(String, String)</function-signature>
</function>
```

B
```
<function>
  <function-name>split</function-name>
  <class>mytags.functions.Functions</class>
  <signature>
    java.lang.String[] splitStr(java.lang.String,java.lang.String)</signature>
</function>
```

C
```
<function>
  <name>split</name>
  <function-class>mytags.functions.Functions</function-class>
  <function-signature>
   java.lang.String [] splitStr(java.lang.String, java.lang.String)</function-signature>
</function>
```

D
```
<function>
  <name>split</name>
  <function-class>mytags.functions.Functions</function-class>
  <method-signature>
   java.lang.String [] split(java.lang.String, java.lang.String)</method-signature>
</function>
```

15

Exhibits

Q.12

```
<% pageContext.setAttribute("list", new java.util.ArrayList(5)); %>
<% pageContext.setAttribute("num", new Integer(6)); %>
<% request.setAttribute("num", new Integer(3)); %>
Statement is
${ !(empty list) ? num+6<10 && num>3 : empty 0 && num < 5 || num > 2 }
```

Q.21

```
public static int length(Object o) {
    if(o instanceof Collection) {
        return ((Collection)o).size();
    }

    if(o instanceof String) {
        return ((String)o).length();
    }
    return 0;
}
```

Q.22

```
package mytags.functions;

public class Functions {
    public static String[] splitStr(String input, String delims) {
        if(input == null) {
            return new String[0];
        }

        /*
         * We use regex here; the actual fn:split uses the semantics
         * of the legacy java.util.StringTokenizer.
         */
         return input.split(delims);
    }
}
```

Answers to Revision Questions

1 **Correct answers: B, D**

A is incorrect as it uses the wrong opening delimiter; B coerces the value of the counter object (whatever that might be) to an integer and performs arithmetic; C will always result in a runtime exception because the string 'counter' cannot be coerced into an integer–recall that EL doesn't support string concatenation, so this won't give you 'counter5'; the lack of concatenation also makes E invalid. D coerces the string '25' to an integer, then performs addition.

2 **Correct answers: B, C E**

D is almost correct, except isELIgnored should be true to disable parsing, not false.

3 **Correct answer: A**

There is nothing wrong with the structure and syntax of this page–it is perfectly valid. However, there is no request implicit object (there is however a request*Scope* object), and we haven't declared one in the page either. Hence *request* is null; but the EL suppresses most occurrences of null pointers, so the output of the expression is actually null–which is coerced to an empty string because a string is expected (since the expression is used in template text).

4 **Correct answer: E**

This throws a translation error; any attempt to access any session scopes (even indirectly through request.getSession() or using EL) raises an error when the session="false" declaration in the page directive is used.

5 **Correct answers: C, E, F**

A is incorrect as this references a hitcount *scripting variable* which doesn't exist. B is incorrect as it is terminated by a semicolon; C is correct, using the PageContext API to retrieve the ServletContext, then the attribute value; D is incorrect as there is no application implicit object; E and F both make use of the applicationScope implicit object and the property and collection access operators (note also the valid use of single quotes in E).

15

6 **Correct answer: B**

The point of this question is to enforce that EL expressions in JSP 2.0 can only *retrieve* data, never set it. Therefore, all the expressions C through to E are incorrect as they use an = for assignment (although EL 2.1 uses the = assignment operator, EL 2.0 doesn't even define it). This explains why the answer has nothing to do with EL, but instead resorts to the traditional scripting–setting variables has to be done programmatically, not through EL. Note also that A is incorrect as this would set a method-local programming variable, and not a scoped attribute. I've mentioned that EL 2.0 in JSP 2.0 only supports reading data, but deferred expressions in the new EL 2.1 (not covered in the SCWCD exam) also support writing data in a limited set of circumstances.

7 **Correct answers: A, B**

The only really correct syntax is A, but for B the container coerces the string '0' into an integer, then uses A anyway! C and D are incorrect, as you can't use the property access operator for numerical indices; E is incorrect, as it attempts to reference a method *on an object*, which is not supported in EL (the only similar constructs are functions, but these aren't executed on an object). Remember: *this isn't Java*!

8 **Correct answer: D**

All of these except C and E use valid syntax; both of these expressions attempt to invoke a method by declaring xxx(), and EL cannot be used to invoke methods (also, functions *cannot* be invoked on objects). Furthermore, it is wrong to use the 'get' in any accessor name, because EL adds the 'get' for you. The only correct expression is D, which obtains the PageContext, invokes its getRequest method, then invokes that object's getRequestURI(). This will return the URI used to request this page, and is quite useful. Note that if the method had a *non-standard accessor* name, for example, requestURI() instead of getRequestURI(), we couldn't have used EL to invoke it.

9 **Correct answer: D**

Only the paramValues implicit object holds a reference to a String[] of all request parameter values.

10 **Correct answers: C, E**

Recall that there is no implicit object called scopes, so A and B are incorrect. Also, it is illegal to invoke any method directly, so D will cause a translation-time EL parsing exception to occur. C is correct; the default EL 2.0 behaviour for any named variable is to search each scope in turn. E is correct; it uses the PageContext API, and the findAttribute method in JspContext, and this is exactly how EL 2.0 variable resolution works.

15

11 **Correct answer:** page, request, session, application.

12 **Correct answer: A**

This question puts together just about as much as it can from EL operators! Firstly, you need to realise that since variables are searched starting with page scope, the assignment on line 3 is effectively ignored by the references to num in the expression. That means that references to num actually hold the value 6. The ArrayList is actually empty – its initial capacity was initialised to 5, but it still contains no entries. So the statement 'empty list' returns true, hence '!(empty list)' is false. Therefore we only need examine the second conditional part, putting in brackets for precedence:

```
((empty 0) && (num < 5)) || (num > 2)
```

Recall that the empty operator returns false unless the thing it is acting on is null, an empty string, or an empty Collection type. Since the integer is none of these, 'empty 0' returns false. Hence, the first part returns false. The second part returns true because 6 > 2, and this is sufficient to send the OR to true. So overall this expression is true. Try also examining the first part by putting in the brackets, and you should obtain false as the answer: ((num + 6) < 10) && (num > 3)

13 **Correct answer:** [], (), empty, %, +, ge, ne, &&, or, ? :.

14 **Correct answer: B**

Disabling EL means the container interprets any EL expressions as template text. This means it passes them verbatim to the response (the opposite behaviour to scripting expressions, which when disabled cause a translation error if used). So B is correct.

15 **Correct answer: D**

Although it is legal to have EL expressions as the contents of <jsp:text> elements, it is illegal XML to use the '&' character when it isn't an entity reference. Hence a validation error occurs as part of translation. '&&' should be written either as the keyword 'and' or as the XML entity alternative '&&' (both are equally valid, but perhaps the first is 'cleaner').

16 **Correct answers: B, E**

17 **Correct answer: E**

There is no easy EL mechanism for accessing servlet parameters; initParam contains a map of context initialisation parameters. You would first need to obtain the parameter and store it in a scoped attribute using scriptlet code or a Front Controller servlet.

18 **Correct answer: B**

<jsp:text> always strips the CDATA syntax it contains, making C incorrect; A is also wrong, as the CDATA section acts as an escape mechanism for the contents of <jsp:text>. There is nothing syntactically incorrect with this example, so D is incorrect.

19 **Correct answers: D**

We only want to obtain the *single first* header, so C is incorrect (although valid). A is incorrect since it uses a Java method syntax which is illegal in EL. E is incorrect as 'Accept-Language' is not a valid Java identifier (the – makes it illegal); the . operator must have valid operators both sides, but as it stands, this would be interpreted as: ${ (header.Accept) – Language }, in other words, the subtraction of the Language variable from the value of the Accept header. Option B is incorrect because pageContext. request is an object of type ServletRequest (and usually HttpServletRequest), but there is no zero-argument getHeader() method on that interface (or class). Hence it cannot be searched using the [] EL operator.

20 **Correct answer: B**

Note that implicit objects take precedence over any scoped attributes, so the page-scoped attribute is ignored. Hence the returned value is the request parameter.

21 **Correct answer: D**

All functions use parentheses as delimiters, making B and E incorrect. A is illegal EL syntax, as you can't nest expressions. Finally, C is incorrect, as EL, unlike Java, never has line-terminating semicolons. Note also that the prefix fn is required to associate the function with a particular library. This means that we could have both fn:length and my:length in the same expression, two functions with the same name, but their prefix determines which library they are actually associated with.

22 **Correct answer: C**

The key things to remember are: the elements are <function>, <name>, <function-class> and <function-signature>; the signature must contain *fully-qualified* class names and <function-signature> refers to the *Java method name* and not the EL function.

In this chapter you'll:

- Learn what actions are how to use them in JSPs.
- Review the concept of JavaBeans, and see how these interact with actions.
- Be introduced to the standard actions which may appear on the exam.
- Summarise other useful actions which are non-examinable.

16 Standard Actions & JavaBeans

This chapter acts as an introduction to one of the trickiest areas of the exam, actions and tag libraries, which collectively will be introduced over the next three chapters. We take a slower pace throughout this section of the book, since many of the objectives were new for the previous SCWCD 1.4 version of the exam and the APIs are substantial.

The Basics of Actions

Actions, often called **tags** as a result of their syntax, provide a way to separate web page-specific template text and common programmatic (scripted) requirements in a JSP. Actions promote code reuse and scalability of applications; in addition, they enforce the clean separation between a JSP's role as a textual content provider, and the other servlet and EJB components responsible for doing processing work. Recall that the purpose of a JSP is to provide a template for a dynamically-derived web page, not to include lots of scripting code which would be better located in an EJB or servlet.

Unofficially, there are two types of action:

- The first type results in *content* being added to the current JSP output stream, and hence returned to the client. This content can be dynamically interpreted, based on the values of helper beans or EJBs, or indeed any scoped variable.
- The second type is *programmatic*, causing variables or JavaBeans to be updated with new values (this functionality does not exist in the expression language remember).

A classic example falling in the first category is the `<jsp:plugin>` action, which is used to dynamically insert *browser-dependent* HTML code for applets into the response stream. This action makes a decision about whether to use the `<object>` or `<embed>` HTML elements, depending on which browser the client is using (unfortunately different browsers support different constructs for embedding objects/applets). By using an action of this type, we avoid cluttering up the JSP with ugly scripting code which checks the client's browser type and outputs the correct HTML code: this promotes *extensibility* since if the HTML code needs to be changed in the future, the code comprising the action can be changed without requiring any changes to the potentially hundreds of JSPs which use it. Additionally, since we can use the simple

`<jsp:plugin>` construct anywhere in the JSP, we can declare *several* applets to be dynamically inserted into the *same* response, without having to repeat the code necessary for each applet separately: code is being *reused* and is *scalable* to any size of JSP-based application.

An example residing in the second category of action would be the `<jsp:useBean>` action, which declares the JSP as requiring the use of a JavaBean component stored in one of the variable scopes; it subsequently stores the retrieved object in a local scripting variable for ease of reference by traditional JSP scripting elements. The other behaviour of this action is to ensure that a certain bean exists already, and if not, instantiate a new one to take its place – thus ensuring that a bean always exists in the specified scoped attribute.

Benefits of Actions

We've already said that actions provide a way for an application to have reusable code, and to be scalable and extensible. A change in code to an action will be reflected by a change in code to all JSPs where that action is used. As a bonus, if an action is redeployed independently of the JSPs which reference it, it doesn't matter – the JSPs are still updated because they call the action dynamically at *request time* and do not have code hard-coded into the JSP itself. For actions which insert dynamic content into a web page, this is a similar process to including a resource using the `RequestDispatcher` mechanism.

One benefit of actions which we haven't considered yet is the primary advantage of the expression language: actions are simple to understand if they are well documented, and since they resemble XML elements (see next section), any JSP author who is *not versed in Java* can use them effectively. This explains why actions replace scripted code; now all a JSP author needs to know to build effective web pages is the basic JSP syntax, the expression language and the set of actions available to them (all of which resemble familiar languages like JavaScript and XML). Since EL and actions decouple a web page from its logic, leaving the programming of actions to the Java EE Web Developers in the team, authors no longer needs to concern themselves with *any* Java code – instead they just ask their friendly, already overworked and underpaid, Java EE colleagues to whip up a new custom action to achieve a particular goal. This new action can then be used across the entire application, and in other applications as well if required. Building an action to solve a problem really is a one-stop solution.

Action Syntax

We will not see how actions work behind-the-scenes until Chapter 18, when we discuss how to construct our own *custom* actions. However, we don't need to know what actions are in order to use them, and making use of the standard JSP and JSTL actions will be the subject of both this and the next chapters.

Believe it or not, we've already seen actions being used (in action, as it were!) in the form of document scripting elements like `<jsp:scriptlet>`. All actions are well-formed XML elements, both in JSP pages and documents. This provides a common syntax across both types of JSP, which is a little less confusing than it otherwise might have been. In general, an action looks like this:

```
<prefix:action_name attr1="val1" attr2="val2" ...>
  body content or other elements
</prefix:action_name>
```

Alternatively, if an action does not contain body content, it is written as an XML empty element:

```
<prefix:action_name attr1="val1" attr2="val2" ... />
```

Don't worry about the syntax yet, if these pseudocode examples don't make much sense. Before long we'll be immersed in such a depth of actions, it will be hard not to see and remember the pattern!

JavaBeans: Ground Coffee?

Actions, as well as servlets and JSPs themselves, often make use of **JavaBean** components, sometimes called **beans** for short. Some Web developers aren't really sure what a JavaBean is, because they haven't met them before or can't see where the name 'bean' comes from? If you've seen the Java logo, you'll know that it is a steaming cup of coffee, of the Java variety. Coffee beans make up ground coffee, and JavaBeans make up a good Java application–the nomenclature connection should now be pretty clear. Note that JavaBeans have a well-defined place in stand-alone client applications as well as on the Enterprise platform.

In fact, while there is a convention describing how JavaBeans should be structured, there is no strict definition like an interface to be implemented. Instead, it is up to the intuition and experience of the bean developer to build a compliant class. This section will demonstrate the stages involved in constructing a bean. This is all background information; a detailed knowledge of programming JavaBeans (even though they are simple) is not required for the exam.

The basic goal of a JavaBean is to be a reusable component written in a standard format. The original intention for JavaBean components was in GUI and event systems, but their popularity has grown and they are now a widespread design pattern. The JavaBeans API consists of the `java.beans` and `java.beans.beancontext` packages. Most classes in these packages are used to investigate the nature of a bean at run time.

One key design goal of beans is that they should be modular and accessible in a uniform manner through the JavaBeans API. Although in practise this is often bypassed, the beans specification requires all instantiation, casting and `instanceof` tests to be performed through the API and not through direct tests. For example, using the `getInstanceOf` method on `Beans` returns a view of the `Object` in type `Class` (effectively performing a class cast), or the original `Object` if that is not possible. This is treated as *obtaining a different view of the same bean*, and not as casting. The distinction is that in the future some applications may obtain completely different `Object`s as different views of the same bean – a view need not necessarily be in the same class hierarchy as the original component. This is extremely flexible, but is not yet implemented (the API documentation for `Beans` states 'this method is provided ... to allow ... more flexible bean behaviour in the future'). Similarly, the `instantiate` methods on `Bean` allow instances of the beans to be obtained. The `isInstanceOf` method is used as an alternative to the `instanceof` test.

The `java.beans.BeanInfo` interface can be implemented by any developer of a bean who wishes to provide specific information about their bean at run time. This interface can be used to explicitly map properties to methods.

Fortunately we don't have to use the `BeanInfo` interface to develop a new bean; instead, we can rely on the default `Introspector` mechanism, which uses reflection to determine the methods on the bean at run time. From this, the `Introspector` uses simple design patterns to determine the properties exposed by the component, and how to access and modify them.

Constructors

Since beans are designed to be instantiated using the `instantiate` methods on `Beans`, we need a uniform constructor design. Since it isn't possible for reflection to determine what the parameters of an object's constructors *represent* (although reflection can determine their data types), it is clearly a pointless exercise to design a bean whose constructors take arguments. Instead, we always provide a default no-argument constructor, and it is this single constructor which is always invoked to create a new instance. Note that this is identical behaviour to the `newInstance` method in `Class`. All beans therefore only require the default no-argument constructor; omitting a constructor from a class will cause the compiler to insert a nullary constructor anyway, which is suitable if your constructor would otherwise be an empty implementation.

Since constructors cannot be used to configure beans, we must always use the property methods exposed by the bean to modify its properties instead.

Properties and the Default Introspector

In order to make use of the default introspector, we must obey this contract:

- All property accessors (those methods used to obtain property data about the bean) must be named `getXxx()` for a property with name `xxx`. The return type must be the data type of the property and it must not have any parameters. If that property is of `boolean` data type, the method name may optionally be `isXxx()` instead.
- All property modifier/mutator methods must be named `setXxx` (for a property called `xxx`) and must have a single argument of the data type for that property. The return type must be `void`.

The actual storage of properties can be achieved in any way you wish – the JavaBeans specification imposes no constraints on the underlying data model used by your beans. The most usual pattern is to have private instance variables with the same names and data types as the exposed properties. For example, if our bean had a `boolean` property called `loaded` (perhaps indicating whether a certain feature has been loaded already), our bean class would look a little like this:

```
public class MyBean {
    /* private instance storage */
    private boolean loaded;

    /* Could also be called isLoaded() */
    public boolean getLoaded() {
        return loaded;
    }

    public void setLoaded(boolean loaded) {
        this.loaded = loaded;
    }
}
```

16

Now the `Introspector` will find, by reflection, methods named `getLoaded` and `setLoaded` and will determine from these names that the bean exposes a property called `loaded`. This exact method-to-property name conversion is achieved by first removing the `get`, `set` or `is` prefix, and then using the `Introspector`'s `decapitalize` method, which is implemented as follows:

- If the first two characters are both capitals, leave the name alone. This allows, for example, `getURL()` to be interpreted as a property called `URL`, rather than `uRL`.
- Otherwise, convert the first character to a lowercase letter; for example, `getLoaded()` is converted to `Loaded`, which is `decapitalized` into `loaded`. (which by happy coincidence is the name of our property!).

NOTE: It follows from the above `decapitalize` process that ideally property names should either begin with a lowercase letter, or should be all capitals. Also, it follows that a property name should always begin with a letter (or perhaps underscore), and *never* with a numeral. If we stick to the guidelines, we will be forced to assume this naming convention anyway, since the private instance variable (as with any Java identifer) cannot begin with any character other than a letter or underscore.

Note that if a class is designed to be overridden by a subclass, it is sometimes convenient to have the instance variable with visibility `protected` rather than `private`. However, this shouldn't strictly be necessary as the accessor and mutator methods should be sufficient for access to the property variable.

Other Methods

16

It is possible for a bean to declare methods other than the property accessors. These will not be treated as properties by the default `Introspector` unless they obey the property naming convention above and appear as `setXxx()` and `getXxx()` or `isXxx()`. The default behaviour can be overridden by the bean implementor by using the `BeanInfo` interface, so in theory properties do not have to follow the `get`/`set` pattern (although this is highly recommended).

Sometimes it is convenient to have methods local to the class for the sole purpose of doing local work, perhaps encapsulating logic used by several other methods to provide maximum reuse of code. Where this is the case, those methods should have private (or protected) visibility. A bean class may also need to implement one or more interfaces, and therefore will have to expose public methods which do not follow the property naming convention.

Standard Actions for the Exam

The actions presented in this section need to be learnt in their entirety, both in function and syntax; the exam likes to ask questions on standard actions, so knowing everything here verbatim can guarantee you correct and quick answers to those questions (leaving you longer to think about the more complex topics they love to throw at you!).

All of the standard actions belong to the default JSP namespace, which as we said in Chapter 14, is usually given the prefix `jsp`. It is this prefix which we will use throughout the chapter. All standard actions appearing in JSP *pages* must have the prefix `jsp`, but the authors of JSP *documents* can choose any prefix they wish, provided it is mapped to the JSP URI (`http://java.sun.com/JSP/Page`).

Working with JavaBeans

<jsp:useBean>

When authors create a JSP component, they will often need to make use of JavaBeans within the application–for example, a JavaBean object containing the client's shopping basket contents stored in the session scope. To make sure that the object is available to subsequent code, we use this standard action. A basic description of its semantics is:

- If a bean of the required description can already be found, then the reference to that bean is copied to a local variable within the JSP. This improves access time and prevents multiple statements in the JSP from having to query the object at the appropriate scope.
- If a bean of the required description is not found, a new bean which matches that description is instantiated, and the reference to this new bean is stored in a local scripting variable in the JSP, as well as in an attribute of the appropriate scope.

The exact semantics depend on the attributes provided by the author (see below), but regardless, the end result of using the `<jsp:useBean>` action is that a bean will be ready to be accessed by subsequent code (either traditional scripting or EL) and by further actions in the JSP. For some applications, having a *guarantee* that a bean is available for use is particularly important.

The general format of this action is:

```
<jsp:useBean id="var_name" scope="var_scope" attrList />
```

The value of the `id` attribute should be the attribute name which is to be searched in the specified `scope`; this name also doubles as the local variable name. *`var_scope`* should be one of `page`, `request`, `session` or `application` (one of the scopes we already know lots about!). The `id` attribute is *mandatory*; the `scope` attribute is optional, and if omitted, its default value is `page`.

We will see the purpose of *`attrList`* in just a minute; to explain everything so far, assume the following code snippet:

```
<jsp:useBean id="basket" scope="session" ... />
<%= basket.toString() %>
```

The basic idea of this code example is that a variable called `basket` (containing a shopping basket object) is to be found in the session scope; this is made available locally to scripting elements through a local variable of name `basket`. The scripting expression just outputs the string representation of the basket to the response stream.

This is all very well, but the purpose of using the `<jsp:useBean>` action is that we can't already guarantee that the `basket` variable exists in the session scope (or in any scope for that matter). What we have excluded from the above example is a way for the action to instantiate a new bean, should the `basket` variable not already exist. Essentially what the action needs to know is what class the object needs to be, so it can happily instantiate a new instance. What we need are some extra attributes which go in the *`attrList`* placeholder in the general syntax given previously; the combinations of valid attributes are:

- **`class="`*`class_name`*`"`**
  Specifies the class type that the bean is, or should be, an instance of. *`class_name`* must be a *fully-qualified* class name.

- **`class="`*`class_name`*`" type="`*`generalised_class`*`"`**
  Specifies the class type that the bean should be instantiated as, and the type of class that is assigned to the local variable. *`generalised_class`*, as well as being a fully-qualified class name, must be either the *same class* type or a *superclass of* `class_name`. This allows for the local scripting variable to be defined as a parent of the instantiated implementation class type (although why you would need to do this is yet to be seen).

- **`beanName="`*`bean_class`*`" type="`*`var_type`*`"`**
  This mechanism instantiates a new bean using the static methods of the `java.beans.Beans` class. *`bean_class`* should be the fully-qualified name of the JavaBean to be instantiated; *`var_type`* should be the fully-qualified (generalised) class type of the object: *`var_type`* should be the *same class*, or a *superclass of* the `bean_class`. The `Beans` class first attempts to retrieve the bean from a serialised object before instantiating a new instance; if

bean_class has the value `a.b.c`, `Beans` first tries to load `a/b/c.ser` before instantiating a new `a.b.c` instance.

- **`type="`*`class_type`*`"`**
  Specifies the fully-qualified class name of the bean that is to be found in the scope as an attribute with name `id`. Note: if this attribute combination is used (i.e. if the `class` and `beanName` attributes are omitted), the relevant scope will be queried, but a new bean *will not be instantiated.* If the object is not available in the scope to be used, an `InstantiationException` is thrown at request time.

The local variable will always be of the class type given by the `type` attribute; the default value of the `type` attribute, if it is omitted, is that of the `class` attribute. An interface is classified as a superclass for the purposes of the above list: i.e. `type` may also be an interface of the implementing `class`. If the object is not assignable (cannot be cast) to the required type, a `ClassCastException` is thrown at request time.

Notice that *only one* of `class` *or* `beanName` may be declared. It is illegal to use both, since they perform the *same function* (with identical end results) but using different mechanisms in the process, and it doesn't make sense to try to do the same thing two different ways at the same time!

That's it for this action, but one quick note about the content of the action, which needn't be empty as we've assumed so far. The following general syntax is also allowed:

```
<jsp:useBean id="var_name" scope="var_scope" attrList>
  body
</jsp:useBean>
```

body can be anything (template text, other actions or scripting elements), but most usually any body content of the `<jsp:useBean>` action will be used for the configuration of the newly established (either located or instantiated) bean. The body will only be invoked if the bean established by the action is newly created. The configuration can be performed using the next action. 16

<jsp:setProperty />

This provides a way to set the properties contained in a bean which has already been established (usually using `<jsp:useBean>`). Properties can be set by one of:

- Using hard-coded string literals for the values;
- Using the value(s) of request parameter(s);
- From an evaluated request-time expression.

The general syntax is:

```
<jsp:setProperty name="var_name" property="property_name" ... />
```

where `var_name` is the name of the local scripting variable created by the `<jsp:useBean>` action when the bean was established; this will be identical to the `id` attribute value of that `<jsp:useBean>` declaration. The `property` attribute will have different values depending on the usage of the action:

- **`property="*"`**
  The action will iterate over all *request parameters*, matching parameter names with the bean's property names, and updating the property values accordingly. This acts as a convenient form of rapid synchronisation. This is particularly useful when the bean is *designed* specifically for storing all the information coming from the client in the request – for instance, as a result of the submission of a form as part of a registration process.

- **`property="property_name"`**
  In the case where the attribute has the name of a specific bean property (`property_name`), only this property's value will be modified.

The former declaration warrants no further attributes. However, if the action is declared with the latter attribute, it needs to know what the new value of that property is to be. As a result, there are two more attributes declared:

- **`value="val"`**
  Provides a way to set the value of the parameter to a hard-coded string literal, which would be typed by the JSP author as `val`. Alternatively, `val` may be a dynamic EL or scripting expression (assuming scripting is enabled).

- **`param="req_param"`**
  Sets the property to the value of the request parameter with name `req_param`. If this value does not point to a valid request parameter, then the bean's property is *not modified* (see next paragraph).

16

The value of either attribute must resolve to a value *compatible with the property type* in the bean. For example, if an `int` type is required by the bean, then it must be possible for `String`s (from request parameters or EL expressions) to be converted to `int`s, and any evaluated scripting elements must return an `int` directly. Any conversion failure will result in a translation or request-time error.

These *cannot appear together* in an action declaration: there can only be one, which is pretty obvious since they both achieve the same thing but using different processes. If *neither* is declared for a named property, or if either evaluates to an empty string or `null`, then that property is not modified. For example:

```
<jsp:setProperty name="abean" property="stock" />
```

does not change the value of the `stock` property, while:

```
<jsp:setProperty name="abean" property="stock" param="counter" />
```

sets the value of the `stock` property to the value of the `counter` request parameter, assuming that this request parameter evaluates to a valid data type at request time—otherwise the `stock` property does not change.

The `name` and `property` attributes are *mandatory*. The others are optional.

<jsp:getProperty />

This action is used to retrieve a property from an available bean, which has usually been established using the `<jsp:useBean>` action (although this doesn't *have* to the be the case). It has the following general syntax:

```
<jsp:getProperty name="var_name" property="prop_name" />
```

The all-important attributes are:

- **name="*var_name*"**
  var_name should be the local scripting variable name of the bean, as declared in the `id` attribute of the `<jsp:useBean>` action.
- **property="*prop_name*"**
  prop_name is the property name in the bean to be retrieved.

Both attributes are *mandatory*. The element is *always empty*—it never contains body content.

The value retrieved by this action is coerced to a `String`, for example by calling `toString()` on an object, and then written directly into the `out` implicit object.

Working with Other Pages

<jsp:include>

This action replaces the need to use `RequestDispatchers` in scriptlets—it functions in exactly the same way, delegating control to the `include` methods of `PageContext` behind the scenes. The two attributes are:

- **page**
  The value should be a relative URL string, pointing to the resource to be included. If this string starts with a forward slash (/), the URL is interpreted relative to the context root; otherwise it is relative to the location of the JSP in which the action is defined.

- **flush**
  Determines whether the response stream buffer is flushed before inclusion of the external resource. This is useful if the resource is large, since it prevents a buffer overflow from occurring. The value should be true if flushing is required, or false otherwise.

The page attribute is *mandatory*; the flush attribute is optional, with a default value of false should it be omitted.

For example, to include a resource at the path /banners/head.html (relative to the context root):

```
<jsp:include page="/banners/head.html" />
```

Alternatively, to include the toc.html resource (residing in the same directory as the current JSP) in the output:

```
<jsp:include page="toc.html" />
```

NOTE: The include *directive* in traditional JSP has the file attribute, while the <jsp:include> *action* has the page attribute. It is easy to get these confused, so be careful!

This action may either be empty (as in the above examples), or contain one or more <jsp:param /> tags which pass additional request parameters to the included resource, as we shall see shortly.

<jsp:forward>

This action is even simpler than the last, since it has only one mandatory form:

```
<jsp:forward page="rel_URL" />
```

where *rel_URL* is the path (either context-relative with a starting /, or relative to the current JSP otherwise) to the external resource to be forwarded to.

This action uses the forward method of PageContext to achieve its goal; it may either be empty (as in the above general syntax), or specify additional request parameters by containing one or more <jsp:param /> tags.

<jsp:param />

This is a special type of action: unlike most of the others we've met so far, this action doesn't actually do anything to the response or provide us with variables or scoped attributes. Instead, it's sole purpose in life is to provide supplementary information to its parent tag. See also *Nested Tags and Cooperating Actions* in Chapter 18.

This tag is used to provide extra information to relevant actions, in the form of name/value pairs which are merged with the current *request parameters*. It has two mandatory attributes:

- **`name`**
  The name of the parameter to be set.
- **`value`**
  The value of the new parameter. The value may be a hard-coded string literal, an EL expression, or a request-time scripting expression.

The use of this tag is best seen with an example. The actions which can have this tag as body content are `<jsp:include>`, `<jsp:forward>` and `<jsp:params>`. Since we have already seen the former (and need to know how to use them for the exam), we will look at an example using parameters:

```
<jsp:include page="/banners/footer.jsp">
  <jsp:param name="dateModified" value="${ modDate }" />
</jsp:include>
```

This example assumes that the `modDate` attribute, containing the date that the web page was last modified, is already bound into a scoped attribute. It includes a dynamic footer (`/banners/footer.jsp`) into the JSP, and 'creates' a new `dateModified` parameter in the request. Should a parameter with this name already exist, it is (temporarily) overridden with the new value. Note that the enclosing tag uses a `ServletRequestWrapper` subclass to achieve this, returning parameters set using `<jsp:param />` from its `getParameter` method in preference to those in the original request. Hence these request parameters revert to their previous values after the `include` invocation, or silently 'disappear' if they didn't exist before.

NOTE: When used with `<jsp:include>` or `<jsp:forward>` actions, the attributes bound into the request using `<jsp:param />` tags will not exist after that call returns. This is the same behaviour as exhibited by the include and forward additional request attributes used by the `RequestDispatcher` mechanism (see Chapter 6), but those are request-scoped attributes while `<jsp:param />` modifies *parameters*!

Other Standard Actions (Not an Exam Objective)

As I've said all along, this book doubles up as a handy reference to Web application development. While all the content in this section does not need to be learnt for the exam, it provides explanations of some of the less commonly used, and yet just as important, actions. I think it is important to introduce these, otherwise you might end up pointlessly constructing custom actions when appropriate standard actions already exist–and why waste precious development time reinventing the wheel? We only discuss actions used in JSPs here; those which are applicable only to tag files (`<jsp:invoke>` and `<jsp:doBody>`) are deferred until Chapter 19.

Supporting Applets

<jsp:plugin>

Inserting an applet into a web page can be difficult, even with several revisions of the HTML and XHTML standards behind us. Some browsers still refuse, or at least seem to find it difficult, to comply. Some browsers use the `<object>` element, which has been adopted in the new standards, but other legacy browsers are still stuck with the now deprecated `<embed>`.

If we had to write logic to determine the type of browser and which element to insert in the web page every time we wanted to include an applet (which the JSP standard action authors seem to think will be quite often), we would soon end up going mad. To save our sanity, we have the `<jsp:plugin>` element which automatically generates the correct HTML code for the browser, so that it will either run the applet, or begin download of the applet plug-in software from Sun.

This action takes the following attributes:

- **`type`**
  Must be one of `applet` or `bean`. This attribute identifies the type of Java object being used in the web page.
- **`code`**
  This has the same meaning as the HTML `code` attribute: it specifies the class that contains the `main` driver method for the applet.
- **`codebase`**
  As in HTML, this specifies the URL of the path containing the applet code.
- **`align`**
  Horizontal alignment: must be one of `left`, `center` or `right`.

- **`archive`**
  A space-separated list of URIs for archives containing resources required by the object. Including this information up front may improve load times.
- **`height`**
  The height of the applet in the web page, in pixels; the value may be the result of a request-time expression.
- **`width`**
  Specifies the width of the object in the web page, in pixels; the value may be the result of a request-time expression.
- **`hspace`**
  The amount of whitespace to be inserted on the left and right of the object–deprecated as of HTML 4.01.
- **`vspace`**
  The amount of whitespace to be inserted on the top and bottom of the object–deprecated as of HTML 4.01.
- **`jreversion`**
  The version of the JRE that the applet requires; the default is Java2, JRE 1.2.
- **`name`**
  Associates the applet with a name, allowing other applets in the same web page to find, and communicate, with each other.
- **`title`**
  A brief title for the applet–this is one of the common (X)HTML attributes.
- **`nspluginurl`**
  The URL of the JRE plug-in which can be downloaded for Netscape-compatible browsers. The default value is Java EE-implementation specific. This can either reference Sun's website, or a local copy of the plug-in on your own server (or any other server if you wish).
- **`iepluginurl`**
  The URL of the JRE plug-in which can be downloaded for Internet Explorer browsers. The default value is Java EE-implementation specific. This can either reference Sun's website, or a local copy of the plug-in on your own server (or any other server if you wish).
- **`mayscript`**
  Valid values are true, to indicate that the applet is permitted to interact with JavaScript client-side scripting in the web page, or false otherwise. Note that this attribute was never officially adopted by the W3C into HTML standards, and support is limited to the Netscape browser. Avoid if possible.

type, code and codebase are mandatory; all others are optional. In addition to these attributes, a <jsp:plugin> may optionally contain one <jsp:params> tag and/or one <jsp:fallback> element. An entire plug-in snippet could be:

```
<jsp:plugin type="applet" code="Clock.class"
            codebase="/applets">
  <jsp:params>
    <jsp:param name="starttime" value="12:00:00" />
  </jsp:params>
  <jsp:fallback>
    <p>Sorry, you have been unable to load the applet!</p>
  </jsp:fallback>
</jsp:plugin>
```

<jsp:params>

Use this tag to provide parametric information to the <jsp:plugin> action. A <jsp:params> tag contains one or more <jsp:param /> tags (note the possibility for confusion with the names here), each of which declares a new applet parameter. In the example above:

```
<jsp:params>
  <jsp:param name="starttime" value="12:00:00" />
</jsp:params>
```

This declares one parameter, with the name starttime, and the value 12:00:00. More parameters are added simply by inserting additional <jsp:param /> tags.

The parameters declared here are written as output into the rendered web page as HTML-formatted parameter information.

<jsp:fallback>

Sometimes an applet cannot be loaded, usually because a user has refused to have the applet plug-in installed (this is particularly a problem in networked organisations that block what employees are permitted to download).

This tag can be used to specify the HTML code to be used should the plug-in fail to load for any reason. In the example given previously, we had:

```
<jsp:fallback>
  <p>Sorry, you have been unable to load the applet!</p>
</jsp:fallback>
```

This will display the body content given (in this example, formatted as an HTML paragraph) in the event of failure to load the applet. It is useful to supply a message, since otherwise the user may assume that nothing was *supposed* to load, as opposed to the applet actually failing to materialise.

Creating XML-Compliant Documents

<jsp:element>

This action is used to dynamically generate XML elements in the response, such that the element names, attributes, attribute values and body do not have to be hard-coded (and as such could be the result of evaluating an expression).

This action has one mandatory attribute:

- **name="*element_name*"**
  The name of the element to be inserted, in the form `<element_name ...>`.

Actions of this type may contain one or more `<jsp:attribute>` actions, which specify the attribute names of values that the element possesses, and optionally one `<jsp:body>` element which specifies the body. If no `<jsp:body>` is given, then the element is written as an empty one.

Thus:

```
<jsp:element name="mytag" />
```

will be converted to:

```
<mytag />
```

While:

```
<jsp:element name="sometag">
    <jsp:attribute name="attr1">something</jsp:attribute>
    <jsp:body>A paragraph of text</jsp:body>
</jsp:element>
```

is converted to:

```
<sometag attr1="something">
  A paragraph of text
</sometag>
```

The next sections look at the methods for inserting attributes and bodies in more detail, but you should be able to see from the above examples how flexible and useful this system could be. You may also recall the problem of inserting JSP scripting elements into attribute values within JSP documents from Chapter 14 – this problem can be solved either using XML CDATA sections, EL (we've already seen both) or by using `<jsp:element>` in conjuction with `<jsp:attribute>`.

16

<jsp:attribute>

This action actually has two purposes: the first follows on from the previous section, while the second might seem slightly obscure.

When used in a `<jsp:element>` action, a `<jsp:attribute>` acts to supply attribute data for the element being dynamically created for the response. An example of this is shown in the previous section. It has two attributes (which might seem a little ironic, considering that is its purpose):

- **`name`**
  The name of the attribute specified by this action.
- **`trim`**
  Determines whether leading (before first character) and trailing (after last character) whitespace should be ignored or not. If `true`, the whitespace is removed, leaving the first and last characters as non-whitespace ones. If `false`, then the entire contents of the action are used verbatim.

A `<jsp:attribute>` may either have content (the normal case), or be empty. If the element is empty, this is equivalent to writing `""` as the attribute value (i.e. an empty value).

This action also has a second use; it can provide attributes and values to *other actions*, instead of coding for those attributes in the action's tag. For example:

```
<jsp:useBean>
  <jsp:attribute name="id">bean_name</jsp:attribute>
  <jsp:attribute name="scope">scope</jsp:attribute>
  <jsp:attribute name="class">class_name</jsp:attribute>
</jsp:useBean>
```

16

is functionally equivalent to:

```
<jsp:useBean id="bean_name" scope="scope" class="class_name" />
```

The semantics of both approaches are the same, in that if an attribute is expecting the result of a request-time expression, then the container will evaluate the contents of the `<jsp:attribute>` action; otherwise, if the body content of `<jsp:attribute>` is a request-time expression, a translation exception will be thrown. However, this action is useful when we need to keep a JSP document well-formed (since using JSP scripting elements or other actions in an attribute value consitutes malformed XML). For example:

```
<jsp:forward page="<%= "/"+locn %>" />
```

is fine for a JSP page, but the equivalent document syntax is malformed XML:

```
<jsp:forward page="<jsp:expression>"/"+locn</jsp:expression>" />
```

This fails on two counts: firstly it is malformed to place an element within an attribute value; secondly, the quotations used in the `<jsp:expression>` interfere with the `page` attribute's quotation marks. The valid alternative is:

```
<jsp:forward>
  <jsp:attribute name="page">
    <jsp:expression>"/"+locn</jsp:expression>
  </jsp:attribute>
</jsp:forward>
```

One note of caution: you cannot use the `<jsp:attribute>` action to specify the `name` or `trim` attributes of a `<jsp:element>`, since in this context the action is used to provide the values for the *generated* element. Additionally, a `<jsp:attribute>` cannot be used to provide the value of an attribute of another `<jsp:attribute>` action (which would just be plain daft!).

<jsp:body>

This has a similar purpose to the `<jsp:attribute>`, in that it either defines the body content for a generated response element (when used inside `<jsp:element>`), or the body of another action.

For example:

```
<jsp:useBean ...>
  <jsp:body>
    <jsp:setProperty ... />
  </jsp:body>
</jsp:useBean>
```

is functionally equivalent to:

```
<jsp:useBean ...>
  <jsp:setProperty ... />
</jsp:useBean>
```

16

This might seem pretty pointless; the real value of this action is when used in conjunction with `<jsp:attribute>` actions:

```
<jsp:useBean>
  <jsp:attribute name="id">bean_name</jsp:attribute>
  <jsp:attribute name="scope">scope</jsp:attribute>
  <jsp:attribute name="class">class_name</jsp:attribute>
  <jsp:body>
    <jsp:setProperty ... />
  </jsp:body>
</jsp:useBean>
```

This makes it clear what is an attribute, and which bit is the body content.

Another note of caution: as with `<jsp:attribute>`, this action has different semantics depending on whether it is contained in a `<jsp:element>` or any other action. Additionally, it is illegal to use `<jsp:body>` to supply the body for another `<jsp:body>`, as you would expect.

<jsp:output />

Unlike most actions, this can only be used in JSP documents and tag files; using it in a JSP page (with traditional syntax) will result in a translation error. An action of this type is used to modify the structure of an XML-formatted document returned to the client; this explains why it is of no use in a JSP page, which is usually assumed not to contain strict XML, unlike JSP documents.

In particular, this action can be used to control the automatic prepending of the XML and DOCTYPE declarations. Since these declarations are usually the very first in a document, it is normal to include a `<jsp:output />` action near the top of a JSP or tag file. This action cannot contain a body.

If configuring the XML declaration is what you want, you'll need this attribute:

- **`omit-xml-declaration`**
  If set to `true` or `yes`, the container will not automatically add the XML declaration to the beginning of the response. This would only normally be used if the return type of document is not to be strict XML (even though a document is likely to be XML given where this action can actually be used). If the value is `false` or `no`, the container will add the XML declaration (see below).

The XML declaration must be first line in a valid XML document; it looks like:

```
<?xml version="1.0" encoding="encType" ?>
```

16

where *`encType`* is the character encoding used in the response. Note that 1.0 is the current XML standard; future versions of the container specification may update this.

The other three attributes can be used to control the automatic generation of a `DOCTYPE`, which specifies the location of the Document Type Description (DTD) for the generated response. These attributes are:

- **`doctype-root-element`**
  Use this to set the root element of the document in the `DOCTYPE` declaration. The value should be a string identifying the name of the root element.

- **`doctype-public`**
  Specifies the public URI of the DTD describing the response document.

- **`doctype-system`**
  Specifies the local (system) URI of the DTD.

The format of the `DOCTYPE` declaration will depend on the presence and values of each of the above attributes. All can be omitted if no `DOCTYPE` is required at all. However, if you do want an automatically generated declaration, then these conditions must be satisfied:

- The `doctype-root-element` attribute is *mandatory*.
- The `doctype-system` attribute is *mandatory*.
- The `doctype-public` attribute is optional.

If `doctype-public` is omitted, the generated declaration is of the form:

```
<!DOCTYPE root_element SYSTEM "system_URI">
```

where *root_element* is the value of the `doctype-root-element` attribute, and *system_URI* the value of the `doctype-system` attribute.

If the `doctype-public` attribute is present, the declaration is of the form:

```
<!DOCTYPE root_element PUBLIC "public_URI" "system_URI">
```

where *root_element* is the value of the `doctype-root-element` attribute, *public_URI* the value of the `doctype-public` attribute, and *system_URI* the value of the `doctype-system` attribute.

Revision Questions

1 **What are the effects of declaring the following in a JSP page?** **(choose two)**

```
<jsp:useBean id="order" class="net.beans.MyOrder" />
```

A If the bean can already be located in any one of the scoped attributes called order, it is stored in a local scripting variable called order.

B If the bean can already be located in the page-scoped attribute called order, it is stored in a local scripting variable called order.

C If the bean cannot be located, a new object of class net.beans.MyOrder is created, and the order scripting variable is left null.

D If the bean cannot be located, a new object of class net.beans.MyOrder is created, and this new bean assigned to the order scripting variable

E If the bean cannot be located, nothing happens.

2 **Which of the following are valid attributes on <jsp:useBean>?** **(choose three)**

A id

B name

C class

D bean

E type

3 **What possible effects does the following have in a JSP page?** **(choose two)**

```
<% request.setAttribute("list", null); %>
<jsp:useBean id="list" class="java.util.List"
             type="java.util.ArrayList" scope="request" />
```

A The list scripting variable is set to the value of the request-scoped attribute called list.

B A new List object is created and assigned to both the list scripting variable and the list page-scoped attribute.

C A new List object is created and assigned to both the list scripting variable and the list request-scoped attribute.

D A runtime exception is thrown.

E A translation error occurs

4 **What possible effects will the exhibit have in a JSP page?** **(choose two)**

EXHIBIT

A The scripting variable called connection is declared, of type ConcreteConnection, and initialised to the value of the page-scoped attribute called connection.

B The scripting variable called connection is declared, of type AbstractConnection, and initialised to the value of the page-scoped attribute called connection.

C The scripting variable called connection is declared, a new ConcreteConnection instantiated and assigned to both the scripting variable and page-scoped attribute called connection.

D A runtime error occurs on line 2.

E A compilation error occurs on line 2.

5 **What is the difference between these two tag declarations?** **(choose one)**

```
<jsp:useBean id="user" class="org.mysite.Person" />
<jsp:useBean id="user" beanName="org.mysite.Person"
           type="org.mysite.Person" />
```

A There is no difference; these are identical statements.

B The first statement instantiates a new instance if one isn't available in the scoped attribute, while the second throws a runtime exception.

C The first statement tries to retrieve the object from serialised form before instantiating a new instance.

D The second statement tries to retrieve the object from serialised form before instantiating a new instance.

E The first statement sets the JSP scripting variable called user while the second does not.

6 **What is the result of compiling and executing the following, assuming the logbean scoped attribute does not already exist?** **(choose one)**

```
<jsp:useBean id="logbean" beanName="net.beans.LoggingBean" />
```

A The bean is obtained and instantiated from a serialised object; the JSP scripting variable is set to this value, but the page-scoped attribute is left empty.

B The bean is obtained and instantiated from a serialised object; the logbean JSP scripting variable and page-scoped attribute called logbean are both set to this value.

C A new instance of the net.beans.LoggingBean class is created, stored in both the page-scoped attribute called logbean and the JSP scripting variable called logbean.

D A ClassCastException is thrown at run time.

E A translation error occurs.

7 **What is the effect of compiling and executing the following, assuming the product attribute does not already exist?** **(choose one)**

```
<jsp:useBean id="product" beanName="org.myonlineshop.ProductBean"
             class="org.myonlineshop.ProductBean" />
```

A The bean is obtained and instantiated from a serialised object, or if that serialisation does not exist, creates a new instance of the class.

B The bean is instantiated from a new instance of the class.

C An InstantiationException is thrown at run time.

D A ClassCastException is thrown at run time.

E A translation error occurs.

8 **What is the result of compiling and executing this JSP page?** **(choose one)**

```
<jsp:useBean id="item" beanName="com.myshop.Item" scope="request"
             type="org.mysite.Person" />
<jsp:useBean id="item" class="com.myshop.Item" scope="page" />
<%= item.toString() %>
```

A Instances of the com.myshop.Item class are placed in the request-scoped and page-scoped attributes called item.

B Instances of the com.myshop.Item class are placed in the request-scoped and page-scoped attributes called item, and a new JSP scripting variable created to store the value of the request-scoped attribute.

C Instances of the com.myshop.Item class are placed in the request-scoped and page-scoped attributes called item, and a new JSP scripting variable created to store the value of the page-scoped attribute.

D A translation error occurs.

E A compilation error occurs.

16

9 **The request-scoped attribute datastore contains a java.util.ArrayList of values. What is the result of compiling and executing this JSP page?** **(choose one)**

```
<jsp:useBean id="datastore" scope="request" class="java.util.HashMap" />
```

A The datastore JSP scripting variable is created and set to the ArrayList value of the request-scoped attribute.

B The scoped attribute is replaced with a new HashMap instance, and the JSP scripting variable created to hold this value.

C A ClassCastException is thrown at run time.

D An InstantiationException is thrown at run time.

E A translation error occurs.

10 **What is the result of compiling and executing the exhibit, assuming the com.mystore.Item class is on the classpath and has a default no-argument constructor?** **(choose one)**

EXHIBIT

- A The output is empty.
- B The text 'We're here!' is written to the response.
- C An InstantiationException is thrown at run time.
- D A ClassCastException is thrown at run time.
- E A translation error occurs.

11 **Which are possible outcomes resulting from using this code in a JSP document declared as scriptless in the deployment descriptor?** **(choose one)**

```
<jsp:useBean id="mybean" class="net.bean.MyBean" />
```

- A The page-scoped attribute called mybean is retrieved and its value stored in a JSP scripting variable called mybean.
- B All scopes are searched for an attribute called mybean, whose value is then stored in a JSP scripting variable called mybean.
- C If there is no mybean page-scoped attribute, a new one is created containing a deserialised instance of net.bean.MyBean.
- D If there is no mybean page-scoped attribute, a new one is created containing a new instance of net.bean.MyBean.
- E A translation error occurs.

12 **What of the following statements sets the orderID property of the order bean to the value W0601?** **(choose one)**

- A <jsp:setProperty id="order" name="orderID" value="W0601" />
- B <jsp:setProperty id="order" property="orderID" value="W0601" />
- C <jsp:setProperty name="order" prop="orderID" value="W0601" />
- D <jsp:setProperty name="order" action="orderID=W0601" />
- E <jsp:setProperty name="order" property="orderID" value="W0601" />

16

13 **Which of these statements sets all the properties of a bean stored in mybean to the values of matching request parameters?** **(choose one)**

- A <jsp:setProperty id="mybean" name="*" value="*" />
- B <jsp:setProperty name="mybean" value="*" />
- C <jsp:setProperty name="mybean" value="${ paramValues }" />
- D <jsp:setProperty name="mybean" property="*" />
- E <jsp:setProperty name="mybean" property="${ paramValues }" />

14 **Which of the following statements invokes the setLanguage method of a bean named dictionary, passing the value of the Accept-Language request parameter as the argument?** **(choose one)**

A <jsp:setProperty name="dictionary" property="setLanguage" />

B <jsp:setProperty name="dictionary" property="language"
value="${ param["Accept-Language"] }" />

C <jsp:setProperty name="dictionary" property="language"
value="Accept-Language" />

D <jsp:setProperty name="dictionary" property="language"
param="Accept-Language" />

E <jsp:setProperty name="dictionary" property="*" />

15 **What are the possible outcomes of compiling and executing this JSP page?** **(choose three)**

```
<jsp:useBean id="item" scope="request" class="com.mystore.Item">
  <jsp:setProperty name="item" property="num" value="501" />
</jsp:useBean>
```

A The JSP scripting variable called item is set to the value of the item request-scoped attribute, and the property setting is ignored.

B The JSP scripting variable called item is set to the value of the item request-scoped attribute, and its num property is set to '501'.

C If the request-scoped attribute does not already exist, a new Item instance is created and added to the item request-scoped attribute and JSP scripting variable, and the property setting is ignored.

D If the request-scoped attribute does not already exist, a new Item instance is created, its num property is set to '501', and the object is added to the item request-scoped attribute and JSP scripting variable.

E A runtime exception occurs.

16 **What is the purpose of the <jsp:getProperty> standard action?** **(choose one)**

A To retrieve the value of a named property and place it in a scoped attribute.

B To retrieve the value of a named property and place it in a JSP scripting variable.

C To retrieve the value of a named property and place it in both a scoped attribute and a JSP scripting variable.

D To write the value of a named property directly to the out implicit object.

E To throw an exception if the property is nonexistent on the bean.

17 **Which of the following are valid statements?** **(choose one)**

- A <jsp:getProperty id="mybean" name="myprop" />
- B <jsp:getProperty name="mybean" value="myprop" />
- C <jsp:getProperty name="mybean" property="myprop" />
- D <jsp:getProperty name="mybean" property="myprop" default="novalue" />
- E <jsp:getProperty name="mybean" param="myprop" />

18 **Which of these perform dynamic inclusion of the resource whose path is located in the dispatch page-scoped attribute?** **(choose two)**

- A <%@ include file="${ dispatch }" %>
- B <jsp:include file="${ dispatch }" />
- C <jsp:scriptlet>pageContext.include(pageContext.getAttribute("dispatch"));
  </jsp:scriptlet>
- D <jsp:include page="<jsp:expression>request.getAttribute("item")
  </jsp:expression>" />
- E <jsp:include page="${ dispatch }" />

19 **Which of the following are valid page inclusion mechanisms?** **(choose two)**

- A <%include file="/mypage.jsp" %>
- B <jsp:directive.include file="/mypage.jsp" />
- C <jsp:directive.include page="/mypage.jsp" />
- D <jsp:include page="/mypage.jsp" />
- E <jsp:include file="/mypage.jsp" />

16

20 **The exhibit shows a JSP page called /WEB-INF/userid.jsp. What is the effect of executing and compiling this JSP?** **(choose one)**

EXHIBIT

```
<%@ page contentType="text/html" %>
<jsp:include page="/WEB-INF/userid.jsp" />
```

- A The value of the userid session-scoped attribute is sent to the response
- B The response is always empty.
- C An IllegalStateException is thrown.
- D A translation error occurs.
- E A compilation error occurs.

21 **What line should be inserted in the following to set a new request-scoped attribute before forwarding to the /catalogue.jsp resource?** **(choose one)**

```
<jsp:forward page="/catalogue.jsp">
  <!-- insert here -->
</jsp:forward>
```

A <jsp:param name="category" value="java" />

B <jsp:param name="category">java</jsp:param>

C <jsp:param>
  <jsp:name>category</jsp:name>
  <jsp:value>java</jsp:name>
</jsp:param>

D None of the above.

Exhibits

Q.4

```
1. <% pageContext.setAttribute("connection",
                                   new com.mybeans.ConcreteConnection()); %>
2. <jsp:useBean id="connection" class="com.mybeans.ConcreteConnection"
                 type="com.mybeans.AbstractConnection" scope="page" />
```

Q.10

```
<%-- Assume the com.mystore.Item() is valid --%>
<% request.setAttribute("item", new com.mystore.Item()); %>
<jsp:useBean id="item" scope="request" class="com.mystore.Item">
  We're here!
</jsp:useBean>
```

Q.20

```
<%@ page contentType="text/plain" %>
${ sessionScope['userid'] }
```

Answers to Revision Questions

1 **Correct answers: B, D**

Note that the default scope is page if the scope attribute is omitted, so this rules out A, and if not found there, a new class is instantiated, saved in that scope and the JSP scripting variable is set (unless an exception occurs because the class cannot be found or instantiated). C is incorrect because a order scripting variable will always be created and initialised (except in a scriptless page). E is plainly incorrect; the entire point of this action is that if the bean cannot be located, a new one is created.

2 **Correct answers: A, C, E**

3 **Correct answers: D, E**

ArrayList implements List, which cannot be instantiated (as it is an interface) and cannot be cast to a subclass type like ArrayList. The specification leaves the actual behaviour undefined–such errors could result in either runtime exceptions (such as ClassCastException, InstantiationException or ClassNotFoundException) or translation errors. Regardless, certainly none of A to C will be correct.

4 **Correct answers: B, D**

We aren't told anything about the classes; however, from the names we guess that there is an AbstractConnection bean class with a ConcreteConnection subclass. Note that the need to make such assumptions in the exam is a possibility. If we are incorrect in our assumption, D happens because a ClassCastException occurs. Since none of the possible answers are 'compilation error on line 1', we may assume that ConcreteConnection exists on the classpath and has a default no-argument constructor suitable for instantiating the bean. Since line 2 won't cause a compilation error, we may ignore E. A is also wrong, as the declared type of the scripting variable is the same as the type attribute if present (otherwise the container uses the class attribute). C is incorrect, as a ConcreteConnection instance already exists in that variable, so another won't be instantiated.

5 **Correct answer: D**

Provided the user attribute doesn't already exist, D uses the beanName variant and therefore first attempts to load the bean from its serialised form at path org/mysite/Person.ser; only if it fails will it then create a new instance.

6 **Correct answer: E**

E is correct because the tag is missing the type attribute, which is required if beanName is being used instead of class.

7 **Correct answer: E**

E is correct; it is illegal (and nonsense) to declare both class and beanName attributes.

8 **Correct answer: D**

It is illegal to specify two <jsp:useBean> elements with the same id in the same 'translation unit' (a JSP source file and any files included using the include directive). This is logical when using JSP scripting variables, since then where should the item scripting variable refer to? We can't declare it twice, because that would lead to a compilation error, so which scope should it contain the value of – the request or page? Note that this problem also applies to including resources.

9 **Correct answer: C**

Since there is already a scoped attribute in existence, a new value will not be assigned – making B incorrect. However, the JSP scripting variable declared will be of data type java.util.HashMap, which is incompatible with ArrayList. Therefore a ClassCastException is thrown at run time.

10 **Correct answer: A**

There is nothing erroneous here, so none of C to E will happen. The answer is A because <jsp:useBean> only evaluates its body if it creates a *new instance* of the object, not if it obtains a reference to an existing one.

11 **Correct answer: D**

Note that this is a *scriptless* page, and as a result, no scripting variable is created (this behaviour is dictated for the <jsp:useBean> tag in the specification). Hence A and B are wrong. C is wrong because only the beanName attribute can be used to retrieve an object from serialised form. D is correct; the only use for <jsp:useBean> in a scriptless environment is to ensure a scoped attribute exists.

12 **Correct answer: E**

13 **Correct answer: D**

A is invalid because it uses the id attribute. B and C are invalid, using the value attribute without the corresponding property scoped attribute. E is incorrect since it tries to set the property called ${ paramValues }, which is a Map not a name, and hence is useless (note that it is valid to use a request-time expression in the property attribute value).

14 **Correct answer: D**

Using the param attribute is the correct mechanism. Note that B is incorrect, as it uses an EL expression containing double quotes, and this will interfere with the quotes on the attribute itself; in fact, B would cause a translation error. A is incorrect – not only does it omit any attribute for setting the value, but it references the setLanguage property, which according to JavaBeans would have the method name setSetLanguage, which is incorrect. C sets the value to the property to the literal 'Accept-Language'. E is incorrect as the language property doesn't map to the language request header – instead it maps to the Accept-Language header – so this 'quick-set' method cannot be used.

15 **Correct answers: A, D, E**

The key to answering this question is that the body of the <jsp:useBean> is only executed if the object is *newly* created, making the body the ideal place to initialise the values of a new bean. Hence, B is wrong because if the bean already exists, the body of <jsp:useBean> is ignored; C is wrong because if the bean is newly created, the body is evaluated and the properties set. Note that E is possible if the class cannot be found, cannot be instantiated, or a casting error occurs.

16 **Correct answer: D**

17 **Correct answer: C**

A, B and E are plainly incorrect; C is correct, while D uses a default attribute which is invalid–such an attribute might be useful to provide a default value if the property is nonexistent or null, but this attribute is invalid nonetheless!

18 **Correct answers: C, E**

A performs static inclusion and is invalid anyway because of the EL expression. B is incorrect as it declares the nonexistent file attribute. C is a manual way to include the resource. D is incorrect, as it illegally declares an element inside another attribute, and represents malformed XML. E is correct, using the much tidier EL syntax to retrieve the scoped attribute's value.

19 **Correct answers: B, D**

Remember on which tags the file and page attributes go! Note also that A has an invalid delimiter, using <%include rather than <%@ include.

20 **Correct answer: A**

Note that using the static include would cause a translation error, due to the redefinition of the contentType page directive with a different value. However, using dynamic inclusion isn't so temperamental because each page is processed individually as and when required. In fact, the /WEB-INF/userid.jsp page's attempt to set contentType to text/plain is ignored, as any attempt to modify headers during a RequestDispatcher forward is ignored. Therefore, no errors are raised and the correct answer is A.

21 **Correct answer: D**

This is correct, because the question asks about request-scoped *attributes*, which cannot be modified using any shortcuts. The use of <jsp:param> sets a request *parameter* with the name and value supplied–if request parameters were what we wanted to set, A would be correct. It actually uses a ServletRequestWrapper to achieve this, overriding the request parameter methods to supply the <jsp:param> values in preference.

In this chapter you'll:

- Be introduced to tag libraries.
- Deploy tag libraries into Web applications.
- Utilise tag libraries in JSPs.
- Appreciate the different versions of the JSTL and which to choose.
- Learn the key tags in the JSTL core library which may appear on the exam.

17 Tag Libraries and the JSTL

In the last chapter we looked at the standard actions, associated with the JSP namespace. In this chapter, we take a step back to look at using tag libraries in general and then we take a sidestep to delve into the **JSP Standard Tag Library** (**JSTL**).

Tag Libraries in JSPs

For the moment it is appropriate to think abstractly. Until we can see exactly how a tag library is composed and configured, it is sensible to consider a tag library simply as an abstract collection of (possibly related) actions. The model we will envisage, which is by far the most popular but not the only one, is that a tag library is contained inside a JAR file: use of a new library in an application requires that library's JAR to be present on the `classpath`, and the JAR file contains all the code necessary to implement the tag library. We can therefore picture tags as being 'bundled' into a single JAR file, perhaps being made available to download from the Internet.

Deploying a Tag Library

In order to use a tag library we must somehow make its JAR file available to the classpath (for example by deploying to `/WEB-INF/lib/` or to a shared path in the container).

Alternatively, as we shall see in Chapter 20, individual tags outside of a JAR library can be deployed directly into the application's WAR (tag files into `/WEB-INF/tags/` and tag handler classes into `/WEB-INF/classes/`). In this case, a **Tag Library Descriptor** (**TLD**) must also be deployed into the application, into `/WEB-INF/`. This individual method of deployment is suitable only for development stages. All production systems use JAR libraries as they provide a more compact solution and we will therefore only concern ourselves with the JAR deployment model for now.

If you are using a recent Java EE server, all the standard tag libraries in this chapter will already be installed in your Web container for your applications to use. If not, you will first need to obtain and deploy the tag libraries. At the time of writing, implementations of the JSTL libraries could be downloaded from the JCP Standardized Tag Libraries section of the Jakarta-Taglibs Project:

`http://jakarta.apache.org/taglibs/`

NOTE: As commented below, if you have a JSP 2.0 container, you actually only need the 1.1 version of the JSTL libraries (a JSP 2.1 container should use the 1.2 version).

Once you have the JARs, the easiest way to start using the libraries is simply to copy them into the `/WEB-INF/lib/` of each application you deploy. The more permanent solution is to deploy them to the container's shared path, but this will depend on your particular container. GlassFish uses *SERVER_ROOT*`/lib/` for server-wide libraries and *SERVER_ROOT*`/domains/`*domain_name*`/lib/` for domain-wide libraries (where *domain_name* is the name of the individual domain).

The taglib Directive

Once we've made sure the library implementation is available in the classpath, we need to import that library into each JSP which uses it.

A tag library, in whatever form, is made available to the JSP page or document using the `taglib` directive which we mentioned all the way back in Chapter 13, but haven't yet used; Chapter 14 discussed the equivalent method for importing tag libraries into JSP documents using XML namespaces. As a refresher, the `taglib` directive takes these three attributes:

- **`uri`**
  This should uniquely identify or point to the TLD for the library being used; it should be either an absolute or relative URI for the descriptor. For libraries which you have obtained, and not developed yourself, this will probably be specified in the documentation. We list the URIs for the JSTL libraries shortly.

17

- **`tagdir`**
  A path which points to the location of the tag files in the `/WEB-INF/tags` directory of the WAR. Note that the path must begin with `/WEB-INF/tags/`, and the directory must exist in the WAR, or a translation error will occur. We will not be using tag files until Chapter 19. In a JSP document, use a namespace URI of the form `urn:jsptagdir:/WEB-INF/tags/`*path*.

- **`prefix`**
  Defines the XML namespace prefix that is to be used by actions from this library in the JSP.

NOTE: *Only one* of `uri` or `tagdir` should appear in the declaration.

We should also mention briefly that the URI is determined by the tag library you want to use, and will most likely be chosen by the tag author, but the prefix is always chosen *by the author* of the JSP. Provided we avoid namespace clashes, the name of the prefix is irrevelant provided it references the correct URI in the `taglib` directive. For example:

```
<%@ taglib uri="http://mysite.com/" prefix="mytags" %>
<mytags:tag1 />
```

Invokes the `tag1` action from the library with URI `http://mysite.com/`. We use the `mytags` prefix to make referencing the library easy. However, this prefix could equally well be anything else; for example in a JSP document:

```
<blogs:tag1 xmlns:blogs="http://mysite.com/" />
```

is perfectly valid and will do exactly the same as the previous example (note that this is *document*, not page, syntax, and we could instead have declared the namespace and prefix using an `xmlns` on *any parent* element). To avoid confusion, it is best to pick a useful and memorable prefix for a particular tag library and stick with it throughout all your JSPs. In some cases, the recommended prefix is prescribed by the tag author (for example, `c` is used for the *core* JSTL library we discuss next).

JavaServer Pages Standard Tag Library (JSTL)

The JSTL itself, at the time of writing in version 1.1, is one of the most comprehensive tag libraries around, so much so that it has been broken into four further tag libraries:

- Core actions
- XML processing
- Internationalisation formatting
- SQL-related (database) actions

The core tag library focuses on fundamentals: flow control and conditional statements, iterative loops and URL formatting; the XML library concentrates (oddly enough) on parsing and writing XML well-formed document structures; the internationalisation library includes options for formatting dates and times, and generating locale-dependent responses; the SQL library provides (you've guessed it) support for making calls to databases.

Thankfully for the exam, we don't have to learn all four libraries (and its just as well that the JSTL is subdivided, or we might end up learning the lot anyway!). Instead, the exam mandates knowledge of only the core actions, so that is all we shall discuss. I don't intend to get bogged down in the detail of the other actions we don't need to know about (given that there are so many of them), so if you are interested in the others available, please see the JSR-52 expert group (the maintainers of the JSTL) at the Java Community Process website: `http://www.jcp.org`.

Dynamic vs. Static Attributes

Dynamic attributes, as referred to in the JSTL specification, are any attributes which can accept a **request-time expression** instead of a hard-coded literal value. Most, but not all, attributes are of this category. Those which are not are called **static attributes**, and will not evaluate the content at request time, but instead will throw a translation exception (unless you use EL expressions in JSTL 1.0 RT tags, which don't support EL, and actually don't understand *it is* EL you're trying to use!).

For example, consider the following action with a dynamic attribute:

```
<action dynAtt="${ someFunc() }" />
```

This action will parse the EL expression (which in turn calls the `someFunc()` function), and use the *evaluated result* as the attribute's value. JSTL 1.0 RT tags do not support EL and would therefore interpret the value as the literal `${ someFunc() }` (see the next section to clarify this).

However, with a static attribute:

```
<action statAtt="${ someFunc() }" />
```


Using this action in a JSP will cause a translation exception to be raised, because we are attempting to use a runtime expression in a static attribute. Tags in the JSTL 1.0 RT library take the value of the `statAtt` to be the string literal `${ someFunc() }`, merely because they do not support the processing of EL expressions. Note that if the value of the attribute was a traditional JSP scripting element, it would always throw a translation exception regardless of the version of JSTL used.

JSTL Versions and Libraries

The JSTL currently exists in two versions, 1.0 and 1.1. JSTL 1.0 is the original version of the library, designed for use with *pre-JSP 2.0* containers, where the Expression Language is unrecognised by the container. In JSTL 1.0, the tags themselves are responsible for parsing and evaluating EL code, and not the container. Within JSTL 1.0, two editions of tags ship with the library:

- **RT-based tags**
  These include support for traditional JSP scripting elements; where appropriate, the tag attributes and bodies are declared in the TLD to accept container-parsed and -evaluated runtime values as well as static text.
- **EL-based tags**
  In a pre-JSP 2.0 container, the container doesn't support the Expression Language. This tag library provides support for using EL syntax within tag attributes (but never tag bodies). Since EL is not recognised by the container, these attribute values will simply be interpreted as plain text and not as container-evaluated runtime values. It is then the responsibility of the tag itself to evaluate the EL expression. When using EL-based libraries, it is illegal to include any JSP scripting elements within attribute values.

NOTE: In pre-JSP 2.0 containers, the Expression Language can be used *only with JSTL attribute values* and nowhere else (not in template text, tag bodies or other actions' attributes).

So, in JSTL 1.0 there was a choice: use traditional JSP scripting elements *or* use the new Expression Language (which was originally designed by the JSTL expert group for this exact purpose).

JSTL 1.1 relies on a JSP 2.0-compliant container to work correctly, since 1.1 tags leave the evaluation of Expression Language statements to the container. However, JSTL 1.1 tags accept *both* traditional JSP scripting elements *and* EL expressions as the values of any dynamic attributes, without any further consideration on our part. It's even possible to mix the two types of expressions in the same attribute value!

17

The difference in behaviour between the two libraries can be explained by looking at the TLDs for each (TLDs are covered in Chapter 20). Since in pre-JSP 2.0 containers the Expression Language is treated only as plain text (and not as a 'request-time expression'), the TLDs for each of these types of library have the `rtexprvalue` values configured as shown in Table 17.1.

Note that *all* versions of the libraries may use `bodycontent` values of `JSP`, `tagdependent` or `empty` regardless of whether their *attributes* may take traditional JSP scripting elements or not. This is a result of EL expressions only being valid *within attribute values* when using JSTL 1.0 EL and a pre-JSP 2.0 container.

Table 17.1 JSTL TLD Request-Time Attribute Settings

JSTL Version	TLD rtexprvalue Configuration
1.0 EL	`rtexprvalue=false` for all attributes.
1.0 RT	`rtexprvalue=true` for attributes which accept traditional JSP scripting elements.
1.1	`rtexprvalue=true` for attributes which accept 'runtime expressions' (either EL expressions or traditional JSP scripting elements).

Which Library do I Use?

JSTL 1.1 is completely backward-compatible with JSTL 1.0, which means that any JSPs designed to work with JSTL 1.0 will also work with the 1.1 edition.

However, if you know that you're using a JSP 2.0 container, it is good practise to always use the JSTL 1.1 version of the library. The servers I recommended in the Preface are both JSP 2.0 compliant and already contain both the 1.0 and 1.1 editions of JSTL installed.

It may not always be the case that JSP applications you design will be installed in a JSP 2.0 container, and for that reason, you may find that you need to use the JSTL 1.0 libraries. You then have to make a concious decision: use the RT libraries if your tag values contain JSP scripting elements, or use the EL libraries if you prefer the Expression Language. Another important factor to consider is that, while the use of EL within attribute values in JSP documents doesn't constitute malformed XML, the use of JSP scripting elements does – one of the many advantages of EL is that it is a more compact syntax which can be used in a wider variety of situations.

One point to make is that if you intend to use EL within attribute values within a JSP 2.0 container, but still opt to use the JSTL 1.0 libraries, you *must* use the RT version of the library. This is because JSP 2.0 containers interpret EL expression *as request-time expressions* and not as plain text (as pre-JSP 2.0 containers do), and it is only the RT libraries which are configured to accept request-time expressions as attribute values. Alternatively, you can use the 1.0 EL libraries if you disable EL evaluation for the entire JSP (see Chapter 15, *Evalution of EL Expressions in JSPs*).

Table 17.2 Java Standard Tag Library URIs

JSTL Version	Library	Usual Prefix	URI
1.0 EL	Core	`c`	`http://java.sun.com/jstl/core`
	XML Processing	`x`	`http://java.sun.com/jstl/xml`
	Internationalisation	`fmt`	`http://java.sun.com/jstl/fmt`
	Relational DBs (SQL)	`sql`	`http://java.sun.com/jstl/sql`
1.0 RT	Core	`c`	`http://java.sun.com/jstl/core_rt`
	XML Processing	`x`	`http://java.sun.com/jstl/xml_rt`
	Internationalisation	`fmt`	`http://java.sun.com/jstl/fmt_rt`
	Relational DBs (SQL)	`sql`	`http://java.sun.com/jstl/sql_rt`
1.1	Core	`c`	`http://java.sun.com/jsp/jstl/core`
	XML Processing	`x`	`http://java.sun.com/jsp/jstl/xml`
	Internationalisation	`fmt`	`http://java.sun.com/jsp/jstl/fmt`
	Relational DBs (SQL)	`sql`	`http://java.sun.com/jsp/jstl/sql`
	Functions (EL)	`fn`	`http://java.sun.com/jsp/jstl/functions`

Java Standard Tag Library URIs

Both JSTL versions contain four individual libraries which each contain specific functionality; these are the four presented in the previous section. JSTL 1.1 also adds the Functions library, which contains a set of EL functions representing common string-modification requirements (like `trim()` and `toUpperCase()`). The URIs for JSTL 1.0 are different from those for JSTL 1.1, due to the different nature of the tags in each. Table 17.2 contains a summary of all the URIs used for each of the three editions of the library.

The JSTL Core Library

As with all tag libraries, the core library must be associated with a URI; the different URIs are shown in Table 17.2. To avoid having to discuss particular JSTL editions and thus refer to different URIs, we will use `c` (for 'core') as the library prefix throughout. Since the JSTL specification uses the `c` prefix consistently, we (as does the exam) shall stay with it to avoid confusion.

Output Parser: <c:out>

The contents of this action are dynamically evaluated before being written to the response stream. The evaluation of any nested scriptlets or EL expressions is performed first, before the final text is evaluated. This action is useful when the content is known to be *pure template text*–i.e. it does not contain any XML elements for the document. The reason for its use is that it automatically converts characters which would be illegal in XML character data into entity references; for example, the opening and closing tags < and > are converted to their references `<` and `>`, respectively. This can be useful for two reasons: firstly, it means we don't have to type the entity references directly (and these can seriously clutter up the JSP if there are lots of them), and secondly it works dynamically, so even if the evaluated dynamic expression returns some text containing the illegal characters, these will still be converted to entity references.

Of course, if you don't want the action to replace illegal characters and tags with entity references you can disable that stage of the parsing, but there isn't overly much point to having this action if that's what you intend to do.

As well as parsing strings to ensure they are well-formed character data, this action can be used to provide a default value, in the situation that the parsed value returns `null` (or is an empty string). This can be useful if you intend to output a list, but there turns out to be nothing in the list at request-time; instead, the default value could say 'No items in the list' or similar.

The attributes used to achieve this are:

- **`value`**
  The expression to be parsed before being outputted; the evaluated expression will be coerced to a `String` object before parsing begins. This is a dynamic attribute, so the value may be either a literal or a request-time expression (either EL or scriptlet). This attribute is *mandatory*.

- **`escapeXml`**
  Determines whether illegal character data is to be converted to XML entity references or not. If `true`, then conversion takes place, while using `false` as the value leaves all illegal characters in the response. The value may be dynamically derived by the evaluation of an EL expression or scriptlet. This attribute is optional, with a default value of `true` if it is omitted.

- **`default`**
  Specifies the default value to be output if the result of parsing the value attribute is `null` (or an empty string). This is an optional attribute, with the default value being an empty string.

If a body is specified, this takes on the role of the `default` attribute: i.e. the body of a `<c:out>` action is the default text to be written to the response should the value attribute resolve to `null`.

The character conversions which take place, while they do not need to be learnt for the exam, are shown in Table 17.3.

Table 17.3 <c:out> Entity Replacements

Character	Entity Reference Replacement
<	<
>	>
&	&
'	'
"	"

Exception Handling: <c:catch>

This action is used as a wrapper for suppressing exceptions which arise in the JSP. Specifically, it suppresses exceptions which occur as a result of the evaluation of its contents. If any nested actions of `<c:catch>` throw an exception, the action simply wraps the exception object in a page-scoped attribute and ignores it, leaving processing to continue to the rest of the JSP after the closing tag.

The syntax is:

```
<c:catch var="page_var_name">
  nested actions
</c:catch>
```

Where `var` is an optional attribute specifying the name of the page-scoped attribute into which the `Throwable` object will be placed. This can be used by subsequent code to supply a short warning to the client, log the exception in the server's log or whatever; in many cases, the attribute is just ignored. If `var` is not declared, the exception is suppressed by the action, but the `Throwable` object is not kept. Note: `var` is a *static attribute*, and as such its value cannot be the result of a request-time evaluation of an expression, but instead must be hard-coded literally.

This action is only useful where the presence of an exception would be an annoyance and it is useless to display an error page. However, for most actions or scriptlets which throw an exception, it is recommended to let the container handle the exception using the error page mechanism. Allowing processing of the JSP to continue without handling an exception correctly may cause further errors later in the JSP. For this reason, use this action cautiously.

Scoped Attribute Modification: <c:set> and <c:remove />

These JSTL actions provide a similar facility to the bean modifiers provided by the JSP standard actions, except they only affect scoped attributes and not local scripting variables. The `<c:set>` action is used to set an attribute in a scope, or a property of a known target object. The `<c:remove />` action is used to remove an attribute from its scope.

The syntax of the `<c:remove />` action is simple:

```
<c:remove var="var_name" scope="var_scope" />
```

var_name should be the name of the scoped attribute to be removed, while *var_scope* specifies the scope in which that attribute resides. The `var` attribute is *mandatory*, whilst `scope` is optional. If `scope` is omitted, the attribute is removed according to the semantics of `JspContext`'s `removeAttribute(String)` method, which is implement to remove the named attribute from *all scopes* in which it is found. If an attribute with name *var_name* cannot be found in any scope, this action does nothing. `var` and `scope` are *static attributes*, so their values must be hard-coded.

The `<c:set>` action is slightly more complex, because it can be used for two purposes. The first use of `<c:set>` is to set the value of a scoped attribute. This might seem to be the same action as performed by `<jsp:setProperty>`, but the `<c:set>` action sets the value of an *entire attribute* and not just one property from a bean variable. Its general syntax for this purpose is:

```
<c:set var="var_name" scope="var_scope" value="var_value" />
```

or

```
<c:set var="var_name" scope="var_scope">
  var_value
</c:set>
```

17

where *var_name* is the name of the attribute, residing in the *var_scope* scope, to be set to the value *var_value*. The `var` attribute is *mandatory*, while the `scope` attribute is optional with a default value of `page`. If the action is declared as an empty element, the `value` attribute is required, specifying the value that the attribute will take. Otherwise, the body content is interpreted as being the new value of the attribute. Either way, the type of attribute will match the type of the value expression when evaluated–i.e. if a *var_value* EL expression evaluates to `true`, then the new attribute will be of type `boolean`.

The second use of the `<c:set>` action is to modify the value of a property on a target object. This is practically the same behaviour as supplied by the `<jsp:setProperty>` action, so we'll just look at its syntax:

```
<c:set target="obj_target" property="prop_name" value="value" />
```

or

```
<c:set target="obj_target" property="prop_name">
  value
</c:set>
```

`obj_target` is the object containing the property, called `prop_name`, to be set to the value `value`. In general, the value of the `target` attribute will be a request-time expression (either scriptlet or EL) which resolves to a valid JavaBeans or `Map` object. Both the `target` and `property` attributes are *mandatory*, with the `value` attribute being required only if there is an empty body. All of the attributes may take dynamic values–i.e. the results of evaluating request-time expressions. Since, in this situation, we are specifying an actual object in existence (and not an attribute name in a scope), clearly the `var` and `scope` attributes should be omitted. Let's look at an example:

```
<c:set target="${ basket }" property="itemTotal" value="12" />
```

This sets the `itemTotal` property to `12` by calling `setItemTotal(12)` on the JavaBeans object retrieved by the EL expression `${ basket }`.

This example alters an entry in a `Map` (the `counterMap` attribute), by changing the entry with the key counter to the result of the expression `${ oldCounterValue + 1 }`:

```
<c:set target="${ counterMap }" property="counter">
  ${ oldCounterValue + 1 }
</c:set>
```

Conditional Evaluation: <c:if>

Most dynamic components require some form of conditional logic and execution branching at one time or another. To avoid the use of untidy scriptlet code, the `<c:if>` action can be used. This takes a dynamic expression, which must evaluate to a Boolean type. This expression is known as the **test condition**; if it resolves to `true` at request time, then the body of the action is included in the response; otherwise, the body content is ignored.

17

Optionally, the Boolean result of the test condition may be stored in a scoped attribute for further processing. The body of the action may be omitted, in which case it is likely that the only purpose of the action is to store the result of the expression in the scoped attribute.

In general, the syntax is:

```
<c:if test="test_cond" var="var_name" scope="var_scope" />
```

if the action is empty, in which case the result of `test_cond` will be stored in the attribute `var_name` in the specified `var_scope`. In this situation, `scope` is optional while `var` is *mandatory*.

Alternatively:

```
<c:if test="test_cond" var="var_name" scope="var_scope">
  output
</c:if>
```

Here, `output` will only be written to the response should `test_cond` evaluate to `true`. In this situation, *both* `var` *and* `scope` *are optional*, but if `scope` is declared `var` should also be given (it doesn't make much sense to have a scope without an attribute after all!).

A summary of the attributes:

- **test**
  Supplies the action with the test condition expression; this is likely to be either an EL or scriptlet expression which is evaluated dynamically at request time. This attribute is mandatory.

- **var**
  Supplies the name of the attribute in which to store the Boolean result of evaluating the test condition. This is a *static attribute*, so its value must be hard-coded. This attribute is optional when a body is supplied to the action, but mandatory if the action is empty.

- **scope**
  Specifies the scope which the attribute `var` resides in. This attribute is optional, but if declared `var` must also be declared. The value must be one of `page`, `request`, `session` or `application`, with the default being `page` should it be omitted completely.

Conditional Choice: <c:choose>, <c:when>, <c:otherwise>

17

The JSTL does not contain any `else` actions, so we cannot construct `if...else` statements. As an alternative, we can use a JSTL construct which is similar to Java's `switch` statement. Let's look at a simple structure:

```
<c:choose>
  <c:when test="cond_1">
    ...
  </c:when>
  <c:otherwise>
    ...
  </c:otherwise>
</c:choose>
```

The effect is that if `cond_1` evaluates to `true`, then the first block is executed; if `cond_1` is `false`, the `otherwise` block is executed. This is similar, and the alternative to, an `if...else` construct. The difference comes in when we have multiple `<c:when>` statements like this:

```
<c:choose>
  <c:when test="cond_1">
    ...
  </c:when>
  <c:when test="cond_2">
    ...
  </c:when>
  <c:when test="cond_3">
    ...
  </c:when>
  <c:otherwise>
    ...
  </c:otherwise>
</c:choose>
```

This code acts like `if...else if...else`; here's how the above is executed:

- If *cond_1* evaluates to `true`, then the first block will execute, following which execution jumps out of the `<c:choose>` action completely. If *cond_1* is `false`, then *cond_2* is evaluated.
- If *cond_2* is `true`, then the second block executes, followed by control jumping out of the `<c:choose>` action. If *cond_2* is `false`, then *cond_3* is evaluated.
- If *cond_3* is `true`, then the third block executes, followed by control breaking out of the `<c:choose>` action altogether. If *cond_3* is `false`, then control passes to the `<c:otherwise>` action.
- If all else fails, the `<c:otherwise>` action will be executed. This is similar to the `default` block in a Java `switch` statement.

Thankfully, there are very few rules to know:

- `<c:choose>` takes *no attributes* but must contain one or more `<c:when>` actions and an optional `<c:otherwise>` action in its body.
- `<c:otherwise>` takes *no attributes*, but must be the *last* nested action in a `<c:choose>` block.
- `<c:when>` only has the `test` attribute, which has the same semantics as the `test` attribute of the `<c:if>` action.

17

Before leaving this section (which, let's face it, was pretty straightforward), make sure you know that *only one* `<c:when>` or `<c:otherwise>` statement will ever be executed for a given `<c:choose>` block. This will always be the first block whose test condition evaluates to `true`. This is exactly the same behaviour as with an `if...else if... else` construct, where the if and else if blocks are supplied by

<c:when>s and the else by a <c:otherwise>.

NOTE: The behaviour described above is the correct one. However, one implementation of the JSTL exists (in one version of the GlassFish server) which causes all <c:when> elements with conditions evaluating to true to be executed, not just the first. This is however a bug and therefore is erroneous, but if you do encounter it during practical trials, you may wish to upgrade to a newer version of your server or download another JSTL implementation.

Looping: <c:forEach>

Let's get loopy... Clearly aside from conditional operators, a program may also need to iterate through a loop as well. The <c:forEach> action provides two types of iteration: the enumeration of a Collection or array of primitives or objects, and fixed counter-based iterations. We will look at the latter type first, since it is more basic. We will then go on to look at the former type of iteration.

A basic requirement of a programming language is to be able to repeat a set of instructions a finite number of times. This is provided through the following syntax:

```
<c:forEach begin="index1" end="index2" step="step_length">
  body content
</c:forEach>
```

The begin attribute sets the index at which the loop will start, while the end attribute sets the index at which the iteration terminates. The action maintains an internal counter variable, which is incremented by *step_length* (the default value of the step attribute is 1) on each new iteration of the loop. For example, to run though a loop six times, we might write:

17

```
<c:forEach begin="0" end="5">
  Body text or something
</c:forEach>
```

Note that the counter is updated at the end of each iteration, and the loop terminates at *finish_index* ***inclusive***. Hence in the above example, exactly six iterations are performed from 0 through to (and including) 5. Six iterations are also performed in this loop, which increments the counter by 3 every time:

```
<c:forEach begin="0" end="15" step="3">
  Body text or something
</c:forEach>
```

It may also be useful for the inside of the loop to have access to the current counter value. However, the counter is internal to the action, so how can we get hold of it? The answer lies in the var attribute, which by now should seem pretty familiar. The *static* var attribute specifies the name of an attribute in which to store the current counter value. This attribute is accessible only within the action's body, and doesn't have an associated scope like most other attributes (its scope could be considered to be 'action-local' but this isn't an official designation). *Outside of the action, the attribute doesn't exist.* For example:

```
<c:forEach begin="0" end="5" var="countvar">
  Iteration number ${ countvar }
</c:forEach>
```

will output the following text when executed:

```
Iteration number 0
Iteration number 1
Iteration number 2
Iteration number 3
Iteration number 4
Iteration number 5
```

What we haven't said so far is that the attribute created by var must be of type Object, and not int (for reasons which we will see shortly). Thus, the counter value is actually stored as an instance of the Integer class, and not as a primitive. In the above example this wasn't important, since the toString() method was called by the EL evaluator to obtain a String representation of the integer, and everything worked out fine.

When we want to perform mathematical operations on the counter, we need to be wary that it is an Object. Another advantage of the expression language is that, when using the + operator, it automatically coerces every item being added into an integer primitive from whatever form its already exists as. Thus, if we wanted to add 24 to the counter in EL, we just write:

```
<c:forEach begin="0" end="5" var="countvar">
  Iteration number ${ countvar + 24 }
</c:forEach>
```

17

which isn't much different from before; the code is still pretty clear. However, consider the alternative using the JSP scripting expression:

```
<c:forEach begin="0" end="5" var="cv">
Iteration number
<%= ((Integer)(pageContext.findAttribute("cv")).intValue()+24 %>
</c:forEach>
```

The code shown in bold is the extra code required to add the number: basically, the attribute (in its Object form) has to be retrieved from the pageContext, cast to an Integer, and then the int primitive has to be obtained by a call to intValue(). Only then can the 24 be added. It should be pretty clear why the EL is the language of choice of the modern Web developer.

Now let's turn our attention to the second use of this action: to cycle through the elements of an array or Collection. Quite often, a loop in Java is used to iterate through all the entries of a container such as a primitive or Object array, or one of the collection types (List, Set or Map). To save us having to use scriptlet code inside the body of a fixed-counter loop (and we've just seen how messy this can be), we can let the action take care of the gory details of iterating through the elements for us. At its simplest:

```
<c:forEach items="collection_obj">
  Body content
</c:forEach >
```

This form introduces an extra attribute, items, whose value should be a Collection object or an array. The action will iterate over each item in the object until there are no more left, at which point execution terminates. Clearly, it would be useful to get hold of the current element in the collection inside each iteration of the loop; the action exposes the current element through the use of the *static* var attribute again. The value of var should be a string which specifies the name of the scoped attribute to contain the current collection element. This scoped attribute is local to the body of the action. The type of attribute will depend on the type of collection being accessed, and the type of the current element:

- **For primitive arrays**
  The current element will be encapsulated in its appropriate wrapper class (e.g. int wrapped inside Integer); it is this wrapper which is exposed to the var attribute.

- **For Object arrays**
  Each element is returned 'as is' in its Object form.

- **For Collection types** (other than Map)
  An Iterator is used to loop through the collection; as such, each element is exposed as an Object.

17

- **For Map types**
  An Iterator is used to loop through the collection, but the type exposed to the var attribute is of class Map.Entry, allowing access to both the entry's *value and key*. To obtain the value itself, call getValue() on the exposed Map.Entry; to obtain the key, call getKey(). In EL, you can use the collection or property operators with the property name value.

- **For Strings**
  If the items attribute value is a String containing a *comma-separated list* of values, this action iterates through each item in the list, exposing it to the var attribute as a String. Consider the <c:forTokens> action as an alternative.

It is highly unlikely that you need to know any of these types for the exam, but they are pretty self-explanatory. Regardless, they suit this book's secondary purpose as a comprehensive reference. Note that since EL coerces all of the above values to the appropriate form for any operations (like arithmetic or logic operators, or method calls), it is unlikely that the type of `var` attribute will be much of an issue (unless it is of class `Map.Entry`, which requires further EL code to access the key and value).

Finer control can be gained over the iteration process using the attributes we have already seen:

```
<c:forEach items="collection_obj" var="var_name"
    begin="start_index" end="finish_index" step="step_length">
  Body content
</c:forEach>
```

When used, `begin` gives the index of the element in the collection object at which to begin the iteration while `end` specifies the index (inclusive) at which to finish. If `end` would cause the iteration to spill over the end of the collection (i.e. if `end` is larger than the size of the collection), the action simply stops after the last entry. The `step` attribute can be used to control the number of objects skipped during iteration: for example, a value of `1` does not skip any elements (the internal counter is incremented to each element in turn) while a value of `3` causes 2 elements to be skipped etc.

In addition to everything we've seen, we should look at one the last attribute: `varStatus`. This specifies an attribute in which to insert an object of type `javax.servlet.jsp.jstl.core.TagLoopStatus`. This attribute is accessible only *from within the action's body*. This class exposes several properties (as Java methods) which could be useful during an iteration:

- **`Object getCurrent()`**
  Retrieves the current item in the iteration, as found in the `var` attribute.

- **`int getIndex()`**
  Returns the current counter value. For collections, this is 0-based.

- **`int getCount()`**
  Returns the number of iterations that have already been performed, beginning at 1. For example, during the first iteration (regardless of the counter index value), this will return `1`. During the second iteration, it returns `2` etc.

- **`boolean isFirst()`**
  Returns `true` if this is the first iteration (i.e. if `getCount()` returns `1`).

- **`boolean isLast()`**
  Returns `true` if this is the last iteration for the action.

- **`Integer getBegin()`**

Returns the value of the begin attribute – i.e. the start index for the counter.

- **Integer getEnd()**
  Returns the value of the end attribute – i.e. the last (inclusive) index for the counter.

- **Integer getStep()**
  Returns the value of the step attribute – i.e. the amount by which the counter will be incremented between iterations.

That's all on this action (and about time too!).

Token Iteration: <c:forTokens>

<c:forEach> provides a simple mechanism for iterating over a *comma-separated* list contained in a String. However, <c:forTokens> provides exclusive support for iterating over items in a String, separated with *arbitrary* delimiters. For example, it could be used to enumerate over the items in the following string:

```
item1;%:item2;%:item3;%:item4
```

Using the (rather peculiar) delimiter ;%: the items are interpreted as expected:

```
item1
item2
item3
item4
```

Each of these items is known formally as a **token**. The basic syntax is:

```
<c:forTokens items="token_string" delims="separator_sequence">
  Body content
</c:forTokens>
```

where items provides the String to be examined, and delims is the delimiter sequence of characters. Using the previous example as a guide:


```
<c:forTokens items="item1;%:item2;%:item3;%:item4" delims=";%:">
  Iteration Body
</c:forTokens>
```

If executed, this would output the following:

```
Iteration Body
Iteration Body
Iteration Body
Iteration Body
```

The loop has iterated four times, in accordance with there being four items in the list. By now you've probably figured this out, but to get access to the current String token in the body of the action, we use the *static* var attribute. This specifies the name of the scoped attribute used *inside the body* (this attribute is not visible outside the action's body) to store the current token in the String. Taking the previous example a little further then:

```
<c:forTokens items="item1;%:item2;%:item3;%:item4" delims=";%:"
             var="currentToken">
  Iteration now on: ${ currentToken }
</c:forTokens>
```

This results in the output:

```
Iteration now on: item1
Iteration now on: item2
Iteration now on: item3
Iteration now on: item4
```

Additionally, as for <c:forEach>, <c:forTokens> can accept these attributes:

- **begin**
  Specifies the index at which iteration should start; the first token has index 0.
- **end**
  Specifies the final (inclusive) index of the iteration counter.
- **step**
  The amount by which the counter is incremented between iterations.
- **varStatus**
  Name of the scoped attribute to which the LoopTagStatus object for the loop will be stored. This attribute is accessible only within the body of the action, and does not exist outside it. See the last section on the <c:forTokens> element for more details of this class.

URL Formatting: <c:url>

A requirement of most URLs in a document is to be rewritten, the process whereby the session ID (jsessionid) is included in the URL to provide persistence of sessions where cookies are disabled. We first looked at this in Chapter 9. Additionally, an important but often overlooked requirement is for all URLs to be encoded, by which we mean converting special characters (like whitespace and symbols) into character codes which are recognised by the encoding standard. As an example, single spaces are usually converted to either a shorthand + sign, or their Unicode hex representation %20. Thus:

`http://domain.ext/my page.html`

becomes either:

`http://domain.ext/my+page.html` or `http://domain.ext/my%20page.html`

More details of the encoding process are available in RFC 2396 (http://www.

ietf.org/rfc/rfc2396.txt), but since this action takes care of it all for us anyway, do we really care?!

The action only *rewrites relative* URLs (which must be local to the container by definition) to avoid exposing the session ID to external resources specified using an absolute URL. It does however *encode both* relatives and absolutes. A relative URL is defined to be one which is relative to the context root of the application (if it begins with the forward-slash, /) or the current URL of the component (no / at start). An absolute URL would begin with a valid scheme (e.g. http://).

The URL to be encoded (and rewritten if applicable) is supplied via the *mandatory* value attribute, which may contain a request time expression:

```
<c:url value="url_expression" />
```

You might think we've got a dilemma here: absolute URLs don't cause rewriting to occur for security reasons, but we might want to use a resource from another application for which a relative URL cannot be created. For this reason, the action also provides a way to specify the context root of a foreign application in which the specified resource URL resides. In this case, the value would be the relative URL of the component in the foreign application (relative to the application's context), which is appended to the foreign application's context root specified using the context attribute. For example, suppose we have an application A deployed at context /appA and an application B deployed at context /appB. Now assume a JSP component in A creates a URL to point to the /includes/banner.jsp file in application B; it can do this using:

```
<c:url value="/includes/banner.jsp" context="/appB" />
```

which encodes and rewrites the URL into something similar to:

```
/appB/includes/banner.jsp
```


If this were included in a hyperlink, for example, the client would be pointed towards the appB application under the current server's root; for example, if the Java EE root were http://www.domain.ext/root/, the URL would actually be:

```
http://www.domain.ext/root/appB/includes/banner.jsp
```

The context attribute is clearly very useful. In addition, we can use two more attributes available. These act to store the resultant URL in a scoped attribute, and not output it to the output stream writer directly (which is the default behaviour of the action). These should seem familiar by now:

- var
  Specifies the attribute name in which to store the encoded (and rewritten, if applicable) URL. The type of attribute is String.

- `scope`
  Specifies the scope in which `var` should be stored.

It is logical that behind the scenes, this action should use the Servlet API: in particular the `HttpServletResponse`'s `encodeURL` method handles the URL encoding (see Chapter 5). Using this action saves us having to resort to JSP scripting elements, which is always a good thing if possible!

This action can either be empty or contain one or more `<c:param>` tags which are used to encode the HTTP query string (name/value parameter pairs) into the URL.

Importing Resources: <c:import>

This action is used to include a resource, specified by a URL, into the current output stream. For all resources in the container (either the current or a foreign application), the `RequestDispatcher` mechanism is used. For resources specified by an absolute URL, an `InputStream` is used to buffer the data byte-by-byte into the response. The normal requirement when using this action is to transfer the included data directly into the `out` (implicit object) stream; if so, we can use this basic syntax:

```
<c:import url="resource_url" />
```

The resource residing at *`resource_url`* is included in the JSP, or a `JspException` thrown if it could not be found, or an `IOException` thrown if a stream error occurs. These would typically cause a JSP error page to be displayed, as with any other exceptions thrown during the course of a resource servicing requests. Relative *`resource_url`* values refer to a component in the container, while absolute *`resource_url`* values refer to components on others servers etc. As with `<c:url>`, we can use the `context` attribute to import a resource from a foreign application inside the same container:

```
<c:import url="resource_url" context="app_context" />
```

The `context` attribute's value should be the name of a valid context root (beginning with a forward-slash, `/`), or a `JspException` is thrown. The `url` attribute's value should be a context-relative URL (also beginning with a `/`) for the resource in the foreign application.

Aside from writing the retrieved resource directly to the response output stream, the resource can be written to a `String` attribute in a specified scope. This uses the `var` and `scope` attributes, which I'm sure we've seen just a couple of times before now! In addition, this action provides one more option because the data being stored is likely to be large. This comes in the form of a `Reader` object, whose name is specified via the `varReader` attribute and which is accessible *only within the body* of the `<c:import>` action. Scripting code can be used to read the data byte-by-byte from the `Reader`; for example:

```
<c:import url="/banner/header.jsp" varReader="myReaderObj">
  <% Reader r = (Reader) pageContext.getAttribute("myReaderObj");
     int thisByte = 0;
     while((thisByte = r.read()) != -1) {
       // Do something with the data
     }
  %>
</c:import>
```

The scriptlet code first obtains and casts the `Reader` object from the page-scoped attribute called `myReaderObj`, then iterates through the stream until there are no more bytes left. What the code then does with that data is not stated. If you really wanted to, the scriptlet code could copy the `Reader` from its temporary page-scoped attribute (which is removed after the action completes processing) into a permanent scoped attribute, for example to be used further down the JSP; that's just one idea to keep your brain ticking over.

One more attribute to mention briefly without discussion: `charEncoding` can be used to explicitly specify the character encoding of the resource to be included. This allows the encoding for the data contained in the `Reader` and `String` to be set. If omitted, the character encoding given by the resource is used, or failing that the container's default encoding.

Redirection: <c:redirect>

17

This action can be used to redirect a client to another URL. A typical implementation might call `sendRedirect()` on the current `HttpServletResponse` object, aborting evaluation of the rest of the JSP. Following the semantics of this method, it is important that no content has already been written to the response, otherwise an exception will be thrown and you'll end up with an error page which you didn't really want to see. The syntax for this action is simple:

```
<c:redirect url="redirect_url" context="app_context" />
```

This causes the client to be redirected to *`redirect_url`*. In the case that *`redirect_url`* is a context-relative URL from a foreign application, `context` can be used to specify the root of that application (as we've already seen, several times now). *`redirect_url`* may be either absolute or relative (based on the context or current component's URL).

A typical use of this action is as part of a conditional; in the following example, the `<c:if>` action is used to confirm that `var1` exists in the request scope, and if not redirects the client:

```
<c:if test="${ empty requestScope['var1'] }">
  <c:redirect url="failed.jsp" />
</c:if>
```

If `var1` cannot be found (and hence resolves to `null`), the client is redirected to the `failed.jsp` resource. Notice that we've used the `empty` EL operator to test for a null value (or equivalently an empty list).

Request Parameters: <c:param>

This is the last tag we must look at (do I hear a sigh of relief?); it's another cooperating action (see *Nested Tags and Cooperating Actions* in Chapter 18) which doesn't appear to do anything but instead is used to specify extra request parameters to be included in the results of other actions. It can be used in any of the three actions we have just seen, i.e.: `<c:url>`, `<c:import>` and `<c:redirect>`.

The syntax of `<c:param>` is:

```
<c:param name="param_name" value="param_value" />
```

or

```
<c:param name="param_name">
  param_value
</c:param>
```

Both `name` and `value` are *dynamic attributes*: they can take request-time expressions as values.

The syntax and semantics of this action are similar to those of `<jsp:param>` in the last chapter, with the exception that `<jsp:param>` must be an empty element, whereas `<c:param>` may have content which then represents the value. This distinction is a subtle one which a cruel examiner might nevertheless throw in to throw you! Even though it's unlikely that they will test such obscure syntactic details (they generally like to know that you *understand* everything and not that you necessarily know it by heart), try not to be caught out.

Let's look at one short example:

```
<c:import url="/widgets/menu.jsp">
  <c:param name="style" value="sunrise" />
</c:import>
```

This code includes the `/widgets/menu.jsp` resource into the current output, specifying the value of a request-time attribute called `style`. For this hypothetical example, we'll suppose that `sunrise` is the name of a 'skin' (i.e. presentation style) for the menu bar widget. The `menu.jsp` resource looks at the `style` request parameter and applies the appropriate colour schemes depending on its value (presumably in this example we'd be looking at a mix of dawn colours).

Revision Questions

1 **Which of the following used in JSP pages or documents are valid ways to declare usage of the JSTL v1.1 core tag library with prefix c?** **(choose two)**

- A <%taglib url="http://java.sun.com/jsp/jstl/core" prefix="c" %>
- B <jsp:directive.taglib uri="http://java.sun.com/jsp/jstl/core" prefix="c" />
- C <c:set xmlns:c="http://java.sun.com/jsp/jstl/core" ... />
- D <%@ taglib uri="http://java.sun.com/jsp/jstl/core" prefix="c" %>
- E <jsp:taglib uri="http://java.sun.com/jsp/jstl/core" prefix="c" />

2 **What is the result of compiling and executing the following lines in a JSP page?** **(choose one)**

```
<% pageContext.setAttribute("var", "Facts & figures: 5 < 6"); %>
<c:out value="${ var }"> Nothing to say</c:out>
```

- A The response contains the text 'Facts & figures: 5 < 6'.
- B The response contains the text 'Facts & figures: 5 < 6 Nothing to say'.
- C The response contains the text 'Facts & figures: 5 < 6'.
- D The response contains the text 'Facts & figures: 5 < 6 Nothing to say'.
- E The response contains the text 'Nothing to say'.

3 **What is the effect of compiling and executing the exhibited JSP page?** **(choose one)**

EXHIBIT

- A The response is empty.
- B The response contains the text 'An error occurred'.
- C The RuntimeException is propagated to the container.
- D A translation error occurs.
- E A compilation error occurs.

4 **What is the effect of deploying and executing the exhibited JSP?** **(choose one)**

EXHIBIT

- A The <c:catch> suppresses the exception and the response is empty.
- B The <c:catch> suppresses the exception and the response contains the exception message.
- C The <c:catch> suppresses the exception and the response contains the text 'My message'.
- D The <c:catch> propagates the exception to the container returning an error page.
- E A translation error occurs.

5 **What types of exceptions does <c:catch> handle?** **(choose one)**

- A java.lang.Exception subclasses only.
- B java.lang.Error subclasses only.
- C java.lang.RuntimeException subclasses only.
- D java.lang.Exception and java.lang.Error subclasses.
- E All java.lang.Throwable subclasses.

6 **Which of the following sets the value of the item page-scoped attribute to 'W0601'?** **(choose one)**

- A <c:set var="item" value="W0601" />
- B <c:set name="item" value="W0601" />
- C <c:set var="item" scope="page" property="W0601" />
- D <%! pageContext.setAttribute("item", "W0601"); %>
- E <jsp:setProperty name="item" value="W0601" />

7 **What is the result of the following?** **(choose one)**

```
<% request.setAttribute("code", new Integer(10)); %>
<c:set var="code" value="5" />
${ code + 2 }
```

- A The response is the text '10'.
- B The response is the text '12'.
- C The response is the text '7'.
- D The response is empty.
- E A runtime exception is thrown.

17

8 **Which JSTL action declarations are equivalent to the following standard action?** **(choose two)**

```
<jsp:setProperty name="dictionary" property="language" value="en" />
```

- A <c:set name="dictionary" property="language" value="en" />
- B <c:set id="dictionary" property="language">en</c:set>
- C <c:set target="dictionary" property="language">en</c:set>
- D <c:set id="dictionary" value="language=en" />
- E <c:set target="dictionary" property="language" value="en" / >

9 **What is the result of compiling and executing the exhibited page?** **(choose one)**

EXHIBIT

- A The response is the text 'Condition 1 was true true'.
- B The response is the text 'Condition 2 was true false'.
- C The response is the text 'The conditions were false false'.
- D The response is the text 'false'.
- E A translation error occurs.

10 **Which of the following are attributes of <c:when>?** **(choose one)**

- A condition
- B when
- C test
- D var
- E break

11 **What is the result of compiling and executing the following?** **(choose one)**

```
<%@ taglib uri="http://java.sun.com/jsp/jstl/core" prefix="c" %>
<c:choice>
  <c:when test="${ false }">Case 1</c:when>
  <c:when test="${ 6 < 5 }">Case 2</c:when>
</c:choice>
```

- A The response is the text 'Case 1'.
- B The response is the text 'Case 2'.
- C The response is the text 'Case 1 Case 2'.
- D The behaviour is indeterminate.
- E A translation error occurs.

17

12 **Which of the following lines inserted in place of the comment will cause the sequence '1 2 3 4' to be output?** **(choose one)**

```
<!-- insert here -->
  ${ index }
</c:forEach>
```

- A <c:forEach start="${ '1' }" end="4" var="index">
- B <c:forEach start="1" finish="4" var="index">
- C <c:forEach begin="1" end="5" var="index">
- D <c:forEach begin="1" end="${ '4' }" var="index">
- E <c:forEach start="1" end="5" var="index">

13 **Which of the following is the JSTL tag used to loop over arbitrary collections of objects?** **(choose one)**

- A <c:loop>
- B <c:iterate>
- C <c:forEach>
- D <c:for>
- E <c:tokens>

14 **What is the result of compiling and executing the JSP shown in the exhibit?** **(choose one)**

EXHIBIT

- A The text 'Entry A' is written to the response.
- B The text 'Entry A Entry B Entry C' is written to the response.
- C The text '1' is written to the response.
- D The text '1 2 3' is written to the response.
- E A translation error occurs.

15 **What is the effect of compiling and executing the exhibit?** **(choose one)**

EXHIBIT

- A The response is the text '9 8 7 6 5'.
- B The response is the text '0 1 2 3 4'.
- C The response is the text '1 2 3 4 5'.
- D The response is empty.
- E A translation error occurs.

16 **Which of the following inserted in this JSP will give the output 'apples bananas celery'?** **(choose one)**

```
<!-- insert here -->
  ${ token }
</c:forTokens>
```

- A <c:forTokens string="apples,bananas,celery" delim="," var="token">
- B <c:forTokens value="apples,bananas,celery" delims="," var="token">
- C <c:forTokens items="apples,bananas,celery" delim=";" var="token">
- D <c:forTokens items="apples,bananas,celery" delim="," var="token">
- E <c:forTokens items="apples,bananas,celery" delims="," var="token">

17 **Which of the following performs URL rewriting on /catalogue/item.jsp and writes the result to the out implicit object?** **(choose one)**

- A <c:url url="/catalogue/item.jsp" />
- B <c:url value="/catalogue/item/jsp" />
- C <c:url value="/catalogue/item/jsp" var="url" />
- D <c:rewrite url="/catalogue/item.jsp" />
- E <c:rewrite value="/catalogue/item.jsp" />

18 **Which of the following can be used to perform dynamic inclusion?** **(choose two)**

- A <jsp:include />
- B <jsp:import />
- C <c:include />
- D <c:import />
- E <c:forward />

19 **Which of the following are attributes of <c:import>?** **(choose two)**

- A value
- B page
- C file
- D url
- E context

20 **Which of the following can be used to include the /index.jsp page from the application deployed at context mainApp into the current JSP?** **(choose one)**

- A <c:import value="/index.jsp" app="/mainApp" />
- B <c:import page="/index.jsp" context="/mainApp" />
- C <c:import url="/index.jsp" context="/mainApp" />
- D <jsp:include path="/index.jsp" context="/mainApp" />
- E <c:import path="/index.jsp" context="/mainApp" />

21 **What is the result of invoking the exhibited JSP?** **(choose one)**

EXHIBIT

A If the code request parameter does not exist, a redirect request is sent for the nocode.jsp page relative to the application's context root.

B If the code request parameter does not exist, a redirect request is sent for the nocode.jsp page relative to the current page's location.

C If the param implicit object is empty, nothing happens.

D A runtime exception is thrown.

E A translation error occurs.

22 **What is the effect of the exhibited JSP page?** **(choose one)**

EXHIBIT

A The /catalogue/item.jsp source code is included in the response.

B The request-scoped attribute called code is set to the value 'W0601' and the /catalogue/item.jsp page is evaluated.

C The request parameter called code is set to the value 'W0601' and the /catalogue/item.jsp page is evaluated.

D A translation error occurs.

Exhibits

Q.3

```
<%@ taglib uri="http://java.sun.com/jsp/jstl/core" prefix="c" %>
<c:try>
  <% throw new RuntimeException("Something bad happened!"); %>
</c:try>
<c:catch>
  An error occurred
</c:catch>
```

17

Q.4

```
<%@ taglib uri="http://java.sun.com/jsp/jstl/core" prefix="c" %>
<% request.setAttribute("theexception", new Exception("My message")); %>
<c:catch var="theexception">
  <% int i=1; %>
  <%= 100/(i-1) %>
</c:catch>
${ theexception.message }
```

Q.9

```
<%@ taglib uri="http://java.sun.com/jsp/jstl/core" prefix="c" %>
<c:if test="${ 6 < 5 }" var="condition1">
  Condition 1 was true
</c:if>
<c:if test="${ 3 < 9 }">
  Condition 2 was true
</c:if>
<c:else>
  The conditions were false
</c:else>
${ condition1 }
```

Q.14

```
<%@ page import="java.util.*" %>
<%@ taglib uri="http://java.sun.com/jsp/jstl/core" prefix="c" %>
<%
  ArrayList list = new ArrayList();
  list.add("Entry A");
  pageContext.setAttribute("list", list);
  list.add("Entry B");
  list.add("Entry C");
%>
<c:forEach items="${ list }" var="counter">
  ${ counter }
</c:forEach>
```

Q.15

```
<%@ taglib uri="http://java.sun.com/jsp/jstl/core" prefix="c" %>
<% pageContext.setAttribute("arr", new int[]{ 9, 8, 7, 6, 5 }); %>
<c:forEach items="${ arr }" varStatus="status">
  ${ status.index }
</c:forEach>
```

17

Q.21

```
<%@ taglib uri="http://java.sun.com/jsp/jstl/core" prefix="c" %>
<c:if test="${ empty param['code'] }">
  <c:redirect url="nocode.jsp" />
</c:if>
```

Q.22

```
<%@ taglib uri="http://java.sun.com/jsp/jstl/core" prefix="c" %>
<c:import url="/catalogue/item.jsp">
  <c:param name="code">W0601</c:param>
</c:import>
```

Answers to Revision Questions

1 **Correct answers: C, D**

C is used in JSP documents, where the XML namespace is used to bind the prefix to the URI of the tag library; in this particular example, we've localised the namespace definition to one particular tag, but using the same 'xmlns:c' declaration on <jsp:root> or any other root of the document will bind the namespace for all elements. D is the correct page version.

2 **Correct answer: C**

The content of a <c:out> is only output to the response if the value attribute resolves to null. Otherwise, the content of the value attribute is escaped (since we omitted the escapeXml attribute whose default is true) in order to be XML compliant. Hence '&' is replaced by '&' and '<' by '<'.

3 **Correct answer: D**

There is no element called <c:try>!

4 **Correct answer: B**

The Throwable which caused the exception is stored in a *page*-scoped attribute, which in this example is called theexception. Execution then continues after the block that catches the exception.

5 **Correct answer: E**

6 **Correct answer: A**

A uses the correct syntax, where scope has a default value of page; B uses an illegal name attribute, C uses an illegal property attribute, E is used for setting bean properties and so is not appropriate here (where we want to set entire scoped attributes), and D is wrong because it is a declaration and not a scriptlet (in that case it would be correct).

7 **Correct answer: C**

The <c:set> has the default scope of page, so in this example we set the code page-scoped attribute to 5. Since the expression then searches the scope in order starting with page, the value 5 is obtained, 2 added, and the result 7 returned.

8 **Correct answers: C, E**

Note that the body content of <c:set> represents the value if no value attribute is specified. The id and name attributes don't exist, making A, B and D illegal. Also, the 'language=en' assignment in D is illegal; you should use the separately property and language attributes.

9 **Correct answer: E**

<c:else> is not a valid JSTL tag.

10 **Correct answer: C**

This is the only attribute of <c:when>

11 **Correct answer: E**

The outer tag should be <c:choose> not <c:choice>.

12 **Correct answer: D**

Note that end is *inclusive* and that the attributes are named begin and end; any Strings in an EL expression will be coerced to an integer value automatically.

13 **Correct answer: C**

14 **Correct answer: B**

Note that since it is the *reference* to the list stored in the page-scoped attribute, any changes to the list after binding to the scope still take effect. Therefore, there are 3 entries in the list; the loop then iterates over each, and on each iteration stores the value of that list entry in the counter variable. Hence the output is B; if you want to obtain the numerical counter value on each iteration, you will need to use a TagLoopStatus object.

15 **Correct answer: B**

We've used the TagLoopStatus object to keep track of the current counter value; for collections, this is 0-based, so B is correct.

16 **Correct answer: E**

The others use an illegal set of attributes.

17 **Correct answer: B**

Note that C is also valid, but incorrect, because it writes the rewritten URL into the url page-scoped attribute and not to the current (out) JspWriter.

18 **Correct answers: A, D**

19 **Correct answers: D, E**

20 **Correct answer: C**

Note that a useful feature of <c:import> is that it can be used to import resources from foreign applications and also resources from other websites and absolute URLs.

21 **Correct answer: B**

Note that C is false because if param were null (and it never should be), the entire param['code'] expression returns null, and empty null returns true. Therefore the client would be redirected.

22 **Correct answer: C**

The use of <c:param> is the same as for <jsp:param>: it sets a request parameter with the name and value supplied, using a request wrapper to achieve this.

In this chapter you'll:

- Be introduced to the Tag Extension API.
- Create custom tags by implementing Tag, IterationTag and BodyTag.
- Use convenience classes TagSupport and BodyTagSupport.
- Learn the Simple Tag API and how it differs from classic tags.
- Understand the lifecycles of both classic and simple tags.
- Use JSP Fragments in the Simple Tag API.
- Add attributes and dynamic attributes to a custom tag.
- Create nested and cooperating custom tags.
- Expose scripting variables and scoped attributes from tags.

18 Custom Tags

We've already seen plenty of examples of the standard and JSTL tags available to us, what they do, how they do it and when best to use them–which, frankly, is everywhere to replace JSP scripting elements. Using libraries of existing tags is perfectly fine until you need more functionality from what tags offer; iterating through lists and using JavaBean properties is all very well, and absolutely essential in a well-designed JSP, but there will always be circumstances when the standard tags are just not sufficient, or indeed are too generic. When this is the case, you must look towards creating your own application-specific tags which do useful things, like querying an EJB or database in the Java EE application, or looking up data from a configuration file, both of which require a fair amount of logic and which you might need to share across many JSPs. Hard-coding the same code into each one is highly undesirable; it is inextensible, not scalable, and increases maintenance costs, but just the amount of typing or copying/pasting puts me off. Tags of this type are referred to as **custom tags**, since they are built for the individual needs of every application.

This chapter begins by introducing the basic theory of the Tag Extension API, and gives details of the interfaces a classic tag handler class must implement. We then move on to discuss the Simple Tag API. Finally, we add further complexity to our tag handler classes by adding attributes to our custom tags. Unfortunately, the addition of attributes to a custom tag is not an obvious exam requirement, and yet the vast majority of tags do have attributes (just look at the JSTL core library and see how many of those tags don't have attributes). Furthermore, all the examples referred to in this chapter define at least one attribute; since these examples rely on all the content discussed in this chapter, and are quite long, they can be downloaded as part of the download bundle (see the Preface). We refer to individual tag handler class names throughout the chapter to illustrate specific features of the Tag Extension API.

JSP's Custom Tags

This chapter contains some of the most demanding material on the exam–it's the stuff that every developer finds hardest. So, before we go on to look at how custom tags are coded for, let's first take a more advanced introduction into the basics of tags and tag libraries. We will begin with a discussion of the two types of tag available in JSP 2.0, and follow up with the trusty old life cycle.

Classic Tags vs. Tag Files

Like many things in Java, and technology in general, custom tags have a variety of names and conventions associated with them. In particular, custom tags are also known as tag extensions or custom actions. Before JSP 2.0, the only type of custom tag available was coded for as a Java class, and much like servlets they all had to implement a special interface which defined the contract that any tag must fulfil (we will see all the details of this later). JSP 2.0, on which this exam is based, gave the specification for a new type of custom tag which was not constructed as a class, but as a JSP itself. This takes tags to a new level: no longer must a tag be bound to a Java platform and no longer must JSP authors rely on a Java programmer in a team. Recall from Chapter 13 that this was the primary goal of JSPs in the first place.

The older tags, created as classes, are known now as **classic tags** (or classic *actions*, or classic *tag extensions*–anything that makes them sound antique really), while the newer JSP-based tags are known as **tag files**. Just to be even more confusing, the actual *classes* which implement and define the behaviour of both classic tags and tag files are known as **tag handlers**. Of course, with tag files as with JSPs, the implementation class is created by the container as part of the tag file's translation, so you won't actually see the handler class or even care about it; in contrast, classic tag handlers must be programmed directly as classes by the tag author.

We will examine the two types of tag chronologically; this chapter looks at classic tags, starting with the original classic tag extensions and moving on to the newer `SimpleTag`. The next chapter is dedicated to tag files.

Tag Life Cycles

18

Unfortunately, both types of tag have a slightly different life cycle due to their differences in nature (one is a compiled class, while the other is a JSP). See also Figure 18.5 and the next chapter.

Classic Tag Extensions

Depending on what you want to do with a classic tag, there are a number of different interfaces available to be implemented. At their most basic, all tags must implement the `javax.servlet.jsp.tagext.JspTag` interface; if you look at the

API definition for this interface, you'll find that it has an empty definition (i.e. no methods or fields) and that it was specified first in JSP 2.0, which at the time of writing is the latest version. This interface was in fact added in JSP 2.0 to provide a base type for a new tag handler, `SimpleTag` which we examine later on.

When looking at classic tag handlers, we are primarily interested in the `javax.servlet.jsp.tagext.Tag` interface, and all its subinterfaces, so let's look at this first and work through the available tag handler types in increasing complexity (and hence, flexibility of course). Unless otherwise stated, all tag-related interfaces and classes reside in the `javax.servlet.jsp.tagext` package.

The Tag Interface

Custom tags created by implementing just the `Tag` interface provide the solutions to three possible problems:

- When a tag is required to perform a singular atomic action which writes content to the current output stream, for example, inserting the name of a database field into the JSP. These are typically shown as *empty action* tags in the JSP–they don't require content since they perform their own self-contained process.
- To make a new scripting variable or scoped attribute available to the JSP. The JSTL `<c:set />` action is a typical example, which when used creates a new scoped attribute which can then be accessed by subsequent code. We look more closely at actions which create scripting variables and scoped attributes later in the chapter.
- When content needs to be inserted into the JSP conditionally–i.e. the content of the action should only be written to the response stream when a certain set of conditions are true.

The methods declared in the `Tag` interface are:

- **`void setParent(Tag)`**
  The container invokes this method to set the `Tag` which encloses this tag in the document. This is useful when using cooperating nested tags, a topic featuring later in the chapter.
- **`void setPageContext(PageContext)`**
  Called by the container when the tag handler is invoked as a result of its custom tag being encountered in a JSP. The `PageContext` argument can be stored in the tag handler and used to access scoped variables and JSP implicit objects.

- **`Tag getParent()`**
  Returns the enclosing `Tag` which was set using the `setParent` method by the container.

- **`void release()`**
  Called on the tag handler by the container to provide it with an opportunity to remove/destroy any resources it has a handle on; this is semantically similar to the `destroy` method found on servlets and filters. When called, it is typical that the parent `Tag` and `PageContext` objects will be in an unpredictable state (they may even have been released for garbage collection already). You should therefore not rely on or invoke these objects during the execution of `release()`.

Those are all life cycle methods which alone don't allow us to write tags; for this we must look more closely at these methods:

- **`int doStartTag()`**
  This is invoked when the *opening tag* of the action is encountered in the JSP. At this time, the body of the action (if there is any) has not been examined.

- **`int doEndTag()`**
  Called when the *closing tag* of the action is encountered in the JSP. This method will always be evaluated, regardless of whether the tag is empty (i.e. has no content).

Each method must return an integer matching the constants declared in the `Tag` interface. This integer acts as a flag, informing the container of what action should now be taken. For the `doStartTag` method, these constants are:

- **`EVAL_BODY_INCLUDE`**
  Tells the container to parse and evaluate the content of the tag.

- **`SKIP_BODY`**
  Tells the container not to parse and output the body of the tag. If the tag is declared such that it must *always be empty* (this can be done through the TLD), then this value must be returned. If the action is not declared as always being empty, but in this instance is anyway, then either value will result in the same output.

Thus, using the above we can easily control (conditionally) whether the body of an action is included in the response, in which case `EVAL_BODY_INCLUDE` is returned, or omitted, when the return value should be `SKIP_BODY`. The `doEndTag` method has two other constants:

- **`EVAL_PAGE`**
  Informs the container that it should continue processing the rest of the JSP.

- **SKIP_PAGE**
  Causes the container to stop processing the JSP component. This will send all processing of the calling JSP until this point to the current output stream. If this JSP was the result of a `RequestDispatcher forward()` or `include()`, only processing of *this JSP* is halted, allowing calling components to carry on executing.

In general, the `SKIP_PAGE` flag should be treated with the utmost care and used rarely. Using it will almost certainly result in incomplete output, which in the case of strict and well-formed languages like XML and XHTML equates to disaster. There's guaranteed to be a better way to achieve conditional rendering without resorting to this return value. For this reason, the majority of tag handlers will return `EVAL_PAGE`.

Now, knowing the four life cycle methods and two service methods which we need to implement, it should be straightforward to walk through the coding of an example custom tags. For this explanation we use the `mytags.MyConditionalTag` tag handler class found in the download bundle (see the Preface). This is effectively an implementation of the `<c:if>` JSTL tag; hopefully seeing this type of tag twice will enforce its syntax—perhaps also seeing how such a tag works will help you understand why and how it does what it does.

Firstly, we notice that we've implemented the `Tag` interface and provided private instance storage of the `PageContext` and parent `Tag` for this handler. In this class, we don't actually use either of these objects, so it might be tempting to omit storage of them. However, it may be the case that a nested tag uses properties of its parents, perhaps searching for a specific ancestor, and it may be a nested tag relies on `getParent()` to achieve this goal. As a result, we should always supply a complete implementation.

Next, we rely on the `test` attribute to tell us whether to evaluate the body of the tag or not. We won't worry about the details of how the attribute is set up here (it uses the `setTest` mutator method), but instead we guarantee that the instance `test` variable stores the evaluated state of the `test` attribute.

Since we only want to include the body if the `test` attribute is `true`, we implement the `doStartTag` method to return `SKIP_BODY` only if `test` is `false` (otherwise we return `EVAL_BODY_INCLUDE`).

In this handler, the `doEndTag` method does nothing, so we simply return `EVAL_PAGE`.

Figure 18.1 summarises the execution flow for a `Tag` implementation.

All tags require a single no-argument constructor so they can be instantiated by the container (like JavaBeans, which also require a no-argument constructor). Note

Figure 18.1

Tag Execution Flow (Life Cycle)

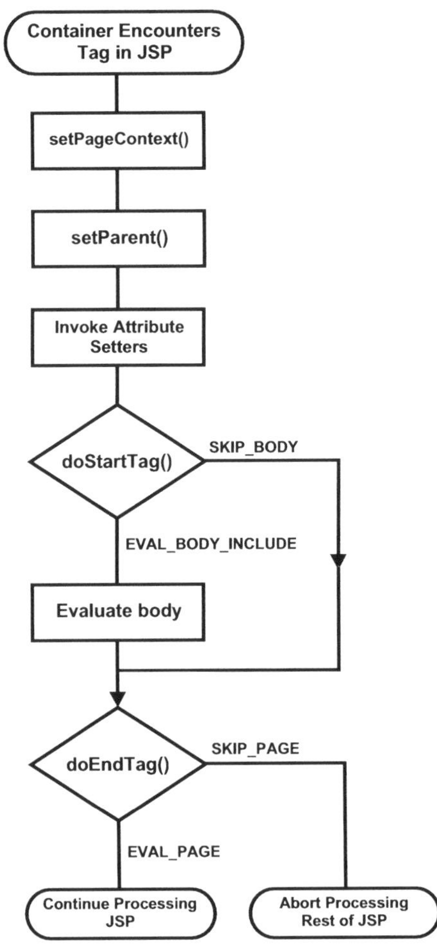

that we've omitted all reference to a constructor, but recall that the compiler will automatically insert a public no-argument empty constructor when one is omitted from the class code, so this won't be a problem. All the tag handlers located in the download bundle (the Preface contains download details) omit an explicit constructor.

18

If you think the `MyConditionalTag` handler looks like a pretty straightforward implementation, that's good: the only thing the examiners really want to know is whether you have an appreciation for the methods and invocation procedures of tags, and can put that understanding to use. If you can understand the purpose and syntax of the `Tag` interface (and even better if you've already learnt the method signatures and constant names by heart) then you're already on the way to passing this area of the exam. We will now proceed to create more complex tags, so make sure that you are confident with the basics now.

Note that the mytags.MyIncludeTag is a second implementation of Tag, but it extends TagSupport (see later in this chapter) to avoid us having to explicitly code all the 'housekeeping code' for the PageContext and Tag objects.

The IterationTag Interface

The use cases for tag handlers based on Tag are limited; we mentioned three in the previous section, and scraping around you might be able to find a few more. In some cases it may be necessary to include the body content of the action *multiple times*, for example when rendering rows in a table. The IterationTag interface, which extends Tag, fills this use case.

IterationTag defines one more method, *in addition* to all those provided by Tag:

- **int doAfterBody()**
  This method is called by the container after every evaluation of the tag's body content. The return value will determine whether the body should be evaluated once more, or whether control should now jump to the doEndTag method.

The returned integer must be one of the constants:

- **SKIP_BODY**
  Causes execution to jump immediately to the doEndTag method.
- **EVAL_BODY_AGAIN**
  Causes the container to evaluate the body content once more.

Should the action's body by empty anyway, execution jumps straight from doStartTag() to doEndTag() (bypassing doAfterBody()) regardless of the return value of doStartTag().

The simplest possible example of a tag which iterates is a loop—mytags.MyForTag is a tag handler class which acts as a simple for loop (this is a simpler version of <c:forEach>; our version doesn't handle iteration of Collections). MyForTag is a tag which takes start and end attributes, specifying the integer indices to begin and finish at, an optional integer step attribute which specifies the amount by which the internal counter should be incremented on each count, and the optional var attribute gives the name of the page-scoped attribute and scripting variable in which the counter value should be stored on each iteration. Note that these attributes are the same as those of <c:forEach>.

18

Once again, we shall ignore the mechanics of setting attributes on the tag, and simply take for granted the fact that the instance attributes store the state of the attributes. We note also that this class doesn't define any 'housekeeping code' as required by implementations of the `Tag` interface; this is because this class extends `TagSupport` (see next section) which does all the standard 'housekeeping' for us, leaving us to concentrate on the custom implementation.

The first method executed on the tag is always `doStartTag()`, so we implement this to do the following:

- If the `step` attribute was not declared, we set `step` to the default value of 1.
- We test to see if this loop will definitely terminate; if it goes on forever, we throw a `JspException` rather than letting it run and consume resources needlessly.
- Next we initialise the private `counter` variable to `start`.
- Finally we update the page-scoped attribute if the `var` attribute is declared.

We've used the `runLoop` method to encapsulate the logic to determine whether the loop should terminate or not. This test is complicated slightly by the possibility that `step` be negative (and the loop count down) as well as positive. `runLoop()` returns `true` if the loop should continue to the next iteration, or `false` to halt it.

We implement `doAfterBody()` to:

- Increment the internal `counter` by the `step` amount.
- Update the page-scoped attribute if the `var` attribute is declared.
- Determine whether to continue to the next iteration (returning `EVAL_BODY_AGAIN`) or to stop here (returning `SKIP_BODY`).

Finally, our `doEndTag()` resets the state of the tag and removes the page-scoped attribute (if it existed in the first place).

NOTE: One issue we haven't addressed in any tag handler examples is a conflict of scoped attributes. For example, what if an attribute of the name given by `var` already exists in the page scope? At the moment, calling `removeAttribute()` in the `doEndTag` method will remove it permanently. We might like to make a copy of the original value in `doStartTag()` and *restore* (rather than remove) the attribute in `doEndTag()`. This is left as an exercise.

18

The TagSupport Class

As we said in the previous sections, it gets tiresome to write the 'housekeeping code' into the tag handler classes – it's always the same, and doesn't add anything to the handler's implementation.

Thankfully, the Tag Extension API provides the `TagSupport` class which implements the `IterationTag` interface, and by implication the `Tag` interface also, taking care of all that boring state-saving for us. In fact, all methods are concrete, and even the class isn't marked as abstract! All you need to do is implement the methods that concern you. This is the same as the adapter pattern used frequently in the AWT and Swing (Event) APIs, if you are familiar with them. The default return values from the methods skip the body, prevent further body evaluations and continue with evaluation of the calling JSP:

- `doStartTag()` returns `SKIP_BODY`
- `doAfterBody()` returns `SKIP_BODY`
- `doEndTag()` returns `EVAL_PAGE`

While we're here, one extra bonus worth mentioning is that, although it is advisable to include a constructor in your code for clarity, you don't actually have to in this case. Omitting a constructor will cause the compiler to generate a default no-argument one which calls the `TagSupport` class's default no-argument constructor (which is what the API expects to happen). Your tag handler classes can now be really compact, containing at a minimum one method implementation; this is elegant code indeed!

A more detailed example of a `Tag` is the `mytags.SelectCountryTag`. This custom tag is designed to be used in an HTML document. Wherever the tag appears in the JSP, it is replaced by an (X)HTML `<select>` drop-down list of countries. The entries are automatically generated by Java's `Locale` class; using the `lang` attribute, it is possible to change the language in which the countries are displayed. For example, a value of `en` (the default) shows country names like United Kingdom, United States and France, while a value of `fr` shows Royaume-Uni, Etats-Uni and France as the country names. This allows the JSP author to (dynamically) change the language which the list is displayed in with ease. We've significantly reduced the amount of code by extending `TagSupport` (and using its default implementation of `doAfterBody()`) rather than implementing `IterationTag` directly.

Figure 18.2 summarises the execution flow for implementations of `IterationTag` (and hence `TagSupport`).

Figure 18.2

IterationTag and TagSupport Execution Flow (Life Cycle)

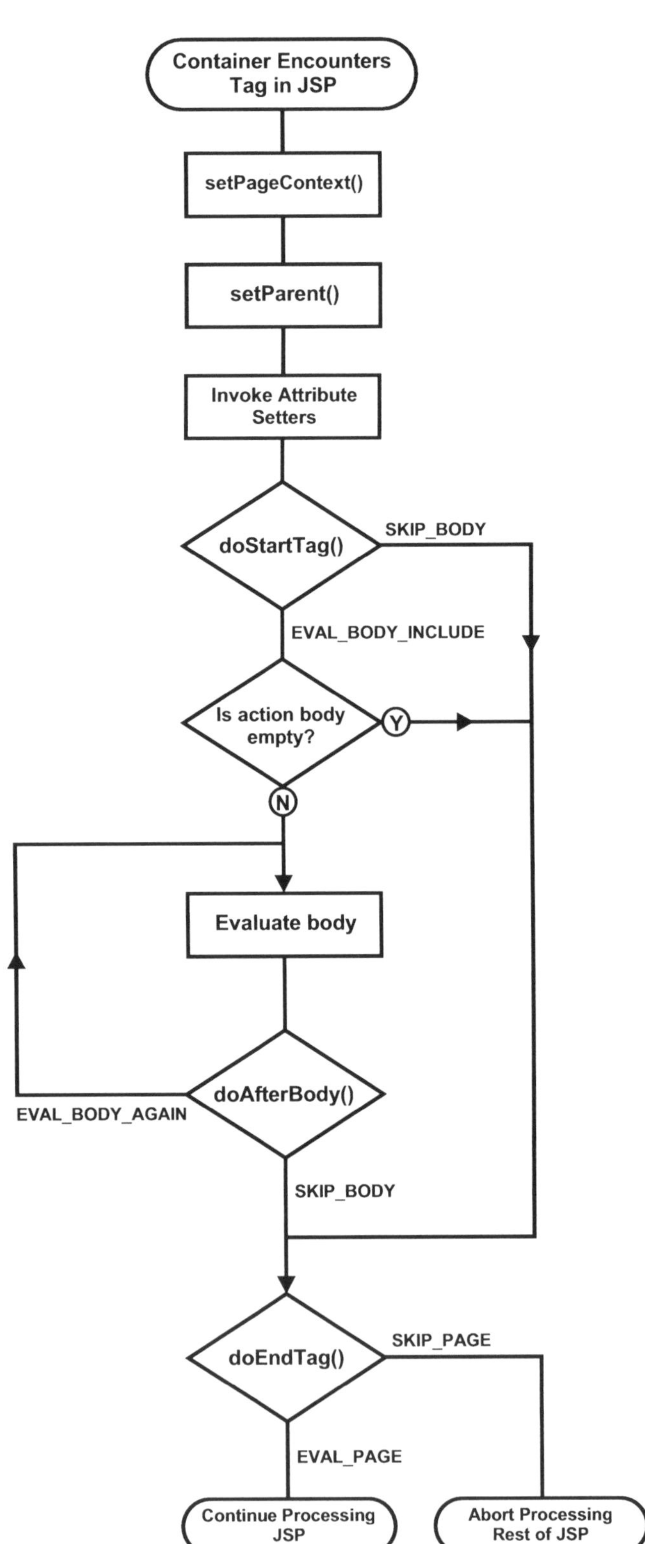

18

The BodyTag Interface

Both `Tag` and `IterationTag` write the content of the action's body to the response stream straight away, as soon as the content is evaluated. This doesn't give the tag handler any chance to evaluate the content for itself. Using the return value from the `doStartTag` method, a handler can decide whether to render the body or not, and by using the `IterationTag`'s functionality the body can be repeatedly output, but we have not yet seen a way for a tag to *modify* the body content. As an example, suppose that we are implementing a guestbook system with visitor's comments. We design a custom tag to obtain their comments from a database and write them to the output; it looks like `IterationTag` could be the solution. Now I'll impose another restriction: we want to *moderate* the visitor's comments to prevent rude words about our site (such as 'useless', 'uninformative', 'rubbish', you know the kind of thing) from showing up. What we need is to be able to edit each entry in the book (or all the entries as a whole) to replace all the 'rude' words with our own delimiters like '***'; for example, 'rubbish' could be converted to 'ru***sh'. The solution is a handler implementing the sophisticated `BodyTag` interface.

`BodyTag` provides a separate buffer (a subclass of `Writer`) to which all evaluated body content is written. Normally, evaluated content is written directly to the `out` implicit object, or to a parent tag's `Writer`, both of which are of class `JspWriter`. The semantics of `BodyTag` are different:

1. When a `BodyTag` is invoked, the calling JSP's implementation invokes `pushBody()` on the `PageContext` object for JSP being executed. This saves the current `Writer` object (which may be the value of `out`) and returns a *new* `BodyContent` object, `BodyContent` being a subclass of `JspWriter`.
2. The result of calling `pushBody()` is that all content written to the output by the tag is *not written to the original* `JspWriter` (either `out` or the parent tag's writer) but to the new `BodyContent` stream instead.
3. Once the tag has finished executing, and `doEndTag()` has returned, the calling JSP's implementation invokes `popBody()` to remove the `BodyContent` writer from the stack and replace it with the original one (which will either be `out` or the parent tag's writer).

The `BodyContent` writer acts as a buffer; the result of executing the tag is written here instead of to the response stream. This allows the tag handler to examine the contents of the buffer before finally writing it to the response–and yes, you do have to *manually* write the contents to the response since the default behaviour is to '*lose*' the contents of the `BodyContent`. Once the `doEndTag()` returns, the `BodyContent` for that tag is cleared (and may be reused by future invocations); its contents are not written automatically to the response – as the saying goes, 'once it's gone, it's gone'. This can be useful: if you want to suppress the data already written to the stream, then simply return from `doEndTag()` without having explicitly copied the data to the parent `Writer`.

Let's look at the two new methods which `BodyTag` introduces:

- **`void setBodyContent(BodyContent)`**
  Called by the container to set the `BodyContent` stream for this tag invocation. This method is only called if `doStartTag()` returns `EVAL_BODY_BUFFERED`.

- **`void doInitBody()`**
  This method is invoked straight after `setBodyContent()`. This allows the tag handler to write some initial content to the stream before evaluation of the action's body content takes place. Note that in `BodyTag` implementations, `doStartTag()` is invoked *before* the `BodyContent` buffer has been established; `doInitBody()` is therefore *the* place to do pre-tag operations on the buffer (since `doStartTag()` cannot access it).

Both of the above will only be invoked should the `doStartTag` method return the constant value `EVAL_BODY_BUFFERED`, and the body content of the action in the JSP is not empty. If the body is empty, execution jumps straight to `doEndTag()`.

NOTE: The following comment appears in the API documentation for `setBodyContent()`: 'This method will not be invoked for empty tags or for non-empty tags whose `doStartTag()` method returns `SKIP_BODY` or `EVAL_BODY_INCLUDE`'. It is a fairly subtle point that if an action is empty, the `BodyContent` object it stores will be `null` since it is never initialised. This can be used as a test to determine if the action is empty at run time, but more importantly, to avoid seeing `NullPointerException`s, you should always assume the `BodyContent` object might be `null`, and test for this case before trying to invoke its methods.

18

The `BodyContent` class is a subclass of `JspWriter` which acts as a buffer not backed by any other stream. As a result, discarding its contents causes them to be omitted from the output stream. In order to make use of the `BodyContent` data correctly, you will need to use one or more of the following methods:

- **`void clearBody()`**
  Clears the `BodyContent` buffer, causing all its contents to be lost.

- **`void flush()`**
  Always throws an `IOException` – we can't flush the buffer since it isn't backed by another stream, and there isn't anything to flush into!

- **`JspWriter getEnclosingWriter()`**
  Used to obtain the parent `JspWriter`; if this tag has a parent `BodyTag`, this will be another instance of `BodyContent`. Otherwise it might be the `out` implicit object.

- **`Reader getReader()`**
  Returns a `Reader` suitable for extracting the contents of this buffer.

- **`String getString()`**
  Returns the contents of the buffer as a `String`.

- **`void writeOut(Writer write)`**
  Writes the entire contents of this stream to the specified `Writer`. This can be any writer of your choice, but perhaps most usually `write` is the parent writer obtained from `getEnclosingWriter()`. It is possible to use the `out` implicit object as an argument here, but bypassing the parent writer may lead to incorrect behaviour (such as not evaluating a conditional parent tag).

The BodyTagSupport Class

`BodyTagSupport` is the concrete convenience implementation of the `BodyTag` interface. `BodyTagSupport` provides the basic `Tag` and `IterationTag` implementations by subclassing `TagSupport`. In addition, it supplies default implementations for each of the `BodyTag` methods. Figure 18.3 summarises the execution flow. Hence, the full header of this class is:

```
public class BodyTagSupport extends TagSupport implements BodyTag
```

The default return values from the service methods are:

- `doStartTag()` returns `EVAL_BODY_BUFFERED` (overridden from `TagSupport`)
- `doAfterBody()` returns `SKIP_BODY` (inherited from `TagSupport`)
- `doEndTag()` returns `EVAL_PAGE` (inherited from `TagSupport`)

18

By default, therefore, all `BodyTagSupport` subclasses evaluate the body *once only*, using the `BodyContent` buffer and continue evaluation of the calling JSP once `doEndTag()` returns.

The `mytags.ModerationTag` handler class is an example of a `BodyTag` which extends `BodyTagSupport` for convenience. This might seem a bizarre tag–but it's designed for a very specific application, in particular a guestbook/feedback display system. The JSP author supplies the tag with a `Map` of entries (`Date`s when the entries were submitted and the text they contain), and the `ModerationTag` iterates through each entry, censoring it to remove any offensive language which

Figure 18.3

BodyTag and BodyTagSupport Execution Flow (Life Cycle)

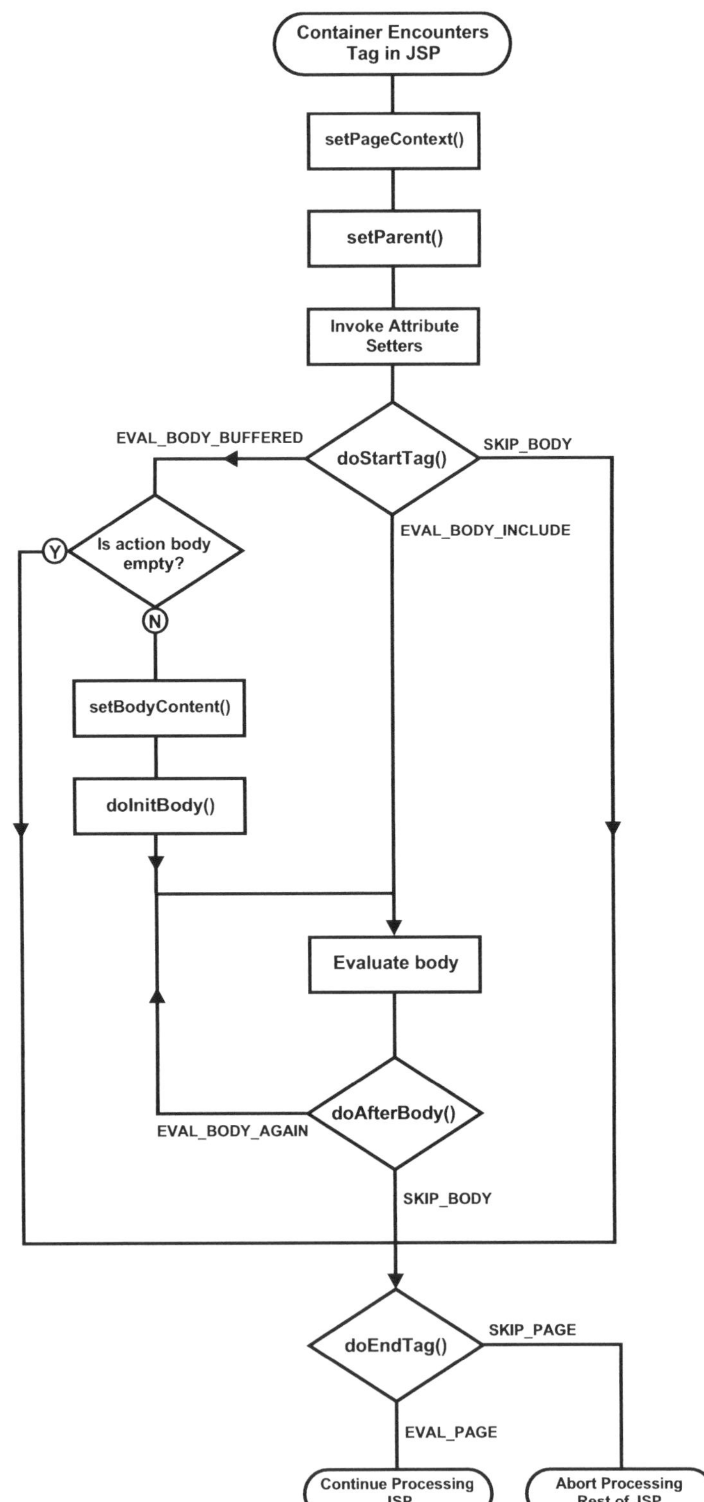

18

unscrupulous visitors may have used. Any entry which contains an excess of 'swear words' is suppressed completely (as obviously that visitor had nothing constructive or sensible to say). The words which are counted as 'swear words', along with what is considered an excess, are configured using attributes of the tag, but we will not concern ourselves with the attributes here.

NOTE: Throughout some of our examples we make use of J2SE 5.0 features such as the for-each loop, generics and autoboxing. If you are not currently familiar with J2SE 5.0 features, I would encourage you to invest some time in upgrading to them: they are extremely powerful and can cut down both the amount of code required, and the number of errors introduced.

The `data` attribute is used to supply the tag with the `Map` of guestbook entries; this is stored in the private instance `data` variable, the `Dates` are sorted in ascending order (using `TreeSet` and the natural order of `Date` instances), and an `Iterator` obtained from the sorted set.

The `doStartTag` method is implemented to:

- Set `swearlimit` to a default of 5 if it was omitted from the tag's attribute list.
- Next, if there are no entries in the `Iterator` at all, we `SKIP_BODY`.
- Otherwise we synchronise the page-scoped attributes (given by the `datevar` and `textvar` attributes) and return `EVAL_BODY_BUFFERED`.

We leave the implementation of `doInitBody()` empty – this method is called after the container has invoked `setBodyContent()`, but before the first iteration of the body. This can be used to add preliminary data into the buffer, if required.

Now the body is invoked for the first time, and the `BodyContent` object is filled with its evaluation. The container next invokes `doAfterBody()` which we implement as follows:

- Firstly it obtains the `BodyContent` that has just been updated, and invokes its `getString()` to obtain a `String` representation of the recently invoked body.
- Next it iterates through each 'swear word' found in the supplied dictionary (specified using the `replace` attribute by the JSP author). We count how many 'swear words' appear, replacing each with its alternative dictionary entry.
- We then call `body.clearBody()` to clear the `BodyContent` buffer, cleaning it for the next body invocation.

- We then decide whether to write out the censored text or not; if the `swearlimit` is exceeded, we suppress the text. Otherwise, we use `BodyContent`'s `getEnclosingWriter()` to obtain the parent `JspWriter`, then invoke its `write` method, passing the censored text as the argument.
- Finally, we decide whether to iterate once more; if there are more entries in the `Iterator`, we go again and update the page-scoped attributes (by calling the `sync` method) and return `EVAL_BODY_AGAIN`. Otherwise we return `SKIP_BODY` and move processing to `doEndTag()`.

Finally, the `doEndTag()` method is implemented to reset the instance variables and remove the page-scoped attributes if they were set. The reset is required since this tag handler may be reused (without being reinstantiated) for later tag invocations, and we don't want the state of the two tag invocations to overlap. The problem of pooled tags is overcome using simple tags.

Simple Tag Handlers

The classic tag handlers we've seen provide an enormous amount of flexibility, and can be used to achieve almost anything. However, the price of power is complexity: no one can deny that tag handlers look horrid, especially to those new to tag libraries. A more intuitive tag handler would only have one method, `doTag()`, which is called when the tag as a whole is encountered in the JSP. This method replaces the need for both `doStartTag()` and `doEndTag()`–and in basic tag handlers you'll probably find yourself implementing only one of these anyway (for example, `doStartTag()` for a conditional output). JSP 2.0 introduced **simple tag handlers** subclassing `SimpleTag`, itself a subclass of `JspTag` (the new base interface for all tags) but *not* `Tag`. `SimpleTag` defines `doTag()` as its service method.

The order of invocation of a simple tag handler (summarised in Figure 18.4) is:

18

1. A new simple tag handler instance is created for each action implemented by a `SimpleTag` class in a JSP.
2. `setJspContext` is called on the `SimpleTag` to set the context.
3. `setParent` is invoked only if the `SimpleTag` has a parent `JspTag`.
4. If the action is not empty–i.e. it has body content–the `setJspBody` method is called to allow the tag handler to get hold of the body content.
5. The `doTag` method is called. This method will use the prescribed body content, set by the container in stage 4, to generate its output. The method may contain code for alteration of the body content, iteration, conditional

output etc. *All processing* associated with the tag is carried out in this method. Note that the return type of this method is `void`; when execution of a `SimpleTag` completes, the handler instance is destroyed and the evaluation of the calling JSP continues – it is not possible to halt evaluation like it is with a classic handler (only by throwing an exception).

Figure 18.4

SimpleTag Execution Flow (Life Cycle)

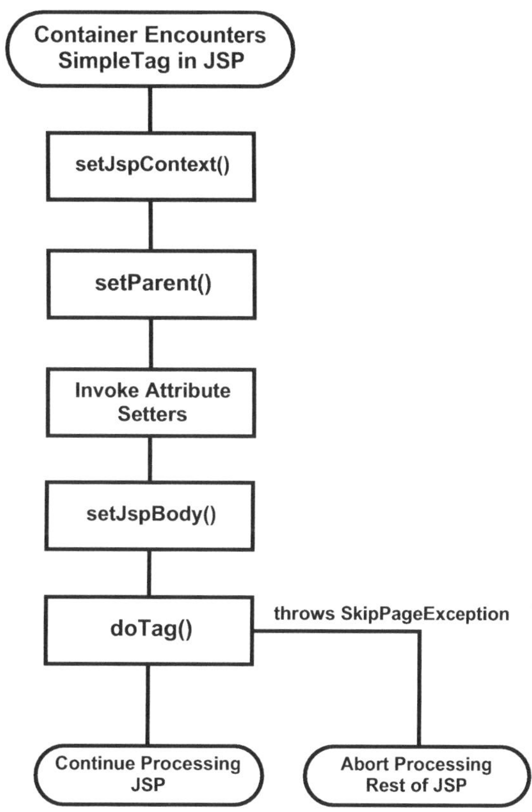

The `SimpleTag` interface methods are therefore (shown in invocation order):

- **`void setJspContext(JspContext context)`**
  Used by the container to set the context for this tag handler. This object can be used primarily by your tag to access and modify scoped attributes during the execution of `doTag()`.

- **`void setParent(JspTag parent)`**
  Used by the container during initialisation to establish the tag enclosing this one in the JSP; this is not called if no parent exists.

- **`JspTag getParent()`**
  Used to retrieve the parent tag set by the container during initialisation.

- **`void setJspBody(JspFragment fragment)`**
  Sets the fragment which encapsulates the unevaluated body contents of this action, as declared in the JSP.

- **`void doTag()`**
  Invoked by the container when the closing tag of the action is encountered in the JSP. This method represents the service method of the tag; all processing should occur here.

NOTE: The following comment appears in the API documentation for `setJspBody()`: 'If the action element is empty in the page, this method is not called at all'. As with `BodyContent` for a `BodyTag`, it is possible that the `JspFragment` object stored will be `null` since it is never initialised. This can be used as a test to determine if the action is empty at run time, but more importantly, to avoid seeing `NullPointerException`s, you should always assume the `JspFragment` object might be `null` and test for this case before trying to invoke its methods.

You will notice how many methods use generic JSP objects and not those specifically related to servlet-based implementations of JSP. For example, `setJspContext()` accepts an argument of class `JspContext` and not `PageContext` (which is the servlet-specific implementation). This is in the continuing move to promote JSP as not being tied to the Java EE platform's servlet model–although in practise this is often the case, at least for the time being. We first looked at `JspContext` and `PageContext` back in Chapter 13, so I don't intend to mention them again. Instead, we're going to look at how the container evaluates simple tags and the classes required along the way.

The SimpleTagSupport Class

As with the classic tag handlers, the API provides a concrete default implementation of the `SimpleTag` interface in the form of the convenience class `javax.servlet.jsp.tagext.SimpleTagSupport`. This includes additional accessor methods for retrieving the `JspContext` and `JspFragment` objects set via `setJspContext()` and `setJspBody()`, respectively.

JSP Fragments

When using simple tags, the container may translate certain parts of the document into **fragments**. Each of these pieces extends the `javax.servlet.jsp.tagext.JspFragment` class. As we shall see momentarily, a fragment represents the unevaluated form of its contents, and can be evaluated by calling its `invoke` method which causes the container to evaluate the contents of the fragment and write it to an output stream. Since the custom tag is in complete control of the fragment, the tag can choose to write all of the fragment to an output stream exactly once, write it several times by iteration, modify its contents or suppress it completely.

More precisely, the following parts of a document are converted into `JspFragments`:

- The bodies of `SimpleTags`;
- Attributes declared using `<jsp:attribute>` and configured in the TLD with a `<fragment>` having value `true`.

NOTE: It is illegal to declare a fragment attribute using normal attribute syntax in the opening tag of the action; all fragment attributes must be declared as `<jsp:attribute>`s. See also the section *Attribute Fragments* later.

Each fragment may contain only template text, embedded EL expressions and nested actions, but must *never* contain JSP scripting elements. Whenever evaluation of a fragment comes across another action, it automatically invokes that action and evaluates it. If a fragment is evaluated repeatedly (as part of an iteration), each time a nested action is encountered for that iteration its *dynamic* evaluation (at the precise point in time at which it is invoked) is inserted into the output stream. The evaluation process not only includes the processing of other, nested, actions but also EL expressions as well. Thus, a fragment containing an EL expression will have different output if the values of variables declared in the EL expression change between fragment invocations.

Like with `BodyTag`, the fragments are *not written directly* to the response, but to a `JspFragment` instance, which acts like a buffer. This allows the `doTag` method of each simple action to choose whether to write the `JspFragment` to the output stream or not, or to repeatedly evaluate it. The next section concentrates on the methods used by this class to control the output of a simple tag handler.

The JspFragment Class

Unlike the `BodyContent` class used by classic tag handlers, `JspFragments` are not themselves `Writers`–they can't be output to another stream per se. This is because a fragment contains the *unevaluated* form of some content: it contains the *code* necessary to call other nested actions and evaluate EL expressions. This allows the fragment to be evaluated dynamically at any period in time; the evaluation it provides is based on the state of variables at the time the evaluation took place. As with classic handlers, this allows us to modify scoped variables between iterations using the same `JspFragment` object and still have different output.

The `JspFragment` abstract class has only two methods, both of which are abstract and which the container creates a concrete implementation class for:

- **`JspContext getJspContext()`**
  Gets the (page) context associated with this action. This is an instance of the more generic `JspContext` and not `PageContext`, which would imply the components are run in a servlet environment.

- **`void invoke(Writer write)`**
  Causes the fragment encapsulated by this `JspFragment` object to be evaluated by the container and written to the supplied `Writer`. Use `null` to write to the `out` stream (this is the parent tag's output stream, or the JSP's stream if there is no parent tag).

There are three choices to make when executing `invoke(Writer)`:

- Use your own `Writer` instance to get a handle on the evaluated fragment content. Your own `Writer` won't be accessible outside the simple tag handler you are writing–and certainly won't be written to the response stream. You can use this technique to parse the evaluated fragment contents for yourself, for example when making conditional output decisions, or when the content needs to be censored or modified before being written to the response.

18

- Use the `out` implicit object, or the special value of `null`, as the argument to cause the method to write the evaluated fragment directly to `out` without your intervention.

- Don't call `invoke()` *at all*: this way, the evaluated fragment isn't written to any output stream. It may be useful to parse the data for yourself beforehand, using the first approach. Alternatively, the conditional output may be based on the values of scoped variables and not on the evaluated body content fragment, in which case you should make use of the `JspContext` obtained via `getJspContext()`.

The `JspContext` contains all the methods necessary for locating, accessing, modifying and removing scoped variables – use it to make decisions based on the values of these variables. The container uses this instance (or an identical one) when evaluating EL expressions in a fragment.

Simple Tag Handlers: Useful or Useless?

Simple tag handlers, as their name implies, are much easier to use and implement: we don't need to worry about where to do the processing (start or end tag?), or what the invocation procedures are. Buffers and return flags are also not an issue. In all probability, simple tag handlers match up with a beginner's views about what a tag handler should be: a Java class with a single method to which common processing and computation requirements are delegated, rather than cluttering up a JSP with frequent infusions of the same scripting code.

However, simple tag handlers have their drawbacks as well; unfortunately, with simplicity and a minimal interface, simple handlers don't have the power offered by their classic handler counterparts. For example, simple tag handlers are forbidden to contain JSP scripting element code, leaving EL as the only alternative. The reasoning is clear enough: using JSP scripting elements in bodies requires synchronisation between the scripting elements in the current JSP and the body of the current action being invoked. Classic handlers provide the container with a way to initialise and terminate scripting variables in the JSP; they do this via their extensive set of methods, each of which represents a singular task. For example, `doStartTag()` instructs the container to create the variables, `doEndTag()` instructs it to destroy `NESTED` variables, while both `doInitBody()` and `doAfterBody()` instruct the container to resynchronise all the external scripting variables again. However, consider doing multiple iterations of a simple tag: the container cannot synchronise scripting variables because it only knows about the singular `doTag()` method, which doesn't give enough detail for it to know where to create, destroy and resynchronise the scripting variables declared. To reinforce this, the `JspFragment` class, which you'll recall is used to encapsulate the pre-evaluated form of an action's body, is defined to only contain *template text* (which includes EL expressions) and other JSP actions, and never JSP scripting elements.

18

Just to be confusing though, simple tag handlers do accept JSP scripting elements as attribute values, provided that the attribute accepts a runtime expression (`rtexprvalue` is `true` in the TLD) and is not of data type `JspFragment` (`<fragment>` has value `false` or is omitted from the TLD). The reasons for this discrepancy lie in the container's treatment of tag contents vs. tag attributes. Attributes, regardless of which interface the handler implements, evaluated before the tag instance is invoked (and never need to be repeatedly evaluated) and are always set via the JavaBean setter methods for that handler – thus a generic way to set attributes exists for any type of handler.

In summary:

- All types of `JspTag` support template data and EL expressions in action bodies and in attribute values: EL really is that useful!
- Classic `Tag` handlers support traditional JSP scripting elements as part of both tag bodies and as attribute values (provided that `<body-content>` has the value `JSP` in the TLD).
- `SimpleTag` handlers never support traditional JSP scripting elements *in their bodies*, but do sometimes allow them as attribute values (provided the attributes aren't declared as `JspFragment` types and that they do accept runtime expressions).

SimpleTag vs. Tag Life Cycles

When an action is encountered in a JSP, the container needs to use an instance of the tag handler to process the action. For a `SimpleTag` handler, the container *always instantiates a new instance* for *every* action encountered in a JSP. This means that any instance variables in the `SimpleTag` implementation will be cleared between invocations of tags with the same handler class.

`Tag` handlers, on the other hand, may be *pooled* by the container for efficiency. This means that the same `Tag` instance could be used to service multiple actions in the same JSP, or even in different JSPs. This increases performance since it reduces both the processor and memory overheads associated with creating new handler instances. However, it does mean that you have to be careful about the use of variables. The container guarantees that the same handler instance will not be invoked multiple times until it has *fully completed its execution* – i.e. you can be guaranteed that execution will flow from `setParent()` right through until `doEndTag()` with no multithread or multiservice interference. However, by the time `release()` is reached, the `Tag` handler may have been invoked several times from applications of the action in different places. Hence, you can always rely on class-scoped instance variables being consistent when used between the `setParent` and `doEndTag` methods – but if their values need to be distinct for each invocation of the same handler, care must be taken to ensure they are *always reset*, either at the start of each invocation, or at the end of the previous one. You can then be sure that their state isn't 'left over' from a previous invocation.

For example, the following `Tag` uses its default constructor to set the value of an instance variable:

Figure 18.5

Tag (left) vs. SimpleTag (right) Instance Life Cycles

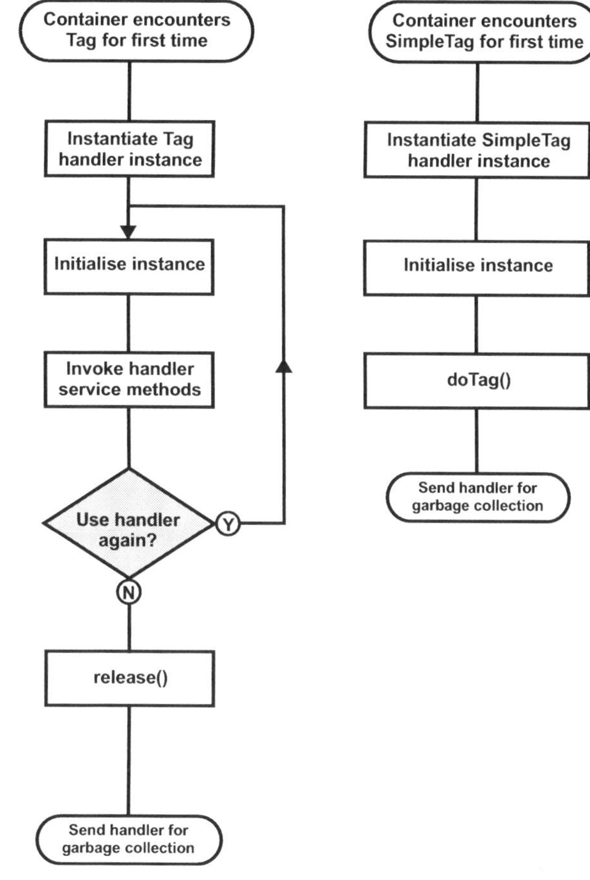


```
public class MyClassicTag extends TagSupport {
    private int startIndex;

    /* Here, the constructor is used to initialise startIndex */
    public MyClassicTag() {
        startIndex = 0;
    }
    public int doStartTag() {
        pageContext.getOut().write("Tag invoked\n");
        return EVAL_BODY_INCLUDE;
    }
    /* Use the doAfterBody() to count up to 3 (inclusive) */
    public int doAfterBody() {
        out.write("Iteration counter: " + startIndex + "\n");
        startIndex++;
        if(startIndex > 3) {
            return SKIP_BODY;
        }

        /* Otherwise, go for another iteration */
        return EVAL_BODY_AGAIN;
    }
}
```

Now, suppose we invoke this handler using these two actions in the same JSP:

```
<mytags:classictag />
<mytags:classictag />
```

You would expect this to write the same sequence twice:

```
Tag invoked
Iteration counter: 0
Iteration counter: 1
Iteration counter: 2
Iteration counter: 3
Tag invoked
Iteration counter: 0
Iteration counter: 1
Iteration counter: 2
Iteration counter: 3
```

However, in practise, you may find that this is the output:

```
Tag invoked
Iteration counter: 0
Iteration counter: 1
Iteration counter: 2
Iteration counter: 3
Tag invoked
Iteration counter: 4
```

The second iteration block is missing; the reason: the instance variable `startIndex` is not reset between different invocations of the same handler object. The container pools the `MyClassicTag` object it creates during the first invocation of the action, and doesn't release it for garbage collection. As a result, after the first action completes, `startIndex` has the value `4` (as is to be expected from the code in `doAfterBody()`). When the second action is encountered, the container will call `doStartTag()`, followed by `doAfterBody()`. The value of `startIndex` will *still* be `4`, since no code has been written to reset it to `0`, so the value `4` will be written out, and since `4 > 3`, the second action will terminate there. I somewhat doubt this would be the desired behaviour—and even if it was, we can't guarantee how many times the container will use the same handler instance, so you should *never rely on instance variables in a handler class being shared between handler invocations.*

18

The error in the previous code came when we used the constructor to set `startIndex = 0`. Since the constructor is called only once, when the handler is instantiated, and not at the beginning of every tag invocation, `startIndex` is never reset. We really should have included the code for resetting it in the `doStartTag()` implementation, which *is called for every new invocation* of the tag:

```
public int doStartTag() {
    startIndex = 0;
    return EVAL_BODY_INCLUDE;
}
```

Alternatively, we could insert `doEndTag()` to do the resetting at the end of the *previous* invocation:

```
public int doEndTag() {
    startIndex = 0;
    return EVAL_PAGE;
}
```

With either of these modifications, the output is as we would expect, and is *consistent* regardless of any pooling used by the container:

```
Tag invoked
Iteration counter: 0
Iteration counter: 1
Iteration counter: 2
Iteration counter: 3
Tag invoked
Iteration counter: 0
Iteration counter: 1
Iteration counter: 2
Iteration counter: 3
```

As we said earlier, this problem doesn't arise with `SimpleTag` handlers, since one instance represents exactly one invocation of an action and instances of *`SimpleTag` are never pooled.* Thus, it would be safe in this case to use an instance variable (but would it necessarily be desirable?).

In many cases, the use of an instance variable is to be strongly discouraged – instance variables are accessible neither within nor outside the action in the JSP, since they aren't bound into any particular scope. As a result, such a variable can't be queried by EL expressions or even scripting elements; normally, the purpose of such a custom tag is to allow the JSP to access variable data, so a valid alternative to using an instance variable in the handler would be to bind a variable into the page scope. Figure 18.5 summarises the two life cycle paths which a `Tag` and a `SimpleTag` instance may follow.

NOTE: The problem of variable reuse arises only for variables maintained *at the class level of the handler*; method-local variables are immune from such issues due to the way in which the Java Virtual Machine allocates them memory (each execution of a method creates new variable references rather than reusing old ones from a previous execution).

18

Using Simple Tag Handlers

To weigh up the relative benefits of simple tag handlers, we're going to reimplement some of the tags we created using classic tag handlers and compare the clarity and amount of code which it took to achieve.

We'll first look at the `mysimpletags.MyConditionalTag` class, which is the `SimpleTag` version of the classic `mytags.MyConditionalTag` we saw earlier. This class implements `SimpleTag` directly, and provides all the necessary 'housekeeping code' (shown under the comment `STANDARD IMPLEMENTATION`). The implementation is very simple: the `test` attribute (and, as before, we won't worry about how that attribute is set up) is a `boolean` and the `doTag` method is implemented such that:

- If `test` is `true`, the `JspFragment`'s `invoke` method is called. We pass `null` as the argument so that the fragment evaluation is written to the parent tag's `Writer` (or directly to `out` if there is no parent).
- If `test` is `false`, the `doTag` method does nothing and simply returns; the `JspFragment` is never invoked, and so the body content is never written out.

And that's it–we didn't need to mess around with integer constants returned from methods, and we only had to implement a single `doTag` method. But have we really gained anything? Certainly by using a `SimpleTag` we have lost the ability to place JSP scripting elements in the body of the action; if we compare the amount of code from `mysimpletags.MyConditionalTag` with the class `mytags.MyConditionalTag`, we find that we haven't really saved anything by using a `SimpleTag`. All we've done is skirt round the issue of using a return constant from the `doStartTag` method, but instead replaced it with the `fragment.invoke(null)` line. All in all, I prefer the classic version here, since it allows JSP authors to use scripting elements if they wish.

The next example is the `mysimpletags.MyForLoop` simple tag, compared with the `mytags.MyForLoop` classic tag. My first impression is that each took roughly the same number of lines of code to write (neglecting empty lines and comments, the simple tag is 41 lines while the classic handler is 55 lines long). Note that in the simple tag version we managed to remove both the `syncCounter` and `runLoop` methods; these were advisable (but not required) in the original tag because they were invoked from both `doStartTag()` and `doAfterBody()`, and encapsulating and reusing code in this way is essential to designing a maintainable class. We've managed to do away with these methods because all our functionality is now in `doTag()`, so both these methods would be called only from the `for` loop in `doTag()`, and so new methods are not required to ensure maintainability. We also no longer require the reset code in the `doEndTag` method, since simple tags are never pooled. Otherwise, the only distinction is that perhaps the obvious `for` loop in the simple tag makes the code easier to follow and debug, but once again we lose the ability to include JSP scripting elements in the body content.

Finally we look at the somewhat complex `mysimpletags.ModerationTag` (92 lines) against the classic `mytags.ModerationTag` (73 lines). We observe that we've saved about 20% in the amount of code required. We notice however that the `BodyContent` code, occupying just 2 lines, has been converted to the equivalent `JspFragment` code, occupying 4 lines. Only the cleanup reset code in the `doEndTag` method makes the difference between the two tags. Again, the only real difference between the two is that the simple tag is easier to follow and debug; in the simple tag we only use one `while` loop to iterate through all the entries, while in the classic tag we have to do one test in the `doStartTag` method (to determine whether to do the *first* iteration or not), and then a second test in `doAfterBody()` to decide whether *future* iterations are necessary. Otherwise, we've lost the ability to use JSP scripting elements without any real advantages, except clarity of code.

In conclusion: `SimpleTag` handlers may be useful for much larger examples which are orders of magnitude more complex than those presented here, and where debugging would be a nightmare if the code wasn't obvious to follow. Otherwise, the classic model is more robust and flexible.

In addition, all the requirements and limitations we have seen here apply to tag files, since these are also translated and compiled into `SimpleTag` handlers, as we shall see in the next chapter.

Advanced Tag Functionality

Actions with Attributes

Attributes are the name/value pairs of supplementary data which can be used to configure the behaviour of actions at run time. So far, I've avoided becoming bogged down in a discussion of them, despite the fact that we used them in every example. Attributes appear absolutely everywhere; we've seen countless examples such as those used with the JSTL tags like:

18

```
<fmt:setTimeZone value="timeZone" />
```

The `value` attribute is used to supply the time zone (such as 'GMT-8' which indicates 8 hours behind GMT). By default (omitting the `var` and `scope` attributes for a moment), this action stores the supplied time zone in the page-scoped attribute `javax.servlet.jsp.jstl.fmt.timeZone`, making it the default time zone in that scope which is useful for formatting dates and times using JSTL. The use of an attribute here could be considered optional: why not use the content of the tag to specify the resource URL, like the following?

```
<fmt:setTimeZone>
  timeZone
</fmt:setTimeZone>
```

This is semantically bad: firstly, body content of actions should be content which is ultimately *intended for the response stream*. Secondly, what happens when we introduce the other attributes (`var` and `scope`)? If we were to use the content, we would have to write something similar to:

```
<fmt:setTimeZone>
  <value>GMT-8</value>
  <var>myzone</var>
  <scope>request</scope>
</fmt:setTimeZone>
```

When we compare this to the alternative which uses attributes, we can see that using attributes wins hands down, with such a concise and unambiguous meaning:

```
<fmt:setTimeZone value="timeZone" var="var" scope="scope" />
```

In fact, attributes are even simpler to declare and use in tag handlers than manipulating body content would be. The key lies behind the tag handler being a JavaBean (or almost a JavaBean, since we may choose to omit the `get` accessor methods); as such, it must have setter methods named after all the properties it contains. As it happens, when considering tag handlers, attributes are considered to be *the JavaBean's properties*. As an example, the tag handler class for the `<fmt:setTimeZone />` JSTL action has the following methods:

- **`void setValue(Object value)`**
  Sets the time zone data from the `value` attribute.

- **`void setVar(String var)`**
  Sets the name of the variable to be exported as the scoped attribute, as specified by the `var` attribute on the tag.

- **`void setScope(String scope)`**
  Sets the name of the scope of the exported attribute, as specified by the `scope` attribute on the tag (this defaults to `page` if the supplied value is invalid).

Now, when an action is encountered and the correct tag handler initialised to evaluate it, the container will call the `setXxx` methods for each of the attributes `xxx` declared in the action's opening tag (casting the argument to the required type). This *always occurs before* the invocation of `doStartTag()` (for a `Tag`) or `doTag()` (for a `SimpleTag`). You might think this is a bit haphazard: what happens if there is no setter method for an attribute supplied in the opening tag? The solution to this problem relies on the TLD, in which all tags and tag handlers are declared. The TLD is also the place to store information about the attributes which an action takes, and whether they are optional or mandatory. However, the TLD does not provide a mapping between attribute names and method names: the container still relies on the JavaBeans properties contract being in place and will expect to find methods called `setXxx()` for all attributes `xxx` declared in the TLD.

You will also notice that our attribute setters in the previous example have different parameter types: two take `String`s while the other takes an `Object`. While attribute setters must all have only one parameter (it wouldn't make sense to have more than one parameter to set a single property), that parameter can be of any primitive or object type. The type found in the handler's method declaration must match the attribute `<type>` declared in the TLD. The container then performs all the necessary casting before passing the attribute value to the appropriate tag handler's setter method. If, during validation of the JSP, type casting cannot be performed, for example, because a `boolean` attribute is in fact a numerical value, the JSP will not be compiled and an error will be raised.

Dynamic Attributes

In the last section we said that attributes had to be declared in the TLD before they could be used; using an attribute not declared in the TLD would cause an error to occur during validation. Declaring an attribute called `xxx` in the TLD was synonymous to saying 'the tag handler bean has a property `xxx` with a method `setXxx` which must be configured before the handler is used'.

It can also be useful to provide support for attributes which can be declared *by the JSP author* and not by the tag author. Clearly, the name and permissible values of these attributes cannot be known by the tag author, the tag handler or the TLD up-front. Attributes which can be added individually on a per-tag and per-JSP-author basis are known as **dynamic attributes**. A typical use for these is when a custom tag mimics the behaviour of an (X)HTML element; for example, a tag which declares an HTML table and iterates through the rows might look like this at its most basic:

```
<mytags:table>
  <tr><td>A row</td></tr>
</mytags:table>
```

18

The `<mytags:table>` action may create the opening HTML `<table>` tag in the `doStartTag` method of the handler, and iterate over the body which represents a single row in the table any number of times before adding the closing `</table>` tag in the `doEndTag` method. However, the HTML `<table>` element itself may take a varying number of different attributes; it is up to the JSP author to decide which to use. It is also up to the JSP author to decide which version of the (X)HTML specifications they are conforming to – if they're not using a hybrid 'tag soup', that is. It would be inappropriate for the JSP tag author to specify the attributes in the TLD up front: it is simply impossible to say what the HTML author will require, which attributes are mandatory in one version of an (X)HTML specification but optional in another, or which new attributes have been added in a version of the (X)HTML specification created after the tag library.

This example is a typical use case for dynamic attributes: they can't really be used to *configure* an action's behaviour because the action doesn't know what to expect, but they can easily be 'passed through' from their declaration in the JSP directly to the response stream. This provides flexibility, and ultimately power, over how content is rendered. Dynamic attributes also save having to type a new `<table ...>` start tag and a `</table>` end tag, since the tag handler will take care of that much more efficiently for us.

A tag handler which supports dynamic attributes must implement the `javax.servlet.jsp.tagext.DynamicAttributes` interface, providing an implementation of this method:

- **`void setDynamicAttribute(String ns, String name, Object value)`**
  Called by the container to set the dynamic attribute `name` to `value`. If the attribute name was preceded by a namespace qualifier, `ns` will contain the value of this namespace; otherwise, if no qualifier is given, the attribute is assumed to be in the default namespace and `ns` will be `null`.

Additionally, if a tag handler supports dynamic attributes, it must be configured as such in the TLD. If the container encounters an attribute which it does not recognise for an action, it will first check the action's dynamic attribute setting in the TLD. If the action is configured to accept dynamic attributes, everything will be okay and the JSP will translate and compile. If the action cannot accept dynamic attributes, a validation error will occur.

Attribute Fragments

18

When configured in the TLD, attributes must be assigned a data type (a class type into which they will be resolved, using `<type>`) and must be configured to accept runtime expression values or not (`<rtexprvalue>`). However, attributes may also be configured so they are converted into `JspFragment`s which can be invoked to process their contents, rather than any other regular `Object` type. This is accomplished using `<fragment>true</fragment>` in the TLD. Should you choose to have the attribute presented to the tag as a `JspFragment`, you will need to supply the attribute value as a `<jsp:attribute>` child and *not* as a normal attribute–for example:

```
<mytag:action1 attr1="My fragment is ${ status }">
  This body (also a fragment for a SimpleTag) is ${ bodyStatus }
</mytag:action1>
```

is illegal, and will result in a translation error. The alternative, using `<jsp:attribute>`, should always be used for a fragment attribute:

```
<mytag:action1>
  <jsp:attribute name="attr1">
    My fragment is ${ status }
  </jsp:attribute>
  <jsp:body>
  This body (also a fragment for a SimpleTag) is ${ bodyStatus }
  </jsp:body>
</mytag:action1>
```

This discrepancy is a result of the way the container treats normal attributes compared with the contents of `<jsp:attribute>` actions.

The `JspTag` handler for tags with fragment-attributes requires a JavaBean setter method for each fragment attribute, just as for any other fixed attributes which the tag takes. The parameter to this setter method must be of type `javax.servlet.jsp.tagext.JspFragment`. Thus, in this example the tag handler class would require a `setAttr1()` method with `JspFragment` as its only parameter.

NOTE: A fragment (including the body of a `SimpleTag` or tag file, which are `JspFragment`s by default) may *never* contain JSP scripting elements; attempting to include a JSP scripting element in any fragment will cause a translation-time error.

Introducing Scripting Variables into a JSP

An action may not necessarily have to, or even want to, be responsible for outputting content; instead, its purpose may be to introduce useful scripting variables into the JSP (or it might do both). Take as an example the `<jsp:useBean>` action, whose purpose is to ensure that the specified bean is available in the JSP thereafter–if it cannot retrieve a scoped attribute with the name supplied by the `id` attribute, the action creates a new bean matching the description and adds it to the scope. It then creates a Java programming variable in the JSP (or in fact in the translated servlet) with the same name as the `id` attribute's value. This programming variable can then be accessed by JSP scripting element code. For example, let's suppose we have this action in the JSP:

```
<my:useBean id="mybean" scope="request" class="MyBeanClass" />
```

NOTE: Unfortunately, no JSTL tags expose scripting variables, so we can't use JSTL tags as examples here. Instead, we'll resort to using a JSP standard action as a model. In reality, all `jsp` standard actions are in fact optimised by the container and embedded directly into the translated servlet code, without using separate handler instances, so our comparison is a little false but I hope still instructive.

For demonstration, we'll assume this action is implemented as a classic tag, using the Tag Extension API. We'll assume that we have a handler class (perhaps called `UseBeanTag`) which creates a new `MyBeanClass` instance if one does not already exist in the request-scoped `bean` attribute, and adds the new instance to that scoped variable. This action does nothing if the attribute already exists. So, after executing our `UseBeanTag`, we know that the scoped attribute will exist. But, in order to access it from JSP scripting element code we'll need something like:

```
<my:useBean id="bn" scope="request" class="MyBeanClass" />
<%= ((MyBeanClass)request.getAttribute("bn")).getName() %>
```

We've assumed that `MyBeanClass` has a `getName` method which we write out using an expression scripting element. This code is a little cumbersome, especially if we want to use the `bean` variable every time; we might instead want to write:

```
<my:useBean id="bn" scope="request" class="MyBeanClass" />
<% MyBeanClass bean=(MyBeanClass)request.getAttribute("bn"); %>
```

which then enables us to use the `bean` *variable* (my convention is to use 'variable' to mean the Java programming variable inserted into the translated servlet, and 'attribute' to refer to the scoped attribute) in scripting element code without having to refer to the scoped attribute each time:

```
<%= bean.getName() %>
<% bean.setAmount(10.5f) %>
<%= bean.getAmount() * 1.5 %>
```

18

You will note that since `bean` is now a programming variable in the JSP (or more correctly in the translated servlet), making use of it is a much simpler task; our code is much tidier than it would be if we referenced the `request.getAttribute` method each time, along with the required casting.

Even better still, we can let the container do all the hard work, providing us with the `bean` programming variable without having to use an explicit scriptlet ourselves. This is called variable **synchronisation** – the container updates the variable in the JSP (or translated servlet) to follow the value of a scoped attribute. Underneath, it is *always* the scoped attribute which is modified by the tag, but the synchronisation causes the container to copy the value of the scoped attribute into the scripting variable, conveniently integrating JSP scripting elements with the tag.

NOTE: Both classic and simple tags can expose scripting variables for synchronisation, but only classic tags can make use of them in their bodies (since simple tags and `JspFragment`s cannot contain JSP scripting).

To declare synchronisation, we use the `<variable>` element in the TLD (see Chapter 20 for more details). We then have to choose the scope for the scripting variable; this must be one of the values `AT_BEGIN`, `NESTED` or `AT_END`. Note that the *scope of a (synchronised) scripting variable* is completely different from the *scope of an attribute*!

In essence, `AT_BEGIN` variables are created in servlet code before the action is invoked, synchronised throughout the tag's life, and remain in existence after the tag completes processing. `NESTED` variables are created before the action is invoked, and removed when the action terminates. `AT_END` variables are created just after the tag finishes its invocation.

It can also be instructive to examine typical translated servlet code; the following snippets are skeleton models of servlet code taken from the J2EE 1.4 Reference Implementation (Sun AppServer 8.0). We assume that the variable is of type `MyClass` and has name `myvar`. We also assume that the handler implements `IterationTag` to show how synchronisation occurs between iterations (implementing `BodyTag` doesn't add anything to the synchronisation pattern, and will only clutter up our code).

- **`AT_BEGIN`:**

```
/* Declare variable */
MyClass myvar = null;
/* Initialise handler instance */
IterationTag handler = ...;
if(handler.doStartTag() != Tag.SKIP_BODY) {
 /* Synchronise just after doStartTag() */
 myvar = (MyClass) pageContext.findAttribute("myvar");
 do {
   // Process body
   /* Now resynchronise after body has processed */
   myvar = (MyClass) pageContext.findAttribute("myvar");
 } while(handler.doAfterBody()==IterationTag.EVAL_BODY_AGAIN);
}
if(handler.doEndTag() == Tag.SKIP_PAGE) {
 return;
}
/* Resynchonise after doEndTag() */
myvar = (MyClass) pageContext.findAttribute("myvar");
```

- **NESTED:**

```
/* Initialise handler instance */
IterationTag handler = ...;
if(handler.doStartTag() != Tag.SKIP_BODY) {
 /* Declare NESTED variable here, local to the block */
 MyClass myvar = null;
 /* Synchronise just after doStartTag() */
 myvar = (MyClass) pageContext.findAttribute("myvar");
 do {
    // Process body
    /* Resynchronise after body has processed */
    myvar = (MyClass) pageContext.findAttribute("myvar");
 } while(handler.doAfterBody()==IterationTag.EVAL_BODY_AGAIN);
}
if(handler.doEndTag() == Tag.SKIP_PAGE) {
 return;
}
/* Can't synchronise at end
 *(NESTED variable doesn't exist here) */
```

- **AT_END:**

```
/* Initialise handler instance */
IterationTag handler = ...;
if(handler.doStartTag() != Tag.SKIP_BODY) {
 do {
    // Process body
 } while(handler.doAfterBody()==IterationTag.EVAL_BODY_AGAIN);
}
if(handler.doEndTag() == Tag.SKIP_PAGE) {
    return;
}
/* Declare AT_END variable here, after doEndTag() is done */
MyClass myvar = null;
myvar = (MyClass) pageContext.findAttribute("myvar");
```

18

Note in particular that each tag executes in its own block (i.e. between `{` and `}`), and recall that Java variables are scoped to the closest outside block from where they are originally declared, whether that be a class, method, conditional, loop, synchronisation block, or just your own `{...}` block. Since `NESTED` variables are declared inside the block for the tag, they *do not exist* outside the tag invocation, making them truly nested.

It is possible to encounter a translation error if a variable already exists in the JSP with the same name as the new variable. In general, using two identically-named variables presents a naming conflict. However, since `NESTED` variables are local to their tag invocation block, it is safe (but perhaps not advisable) to declare an identically-named variable *after* (but never before) the tag's invocation.

Most tags request that the container create new scripting variables for each invocation. However, there may be some tags which need to update the state of a scripting variable which is *already* guaranteed to exist in the JSP; if this is the case, to prevent a naming conflict, use a value of `false` for the `<declare>` element in the TLD. This causes the container to re-initialise, but not redeclare, the variable in question, and therefore prevents naming conflicts caused by excess declarations. The caveat is that in order to use `false` for `<declare>`, you must be certain that the variable has already been declared, or the translator's compiler will complain about 'cannot find symbol [myvar]...' In general, it is best to avoid conflicts in naming by always naming variables with different names.

In addition to naming conflicts, scopes can cause problems. As you can see from the previous code snippets, the container always uses the `PageContext`'s `findAttribute()` method to locate the variable to use for synchronisation. Since this always searches in the order page, request, session, application, problems can arise by having variables with the same name in different scopes. For example, suppose we have a loop which also stores its counter value in a scoped variable, with name given by the `var` attribute, and scope specified by the `scope` attribute. Then:

```
<mytag:loop start="0" end="3" var="myvar" scope="request">
  <%= myvar %>,
</mytag:loop>
```

will output `0,1,2,3,` as expected. Now consider:

```
<% pageContext.setAttribute("myvar", new Integer(6)); %>
<mytag:loop start="0" end="3" var="myvar" scope="request">
  <%= myvar %>,
</mytag:loop>
```

This outputs `6,6,6,6,` which is not what we expected; this is because the variable synchronisation uses the `PageContext`'s `findAttribute` method, which examines the page scope in priority to the request scope. Hence, `findAttribute()` always returns the `Integer` 6 configured in the scriplet, rather than the counter value.

So how useful is synchronisation? I know that I now use EL almost exclusively (rather than scripting elements), so the synchronisation service doesn't really apply anymore. I also know that JSTL tags don't provide synchronisation, forcing us to either do the synchronisation ourselves, or use EL. Of course, as a tag library author, you've got a choice: do you provide synchronisation or not? Some JSP authors who use your tag library may still make use of scripting elements, so provision for synchronisation is probably a good idea wherever possible.

NOTE: Synchronisation is only an issue when considering traditional JSP scripting elements, when variables in the compiled servlet are synchronised with the relevant scoped attribute after every iteration etc. If you're now in the good habit of using only EL, then as a JSP author, synchronisation doesn't really become a consideration.

Tag files have a slightly different synchronisation mechanism, which refers to the sychronisation between scoped attributes in the calling JSP and scoped attributes in the tag file. The next chapter looks at this distinction.

Configuration of Scripting Variables for a Tag

The TLD is the primary location used to configure scripting variables and synchronisation details. See Chapter 20 for details of the TLD. Tag files, discussed in the next chapter, use the `tag` directive to specify the variables they expose.

Nested Tags and Cooperating Actions

Sometimes it is necessary to use actions in a manner in which they can communicate with each other. We've already seen some examples: `<jsp:attribute>` and `<jsp:body>` set the attributes of their direct parent and `<c:param>` is used to provide additional data to parent `<c:import>`, `<c:url>` and `<c:redirect>` actions. These are technically referred to as **cooperating actions**, since they work very closely together to achieve their collective goal.

There are two ways for tags to cooperate:

- Tags communicate using page-scoped attributes stored in the `JspContext` object. Objects exposed in this way are available to both tag handlers and the JSPs in which they are used.
- Tag handlers expose public methods which allow other tags to change their properties. Only classes from that particular tag library implementation will be aware of the exact API exposed by each handler. This design is only useful for nested cooperating tags.

18

An important property about tags is that they define unidirectional relationships: a tag can communicate with its parent (and its parent's parent, and its parent's parent's parent etc.) tag, but it never knows anything about its children. This is an important design consideration, as any tag which needs to expose an object to *arbitrary* children will have to use the former method.

As we already know, both `Tags` and `SimpleTags` expose their parent through their getParent method. However, the return type for Tag's method is Tag, while for SimpleTags the return type is the more general JspTag. Ideally we would like both to return JspTag, which is the supertype for both classic and simple tags, but in order to provide backward compatibility with pre-JSP 2.0 applications, this isn't possible.

We therefore have a small problem: how can a SimpleTag be a parent to a Tag, if setParent() and getParent() accept only Tags? There is in fact no real answer to this question, just a work-around in the form of the TagAdapter class. This is a wrapper implementing Tag which is used to contain a SimpleTag. All of the service methods throw UnsupportedOperationException, leaving just two methods of interest:

- **Tag getParent()**
  Returns the parent of the wrapped SimpleTag, as another TagAdapter if that parent is not already an instance of Tag.
- **JspTag getAdaptee()**
  Returns the SimpleTag which is being wrapped by this adapter.

If we're navigating through the hierarchy of tags using getParent() on a Tag instance, we need to be careful about whether we've actually got a Tag instance or a TagAdapter (indicating a wrapped SimpleTag).

Sometimes it's necessary to find a tag which is arbitrarily far away from the current tag, but implements a certain tag handler class. When this is the case, we can use one of the findAncestorWithClass methods:

- **TagSupport**:
  `public static Tag findAncestorWithClass(Tag from, Class klass)`
- **SimpleTagSupport**:
  `public static JspTag findAncestorWithClass(Tag from,Class klas)`

The only difference is the return type; both methods start at the from tag, and travel up through the parents, returning the first parent tag encountered of the required class type (or a subclass). The only implementation difference is that if the SimpleTagSupport method matches a TagAdapter during traversal, it invokes getAdaptee to obtain the actual SimpleTag instance; in contrast, TagSupport will return the TagAdapter wrapper. Since both are static, we can invoke them from any code we wish; it is therefore recommended that SimpleTagSupport be used in case SimpleTags are present in the parent hierarchy.

18

To gain more familiarity with cooperating tags, we shall implement our own version of the <c:choose>, <c:when> and <c:otherwise> JSTL actions, suitable for deployment to a JSP 2.0 container. We will implement both classic and simple tag versions for experience.

NOTE: Although we implement both versions of the tags, in order to show that they can cooperate together provided we are careful with the handler implementation, they *must reside in the same tag library.* Although logically there is no reason why tags from different libraries cannot attempt to communicate, the Reference Implementation container, and perhaps others, have problems providing communication between tags (for example, `getParent()` returns `null` if the parent tag is not in the same library).

We implement both `mytags.MyChooseTag` and `mysimpletags.MyChooseTag` in the same way: they both maintain a flag (`childInvoked`); this is set by the first `<when>` or `<otherwise>` child which is executed, and is tested by all other children to see whether they should execute or not. The `choose` tag evaluates its contents by default.

The `mytags.MyWhenTag` and `mysimpletags.MyWhenTag` both check to see (a) if the `childInvoked` flag is set, indicating that a `<when>` has already been executed and (b) the state of the `test` condition. They evaluate the contents (returning `EVAL_BODY_INCLUDE` or by invoking the `JspFragment`) only if `childInvoked` is `false` and `test` is `true`.

The `otherwise` tags execute only if the `childInvoked` flag is still `false` when they are encountered.

Note the only real difference between the classes is that the classic tag variants include code for testing whether the parent is a `TagAdapter`, and therefore need to extract the `SimpleTag` adaptee. The `SimpleTag`'s `getParent` method of course avoids this problem by returning `JspTag` directly.

Revision Questions

1 **What is the base interface implemented by all tag handler classes?** **(choose one)**

- A javax.servlet.jsp.Tag
- B javax.servlet.jsp.tagext.Tag
- C javax.servlet.jsp.tagext.JspTag
- D javax.servlet.jsp.tagext.TagHandler
- E javax.servlet.jsp.tagext.JspTagHandler

2 **What is the base interface implemented by all classic tag handler classes?** **(choose one)**

- A javax.servlet.jsp.Tag
- B javax.servlet.jsp.tagext.Tag
- C javax.servlet.jsp.tagext.JspTag
- D javax.servlet.jsp.tagext.TagHandler
- E javax.servlet.jsp.tagext.JspTagHandler

3 **Which of the following interfaces are found in the javax.servlet.jsp.tagext package?** **(choose three)**

- A Tag
- B TagHandler
- C LoopTag
- D SimpleTag
- E BodyTag

4 **Arrange the following in the order they are executed during the life cycle of an IterationTag (assuming all stages are executed).**

doStartTag()	setPageContext()	doAfterBody()
doEndTag()	setParent()	Invoke attribute setters

5 **Arrange these in the order they are executed during the life cycle of a SimpleTag.**

setJspContext()	Invoke attribute setters	Destroy handler	
setParent()	doTag()	Instantiate	setJspBody()

18

6 **Which of the following are correct statements?** **(choose two)**

- A Classic tag handlers are pooled for efficiency.
- B SimpleTag handlers are pooled for efficiency.
- C Classic tag handlers are never pooled.
- D SimpleTag handlers are never pooled.
- E Tag handlers implementing DynamicAttributes are never pooled.

7 **Which of the following are methods in JspTag?** **(choose one)**

- A JspTag getParent()
- B void setParent(JspTag)
- C int doStartTag()
- D void doTag()
- E None of the above

8 **Which of the following are methods in Tag?** **(choose two)**

- A void doStartTag()
- B int doStartTag()
- C void doTag()
- D void doEndTag()
- E int doEndTag()

9 **Which of the following are valid return values from the doStartTag() method in a classic tag handler?** **(choose two)**

- A EVAL_BODY
- B INCLUDE_BODY
- C EVAL_BODY_INCLUDE
- D IGNORE_BODY
- E SKIP_BODY

18

10 **Which of the following combinations are valid return values from the doInitBody() method?** **(choose one)**

- A EVAL_BODY, SKIP_BODY
- B EVAL_BODY_BUFFERED, EVAL_BODY_INCLUDE
- C EVAL_BODY_BUFFERED, EVAL_BODY_INCLUDE, SKIP_BODY
- D EVAL_BODY_AGAIN, SKIP_BODY
- E None.

11 **An object of which class is invoked to evaluate the body of a BodyTag?** **(choose one)**

- A TagBody
- B BodyContent
- C TagBodyContent
- D TagBody
- E JspFragment

12 **An object of which class is invoked to evaluate the body of a SimpleTag?** **(choose one)**

- A SimpleTagBody
- B TagFragment
- C JspFragment
- D BodyFragment
- E BodyContent

13 **The exhibit shows the tag handler class for <mytags:loop>. What is the effect of compiling and executing the tag handler class and this page?** **(choose one)**

EXHIBIT

```
<% pageContext.removeAttribute("counter"); %>
<mytags:loop>Count ${ counter }</mytags:loop>
```

- A The response is the text 'Count 0 Count 1 Count 2 Count 3'.
- B The response is the text 'Count Count Count Count'.
- C The response is empty.
- D The response is indeterminate.
- E A compilation error occurs in the tag handler class.

14 **Which of the following methods on BodyContent must be invoked from a BodyTagSupport subclass to write the contents of the buffer to the out implicit object?** **(choose one)**

- A void writeTo(null);
- B void copyTo(pageContext.getOut());
- C void writeOut(pageContext.getOut());
- D void flushTo(null);
- E void writeOut(null);

15 **Which of the following methods in IterationTag is invoked between evaluations of the body content of the tag?** **(choose one)**

- A void afterBody()
- B int doBody()
- C int doBeforeBody()
- D int doAfterBody()
- E void releaseBody()

16 **The exhibit shows the tag handler class for <mytags:item>. What is the effect of compiling and executing the tag handler class and JSP page?** **(choose one)**

EXHIBIT

```
<mytags:item>Item code: ${ item }</mytags.item>
```

- A The response is the text 'Item code: 0301'.
- B The response is the text 'Item code: '.
- C The response is empty.
- D A compilation error occurs in the tag handler class.

17 **The tag <my:conditional> is written as a SimpleTag; its body content is written only if the value of the when attribute resolves to true using Boolean.valueOf(String) method. What is the result of compiling and executing this JSP?** **(choose one)**

```
<% String name = "John"; %>
<my:conditional when="true">
  <%= name %>, we have success!
</my:conditional>
```

- A The response is the text 'John, we have success!'.
- B The response is the text ', we have success!'.
- C The response is the text '<%= name %>, we have success!'.
- D The response is empty.
- E A translation error occurs.

18

18 **Which of the following methods in JspFragment can be invoked to write the contents of the buffer to the out implicit object?** **(choose one)**

- A void write(null);
- B void writeOut(pageContext.getOut());
- C void invoke(null);
- D void flushTo(null);
- E void evaluate(pageContext.getOut());

19 **The exhibit shows the tag handler class for <my:loop>. What is the result of compiling and executing the tag handler class and JSP page?** **(choose one)**

EXHIBIT

```
<% pageContext.removeAttribute("count"); %>
<my:loop>Counter ${ count }</my:loop>
```

- A The response text is 'Counter 0 Counter 1 Counter 2'.
- B The response text is 'Counter Counter Counter'.
- C The response is empty.
- D The response is indeterminate.
- E A compilation error occurs in the tag handler.

Exhibits

Q.13

```
import javax.servlet.jsp.tagext.*;
public class MyLoopTag extends TagSupport {
    private int counter;
    public int doAfterBody() {
        if(counter++ < 4) return EVAL_BODY_AGAIN;
        return SKIP_BODY;
    }
}
```

Q.16

```
import javax.servlet.jsp.tagext.*;
public class ItemTag extends SimpleTagSupport {
    public void doTag() throws JspException, IOException {
        getPageContext().setAttribute("item", "0301");
        getJspBody().invoke(null);
    }
}
```


Q.19

```
import javax.servlet.jsp.tagext.*;
public class MyLoopTag extends SimpleTagSupport {
    private int index;
    public void doTag() throws JspException, IOException {
        do {
            getJspContext().setAttribute("count", new Integer(index));
            getJspBody().invoke(null);
        } while(++index < 3);
    }
}
```

Answers to Revision Questions

1 **Correct answer: C**

JspTag is the correct answer as of JSP 2.0; previously B would have been correct.

2 **Correct answer: B**

3 **Correct answers: A, D, E**

The only notable absence is IterationTag.

4 **Correct answer:** setPageContext(), setParent(), Invoke attribute setters, doStartTag(), doAfterBody(), doEndTag().

5 **Correct answer:** Instantiate, setJspContext(), setParent(), Invoke attribute setters, setJspBody(), doTag(), Destroy handler.

6 **Correct answers: A, D**

7 **Correct answer: E**

JspTag doesn't contain any methods; it simply acts as a marker for all JSP 2.0 tags.

8 **Correct answers: B, E**

9 **Correct answers: C, E**

The only value missing is EVAL_BODY_BUFFERED.

10 **Correct answer: E**

This method has a void return type, as it doesn't change the flow of execution of the tag (see Figure 18.3).

11 **Correct answer: B**

12 **Correct answer: C**

13 **Correct answer: C**

The response is empty because the default doStartTag() implementation of TagSupport returns SKIP_BODY. Hence the body is never evaluated, even once, making C correct. Note that B would have been correct if we had explicitly re-initialised the counter instance variable to 0 in doStartTag(), guaranteeing 4 iterations for this invocation of the tag. No re-initialisation would have left D as the answer, as on the first invocation of the pooled tag B would be true, but on subsequent invocations of the same instance, there would only be one 'Count ' as output. A is incorrect, as there is no code that sets a scoped attribute in the tag handler.

14 **Correct answer: C**

Note that writeOut in BodyContent cannot take the special value null, as invoke() can in JspFragment.

15 **Correct answer: D**

16 **Correct answer: D**

Note that the class references getPageContext(), which doesn't exist–recall that SimpleTags have access to JspContexts, so the method should be getJspContext(). Furthermore, note that classic tag handlers support classes don't have getPageContext() either–instead you have to access the protected field pageContext!

17 **Correct answer: E**

Simple tags must not contain JSP scripting elements or a translation error is raised (an EL expression would have been successful).

18 **Correct answer: C**

Note that writeOut() in BodyContent cannot take the special value null, but invoke() in JspFragment can–in this case, it means the 'write to the out implicit object'. Another alternative would be invoke(pageContext.getOut()).

19 **Correct answer: A**

On each iteration we first set the page-scoped attribute and then invoke the body fragment. Note that since SimpleTags are never pooled, the fact that index is an instance variable doesn't cause any problems (as it could with classic tags).

In this chapter you'll:

- Learn about tag files and how they compare to simple tags and JSPs.
- Appreciate the basic tag file syntax.
- Use tag file-specific directives to add attributes to the tag.
- Expose variables from the tag and understand variable synchronisation.
- Memorise the implicit objects available in tag files.
- Invoke JSP Fragments using tag file-specific standard actions.
- Examine a complete tag file example, written in both JSP page and JSP document syntax.

19 Tag Files

In the last chapter we made an in-depth examination of classic tags, what they're for, how they work, how to use them and (most importantly) what might be on the exam!

Classic tags and the newer simple tags are incredibly powerful, providing a straightforward way to create and employ reusable components, without the need for large numbers of helper beans. However, programming classes for tag handlers may be unnecessary in some cases. This is especially the case when your custom tag's role in life is to insert mainly content (like HTML code) into the JSP – this is a job handled much better by JSPs and not servlet-style components.

As a result, JSP 2.0 introduced a new type of tag technology, **tag files**. A tag file is a JSP page or document designed to be used as a custom action. The advantage of tag files in JSP syntax is that it's relatively quick to write a custom tag which provides large amounts of *content* to its calling JSP; the disadvantage, as with JSPs in general, is that tag files are pretty hopeless at doing much processing. Tag files cannot hope to replace traditional tag handler classes, but when used correctly they provide an optimal compromise. The trade-off between the two types of components is dictated mostly by the amount of servlet-style processing which the handler must do.

As a general rule, tag files are a good solution if you find yourself using the same JSP content (consisting of template text, scripting elements, EL expressions and other actions) over and over again in lots of different places. For example, you might use some JSTL conditional and iteration actions and EL expressions to generate an HTML table of items in a catalogue. This table might appear on every web page in the catalogue, and it would therefore be appropriate to encapsulate this common table-building code into a tag file. Then, rather than including the same set of JSTL actions and EL expressions in different places, you can use invocations of your new action instead. This has the advantage that changes to the table-building code need only be made in the tag file and not in the many places the action is used, making the exercise much more maintainable. Another advantage of tag files over tag handler classes is that, since tag files use JSP syntax, even a Web developer not familiar with Java can build their own custom actions. This makes custom actions more accessible to Web developers working in a team of Java experts who are not themselves expert with Java.

We will look at how to deploy tag files in the next chapter; in this chapter we concentrate on the syntax, properties and use of this new type of component as a custom action.

Basic Tag File Syntax

A tag file is written in just the same way as a normal JSP, in either (traditional) JSP page syntax or in the newer (XML) JSP document syntax. However, by necessity tag files have different semantics from JSPs; the fact that a tag file can be supplied with extra attribute information declared in the action means that a different invocation procedure is required. This has a minor knock-on effect on some of the syntax usually permitted in a JSP – for example, the `page` directive is replaced by the `tag` directive which provides settings more applicable to a tag handler. The rest of this chapter is devoted to iterating through the differences which arise between JSPs and tag files.

On an implementation level, a JSP is compiled into a `javax.servlet.jsp.JspPage` (which extends `Servlet`) implementation class, with the JSP body being translated into the `_jspService` method. On the other hand, a tag file is compiled into a `SimpleTag` handler class, with the body of the tag file JSP forming the `doTag()` method. Note that since a tag file is in reality a `SimpleTag`, the same restrictions that apply to `SimpleTag`s, such as JSP scripting elements being disallowed in the content of the declared action, also apply to tag files.

We will first look at the 'nuts and bolts', the mechanics, of how tag files are declared, and follow this up with actual examples of tag files being used. You should find most of the content of this chapter familiar, as it incorporates both JSP and custom tag nomenclature and syntax. The examples at the end of the chapter, also available in the download bundle (see the Preface for download instructions), show how similar JSPs and tag files really are.

Tag File Semantics

A tag file is neither a JSP nor a regular tag handler. Instead, while its life cycle is broadly identical to `SimpleTag`'s (of course a tag file must also be translated and compiled), tag files define their own set of semantics. The basic aim of these modified semantics is to present a page scope for attributes which is distinct from the page scope of the calling JSP or action.

- The container passes the tag file the `JspContext` instance it passes to every tag handler, using `setJspContext`. This is called the **Invoking JSP Context**.
- The tag file keeps a copy of the original `JspContext` but creates a *wrapper* of the context (for `PageContext`s, this wrapper must also be a `PageContext`). This is called the **JSP Context Wrapper**. The `getJspContext` method always returns this Wrapper. Nearly all methods on the Wrapper, except those

relating to page-scoped attributes, delegate to the Invoking JSP Context. The Wrapper provides local storage for page-scoped attributes, distinct from those in the Invoking JSP Context.

- JSP Context Wrappers may be pooled for different invocations of the same tag file, but the page scope must be cleared between each invocation. Tag files will always see an empty page scope when invoked (unless attributes are declared, see next point).
- For each attribute declared in the action's opening tag, a new page-scoped attribute is created, with the same name as the declared attribute, and with the attribute's (evaluated) value. Since these will be added to the JSP Context Wrapper and not to the original Invoking JSP Context, these page-scoped attributes are never visible outside the tag file.

Note that since we usually obtain the context by invoking `getJspContext()`, it is the JSP Context Wrapper and not the Invoking JSP Context which we interact with inside a tag file. We can gain direct access to any scopes other than page; the page scope is completely isolated from the calling JSP or parent action, and it is impossible to gain access to the calling JSP's page scope contents. This avoids naming conflicts–especially between multiple, possibly nested, invocations of the same tag file.

The life cycle of a tag file is based on that of a `SimpleTag`:

1. When the tag file is first invoked (or for some servers when it is first deployed), the container translates and compiles it into a new class implementing `SimpleTag`.
2. When the action corresponding to this tag file is invoked, the container creates a new instance of the `SimpleTag` class using a default (no-argument) constructor.
3. The container invokes `setJspContext()` which causes the tag to store the Invoking JSP Context passed as the argument and create the JSP Context Wrapper, then calls `setParent()` if this action has a parent tag.
4. All attributes are initialised by placing them in the tag-local page scope (see discussion above).
5. For all attributes declared as `<jsp:attribute>` child elements, these attributes are added to the tag-local page scope (as described above). If the type of attribute is `JspFragment`, the container parses the body of the `<jsp:attribute>` element into a `JspFragment` instance. These fragments can be invoked in the tag file using `<jsp:invoke />`.

6. The container evaluates the body of the action, either as normal body content or as the content of a `<jsp:body>` element. If the tag is declared to have a body content of `empty` or no body is present, `setJspBody()` is not called; otherwise, the body of the tag is parsed into a new `JspFragment` instance. If the tag is declared to have a `tagdependent` body, the `JspFragment` must reflect the body's content verbatim; otherwise, if the tag is declared to have a `scriptless` body, the `JspFragment` must reflect an unevaluated scriptless body. Note that `SimpleTag` (and hence tag file) bodies *must never* contain JSP scripting element code but may contain EL expressions. Using the `<jsp:doBody />` action in the tag file causes the `JspFragment` for the body to be invoked.
7. Finally, the `doTag` method is invoked by the container. This causes evaluation of the compiled JSP tag file to occur.
8. Once the `doTag` method returns, the tag handler instance is discarded. If `SkipPageException` is thrown, evaluation of the rest of the calling JSP is halted.

Note that for each tag scripting variable declared with synchronisation scopes `AT_BEGIN` or `AT_END`, the appropriate page-scoped attributes are declared in the calling JSP–see also *Variable Synchronisation* later.

Directives

Aside from the `page` directive (which is replaced by the `tag` directive for tag files), all directives used in normal JSPs can be used in tag files. In addition, there are several other directives specific to tag files which can be utilised. You will notice that many of the directive's attribute names seem to reflect properties found in the Tag Library Descriptor (TLD) which we look at in the next chapter (for example, there are elements for giving names and descriptions of the custom action). The reason is that tag files do not have to be associated with a TLD but can 'stand alone', just like JSPs do not need to be declared in the Web application's Deployment Descriptor. As a result, many non-essential attributes have found their way in here. We will discuss each of the directives and all their attributes in detail now, but just make sure you *learn all the important* gruelling details for the exam!

The tag Directive

This directive replaces the `page` directive for tag files, providing tag handler-specific features–for example, the ability to declare that this handler accepts dynamic attributes. `tag` is similar to `page` in that more than one `tag` directive may be declared, but only one occurrence of any given attribute may be declared, unless each occurrence of that attribute has the same value. The `import` and `pageEncoding` attributes are exceptions to this rule, and may appear multiple times.

The `tag` directive may contain the following attributes (all are optional):

- **`display-name`**
  A human-readable name intended to be shown in application deployers and tools. Defaults to the name of the tag file without the file extension.

- **`body-content`**
  This should be one of the values: `empty` if the action must be declared as an empty element, `tagdependent` if the contents are to be supplied to the tag file *verbatim* and interpreted by the tag handler itself, or `scriptless` (the default) if traditional JSP scripting elements should not be placed in the action's body but otherwise the contents should be evaluated. Note that `SimpleTag`s, and therefore tag files, do not permit JSP scripting elements in their body content–in the move away from servlet-environments. As a result, the value `JSP` is *not permitted* for a `SimpleTag` or a tag file, as it would be for a classic `Tag` handler.

- **`dynamic-attributes`**
  The mere presence of this attribute indicates that this tag accepts dynamic attributes. Declaring this attribute forces the container-generated tag handler to implement the `DynamicAttributes` interface (see the previous chapter). The value of this attribute specifies the name of a page-scoped attribute into which a `Map` containing the names (as map keys) and values (as map values) of all the dynamic attributes passed during this invocation should be stored. Note that care must be taken to ensure that no naming conflicts arise between the value of this attribute and any declared attributes (using the `attribute` directive) and local variables (using the `variable` directive) or a translation error will occur.

- **`small-icon`**
  A path specifying the image file containing a small icon which can be used by application deployers or tools to symbolise this tag file. The path should either be context-relative (starting with a forward slash), or relative to the path of this tag file.

- **large-icon**
  A path specifying the image file containing a larger icon which can be used by application deployers or tools to symbolise this tag file. Paths are resolved in the same way as for the `small-icon` attribute.

- **description**
  If declared, the value represents a textual description of this tag file's function.

- **example**
  If declared, this attribute should provide an informal description of a typical use of this action.

- **language**
  Same as the `page` directive: defines the scripting language used in this tag file. The only supported language on the Reference Implementation is `java` (but other JSP-compliant servers may support others).

- **import**
  Provides a language-specific mechanism to declare external dependencies. In Java scripting, this is used for package declarations.

- **pageEncoding**
  Describes the character encoding used in the tag file. This cannot be used for tag files declared in XML syntax as JSP documents inherently specify a character encoding.

- **isELIgnored**
  The value of this attribute should be either `true` (if EL expressions are to be ignored) or `false` otherwise. The default value varies depending on the version of the Java EE server and deployment descriptor you are using, but is determined in the same way as for the page directive.

As with JSP pages, the `tag` directive is declared in traditional JSP syntax:

```
<%@ tag attr_list %>
```

For tag files written in XML syntax (i.e. as JSP documents):


```
<jsp:directive.tag attr_list />
```

The attribute Directive

In the last chapter, we saw that tag handlers receive attribute data declared in the action through their JavaBean setter methods. However, since JSPs shouldn't ideally have many different methods, we must introduce an alternative way to get hold of the attributes and their values specified at run time. The `attribute` directive is used to specify the name and runtime type of all attributes declared by this action. This does not of course include dynamic attributes, which can be optionally established using the `tag` directive. The `attribute` directive replaces the need to configure the tag in the TLD.

This directive accepts six attributes; the first (`name`) is mandatory while all others are optional:

- **`name`**
  The (unique) name of the attribute being declared. A translation error occurs if a naming conflict arises because the name is also specified elsewhere in the `tag` or `variable` directives.
- **`required`**
  The value should be `true` if the attribute being declared is mandatory, or `false` (the default) otherwise.
- **`fragment`**
  Declares whether this attribute is a fragment to be evaluated by the tag handler (in which case a `JspFragment` is used), or whether the attribute is normal. If the attribute is a fragment, use `true`, otherwise use `false` (the default). Setting this attribute to true fixes the `type` attribute's value to `javax.servlet.jsp.tagext.JspFragment` and the `rtexprvalue` attribute to `true`. Declaring either of these attributes under this condition will result in a translation error.
- **`rtexprvalue`**
  Specifies whether the attribute's value may be dynamically calculated at run time. Defaults to `true`.
- **`type`**
  The runtime type of the attribute's value. This must be a fully-qualified class name; specifying a primitive results in a translation error. The default is `java.lang.String`.
- **`description`**
  A brief textual description of the attribute, as would be shown in an application assembly or deployment tool.

19

As with JSP pages, the `attribute` directive is declared in traditional JSP syntax as:

```
<%@ attribute attr_list %>
```

For tag files written in XML syntax (i.e. as JSP documents):

```
<jsp:directive.attribute attr_list />
```

Note that since no setter methods are available, another approach must be taken.

As we mentioned in *Tag File Semantics* earlier in this chapter, attributes are added to the JSP Context Wrapper's page scope. In the tag file, we retrieve the attribute value for an arbitrary attribute called `myAttr` using:

```
getJspContext().getAttribute("myAttr")
```

The variable Directive

The page scope in a tag file is isolated from the page scope in the calling component because of the distinction between the Invoking JSP Context and the JSP Context Wrapper.

This makes tag files with scriptless bodies rather redundant – for example:

```
<mytags:bankinfo>
 <tr><td>${ net }</td><td>${ gross }</td></tr>
</mytags:bankinfo>
```

Here, the `bankinfo` action is used to provide the value of the `net` and `gross` variables (in this example, each iteration of the action's body populates a new row in an HTML table). It is logical, since these are nested variables, to have them stored in the page scope, and we will need to update them before each iteration. However, if they are in the page scope, our tag file cannot update them because it cannot 'see' past its own JSP Context Wrapper's page scope (which is completely isolated from the Invoking JSP Context's page scope). We could of course store the variables in one of the other scopes, but that isn't really where they belong, and we try not to needlessly clutter the other scopes.

We need a way to copy the variables in the JSP Context Wrapper's page scope into the original Invoking JSP Context's page scope; this is in fact provided by the container as part of its **variable synchronisation**.

NOTE: Variable synchronisation for tag files, which effectively copies one page scope to another, is a distinct process from the synchronisation performed by the container for classic tags, which involves updating JSP scripting variables. Unfortunately, both mechanisms have been assigned the same name. Note further that both types of variable synchronisation are unavailable for raw `SimpleTag` implementations because they: (a) only ever access one page scope; (b) cannot contain JSP scripting expressions.

In order to take advantage of the container's variable synchronisation, you need to declare the variables which take part in synchronisation, along with their scopes – these have the same names as for classic variable synchronisation, `AT_BEGIN`, `AT_END` or `NESTED`, even though the tag file synchronisation process is distinct. To do this, we use the `variable` directive, which takes the following attributes:

- **`name-given="`*`output_name`*`"`**
  Declares the name (*`output_name`*) of a scoped attribute to be defined in the JSP currently invoking this tag. This is also the name of the local attribute in the tag file whose value is to be synchronised.
- **`name-from-attribute="`*`action_attribute_name`*`"`**
  Declares the name of a scoped attribute to be defined in the JSP currently invoking this tag. The name of the scoped attribute is determined at run time from the translation-time value of the attribute identified by *`action_attribute_name`*. Note that the name used as the value of this attribute must also be declared using the `attribute` directive which must also have the following attributes set:
  - `required="true"`
  - `rtexprvalue="false"`
  - `type="java.lang.String"`
- A translation error will occur if *`action_attribute_name`* is not already declared at translation time, or if it does not meet the above requirements of the attribute. The `alias` attribute must also be declared alongside this attribute, or a translation error will occur.
- **`alias="`*`local_name`*`"`**
  Declares the name of a locally scoped attribute to hold the value of this variable. The container will synchronise this value with the variable whose name is given by `name-from-attribute`. This attribute is *required along with* `name-from-attribute` when it is declared, and a translation error occurs if it is used otherwise.
- **`variable-class`**
  Specifies the fully-qualified name of the class of this variable. Primitives are not permitted, and the default is `java.lang.String`.
- **`declare`**
  The value should be `true` if we require the container to *create* this variable in the calling JSP, should it not already exist. If you rely on it already existing, use `false` as the value.

- **`scope`**
  This scope refers to the synchronisation given to the defined scripting variable, and *not* to the scope (page, request, session or application) in which the variable is stored – incidentally, page scope is always used for tag file attribute storage. The value of this attribute should be one of `AT_BEGIN`, `AT_END` or `NESTED` (the default). Table 19.1 shows the synchronisation points.

- **`description`**
  A textual description of this variable; this has limited use in application assembly and deployment when declaring the variables this tag exposes.

NOTE: The synchronisation here is different from that discussed in *Variable Synchronisation* in the last chapter – there we had synchronisation between scoped attributes (concurrently available in both the tag handler and calling JSP) and JSP scripting variables in the calling JSP; whereas here we have synchronisation between scoped attributes in the tag file and scoped attributes in the calling page's context. The synchronisation between tag files and calling JSPs has nothing to do with JSP scripting variables!

Table 19.1 Synchronisation Behaviour

Sync. Type	Start of Handler Invocation	Before each Fragment	End of Handler Invocation
`AT_BEGIN`	do nothing	synchronise	synchronise
`NESTED`	save original value	synchronise	restore original value
`AT_END`	do nothing	do nothing	synchronise

NOTE: Synchronisation *always occurs before* any fragment is executed, and *never after* a fragment's execution.

19

synchronise means the container updates the calling page's attribute with the local attribute in the tag file. If it does not exist in the tag file, it is removed from the calling page's context.

save means to store a copy of the calling page's attribute for later restoration. If it did not exist, remember that fact.

restore means to replace the calling page's attribute with the value saved earlier; if it did not exist earlier, make sure it is removed.

All attributes are optional except that either the `name-given` or *both* the `name-from-attribute` *and* `alias` attributes must be declared. `name-given` is used to specify a single, predetermined attribute in the Invoking JSP Context's page scope. In this case, `name-given` will be *both* the name of the Invoking JSP Context's page-scoped attribute *and* the JSP Context Wrapper's page-scoped attribute, local to the tag file. So, for example, specifying:

```
<%@ variable name-given="myvar" %>
```

asks for the local page-scoped attribute (bound into the JSP Context Wrapper) called `myvar` to be synchronised with a page-scoped attribute called `myvar` in the calling JSP (i.e. in the Invoking JSP Context's page scope).

`name-from-attribute` is used to declare an attribute in the Invoking JSP Context's page scope, with a name that depends on the value of a certain attribute in the opening tag of the declared action; we do this for attributes like `var` on JSTL actions, which then expose a scoped attribute which has the same name as the value of the `var` attribute in the opening tag of the action. Since we don't know what the name of the variable is up front, we must also declare `alias`, which is the predetermined name of the local attribute in the tag file. Then, synchronisation copies the value of the local attribute (whose name is the value of the `alias` attribute) to the calling JSP's page scope, into an attribute whose name is the value of the attribute identified by `name-from-attribute`. For example, for a JSTL-style loop, we might declare:

```
<%@ variable name-from-attribute="var" alias="counter" />
```

Then if we use a tag file containing this directive such as:

```
<mytags:forEach start="0" end="2" var="mycount">
  ${ mycount }
</mytags:forEach>
```

the container will synchronise the local `counter` attribute (declared using `alias`) in the tag file with the `mycount` attribute in the calling JSP (declared by referencing the `var` attribute using `name-from-attribute`).

Although this is an obvious point, it is worth noting that a translation error will occur if the name of any variables overlap with any declared attributes. This is because both attributes and variables are stored in the JSP Context Wrapper's page scope, as scoped attributes. This condition is therefore in place to avoid naming conflicts. An error will also occur if any dynamic attributes overlap with the names of declared variables.

19

As with JSP pages, the `variable` directive is declared in traditional JSP syntax as:

```
<%@ variable attr_list %>
```

For tag files written in XML syntax (i.e. as JSP documents):

```
<jsp:directive.variable attr_list />
```

NOTE: Configuration of variables and attributes can only be declared in the tag file, using the `variable` and `attribute` directives respectively. There are no `<variable>` or `<attribute>` elements in an explicit TLD for configuring tag files (unlike tags implemented by tag handler *classes*).

Implicit Objects

Just like JSPs, tag files have access to a set of implicit objects for use in JSP scripting elements; these are inserted implicitly into the tag handler implementation by the translator, typically at the start of the `doTag()` implementation. Note that these are Java variables, accessible only by traditional JSP scripting elements; any EL expressions in the tag file have access to the same implicit objects as any other EL expressions, as first shown in the *Implicit Objects* section in Chapter 15 – this is because the container always resolves variables in EL expressions using a `VariableResolver`, which in turn uses the objects in the `JspContext`, regardless of where, or in what type of components, those expressions occur.

The complete set of JSP scripting element tag file implicit objects, shown below, follows closely those available in a regular JSP component, so I would refer you to Chapter 13 for the descriptions of each; there is one exception, a new object, noted by an asterisk (*) below:

- **`request`**
- **`response`**
- **`jspContext`** *
  The instance of `javax.servlet.jsp.JspContext` for this tag file; this is the JSP Context Wrapper instance. Notice that JSPs have the `pageContext` implicit object defined instead; in the drive to move JSPs away from pure Java platforms, instances of the more generic `JspContext` class (which EL uses) are preferred to the `PageContext` class which is specific to servlet environments. Hence (and we comment more on this in the section *Employing Other Actions* below), tag files should not be designed necessarily with servlet-oriented platforms in mind.
- **`session`**
- **`application`**

19

- **out**
- **config**

The two implicit objects not available from the normal JSP set are `page` and `exception` (with `pageContext` being replaced by `jspContext`). Note that all these implicit objects refer to the same objects as those in the calling JSP, with the exception of `jspContext` which is the JSP Context Wrapper, and `session` which is independent of the setting of the `session` attribute of the calling page's `page` directive (i.e. the tag file `session` object exists regardless of whether this implicit object exists in the calling page).

Invoking Body Fragments via Standard Actions

Recall that a tag file is implemented as a `SimpleTag` handler, and that for a `SimpleTag`, we have an instance of `JspFragment` which represents the unevaluated body content of the action. In a `SimpleTag` handler, all we do is invoke the `JspFragment` programmatically.

However, in a tag file, we have no way to get a handle on the fragment in order to invoke it programmatically–it isn't defined as an implicit object for instance. But, if we can't invoke the fragment, we can't iterate over the body, or even evaluate it once.

The solution to our problem comes in two standard actions (the other standard actions were discussed in Chapter 17); these can be used to invoke both body content fragments and attribute fragments, and therefore provide the JSP (tag file) alternative to calling methods on `JspFragment` directly.

<jsp:doBody />

At its simplest, this action is used to invoke the body and write its contents to the current `out` stream. Behind the scenes, this action calls the `invoke` method on the body's `JspFragment`, passing it the `null` argument (which by default means the content is written to `out`; see the contract for the `invoke` method in the last chapter). 19

However, we needn't necessarily write the body to `out`–instead we might want to put the evaluated contents into our own `Writer`, as we can by passing a `Writer` instance to the `invoke` method. Unfortunately, this behaviour isn't available directly. Instead, we are able to obtain a `Reader` from this action. In fact, a `Reader` usually turns out to be more useful–we are typically interested in obtaining and parsing the content of the evaluated body, not in writing to it further. We can obtain a `Reader` object, filled with the contents of the evaluated body, by using the `varReader` attribute. This specifies the name of a scoped attribute to hold the new `Reader`. Note that this is similar to the `<c:import>` action, which also uses the `varReader` attribute for the purpose of obtaining a `Reader`. Once we've obtained the `Reader`, we are free to examine and modify its contents, buffer them into another `Writer`, write them to `out`, or simply suppress the contents completely by ignoring them. Remember: you must *explicitly* write the contents to `out` or the data will be lost.

```
<jsp:doBody varReader="mybody" />
```

This action, invoked from a tag file, causes the body to be evaluated once, and the result stored in a `Reader` in the `mybody` scoped attribute. By default, this will reside in the page scope; we may want to select another scope using the `scope` attribute, for example:

```
<jsp:doBody varReader="mybody" scope="session" />
```

`scope` takes all the normal values (`page`, `request`, `session` or `application`).

Finally, we might also want to retrieve the result as a `String`, rather than a `Reader`, to aid in examination and manipulation of the contents. When doing this programmatically, the easiest way is to pass a `StringWriter` to `invoke()`, and then use the `toString` method on the writer (as we did for the `mysimpletags.ModerationTag` example in the last chapter). The `<jsp:doBody />` action takes care of this for us by providing the `var` attribute. If declared, this attribute should have as its value the name of scoped attribute in which the evaluated body should be stored as a `String`. So, we might have:

```
<jsp:doBody var="mybodystr" scope="request" />
```

which stores the body as a `String` in the request-scoped attribute called `mybodystr`. The default value, if the `scope` attribute is omitted, is `page`.

A translation error will occur if both `var` and `varReader` are specified; if neither is specified, the evaluated body is written directly to `out` (as we mentioned at the start of this section).

19

If the body of the action causing this tag file to be invoked is empty, according to the specification, this action 'behaves as though a body was passed in that produces no output'. Basically, if the body is empty, this action does nothing!

<jsp:invoke />

This works like `<jsp:doBody />` but is used for invoking *attribute* fragments rather than the body fragment. Using this form:

```
<jsp:invoke fragment="attrname" />
```

causes the fragment for the attribute with name `attrname` to be invoked. Note that, because of the way in which attribute storage works in tag files, this is synonymous with invoking the `JspFragment` stored in the `attrname` page-scoped attribute (where the page scope here refers to the JSP Context Wrapper's scope and not the Invoking JSP Context). By default, without using `var` or `varReader`, this content is written directly to the `out` stream (by passing `null` to the `invoke` method of the fragment).

As with `<jsp:doBody />`, we can also specify up to one of the `var` or `varReader` attributes, which declare scoped attributes into which a `String` or `Reader` (respectively) of the evaluated fragment will be stored. The `scope` attribute can be used to declare the scope of this attribute.

If the fragment is empty or does not exist (i.e. the `attrname` page-scoped attribute is `null`), according to the specification, this action 'will behave as though a fragment was passed in that produces no output'–which translated into regular English, means it doesn't do anything!

Variable Synchronisation

It may be the case that the contents of EL expressions or other actions in the body of the action change over time. Where this is the case, each invocation of the `<jsp:doBody />` or `<jsp:invoke />` actions needs to give rise to different contents (for example, during a loop where each iteration has a different set of variables, perhaps set by the tag file just before each iteration).

The tag file can synchronise its attributes (found in the JSP Context Wrapper's page scope) with those in the calling component's page scope by using the variable synchronisation mechanism we saw previously in this chapter (using either the `variable` directive or configuration in the TLD). What is of importance to us is when the variables are updated, since this will affect whether the body is different for each invocation. The container makes only one guarantee: all synchronisation variables of scope `AT_BEGIN` or `NESTED` will be synchronised *just before* an invocation of either `<jsp:doBody />` or `<jsp:invoke />`. This allows variables to be used in both the body of the action *and* its attribute values. In effect, this means that synchronisation occurs as part of the processing of the action, but before `invoke()`

19

is called on the fragment. Now, we know that any changes to variables between invocations of a fragment will correctly be reflected in changes to the body. This is emphasised in the note below Table 19.1 shown earlier. Note that this behaviour is not required for variables with `AT_END` scope, since these are guaranteed to exist only after the tag has completed execution (and therefore, long after the chance for the tag file to execute its body or attribute fragments has passed).

Employing Other Actions

A tag file may make use of other tags in its implementation. Since a tag file is just a JSP, making use of existing tags like those in the JSTL library is usually the best way to approach a design problem. As with all JSPs, avoiding Java-based scripting code and making the full use of reusable components like tags is becoming increasingly important.

However, we must take some extra care when using other actions in tag files. In the move to make JSP technology independent of the Java EE platform, the new `SimpleTag` extensions, of which tag files are all instances, are not bound to the servlet environment. Classic tags implementing `Tag` rely on the `PageContext` object which is part of the servlet model, while `SimpleTag`s use the `JspContext` which is servlet-independent. As a result of this difference, a `SimpleTag` should not assume that it exists in a servlet environment along with other classic tags. If the `SimpleTag` is in fact running on a non-servlet platform, then the classic tags won't be available for use and an exception will be thrown.

The impact this has on your design decisions will probably be minimal – most, if not all, current JSP Web servers are Java EE-compliant (which is only to be expected since JSP was originally a Java technology!). In general therefore, most JSP platforms will be servlet-based and support classic tags. However, if you plan to distribute your tag extensions, you may wish to issue a 'health warning' to JSP authors that your tags do make use of classic tags and that a servlet environment is required for them to work correctly (and then, if it all goes wrong, they can't blame you!).

An Example

Quite possibly the best way to demonstrate tag files is to work through an example. This section contains all the code and deployment information required to use the code in a real application (the download bundle is also available in deployable form). The code itself incorporates many of the techniques you have learnt so far: JSP basics, scripting elements, the Expression Language, standard and JSTL actions and tag file semantics. The tag file has been written in two variants: one in JSP page syntax (`calendar.tag`) and one in JSP document syntax (`calendarx.tagx`). Also included is a sample JSP (`calendartest.jsp`) which can be deployed and used to test either tag file.

The code as presented requires a JSP 2.0 container running from a JRE 5.0 installation (we use a few features like auto(un)boxing to simplify the code).

This example, when supplied with a year and month, generates a calendar of dates, displayed as a grid. To motivate the discussion, Figure 19.1 shows the final result we aim to achieve, as rendered in a Web browser. Our design allows the starting day of the week to be changed, to allow for customisation for different purposes; for example, a businessman might select Monday as the start of the week, while the default might be Sunday. We also allow notes to be attached to each day, perhaps as reminders of business meeting or anniversaries.

Our tag's only role is to build the basic grid layout, arrange the days of the week in the correct order, and use the `java.util.Calendar` class to place the days in the correct boxes. Our tag doesn't fill the grid by itself: instead, the body of the tag should be used to supply the contents of each table cell. The tag file will invoke the body exactly once for each day of the month, allowing authors to place any content they wish in each day's box.

We use (X)HTML, with a small amount of CSS styling code, as the presentation code. This is not of prime importance to the example; if you are unfamiliar with (X)HTML or CSS, this is not important as far as the SCWCD exam goes. Instead, you should concentrate on the implementation code in the tag file. In the tag file itself, we make use of modular (mod 7) arithmetic such that, for example, the 8th day of the week is also the 1st day of the week. If you are not familiar with the mathematics of modular arithmetic, again don't worry as this does not form the major part of the exercise. I will provide some overview commentary to explain roughly what each implementation does, without providing details.

Figure 19.1

Browser Rendering of Target Result

February 2006

Su	M	Tu	W	Th	F	Sa
			1	2	3	4
5	6	7	8	9	10	11
12	13	14	15	16	17	18
19	20	21	22	23	24	25
26	27	28				

calendar.tag

I've made this part of a custom `mydates` library and deployed it into the sample application under `/WEB-INF/tags/mydates/calendar.tag`.

This is the code:

```
<%@ tag import="java.util.Calendar" %>
<%@ taglib uri="http://java.sun.com/jsp/jstl/core" prefix="c" %>
<%@ taglib uri="http://java.sun.com/jsp/jstl/fmt" prefix="fmt" %>

<%-- Note these directives could be configured in the TLD instead
     but here we use the container's implicit TLD --%>
<%@ attribute name="year" required="true"
  type="java.lang.Integer" description="Year of calendar" %>
<%@ attribute name="month" required="true"
  type="java.lang.Integer" description="Month of calendar" %>
<%@ attribute name="diary" required="true"
  type="java.lang.String[][]"
  description="String[] entries for each day" %>
<%@ attribute name="startofweek" required="false"
  type="java.lang.Integer"
  description="Start day of week (Sunday=1,...,Saturday=7)" %>
<%@ attribute name="varEntries" required="true"
  rtexprvalue="false"
  description="Name for each day's exported entries" %>
<%@ attribute name="varDay" required="true" rtexprvalue="false"
  description="Name for the day's exported number" %>

<%@ variable name-from-attribute="varEntries" alias="entries"
  variable-class="java.lang.String[]" scope="NESTED"
  description="Entries for the particular date" %>
<%@ variable name-from-attribute="varDay" alias="daynum"
  variable-class="java.lang.Integer" scope="NESTED"
  description="Day of the month (1 up to 31)" %>

<%-- Scriplet initialisation code: JSP scripting elements are
     valid as content in tag files, but not in the bodies of the
     actions they represent! --%>
<%
/* Get year and month as ints from page-scoped attributes */
int year=((Integer)jspContext.getAttribute("year")).intValue();
int month=
        ((Integer)jspContext.getAttribute("month")).intValue();

  Calendar cal = Calendar.getInstance();
  /* Set year and month (0 based). Day to 1st of the month */
  cal.set(year, month-1, 1);

  /* Store this in the page-scope to allow EL to access it */
  jspContext.setAttribute("calendar", cal);
  int maxday = cal.getActualMaximum(Calendar.DAY_OF_MONTH);
  jspContext.setAttribute("maxday", maxday);
```

19

```
  /* NOTE: Although we probably shouldn't rely on this,
     Calendar.DAY_OF_WEEK takes the value 1 for Sunday,
     2 for Monday...up to 7 for Saturday. We use this later. */
  int startday = cal.get(Calendar.DAY_OF_WEEK);
  jspContext.setAttribute("startday", startday);

  /* Convert textual 'startofweek' value into number */
  Integer startofweekobj =
      (Integer) jspContext.getAttribute("startofweek");
  int startofweek =
      (startofweekobj ==  null ? 1 : startofweekobj.intValue());
  jspContext.setAttribute("startofweek", startofweek);

  /* The 'startcondition' is an offset representing index of the
    cell just before the first cell to be filled. */
  int startcondition = (startday - startofweek) % 7;
  if(startcondition < 0) {
    startcondition += 7;
  }
  jspContext.setAttribute("startcondition", startcondition);

  /* We need to calculate the final cell number - this is
     'maxday + startcondition' rounded to the next highest
     multiple of 7 */
  int maxcount = maxday + startcondition;
  if(maxcount % 7 != 0) {
      maxcount += 7 - (maxcount % 7);
  }
  jspContext.setAttribute("maxcount", maxcount);
%>

<%-- NOTE: Other than comments, no JSP scripting elements
     follow. We could therefore offload all the previous
     scripting code into a helper class, leaving this tag file as
     a purely scriptless JSP (using EL only). --%>

<table>
  <tr><th colspan="7">
  <fmt:formatDate value="${ calendar.time }"
                  pattern="MMMMMMMMM yyyy" />
  </th></tr>

  <%-- Output the headings - this could also be formatted for
    different languages using another custom or JSTL action --%>
  <tr>
    <c:forEach begin="${startofweek}" end="${startofweek+6}"
               var="counter">
      <th>
        <c:choose>
          <c:when test="${ counter % 7 == 1 }">Su</c:when>
          <c:when test="${ counter % 7 == 2 }">M</c:when>
          <c:when test="${ counter % 7 == 3 }">Tu</c:when>
          <c:when test="${ counter % 7 == 4 }">W</c:when>
          <c:when test="${ counter % 7 == 5 }">Th</c:when>
```

19

```
          <c:when test="${ counter % 7 == 6 }">F</c:when>
          <c:when test="${ counter % 7 == 0 }">Sa</c:when>
        </c:choose>
      </th>
    </c:forEach>
  </tr>

  <%-- Generates cells in the table
       (start top-left with index 1) --%>
  <c:forEach begin="1" end="${maxcount}" step="1" var="counter”>
    <%-- If we are at start of a new week, start a new row --%>
    <c:if test="${ counter % 7 == 1 }">
      <jsp:text><![CDATA[<tr>]]></jsp:text>
    </c:if>

    <td>
    <%-- Only invoke the body if this is a valid day
         (non-empty cell) --%>
    <c:if test="${ counter > startcondition &&
                   counter <= (maxday + startcondition) }">
      <%-- Configure variables for this date,
           then invoke the body --%>
      <c:set var="daynum" value="${counter-startcondition}" />
      <c:set var="entries" value="${diary[daynum]}" />
      <jsp:doBody />
    </c:if>

    </td>

    <%-- If we are at the end of a week, end this row --%>
    <c:if test="${ counter % 7 == 0 }">
      <jsp:text><![CDATA[</tr>]]></jsp:text>
    </c:if>
  </c:forEach>
</table>
```

Now we'll briefly analyse this tag file:

- Firstly, we start with a `tag` directive which imports the `java.util.Calendar` class into the tag file–giving us access to the date facilities it provides.
- We then import a couple of other tag libraries, JSTL Core and Formatting, which we use later in the tag file. We do this with two `taglib` directives.
- We then configure all the attributes for this tag file, using an `attribute` directive for each:
  - `year`–an `Integer` specifying the year we want to display (e.g. 2006).
  - `month`–an `Integer` specifying the month to display; January has index 1, December is 12.
  - `diary`–a `String[][]`. The first dimension is the days of the month; i.e. `diary.length` should equal the number of days in the specified month.

The second dimension is an array of all the entries for a particular day. So, `diary[5]` is a `String[]` of all the entries for the 5th day of the month.

- ▷ `startofweek` (optional) – The starting day of the week, as to be displayed in the calendar. Use 1 for Sunday, 2 for Monday, ..., 7 for Saturday.
- ▷ `varEntries` – For each day in the month, the tag makes the diary `String[]` for that day available. This exported variable has the name of the value of this `varEntries` attribute.
- ▷ `varDay` – This is the name of the exported variable, in which the tag stores the current day number of the month (starting at 1, with a maximum possible value of 31).

- ▶ Then we declare the exported variables for this tag; these have the names given by the `varEntries` and `varDay` attributes, and export `String[]` and `Integer` objects respectively.
- ▶ We then use scriptlet code to extract and manipulate the data from the attributes. In particular, we store page-scoped (local to the tag file) attributes of data we will need later:
  - ▷ We start by obtaining a `Calendar` instance for the current month, with the day set to the 1st of the month. We store this in the `calendar` attribute.
  - ▷ Then we obtain the maximum day in this specific month – a value between 28 and 30. We store this in the `maxday` attribute, and also in a local variable of the same name (it is used later in the scriptlet).
  - ▷ Now, since our `calendar` is positioned at the 1st day of the month, we find the `Calendar` constant representing this day. By convention, we should never rely on the actual values of constants, but to simplify the code here (to avoid doing comparisons and then assigning our own numerical values) we will assume the `Calendar` constants stay constant over time. We set the `startday` attribute to this value, where Sunday is represented by 1, Monday is 2, ..., Saturday is 7.
  - ▷ Next we obtain the `startofweek` attribute value, specifying the day on which the displayed week should begin. We first extract the `int` primitive from its wrapper, then store it in the local `startofweek` variable. If the attribute wasn't declared, we give it the default value of 1 (Sunday).
  - ▷ The `startcondition` attribute stores the (1-based) index of the cell just before the cell at which the 1st of the month will be displayed. This is also the number of cells skipped (left empty) in the first row. For example, in Figure 19.1, this would have the value 3, since we skip over 3 cells.

  - ▷ The `maxcount` attribute will be exactly a multiple of 7. This attribute stores the total number of cells, including the empty ones which fill the end of the table. In Figure 19.1, this attribute would have value 4. The number of empty cells at the end is given by `maxcount - maxday` (here 32 - 28 = 4).

- Now we've done the preprocessing, we are ready to build the calendar grid. You will notice the code from this point on is scriptless–i.e. contains no JSP scripting elements. In fact we have no need for them, since we have already set up our attributes, and EL expressions will do just nicely here!

- We first create the opening `<table>` element and the first row of the table, which specifies the month and year. We use the `getTime()` method of `Calendar` (invoked by the property access expression `${ calendar.time }`) to obtain a `Date` object, which we pass to the JSTL `<fmt:formatDate />` action. The Formatting actions aren't on the exam, but here we use it to generate a textual description of the `Date`, in this case in the form *`month year`* where *`month`* is the ***name*** (rather than number) of the month. In Figure 19.1, this is `February 2006`.

- Next we render the day headings–we've used hardcoded abbreviations like 'Su' (Sunday), 'Tu' (Tuesday) and 'Th' (Thursday). The order in which these are displayed depends on which day the user has configured to be start of the week–as found in the `startofweek` attribute. We use modular arithmetic so that 8 becomes 1, 9 becomes 2 etc. in the loop, which simplifies the code. Note: you might want to customise the short names displayed depending on the client's preferred language, if it isn't English. You could achieve this using an attribute of the tag (specifying an ordered array of abbreviations), a helper class, perhaps an EL function, or even better a helper tag which does the formatting. This is left as an exercise.

- Next we begin to loop through the cells in the table, starting at the top-left, with index 1, working along the top row, then down onto the next row etc. In the loop we:

  - ▷ Write out a `<tr>` tag if the counter value (mod 7) is 1–i.e. if the counter value is 1, 8, 15, 22, ..., which correspond with the indices of the first cells in each row.

  - ▷ If the counter has already moved past (i.e. skipped) `startcondition` cells, then start evaluating the body. We only evaluate the body of the tag when the dates in the calendar are valid, to avoid `NullPointerExceptions` and `IndexOutOfBoundsExceptions` being raised by the body invocation.

  - ▷ Just before this evaluation, we set the `daynum` and `entries` local page-scoped attributes to the current day of the month number and the

19

String[] of entries for this day, respectively. Note that the variable synchronisation uses these as aliases for the exported variables, and copies their values to the Invoking JSP Context's page-scoped attributes before <jsp:doBody /> is invoked.

- Finally, we write out the closing </tr> for the row, only if the counter value is 0 (mod 7) – i.e. has the values 7, 14, 21, 28, ..., which correspond with the indices of the last cells in each row.

- Lastly we exit the loop and write the closing </table>.

That complete's our tag's functionality. If you can't quite see why certain things work, especially those in loops, try writing out a few terms and spot the pattern!

calendarx.tagx

We will now proceed to rewrite calendar.tag into its JSP document counterpart. This is only for practise with the JSP document topics – we won't be altering the implementation details of the tag file. I deployed this file to /WEB-INF/tags/mydates/calendarx.tagx (note the tagx extension denotes a tag file *document* which is XML formatted, just like jspx is the recommended extension for an XML formatted JSP *document* rather than an arbitrarily-formatted page). Here's the code (I've removed all comments from before to keep the code condensed):

```
<jsp:root xmlns="http://www.w3.org/1999/xhtml"
          xmlns:jsp="http://java.sun.com/JSP/Page" version="2.0"
          xmlns:c="http://java.sun.com/jsp/jstl/core"
          xmlns:fmt="http://java.sun.com/jsp/jstl/fmt">

<jsp:directive.tag import="java.util.Calendar" />

<jsp:directive.attribute name="year" required="true"
 type="java.lang.Integer" description="Year of calendar" />
<jsp:directive.attribute name="month" required="true"
 type="java.lang.Integer" description="Month of calendar" />
<jsp:directive.attribute name="diary" required="true"
 type="java.lang.String[][]"
 description="String[] entries for each day" />
<jsp:directive.attribute name="startofweek" required="false"
 type="java.lang.Integer"
 description="Number for start day (Sunday=1,...,Saturday=7)" />
<jsp:directive.attribute name="varEntries" required="true"
 rtexprvalue="false"
 description="Name for each day's exported entries" />
<jsp:directive.attribute name="varDay" required="true"
 rtexprvalue="false"
 description="Name for the day's exported number" />

<jsp:directive.variable name-from-attribute="varEntries"
```

19

```
 alias="entries" variable-class="java.lang.String[]"
 scope="NESTED" description="Entries for the particular date" />
<jsp:directive.variable name-from-attribute="varDay"
 alias="daynum" variable-class="java.lang.Integer"
 scope="NESTED" description="Entries for the particular date" />

<jsp:scriptlet><![CDATA[
int year=((Integer)jspContext.getAttribute("year")).intValue();
int month=
         ((Integer)jspContext.getAttribute("month")).intValue();

  Calendar cal = Calendar.getInstance();
  cal.set(year, month-1, 1);

  jspContext.setAttribute("calendar", cal);
  int maxday = cal.getActualMaximum(Calendar.DAY_OF_MONTH);
  jspContext.setAttribute("maxday", maxday);

  int startday = cal.get(Calendar.DAY_OF_WEEK);
  jspContext.setAttribute("startday", startday);

  Integer startofweekobj =
      (Integer) jspContext.getAttribute("startofweek");
  int startofweek =
      (startofweekobj == null ? 1 : startofweekobj.intValue());
  jspContext.setAttribute("startofweek", startofweek);

  int startcondition = (startday - startofweek) % 7;
  if(startcondition < 0) {
    startcondition += 7;
  }

  jspContext.setAttribute("startcondition", startcondition);
  int maxcount = maxday + startcondition;
  if(maxcount % 7 != 0) {
      maxcount += 7 - (maxcount % 7);
  }
  jspContext.setAttribute("maxcount", maxcount);
]]></jsp:scriptlet>

<table>
  <tr><th colspan="7">
  <fmt:formatDate value="${calendar.time}"
                  pattern="MMMMMMMMM yyyy" />
  </th></tr>
  <tr>
    <c:forEach begin="${startofweek}" end="${startofweek+6}"
               var="counter">
      <th>
        <c:choose>
          <c:when test="${ counter % 7 == 1 }">Su</c:when>
          <c:when test="${ counter % 7 == 2 }">M</c:when>
          <c:when test="${ counter % 7 == 3 }">Tu</c:when>
          <c:when test="${ counter % 7 == 4 }">W</c:when>
          <c:when test="${ counter % 7 == 5 }">Th</c:when>
```

19

```
          <c:when test="${ counter % 7 == 6 }">F</c:when>
          <c:when test="${ counter % 7 == 0 }">Sa</c:when>
        </c:choose>
      </th>
    </c:forEach>
  </tr>

  <c:forEach begin="1" end="${maxcount}" step="1" var="counter">
    <c:if test="${ counter % 7 == 1 }">
      <jsp:text><![CDATA[<tr>]]></jsp:text>
    </c:if>

    <td>

   <c:if test="${ counter gt startcondition and
                  counter le (maxday + startcondition) }">
    <c:set var="daynum" value="${ counter - startcondition }" />
    <c:set var="entries" value="${ diary[daynum] }" />
    <jsp:doBody />
   </c:if>

    </td>

    <c:if test="${ counter % 7 == 0 }">
      <jsp:text><![CDATA[</tr>]]></jsp:text>
    </c:if>
  </c:forEach>
</table>

</jsp:root>
```

You will notice that there are very few changes. We had to replace `<%@ ... %>` with `<jsp:scriptlet>...</jsp:scriptlet>` and the directives with their appropriate XML elements. In JSP documents we do away with the `taglib` directive completely, instead configuring tag library URIs and prefixes as XML namespaces (using the `xmlns` attribute). We also had to put the scriptlet code in a CDATA section to avoid problems caused by < and `&` characters used in the Java code, and replaced EL operators like <, `&&` and > with their literal counterparts (`lt`, with <= becoming `le`, `and`, `gt`) to maintain a well-formed document.

Other than that, because we tried to keep a well-formed document before anyway by using only custom actions and EL expressions in the second half of the document, there were only a few simple modifications.

19

calendartest.jsp

This is a JSP page which can be used to test the two calendars. It provides a few example entries, namely on the 5th and 18th of every month (not very realistic, but adding realism is left as an exercise), shows overview calendars for each month in the year by iterating through all months for that year, and then provides a single, detailed, calendar for one month in question.

Note that the bodies of the `calendar` (or `calendarx`) actions contain the rendering code for the grids. In the first example, the number of the day is rendered, with a link which causes the page to reload with the larger calendar at the bottom showing the month which that day resides in. Any days for which there are entries (i.e. the `myplans` array is non-`empty` on that day) are shown highlighted by a yellow background.

Note that this page also includes support to specify the year, month and starting day of the week using the `year`, `month` and `weekbegins` request parameters, respectively. We provide the user with control over `year` and `weekbegins` by a small HTML form on the page.

I deployed this to `/calendartest.jsp` in the sample application:

```
<%@ taglib uri="http://java.sun.com/jsp/jstl/core" prefix="c" %>
<%@ taglib tagdir="/WEB-INF/tags/mydates" prefix="dates" %>

<%
  /* Initialise example diary entries (for every month) */
  String[][] diary = new String[31][];
  diary[5] = new String[]{ "Anniversary" };
  diary[18] = new String[]{ "Business meeting" };
  pageContext.setAttribute("myplans", diary);
%>

<%-- Obtain the year from a request parameter, or 2006 by
default --%>
<c:set var="year"
   value="${ (empty param['year']) ? 2006 : param['year'] }" />
<html>
<head>
<title>Calendars for year ${ year }</title>
<style>
 table { border-collapse:collapse; border:solid black 0.5pt; }
 table td { width:12pt; height:12pt; border:solid black 0.5pt; }
</style>
</head>
<body>
   <!-- HTML form for changing year/start day -->
   <form method="GET" action="">
   <input type="text" maxlength="4" name="year" value="${year}"/>
      <select name="weekbegins">
        <option value="1">Sunday</option>
        <option value="2">Monday</option>
        <option value="3">Tuesday</option>
        <option value="4">Wednesday</option>
        <option value="5">Thursday</option>
        <option value="6">Friday</option>
        <option value="7">Saturday</option>
```

```
          </select>
          <input type="submit" />
        </form>
        <%-- Show the 12 months --%>
        <c:forEach begin="1" end="12" var="thisMonth">
          <dates:calendar year="${ year }" month="${ thisMonth }"
                 diary="${ myplans }" varDay="todayNum"
                 varEntries="dayEntries"
                 startofweek="${ (empty param['weekbegins']) ?
                                1 : param['weekbegins'] }">
            <%-- Note that splitting the <span> opening element
                 is BAD document syntax, but valid for a page --%>
            <span
               <c:if test="${ !(empty dayEntries) }">
                 style="background-color:yellow;"
               </c:if>
            >
            <a href="?year=${ param['year'] }&month=${ thisMonth }">
                ${ todayNum }
              </a>
            </span>
          </dates:calendar>
        </c:forEach>
        <%-- The main calendar --%>
        <dates:calendarx year="${year}" month="${param['month']}"
               diary="${myplans}" varDay="todayNum"
               varEntries="dayEntries">
          <p><strong>${ todayNum }</strong></p>
          <c:if test="${ !(empty dayEntries) }">
            <c:forEach items="${ dayEntries }" var="thisEntry">
            ${ thisEntry },
            </c:forEach>
          </c:if>
        </dates:calendarx>

      </body>
    </html>
```

You can now use the form to control some of the rendering on the page, clicking a link in the overview calendars to display that month in the main calendar. This isn't the neatest web page ever, but it should have demonstrated how to use tag files effectively, and when a tag file is better than a classic tag handler. You will notice that in this page, we have used both the page-structured tag file (`calendar` action) and the document-structured tag file (`calendarx` action).

The best way to get the ideas concrete is to do some practical examples for yourself–start by adapting the example in this chapter, then move on to implement your own, progressively more complex, ideas. Custom tags are, in my opinion, the most complicated topics in both the exam and in real-world Web development. But, once you've mastered them, they are an extremely powerful, flexible and useful tool which you'll quickly find you can't do without! Believe me, it's worth the effort and time to become familiar with these many ideas now.

Revision Questions

1 **Which of the following are correct statements?** **(choose three)**

- A A tag file can be written as a JSP page.
- B A tag file can be written as a JSP document.
- C A tag file is implemented as a javax.servlet.jsp.JspPage.
- D A tag file is implemented as a javax.servlet.jsp.tagext.Tag.
- E A tag file is implemented as a javax.servlet.jsp.tagext.SimpleTag.

2 **Which of the following are correct statements?** **(choose one)**

- A Tag file handler instances are always pooled for efficiency.
- B Tag file handler instances may be pooled.
- C Tag file handler instances are never pooled.
- D A single tag file handler exists which is accessed concurrently by all tag invocations implemented by that handler.

3 **Which of the following directives cannot be used in a tag file?** **(choose one)**

- A include
- B page
- C taglib
- D tag
- E variable

4 **The tag <my:out> outputs its body content to the out implicit object; it is implemented as a tag file. What is the result of including the following in a JSP page?** **(choose one)**

```
<my:out>Welcome <%= request.getRemoteUser() %></my:out>
```

19

- A The response is the text 'Welcome ' followed by the username.
- B The response is the text 'Welcome '.
- C The response is empty
- D A translation error occurs.
- E A compilation error occurs.

5 **The exhibit shows a tag file, mytag.tag, and a JSP page used by it. What is the result of using the mytag tag file in a page?** **(choose one)**

EXHIBIT

- A The tag outputs the value of the request-scoped attribute called username.
- B The tag makes the request-scoped attribute called username available to the calling page.
- C A translation error occurs on line 1 of mytag.tag.
- D A translation error occurs on line 2 of mytag.tag.
- E A translation error occurs in user.jsp.

6 **Which of the following are available as JSP implicit objects in a tag file?** **(choose two)**

- A request
- B param
- C out
- D pageContext
- E headers

7 **What is the effect of using the session JSP implicit object in a tag file when the invoking page sets the session="false" attribute of its page directive?** **(choose one)**

- A The tag file's session implicit object is never declared by the container.
- B The tag file's session implicit object is always null.
- C The tag file's session implicit object is initialised to the value of the client's current session.
- D A translation error occurs.
- E A compilation error occurs.

8 **Which of the following statements causes the body of the tag be invoked and written to out using a tag file?** **(choose one)**

- A <% getJspBody().invoke(null); %>
- B <% fragment.invoke(null); %>
- C <jsp:invoke />
- D <jsp:invoke var="out" />
- E <jsp:doBody />

9 **Which of the following statements is correct?** **(choose one)**

- A The tag file uses the same JspContext as its calling page.
- B The container creates a second instance of JspContext, containing no page-scoped attributes, for use in the tag file.
- C The container creates a second instance of JspContext for use in the tag file, copying all page-scoped attributes from the calling page.
- D The container creates a second instance of JspContext for use in the tag file, which is kept synchronised with the calling page's JspContext.

10 **The exhibit shows the tag file implementation for the <my:item> tag. What is the effect of compiling and executing the following JSP page?** **(choose one)**

EXHIBIT

```
<my:item>Login information</my:item>
```

- A The response is the text 'Welcome ' followed by the value of the request-scoped attribute called user.
- B The response is the text 'Login information'.
- C A translation error occurs in the JSP page.
- D A translation error occurs in the tag file on line 1.
- E A translation error occurs in the tag file on line 2.

11 **The exhibit shows the tag file implementation for the <my:loop> tag. What is the effect of compiling and executing the following JSP page?** **(choose one)**

EXHIBIT

```
<% request.setAttribute("items", new int[]{ 1, 2, 3 }); %>
<my:loop>Item list</my:loop>
```

- A The response is the text 'Item: 1, Item: 2, Item: 3,'.
- B The response is the text 'Item: , Item: , Item: ,'.
- C The response is the text 'Item list'.
- D A translation error occurs in the tag file.
- E A translation error occurs in the JSP page.

19

12 **The exhibit shows the tag file implementation for the <my:loop> tag. What is the effect of compiling and executing the JSP page?** **(choose one)**

EXHIBIT

```
<% pageContext.removeAttribute("code"); %>
<% request.setAttribute("itemcodes",new String[]{"0152","1934","8832"}); %>
<my:loop>Code: ${ code }</my:loop>
```

A The response is the text 'Code: 0152 Code: 1934 Code: 8832'.

B The response is the text 'Code: Code: Code:'.

C The response is empty.

D A translation error occurs in the tag file.

E A translation error occurs in the JSP page.

13 **What is the correct way to set tag attributes on a tag implemented as a tag file?** **(choose one)**

A Use a declaration in the tag file to create the appropriate setter method.

B Use an instance of TagFileInfo to configure the attributes.

C Declare an attribute directive with the configuration of the attribute.

D Declare the attributes in the deployment descriptor.

E Declare the attributes in the tag library descriptor.

14 **The exhibit shows the tag file implementation for the <my:loop> tag. What is the effect of using this tag file in the following JSP page?** **(choose one)**

EXHIBIT

```
<my:loop>Hello</my:loop>
```

A The response is the text 'Counter 0 Counter 1'.

B The response is the text 'Counter 0 Hello Counter 1 Hello'.

C The response is empty.

D A translation error occurs in the tag file.

E A translation error occurs in the JSP page.

15 **The exhibit shows the tag file for <my:output>. What is the effect of compiling and executing the tag file and JSP page?** **(choose one)**

EXHIBIT

```
<my:output>world</my:output>
Hello ${ requestScope['evaluated'] }
```

A The text 'Hello world' is output.

B The text 'world Hello' is output.

C The text 'Hello' is output.

D The response is empty.

E A translation error occurs.

Exhibits

Q.5

mytag.tag:

```
<%@ tag body-content="empty" language="java" %>
<%@ include file="/user.jsp" %>
```

/user.jsp:

```
<%@ page contentType="text/html" %>
<%= request.getAttribute("username"); %>
```

Q.10

```
<%@ tag body-content="empty" %>
Welcome ${ requestScope['user'] }
```

Q.11

```
<%@ tag body-content="scriptless" %>
<c:forEach items="${ requestScope['items'] }" var="thisItem">
  Item: ${ thisItem },
</c:forEach>
```

Q.12

```
<jsp:root xmlns:jsp="http://java.sun.com/JSP/Page" version="2.0"
          xmlns:c="http://java.sun.com/jsp/jstl/core">
<c:forEach items="${ requestScope['itemcodes'] }" var="thisCode">
  <c:set var="code" scope="page" value="${ thisCode }" />
  <jsp:doBody />
</c:forEach>
</jsp:root>
```

Q.14


```
<%@ tag body-content="JSP" %>
<% for(int i=0; i < 2; i++) {
            out.write("Counter: " + i); %>
            <jsp:doBody />
<% } %>
```

Q.15

```
<%@ tag body-content="scriptless" %>
<jsp:doBody var="evaluated" scope="request" />
```

Answers to Revision Questions

1 **Correct answers: A, B, E**

2 **Correct answer: C**
Tag files are implemented as SimpleTags, and are therefore never pooled.

3 **Correct answer: B**
page is the only directive not applicable to tag files. Note that D and E are not available to normal JSPs.

4 **Correct answer: D**
Tag files are compiled into SimpleTags; it is therefore illegal to include JSP scripting expressions in the body of a tag implemented using a tag file. EL expressions are, however, valid.

5 **Correct answer: D**
The user.jsp page contains the page directive; this is illegal in tag files, and attempting to include any resource into a tag file which contains illegal syntax causes a translation error (it doesn't make sense to set the contentType for a tag anyway, as this is the job of the calling page).

6 **Correct answers: A, C**
Note that param and headers are EL implicit objects, but not JSP ones. Also note that pageContext exists in JSPs, but jspContext exists in tag files.

7 **Correct answer: B**
The tag file uses its JSP Context Wrapper to obtain the session object; this is always non-null except if the calling page explicitly sets session="false" in a directive.

8 **Correct answer: E**
A and B are incorrect (note that a tag file needn't implement SimpleTagSupport, so it needn't have a getJspBody() method); <jsp:invoke /> is used to invoke an *attribute* fragment, so C and D are incorrect.

9 **Correct answer: B**
The container creates a new instance of JspContext (the so-called 'JSP Context Wrapper') which has a page scope isolated from that of the calling page. Tag files don't have access to *page-scoped* attributes in its calling page (but they may expose some, by configuring synchronised variables).

10 **Correct answer: C**
Note that the tag file is declared to have an *empty* body, but we have supplied one. This produces an instant validation (translation) error.

11 **Correct answer: D**

No tag library prefix/URI mapping has been provided for the <c:forEach> tag.

12 **Correct answer: B**

Although the tag file invokes the body of the tag three times, setting a page-scoped attribute in the tag file doesn't automatically set that page-scoped attribute in the calling page. Recall that the container uses a JSP Context Wrapper for the tag file, rather than the original Invoking JSP Context, the purpose being to isolate the page contexts.

13 **Correct answer: C**

This is the *only* way to achieve this; the TLD is not the place to configure attributes for tag files, and therefore no setXxx methods will necessarily be invoked by the container.

14 **Correct answer: D**

Note that 'JSP' is an illegal value for use in the body-content attribute of a tag file (or SimpleTag). Hence a translation error occurs. If the value was in fact 'scriptless', the correct answer would have been B.

15 **Correct answer: A**

Note the var attribute of <jsp:doBody /> stores the evaluated body in a scoped attribute (note that an unsynchronised page-scoped attribute would be accessible only to the tag file). Hence, the body is stored in the request-scoped attribute called evaluated, the template text 'Hello ' written, followed by the value of the evaluated attribute which is 'world' (the body content of <my:output>). Therefore A is correct.

In this chapter you'll:

- Package custom tags and tag files into tag libraries.
- Deploy tags and tag libraries into Web applications.
- Use custom tags and tag libraries in JSPs.
- Create Tag Library Descriptors or use implicit TLDs.
- Memorise the common elements which appear in TLDs.

20 Tag Deployment

Before we go down the road of long and complicated XML syntax and deployment procedures, I must emphasise that none of the TLD syntax in this chapter is in the exam; to that effect, there are no questions at the end of the chapter on this subject. However, since you'll almost inevitably want to use the skills you have with tags at some point in the future, this chapter includes such information as a compact reference to everything you need to know about tag deployment.

In most respects, the assembly and deployment of tags is similar to that of a complete application, differing only in details. A tag library (see next section) should be designed to be reusable, and ideally portable between applications. Tag libraries are self-contained JARs which can easily be 'dropped' in and out of applications as required; this is a similar design strategy to Web applications, which as you'll recall can be 'dropped' in and out of the container, allowing vendors to provide 'pre-built' applications with common functionality. Another similarity between Web applications and tag libraries is the use of an XML descriptor file: WARs have a Deployment Descriptor, while tag libraries have a **Tag Library Descriptor (TLD)**. Finally, Web applications use a context root as a unique URI identifier, while tag libraries are identified and referenced using a similar URI system.

As you can see, many similarities can be drawn between the assembly and deployment of applications and tags and tag libraries, and we will use these to good effect in this chapter.

Tag Libraries

As we glossed over in the introduction, a tag library is a collection of related actions which usually (but don't necessarily) perform some common functionality. A good example is the Core JSP Standard Tag Library (JSTL) which contains actions used for basic flow control and iterative procedures, and replaces the need for traditional JSP scripting.

A tag library is simply a JAR file containing all the classic/simple tag handler classes, tag files and helper classes which comprise the library (Figure 20.1).

Additionally, a tag library must contain a Tag Library Descriptor (TLD) which describes to the container what actions are contained in the library, a description of their purpose, what attributes and body content they take etc.

Traditionally, a tag library JAR was permitted to contain only one TLD for the entire library; this was located at `/META-INF/taglib.tld`. As of version 1.2 of the JSP specification, multiple TLDs are permitted, each one representing a separate tag library. Hence, a single JAR archive may contain more than one tag library, each identified by a unique TLD. All TLDs should end in the extension `.tld` and should be deployed to the `/META-INF` directory, or any subdirectory of it.

Figure 20.1

Tag Library JARs

Assembly and Deployment

Each of the following sections looks at the individual procedures required for the assembly and deployment of tag libraries, tags and tag files respectively, since the procedures are different for each.

Tags and Tag Files in Tag Libraries

20

All tag handler classes are packaged in the normal way, just like normal class files, by being placed into the JAR under a path which maps to their package names. For example, the class file for `com.mydomain.taglibs.MyTag` would be located at `com/mydomain/taglibs/MyTag.class` inside the JAR.

All tag files must be placed in, or in any subdirectory of, the `/META-INF/tags` directory in the JAR. For example, the tag file `MyTagFile.tag` could be deployed directly to `/META-INF/tags/MyTagFile.tag`, or we could choose any subdirectory location such as /META-INF/tags/dirA/dirB/MyTagFile.tag.

Tag files which have been precompiled into tag handler classes are deployed in the same manner as all other tag handler classes.

A tag library descriptor (TLD) must accompany all tag handler classes and tag files in the JAR. Any tags or tag files which are not declared in the TLD will not be recognised or loaded by the container. Tags are declared using <tag> elements while the declaration of tag files is made using <tag-file> elements. Using both types of element in the same TLD allows tags and tag files to be combined in the same library. Each TLD should be deployed into the /META-INF directory or any subdirectory.

The resulting JAR must be deployed into the Web application archive under the /WEB-INF/lib directory as with any JAR used by the application (Figure 20.2).

Figure 20.2

Tag Library Assembly and Deployment

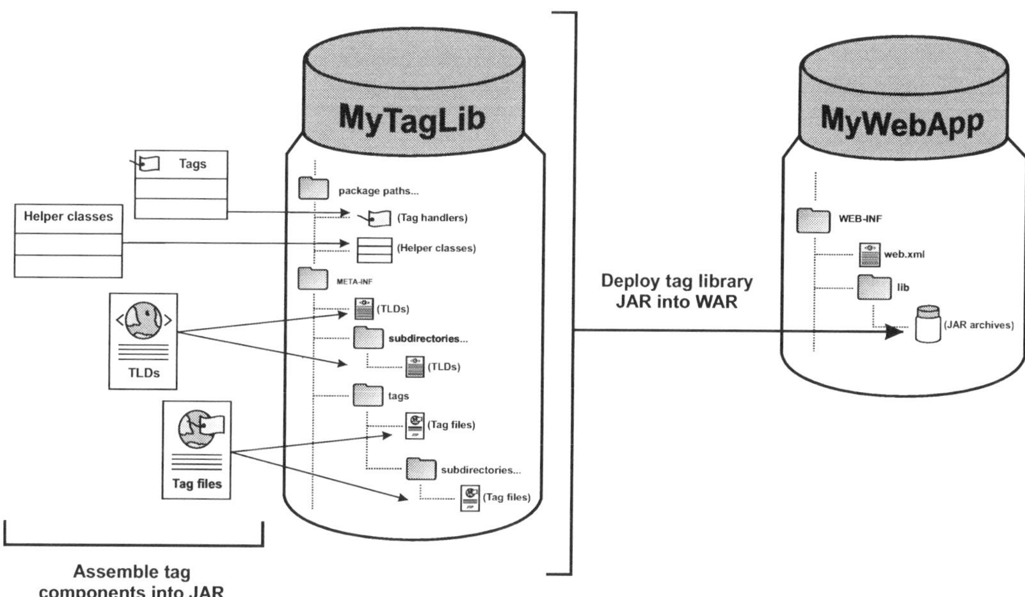

Tags in Applications

During the development stage of a tag, it may be more appropriate to drop the tag handler class file directly into the Web application archive. This can be achieved by deploying the `.class` file to the appropriate subdirectory (with name derived from the package name of the class) of `/WEB-INF/classes/` in the WAR, just as with any other class file which is to be accessible to the application.

All tags deployed in this manner must have one or more accompanying TLDs if they are to be available as tags. These TLDs should have the extension `.tld` and should be deployed to the `/WEB-INF` directory of the WAR, or indeed any subdirectory of `/WEB-INF/`. Multiple TLDs may be deployed, in which case each one represents an atomic library of tags.

Figure 20.3

Tags Deployed in Web Applications

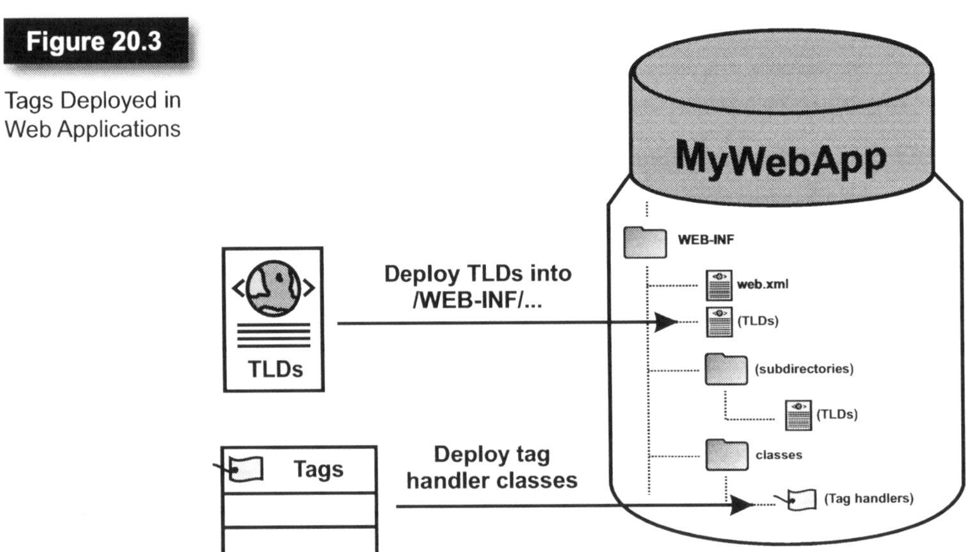

Tag Files in Applications

Tag files were created to make the construction and deployment of tags easier and faster. Like tag handler classes, tag files may also be deployed directly into the Web application archive; in fact, deployment of tag files in this way is easier than deployment in a JAR library, the reason being that *no TLD is required* (although one may optionally be supplied).

All tag files deployed in a WAR must be placed in the `/WEB-INF/tags` directory, or any subdirectory of it. At the same time, all tag files (identified by their `.tag` or `.tagx` extensions) deployed here are assigned an **implicit TLD** by the container.

The implicit TLD is created by the container as and when required, saving the need for the tag file author to write an explicit TLD. In fact, the `/WEB-INF/tags` directory is treated as one tag library, with all subdirectories being treated as individual tag libraries. An implicit TLD is therefore created by the container for each subdirectory, and each subdirectory therefore represents a distinct tag library.

For example, the following paths result in four different tag libraries:

- `/WEB-INF/tags/mytag1.tag`
- `/WEB-INF/tags/mytag2.tagx`
- `/WEB-INF/tags/dir1a/mytag3.tag`
- `/WEB-INF/tags/dir1a/dir1b/mytag4.tag`
- `/WEB-INF/tags/dir2/mytag5.tag`

The four libraries declared here are:

- `/WEB-INF/tags/` (containing 2 tag files)
- `/WEB-INF/tags/dir1a/` (containing 1 tag file)
- `/WEB-INF/tags/dir1a/dir1b/` (containing 1 tag file)
- `/WEB-INF/tags/dir2/` (containing 1 tag file)

Each tag contained in these directories is considered a part of its respective library. An implicit TLD is created for each of these paths. The next section looks at the structure of this TLD.

Additionally, a tag author may choose to create an explicit TLD for any/all tag files, for example to package both tag handler classes and tag files into a single library. Each explicit TLD must have a `.tld` extension and be deployed to the `/WEB-INF` directory, or any subdirectory, of the WAR. It is valid for both an explicit and implicit TLD to reference the same tag file. Each `<tag-file>` element in the explicit TLD must have a `<path>` element which points to the location of the tag file, starting with `/WEB-INF/tags/`.

Deployment of tag files in this manner is highly encouraged due to the truly 'pluggable' nature of the deployment method. Tag files may also be precompiled into tag handler classes, in which case they are deployed as classes with a TLD as discussed in the previous section, *Tags in Applications*.

20

Figure 20.4

Tag Files Deployed in Applications

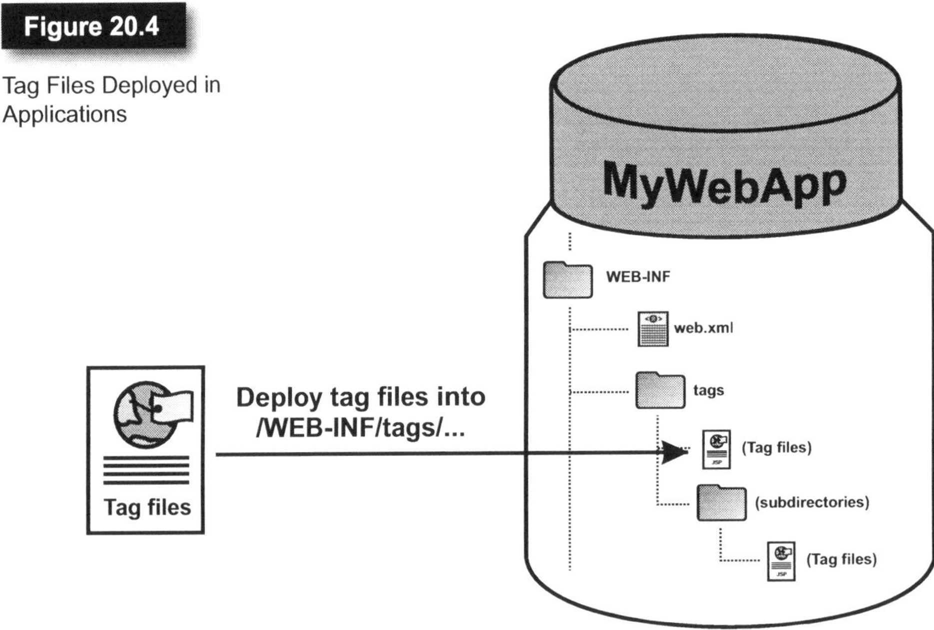

The Implicit TLD for Tag Files

We'll look at the implicit TLD structure here so we can determine whether an explicit TLD needs to be written for any tag files we develop, in order to provide a configuration other than the default.

For each directory a new TLD is created with the following structure:

```
<taglib>
    <tlib-version>1.0</tlib-version>
    <short-name><!-- a name for this library --></short-name>
    <!-- one or more <tag-file> elements -->
</taglib>
```

The `<short-name>` value for the library is derived using the following rules:

20

- If this library's directory is `/WEB-INF/tags/`, the short name is `tags`.
- Otherwise, the short name is the directory name created by removing the `/WEB-INF/tags/` prefix and replacing all subsequent `/` (forward slashes) with `-` (hyphens).

NOTE: `<short-name>` values may not be unique; for example, `/WEB-INF/tags/` has a short name of `tags` while `/WEB-INF/tags/tags/` also has a short name of `tags`. Also, due to the hyphenation replacement, the short name for `/WEB-INF/a/b/` is equivalent to the short name for `/WEB-INF/a-b/`. Although this is unlikely to cause problems since the short name has little programmatic consequence, some JSP authoring tools may use the short name as the XML prefix for actions declared in a JSP; you should therefore be cautious when using tag file paths which have the potential for conflicts.

A `<tag-file>` element is created for each tag file contained in the directory; it has the subelements `<name>`, whose body content is the filename of the tag file without the `.tag` or `.tagx` extension, and `<path>` whose body is the path of the tag file relative to the root of the WAR (i.e. beginning with `/WEB-INF/tags/`).

For example, for the tag file `/WEB-INF/tags/apple/pie/custard.tag`, the implicit TLD generated by the container would be:

```
<taglib>
    <tlib-version>1.0</tlib-version>
    <short-name>apple-pie</short-name>
    <tag-file>
        <name>custard</name>
        <path>/WEB-INF/tags/apple/pie/custard.tag</path>
    </tag-file>
</taglib>
```

When using the implicit TLD, it is the *name of the `.tag` file* that determines the name of the action that must be used in a JSP; if you wish to have different action and file names for a tag file, you will have to create an explicit TLD which specifically provides for this using the `<name>` element for the appropriate `<tag-file>`. Hence, using the implicit TLD, the `custard.tld` tag file will have the action name `custard`, and would be used in a JSP like this:

```
<custard ...>...</custard>
```

Using Tags in JSPs

20

This section revists the `taglib` JSP directive (and the equivalent JSP document configuration for using a tag library) and the `web.xml` deployment descriptor, placing more emphasis on how exactly tags, tag files and tag libraries can be used in applications. We will also see how the TLD is used as the focal point for the library.

The taglib Directive

Let's recap this directive's structure for a JSP page:

```
<%@ taglib ( uri="tagLibURI" | tagdir="tagDir" ) prefix="tagPrefix"
%>
```

The `( ... | ... )` syntax means that *either* the `uri` attribute *or* the `tagdir` attribute should be declared, but not both. For a JSP document, the tag library is identified with a URI by configuring an XML namespace and prefix for that library–for example, by using `xmlns` on `<jsp:root>`:

```
<jsp:root xmlns:jsp="http://java.sun.com/JSP/Page"
          xmlns:c="http://java.sun.com/jsp/jstl/core">
  <c:url value="/css/style.css" />
</jsp:root>
```

The namespace URI may also take the form `urn:jsptagdir:`*`path`* (where *`path`* starts with `/WEB-INF/tags/`) for an implicit tag file library deployed in the application (this replaces the `tagdir` attribute of the `taglib` directive), or the form `urn:jsptld:`*`path`* where *`path`* is the location of an explicit TLD. See also *Directives and Scripting Elements* in Chapter 14.

The `uri` attribute on the `taglib` directive is used to declare a URI (either absolute or relative) which is used by the container to uniquely identify the TLD, which in turn is used to load the tag library (since the TLD is the descriptor for the entire library). We look at what exactly this URI means in the section which follows.

The `tagdir` attribute on the directive is used to identify the path to a *tag file* directory for which an implicit TLD exists. Since all qualifying tag files are deployed into the `/WEB-INF/tags` directory (or a subdirectory), a translation error will occur if the value of this attribute does not begin with `/WEB-INF/tags/` or if it does not point to a valid directory.

The `prefix` attribute identifies the XML namespace prefix which is used to distinguish actions from different tag libraries in the JSP. A translation error will occur if the prefix attribute is omitted or the value is empty.

For example, the JSTL 1.1 core tag library's TLD has a URI of `http://java.sun.com/jsp/jstl/core` and hence, if we choose to use the `c` prefix (although we are free to choose any) then:

20

```
<%@ taglib uri="http://java.sun.com/jsp/jstl/core" prefix="c" %>
```

declares the use of the JSTL core tag library.

If we have a tag file at the location `/WEB-INF/tags/apple/pie/custard.tag`, then we can make use of the implicit TLD generated by the container by using the `tagdir` attribute rather than referencing an explicit TLD using the `uri` attribute:

```
<%@ taglib tagdir="/WEB-INF/tags/apple/pie/" prefix="bananas" %>
```

The `custard.tag` tag file is referenced by the implicit TLD to the action with name `custard`, as discussed in the previous section, so we can invoke our action using the following JSP syntax:

```
<bananas:custard ... />
```

Identifying and Locating Explicit TLDs with URIs

In the previous section we saw that a URI is used to locate the TLD of a tag library. What we didn't however discuss is what format the URI takes, or what it really means.

Every TLD is associated with a URI which is unique to that tag library. This mapping is either found in the TLD itself, or in the deployment descriptor. When the container loads the application, it gathers together all the TLD files it can find and maintains a mapping between TLD files (and hence tag libraries) and URIs. The location of a TLD file is known as its TLD resource path; the mapping which is maintained by the container is known as the **taglib map**. Each TLD resource path is specified as a context-relative path starting with a `/`, while the URI may be relative or absolute.

NOTE: The URI associated with a tag library is *arbitrary*, and can be decided by either the tag library author (preferred) or the application deployer, but it should be *unique* for every different tag library which exists. To avoid naming conflicts, it is recommended that the URI associated with a library broadly follow the URL of the tag author's website, or in the case of a URI chosen by the application deployer, the URL of the website on which the application is running. For example, the JSTL libraries start with `http://java.sun.com/` which is unambiguously the Java site maintained by Sun.

When a JSP requires the use of a tag library, it notifies the container which library to use by referencing the required URI. The container subsequently looks up the TLD resource path in the taglib map in order to obtain the TLD's description of the library; from the TLD, the container is able to determine the precise location of the tag handler classes and tag files used in the library.

Figure 20.5 outlines the process by which the container first builds the taglib map of TLDs, and the method by which JSPs refer (indirectly) to tag libraries using URIs.

The container generates the taglib map by the following rules which are conducted *in this order*:

1. The taglib map *in the deployment descriptor* (`web.xml`) is examined for TLD-to-URI mappings; these mappings are made using `<taglib>` elements (see Chapter 10).
2. Next all TLDs are examined for so-called **implicit map entries** which are made using *the* `<uri>` *element of the TLD*. The container searches both packaged JAR libraries for all TLDs under `/META-INF/`, and all TLDs under `/WEB-INF/` in the application.
3. Implicit map entries *from the container* are added to the taglib map. These are installed by your Java EE server vendor and reference common libraries like the JSTL.

Figure 20.5

Building and Using the Taglib Map

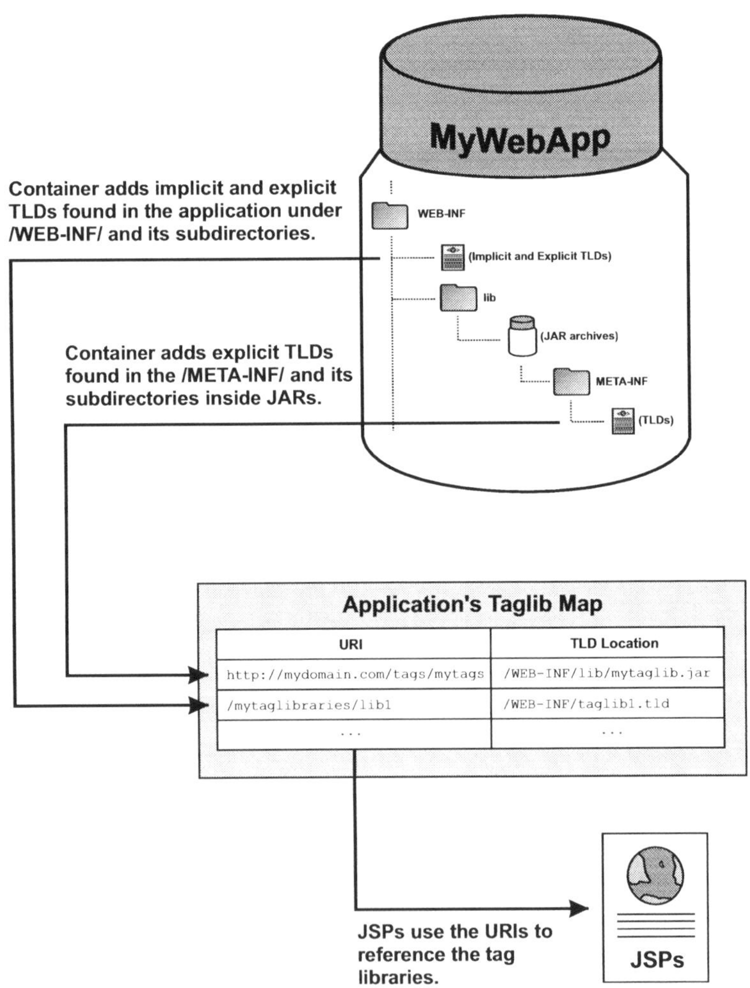

A URI used for taglib mapping may be either absolute or relative, with no restrictions on its format. An absolute URI is defined here to begin with a scheme (e.g. `http://`) and a host; relative URIs contain neither a scheme nor a host. It is valid for multiple URIs to reference the same tag library (for example, one URI from `web.xml` and one from the TLD itself), but not for a single URI to reference multiple libraries; each unique URI declared must point to *only one library*.

If the URI used in a JSP `taglib` directive does not map to any entries in the taglib map then the container uses the **fallback mechanism**:

- If it is an absolute URI, a translation error occurs.
- If it is a relative URI given relative to the context (i.e. starting with a `/`), it is assumed to point to the location of the TLD relative to the application's context.
- If it is a relative URI given with no opening forward-slash (`/`), it is assumed to point to the location of a TLD relative to the JSP in which the directive is used.

For example, suppose mappings exist for the following URIs in the taglib map:

- `http://mydomain.com/tags/mytags`
- `/mytaglibraries/lib1`

The following is a list of URIs used in JSP `taglib` directives; under each, the container's interpretation of the URI is given:

- `http://mydomain.com/tags/mytags`
  This maps to a TLD specified in the taglib map.
- `http://mydomain.com/othertags`
  A translation error occurs; this URI does not exist in the taglib map and is absolute.
- `/mytaglibraries/lib1`
  This maps to a TLD specified in the taglib map.
- `/WEB-INF/lib2.tld`
  This references the TLD located at this context-relative location.
- `../../WEB-INF/lib3.tld`
  This relative URI references a TLD located in the `/WEB-INF` directory contained under the path `../../`. If this is to work correctly (and not result in a translation error), the JSP must be located in, for example, the directory `/a/b/` underneath the application's context.

The deployment descriptor (`web.xml`) syntax for TLD-to-URI mappings (using

20

<taglib>) is discussed in Chapter 10. The syntax for the implicit map entries found in the <uri> elements of TLDs is discussed along with the other TLD syntax below.

Which URI Mechanism Should I Use?

Okay, so there are lots of ways to assemble tags and deploy TLDs – but which one is best? My advice goes a little like this:

- If you're a *tag library author*, all your libraries should be associated with a default URI; as an example, the JSTL 1.1 core library is associated with `http://java.sun.com/jsp/jstl/core` and we know this *always* references the same library – it's highly unambiguous. If page authors choose to use the default URI you provide, then assuming that the library is installed correctly, the Deployer need supply no further mappings in the deployment descriptor. The default URI can be configured as an implicit map entry using the <uri> element of the TLD.
- If you're an *application deployer*, and you know that some libraries assembled in the application don't provide implicit map entries, or some JSPs use URIs which don't match the default URIs provided by the libraries, then configure the URIs using <taglib> elements in the deployment descriptor (`web.xml`).
- If you're a *page author*, and are using tag files which are deployed into the application directly and make use of an implicit TLD, use the `tagdir` attribute of the `taglib` directive to reference those tag files.
- *Never, ever,* rely on the 'fallback mechanism' for URI resolution; using a relative URI in a JSP which is supposed to point to a TLD directly in the application doesn't provide any flexibility. Suppose, for instance, that the name of the TLD for a given library changes – you'll have to go back through *all* the JSPs you created to update the URIs to point to the new file. The preferred alternative is to configure the TLD locations in the deployment descriptor – if the name of the TLD ever changes, you only need to update *one* reference in the deployment descriptor without breaking all your JSP components. Similarly, always avoid using the page-relative URIs (those without an opening `/`) to point to a TLD, since if you move the JSP and not the TLD file, you'll destroy the reference that way as well!

20

Tag Library Descriptor (TLD) Syntax

A TLD is an XML document which describes a tag library and the tags it contains. This section looks at the element syntax and structure of a JSP 2.0 TLD; this version of the TLD is described by an XML Schema while previous versions of the TLD had DTD descriptors. There are some discrepancies between the Schema and DTD implementations, particularly with respect to the multiplicities of elements. Since the new 2.0 Schema implementation added support for tag files, support which is not present in the DTDs, this reference concentrates on the 2.0 TLD format. Consult the JSP specifications or the DTDs provided with your Java EE server for compatibility with JSP 1.1 or 1.2 of the TLD.

General TLD Template

The XML Schema for the 2.0 TLD is:

```
http://java.sun.com/xml/ns/j2ee/web-jsptaglibrary_2_0.xsd
```

Your Java EE server will also probably provide a local copy of the schema; consult your server's documentation for more details.

The general format of a typical TLD will be:

```
<?xml version="1.0" ?>
<taglib xmlns="http://java.sun.com/xml/ns/j2ee"
    xmlns:xsi="http://www.w3.org/2001/XMLSchema-instance"
    xsi:schemaLocation="http://java.sun.com/xml/ns/j2ee/web-
jsptaglibrary_2_0.xsd" version="2.0">

    <!-- taglib child elements (see Figure 20.6) -->

</taglib>
```

NOTE: Either the `version` attribute must be declared in the root element (for a schema-validated document as above), or when using DTD validation, `<jsp-version>2.0</jsp-version>` must appear after the `<tlib-version>` element. Failure to provide this version information will result in an error.

The TLD Elements

Figure 20.6

<taglib> Schema

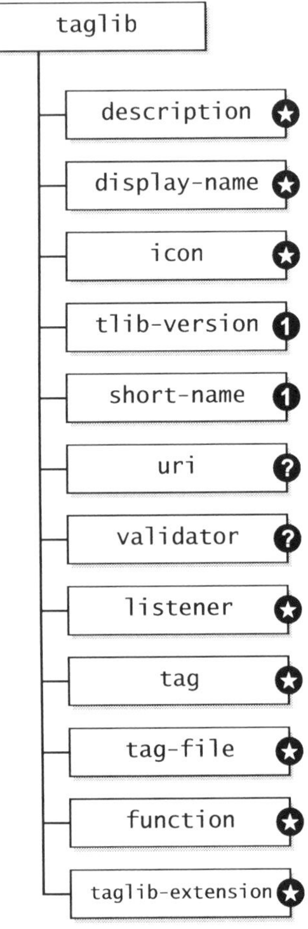

<taglib> Root Element

The `<description>`, `<display-name>` and `<icon>` elements all have the same meaning as they do in the deployment descriptor (see Chapter 10).

The `<tlib-version>` element is used to describe the version of the tag library represented by the TLD; this element allows authors to keep track of different editions of their tag libraries by changing every edition's version number. In general, although the format of this number is not dictated, higher numbers indicate later versions of the same library.

The value of the `<short-name>` element should be a mnemonic value which succinctly describes this library and can, for example, be used by JSP authoring tools to provide the default XML namespace prefix for actions in this tag library.

The optional `<uri>` element can be used by the tag author to associate the tag library with a default URI. This mapping is added to the container's taglib map when the container loads this TLD. If you do not wish to provide a default URI, but instead wish to rely on either the application's `web.xml` mappings or the 'fallback mechanism' used by the container when loading tag libraries from URIs, omit this element. Omitting `<uri>` is a highly unrecommended practice to be avoided where at all possible.

20

<validator>

The `<validator>` element can be used to supply the fully-qualified class name of an appropriate `javax.servlet.jsp.tagext.TagLibraryValidator` subclass. A tag library author will want to create and use a `TagLibraryValidator` when the tag library needs to impose its own strict translation-time validation on the XML view of each JSP in which the library is used. See the Java EE API documentation for details on the `TagLibraryValidator` class.

The value of the `<validator-class>` element should be the fully-qualified class name of the concrete `TagLibraryValidator` subclass to use for validation. The `<init-param>` element can be used to specify zero or more name/value pairs which are used to initialise the validator instance before it is required to validate its first JSP. These initialisation parameters are used in just the same way as those in the deployment descriptor for servlets and filters.

Figure 20.7

<validator> Schema

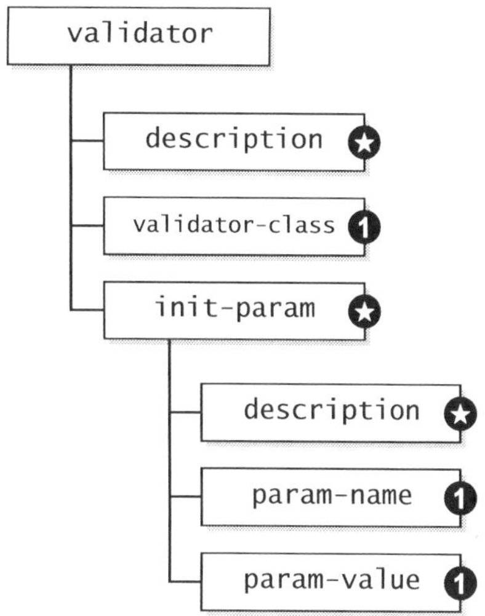

<listener>

The tag library may also listen for servlet-based events which are raised in the container; for example, a tag library may need to know when a session is being destroyed. The tag library author uses zero or more of the TLD's `<listener>` element to specify listeners to be called when changes occur to the servlet environment in the container.

The only child element of significance here is `<listener-class>` which is used to specify the fully-qualified class name of the listener which must be initialised by the container. Note that unlike listeners configured in the deployment descriptor, the container provides no guarantee as to the order in which listeners in TLDs will be registered. The class specified will most likely be an implementation of one of the listener interfaces found in the `javax.servlet` or `javax.servlet.http` packages.

Figure 20.8

<listener> Schema

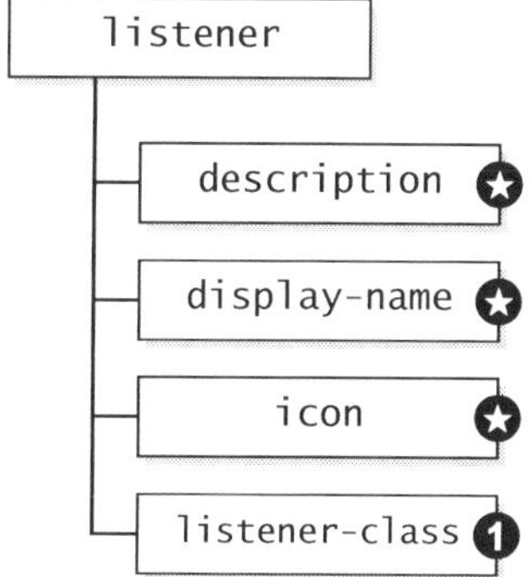

<tag>

Figure 20.9

<tag> Schema

Each instance of the `<tag>` element specifies an individual tag to be found in the library. Each tag may be used as an action in JSPs. Unfortunately, due to the relatively complex natures of tags, there are many subelements to be considered.

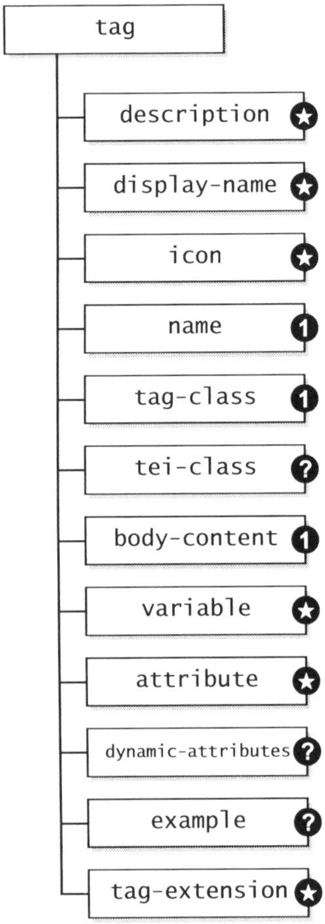

The `<name>` element specifies the action name that will be referenced from JSPs using this tag library; this name should be unique within this tag library. For example, if the value of this element were `action1` and a JSP used the prefix `lib` for this library, then:

```
<lib:action1 ... />
```

is used to invoke this tag in the JSP.

The `<tag-class>` element specifies the fully-qualified class name of the tag handler class implementing `javax.servlet.jsp.tagext.JspTag`.

The `<tei-class>` element is used to provide the fully-qualified class name of an optional `javax.servlet.jsp.tagext.TagExtraInfo` subclass. A `TagExtraInfo` class is used to provide additional translation-time information to the container which is not available from the TLD. For example, it can be used:

- to indicate that the tag defines scripting variables;
- to perform translation-time validation of tag attributes.

Like `TagLibraryValidators`, this provides the library author with more power and flexibility than is offered just by the TLD. Consult the Java EE API documentation for details of the `TagExtraInfo` class.

The `<body-content>` element is used to specify the types of body content which the action used in the JSP may possess. The value of this element may be one of four strings:

- **`empty`**
  The body of the action must be empty.
- **`tagdependent`**
  The body of the action is passed directly to the tag implementation itself without being processed by the container; this allows the body of the action to be in a language not recognised by the container (e.g. SQL). Of course, the content may also just be plain text.
- **`JSP`**
  The body of the action may contain any nested JSP syntax or actions. This will result in an error if applied to `SimpleTags` or tag files.
- **`scriptless`**
  The body must not contain any traditional JSP scripting elements. It may contain template text, EL expressions and nested JSP actions.

The `<variable>` and `<attribute>` elements are used to specify the scripting variables and permitted attributes of the action, respectively, and are discussed separately in the following two sections.

The `<dynamic-attributes>` element, if present, determines whether this tag will accept attributes with dynamic names at run time. If the value is `true`, indicating that dynamic attributes are accepted, the tag handler class must implement the `javax.servlet.jsp.tagext.DynamicAttributes` interface. Otherwise, if the value is `false` (the default if the element is omitted), dynamic attributes are not permitted; an action subsequently attempting to use dynamic attributes will cause an exception to be raised.

The `<example>` element can be used by the tag library author to provide an informal description string of the syntax used by this action; this can be displayed by JSP authoring tools or by appropriately sophisticated containers.

The `<tag-extension>` element can be used primarily by tools to add their own additional information to that already provided in the TLD. The data type assigned to `<extension-element>` is abstract, and hence the data type used for each element should be specified using the `xsi:type` attribute. The namespace attribute essentially identifies the tool to which this extension belongs; the `id` attribute specifies the name of this extension. It is unlikely that tag library authors will need to use `<tag-extension>` directly.

Figure 20.10

<tag-extension> Schema

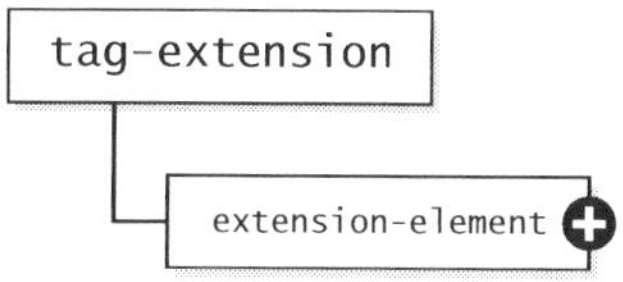

20

<variable>

This element is used to specify the scripting variables exposed by the tag. Using this element in the TLD is the simplest way to specify the variables exposed by the tag; a more sophisticated mechanism uses the `TagExtraInfo` class and the `<tei-class>` subelement of `<tag>`. Most often, detailing the variable requirements in the TLD is sufficient and since it is declarative, is preferred. Consult the API documentation for details of the `TagExtraInfo` class; we discussed `<tei-class>` previously.

Figure 20.11

<variable> Schema

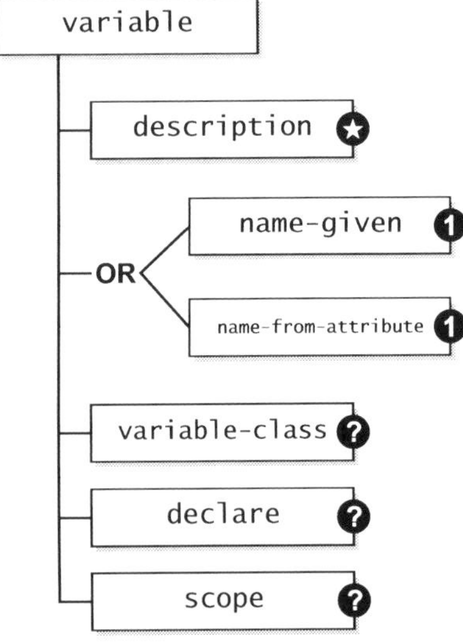

You will recall that a scripting variable can either be given a 'static' name by the tag, in which case it will always expose a variable with this name, or that the variable's name can be dynamically determined from the value of an attribute declared by the JSP author at run time. To declare a scripting variable with a 'static' name, we use the `<name-given>` element with value the name of the variable.

To determine the name of the exposed scripting variable from a supplied attribute, we use the `<name-from-attribute>` element whose body is the name of the attribute from which the variable name is to be extracted. The attribute specified must also be declared in the TLD (as an `<attribute>`) and must have the following properties:

- It must be marked as required.
- It must have a data type of `String`.
- Its value must not be determined at run time from any request-time expression (such as a JSP scripting element or an EL expression).

These rules determine the exact configuration of the `<attribute>` from which this scripting variable's name will be determined:

```
<attribute>
    <name><!-- same as <name-from-attribute> value --></name>
    <required>true</required>
    <rtexprvalue>false</rtexprvalue>
    <type>java.lang.String</type>
</attribute>
```

The <variable-class> element contains the fully-qualified class name of the data type of the exposed scripting variable; primitives are not permitted (consider using one of the primitive wrapper objects instead). The default if the element is omitted is `java.lang.String`.

The <declare> element should have a value of `true` (the default) if the scripting variable should declare a new variable in the calling page; if the variable would not be accessible based on its context (for example, a `NESTED` variable is not much use in a `scriptless` body), the value of <declare> can be `false`.

The <scope> element is used to declare the synchronisation scope of the exposed variable; it must be one of the strings:

- **`NESTED`** (the default)
  This indicates that the scripting variable exists only for the duration of the action's invocation only–i.e. within the action's body, between the start and end tags, only.
- **`AT_BEGIN`**
  This indicates that the scripting variable is available from the start tag of the action until the end of the action's own scope (which may be the end of the entire JSP).
- **`AT_END`**
  This value indicates that the scripting variable is available only after the end tag of the action and until the end of the action's own scope in the JSP.

For more information on synchronisation and scoping, refer back to Chapter 18 where we discussed variable synchronisation in detail.

<attribute> Schema

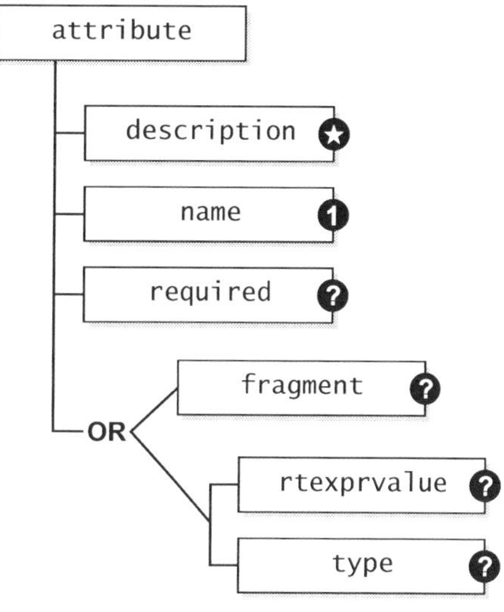

<attribute>

For every attribute that an action may take, a new <attribute> subelement is required in the <tag> describing that action.

The <name> element is used to configure the name of the attribute for which this <attribute> applies.

The <required> element is used to determine whether the attribute is required or not; if the value is `true`, indicating

20

that this attribute is required, and the attribute does not appear in the action at translation time, an error occurs. If the value is `false` (the default if this element is omitted), the attribute may be declared optionally by the JSP author.

The `<fragment>` element is used for `SimpleTag` handlers. If the tag requires the dynamic evaluation of the attribute several times, it will want the attribute's value encapsulated as an object which can be invoked multiple times. It can request that the container encapsulates it in a `javax.servlet.jsp.tagext.JspFragment` object which can then be invoked as required by the `SimpleTag` implementation. We first saw the `JspFragment` mechanism for `SimpleTag` handlers in Chapter 18. If this encapsulation is required by the tag, set the value of the `<fragment>` element to `true`; otherwise it is best to omit the element. Using a value of `true` here implies also that:

- `<rtexprvalue>true</rtexprvalue>`
- `<type>javax.servlet.jsp.tagext.JspFragment</type>`

If `<fragment>` is not used, then both `<rtexprvalue>` and `<type>` may be declared with any valid values.

`<rtexprvalue>` determines whether the attribute is permitted to contain request-time expressions (JSP scripting elements and EL expressions). If `true`, scripting elements and EL expressions are allowed; if `false` (the default if no fragment is used and the element is omitted) and the author includes scripting element or EL code in the attribute's value, a translation-time error is raised.

`<type>` is used to set the fully-qualified class name of the attribute type that is expected; primitives are also permitted—e.g. `boolean` is treated the same as its `Boolean` wrapper. The default value if the element is omitted is `java.lang.String`.

<tag-file>

This element is used to configure each tag file found in the library. To the world outside the library, tag files look just the same as simple tags, but due to their different semantics, they must be configured separately.

20

What might first strike you about the subelement list is that there are no attribute/variable declarations. This is of course deliberate, since attributes and exposed variables are configured *in the tag file* and not in the TLD (see Chapter 19 on tag files). This somewhat simplifies the TLD syntax.

The `<name>` element specifies the action name that authors will use in JSPs; this is the same as for `<tag>`.

The `<path>` element is unique to tag files. It specifies the location of the tag file with extension .tag or .tagx. For tags deployed directly into the application, this path must be relative to the root of the Web application and must begin with /WEB-INF/tags/. For tags deployed in a tag library JAR, this path is relative to the root of the JAR and must begin with /META-INF/tags/.

The <example> element can be used by the tag library author to provide an informal description string of the syntax used by this action; this can be displayed by JSP authoring tools or by appropriately sophisticated containers.

The <tag-extension> element has the same function and syntax as the <tag-extension> subelement of <tag>.

Figure 20.13

<tag-file> Schema

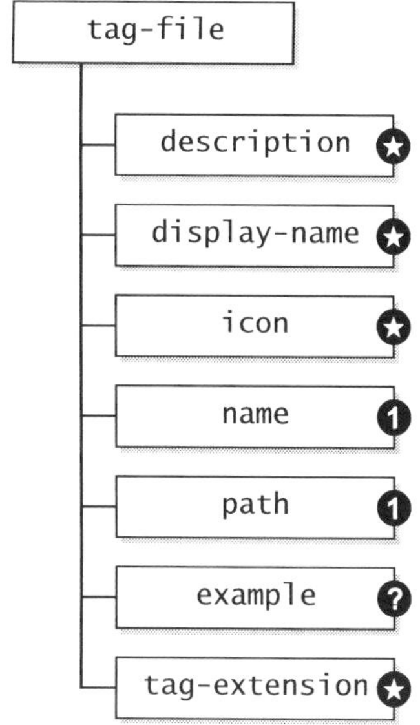

<function>

When we discussed the Expression Language in Chapter 15, we looked at how to use and write EL functions. We also said that the configuration of EL functions is provided for in the TLD and we referred to this chapter. Indeed, it is the <function> element of the TLD that is used to specify EL functions and map them to Java methods.

The value of the <name> element is the name of the exposed EL function. Note that this name does not have to match the name of the Java method used to implement the function.

The <function-class> element specifies the fully-qualified class name which contains the Java method to be invoked when the EL function is called.

The <function-signature> element specifies the partial method signature of the Java method which implements the EL

Figure 20.14

<function> Schema

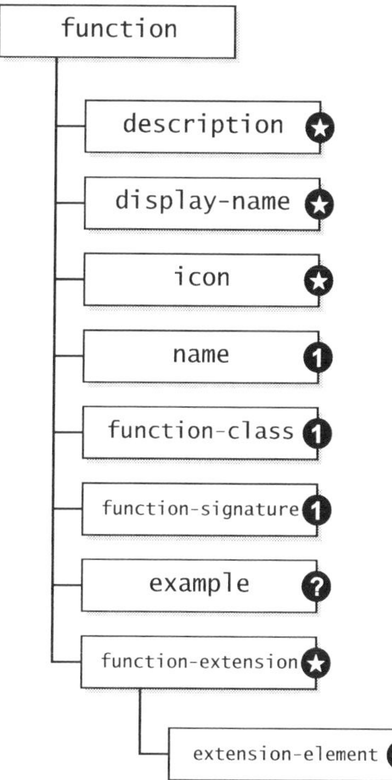

20

function. This method signature should include only:

- The return data type;
- The method name;
- The parameter data types.

While the implementation method must be public and static as well, this is not reflected in the value of the `<function-signature>` element. Referring back to the example first given in Chapter 15:

```
<function>
  <name>exchange</name>
  <function-class>mypackage.MyExchangeClass</function-class>
  <function-signature>
    float exchangeConversion(java.lang.String, java.lang.String,
float)
  </function-signature>
 </function>
```

This specifies an EL function called `exchange` which is implemented by the public and static method `exchangeConversion()` in the class `mypackage.MyExchangeClass`. The return type of the method (and hence of the EL function) is `float` and the parameter data types are `String`, `String` and `float` in that order. The method might be implemented as follows (this was first in Chapter 15):

```
package mypackage;

public class MyExchangeClass {
    public static float exchangeConversion(String from,String to,
                                            float amount) {
        float calculatedAmount = 0.0f;
        // implementation code
        return calculatedAmount;
    }
}
```

Any Java methods returning `void` cause the EL function to return `null`.

The `<example>` element can be used by the tag library author to provide an informal description of the syntax of the EL function.

The `<function-extension>` element has practically the same purpose and syntax as the `<tag-extension>` subelement of `<tag>`. It is typically of little consequence to TLD authors.

20

<taglib-extension>

This element has the same purpose and syntax as the `<tag-extension>` subelement of `<tag>` but is applicable to the entire tag library rather than one individual tag. It is typically of little consequence to TLD authors.

Revision Questions

NOTE: The TLD syntax covered in the chapter is not an exam objective, so there are no questions covering it below. The questions below refer to the deployment of tags and tag libraries only.

1 **A tag library is contained in the MyTagsv1.jar file; where should this be deployed in the application's WAR in order to use the tags in the application?** **(choose one)**

- A /WEB-INF/tags/
- B /WEB-INF/taglib/
- C /WEB-INF/classes/
- D /WEB-INF/lib/
- E /WEB-INF/taglibs/

2 **In what file or to what path in a tag library JAR should a TLD for the library reside?** **(choose one)**

- A Any path.
- B /WEB-INF/web.xml
- C /META-INF/taglib.tld
- D /WEB-INF/taglib.tld
- E /META-INF/ or any subdirectory.

3 **Tag files deployed as part of a tag library JAR should reside in which path of the JAR?** **(choose one)**

- A /tags/
- B /META-INF/tags/
- C /META-INF/tags/ or any subdirectory.
- D /META-INF/tagfiles/
- E /META-INF/tagfiles/ or any subdirectory

4 **Tag handler classes and pre-compiled tag files should be deployed to which path in a tag library JAR?** **(choose one)**

- A /META-INF/compiled
- B /META-INF/lib/
- C /META-INF/tags/
- D /META-INF/classes/
- E None of the above

5 **After deploying a tag library JAR already associated with a URI to /WEB-INF/lib/, what other steps must be taken to ensure the tag library can be used by the application?** **(choose one)**

- A The JAR file URI must be mapped to a Web application local URI in the deployment descriptor.
- B The TLD files in the JAR library must be mapped to local URIs in the deployment descriptor.
- C The TLD files in the JAR must be extracted and placed in /WEB-INF/ or any subdirectory.
- D None of the above.

6 **When an unpackaged tag library is deployed directly into a Web application's WAR, which of the following should be performed?** **(choose three)**

- A Deploy tag handlers to /WEB-INF/tags/
- B Deploy tag files to /WEB-INF/tags/
- C Deploy TLDs to /WEB-INF/tlds/
- D Deploy tag handlers to /WEB-INF/classes/
- E Deploy TLDs to /WEB-INF/
- F Reference the TLDs in the deployment descriptor.

7 **A tag file is deployed directly to the Web application into the file /WEB-INF/tags/library/mytag.tag. Which of the following statements are true?** **(choose two)**

- A A TLD must be created and deployed to /WEB-INF/ or a subdirectory to refer to the new tag file.
- B The tag file must first be translated by the container before it can be used.
- C A JSP page using this tag library with prefix my should declare the following: <%@ taglib uri="/WEB-INF/tags/library/mytag.tag" prefix="my" %>
- D A JSP page using this tag library with prefix my should declare the following: <%@ taglib tagdir="/WEB-INF/tags/library" prefix="my" %>
- E The tag will have the name library-mytag, and therefore can be invoked by <my:library-mytag>.

20

8 **Which of the following is the correct way to associate a tag library with prefix my in a JSP document, where the library is referenced by an explicit TLD deployed directly to /WEB-INF/mytags.tld in the Web application's WAR?** **(choose one)**

- A <jsp:root xmlns:my="/WEB-INF/mytags.tld" ...>
- B <jsp:root xmlns:my="urn:tagdir:/WEB-INF/mytags.tld" ...>
- C <jsp:root xmlns:my="tld:mytags.tld" ...>
- D <jsp:root xmlns:my="urn:jsptld:/WEB-INF/mytags.tld" ...>
- E <jsp:root xmlns:my="urn:tld:/WEB-INF/mytags.tld" ...>

9 **Which of the following is the correct way to associate a tag library with prefix my in a JSP document, where the library is deployed as a set of tag files in /WEB-INF/tags/mylib/?** **(choose one)**

- A <jsp:root xmlns:my="/WEB-INF/tags/mylib" ...>
- B <jsp:root xmlns:my="urn:tagdir:/WEB-INF/tags/mylib" ...>
- C <jsp:root xmlns:my="urn:jsptagdir:/WEB-INF/tags/mylib" ...>
- D <jsp:root xmlns:my="tagdir:/WEB-INF/tags/mylib" ...>
- E <jsp:root xmlns:my="jsptagdir:mylib" ...>

10 **A unpackaged tag library is deployed directly into the Web application's WAR, with its TLD deployed to /WEB-INF/mylib.tld; which of the following are valid ways to associate this library with prefix my in a JSP page?** **(choose two)**

- A Associate the TLD with a URI in the deployment descriptor and use that URI in the JSP page's taglib directive.
- B Associate the TLD with a URI in the deployment descriptor and use that URI in a <jsp-config> element to configure the tag library with a prefix for all pages.
- C Use <%@ taglib uri="/WEB-INF/mylib.tld" prefix="my" %> in the JSP.
- D Use <%@ taglib tagtld="/WEB-INF/mylib.tld" prefix="my" %> in the JSP.
- E None of these are required; all explicit TLDs are automatically associated with prefixes by the container.

Answers to Revision Questions

1 **Correct answer: D**

Like *every* JAR used in a Web application, tag library JARs should be deployed into /WEB-INF/lib/.

2 **Correct answer: E**

For JARed libraries, E is correct. C is more specific, and was the only valid way to specify a (single) TLD before JSP 1.2. A is far too general and is incorrect. B is the deployment descriptor *inside a WAR*, so is incorrect. D would be one possibility, if deploying a tag library and TLD directly into a Web application.

3 **Correct answer: C**

Note that tag files deployed in this way must also be referred to in an explicit TLD inside the JAR in order to be 'visible' to the outside world.

4 **Correct answer: E**

As with normal JARs, class files should be deployed to a directory depending on their package – so for example, com.mytags.MyLoopTag would be deployed to /com/mytags/MyLoopTag.class.

5 **Correct answer: D**

We are told that the tag library is already associated with a URI. This means that the implicit taglib map in the container will be updated to include all tags in this library when the JAR is deployed. All we have to do to use the tags is include a taglib directive pointing to the correct URI in each JSP (or for a group in the deployment descriptor). Note that A and B are completely incorrect and should never be attempted; C is correct only for unpackaged tag libraries deployed directly into the application, and is unnecessary here.

6 **Correct answers: B, D, E**

Note that F is not required because the container automatically searches for TLDs deployed under /WEB-INF/ and therefore no explicit mapping is necessary.

20

7 **Correct answers: B, D**

A is incorrect as no explicit TLD is required – the container creates an implicit TLD; B is correct because a tag file is a JSP, and all JSPs must be translated and compiled before their first invocation; C is incorrect, you should not use the uri attribute; D uses the tagdir attribute correctly; E is incorrect because the implicit TLD gives a tag the same name as its *file* (and not path), and therefore you would actually use <my:mytag>.

8 **Correct answer: D**

9 **Correct answer: C**

10 **Correct answers: A, C**

If you actually ever do deploy a tag library in this way (a far better alternative is pre-packaged in a JAR), it is far better to associate it immediately with an application-specific URI using the deployment descriptor and the <taglib> subelement of <jsp-config>; this is what A achieves. B is erroneous, as all library/prefix associations must be done on a per-page or per-tag file basis using a directive. D is incorrect, as it uses the nonexistent tagtld attribute; C is the correct variant, using the 'fallback mechanism'. E is incorrect, as although the container automatically locates the TLD upon deployment, you must at least associate this with a prefix in each JSP it is used in.

IV PART 4

Further Topics

Chapter Overview

21. Security

Declaritive container- and server-wide security is one of the major advantages of Java EE over other server-side programming languages. This chapter examines how to best make use of this feature, as well as mentionining some of the benefits of programmatic security and citing some useful resources.

22. Design Patterns

Reusing proven code makes a lot of sense. This chapter outlines the key design patterns which can make building Web applications faster and ensure a more reliable result by choosing the right sort of components for each task, and ensuring they cooperate well.

In this chapter you'll:

- Learn the key terms: authentication, authorisation, integrity and confidentiality.
- Understand basic, digest, form and SSL authentication techniques.
- Configure declarative authentication.
- Perform authorisation on application components based on user roles.
- Apply resource constraints for data integrity and confidentiality.
- Review the security-focused deployment descriptor syntax.
- Briefly examine programmatic security (non-examinable).

21 Security

Almost all Web application developers will, at some stage in their career, be concerned about the safety of their application and the data transmitted between it and the client. The immediate concerns which spring to mind would likely cover a broad range of possible infiltration targets: the client and server machines, the transmission channel between the server and client, how data is stored on the server, and how secure passwords are for critical resources like databases. Most of these issues already outlined are the responsibility of the server or network administrators, and as such are not our concern. As application developers, we are primarily interested in the following aspects of security:

- How do we prove that a user really is who they claim to be? This process is called **authentication**.
- Is a user permitted to access a certain resource – are they logged in with a valid username and password? This is known as **authorisation**: is a user authorised to access a resource?
- Can we make sure that data is transmitted without corruption or modification by a third party? This ensures that **data integrity** is maintained.
- Can we secure communications with the client using, for example, Secure HTTP (HTTPS)? This is taking steps to ensure **confidentiality** (**data privacy**) – a third party is unable eavesdrop on our secret or private communications.

These goals lie at the software-level of an application, not with the hardware issues like open ports and the correct use of firewalls. The Java EE platform is incredibly helpful with security issues: using the deployment descriptor for an application, we can specify **declarative security** requirements; being able to do this is the only security-based exam objective. For completeness, we will look briefly at how a finer-grained security model can be built using **programmatic security** – i.e. programming security requirements ourselves using Java code rather than relying on the container's declarative security model, which may not suit every application's needs.

Authentication Basics

Authentication is the process of confirming the identity of a user.

Methods for Authentication

Java EE 5 provides four ways in which to authenticate a user. Three of these rely on a username and password, while the fourth uses more sophisticated encryption technology. Thankfully, we don't need to know anything about the underlying mechanisms for the exam, and I don't propose to discuss the mathematics behind today's cryptography here!

The data used to authenticate a user are known as the **credentials** of that user; **valid credentials** result in a user being authenticated and 'logged in', while **invalid credentials** represent their failure to provide sufficient or correct information. The provision of invalid credentials will prevent the user from being authenticated, and as such they will not be authorised to access restricted resources.

Basic Authentication

At its most basic, authentication relies on the client to ask for a username and password. When using a browser, this normally results in a pop-up window with the requisite fields as shown in Figure 21.1.

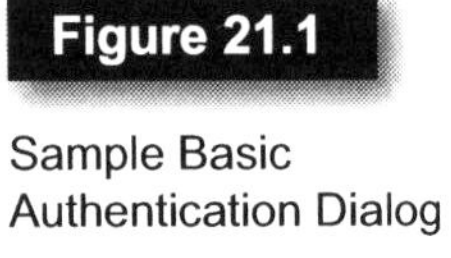

Figure 21.1

Sample Basic Authentication Dialog

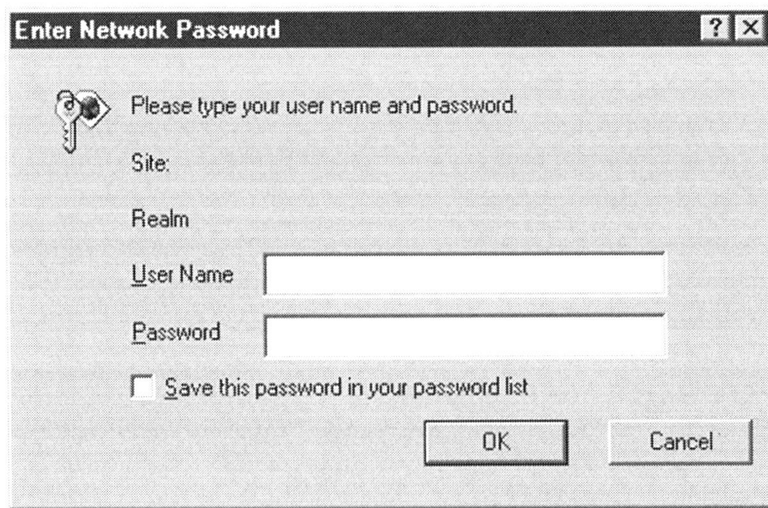

This method of authentication is simple to implement, but provides a platform- and browser-dependent dialog window which may not suit the style of your application. This type of authentication uses HTTP headers to request authentication data from the client and to transmit the input data back to the server.

Digest Authentication

One of the problems with Basic Authentication is that it transmits data in plain, unencrypted, base 64 format. This makes the interception of data by an unauthorised party a relatively simple task: eavesdrop on the HTTP packets and simply read the submitted username and password.

The alternative is to use a form of cryptography known as **hashing**, or more correctly using a **message digest**. A digest is a numerical summary of the transmitted data's contents; the calculations are performed in such a way that every string has a different digest value. What makes this method strong is that hashing a message is a one-way operation only: a digest can be created from a message, but it is computationally infeasible to reconstruct the original message from the digest. The strength of the digest depends on the type of algorithm used, but on the whole the default digests are strong enough for most applications.

Using Digest Authentication causes the password to be hashed by the client (a message digest created from it) before it is sent back to the server. Since the digest cannot be reversed to obtain the original password string, the server must also hash the password it stores using the same algorithm and compare the hashes rather than the original passwords. Since each string hashes to its own unique digest, if the client and server copies of the password are equal, then by definition their hashes must also be equal. Notice that hashing is only performed on passwords: usernames are always sent in plain text (as unencrypted strings).

This still might not seem terribly secure: surely an unauthorised party could eavesdrop on the digest for the password and use that to authenticate themselves, in the same way the real client does? To overcome this, the server passes a **salt** to the client when it requests authentication; this usually comes in the form of the current date and time (or the numerical timestamp). The client incorporates this timestamp in the password string before hashing it. The timestamp will be different for every request for authentication, because the server's clock is constantly changing, so each new password digest created by the client will be different even if the password is the same. Both the server and client use the same salt, and the same combination of salt and password, so if both the salt and password are equal then the client's digest will equal the server's digest and they will be successfully authenticated. Using a different salt for each digest means that using the same password/salt hash in the future will result in a failed authentication. Only someone

Figure 21.2

Using Password Digests

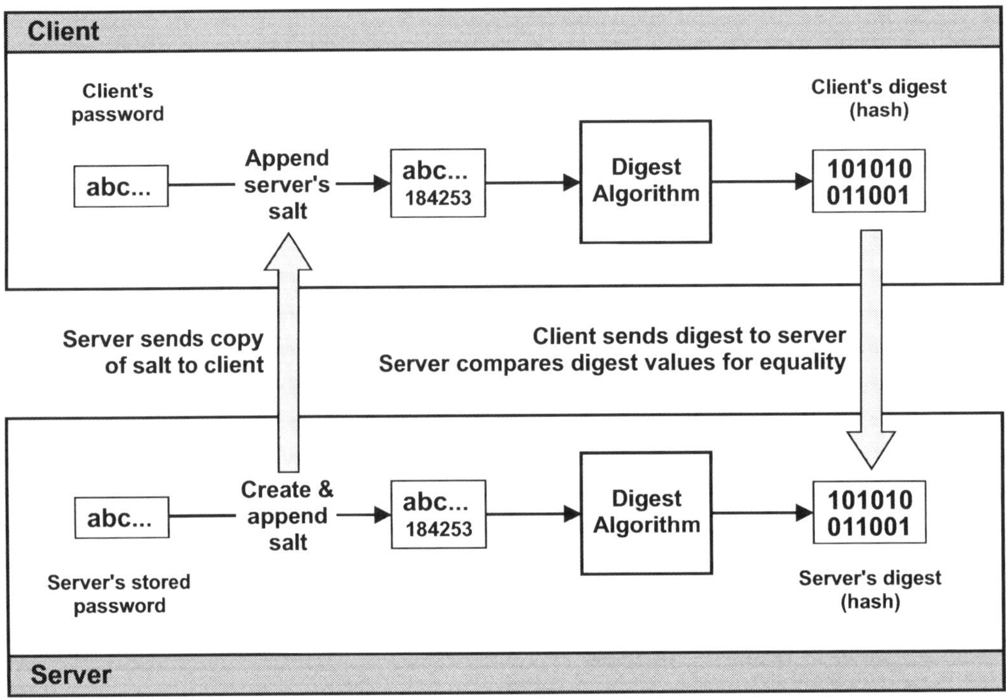

who knows the original password and the current salt can be authenticated. Figure 21.2 shows a summary of the Digest Authentication process, including how the salt created by the server is used.

Java EE-compliant containers are not required to support this authentication method, but must support the other three.

Form Authentication

If you want to integrate the authentication process with the rest of your website, you'll want to use Form Based Authentication. This uses an (X)HTML form, embedded in a web page designed by you, to request the username and password. Since this is just another web page, it can be designed to fit with the rest of the site – it needn't be obtrusive like Basic Authentication.

You could program your own Form Based Authentication mechanism, but the container already provides a template for the layout of the form. Using this default layout allows the container to do declarative authentication, which saves you having to write your own application code. The container's template requires a username and password; it obtains these using (X)HTML input fields:

```
<form method="POST" action="j_security_check">
    <input type="text" name="j_username" />
    <input type="password" name="j_password" />
</form>
```

The key to this template lies not in the HTML code, but the `action` destination which must be `j_security_check`, and the names of the input fields, `j_username` and `j_password`. The action attribute of the HTML `<form>` element is the URL to which the form's data will be submitted; `j_security_check` alerts the container that this is the default authentication form. The container will look for the values of the `j_username` and `j_password` request parameters in the body of the request (since the request uses POST); it uses these as the credentials.

The advantage of this method is that it easily integrates with the rest of the website. The disadvantage is that the data is still sent *unencrypted*, as with Basic Authentication. For true security, you would need to use Form Based Authentication over a Secure HTTP channel, so that all submitted data (the username, and password in particular) are encrypted. This is declared as part of the *confidentiality* requirements of an application, so a discussion is deferred until later in the chapter.

SSL Certificates

As part of the process of establishing a secure channel with the client, both the client and server are required to identify themselves by providing appropriate credentials. This typically occurs by comparing the client's Public Key Certificate (PKC) with a copy stored on the server. This is the most secure form of authentication since it is difficult to fake a certificate.

While Java EE allows us to use SSL certificates for authentication simply by making the appropriate declarations in the deployment descriptor, the theory behind SSL and asymmetric encryption is too involved to discuss here. Bear in mind, however, that there are drawbacks: each client authenticated using this method must have its own PKC, which is not something most of the general public possess. Moreover, the server must already own a copy of the certificate for comparison purposes, which implies that a server administrator has taken the time to establish a database of known certificates. Hence, the use of SSL certificates for authentication is really limited to internal networks and intranets where *both* the client and server machines are under the control of a single authoritative body.

Authentication and Sessions

The container must have some way to track users and their authentication status. It typically does this using either HTTP sessions or SSL sessions. While the latter provide a secure, undisputable, identification of the client through the use of unique certificates, using unencrypted sessions over HTTP can be problematic. For example, what if an unauthorised user were able to obtain (or guess) the `jsessionid` for an authorised user? This could very easily lead to unauthorised (and even unauthenticated) users acting as though they are authorised to access restricted resources. In many cases, applications don't require a totally secure form of authentication, and the use of session timeouts can help to reduce security problems, but for online banking and eCommerce especially, the use of SSL authentication should be a design priority.

Declarative Authentication

Basic, Digest and Client-Cert Authentication

The type of authentication you wish to use, if you don't want to create your own programmatic authentication mechanism, must be configured in the deployment descriptor for the application, using the `<login-config>` element:

```
<web-app>
  ...
  <login-config>
    <auth-method>BASIC</auth-method>
    <realm-name>Restricted zone</realm-name>
  </login-config>
  ...
</web-app>
```

As you can see, `<login-config>` is a direct child of the descriptor's root `<web-app>` element. There may only be one `<login-config>` element per deployment descriptor, so the authentication method you use must be consistent across the *entire Web application*.

The example given above is suitable when HTTP Basic Authentication is required, using the client's or browser's own pop-up dialog window. The `<auth-method>` specifies the name of the authentication type being used: here `BASIC`. `<realm-name>` is specific to the `BASIC` method, declaring the realm name to be displayed in the pop-up dialog window. Realm names are human-readable textual reminders which can help to remind a user what facility they are attempting to access. In Figure 21.1, this name is blank; if that dialog had been produced from this example, the value of `<realm-name>` would be displayed next to the Realm label (above the input boxes).

The declaration for Digest Authentication is the same as for Basic Authentication, since it uses the same HTTP mechanism and client dialog, but specifies the `DIGEST` authentication method flag:

```
<web-app>
  ...
  <login-config>
    <auth-method>DIGEST</auth-method>
    <realm-name>Restricted zone</realm-name>
  </login-config>
  ...
</web-app>
```

Specifying that the client's SSL certificate should be used for authentication is even simpler since it cannot include the optional `<realm-name>` element anyway (the use of a realm name with certificates is meaningless):

```
<web-app>
  ...
  <login-config>
    <auth-method>CLIENT-CERT</auth-method>
  </login-config>
  ...
</web-app>
```

Form Authentication

The configuration for Form Based Authentication is necessarily a little more complex:

```
<web-app>
  ...
  <login-config>
    <auth-method>FORM</auth-method>
    <form-login-config>
      <form-login-page>/login.html</form-login-page>
      <form-error-page>/errors/403.html</form-error-page>
    </form-login-config>
  </login-config>
  ...
</web-app>
```

The `<auth-method>` value must now be the `FORM` flag; notice that `<realm-name>` does not apply to Form Based Authentications so we've omitted it. The key to the configuration lies in the `<form-login-config>` element and its subelements. `<form-login-page>` specifies the *context-relative* URL (beginning with a `/`), to the page containing the login form. If the page is authored using (X)HTML, the form should use the template we saw when we first discussed Form Based Authentication in this chapter. `<form-error-page>` specifies the *context-relative*

URL of the error page to use if authentication fails. Typically this will point to a 'login failed' page.

An interesting idea which I've implemented in the past is to effectively point the error page to the login page–i.e. the error page and login page are (very nearly) one and the same. This means that if login fails, the user gets another chance to enter their details and try to authenticate again. By storing the username in an appropriate scope (namely the session), the form can be auto-completed with the username last used, should authentication have failed. Optionally, by using an appropriately scoped integer variable, you can also keep track of how many times authentication has already failed; after three or so times you could respond with the 'login failed' page instead of another presentation of the login page. If a user has mistyped or forgotten their password, this allows them to attempt login at least three times before receiving an error. This is quite often preferable to jumping straight to an error page, and frequently implemented on websites of varying complexity. HTTP Basic Authentication also characteristically asks for credentials three times before returning an error.

Performing Authorisation

As we've already said, authorisation is about deciding whether a user is permitted to access a resource or not. The question is how do we make this decision? Clearly, authentication is the first step towards authorisation; once a user is 'logged in' we know who they are, and can identify them amongst other users in other sessions. To be useful, we need to make use of authentication for the purposes of authorisation. The design which springs to mind is to maintain a database of users' usernames against the resources they're permitted to access on the server. This allows us to look up the authenticated user's database record to see if the page requested is in the record: if so, then the user is authorised to access the resource, and if not access is denied. Indeed, this is quite possible using programmatic security which we look at briefly at the end of the chapter.

Unfortunately, using usernames per se for authentication is too fine-grained to be practical for the container's model of declarative security. Another suggestion is quite often more realistic; it uses the concept of **roles**, which are *groups* into which users are categorised. Now, instead of permitting access to each individual user in turn, we can assign permissions based on the roles into which users 'fit'. This is easiest seen with an example: take a banking application which is accessed by system-level administrators, bank clerks and customers. Each of these categories represents a distinct role: `administrators`, `clerks` and `customers`. Each role has different levels of access permissions: `administrators` maintain the application so they have unrestricted access, `clerks` have permission to make bank-level transactions and access bank funds as well as check and update customers' accounts, which is the only function `customers` can perform. Most authorisations here can be performed based on the user's role alone, but it would obviously be necessary to restrict `customers` access to their *own account* only and not the collection of all customers' accounts. This would be a job for programmatic security: controlling access to resources based on the *individual user's credentials* rather than roles.

Declaring Security Roles

In order to use roles as part of the container's security, we need to do two things: declare the set of roles that exist in the application, and assign users to those roles.

Security Roles in Applications

We use the `<security-role>` element (a direct child of the `<web-app>` root) in the deployment descriptor to declare a role which exists in the application. *All roles used in the application must be declared* in order to be used as identifiers in the rest of the deployment descriptor and in component code itself. Declaring a role name using this syntax is equivalent to notifying the container up front about the roles it is required to recognise and support:

```
<web-app>
  ...
  <security-role>
    <role-name>customers</role-name>
  </security-role>
  ...
</web-app>
```

While `<security-role>` may only contain one mandatory `<role-name>` subelement, the declaration of multiple `<security-role>` elements is permitted; thus, from the previous example:

```
<web-app>
  ...
  <security-role>
    <role-name>administrators</role-name>
  </security-role>
  <security-role>
    <role-name>clerks</role-name>
  </security-role>
  <security-role>
    <role-name>customers</role-name>
  </security-role>
  ...
</web-app>
```

Roles can also be declared using annotations on any component implementing the `javax.servlet.Servlet` interface. The annotation takes an array of `Strings` which are the role names (or equivalently just a single string if only one role name needs to be specified). For example:

```
import javax.annotation.security.DeclareRoles;
import javax.servlet.*;

@DeclareRoles({"administrators","clerks","customers"})
public class MyServlet implements Servlet {
  // ...
}
```

or to declare just a single role, either of the following can be used:

```
@DeclareRoles({"administrators"})
@DeclareRoles("administrators")
```

Assigning Users to Roles

Users are assigned to roles in a way *specific to each Java EE server.* There's no one generic way to do this assignment, it depends purely on what Java EE server software you've got running. Common methods for the authentication of users include a dedicated file stored in the Java EE server environment, querying a directory service and interrogating the lists of usernames, passwords and user groups native to the operating system on which the Java EE server is running.

You should check your Java EE server's specific documentation before considering implementing security. If you require authentication based on data which is operating-system dependent, or which references an external database or file store, you will most likely need to program your own authentication modules. Your server should provide an API and documentation to enable you to do this. See the section on programmatic security later in the chapter for more details.

Glassfish v3, at the time of writing still in Beta, includes these methods of authentication ('realms'):

- Keyfile realm: stores usernames and hashed (digested) passwords in a file, as well as role names for each username. A similar admin-realm is used for administrative users.
- Retrieval using LDAP from a named directory service.
- JDBC realm, for looking up user credentials from a database—the most useful of the realms.
- Certificate realm: authenticates clients by their SSL certificates. Most useful in high-security environments but can be some hassle to configure. Each client needs their own SSL certificate.

Glassfish allows the usernames and passwords for its file-based storage to be set through its Web-based administration console, which is ideal if the data doesn't change very often, but it doesn't allow changes to be made by anyone other than administrators; the use of a directory or database promotes scalability and extensibility, but you might still find yourself programming your own modules. Thankfully, Glassfish provides an API you can use to extend the available list of authentication realms, should you need custom authentication and authorisation mechanisms.

The standard distribution of the Apache Tomcat Web container includes XML configuration files for lists of users, passwords and their roles, and ships with a JDBC database realm for authentication.

Declarative Authorisation and Confidentiality

For the exam, you will need to know all the deployment syntax which appears in this section, and it isn't that detailed so my best advice is to learn as much of it as possible.

All authorisation and confidentiality security requirements for an application are contained in one or more `<security-constraint>` elements in the deployment descriptor:

```
<web-app>
  ...
  <security-constraint>
    <!-- put the constraint details in here -->
  </security-constraint>
  ...
</web-app>
```

Each `<security-constraint>` element declares security properties only for a specified collection of Web resources, much like `<jsp-property-group>` declares properties for a collection of JSPs. If different security constraints are required for different components in the application, they can each be configured in separate `<security-constraint>` elements. Each `<security-constraint>` may contain zero or more `<display-name>` elements, which specifies human-readable names given to this constraint (if any):

```
<security-constraint>
  <display-name>My Constraint 1</display-name>
</security-constraint>
```

21

We will now look at the other child elements grouped by their function; a summary of all the security-related descriptor elements can be found at the end of this chapter.

Defining Resource Collections

We said that each <security-constraint> applies only to a certain, specified, collection of resources and that this model allows us to have different security constraints for different resources.

Resource collections are specified using one or more <web-resource-collection> elements and their children:

```
<security-constraint>
  ...
  <web-resource-collection>
    <web-resource-name>shoppingbasket1</web-resource-name>
    <url-pattern>/basket/*</url-pattern>
    ...
    <http-method>PUT</http-method>
    <http-method>DELETE</http-method>
    ...
  </web-resource-collection>
  ...
</security-constraint>
```

There may only be one <web-resource-name> element per collection; this element specifies the *logical* descriptor name given to this collection.

There may be one or more <url-pattern> elements, each specifying a pattern to which every incoming request will be matched; if the request matches the pattern, the container will consider the resource to be in this collection and impose the declared security constraints.

Requests may also be filtered by what HTTP method is being used to access the resource, allowing some methods to be blocked while others are allowed through. A typical requirement is to impose access restrictions on the sensitive PUT and DELETE methods (if these are actually implemented) while allowing GET requests to pass through unchallenged. The optional <http-method> is used to specify each HTTP method which should fall under this security constraint for the given URL patterns.

There are therefore two ways to specify a collection:

- Using only the URL pattern(s); every request which matches this pattern(s), regardless of its HTTP method type, will have the specified constraints applied to it.
- Using both the URL pattern and one or more <http-method> elements will apply security constraints only if the request matches both the URL pattern(s) and the declared HTTP method(s).

A resource may belong to more than one <web-resource-collection> in more than one <security-constraint> simultaneously. When this is the case, the container matches each incoming URL to *every* resource collection encountered in the descriptor, and not just the first found. The container then amalgamates all <security-constraint> properties for the requested resource.

Authorisation Constraints

Now that we have selected some (or perhaps all) resources in the application to which the container's security model will be imposed, we have a choice of what security is required: authorisation for these resources only, confidentiality only, or both.

Authorisation is declared using the <auth-constraint> child element of <security-constraint>. Aside from the generic <description> element, this declares only one child element:

```
<security-constraint>
  ...
  <auth-constraint>
    <role-name>role1</role-name>
    <role-name>role2</role-name>
    ...
  </auth-constraint>
  ...
</security-constraint>
```

Each <role-name> declares the name of a role into which the authenticated user can fit if they are authorised to access the resources in the collection. If the user fits into the role name specified here, they are granted access. Otherwise, access is denied. There are some special cases:

- A declaration of the form <role-name>*</role-name> means 'grant access to an authenticated user of any role'. This does imply that the user *has already been authenticated*, but you don't care to which exact role(s) they belong. *Never* mistake the wildcard to mean 'grant anyone access, even if they're not authenticated'. Declaring any other <role-name> elements is redundant since the * wildcard encompasses all roles anyway.
- Omitting all <role-name> elements, or indeed the parent <auth-constraint>, means 'grant access to anyone, authenticated or not'. The emphasis here is that we are allowing *unrestricted* access to resources by not specifying any roles; the user doesn't even have to have been authenticated.

21

In the case that a resource is mapped to more than one <security-constraint> at one time, by virtue of being declared in multiple <web-resource-collection> elements, all role names will be amalgamated at run time for that resource. For example:

```
<security-constraint>
  ...
  <web-resource-collection>
    <web-resource-name>View page</web-resource-name>
    <url-pattern>/basket/view.jsp</url-pattern>
  </web-resource-collection>
  <auth-constraint>
    <role-name>role1</role-name>
    <role-name>role2</role-name>
  </auth-constraint>
  ...
</security-constraint>
<security-constraint>
  ...
  <web-resource-collection>
    <web-resource-name>View page</web-resource-name>
    <url-pattern>/basket/*.jsp</url-pattern>
  </web-resource-collection>
  <auth-constraint>
    <role-name>role3</role-name>
  </auth-constraint>
  ...
</security-constraint>
```

The resource `/basket/view.jsp` falls into both declared security constraints, since its URL matches both the `<url-pattern>`s specified. If the user were to request this resource, the authorised role name set is the union of both `<security-constraint>` instances: `role1`, `role2` and `role3`. If the user is in *any of these three* roles, they will be authorised.

Confidentiality and Data Integrity

The `<security-constraint>` element is also the place for declarations relating to securing communication channels. Confidentiality and data integrity are configured using the `<user-data-constraint>` element as a child of the `<security-constraint>` to which this communication restriction applies. In turn, the `<user-data-constraint>` element only has one child of its own, `<transport-guarantee>` which is mandatory and singular (i.e. may only appear once):

```
<user-data-constraint>
  <transport-guarantee>NONE</transport-guarantee>
</user-data-constraint>
```


The `<transport-guarantee>` element must contain one of the values:

- **NONE**
  Specifies that no security precautions are required on the channel.

- **INTEGRAL**
  Specifies that data integrity should be preserved on the channel by creating a digest for each message sent between the client and server. This digest is normally appended to the message being transmitted as supplementary information.

- **CONFIDENTIAL**
  Declares that complete encryption is required on the channel; on the Web, this is usually implemented using Secure HTTP (HTTPS), which in turn uses Secure Socket Layer (SSL) encryption. Note that encryption systems such as SSL include message digests (hashing) as an inherent part of their cryptography, to ensure the encrypted transmitted data is not modified during transmission. Using a value of `CONFIDENTIAL` often implies that `INTEGRAL` is being used as well, but as part of a more sophisticated form of encryption.

It is only legal to declare one `<transport-guarantee>` and one of the values given above, but as we said `CONFIDENTIAL` implies `INTEGRAL`, and `NONE` stands alone, so there shouldn't be a need to use more than one value anyway.

Servlet Security with Annotations

The Servlet 3.0 specification provides annotations for configuring the declarative security discussed in this chapter, as an alternative (or in addition) to the XML deployment descriptor elements.

Recall that with the descriptor elements, servlets are first mapped to URLs (using `<servlet-mapping>` elements) and then declarative security is applied to those URLs using `<url-pattern>` inside a `<web-resource-collection>` in a `<security-constraint>`.

Whilst annotations are broadly used to similar effect, they work differently: they are applied *directly to servlet components* and not to URL mappings. In a sense, they are less complex and error-prone to configure, provided you want to apply the same policy to all URLs mapped to the same servlet. If you don't, then you still need to use the deployment descriptor as a granular override for the annotations.

All annotations are in the `javax.servlet.annotation` package.

The most fundamental annotation is `@ServletSecurity` defined by:

```
@ServletSecurity {
  HttpConstraint value;
  HttpMethodConstraint[] httpMethodConstraints = {};
}
```

This can annotate any class implementing `javax.servlet.Servlet` interface. Within this annotation we can set two elements:

21

- **`HttpMethodConstraint[] httpMethodConstraints`**
  This should be an array (or single element) defining the protection to be applied to a particular HTTP method (such as GET or POST). For a given HTTP method, there can only be one constraint declared - no duplicates.

- **`HttpConstraint value`**
  This is the *default protection* to be applied to all methods not explicitly provided in the httpMethodConstraints setting. It may be omitted or used exclusively (if protection is the same for every HTTP method).

Let's start with the specific method constraints, which require the annotation:

```
@HttpMethodConstraint {
  String value; // required: the HTTP method name
  String[] rolesAllowed={};
  ServletSecurity.TransportGuarantee transportGuarantee = NONE;
  ServletSecurity.EmptyRoleSemantic emptyRoleSemantic = PERMIT;
}
```

This is a container for the `<http-method>`, `<auth-constraint>` (`<role-name>`) and `<user-data-constraint>` (`<transport-guarantee>`) descriptor elements:

- **`String value`**
  This must be present and must be the name of an HTTP method name - for example `GET`, `POST`, `PUT` or `DELETE`. This element is required.

- **`String[] rolesAllowed`**
  This is an array (or single string) of role names being granted authorisation.

- **`ServletSecurity.TransportGuarantee transportGuarantee`**
  An enumeration value of either `NONE` (default) or `CONFIDENTIAL` (SSL/TLS).

- **`ServletSecurity.EmptyRoleSemantic emptyRoleSemantic`**
  An enumeration of either `PERMIT` (default) or `DENY`. This is only relevant, and should only be declared, if `rolesAllowed` is omitted or empty. It defines the "blanket" (all users) policy to be applied to the method: allow or deny access.

After, or instead of, declaring individual HTTP method constraints, you may want to apply a default policy to the servlet. This is done using the similar annotation:

```
@HttpConstraint {
  String[] rolesAllowed = {};
  ServletSecurity.TransportGuarantee transportGuarantee = NONE;
  ServletSecurity.EmptyRoleSemantic value = PERMIT;
}
```


The purpose of these elements is the same as for `@HttpMethodConstraint`, however notice that the `EmptyRoleSemantic` is now the default `value`. which can be declared independently. For example, the following will permit and deny all authorisation, regardless of user roles, respectively:

```
@ServletSecurity(@HttpConstraint)
@ServletSecurity(@HttpConstraint(DENY))
```

due to `PERMIT` being the default `value`, and the explicit `value=` can be omitted if there is only one element for the annotation. In fact the first can be abbreviated further, as its default `value` is a default `@HttpConstraint`, to just:

```
@ServletSecurity
```

which means "allow all users for all HTTP methods with no other constraints".

Another common example would be to allow read-only access to resources but to only allow `POST`, `PUT` or `DELETE` operations for members of the `admin` role:

```
@ServletSecurity(httpMethodConstraints={
  @HttpMethodConstraints(value="POST",rolesAllowed="admin"),
  @HttpMethodConstraints(value="PUT",rolesAllowed="admin"),
  @HttpMethodConstraints(value="DELETE",rolesAllowed="admin")
})
public class MyProtectedResourceServlet implements Servlet {
  // implementation
}
```

We can achieve similar but more securely using the reverse process - allow all access to GET and to those in the admin role, and deny everything else:

```
@ServletSecurity(
  value=@HttpConstraint(DENY),
  httpMethodConstraints={
    @HttpMethodConstraints(value="GET"),
    @HttpMethodConstraints(value="POST",rolesAllowed="admin"),
    @HttpMethodConstraints(value="PUT",rolesAllowed="admin"),
    @HttpMethodConstraints(value="DELETE",rolesAllowed="admin")
  }
)
public class MyProtectedResourceServlet implements Servlet {
  // implementation
}
```

In general, having a `DENY` default policy and then explicitly allowing only certain roles for particular HTTP methods is the least error-prone approach to security.

NOTE: If a deployment descriptor or fragment contains a constraint mapped by a `<url-pattern>` that is an exact match for a pattern mapped to the servlet, any `@ServletSecurity` annotation must not modify the constraints enforced on that pattern as configured in the descriptor. This ensures backward compatibility and that the deployment descriptor can always override configuration via annotations.

Servlets and Role References

When developers write servlets which incorporate programmatic security, they may query the roles to which an authenticated user belongs, but may not actually know the role name at the time of development. In a large enterprise, this is a common problem since lists of users are maintained by the Administrators while the application is written by the Component Developers and deployed by the Deployer. These three parties may not talk to each other very often, so it can be difficult for Component Developers to know what roles the Administrators are going to be using. This problem is particularly prevalent when your application is to be deployed to *different clients'* systems – for example, if your application or its components are sold under licence.

The deployment descriptor allows role names referenced in servlets to be linked to the proper role names stored in the deployment environment. Servlets do not need to be coupled directly to the environment, which makes them portable. It is the duty of the Deployer to liaise with the Administrator and ensure that the correct role associations are made in the deployment descriptor for the application. This declarative approach decouples the servlet code from the environment, allowing changes to be made to the environment's role names and the descriptor, without having to modify, recompile or redeploy servlet code.

We link up the two via one or more instances of the `<security-role-ref>` subelement of the `<servlet>` element (which itself was covered in detail in Chapter 10):

```
<web-app>
  ...
  <servlet>
    ...
    <security-role-ref>
      <role-name>servlet_role</role-name>
      <role-link>environment_role</role-link>
    </security-role-ref>
    ...
  </servlet>
  ...
</web-app>
```

There may be zero or more occurrences of `<security-role-ref>` in every `<servlet>` element, corresponding to zero or more role names used in the servlet code. The `<role-name>` element is used to declare the name as it appears in the servlet code; the `<role-link>` specifies the associated role name as found in the server environment.

21

The `<role-link>` element is optional; if omitted, it is the responsibility of the application Deployer to provide the association. The Component Developer is only required to declare the list of all role names *used in servlet code*, using the mandatory `<role-name>` element.

The only servlet code which this actually affects is invocations of the `isUserInRole()` method on the `HttpServletRequest` object. Should a `<security-role-ref>` for the supplied role name not be declared for the servlet, the container will check the `<security-role>` elements for the application and attempt to find a match. Thus `isUserInRole()` is implemented as follows:

1. `isUserInRole()` checks for a `<security-role-ref>` mapping for this servlet in the deployment descriptor; if it exists, it performs the mapping and checks to see if the user is in the `<role-link>` role supplied. If the user is in the role, return `true`; otherwise return `false`.
2. `isUserInRole()` checks for a `<security-role>` declaration for the entire application in the deployment descriptor; if it exists and the user is in this role, this method returns `true`.
3. Otherwise return `false`.

NOTE: For each `<role-link>` name supplied, there must be a corresponding `<security-role>` declared (with a `<role-name>` child which has the same value as `<role-link>`) for the application as a whole.

For example, suppose the deployment descriptor contained the following code:

```
<web-app>
  <servlet>
    ...
    <security-role-ref>
      <role-name>shelf_stacker</role-name>
      <role-link>shelf_replenishment_technician</role-link>
    </security-role-ref>
    ...
  </servlet>
  ...
  <!--must also declare the role for the entire application -->
  <security-role>
    <role-name>shelf_replenishment_technician</role-name>
  </security-role>
  ...
</web-app>
```

then the following method invocation in that servlet would return `true` due to the `<security-role-ref>` mapping:

```
request.isUserInRole("shelf_stacker")
```

This next method invocation would also return `true` since the supplied role is declared as a `<security-role>` for the entire application:

```
request.isUserInRole("shelf_replenishment_technician")
```

Deployment Descriptor Syntax Summary

We've covered the entire Java EE security model, but in bits and pieces (rather than bytes and nybbles!) as we've gone along. Figure 21.3 is a collective summary of all the Web application deployment descriptor's syntax relating to security. All other deployment descriptor syntax can be found in Chapter 10.

For the exam, just learn this diagram; there aren't that many elements, and most are named sensibly anyway. Make sure you know all the important security concepts, what they achieve and how to declare them, and not only will you be able to build robust and secure software applications, but you'll be closer to passing the exam as well!

Web Security and EJBs

Using any of the declarative methods for authentication, or indeed creating a correct programmatic authentication procedure, allows security to extend across the entire Java EE platform and not just within the current Web application. In particular, the EJB container is able to use the authentication details for the current user to determine whether they are permitted to access EJB components as well. This presents a two-tier security system: not only can we prevent unauthorised users from *accessing Web resources*, but also from *using services* provided by the business logic layer of a Java EE application.

The deployment descriptor provides a way to interface security between Web and EJB applications and containers. It is important that every developer realise that security, whether declarative or programmatic, but especially the latter, *must* be implemented correctly for this work. A makeshift login system which does not interoperate with the rest of the Java EE platform or the container could just be the weakest link in an application. Declarative security is always implemented correctly by the container.

Another important property of Java EE security is that authentication and the user's credentials are tracked at the *container level*, and not individually at the application level. This means that users authenticated by one Web application are automatically authenticated in all other applications running in the same container. This may be advantageous or not: in some cases it is useful because

Figure 21.3

Security-Related Deployment Descriptor Schema

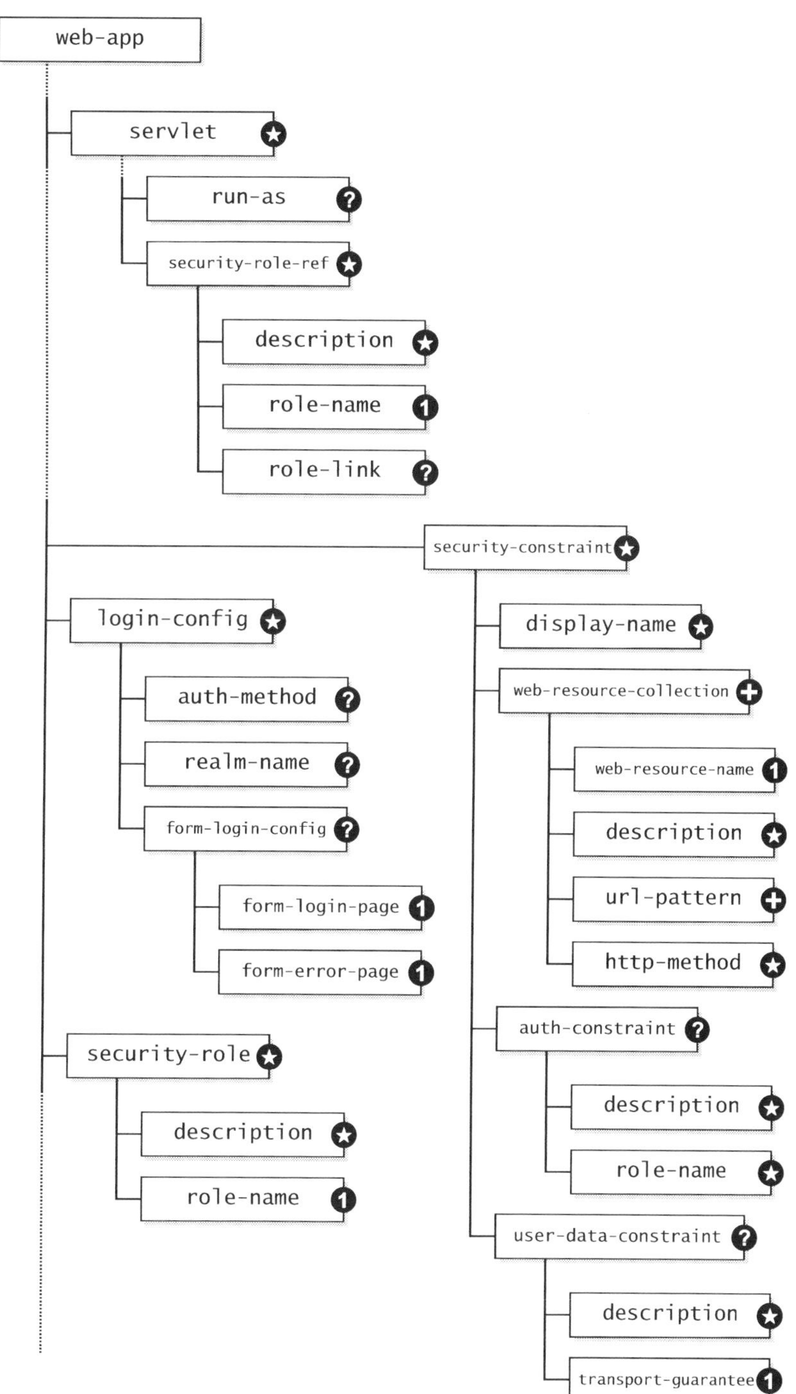

some Web applications run together and are designed to be interoperable. It can be an inconvenience, as well as a possible security issue, if two Web applications contain *the same role names* for authorisation, but are intended to function separately. A user logged in to one of the applications with a role name will be able to access all the resources constrained by that role name in the other application(s) as well, which means unauthorised access in those other applications. To avoid this, you should either run completely separate applications in separate containers (for example, on different physical servers or in different Java EE virtual servers, realms or domains), or ensure that all role names in each deployed application are independent of every other application's.

Note that all invocations of EJBs must be accompanied by a security identity, or principal; by default, the user's principal is used. However, when a servlet grants access to unauthenticated users, or indeed the servlet incorporates its own programmatic security overriding that of the declarative role-based system, using the user's principal becomes inadequate. If this is the case, you can use the `<run-as>` subelement of `<servlet>` in the deployment descriptor to place the *servlet itself* into a role. It is this role which will then be used for security when invoking an EJB from the servlet. This allows the Web developer to build yet another layer of role-based security into the application. Note that if the user is not authenticated and `<run-as>` is not declared for the servlet making the EJB invocation, the 'unauthenticated principal' used for invoking the EJB is undefined by the Java EE specification and will depend on the vendor-specific Java EE implementation.

Programmatic Security (Non-Examinable)

To go down the road of investigating ways to program custom authentication and authorisation methods would take us too far into the realms of the APIs exposed by specific Java EE servers, which is outside the scope of this book. Instead, I would refer you to the following technologies and resources available from Sun:

- Java Authentication and Authorization Service (JAAS) which since J2SE 1.4 comes bundled with the J2SE platform,
- Java Authorization Contract for Containers (JACC) defined in JSR-115,
- Chapter 5, *Securing Applications*, in the GlassFish Developer's Guide (particularly the *Creating a Custom Realm* section).

Whilst the latter is of course platform-specific, based on the Reference Implementation, it provides a readable insight into the methodology behind how similar servers may implement custom security. If you are already running a server from a different vendor, consult their documentation instead.

The APIs exposed by server platforms allow for the complete customisation of authentication and authorisation mechanisms using plug-ins which you create. While these are by far the best way to manage users and authorisation permissions across an entire Java EE application, there is an alternative available to individual servlets (and filters) for authorisation only. Since this interface is part of the core Java EE API, we will investigate it briefly now.

Programmatic Authorisation with Servlets

When we discussed the request mechanism used by the container, we came across four methods in the `HttpServletRequest` interface which at the time might not have made much sense; recapping, these were:

- `String getAuthType()`
- `String getRemoteUser()`
- `Principal getUserPrincipal()`
- `boolean isUserInRole(String)`

The first retrieves a string which describes the method used to authenticate the user. Unless you've programmed custom authentication, this will return one of the values given by these constants, also contained in the `HttpServletRequest` interface:

- **`BASIC_AUTH`**
  This has the value `BASIC`.
- **`CLIENT_CERT_AUTH`**
  This has the value `CLIENT_CERT`.
- **`DIGEST_AUTH`**
  This has the value `DIGEST`.
- **`FORM_AUTH`**
  This has the value `FORM`.

The second method, `getRemoteUser()`, returns the username of the authenticated user; if they are not logged in (i.e. have not yet been authenticated), this method returns `null`.

The third method returns a `java.security.Principal` instance which represents an entity capable of logging into a system – for example, an individual, corporation or another computer terminal. This method returns `null` if the user has not already been authenticated.

The last method tests if the currently authenticated user is in the role specified as the `String` parameter. For example:

```
isUserInRole("admins")
```

will return `true` only if the current user is configured as being in the `admins` role, or `false` otherwise. This method returns `false` if the current user has not yet been authenticated. The role name used as the parameter to this method must be declared in the deployment descriptor inside the `<role-name>` subelement of `<security-role-ref>` for the servlet(s) in which `isUserInRole()` is called, as we've already discussed.

Of these methods, the second and forth will be of most interest to us. The second, `getRemoteUser()`, can be used to find the username of the user. We can then match this against a database of user entries and perform fine-grained authorisation based on that username. The forth, `isUserInRole()`, allows us to make decisions about authorisation based on whether the user is in the specified role. Authorisation by roles is likely to be less useful to us when building additional programmatic security, since these could be declared in the deployment descriptor.

Let's look at the outline for a very simple servlet which does some authorisation based on the username:

```
public class MyAuthorisationServlet extends HttpServlet {
  /* Array of usernames which we permit access this resource */
  private static final String[] allowedUsers = new String[]{
                                              "administrator",
                                              "customer1",
                                              "clerk" };


  public void doGet(HttpServletRequest req,
                    HttpServletResponse resp) {
    String username = req.getRemoteUser();

    /* If the user isn't logged in, leave now with a 401 SC */
    if(username == null) {
      resp.sendError(HttpServletResponse.SC_UNAUTHORIZED);
      return;
    }

    /* Check to see if user is in our "allowedUsers" category */
    boolean permission = false;
    for(String au : allowedUsers) {
      if(au.equals(username)) {
        permission = true;
        break;
      }
    }
```

```
        /* If permission is false, then the user isn't authorised */
        if(!permission) {
          resp.sendError(HttpServletResponse.SC_FORBIDDEN);
          return;
        }

        /* If we get here, the user must be authorised */
        resp.getWriter().write("This user has been authenticated " +
                       "and is authorised for this resource");
    }
}
```

The logic behind this code is explained in the comments. If the user isn't already authenticated and we want to deny them access based on this fact, then we check for `getRemoteUser()` returning `null`, return the 401 ('Unauthorised') status code and terminate processing the rest of the servlet. Otherwise we iterate through the array of permitted usernames. If any matches the current user's username, then we allow them access straight away, and execution effectively jumps to the output writer line which simply sends one line of plain text back to the client telling the user they are authorised. Otherwise, if by the time the loop finishes still no matches have been made, we send the 403 ('Forbidden') status code response and terminate processing of the servlet.

This servlet actually makes use of *both* declarative *and* programmatic security; you'll notice that nowhere have we provided a method to allow a user to login – instead, we've assumed that the container has already authenticated the user by some declarative method. All we're doing is imposing *additional programmatic* security on top of the declarative model provided by the container, since the declarative model based on roles isn't quite up to the requirements of our application. By using the basic declarative security model and adding programmatic security *only where necessary*, we keep all the benefits of container-managed security (such as single sign-on compatibility with EJBs) while being able to extend the model as appropriate.

Obviously this is a crude implementation: having usernames hard-coded in a static array ties the code to a particular application and environment, and should these names change, the servlet would need to be recompiled (I'm sure you can think of other bad practises here as well!). A much better implementation would reference persistent storage such as a database. However, this example should illustrate one way to do programmatic authorisation. If this servlet were to be implemented in the Front Controller pattern or as an Intercepting Filter, both of which we look at in the next chapter, this has the potential to be a very robust application indeed.

Revision Questions

1 **What are the benefits of container-managed security?** **(choose two)**

- A Makes an application more portable.
- B Provides authentication across multiple Web servers.
- C Provides authentication across multiple containers in the same Web server.
- D Reduces programming time.
- E The container always uses a secure connection to process login information.

2 **Which of the following are correct statements?** **(choose two)**

- A Basic Authentication uses plain text for transmission of usernames and passwords.
- B HTTPS Client Authentication is the only mechanism not required to be supported by a J2EE-compliant Web container.
- C Every website should provide a secure login mechanism.
- D Digest Authentication can be seamlessly integrated with existing Web pages.
- E Digest Authentication uses an encrypted password for increased security.

3 **Match the security terms to their correct descriptions.**

Terms	Descriptions
Authentication	The system used to ensure information is consistent between two endpoints, in particular that the information isn't altered by a middleman.
Authorisation	Ensures information is readable only by the intended recipients.
Data integrity	The process of determining the validity of the client's credentials
Confidentiality	The process of determining whether a user has permission to access a resource.

4 **What statement can be used to authorise the user only if their role name starts with 'admin'?** **(choose one)**

A
```
if(request.getUserRoles().startsWith("admin")) {
  // authorise
}
```
B
```
if(request.getRemoteRole().startsWith("admin")) {
  // authorise
}
```
C
```
String[] roles = request.getUserRoles();
for(String role : roles) {
   if(role.startsWith("admin")) {
      // authorise
   }
}
```
D
```
if(request.isUserInRole("admin")) {
   // authorise
}
```
E None of the above.

5 **Which of the following configures Basic Authentication for use in a Web application?** **(choose one)**

A
```
<login-config>
  <method>BASIC</method>
  <realm>Private</realm>
</login-config>
```
B
```
<login-config>
  <auth-method>BASIC</auth-method>
  <realm>Private</realm>
</login-config>
```
C
```
<login-config>
  <method-name>BASIC</method-name>
  <realm-name>Private</realm-name>
</login-config>
```
D
```
<login-config>
  <auth-method>BASIC</auth-method>
  <realm-name>Private</realm-name>
</login-config>
```
E
```
<login-config>
  <method>BASIC</method>
  <realm-name>Private</realm-name>
</login-config>
```

6 **Arrange the following tags in the order they appear inside the deployment descriptor for Form Authentication:**

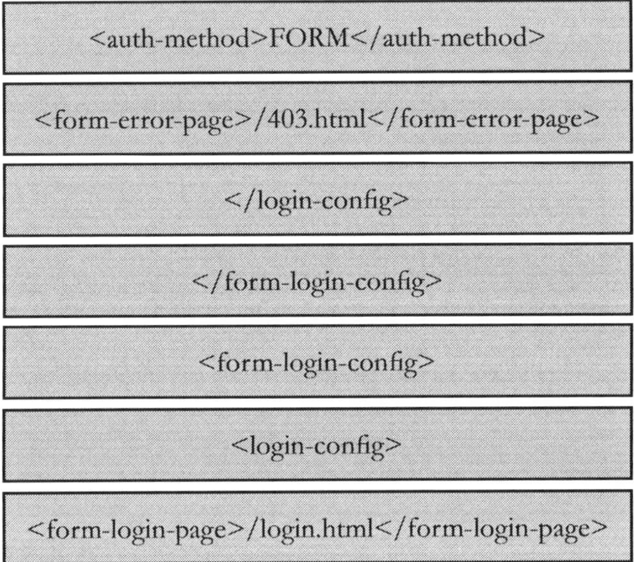
<auth-method>FORM</auth-method>
<form-error-page>/403.html</form-error-page>
</login-config>
</form-login-config>
<form-login-config>
<login-config>
<form-login-page>/login.html</form-login-page>

7 **Which of the following is the correct HTML form template to use when the application is using Form Authentication?** **(choose one)**

A
```
<form method="POST" action="security_check">
  <input type="text" name="user" />
  <input type="password" name="password" />
</form>
```

B
```
<form method="POST" action="security_check">
  <input type="text" name="username" />
  <input type="password" name="password" />
</form>
```

C
```
<form method="POST" action="j_security_check">
  <input type="text" name="j_username" />
  <input type="password" name="j_password" />
</form>
```

D
```
<form method="POST" action="/j_security_check">
  <input type="text" name="j_username" />
  <input type="password" name="j_password" />
</form>
```

8 **What element combination inserted directly into <web-app> in the deployment descriptor declares the security role 'customer' as being used by the Web application?** **(choose one)**

A
```
<security-config>
  <role>customer</role>
</security-config>
```

B
```
<security-role-name>customer</security-role-name>
```

C
```
<security-role-group>
  <role-name>customer</role-name>
</security-role-group>
```

D
```
<security-role>
  <role-name>customer</role-name>
</security-role>
```

E
```
<security-roles>
  <role-name>customer</role-name>
  ...
</security-roles>
```

9 **Which element combination inside a <servlet> declares a mapping between the 'admin' role as declared in the servlet (to invocations of the HttpServletRequest.isUserInRole method), and the 'administrator' role declared in the application?** **(choose one)**

A
```
<role-ref>
  <name>admin</name>
  <link>administrator</link>
</role-ref>
```

B
```
<security-role-ref>
  <role-name>admin</role-name>
  <role-ref>administrator</role-ref>
</security-role-ref>
```

C
```
<security-role-ref>
  <role-name>admin</role-name>
  <role-link>administrator</role-link>
</security-role-ref>
```

D
```
<security-role-ref>
  <servlet-role>admin</servlet-role>
  <app-role>administrator</app-role>
</security-role-ref>
```

E
```
<role-ref>
  <servlet-role>admin</servlet-role>
  <app-role>administrator</app-role>
</ role-ref>
```

10 **Which of these statements in the deployment descriptor configures the /secure path as inaccessible to all unauthenticated users?** **(choose one)**

A
```
<security-constraint>
  <web-resource-collection>
    <url-pattern>/secure/*</url-pattern>
  </web-resource-collection>
  <auth-constraint>
    <role-name>*</role-name>
  </auth-constraint>
</security-constraint>
```

B
```
<security-constraint>
  <url-pattern>/secure/*</url-pattern>
  <auth-constraint>
    <role-name>*</role-name>
  </auth-constraint>
</security-constraint>
```

C
```
<security-constraint>
  <url-pattern>/secure/*</url-pattern>
  <constraint>
    <role-name>*</role-name>
  </constraint>
</security-constraint>
```

D
```
<security-constraint>
  <url-pattern>/secure/*</url-pattern>
  <role-name>*</role-name>
</security-constraint>
```

E Omit any security constraint for this resource.

11 **A website needs to integrate the design of an HTML login page with the rest of its pages. Which of the following authentication methods would be the best one to choose?** **(choose one)**

A Basic Authentication

B Digest Authentication

C Form Authentication

D HTTPS Client Authentication

12 **Which of the following methods in which classes can be used to perform programmatic security?** **(choose two)**

A getRemoteUser() in HttpSession

B isUserInRole(String) in ServletRequest

C getUserPrincipal() in HttpServletRequest

D getAuthType() in ServletRequest

E getRemoteUser() in HttpServletRequest

13 **Which of the following statements in the deployment descriptor configures all resources under the /admin path to be accessible only to users in the 'admin' role?** **(choose one)**

A
```
<security-constraint>
  <web-resource-collection>
    <url-pattern>/admin</url-pattern>
    <role-name>admin</role-name>
  </web-resource-collection>
</security-constraint>
```

B
```
<security-constraint>
  <web-resource-collection>
    <url-pattern>/admin</url-pattern>
  </web-resource-collection>
  <auth-constraint>
    <role-name>admin</role-name>
  </auth-constraint>
</security-constraint>
```

C
```
<security-constraint>
  <web-resource-collection>
    <url-pattern>/admin/*</url-pattern>
  </web-resource-collection>
  <auth-constraint>
    <role-name>admin</role-name>
  </auth-constraint>
</security-constraint>
```

D
```
<security-constraint>
  <web-resource-collection>
    <url-pattern>/admin/*</url-pattern>
  </web-resource-collection>
  <role-name>admin</role-name>
</security-constraint>
```

E
```
<security-constraint>
  <url-pattern>/admin/*</url-pattern>
  <auth-constraint>
    <role-name>admin</role-name>
  </auth-constraint>
</security-constraint>
```

14 **Which of the following statements in the deployment descriptor configures the container to accept only secure connections when a client accesses a resource under the /filestore path?** **(choose one)**

A
```
<security-constraint>
  <url-pattern>/filestore/*</url-pattern>
  <auth-constraint>
    <transport-guarantee>SECURE</transport-guarantee>
  </auth-constraint>
</security-constraint>
```

B
```
<security-constraint>
  <web-resource-collection>
    <url-pattern>/filestore/*</url-pattern>
  </web-resource-collection>
  <auth-constraint>
    <transport-guarantee>SECURE</transport-guarantee>
  </auth-constraint>
</security-constraint>
```

C
```
<security-constraint>
  <web-resource-collection>
    <url-pattern>/filestore/*</url-pattern>
  </web-resource-collection>
  <data-constraint>
    <transport-guarantee>CONFIDENTIAL</transport-guarantee>
  </data-constraint>
</security-constraint>
```

D
```
<security-constraint>
  <web-resource-collection>
    <url-pattern>/filestore/*</url-pattern>
  </web-resource-collection>
  <user-data-constraint>
    <transport-guarantee>SECURE</transport-guarantee>
  </user-data-constraint>
</security-constraint>
```

E
```
<security-constraint>
  <web-resource-collection>
    <url-pattern>/filestore/*</url-pattern>
  </web-resource-collection>
  <user-data-constraint>
    <transport-guarantee>CONFIDENTIAL</transport-guarantee>
  </user-data-constraint>
</security-constraint>
```

15 **Which of the following statements in the deployment descriptor inside <security-constraint> will allow all users, even unauthenticated ones, to access a resource?** **(choose one)**

A
```
<auth-constraint>
  <role>*</role>
</auth-constraint>
```
B
```
<auth-constraint>
  <role-name>*</role-name>
</auth-constraint>
```
C
```
<auth-constraint>
  <role-name>NONE</role-name>
</auth-constraint>
```
D Omit any declarations.

16 **The exhibit shows a servlet used for authorisation. If the user's name is not equal to 'administrator', the servlet must return SC_NOT_AUTHORIZED, and must otherwise forward to the /welcome.jsp page. What is the best statement that should be used on line 7 to achieve this?** **(choose one)**

EXHIBIT

A boolean auth = req.isUserInRole("administrator");

B boolean auth = req.getUsername().equals("administrator");

C boolean auth = req.getRemoteUser().equals("administrator");

D boolean auth = (req.getRemoteUser() == null ? false : req.getRemoteUser().equals("administrator"));

E boolean auth = (req.getUserPrincipal() == null ? false : req.getUserPrincipal().getUsername().equals("administrator"));

17 **The exhibit shows a declaration in the deployment descriptor. What is the effect of this declaration?** **(choose two)**

EXHIBIT

A Provides a constraint on all resources located in the /files directory, preventing any PUT or DELETE operations from occurring.

B Restricts access to all resources in /files/* to users in the 'admin' role.

C Ensures data integrity is maintained.

D Prevents any users other than those in the 'admin' role from using the PUT or DELETE methods.

E Enforces the use of a secure connection.

18 **Which of the following allows only authenticated users to use POST requests for all resources in the application?** **(choose one)**

A
```
<security-constraint>
  <web-resource-collection>
    <url-pattern>*</url-pattern>
    <method>POST</method>
  </web-resource-collection>
  <auth-constraint>
    <role>*</role>
  </auth-constraint>
</security-constraint>
```

B
```
<security-constraint>
  <web-resource-collection>
    <http-method>POST</http-method>
  </web-resource-collection>
  <auth-constraint>
    <role-name>*</role-name>
  </auth-constraint>
</security-constraint>
```

C
```
<security-constraint>
  <web-resource-collection>
    <url-pattern>/*</url-pattern>
    <http-method>POST</http-method>
  </web-resource-collection>
  <auth-constraint>
    <role-name>*</role-name>
  </auth-constraint>
</security-constraint>
```

D
```
<security-constraint>
  <web-resource-collection>
    <url-pattern>*</url-pattern>
    <http-method>POST</http-method>
  </web-resource-collection>
  <auth-constraint>
    <role-name>*</role-name>
  </auth-constraint>
</security-constraint>
```

Exhibits

Q.16

```
import javax.servlet.*;
import javax.servlet.http.*;

public class MyServlet extends HttpServlet {

  public void doGet(HttpServletRequest req,HttpServletResponse resp) {
    // Insert line here
    if(auth) {
      resp.sendError(HttpServletResponse.SC_NOT_AUTHORIZED);
      return;
    }

    /* Otherwise forward */
    RequestDispatcher rd = req.getRequestDispatcher("/welcome.jsp");
    if(rd != null) {
      rd.forward(req,resp);
    }
  }

}
```

Q.17

```
<security-constraint>
  <web-resource-collection>
    <url-pattern>/files/*</url-pattern>
    <http-method>PUT</http-method>
    <http-method>DELETE </http-method>
  </web-resource-collection>
  <auth-constraint>
    <role-name>admin</role-name>
  </auth-constraint>
  <user-data-constraint>
    <transport-guarantee>INTEGRAL</transport-guarantee>
  </user-data-constraint>
</security-constraint>
```

Answers to Revision Questions

1 **Correct answers: C, D**

Note that A isn't necessarily true; only certain features list in the specification must be implemented by containers, others are optional, and there are many proprietary custom authentication mechanisms. In fact, an application developed with its own internal authentication mechanism is more portable than custom authentication mechanisms which integrate with specific containers. B is false, in general, as authentication isn't carried across different Web servers for security reasons. C is true, allowing a Web application to do authentication and an EJB container to use that authentication information. D is certainly true; using declarative security takes only a few minutes to configure in the deployment descriptor and in your server's configuration. E is incorrect; you can *opt* to have a secure connection but it is not mandatory.

2 **Correct answers: A, E**

B is incorrect because all J2EE-compliant containers must support HTTPS Client Authentication; Digest Authentication is the only optional mechanism. C is incorrect because often it is inappropriate to use SSL certificates – for example, a public forum might use a login only to track which members create each thread, and to encourage people to register; since this data isn't 'sensitive', it is unlikely that the author would want to go to the trouble and expense of obtaining a Public Key Certificate and configuring SSL. D is incorrect because this method causes a browser-dependent pop-up window to be used; Form Authentication is the only mechanism which can be integrated with an existing website design.

3 **Correct answer:**

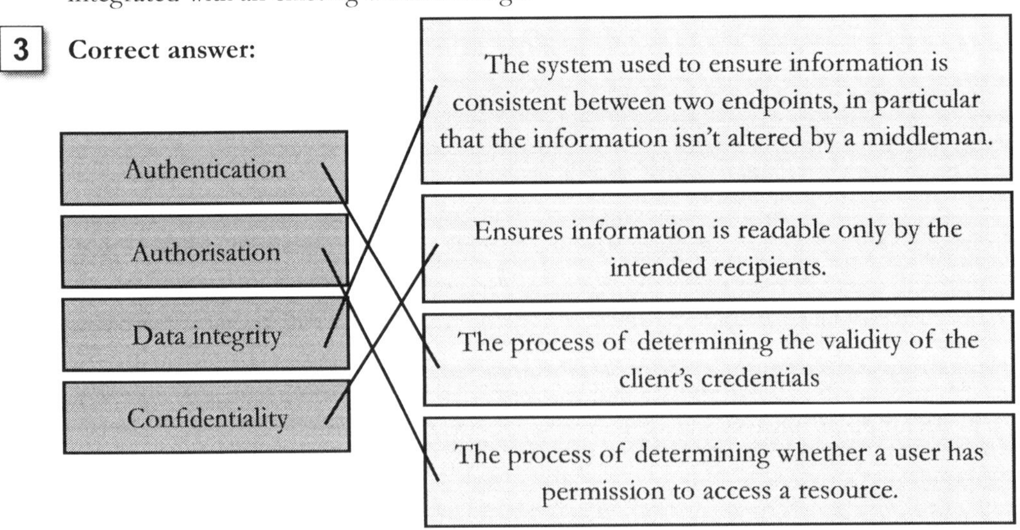

4 **Correct answer: E**

In fact, there is no portable way to determine the roles the user belongs to; the best hope is to access the Principal returned from getUserPrincipal(), but the exact object returned and the methods available on it will be container-dependent. Note that D would be correct if we just wanted to test if the user was in the role 'admin', rather than testing if any of their roles start with that token.

5 **Correct answer: D**

6 **Correct answer:**

```
<login-config>
<auth-method>FORM</auth-method>
<form-login-config>
<form-login-page>/login.html</form-login-page>
<form-error-page>/403.html</form-error-page>
</form-login-config>
</login-config>
```

7 **Correct answer: C**

Note that the path to post the form to, j_security_check, is relative to the current path and not to an absolute resource. When the request is submitted by the client, the container checks to see if the request URI ends with j_security_check; if so its authentication mechanism is automatically engaged. All parameter names start with a 'j_'.

8 **Correct answer: D**

Note that only one <role-name> may be declared per <security-role>, and it is the only useful child element – unless additional subelements of <security-role> are added at a later date, there is practically always vast redundancy here.

9 **Correct answer: C**

10 **Correct answer: A**

A is the correct syntax; B to D are all incorrect. Note that E is incorrect as this would allow *all* users, even unauthenticated ones, to gain access to /secure.

11 **Correct answer: C**

12 **Correct answers: C, E**

Note that all the programmatic security methods are found in HttpServletRequest.

13 **Correct answer: C**

Note that only B and C have the correct syntax, but B maps only to the single /admin resource, whereas C maps to all resources matching /admin/*, which are all resources inside the admin directory.

14 **Correct answer: E**

15 **Correct answer: D**

The only way to allow all users through is to *not* declare any elements; declaring a <role-name>*</role-name> is equivalent to allowing *any authenticated* user to access the resource.

16 **Correct answer: D**

Note the requirement to check whether getRemoteUser() returns null, otherwise trying to invoke equals() on that will cause a NullPointerException. A is incorrect, as it attempts to check the role the user is in, and not the username. B is incorrect because the method doesn't exist. C isn't the best statement because it could throw the NullPointerException. E is incorrect; there is no method called getUsername() on java.security.Principal.

17 **Correct answers: C, D**

A is incorrect, as this constraint allows PUT or DELETE operations *from users in the admin role* (it doesn't prevent all operations from occurring); B is incorrect, as it doesn't actually restrict access – clients using GET or POST could still access the resources; this constraint is designed to prevent the use of the potentially more dangerous HTTP methods. E is incorrect, as INTEGRAL ensures that some form of data integrity test (such as digests) is being used, but doesn't mandate that a completely secure connection such as SSL is required.

18 **Correct answer: C**

Note that using '*' for a <url-pattern> is invalid; you should use /*. In addition, note that there must be one or more <url-pattern>s per <web-resource-collection>; it is insufficient to provide only an <http-method>.

In this chapter you'll:

- Understand the requirement for re-usable and proven design patterns.
- Learn the key patterns for the presentation tier: MVC, Front Controller and Intercepting Filter.
- Learn the key patterns for the business logic layer: Business Delegate, Service Locator, Transfer Object.
- Briefly look at other non-examinable enterprise patterns.

22 Java EE Patterns

Time has proven that the most robust enterprise applications to be developed have had at least four common goals: to be portable, maintainable, scalable and extensible. Portability is about creating truly platform-independent code, such that if the network's hardware or operating systems are upgraded, the code still works without major modifications which would be terribly time consuming and costly. So long as you don't use native code in your applications, Java goes most of the way to ensuring your code is portable. Maintainability is about the ease with which the application can be kept running: you don't want to hard-code properties which change often, for example, because this limits the ease with which modifications can be made and would require recompilation and redeployment. Instead, consider a separate data store such as a database to allow others to change the code as well. Maintainability is also about creating code which is clear in its intentions – commenting source code is a must. Finally, maintainability implies an aspect of providing debugging support – writing exceptions to log files for example. The last two goals, scalability and extensibility, tend to go hand in hand. The former means literally ensuring that an application can grow with the demand for it, a typical example being an online e-business such as Amazon or eBay which have grown gracefully over time. The latter means ensuring that code can easily be added to the application to provide for future expansion or further customisation. The custom security modules which can 'plug-in' to the Java EE server are an example of the server's extensibility support. By conforming to the above, considerable effort and resources can be saved, especially with respect to the growth of applications – good design from the outset is essential.

With this in mind, and with most applications striving to meet these goals, a number of common design requirements have surfaced over the years, each of which has been addressed with a, now established, solution. Such a solution is called a **pattern**, a design strategy which is reusable across applications of any scale or task. The oldest patterns exist for stand-alone client applications that run solely on users' desktop machines, but as server systems have grown, enterprise patterns have emerged as well. The exam requires us to know a small selection of Java EE patterns, totalling six, but we will also look at the other standard patterns relating to the Web tier in a separate section.

Examinable Patterns

This section looks at the patterns which may appear on the exam. Any pattern not listed in this section will never be the correct answer to any exam question, so you can consider any such pattern a wrong answer to a multiple-choice question.

Model-View-Controller (MVC) Pattern

The motivation and design solution for the MVC pattern have been around since the dawn of 'object time', by which I mean since the concept of OO programming was first introduced. MVC is about separating computation processing from presentation; a typical Java application client has:

- An object model which represents a real-world construction. This is the **model** for the application, describing what the application *is* (the data it contains) and what it *does* (the services it offers).
- An AWT or Swing GUI to provide the user with interaction capabilities. This makes up the **view**, the interface that the user sees and works with. View components allow interaction, but do not themselves describe anything about the application—as a result they are often portable enough to be used in an entirely different application.
- Listeners to provide a communications link between what the user does with the view, and how the model responds. This comprises the **controller**, which is a layer responsible for receiving events fired by the user's interaction with the view, and make changes to the model accordingly.

While arguably the model layer is the most important, maintaining the data storage, each layer has an equal part to play in the life of an application. By providing logical divisions between the model and views, we give ourselves the opportunity to change the model code without having to change the view; similarly the converse is true.

Application Tiers

On an enterprise platform, the design strategy is usually unavoidably more complex. Each *client* application can be split into the *three* **tiers** as shown above, each tier having its own level of responsibility. A good enterprise application is also decomposed into multiple tiers—in general we call these **n-tier architectures**. The most common example is a 3-tier strategy:

- Databases, persistent file stores, directories and the like provide **data storage** capabilities.
- Enterprise JavaBeans (EJBs), or in small applications even just JavaBean components, provide the data processing and services required by the application, collectively referred to as the **business logic**.
- Servlets and JSPs, possibly with the help of JavaBeans, provide the **presentation** for the application. This layer could also be a Java client, a desktop application run on the client machine which interfaces directly with the business logic layer via remote calls, e.g. using Java's Remote Method Invocation (RMI) protocol.

The similarities between a 3-tiered enterprise architecture and a simple MVC design should be clear. Data storage does not typically map precisely to an object model, but certainly the business logic tier corresponds with the MVC controller, and the presentation tier with the MVC view.

Larger, more sophisticated, Java EE applications may require even more tiers: *n*-tiers for an *n*-tier architecture. In general, each tier represents the logical partition between application components brought about by their separation into *different physical processes*, such as being in a different container or JVM instance, or on *different physical machines*.

In the subsequent sections we will split patterns into the categories of business logic or presentation as appropriate, and examine each tier of patterns in turn. Note that we will not look at data storage patterns. Some patterns required for the exam will touch on EJB and the business logic tier despite the fact that this is a Web presentation-centric exam! We will look at all patterns required for the exam, regardless of their tier, but will then concentrate solely on those patterns designed for presentation which do not fall in the remit of the exam.

Patterns for the Presentation Tier

Front Controller

Some applications are best maintained if they provide a common central gateway through which all requests and responses pass. Using a central component to handle all requests and responses provides a single location from which to control all logic decisions relating to security, content retrieval and view management. In this pattern, a single component known as the **Front Controller** moderates all requests and responses, either for one region of the site (such as a catalogue) or for the entire site. This component can replace the need for mapping other components to URLs in the deployment descriptor, and can instead query a persistent data store to determine the location of the required resource dynamically at *request time* (rather than being fixed from deployment time). This is useful when sites change frequently and resources are constantly 'coming and going'.

Since the Front Controller usually represents a logic processor, it is best implemented with a servlet. All URLs which this Front Controller is required to handle are mapped to this servlet in the deployment descriptor. The servlet may then delegate processing to other resources based on the format and validity of the request URI. The sequence of events are shown in Figure 22.1:

Figure 22.1

Front Controller Pattern

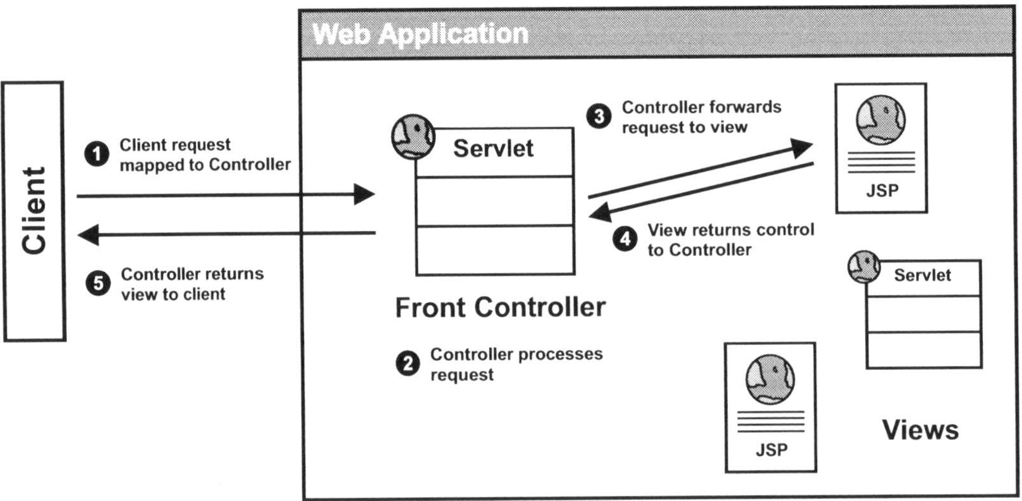

The delegation to other resources normally includes invocations of the `RequestDispatcher` mechanism, or in the case of static files (such as images, audio tracks and movies) may include the manipulation of raw streams of data.

This pattern is best implemented by using more than one Front Controller per application, with each Controller servlet being designed to handle the requirements of specific request types. For example, an e-commerce application might consist of the following Controllers by default:

22

- One to control access to the user's own shopping basket. This might be mapped to the `/basket/*` URL for example.
- An entry point into the catalogue which interprets a product ID and displays the page for that product; the page is derived dynamically at request time by

the Controller, so details of products can be added or modified at any time without having to redeploy the application. E.g. mapping to `/catalogue/*`.

- A payment supervisor, mapped to `/catalogue/buy/*` for example.
- A search engine Controller for the site, mapped to `/search/*`.

Each mapping helps to clearly define each Controller's role in the application. A more abstract example of the Front Controller pattern is exhibited by the Web container itself: all requests to files with extensions `*.jsp` and `*.jspx` are passed by the container to the JSP engine for translation and execution and are not returned directly. A Front Controller could easily be created to emulate this behaviour, delegating all requests to an appropriate JSP translation engine, by mapping the Controller to the URL patterns `*.jsp` and `*.jspx` in the deployment descriptor.

NOTE: Following this pattern, the Apache Tomcat Web container, part of the Reference Implementation, uses the `org.apache.jasper.servlet.JspServlet` servlet mapped against `*.jsp` and `*.jspx` to invoke the JSP translation engine at request time.

Intercepting Filter

This pattern, established after the introduction of filters in the Servlet specification, uses one or more filters 'plugged-in' to the current application to impose services on the requests and responses. Such services include authorisation, logging and encryption and compression, all of which we first mentioned in Chapter 7 when we discussed the use of filters.

Since this pattern is pretty elementary, given what you should already know about filter components, a simple diagram (Figure 22.2) should suffice.

The key reasons to use filters are when:

- Pre- or post-processing capabilities are required.
- The service should be transparent with respect to both the other server components and the client: i.e. neither the client nor other server components should depend on the filters to function correctly.
- The filters are 'pluggable' by design: their addition or removal does not affect the operation of other components or resources.

This pattern is also useful when an existing (possibly legacy) application requires extra request/response processing to be interposed, and the modification of existing code is unsuitable (or more costly or time consuming than simply plugging in a new filter).

Figure 22.2

Intercepting Filter Pattern

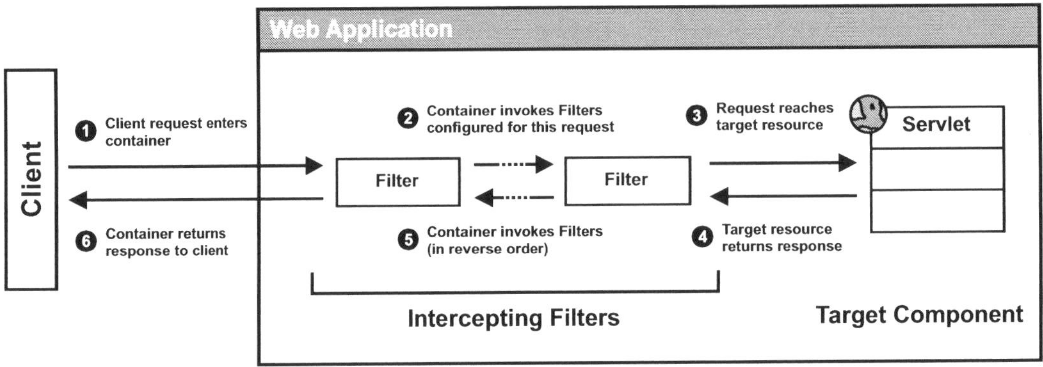

Patterns for the Business Logic Tier

Patterns in this section rely on a partial, but very elementary, knowledge of EJBs, namely what they are and what they do. We will, however, concentrate only on descriptions of what the patterns do for us, and on how these patterns interact with the presentation tier. We will not pursue EJB programming or good practises here–if that's what interests you, consider studying for the Sun Certified *Business Component* Developer (SCBCD) objectives and exam, after you've passed the SCWCD that is!

Business Delegate

The EJB container provides many declarative services which make programming business logic components easy–for example, Container Managed Persistence (CMP) automatically synchronises the contents of a data-centric EJB with the values held in a persistent storage device such as a database. This makes EJBs excellent for encapsulating logic and providing an interface between the data itself, and entities which require that data (such as components in the Web container).

However, as with any good object model, to allow access to every EJB's methods and attributes from the outside world can overly complicate the exposed API, and in some cases can present security concerns. As a result, one or more Business Delegate components are used much like Front Controllers but in the business logic tier. Each Delegate provides a course-grained, minimalist, API which provides the required data and services without exposing any other EJBs it uses in the process.

For example, suppose that one of the methods on a Business Delegate EJB returns a complete order (as a custom object) from a given order ID number argument. This order object may have to be constructed from several different sources: for example, some of it may be contained in an XML serialisation, while the customer's details might be contained in a database. In the simplest of enterprise applications, the Delegate is responsible for assembling the final order object by looking up and gathering together all the required fragments of data, a process which inevitably requires calling multiple methods on other EJBs. The calling code, for example a component in the presentation tier, doesn't have to worry about where or how the data for the order is assembled; all it 'sees' and cares about is the complete object. The sequence for this activity might be something like that in Figure 22.3:

Figure 22.3

Business Delegate Pattern

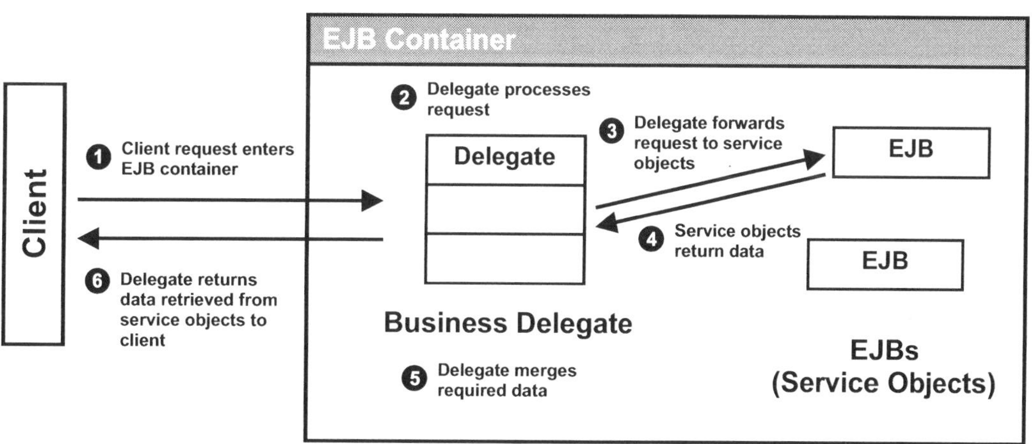

As long as the Delegate's exposed method signatures don't change, the other EJB components and the Delegate's method implementations can be changed without affecting the presentation component's code, which only knows to call the correct method and doesn't care about how it's implemented.

There is one other important consideration which this pattern addresses. There is a substantial performance overhead associated with remote calls to components in the EJB container from the outside world. This is due to the serialisation of parameters and return values which takes place, as well as the need to open sockets to and locate the EJB components themselves. Calls between EJBs in the same container clearly do not involve such performance-hindering operations since calls can be made locally without serialisation. Reducing the number of remote calls made is of a premium. By using a Business Delegate, only a single method to which a remote call can be made is exposed, and by doing the other processing locally we drastically increase performance.

Service Locator

Using EJBs is not as straightforward as using object instances from a local object model. Since requests to EJBs can come from anywhere, inside or outside the container, and from any client or any other executing Java code, this makes them rather difficult to find or create instances for. A stand-alone desktop application uses the static `main` method in the application driver class to start the software. Every object after that is either created by a thread which is executing under this main thread somewhere, or is located from another known object in the model. Once an object is no longer referenced by any other objects, it is marked for garbage collection by the JVM in order to save on memory.

By requirement, EJB management has to work differently on the Enterprise platform – it's no good disposing of EJB objects once all references to them are lost, because their services may be required by a different client at a later date. If the container began to destroy EJB instances storing valuable data just because they were no longer referenced, the application would quickly loose its integrity. Additionally, since EJBs are only really 'seen' by the container, how does any client actually get hold of the EJB classes and instances available to it?

To answer this question would send us too far into the territories of EJB programming to be of any worth here. However, if you've worked with EJBs you'll know how the look-up process for EJBs works, and if you haven't, trust me when I say you don't want to know just yet (it involves JNDI, RMI and all the other acronyms you didn't want to know about, so save it until *after* you've passed the SCWCD)!

A Service Locator is a JavaBean, but not an *Enterprise* JavaBean, component which abstracts the look-up process for EJBs into a single interface. As long as you can get hold of an instance of the Service Locator class, you can get instances of *any other bean*. This is advantageous since the look-up process for EJBs is the same regardless of the type of bean, so calls to the Locator help to reduce redundancy in code which creates instances of EJBs directly (either in the logic or presentation tiers). Any future changes to the look-up mechanism would only involve changing the code in this one Locator. In addition, since the Service Locator normally follows the Singleton pattern as well (i.e. there is only ever one instance of the Locator existing at one time), a reference to the JavaBean class (and not any specific instance) is usually all that's required. Yet another advantage which this pattern offers is the ability of the Service Locator to cache recently retrieved EJB instances, thus improving performance by reducing the volume of remote network

Figure 22.4

Service Locator Pattern

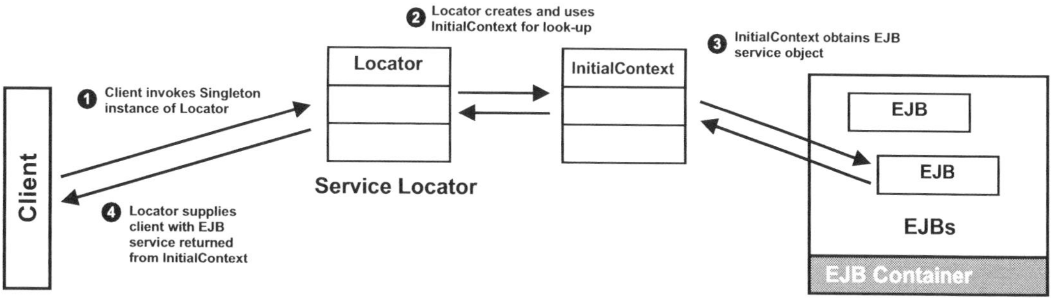

calls which need to be made. Figure 22.4 summarises this.

It is important that the Service Locator is not itself an EJB, since if it were, the calling code would have to go through the EJB look-up procedures to get an instance of the Locator, which seems just a little contradictory! Instead, the Locator is just a plain old Java object which can be deployed with client applications, made available as a JavaBean helper in Web applications, or deployed along with EJBs in EJB applications. This allows the component to be reused in a variety of situations where obtaining EJB instances is necessary. Should you require even more abstraction, a single EJB 'Service Factory' can be placed on the server. The client's Locator makes all EJB calls to this Factory, which in turn returns the EJB instance required by the original client code. Figure 22.5 summarises this somewhat convoluted process.

This pattern helps to make code in the presentation tier and in application clients much simpler. However, it should be noted that in a well designed enterprise application, presentation tier components will only access a Business Delegate component. The Delegate instance may be obtained using the Service Locator class. Delegates will likely, in turn, make use of the Service Factory available to them as well. It is generally bad practise for client code to make any direct connection to any EJBs other than the Delegates, even though this pattern may present this as a more viable option.

Figure 22.5

Service Locator Pattern (with Service Factory EJB)

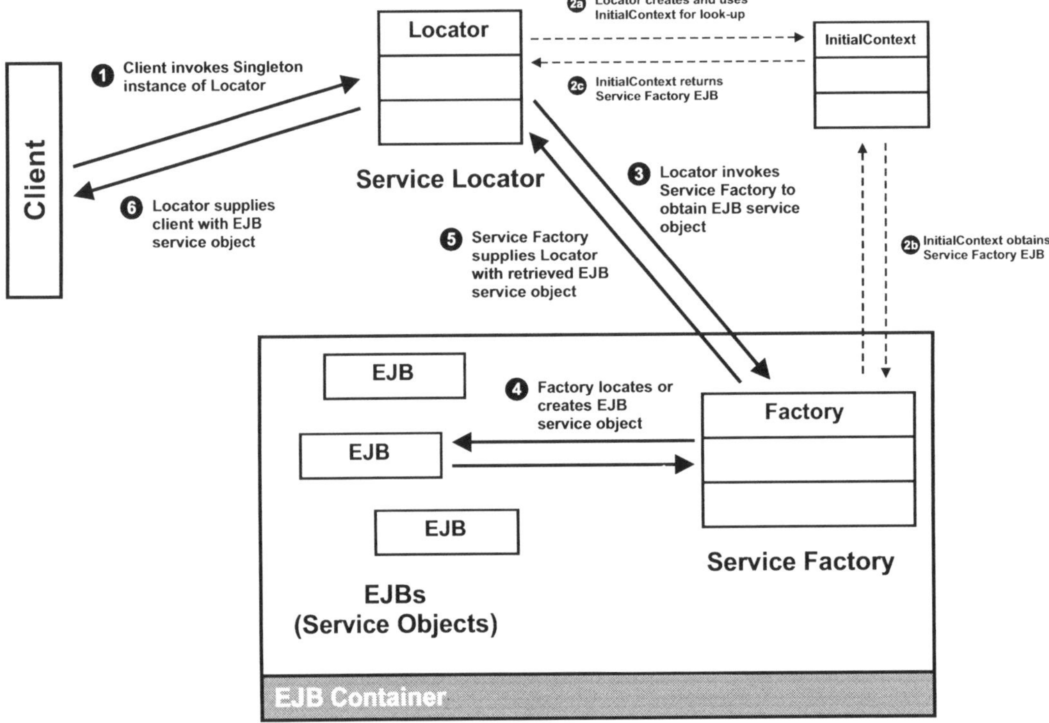

Transfer Object

When we discussed the Business Delegate pattern above, we said how important it is to reduce the number of network calls made between the client and EJBs on the server. Each remote method call has its associated overhead, which it is desirable to avoid if at all possible. We gave an example in that section illustrating the purpose of a Business Delegate as an EJB which encapsulates the services offered by the rest of the EJBs in a course-grained manner; this example was of a customer's order being assembled from various different sources (e.g. databases and XML files).

What we failed to address sufficiently was the actual object which gets sent; we mentioned that it would be an object composed of all the fragments of data collated from all the EJBs, but with no further detail. In fact, this object is the subject of the Transfer Object pattern. Each Transfer Object is a `Serializable` object which contains all the data that needs to be transferred between server and client. Thus, the complete order object would be an example of a Transfer Object.

NOTE: For reasons which will become clear, the Transfer Object pattern is sometimes referred to as the Value Object pattern in older literature.

Transfer Objects have a number of key properties:

- They encapsulate all the related data from a single method call which reduces the number of remote calls which need to be made – a Transfer Object is assembled locally on the server before being sent to the client.
- They must not be EJBs, but like the Service Locator, just plain old Java objects or, optionally, JavaBeans.
- They, and all their attributes (or 'fields' if you prefer), must be `Serializable`.

The reason for the second and third points is that, in order for this pattern to work, the object must be sent *by value*. Normally, objects in Java are passed by reference, but remote calls using RMI serialise both the arguments and the return values of methods, transmit them 'over the wire' in serialised form, and then convert them back into instances at the other end.

There are some advantages to passing by value here: namely that changes made to the Transfer Object by the client do not affect the object on the server. Similarly, changes made to the object on the server do not affect the client's copy. This means that the server is free to use a single Transfer Object instance (or a small pool of them) and just modify its attributes before returning it to each client. This means no overhead on the server associated with creating new instances for each method invocation.

The Transfer Object can expose its data as public attributes, or by providing JavaBean-compliant public accessor ('getter') methods. Either is a valid approach, although the JavaBeans construction is preferred.

Figure 22.6 summarises the Transfer Object pattern when used in conjunction with the Business Delegate pattern.

Figure 22.6

Transfer Object Pattern

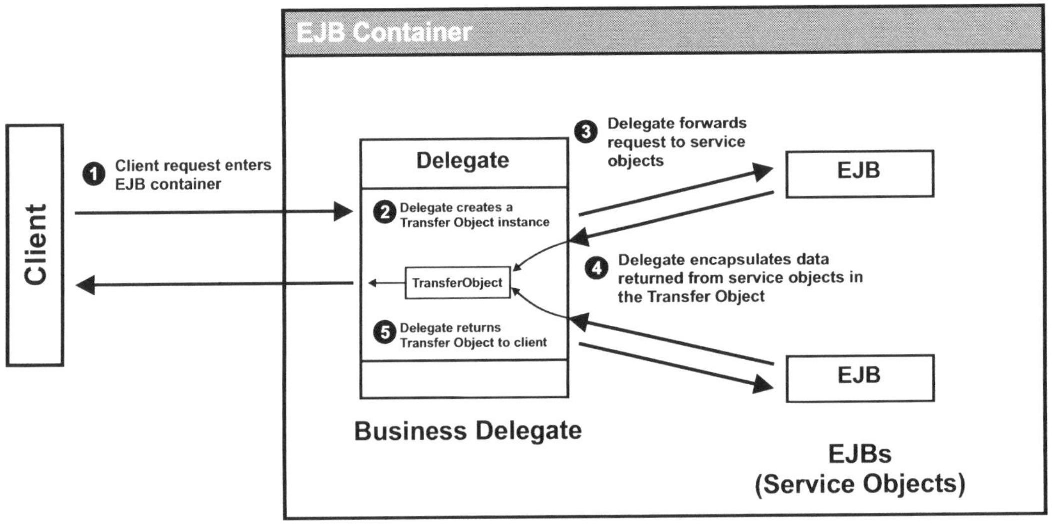

Non-Examinable Patterns

Patterns in this section are generally useful but will not be examined and can quickly be ruled out as correct answers to multiple-choice questions.

Patterns for the Presentation Tier (Non-Examinable)

View Helper

Dynamic view components in the presentation tier nearly always depend on data obtained at request time from another source, such as from a database or by using EJBs in the business logic tier. While it is recommended that most components that return content are implemented as JSPs, these types of components do not lend themselves to the large amounts of processing (logic) code often required to build a truly dynamic page. While servlets may seem like the rational alternative when substantial logic is required, servlets containing large amounts of template text are also not desirable. Servlets are also less portable, given that one of the JSP design goals is platform-independence: no longer should JSPs necessarily be reliant on the servlet model.

The solution is to separate the presentation components from the processing components; this is usually achieved using a View Helper, which is a JavaBean or Custom Tag used by the page to assist with processing functionality. Both JavaBeans and Custom Tags implemented as handler classes lend themselves to doing logic processing. Both are designed as Java classes and as a result provide full programming capabilities with no limitations. A JSP or servlet can use a View Helper component to reduce the amount of code required to build these presentational components. This helps to separate, even in the presentation tier, views from models. With servlets or JSPs prior to the JSP 1.0 specification, the recommended mechanism is to implement the View Helper as a JavaBean component deployed with the application. For JSP 1.1 specifications or greater, the recommended mechanism is to use custom tags.

A special kind of JavaBean, known as a **value bean**, can be used to store data maintained over the lifetime of a request, session or application, or as a storage mechanism for data retrieved from EJB services. There is nothing actually special about the bean in terms of its class structure, but the emphasis is slightly different: the purpose of a value bean is only *to store data*, while a normal JavaBean may also do processing.

Using a separate View Helper provides the following benefits:

- Using a separate Helper promotes code reuse; the same Helper can be invoked from multiple different servlets or JSPs, or indeed from other JavaBean components, possibly Helpers themselves.
- Changes made to the processing code are centralised: only one component needs to be modified, and we know exactly where that component is located.
- Removing processing code from the view creates a clean separation between the roles of the web page author, who for example works only with (X)HTML or XML, and the Java programmer.
- A Helper can double-up as a Service Locator, which in turn could be used by pages directly, or by other Helpers.
- A Helper can correlate data from many sources, including multiple calls to a Business Delegate should one exist. The Helper can assemble all requisite data, and in the case of Custom Tags, can also compile the view code (e.g. HTML) to display that collated data.

When used in conjunction with a Business Delegate, the power of a View Helper really becomes apparent. Changes to the EJB implementation can be compensated for just with changes to the Delegate's method implementations, but without changing the method signatures, so all view components still 'see' the same services. Changes in the method signatures of a Delegate could require the rewriting of

Figure 22.7

View Helper Pattern

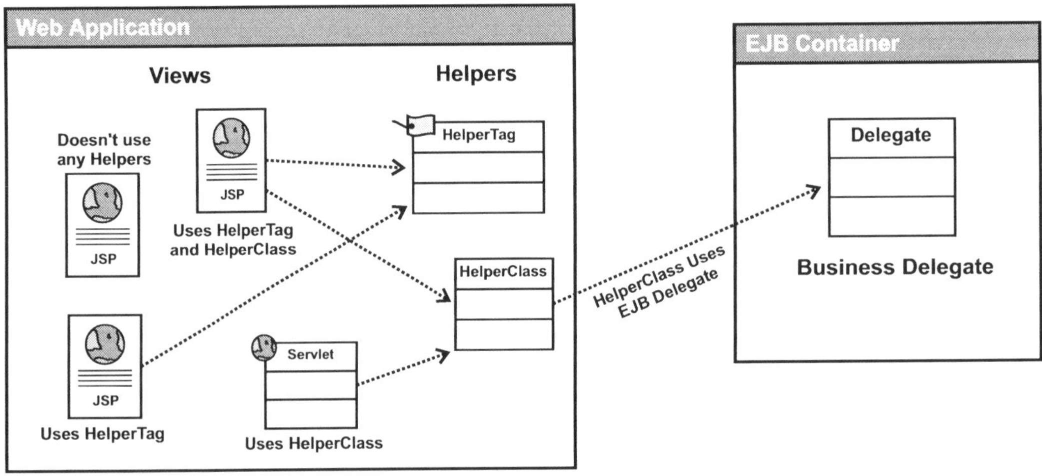

large sections of presentation code if they were invoked directly from JSPs and servlets. However, with a View Helper, changes to Delegate method signatures involve only a change in a central Helper class or tag. This is a very robust model: despite any changes in the logic code provided by the EJB implementation, the view component code never needs to be changed! This gives us scalability: we can add extra services, or upgrade others, without affecting the interfaces that clients interact with.

Figure 22.7 shows usage of both View Helper and Business Delegate patterns.

Composite View

Often, every page on a website contains a set of common components: menu bars and navigation facilities, advertisement banners and footers which are static, or display the date and time that page was last modified. Amongst these, each page will add its own specific content. Let's look at an example schematic of a a typical layout (Figure 22.8). Down the left-hand side we've got a site navigation menu, which will be the same across all pages. At the top we're including an advert banner, presumably to strike up some extra revenue! Both of these components don't change across

Figure 22.8

Typical Composite Layout Schematic

the site's design: they are used in *every* page. To manually type the code for them into each page would be far from maintainable and plainly ridiculous. A better solution would be to keep the navigation bar and banner as two separate JSPs, and use the `RequestDispatcher` mechanism to include them in every other page. This still isn't perfect: a change to the name or location of the resource would entail possibly weeks of work to change the inclusion calls in every other page. The best possible solution is provided by the Composite View pattern, which consists of a single component (typically a JSP) which assembles the view from many different fragments before returning the completed page to the client. The Composite View component is responsible for managing the layout of all pages on the site, separating the layout and style of the site away from that of each page. To demonstrate this, let's look at an example use of this pattern.

We could implement the Composite View component as a JSP page with the following syntax:

```
<html>
  <head>
    <title><mytags:title page="${ viewPath }" /></title>
  </head>
  <body>
    <div id="navigation">
      <%@ include file="/WEB-INF/includes/nav.jsp" %>
    </div>
    <div id="banner">
      <%@ include file="/WEB-INF/includes/advert.jsp" %>
    </div>
    <div id="pagebody">
      <jsp:include page="${ viewPath }" />
    </div>
  </body>
</html>
```

The idea with this page is to include each of the following in the layout:

- The `<mytags:title />` custom tag is used to obtain the title of the page which is actually being requested by the client. We've omitted details of the implementation of this tag, and how the library is imported with a `taglib` directive, since that isn't necessary here – try it out as an exercise if you're ever bored!
- The navigation bar resource (`/WEB-INF/includes/nav.jsp`).
- The advertisement banner (`/WEB-INF/includes/advert.jsp`).
- The page body, which is the resource located at the URL stored by the `viewPath` variable. We assume this variable has been bound into a scope (most likely, request) by a component which has performed prior request processing – e.g. a servlet following the Dispatcher pattern (see next section).

In order for this to pattern to work, the Composite View (Figure 22.9) must receive all requests applicable to this layout template. It can do this in one of two ways. The first uses the deployment descriptor to map *all* incoming requests to the Composite View component; this solution is not ideal since many requests will require logic evaluation (for example by a Front Controller) before displaying the view. The second method uses a Front Controller or Dispatcher (see next section) which delegates view processing here. Either way, the end result should be the same: the intended resource identified by the client's request is embedded in a site-wide template before being returned.

Figure 22.9 Composite View Pattern

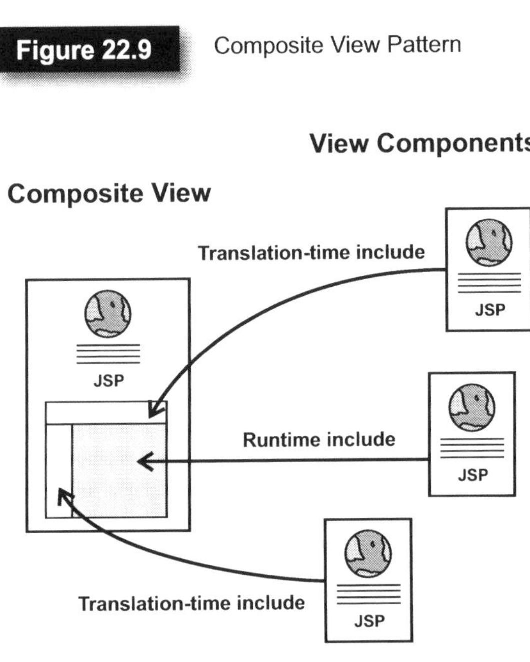

Inclusion of resources into the template can be performed either statically at translation time, or dynamically at run time. The so-called **Early-Binding Strategy** includes one or more of the resources into the template at *translation time*–this is advantageous when the other resource changes infrequently (for example, a navigation or menu bar which tend to always display the same items). This strategy is accomplished using JSP's static `include` directive–for example:

```
<%@ include file="/WEB-INF/includes/nav.jsp" %>
```

The alternative **Late-Binding Strategy** includes one or more of the resources into the template at *run time*. This uses the `<jsp:include />` action–for example:

```
<jsp:include page="/mainPage.jsp" />
```

Dispatcher View (Composite)

This is an example of a **composite** pattern, one which incorporates other individual patterns to form a common strategy. Specifically, this design is assembled from the Front Controller and View Helper patterns we've already seen. Using a Dispatcher View pattern nearly always implies the use of Front Controller and View Helper and as such usually negates the need for these strategies to appear elsewhere in your design.

In some applications, components are not requested directly by the client as resources: instead, they may exist as servlets or JSPs inside the container without the outside world knowing about them. Other components, such as a Front Controller or Composite View incorporate these 'hidden' components into the response using the `RequestDispatcher` mechanism (or similar); the only direct point of contact for the client is with the limited set of controller components which lie at the very front of the application.

The simplest way to use a Front Controller or a Composite View is to hard-code the locations of 'hidden' resources which are to be utilised. Then, upon receipt of a request, the Controller or Composite View knows which page to include or forward execution to. However, while being the simplest, it isn't the most scalable. An application may have more than one Front Controller or Composite View which reference the same set of 'hidden' components; if one of these 'hidden' resources changes purpose or location, all the Controller components would need to be changed to compensate. A strong coupling between any two components is what we're trying to avoid in all Java EE applications: a change to one area of an application affects only a small *localised* area of the rest.

The problem is overcome using a Dispatcher, which put simply is a component which forwards requests for resources with *logical* names to the *physical* components in the application. For example, a Dispatcher might receive a request from a Front Controller destined for `BasketView` (a logical name) but actually forward to `/baskets/view.jsp` (a physical component). Even if the location or name of the `view.jsp` resource changes, its logical name (`BasketView`) can, and should, remain the same. The mapping between logical names and physical resources is made by the Dispatcher. Any changes to the physical component entail only a change in the mapping in the Dispatcher, and nothing else. Since the Dispatcher is only one component, changing the mapping between logical and physical names is highly localised. In effect, we've decoupled the responsibility of requesting a resource (the requirement of a Front Controller or Composite View) from knowing where that resource is (the Dispatcher's role). The sequence of events for such a request is shown in Figure 22.10.

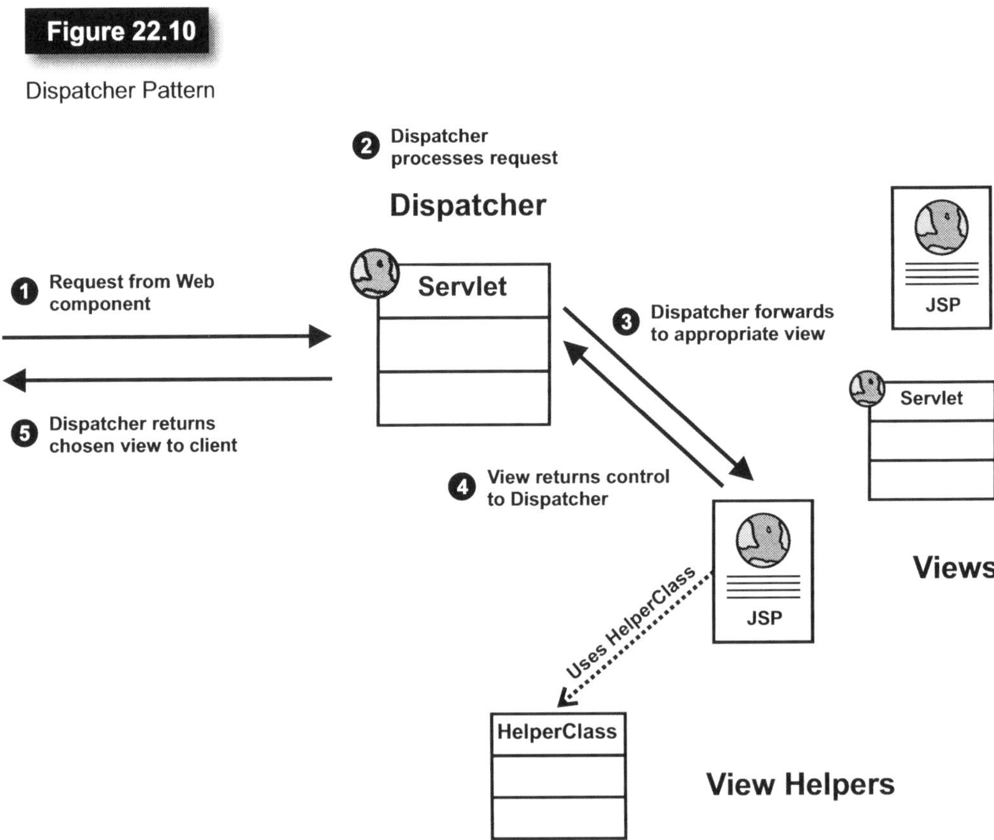

Service to Worker (Composite)

The Service to Worker pattern is essentially the same as the Dispatcher View pattern, but with a different emphasis–it includes all the same components as the Dispatcher View, but each component is responsible for different things. There is much debate over the differences between the Dispatcher View pattern, and the Service to Worker pattern. For a given implementation of either pattern, it can be purely subjective which name to give it.

One explanation of the difference is that the Dispatcher View represents a component (the Dispatcher) which does simple processing (such as consulting a hard-coded map) to determine which resource to forward control to, while the Service to Worker completes more complex code before forwarding onward. We said that the two patterns represented different emphases: the Dispatcher component in the Dispatcher View pattern only maps requests to resources, but the Dispatcher in the Service to Worker may do more processing before forwarding–for example, calling an EJB method to determine properties about the request before deciding on the appropriate view component.

Figure 22.11 shows the Service to Worker pattern in action. Compare this with the Dispatcher View pattern diagram to see the trivial differences.

As you can see, the major difference is that, here, the Dispatcher component decides which view to use for the request based on various properties it processes from JavaBean helpers (and/or EJBs). In the Dispatcher View pattern, the Dispatcher knew *internally* how to forward the request, leaving the view itself to query the JavaBeans and decide what content it wanted to display.

The line between these two patterns is difficult to draw; unfortunately, there's nothing much clearer than to say that Dispatchers in Dispatcher Views do less work and never make use of helpers. Of course, many developers couldn't care less what a pattern's called as long as it works!

Figure 22.11

Service to Worker Pattern

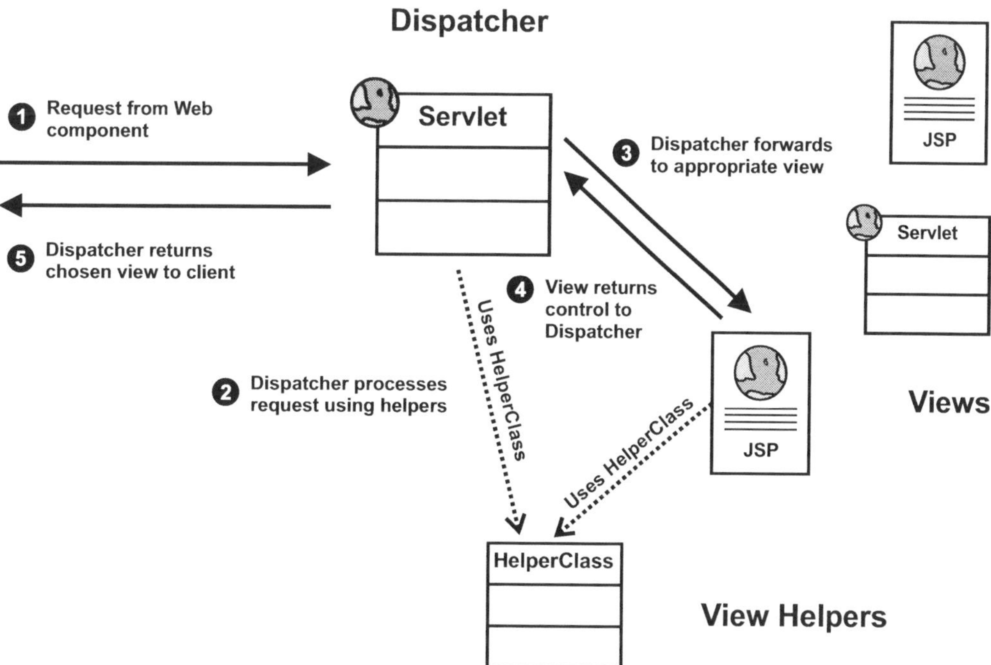

Revision Questions

1 **The National Banking Company wants to add additional logging to their Java EE website to monitor both authorised and unauthorised requests to all pages. Which would be best pattern to implement?** (choose one)

- A Front Controller
- B Intercepting Filter
- C Business Delegate
- D Model-View-Controller

2 **The Sweetastic online store sells confectionary products. They use an SQL database to store a list of all products they sell, and intend to use JSP pages to display the data to the customer. They use a shared Web server with no EJB container. What would be the best pattern to implement here?** (choose one)

- A Front Controller
- B Service Locator
- C Model-View-Controller
- D Business Delegate

3 **A corporate IT body stores technical documents relating to the computer parts it sells. Due to the fast turn-around of such products, many of their documents go out-of-date and are removed very quickly. The corporation is frustrated with users receiving 404 ('Not Found') responses after requesting nonexistent pages from following old hyperlinks on other websites, and wants to implement a more user-friendly search facility so users are presented with 'similar products' matching the terms in the URL. What pattern would you use to accomplish this?** (choose one)

- A Front Controller
- B Intercepting Filter
- C Model-View-Controller
- D Transfer Object

4 **The Really Great Forums open source project is designing a forum which runs exclusively in the Java EE Web container. As part of this forum, users can edit their own posts, and moderators are permitted to modify any posts within the particular forum they moderate. What would be the best pattern to implement to prevent unauthorised users from moderating posts?** **(choose one)**

- A Front Controller
- B Intercepting Filter
- C Business Delegate
- D Service Locator

5 **An online retailer uses various EJBs to construct their catalogue and maintain stock counts, retrieving the item codes, prices and stock levels singularly. They have recently been delivered a custom-built website, but the developers forgot to ask what data storage mechanism they were using and therefore supplied them only with a set of helper beans and some database drivers. What combination of patterns would you use to interface the helper beans with their EJB application?** **(choose two)**

- A Model-View-Controller
- B Business Delegate
- C Service Locator
- D Intercepting Filter
- E Transfer Object

6 **A doctors' practice is upgrading its infrastructure, allowing patients to book appointments online, clerical staff to access records through a desktop client application, and doctors and surgical staff to maintain patients' records. The data is stored as EJBs, backed by a database. Patients and clerical staff only ever access appointment times and patient address details, while surgical staff require access to entire patient records. Which collaborative patterns would you implement in the EJB tier to allow both client applications and Web applications to access the data?** **(choose two)**

- A Front Controller
- B Business Delegate
- C Service Locator
- D Transfer Object

7 **A Web application needs to use programmatic security to protect some of its resources. Which of these patterns would best achieve this goal?** (choose two)

- A Front Controller
- B Intercepting Filter
- C Model-View-Controller
- D Business Delegate

8 **A computer company decides to make a certification exam available for all consumers of its new product, and to administer this in new Web-based exam software. The questions are modelled as Java classes, and are shown in JSP pages; the site includes a navigation mechanism to travel from question to question. What combination of patterns would best achieve this?** (choose two)

- A Front Controller
- B Intercepting Filter
- C Model-View-Controller
- D Transfer Object
- E Service Locator

9 **A bookshop is planning to sell its products online, and to expand its IT infrastructure to also log transactions in-store. They have suggested using EJB technology in conjunction with a Web application. What single pattern would best be used to ensure their EJB catalogue system can be interfaced with the Web application?** (choose one)

- A Intercepting Filter
- B Business Delegate
- C Service Locator
- D Transfer Object

10 **An airline sells tickets online. It first allows customers to select their airport, input a destination and a departure time; a servlet processes this result, but must access an EJB application in order to create a list of all suitable flights before forwarding to a JSP view. Which two patterns combined would be best implemented here?** (choose two)

- A Model-View-Controller
- B Service Locator
- C Business Delegate
- D Transfer Object

Answers to Revision Questions

1 **Correct answer: B**

An Intercepting Filter would give the best solution, as it can immediately be deployed to monitor all requests to all resources without having to change existing code. A would work, but is not the best approach due to its tight coupling with the rest of the application's code. C should be used for data access, so is inappropriate. D describes a basic pattern often employed by JSP pages (views) accessing data stores, and is inappropriate here.

2 **Correct answer: C**

MVC is excellent for separating data from view – in this case, we have a database as a model, perhaps some JavaBean helpers as controllers and a set of JSPs implementing the view. The JSPs communicate with the JavaBeans which retrieve the data and keep the JSPs up-to-date; the helpers might even cache the data to save having to retrieve it from the database every time the same information is requested. A is incorrect, as a Front Controller is a single component, typically a servlet, which should be used to perform a processing task such as moderation; although all the database retrieval could be done here, this limits the servlet's use as a database accessor to one or two pages only. B and D are incorrect, as these patterns are typically used for interfacing a Web or client application with EJBs, but our application doesn't use EJB technology.

3 **Correct answer: A**

A Controller could easily be mapped to become a 404 error page. The servlet receives the old request URI through the additional request attributes placed in the request object by the container upon forwarding to the error page, and uses those attributes to construct a list of similar but valid URLs on the server. It stores these in a request-scoped attribute and forwards to a JSP view which displays those results to the client. B alone is incorrect, as a filter should not represent an accessible *resource*; instead, it should be transparent to the client. There is little, if any, data being accessed from a model here, so C wouldn't be immediately helpful (although it could be used in conjunction with the Controller to get access to a database of known resources). D is incorrect, as we aren't transferring any data between resources here.

4 **Correct answer: B**

An Intercepting Filter is the easiest; the target page is the 'edit page' for the forum, allowing users to edit their own posts or a moderator to change another user's post. The filter is configured simply to check by username and role name: if the username matches the user who originally made the post, or the user's role is 'moderator' and they belong to this forum's moderation group, allow them to see the 'edit page'; otherwise return an SC_UNAUTHORIZED response, which would in turn present some custom error page. A is inconvenient, as a Controller would have to do the deciding then forward to the correct page; in addition, there may be different pages depending on who is going to edit the post–a moderator might have more privileges when editing than the original user, or vice versa. Using a filter rather than a servlet allows these changes to be made in different filters and easily 'plugged in' as required. C and D are incorrect as they are intended for data access in the EJB tier, and we are told this is 'exclusively' a Web container project.

5 **Correct answers: B, C**

A Service Locator can be used by the helper beans to obtain a reference to the Business Delegate, which can then be used to access the appropriate EJBs and return a response. It is unwise to access the entity EJBs directly, in case of name or implementation changes. A is incorrect, as we are told implicitly, by the fact that helpers are present, that an MVC architecture is already being used. D is incorrect; a filter wouldn't help any application interface with EJBs. A Transfer Object might be used in making invocations of the EJB, but in this case is unnecessary, as we are told that the data is accessed 'singularly' in the question.

6 **Correct answers: B, D**

The Business Delegate can be used to control access to the other EJBs through Java EE's declarative security model, as well as providing a single interface for both client and Web applications. Since some staff need entire records, it is sensible for the Delegate to collect this data together into a single Transfer Object when sending large amounts at once; other staff and patients accessing only one or two pieces of data may not require a Transfer Object. A is incorrect, as a Front Controller can only be used in a Web application, and C is incorrect, as a Service Locator is used by (and distributed in) a Web application or desktop client application in order to obtain a reference to a remote EJB such as a Delegate; therefore C is not implemented in the EJB tier.

7 **Correct answers: A, B**

A Controller can be used to protect one or two resources and is good for programmatic *authentication* purposes, while a Filter is the most scalable solution to implement programmatic *authorisation*. C is incorrect; we don't necessarily have any need for a view here. D is incorrect, as we aren't using EJBs.

8 **Correct answers: A, C**

MVC is an obvious choice for where questions are encapsulated in Java(Bean) classes, and JSP pages are rendering the view. The Front Controller can be used to provide navigation, communicating both with the JSP (forwarding to the correct view), and updating the JavaBeans with any submitted information.

9 **Correct answer: B**

Abstracting all the details away from the actual EJB implementation into a single Delegate allows for future change. This would best be coupled with a Service Locator, but this isn't the most important single part of the design, making C incorrect. A is incorrect, as a filter won't help interfacing with EJB. D is incorrect as we aren't necessarily interested in transferring lots of data – at least not in the provided specifications.

10 **Correct answers: C, D**

A Delegate provides a uniform way to access the EJB data, while a Transfer Object is used to transfer details about all the available flights at the same time. A is incorrect, as MVC is already being used by the presence of a servlet (Controller), JSP view and the EJB model. B is incorrect, as although the Web application may use a Service Locator for convenience, the other two patterns provide the significant interface with EJBs.

Index

Symbols

A

B

C

D

E

F

G

H

I

J

Made in the USA
Lexington, KY
27 December 2012